ROBERT PAYNELL'S
KING'S BENCH REPORTS
(1625-1627)

MEDIEVAL AND RENAISSANCE
TEXTS AND STUDIES

VOLUME 369

ROBERT PAYNELL'S
KING'S BENCH REPORTS
(1625-1627)

EDITED BY

W. H. BRYSON

ACMRS
(Arizona Center for Medieval and Renaissance Studies)
Tempe, Arizona
2010

Library of Congress Cataloging-in-Publication Data

Paynell, Robert, 1602-
  Robert Paynell's King's Bench reports (1625-1627) / edited by W.H. Bryson.
    p. cm. -- (Medieval and renaissance texts and studies ; v. 369)
  Includes index.
  ISBN 978-0-86698-417-1 (alk. paper)
  1. Law reports, digests, etc.--England. I. Bryson, William Hamilton, 1941-
II. England and Wales. Court of King's Bench. III. Title. IV. Title: King's
Bench reports.
  KD2001625.P39 A24
  348.42'046--dc22

                                                    2009020933

∞
This book is made to last.
It is set in Adobe Caslon Pro,
smyth-sewn and printed on acid-free paper
to library specifications.
Printed in the United States of America

This book
is dedicated to the memory of
CONWAY ROBINSON
of Richmond, Virginia,
a most distinguished lawyer,
law reporter,
and legal historian.

PREFACE

I would like to thank personally the librarians and their staffs of the British Library manuscripts department, Lincoln's Inn, the University of Richmond School of Law, the University of Virginia School of Law, and the Yale University School of Law for their unfailing kindness and helpfulness.

INTRODUCTION

None of the reports of cases from the Court of King's Bench from the first two years of the reign of Charles I is very good, but, on the other hand, none of them is totally useless. Many of these reports have been insulted by later judges, but, as time has gone by, they have been regularly cited, being the best evidence available of the law at the time. The optimal use of them is to read all of the reports of the same case, both those in print and those still in manuscript, plus the record of the case, which is in the archive of the court in the Public Record Office, in order to have the maximum information. Ideally, each of these reports and records of the cases would be translated into English and printed together *seriatim*, similarly to Eagle and Younge's reports of tithe cases.[1] Such a project is beyond the resources of the present editor; however, this present publication is offered as a small contribution to the greater effort.

The reports that have found their way into print are not necessarily the best, although they are now, of course, the ones that are the most familiar. As will be discussed, many of the attributions of authorship are dubious or false. However, the anonymity to the present generation of lawyers and judges should not by itself detract from their validity. This is because the preservation and printing of law reports in the seventeenth century was quite haphazard, being undertaken more often than not by printers acting without any help or advice from lawyers.

Modern editions of the law reports of this period, 1625 to 1627, will shed much light on the obscurity of the sources of this period of legal history. The following discussion centers on the individual sets of King's Bench law reports from this time.[2]

---

[1] F. K. Eagle and E. Younge, *A Collection of the Reports of Cases . . . Relating to Tithes* (1826), 4 vols.

[2] See generally J. G. Marvin, *Legal Bibliography* (1847); J. W. Wallace, *The Reporters* (4th ed. 1882); W. S. Holdsworth, *History of English Law*, vol. 5 (1924), pp. 355–378; J. H. Baker, "The Dark Age of English Legal History, 1500–1700" in *The Legal Profession and the Common Law* (1986), pp. 435–460.

Robert Paynell

Robert Paynell was born in 1602, the son of Henry Paynell, Esquire, of Belaugh in the County of Norfolk. His mother was Bridget Walpole, the daughter of John Walpole of Houghton in Norfolk.[3] In December 1617, he matriculated at Christ's College, Cambridge.[4] He was admitted to Gray's Inn on 2 June 1619,[5] called to the bar on 8 November 1626, and made an utter barrister on 24 November 1645.[6] In 1640, he participated in the creation ceremony of Francis Bacon (d. 1657) as a serjeant by distributing the customary gold rings.[7] Bacon was from King's Lynn and a member of Gray's Inn, and he was the son of Paynell's aunt, Elizabeth.[8] It is possible that this connection was the reason that Paynell chose to join Gray's Inn. Paynell sat regularly as a justice of the peace in Norfolk from 1650 to 1657; however, he sat in the Norwich sessions only.[9] In 1642, he married Judith Duke, the daughter of John Duke, M.D., of Colchester, and they had two sons, Robert Paynell, who died in 1677, and John Paynell. Robert Paynell died in 1658 and was buried in the Church of St. John the Baptist in Norwich.[10] Paynell reported cases in the courts of King's Bench and Exchequer.

Paynell's King's Bench reports are now first published herein. The best manuscript, and the one used for this edition, is British Library MS. Add. 35961, ff. 2–66. There is another copy in British Library MS. Lansdowne 1083, ff. 3–104. Both of these are in law French. Robert Paynell is identified as the reporter of these King's Bench cases at British Library MS. Add. 35961, ff. 13, 52, and British Library MS. Lansdowne 1083, ff. 16v, 80. It is clear that Paynell was the creator, rather than the copier, of these reports in that he explains the absence of cases from two terms in 1625 by the adjournment of the court to Reading to avoid the outbreak of the plague.[11] The inference is that he did not personally attend these sessions. If he was merely copying other reporters, this note would have been superfluous. Also, at the end, he adds three cases which he acknowledges that he missed because he was absent from court on the day that they were argued.[12]

---

[3] W. Rye, *Norfolk Families* (1913), p. 657; F. Blomefield, *History of the County of Norfolk* (1806), vol. 4, p. 295.

[4] J. Peile, *Biographical Register of Christ's College* (1910), vol. 1, p. 321.

[5] J. Foster, *The Register of Admissions to Gray's Inn* (1889), p. 154.

[6] R. J. Fletcher, *The Pension Book of Gray's Inn* (1901), vol. 1, pp. 274, 354.

[7] J. H. Baker, *Order of Serjeants at Law* (1984), pp. 440, 498.

[8] G. V. Benson and J. M. Blatchly, "Sir Francis Bacon (c. 1587–1657)," *Oxford Dictionary of National Biography* (2004), vol. 3, p. 145.

[9] D. E. H. James, *Norfolk Quarter Sessions Order Book 1650–1657* (1955), passim.

[10] W. Rye, *supra*; F. Blomefield, *supra*; J. Venn and J. A. Venn, *Alumni Cantabrigienses* (1924), part 1, vol. 3, p. 324; C. E. Wright, *Fontes Harleiani* (1972), p. 271.

[11] See Note, No. 19.

[12] See the note preceding case No. 285.

Although Paynell's King's Bench reports have survived in only two manuscripts, some individual cases have been incorporated into other collections of cases. Paynell's reports were part of a large body of manuscript law reports that circulated among the legal profession in the seventeenth century. The various manuscript collections (some large, some small) were lent, copied (in whole or in part), paraphrased, vouched (i.e. cited) in court, and randomly printed. Thus did the law students, practitioners, and judges create their own personal professional libraries. The evidence that Paynell's King's Bench reports were included in this amorphous body of law reports is that some of his cases appear in the other collections. For example, his report of one of the hearings of *Cole v. Shury* (1626), No. 168, was used in Latch 264, 82 E.R. 378. Paynell's report of *Rex v. Beverley* (1626), No. 28, was the basis of Latch 224, 82 E.R. 357. *Bowyer v. Rivet* (1626), Popham 153, 79 E.R. 1252, is based on Paynell's report, below, No. 26.

In Easter term, 1627, Paynell reported a case from the Court of Exchequer.[13] The next term, he began his Exchequer reports, leaving the King's Bench reports to his old friend from Christ's College, Cambridge, and Gray's Inn, Thomas Widdrington.

New Benloe

Les reports de Gulielme Bendloes, serjeant de la ley: des divers resolutions et judgments donne par les reverendes judges de la ley: de certeine matieres en la ley en le temps del raigne de roys et roignes Hen. VIII. Edw. VI. Phil. et Mar. et Elizab. Avecque autres select cases en la ley adjudges et resolves en le temps del regne de tresillustres roys Jaqves et Charles le Premier: jammais par cy devant imprimee. Ovesq; un table bien perfaict de matieres notables contenues en les dits reports et cases. Et auxsi un auter table de nosmes del cases contenues en yceaux. Publies en le XIII. au [sic] de treshaut et renosmes Charles le Second. London: Printed for Timothy Twyford, 1661. 5 p. l., 204 (i. e. 179), [10] p. 29 cm.
Second edition: 73 *English Reports* 931–1060 (1907).
Cambridge U.L. MS. Gg.2.30, ff. 1–79, is a manuscript copy of the second part of New Benloe, pp. 89–204, 73 E.R. 962–1060.[14]

This set of reports is usually referred to as New Benloe. At the end of the Elizabethan cases, at page 41, is written "*Finis*," and the next case, which is from Easter term of 19 James I, 1621, begins on the next page, which is page 89, there being no pages 42 through 88 in the book. This suggests that the compositor was given two separate and completely unconnected texts to put into print or that there were two compositors working quite independently. William Bendlowes

---

[13] *Swinerton v. Wolstenholme* (1627), 118 Selden Soc. 503.
[14] J. H. Baker and J. S. Ringrose, *A Catalogue of English Legal Manuscripts in [the] Cambridge University Library* (1996), p. 264; see generally J. W. Wallace, *Reporters*, p. 135.

died in 1584, and thus there can be no possible connection between him and the cases from the reigns of James I and Charles I.[15] The title of the book and the preface also make it clear that the latter text was added by the editor or the publisher. These cases are only said to have been "collected by a skillful hand."

There are 135 cases dating from Pas. 1 Car. I to Pas. 3 Car. I, 1625–1627: Benloe 146–204, 73 E.R. 1014–1060, Cambridge U.L. MS. Gg.2.30, ff. 73–79.

Edward Bulstrode

The Third Part of the reports of Edward Bulstrode . . . Of divers resolutions and judgments, given . . . by the grave, reverend, and learned judges, and sages of the law. Of . . . cases and matters in law: with the reasons and causes of their said resolutions and judgements, given in the Court of King's Bench in the time of the late reign of King James and the beginning of King Charles. London: Printed for W. Lee, D. Pakeman, and G. Bedell, 1659. 29 cm.

These reports were prepared for the press by Bulstrode himself; "The Epistle Dedicatory" is signed by Edward Bulstrode.

There are 24 cases dating from Mich. 1 Car. I to Pas. 2 Car. I, 1625–1626; they are printed at 3 Bulstrode 295–341, 81 E.R. 245–282 (1908).

Sir George Croke

The reports of Sir George Croke, knight; late, one of the justices of the Court of King's-Bench; and formerly, one of the justices of the Court of Common-Bench, of such select cases as were adjudged in the said courts . . . Collected and written in French by himself; revised and published in English, by Sir Harebotle Grimston, baronet. London: Printed by R. Hodgkinsonne, 1657.

The reports of Sir George Croke (1560–1642) for the period of the reign of Charles I were made by Croke himself while he was a judge. Although they were published posthumously, they were prepared for the press by Sir Harbottle Grimstone (1603–1685), Croke's son-in-law, who was a scholarly lawyer. This volume is today referred to as Cro. Car.; however, in the older law books, it was sometimes referred to as 1 Cro. because it was the first of Croke's reports to be published, as it contained the more recent cases. These reports are good, and there were several editions before the last one in the *English Reports*, vol. 79, pp. 609–1124 (1907).

---

[15] For William Bendlowes (1514–1584), see L. W. Abbott, *Law Reporting in England 1485–1585* (1973), pp. 62–103, esp. 83–84.

John Godbolt

Reports of certain cases, arising in the severall courts of record at Westminster: in the raignes of Q. Elizabeth, K. James, and the late King Charles . . . Collected by very good hands, and lately re-viewed, examined, and approved of by the late learned Justice Godbolt, and now published by W. Hughes. London: Printed by T.N. for W. Lee, D. Pakeman, and Gabriell Bedell, 1652. 4 p. l., 451 (i.e. 439), (11) p. 22 x 18 cm.
78 *English Reports* 1–265 (1907).

The reports currently attributed to John Godbolt (d. 1648), a justice of the Court of Common Pleas from 1647 to 1648, were edited by William Hughes of Gray's Inn and published posthumously in 1652. This book has no preface. After the *"Finis"* of Godbolt's reports at page 451, below a line of printer's ornaments, is added "I have perused this Collection of Reports, and think them fit to be printed. Per me Johannem Godbolt, Unum Justiciar' de Banco 18. Jun. 1648." Thus, a close reading of the title and this colophon discloses that these reports were not composed by Godbolt himself.

Sir William Jones

Les reports de Sir William Jones, Chevalier . . . De divers special cases cy bien in le Court de banck le roy, come le Common-banck in Angleterre. Cy bien en le darreign temps del' reign de roy Jaques, come en l'anns de roy Charles I. Queux fueront adjudge en les dits courts en le temps en que il fuit justice en ceux. Colliges par luy mesme, et imprimee per l'original south son maine propre en francois remanent in les maines de Dorothy Favlconberge, & Lvcy Jones, files & executrices del' dit justice. London: Printed by T.R. and N.T. for Thomas Basset and Richard Chiswel, 1675. 6 p. l., 463, [22] p., 1 l. front. (port.) 31 cm.
Second edition: 82 *English Reports* 1–243 (1908).
British Library MS. Hargrave 317 is an English translation made by Francis Hargrave (d. 1821).

These reports of cases dating from Mich. 18 Jac. I to Mich. 16 Car. I, 1620–1640, were made by Sir William Jones (1566–1640) while he was a judge. After his death, his manuscript was given to the printer by his two daughters, his co-executrices, for publication in 1675. It being published posthumously, there is the usual doubt as to whether the manuscript was of Jones's composition or merely of Jones's ownership.

Jones appears to have made the reports in Harvard Law School MS. 1235 (formerly 5030) (20 Jac. I through Mich. 4 Car. I, 1622–1628),[16] some of which were printed in Latch's reports.[17]

---

[16] J. H. Baker, *English Legal Manuscripts in the U.S.A.* (1990), part 2, p. 182, no. 790(d).

[17] See below.

Sir William Noy

Reports and cases taken in the time of Queen Elizabeth, King James, and King Charles collected and reported by that learned lawyer, William Noy . . . now translated into English; with two necessary tables of the cases and contents, for the readers ease and benefit. London: Printed by F.L. for Matthew Walbancke . . . and T. Firby . . . 1656. [13], 185, [10] p.; Errata: p. [9] at end.

Reports and cases taken in the time of Queen Elizabeth, King James, and King Charles collected and reported by that learned lawyer William Noy . . . Containing most excellent matter of exceptions to all manner of declarations, pleadings, and demurrers, that there is scarce one action in a probability of being brought, but here it is thoroughly examined and exactly laid. 2d ed., cor. and amended. With two necessary tables of the cases and contents for the readers ease and benefit. London: Printed by T.R. for Samuel Heyrick, 1669. 2 p. l., 185, [15] p. 29 cm.

Third edition: 74 *English Reports* 973–1141 (1907).

The reports which have been attributed to Sir William Noy (1577–1634) could not possibly have been made by him. This is because the first case in this set of reports is dated 1559; Noy was born in 1577; Noy died in 1634; and the last case reported is dated 1639. Moreover, these reports were first printed posthumously in 1656. Most of the cases date from the latter part of the reign of Queen Elizabeth I and from the time of King James I. They are not printed in strict chronological order, which suggests that they were copied from various sources.

There is a block of 75 King's Bench cases from the first three years of the reign of King Charles I, 1625 to 1628, printed in the middle of Noy's reports at Noy 75–97, 74 E.R. 1042–1063.

Sir John Popham

Reports and cases collected by the learned, Sir John Popham, knight . . . Written with his own hand in French, and novv faithfully translated into English. To which are added some remarkable cases reported by other learned pens since his death. With an alphabeticall table, wherein may be found the principall matters contained in this booke. London: Printed by Tho: Roycroft for John Place, 1656. 4 p. l., 212, [7] p. 29 cm.

Second edition: 79 *English Reports* 1125–1300 (1907).

Sir John Popham died in 1607, and his reports were published posthumously in 1656. Thus he could not have been responsible for the reports of the cases from the time of Charles I. This is clearly acknowledged on the title page and in the preface. Moreover, at the end of the Elizabethan cases, on page 123 (79 E.R. 1228), is written "Here ends the Lord Popham's Reports." Page 124 is blank. Page 125, the first folio of quire KK, begins with "An Addition of Certain Select Cases in the Time of King James and King Charles." The editor states in the preface that the later cases "were taken by judicious pens."

Popham 153–212, 79 E.R. 1252–1300, reports 54 cases dating from Hil. 1 Car. I to Hil. 2 Car. I, 1626–1627.

John Latch

Plusieurs tres-bons cases, come ils estoyent adjudgees es trois premiers ans du raign du feu Roy Charles le Premier en la Court de Bank le Roy, non encore publiees per aucun autre: colligees per le feu scavant & tres-erudite homme monsieur Jean Latch . . . Avec deux tables . . . publiees per Edward Walpoole. London: Printed by T.R. for H. Twyford, T. Dring, and J. Place, 1662. [12], 275, [18] p.; 29 cm.

Cases determined in the Court of King's Bench, during the I, II, & III years of Charles I collected by John Latch . . . first published, in Norman-French, by Edward Walpoole . . . translated into the English language, by Francois-Xavier Martin. Plusieurs tres-bons cases, come ils estoyent adjugees es trois premiers ans du raign du feu roy Charles le premier en la Court de bank le roy. Newbern, [N.C.]: From the translator's press, 1793. [8], 2–275 (i.e. 215), [21] p.; 20 cm. (8vo).

Cambridge U.L. MS. Ll.3.13 (Pas. 1 Car. I through Hil. 3 Car. I, 1625–1628). Many of these cases are the same reports as Latch's.

Cambridge U.L. MS. Hh.2.1, ff. 181 *et seq.*, are some of the cases in Latch 54 *et seq.*, *Batho v. Salter et seq.*

Harvard Law School MS. 1197 (formerly 2074), ff. 1–117 (Pas. 1 Car. I through Mich. 3 Car. I, 1625–1627). These cases are in Latch 49–263, 82 E.R. 269–377, but Latch has other cases in addition.

Harvard Law School MS. 1235 (formerly 5030) (20 Jac. I through Mich. 4 Car. I, 1622–1628). These reports appear to have been made by Sir William Jones (1566–1640),[18] but they are not the same collection as those printed in 1675 as W. Jones' reports.[19] Some of the reports in this manuscript are printed in Latch's reports.

Yale Law School MSSG R29, no. 23, part 1 (Pas. 1 Car. I through Hil. 3 Car. I, 1625–1628).

There were two printed editions of the reports attributed to John Latch (d. 1655), a barrister of the Middle Temple, before the *English Reports*, volume 82 (1908). The first edition was given to the press for publication by Edward Walpole in 1662.

Latch's reports appears to be two sets of reports printed together. The first set ends on page 224 with *Beverly's Case* (Latch 224, 82 E.R. 357) and the word "*Finis*"; the second set begins with *Reynell v. Kelley* on page 225 (Latch 225, 82 E.R. 357).[20] Page 225 is the first page of quire Hh. Thus, it appears that the

---

[18] J. H. Baker, *English Legal Manuscripts in the U.S.A.* (1990), part 2, p. 182, no. 790(d).

[19] See above.

[20] J. W. Wallace, *Reporters* (1882), p. 265.

printer's compositor was given two separate sets of reports to set up in print or that there were two compositors working independently.

John Latch did not compose either of these sets of reports, but merely owned them. They were found in his possession and printed after his death with his name used as the author. The editor, Edward Walpole, states in his preface that the original manuscript "was all written by [Latch's] own hand wherein (as I apprehend) it received as much the stamp of his approbation and judgment as if he had composed it." The judges' certificate says that Latch collected and copied them from various sources. It states "These reports are all of Mr. Latch's hand, but, as we conceive, not originally taken by him, but excerpted out of some other manuscript." The judges, in 1662, thought them worth publishing to fill a gap in Croke's reports.

The editor of Geoffrey Palmer's reports later claimed that Palmer was the true author of 120 of these case reports and that Palmer had lent his manuscript to Latch.[21] It is to be noted that both Latch's reports and Palmer's reports were printed posthumously.

Francis Xavier Martin (1764–1846), a Frenchman, who was living in North Carolina at the time, translated these reports into English in 1793. However, he omitted some of the cases relating to ecclesiastical matters, which he mistakenly thought would be useless to his American readers.

The modern edition of 1908 is based on the first edition of 1662 and, like it, is in French.

Sir Geoffrey Palmer

Les reports de Sir Gefrey Palmer, chevalier & baronet Attorney General . . . Imprime & publie per l'original. Ovesque deux tables, l'un des nosmes des cases, l'auter des principal matters conteinus en yceux. London: Printed by the assigns of R. and E. Atkyns, Esquires, for Robert Pawlet, 1678. 2 p. l., 567 (i. e. 559), [43] p. front. (port.) 32 cm. Although some title pages bear the dates of 1688 and 1721, there was only one printing of this book.

81 *English Reports* 949–1223 (1908).

Cambridge U.L. MS. Hh.2.1, ff. 181–255v. Pas. 1 Car. I through Mich. 2 Car. I, 1625–1626: some cases are in Palmer, some not; Pas. 4 Car. I through Mich. 4 Car. I, 1628: Palmer 522–567, 81 E.R. 1201–1223.

Cambridge U.L. MS. Mm.6.66 (Trin. 17 Jac. I through Hil. 20 Jac. I, 1619–1623). The second case in this manuscript is *Godfrey v. Dixon* (f. 13v), which is printed at Palmer 13, 81 E.R. 955, and the last case in this manuscript is *Snag v. Fox* (f. 268v), which is printed at Palmer 342, 81 E.R. 1114. (Palmer's printed reports continue on to page 567, 81 E.R. 1223.)

---

[21] G. Palmer, *Reports* (1678), "Preface to the Reader."

British Library MS. Hargrave 21, ff. 10v-420v (Pas. 17 Jac. I through Hil. 20 Jac. I, 1619–1623); Palmer 1–343, 81 E.R. 949–1115 (the last case is *Snag v. Fox*). British Library MS. Lansdowne 1080 (Hil. 15 Jac. I through Mich. 21 Jac. I, 1617–1623). Edward Umfreville (d. 1786) connected these reports with Robert Godfrey;[22] Umfreville said that this manuscript book was owned by Sir Geoffrey Palmer and printed after Palmer's death. There is not much congruence between this manuscript and Palmer's printed reports, but many of the cases are the same, e.g. the next to the last case in this manuscript is *The Bricklayers and Tylers v. The Company of Plasterers* (1623), Palmer 395, 81 E.R. 1140.

These reports attributed to Sir Geoffrey Palmer (1598–1670) were printed posthumously from a manuscript of reports perhaps made or perhaps owned by Robert Godfrey. The preface claims that John Latch used more than 120 of Palmer's manuscript cases and, thus, those cases were not reprinted in Palmer. This is curious since Palmer's cases were taken from a manuscript of Godfrey. Perhaps, none of these reports is of the authorship of any of these men, but were simply owned by them. Palmer had an extensive law library; the manuscript from which the first edition of Sir Francis Moore's reports was printed in 1663 was owned by Palmer.[23] Thus, perhaps, all of these books were based on the manuscripts in Palmer's library, which he lent generously to others.

Edward Umfreville, L. W. Abbott, and Sir John Baker doubt whether they were composed, rather than collected, by Godfrey.[24] The time span is too great for any single person to have been in court personally taking notes. However, the histories of the law reports of Godfrey, Latch, and Palmer are interconnected. Note that the cases of *Fish v. Wiseman, Marget v. Harvey*, and *Man's Case* (Pas. 3 Car. I, 1627), Latch 192–194, 82 E.R. 341–342, Palmer 447–450, 81 E.R. 1164–1165, are the same reports with only minor variations. In general, however, the cases in Latch and Palmer are not printed in the same order.

Sir Thomas Widdrington

British Library MS. Add. 35961, ff. 71v-80, 97–123, 129v-142v, 150–164, 189-end (Trin. 3 Car. I through Trin. 4 Car. I, 1627–1628). Widdrington is identified as the reporter of these cases at ff. 71v, 97, 129v, 142v, 150, 252v.

---

[22] Some reports from the time of Elizabeth I are also associated with Godfrey: BL MS. Hargr. 12; CUL MS. Mm.4.35; and HLS MS. 5063. L. W. Abbott, *Law Reporting in England 1485–1585* (1973), pp. 243, 272, 292. Abbott suggests Richard Godfrey of Lincoln's Inn as the reporter.

[23] This is stated on the title page: F. Moore, *Reports* (1663), t.p.; 72 E.R. 397.

[24] BL MS. Lansdowne 1080, f. 1; L. W. Abbott, *Law Reporting in England 1485–1585* (1973), p. 243; J. H. Baker and J. S. Ringrose, *A Catalogue of English Legal Manuscripts in [the] Cambridge University Library* (1996), pp. 488–489, 518.

British Library MS. Lansdowne 1083, ff. 118v-140v, 167–201, 210v-225v, 234v-249, 279–356 (Trin. 3 Car. I through Hil. 4 Car. I, 1627–1629). Widdrington is identified as the reporter of these cases at ff. 118v, 167, 210v, 225v, 356.
Philadelphia Free Library MS. LC 14.62, ff. 282–304v (Pas. 4 Car. I, 1628). These are the same reports as British Library MS. Add. 35961, ff. 154–164.
Sir Thomas Widdrington (d. 1664), was a barrister of Gray's Inn when he made these King's Bench reports. He was later a Lord Commissioner of the Great Seal (1648–1649, 1654–1655, 1660) and Lord Chief Baron of the Exchequer (1658–1659).[25]

British Library MSS. Hargrave 38 and 39

These two volumes are one continuous set of King's Bench reports dating from Pas. 1 Car. I through Trin. 7 Car. I, 1625–1631, and Pas. 9 Car. I, 1633. Edward Umfreville (d. 1786) mistakenly believed that these reports were made by Sir Thomas Widdrington. However, a comparison of these cases from Trinity term 3 Car. I, 1627, with those in British Library MS. Add. 35961 shows that these reports are not by Widdrington. There are two Exchequer cases here, *Attorney General v. Bacon* (1627) and *Whitmore v. Porter* (1627), which are the same reports as in British Library MS. Lansdowne 1092;[26] otherwise, the King's Bench reports in this latter manuscript are different.

British Library MS. Lansdowne 1092

Pas. 1 Car. I through Hil. 3 Car. I, 1625–1628. Edward Umfreville (d. 1786) mistakenly believed that these reports were made by Sir Thomas Widdrington. However, a comparison of these cases from Trinity term 3 Car. I, 1627, with those in British Library MS. Add. 35961 shows that these reports are not by Widdrington.

Harvard Law School MS. 1063, ff. 1–71v

Mich. 3 Car. I through Pas. 4 Car. I, 1627–1628. These King's Bench reports do not appear to be in print.

---

[25] J. Peile, *Biographical Register of Christ's College*, vol. 1 (1910), pp. 313–314; J. Foster, *Register of Admissions to Gray's Inn* (1889), p. 153; J. Venn and J. A. Venn, *Alumni Cantabrigienses*, part 1, vol. 4 (1927), p. 401; E. Foss, *Judges of England*, vol. 6 (1857), pp. 513–518; D. Scott, "Widdrington, Sir Thomas," *Oxford Dictionary of National Biography* (2004), vol. 58, pp. 820–22.

[26] They are also found in Yale Law School MSSG R29, no. 23, part 1, ff. 254, 266v, and in CUL MS. Ll.3.13, ff. 279, 295, and printed at *Robert Paynell's Exchequer Reports*, pp. 394, 368.

Harvard Law School MS. 1196, ff. 1–86

Trin. 2 Car. I through Trin. 16 Car. I, 1626–1640. These King's Bench reports do not appear to be in print.

Trinity College Dublin MS. 718, part 1

Mich. 22 Jac. I through Trin. 2 Car. I, 1624–1626.

Conclusion

At the beginning of the reign of Charles I, only the yearbooks and a few more recent law reports were in print. However, there was a vast corpus of reports of cases which circulated in manuscript amongst the legal community of England. Perhaps this paucity of printed reports was due to the attempted governmental control over the printing community of England, which was thought necessary in order to control and suppress sedition and heresy.[27] With the fall of the royal government in the 1640s and the restrictions on printing being removed, the production of printed books flourished, including the printing of law reports.[28]

Although the quantity of law publishing in the 1640s and later improved, the quality of editing and printing did not get better. In fact, the quality of law book production at this time was quite poor. We have seen that there was in many instances no connection between the actual person and the reports attributed to him. Godbolt, Latch, Noy, and Palmer were not the authors of the reports sometimes attributed to them, and the appendices of later cases added to the reports of Bendlowes and Popham could not possibly have been of their authorship.

However, the author of this present set of law reports is identifiable. Moreover, there are numerous cases reported here that are not elsewhere in print. Those cases that have been in print for several centuries are now clarified and enhanced by another version that is in English. And, therefore, Robert Paynell's King's Bench reports are now published here.

Editorial Principles and Practices

The headnotes, or syllabi, which are in italics at the beginning of each case, are the product of the present editor. The purpose of these headnotes is not to provide a complete legal analysis of the reports which they accompany, but, rather, they are intended to serve as an indication of the general subjects of the case.

---

[27] H. S. Bennett, *English Books and Readers 1603 to 1640* (1970), chap. III, "The Regulation of the Book Trade," pp. 40–58.

[28] W. H. Bryson, "Law Reports in England from 1603 to 1660," in C. Stebbings, ed., *Law Reporting in England* (1995), pp. 113–122.

Most of these cases have been reported in print elsewhere; therefore, when the case is presently generally known by another style than that used by Paynell, I have used that other style. This is primarily a matter of using a different form of a party's name. The reason for the variations is that the reporters were in court hearing the names being orally pronounced by the judges and the counsel.

Square brackets have been used to enclose matter added by the editor; such matter are words added where there has been a deterioration in the original manuscript or a blank left in a citation. Most frequently, however, they are words added to aid the flow of the text or to make an abbreviated note into a grammatical sentence. Ellipses set off by square brackets indicates that the editor could not decipher a word or several words in the manuscript but declined to speculate on what is missing. A question mark between square brackets warns the reader that the editor was unsure of the correctness of the preceding word.

Marginalia, endorsements, erasures, and cancellations have not been transcribed as a general rule. Those erasures that have been transcribed are enclosed within angle brackets.

Dates are all given in the Old Style, with the new year beginning on January 1; the New Style was not adopted in England until 1752.[29]

In making footnotes to the citations to authority in the cases transcribed, I have given parallel references to the *English Reports Reprint* since this is the edition that is most widely available today, but the statutory references are limited to the *Statutes of the Realm*. Where a case or a statute is referred to more than once in a particular case, only the first reference has been identified in a footnote.

---

[29] Stat. 24 Geo. II, c. 23, s. 1.

TABLE OF CASES REPORTED

[These references are to case numbers, not page numbers.]

Abrahall ads. Godfrey (1626)	56
Alden ads. Bellamy (1626)	53
Alden ads. Jacob (1627)	282
Allen ads. Marshall (1625)	7
Alston's Case (1627)	236
Anonymous (1625)	11
Anonymous (1626)	25, 36, 41, 43, 46, 50, 66, 74, 90, 92, 99, 114, 121, 123, 130, 132, 191, 201, 209, 212, 214, 220, 221
Anonymous (1627)	246, 247, 256, 263, 268, 272, 283
Anonymous ads. Boulsted (1626)	219
Anonymous v. Browning (1626)	107
Anonymous ads. Button (1626)	108
Anonymous ads. Cary (1626)	128
Anonymous v. Davis (1626)	207
Anonymous v. Lady Molineux (1625)	13
Anonymous ads. Piburne (1626)	173
Anonymous ads. Regis (1627)	230
Apsley v. Knowles (1626)	169
Arnold v. Dichton (1626)	145
Ashfield v. Ashfield (1626)	172
Askwith ads. Evans (1626)	101
Attorney General v. Inhabitants of Hunts. (1626)	179
Attorney General v. Lane (1626)	133
Atwood ads. Pierce (1625)	6
Audley v. Joy (1626)	80
Ayleworth v. Crompton (1627)	269
Bacon ads. Gouldsmith (1627)	254
Baker's Case (1626)	82
Baldock v. Cleyland (1626)	180
Balthorpe ads. Bellamy (1627)	234

Barchy ads. Regis (1626)   35
Barker v. Beckham (1626)   164
Barker v. Ringrose (1626)   146
Barman ads. Hudson (1626)   47
Barneloe v. Glarsedge (1626)   84
Barrell ads. Regis (1627)   273
Barry v. Styles (1626)   96
Batho v. Salter (1625)   1
Bayly v. Bugs (1626)   83
Beckham ads. Barker (1626)   164
Bell ads. Regis (1626)   105
Bellamy v. Alden (1626)   53
Bellamy v. Balthorpe (1627)   234
Bellow v. Griffin (1626)   32
Bengor ads. Edsol (1626)   138
Betts ads. Locking (1626)   213
Beverley ads. Regis (1626)   28
Bevin v. Coolmer (1626)   142
Bingley ads. Calfe (1626)   149
Binion ads. Evans (1626)   116
Bird v. Robinson (1626)   54
Blackaller ads. Hawkes (1626)   125
Blackston v. Martin (1625)   15
Blage v. Lamb (1626)   103
Boulsted v. Anonymous (1626)   219
Bowry v. Wallington (1625)   8
Bowyer v. Rivet (1626)   26
Bradbery ads. Regis (1626)   34
Brantingham ads. Payman (1627)   284
Bray ads. Randall (1626)   110
Brooker ads. Regis (1627)   264
Brown's Case (1626)   178
Brown v. Stroud (1626)   188
Browne v. Dixe (1626)   21
Browne ads. Shury (1626)   30
Browning ads. Anonymous (1626)   107
Buck ads. Ratcliff (1626)   158
Budden ads. Lisle (1626)   33
Bugs ads. Bayly (1626)   83
Busher v. Earl of Tullibardine (1626)   141
Button v. Anonymous (1626)   108

Cadiman v. Grendon (1627)   235

Calfe v. Bingley (1626)   149

Carleton v. Hutton (1626)   51

Carlisle, Dean of ads. Dunn (1627)   266

Carter ads. Lowly (1626)   211

Cary v. Anonymous (1626)   128

Chapman v. Chapman (1626)   161

Charles v. Jenkins (1626)   120

Chelely's Case (1626)   97

Clapham v. Middleton (1627)   232

Clare ads. Delavall (1626)   111

Clarke v. Login (1625)   14

Clarke ads. Saul (1626)   118

Clempson v. Poule (1626)   124

Cleyland ads. Baldock (1626)   180

Clobury ads. Constable (1626)   58

Cobb ads. Kinly (1626)   184

Cobb ads. Markham (1626)   102

Codner ads. Henderson (1626)   157

Coles v. Shury (1626)   68

Collier v. Ludkins (1625)   2

Constable v. Clobury (1626)   58

Coolmer ads. Bevin (1626)   142

Cornwallis v. Hamond (1625)   12

Covert v. Wilcocks (1626)   79

Crab v. Tooker (1626)   205

Cranshaw ads. Smith (1626)   20

Cremer ads. Stileman (1626)   112, 113

Cremer v. Tookley (1627)   262

Crompton ads. Ayleworth (1627)   269

Dale ads. Secheverell (1626)   177

Daniel v. Upley (1626)   52

Davis ads. Anonymous (1626)   207

Davy ads. Regis (1626)   95

Dawberne v. Martin (1626)   81

Dean v. Steel (1627)   244

Delavall v. Clare (1626)   111

Dichton ads. Arnold (1626)   145

Dickenson v. Greenehaw (1626)   27

Dixe ads. Browne (1626)   21

Dixon ads. Mason (1627)   228

Dole ads. Mulleyn (1627) 279
Dow ads. Hall (1626) 156
Dowse v. Shelly (1626) 208
Drope v. Thaire (1626) 87
Dunn v. Dean of Carlisle (1627) 266
Edsol v. Bengor (1626) 138
Elworthy ads. Reynell (1626) 67
Errington ads. Harrison (1626) 196
Evans v. Askwith (1626) 101
Evans v. Binion (1626) 116
Evers v. Owen (1627) 253
Ewer ads. Griffin (1626) 117
Ewins v. Pound (1626) 183
Faudry ads. Millen (1626) 59
Featherston ads. Regis (1626) 222
Felton v. Weaver (1626) 127
Fish v. Wiseman (1627) 252
Foster v. Taylor (1626) 210
Fox ads. Gray (1626) 61
Frampton v. Haughton (1626) 45
Fulcher ads. Hayward (1626) 73
Galthorp v. Reynell (1626) 136
Gerard ads. Hall (1625) 5
Glarsedge ads. Barneloe (1626) 84
Godfrey v. Abrahall (1626) 56
Good v. Laurence (1627) 231
Goodwin v. Willoughby (1626) 76
Gouldsmith v. Bacon (1627) 254
Gransgrove Churchwardens ads. Wilks (1626) 182
Gray v. Fox (1626) 61
Green v. Moody (1627) 259
Greene v. Iwyn (1626) 171
Greenehaw ads. Dickenson (1626) 27
Gregory ads. Regis (1627) 243
Grendon ads. Codiman (1627) 235
Griffin ads. Bellow (1626) 32
Griffin v. Ewer (1626) 117
Grise ads. Lyon (1626) 122
Gunter v. Gunter (1627) 285
Hall v. Dow (1626) 156
Hall v. Gerard (1625) 5

Hall v. Huggen (1625)   18
Hallet v. Keymor (1626)   153
Hamond ads. Cornwallis (1625)   12
Hamond v. Slade (1627)   281
Hamond v. White (1626)   139
Harding ads. Warner (1625)   3
Harris's Case (1627)   270
Harrison v. Errington (1626)   196
Harvey ads. Marget (1627)   275
Harvey v. Reynell (1626)   170
Harvey ads. Rose (1626)   176
Haughton ads. Frampton (1626)   45
Haviland ads. Hungerford (1626)   98
Hawkes v. Blackaller (1626)   125
Hayly ads. Sparkes (1627)   240
Hayward v. Fulcher (1626)   73
Henderson v. Codner (1626)   157
Herne v. Stuble (1627)   258
Hoarde v. More (1626)   126
Hobson ads. Petty (1626)   143
Hodgekin ads. Taylor (1627)   286
Hodges v. Moore (1626)   65
Holland ads. Luther (1626)   93
Hollet v. Parker (1626)   134
Holmes v. Winegreen (1627)   248
Hudson v. Barman (1626)   47
Huggen ads. Hall (1625)   18
Hungerford v. Haviland (1626)   98
Huntingdonshire Inhabitants ads. Attorney General (1626)   179
Hutton ads. Carleton (1626)   51
Iwyn ads. Greene (1626)   171
Jackson ads. Spademan (1627)   242
Jacob v. Alden (1627)   282
Jegon v. Purkas (1626)   162
Jenkins ads. Charles (1626)   120
Jenkins v. Vivian (1626)   194
Jermin v. Randall (1626)   78
Jerome v. Stiffe (1625)   16
Jobson's Case (1626)   147
Johnson's Case (1626)   38
Jones ads. Regis (1626)   57

Joy ads. Audley (1626) — 80
Keckhall ads. Rochester (1626) — 198
Kedgewin ads. Ward (1625) — 4
Kelley v. Reynell (1626) — 63
Keymor v. Hallet (1626) — 153
King v. Merrick (1627) — 233
Kinly v. Cobb (1626) — 184
Knowles ads. Apsley (1626) — 169
Lamb ads. Blage (1626) — 103
Lamb ads. Regis (1626) — 160
Lane ads. Attorney General (1626) — 133
Laurence ads. Good (1627) — 231
Laycock v. Wiltshire (1627) — 237
Leith ads. Wingfield (1626) — 159
Lewis v. Whitney (1626) — 155
Lichfield v. Melhurst (1627) — 277
Lindley's Case (1627) — 239
Lisle v. Budden (1626) — 33
Litherland ads. Palmer (1626) — 166
Locking v. Betts (1626) — 213
Login ads. Clarke (1625) — 14
Lowly v. Carter (1626) — 211
Lucas v. Warren (1626) — 86
Ludkins ads. Collier (1625) — 2
Luther v. Holland (1626) — 93
Lyon v. Grise (1626) — 122
Maidstone, Town of ads. Regis (1626) — 131
Man ads. Regis (1627) — 276
Man ads. Smith (1626) — 223
Marget v. Harvey (1627) — 275
Mariton ads. Saunders (1626) — 190
Markham v. Cobb (1626) — 102
Marsh ads. Newman (1626) — 60
Marshall v. Allen (1625) — 7
Martin's Case (1626) — 42
Martin ads. Blackston (1625) — 15
Martin ads. Dawberne (1626) — 81
Mason v. Dixon (1627) — 228
Matchet ads. Regis (1626) — 62
Melhurst ads. Lichfield (1627) — 277
Mellhuishe v. Newcot (1626) — 216

Merrick ads. King (1627)	233
Methold v. Peck (1626)	24
Middleton ads. Clapham (1627)	232
Millen v. Faudry (1626)	59
Mitchell ads. Ramsey (1626)	55
Molineux, Lady ads. Anonymous (1625)	13
Moody ads. Green (1627)	259
Moore ads. Hodges (1626)	65
Moore ads. Morgan (1626)	119
More ads. Hoarde (1626)	126
Morgan v. Moore (1626)	119
Mountford v. Sydley (1626)	37
Mulleyn v. Dole (1627)	279
Mulsor v. Note (1626)	77
Newcot ads. Mellhuishe (1626)	216
Newman v. Marsh (1626)	60
Newsam ads. Parker (1626)	181
Note (1625)	17, 19
Note (1626)	22, 23, 48, 85
Note (1627)	250
Note ads. Mulsor (1626)	77
Noy ads. Powell (1626)	148
Orford, Parson of, Case of (1626)	200
Owen ads. Evers (1627)	253
Oxford, Mayor of ads. Regis (1627)	270
Palmer v. Litherland (1626)	166
Parker ads. Hollet (1626)	134
Parker v. Newsam (1626)	181
Payman v. Brantingham (1627)	284
Peck ads. Methold (1626)	24
Petty v. Hobson (1626)	143
Petty v. Robinson (1626)	197
Piburne v. Anonymous (1626)	173
Pierce v. Atwood (1625)	6
Pigot ads. Shury (1626)	69
Pincent v. Sheiris (1626)	199
Plowden ads. Regis (1626)	215
Plunket ads. Powell (1625)	10
Poule ads. Clempson (1626)	124
Pound ads. Ewins (1626)	183
Powell v. Noy (1626)	148

Powell v. Plunket (1625)   10
Purkas ads. Jegon (1626)   162
Ramsey v. Mitchell (1626)   55
Randall v. Bray (1626)   110
Randall ads. Jermin (1626)   78
Ratcliffe v. Buck (1626)   158
Redfern v. Umphry (1627)   251
Rex v. Anonymous (1627)   230
Rex v. Barchy (1626)   35
Rex v. Barrell (1627)   273
Rex v. Bell (1626)   105
Rex v. Beverley (1626)   28
Rex v. Bradbery (1626)   34
Rex v. Brooker (1627)   264
Rex v. Davy (1626)   95
Rex v. Featherston (1626)   222
Rex v. Gregory (1627)   243
Rex v. Jones (1626)   57
Rex v. Lamb (1626)   160
Rex v. Maidstone, Town of (1626)   131
Rex v. Man (1627)   276
Rex v. Matchet (1626)   62
Rex v. Oxford, Mayor of (1627)   270
Rex v. Plowden (1626)   215
Rex v. Savile (1626)   129
Rex v. Taylor (1626)   40
Rex v. Wheelehouse (1626)   137
Reynell v. Elworthy (1626)   67
Reynell ads. Galthorp (1626)   136
Reynell ads. Harvey (1626)   170
Reynell ads. Kelley (1626)   63
Richards ads. Tindall (1627)   241
Rideout's Case (1626)   144
Ringrose ads. Barker (1626)   146
Rivet ads. Bowyer (1626)   26
Robinson ads. Bird (1626)   54
Robinson ads. Petty (1626)   197
Rochester v. Keckhall (1626)   198
Rolt ads. Sharp (1626)   140
Rose v. Harvey (1626)   176
Sacheverell v. Dale (1626)   177

Salter ads. Batho (1625) 1
Saul v. Clarke (1626) 118
Saunders v. Meriton (1626) 190
Savile ads. Regis (1626) 129
Sharp v. Rolt (1626) 140
Sheiris ads. Pincent (1626) 199
Shelly ads. Dowse (1626) 208
Shury v. Browne (1626) 30
Shury ads. Coles (1626) 68
Shury v. Pigot (1626) 69
Sikes ads. Stokes (1627) 255
Slade ads. Hamond (1627) 281
Smith v. Cranshaw (1626) 20
Smith v. Man (1626) 223
Spademan v. Jackson (1627) 242
Sparkes v. Hayly (1627) 240
Steel ads. Dean (1627) 244
Stiffe ads. Jerome (1625) 16
Stileman v. Cremer (1626) 112, 113
Stokes v. Sikes (1627) 255
Stokley ads. Wood (1626) 204
Stroud v. Brown (1626) 188
Stuble ads. Herne (1627) 258
Styles ads. Barry (1626) 96
Sutton's Case (1627) 267
Sydley ads. Mountford (1626) 37
Taylor ads. Foster (1626) 210
Taylor v. Hodgekin (1627) 286
Taylor ads. Regis (1626) 40
Taylor v. Tolwin (1627) 261
Thaire ads. Drope (1626) 87
Thursby v. Warne (1626) 202
Tindall v. Richards (1627) 241
Tolwin ads. Taylor (1627) 261
Tooker ads. Crab (1626) 205
Tookley ads. Cremer (1627) 262
Tullibardine, Earl of ads. Busher (1626) 141
Umphry ads. Redfern (1627) 251
Upley ads. Daniel (1626) 52
Vessy ads. Walden (1626) 72
Vigors v. Wood (1626) 154

Vivian ads. Jenkins (1626)   194
Walden v. Vessy (1626)   72
Wallington ads. Bowry (1625)   8
Ward v. Kedgewin (1625)   4
Warner v. Harding (1625)   3
Warren ads. Lucas (1626)   86
Watkins's Case (1626)   49
Weaver ads. Felton (1626)   127
Weston ads. Whitton (1626)   29
Wheelehouse ads. Regis (1626)   137
White ads. Hamond (1626)   139
Whitney ads. Lewis (1626)   155
Whitton v. Weston (1626)   29
Wilcocks ads. Covert (1626)   79
Wilks v. Gransgrove Churchwardens (1626)   182
Willoughby ads. Goodwin (1626)   76
Wiltshire ads. Laycock (1627)   237
Winegreen ads. Holmes (1627)   248
Wingfield v. Leith (1626)   159
Wiseman ads. Fish (1627)   252
Witherick ads. Wood (1627)   238
Wood v. Stokley (1626)   204
Wood ads. Vigors (1626)   154
Wood v. Witherick (1627)   238

1

Batho v. Salter

(K.B. Pas. 1 Car. I, 1625)

A contract with a sheriff to perform his official duty is void and unenforceable.

BL MS. Add. 35961, f. 2, pl. 1

Between Batho, plaintiff, and Salter, defendant, in an action upon the case, the case was thus. Salter, the defendant recovered in [an action of] debt against one and had a *capias ad satisfaciendum*. The sheriff returned *non est inventus*. And afterwards, he was outlawed, and the plaintiff, upon a *capias utlagatum* which being thus sued, he promised to the plaintiff that, if he would be a special bailiff to the sheriff and arrest the defendant in debt, that he would give to him 40s. And for the non-performance, he brought this action upon the case. And by the count, the matter above appeared. And in Michaelmas [term] 22 Jac. [1624], it was argued by the counsel of the plaintiff.

And Justice DODDERIDGE [held] that the action is maintainable because it is not within the letter of the Statute of 23 Hen. VIII, ca. 10,[1] because this speaks only of money of someone in custody[2] or that he will be in custody. But here, the person of whom it was taken was the plaintiff and he is not within the equity of it because, here, it is entirely another thing that it is against than is provided by the Statute. And it is not against the common law because it is in advancement of justice because, at this day, if one does not give more than the common fees, it will be hard to come to the execution, which is the end of the law and the fruit of the suit. But they granted, if it was the sheriff himself, as was adjudged in Audlie's case, 7 Jac. in the [court of] common bench, that if he contracted with him, it was void because he, by virtue of his office, is bound to do this. And a contract with one to do this by his office is void, and also, he is the minister appointed to it and the people are constrained to go to him. And on account of this, if he contracts with him to give to him for his office, it will make it void. It breeds extortion and opens a gap to this grievance.

---

[1] Stat. 23 Hen. VI, c. 10 (*SR*, II, 336–337).

[2] en gard *MS*.

And thus, it is if a contract with another officer of the sheriff, *viz.* a bonded bailiff.[1] And among the *capitula itineris* in Fleta,[2] it is one of the articles inquirable *de vicecomitibus et aliis ministris regis capientibus munera vel mercedem pro officiis suis exequendus.*[3]

And also, it is ordained by the Statute of Westminster I[4] that no minister of the king will take rewards for doing his office. But he said that, here, Batho was not an officer of the king at the time of the promise, nor was he bound by his office to make the arrest, but himself worked and took labor upon this promise, which he was not bound to do. And thus, this is the reason that he will be satisfied for his efforts and hazard.

And this contract is not against the law. And it is not similar to the cases of 2 Hen. IV, 9, and Dyer 224, Wise[ham], Dyer 355, Onlye's case,[5] because, there, the condition was against the law, but here [it is] for the advancement of justice.

But yet, DODDERIDGE said that this is a means to open a gap to extortion to the sheriffs. And on account of this, he did not deliver his opinion peremptorily.

And it was argued by the other party.

And now this term, [it was] resolved and adjudged by the court, *viz.* Chief Justice CREWE, DODDERIDGE, JONES, and WHITELOCKE, justices, that the plaintiff will be barred because they resolved (and thus it had been resolved before in Sherley and Packer's case, 13 Jac.[6]) that if one makes a contract with the sheriffs or their ministers and promises to them money beyond the fees to make an execution or other part of his office, that this promise is void because it is against the common law and the statute law that they will perform[7] this, as appears before. And also, it is expressly provided against this by 29 Eliz., ca. 4.[8] Also, they resolved that, even though, here, at the time of the promise, Batho was not a minister of the king nor to the sheriff, yet after he was made a bailiff to the sheriff and by force of this had made this arrest and then he could not take anything for the performance of that his office which, then, he was bound to do even though the contract was before. And if it will be admitted that the promise is good and that a special bailiff will take to make execution, it is as great an inconvenience as if the sheriff himself or a bonded bailiff can take it. And also a great gap opens to extortion as if the sheriff or his bonded officer could immediately take such hire

[1] bayly conus *MS.*

[2] *Fleta*, c. 20 (H. G. Richardson & G. O. Sayles, edd., 1955), 72 Selden Soc. 51.

[3] of sheriffs and other ministers of the king taking rewards or fees for executing their offices.

[4] Stat. 3 Edw. I, c. 26 (*SR*, I, 33).

[5] YB Mich. 2 Hen. IV, f. 9, pl. 44 (1401); *Ligeart v. Wiseham* (1573), 3 Dyer 323, 324, 73 E.R. 732; *Onely v. Earl of Kent* (1577), 3 Dyer 355, 73 E.R. 797.

[6] *Sherley v. Packer* (1616), 1 Rolle Rep. 313, 81 E.R. 509.

[7] preveignora *MS.*

[8] Stat. 29 Eliz. I, c. 4 (*SR*, IV, 769).

and pay. But yet he agreed that, if one promise to another in consideration that he will procure the execution to be duly made and this [. . .] at his own costs and his trouble and he is not nor ever becomes an officer to the sheriff, that this is good, and an action [is] maintainable upon it.

And DODDERIDGE said, if one promise one that, if he will be aiding to the sheriff to make an arrest, that he will give to him 20s., this is good.

But CREWE doubted because he should not intrude himself without being called by the sheriff and, when he is called, it is his office to aid him.

And thus judgment was given against Batho. See Michaelmas [term] 22 Jac., common bench, 5.

[Other reports of this case: Benloe 138, 147, 73 E.R. 1009, 1015, CUL MS. Gg.2.30, ff. 42v, 47v; W. Jones 65, 82 E.R. 34, BL MS. Hargr. 317, f. 89; Latch 54, 82 E.R. 271, HLS MS. 1235, f. 2v; Noy 76, 74 E.R. 1043; BL MS. Hargr. 38, f. 3; BL MS. Lansd. 1092, f. 5v; CUL MS. Hh.2.1, f. 181; CUL MS. Ll.3.13, f. 6; HLS MS. 1197, f. 2v; Trinity College Dublin MS. 718, part 1.]

2

Collier v. Ludkins

(K.B. Pas. 1 Car. I, 1625)

In this case, the words spoken of the plaintiff were defamatory.

BL MS. Add. 35961, f. 2, pl. 2

Collier brought an action upon the case for scandalous words against Ludkins. And he alleged that, where he was a minister and preacher and [was] always of good and honest fame, that the defendant, endeavoring to defame him, both maliciously and falsely, *haec Anglicana verba propalavit* 'Collier is a base fellow and is full of the pox and keeps one Mrs. Sugar and got them of her or she of him, And, if I be questioned for these words, it will cost me but a journey to Mr. Catline in Suffolk, chaplin to my Lady Gawdy, who will justify my words and asked me if Collier did not look pale and marvelled that he was yet alive and that he did not spoil his wife.' And upon [a plea of] *non culpabilis*, it was found for the plaintiff.

And it was moved in arrest of judgment that these words be not actionable because they could have another intent without scandal because he could have the smallpox and he could [have] contracted it from another or infected another with them and the keeping of a woman could be meant a legal and honest keeping of her, and thus they could have a good construction, not scandalous.

And of the other part, it was said and argued by the court, DODDERIDGE, JONES, and WHITELOCKE, that the words cannot be intended of other than of the French pox because he said that he marvelled that he lived, where the smallpox was not such a lingering disease but that it speedily and in a short time ends or kills the party infected with them. And also, it is the nature of the French pox to take away the color. And thus, it was not the smallpox. Also, by the words that he marvelled that it did not spoil his wife, it appears sufficiently what he intended by the words. And they said that as words coming after could make scandalous words not scandalous, as if one [is] called a thief because he had robbed his orchard, or, in speaking of hunting, said that one is a murderer because he had killed so many hares, here, the subsequent words show that he did not intend[1] felonious theft or murder. Thus, subsequent words can show the intent of the words themselves not scandalous is to make them scandalous.

And for this, the counsel cited a case, Hil. 8 Jac., rot. 491, Holland's case,[2] where the defendant said of the plaintiff that he had taken [?] his purse by the wayside and that he deserved to be hanged for it. And even though, here, the first words were not of themselves scandalous because he could take his purse and yet [it be] no felony, yet inasmuch as, by the last words that he deserved to he hanged for it, his intent appears that he intended a felonious taking and no other taking could be intended upon all of the words; it was adjudged maintainable.

And DODDERIDGE [held] that, if one said that such [a one] had the pox and that they have eaten his wife, that these words are actionable because the latter words make the former, which could not be otherwise intended, but of the French pox.

And JONES said that it has been adjudged that, for saying that A. 'has the pox and has been in Cornelius' tub for them', that an action was maintained because this was the common remedy then that the said Cornelius cured this disease with.

And they said that, if one speaks words of one that, in the place where they are spoken, carry a scandalous sense even though, here, they do not have the same meaning, they are actionable. And on account of this, they said that it has been adjudged that, if one *circa* Durham and those north parts say of one that he is 'mansworn', that an action lies because, there, this bears the force of perjury. And Trin. 38 Eliz. in the common bench;[3] one said that such a one did strain a mare, and because, in the place where this [was] spoken, the common taking of it was that he buggered a mare, it was adjudged actionable.

And JONES said that, here, even though he spoke of the relation of another and that such a one said thus to him, yet, whether Catline did not relate it to him, they will be taken [to be] his own words. And he cited Dame Morrison's case, 4 Jac.,[4] where one said that the blackamore told him that he had the use of the lady's body and the blackamore did not say the words. And it was adjudged even

---

[1] extend *MS*.

[2] *Stowe v. Holland* (1611), 1 Bulstrode 112, 80 E.R. 808, *rev'd sub nom. Holland v. Stoner* (1612), Cro. Jac. 315, 79 E.R. 270.

[3] *Coles v. Haveland* (1591), Cro. Eliz. 250, 78 E.R. 505.

[4] *Morison v. Cade* (1607), Cro. Jac. 162, 79 E.R. 142.

though he did not speak it directly but by way of a relation of another, yet inasmuch as the other did not say it, the action was maintainable for those words.

And JONES said that though it is not actionable for reports that one said such words of one where, in fact, they said them, yet it is a matter for the [court of] star chamber because, there, one will be punished for relating what such a one told him.

And DODDERIDGE asked what is the true definition of a scandal.

And WHITELOCKE answered that, for slander, it is *in malam famam ponere*.

And DODDERIDGE added *et probare occasionem ruinae*.

And a further day was given to advise of the matter.

[Other reports of this case: BL MS. Hargr. 38, f. 24.]

3

Warner v. Harding

(Part 1)
(K.B. Pas. 1 Car. I, 1625)

The question in this case was whether the exercise of the power in issue was so personal to the original holder that it could not have been exercised by an assignee or attorney.

BL MS. Add. 35961, f. 2v, pl. 3

Between Warner and Harding in [an action of] *ejectione firmae* which began in Hilary [term] 19 Jac., rot. 1353, upon *non culpabilis* pleaded, it was found by a special verdict that William Shelley was seised of the manor of B., of which the land in question is a part, and, so seised, 16 January 23 Eliz. [1581] by an indenture between him and Hungerford and others, agreed to convey it to covenantees to the use of himself and the heirs male of his body, the remainder to his brother and the heirs male of his body, with a proviso that, if William Shelley give, deliver, or offer to the covenantees or to their heirs a ring of gold or a pair of gloves of the price of 12d. or 12d. in money, the said William Shelley then declaring that the intent of the gift is to frustrate and [. . .] the uses, that then the uses will be void. William Shelley levied a fine accordingly. And afterwards, he was attainted of treason, and it was enacted that he will forfeit all of his lands, tenements, rights, conditions, and hereditaments, saving to all others that William Shelley and his heirs all rights etc.[1] William Shelley died without issue. J. Shelley, his brother, in remainder, two years afterwards according to the Statute entitled to avoid fraudulent conveyances by traitors,[2] brought into the exchequer the deed by which the remainder was limited to him, which was enrolled there. The queen

---

[1] Stat. 29 Eliz. I, c. 1 (*SR*, IV, 766–767).
[2] Stat. 29 Eliz. I, c. 3 (*SR*, IV, 767–768).

authorized Sir John Fortescue to tender the ring at the door of Hungerford and to declare the intent that it was this. And Hungerford accepted it. Sir John returned the commission and that he had done accordingly. J. Shelley, brother of William Shelley, had issue, J. Shelley, who was found to be a person not excepted by the Statute. The queen demised the manor to Hardwyn[1] in tail, the remainder over. [In] 6 Jac. [1608 x 1609], Sir John Shelley exhibited his *monstrans de droit* and had a judgment, and he entered and bargained and sold to Warner, who leased to George Warner, the plaintiff. And whether this condition, as the case here is, was given to the queen by the Statute of 33 Hen. VIII[2] or by the private statute was the sole question.

And it was argued in the time of the late King James and also this term by *Bridgman* that the condition was not given to the queen. And his reason was because it was so inseparably annexed to the person of William Shelley that no other could perform it and that things thus in privity cannot be given by general words. He cited the case of 3 Edw. III,[3] where [by] the Act that gave all the possessions of the Templars to the Hospitalers[4] [it was held] that impropriate advowsons did not pass; and 35 Hen. VI, 56,[5] that a tenure in frankalmoigne will not pass to them by the same words; and 33 Hen. VI, 55,[6] a father who had the wardship of his heir apparent will not forfeit it by outlawry; and other cases which all will find, Coke 7, 11, in Englefield's case.[7] And he said that, here, the condition was inseparably annexed to the person of William Shelley because in the condition it is considerable.

(1) The reason of the declaration of the intent that the uses will be void; and this was made for cause; a ring or such a gift could easily pass between such friends, as the covenantor and the covenantee were, and on account of this, he limits that, upon the gift of a ring, the estate will not be void without declaring that his intent was thus.

(2) The time; because the declaration must be at the same time as the delivery, similarly to the case of 27 Hen. VI, 8,[8] upon Westminster II, ca. 11;[9] the commission of the auditors in an account [. . .] found in arrears must be maintained.

---

[1] I.e. Harding.

[2] Stat. 33 Hen. VIII, c. 20, s. 4 (*SR*, III, 857).

[3] *Rex v. Prior of the Hospital of St. John* (1335), YB Trin. 9 Edw. III, f. 25, pl. 24.

[4] Stat. 17 Edw. II, stat. 2 (*SR*, I, 194–196).

[5] YB Pas. 35 Hen. VI, f. 56, pl. 2 (1457).

[6] YB Mich. 33 Hen. VI, f. 55, pl. 49 (1454).

[7] *Regina v. Englefield* (1591), 7 Coke Rep. 11, 77 E.R. 428, also Moore K.B. 303, 72 E.R. 595, 4 Leonard 135, 169, 74 E.R. 779, 800, Popham 18, 79 E.R. 1139, 1 Anderson 293, 123 E.R. 480.

[8] YB Hil. 27 Hen. VI, f. 8, pl. 7 (1449).

[9] Stat. 13 Edw. I, c. 11 (*SR*, I, 80–81).

(3) The person; and this is William Shelley and no other because, where a person is limited by Parliament or by the act of the parties, their authority is not transferrable over. 14 Edw. IV, 1;[1] it was enacted that the chancellor, calling to himself the justices, will award a subpoena; and, there, the chancellor alone cannot do it. Coke 5, Garnon's case;[2] arbitrators cannot assign their authority over; it is inseparable from them.

(4) The matter of the declaration; and this is the intent of William Shelley, that no one can do, being a secret thing, but himself, which all four things show the intent was that William Shelley only will make the tender.

And for a case in point, he cited the duke of Norfolk's case,[3] cited in Englefield's case. And he said that Englefield's case was doubted and confirmed by Parliament for fear of a writ of error. And he showed the record exemplified where this same question between the same parties was [in] 14 Jac. [1616 x 1617] in the common bench adjudged, as he argued, upon the same reason as he said.

And on the other part, it was argued by *Yelverton*, now justice of the common bench, and this term by Serjeant *Hetley* that the condition was given to the queen. And *Hetley* held without question that though the performance will be admitted not given to the queen, yet the benefit of the performance is given. And on account of this, if, here, after the attainder, William Shelley had tendered the ring in the manner above, the queen would [have] had the advantage.

And as to that which was said that, if the condition was given, yet the queen cannot make the declaration, he argued that this is incident to the delivery of the ring; as attorney to make livery, he can declare for what the livery was made. Thus, the law gives the performance to the second feoffee where the condition is that the feoffee will pay money, and, as incident to this, there, the law allows him to declare the intent of the tender of the money. Also, this condition could have been performed by an attorney [in fact]; therefore, [it is] not so inseparable as it has been urged.

And the last reason, and it is upon which the count most relies was because, there, the law employs this declaration and, being no more than the law intends, it is as if it had not been express because *expressio eorum tacite etc.* And upon this clause, it has been outside. Thus, without question, the queen could have performed the condition.

And DODDERIDGE said the other cases do not go to the point of the case because it is said the prime question [is] whether, there, the law has not implied the condition without [its] being express. And he put this case, if a tenant for life is ousted by the lessor who makes a feoffment and the tenant commands his servant to enter, who does it, it is an attornment, thus the attorney [acts] by attorney.

---

[1] YB Mich. 14 Edw. IV, f. 1, pl. 1 (1474).

[2] *Layton v. Garnon* (1598), 5 Coke Rep. 88, 77 E.R. 188, also Moore K.B. 566, 72 E.R. 762, Cro. Eliz. 706, 78 E.R. 941.

[3] *Duke of Norfolk's Case*, 7 Coke Rep. 13, 77 E.R. 43.

And JONES put the case of Burrowes, Coke 4,[1] and also a case adjudged, as he said, in the exchequer, of the Abbot of Strata Mercella's case,[2] of tithes rendering rent upon condition that, if it was demanded and not paid, that the lease will be void, the abbey was dissolved and came to the king, and whether the king must demand was the question, and it was adjudged not, and the reason was because the demand was incident to the condition and not more than the law implies and therefore not of more force than if it had been left out, in which case the king will not demand.

And they adjourned in the principal case. See more [*blank*] afterwards.[3]

4

Ward v. Kedgewin

(Part 1)
(K.B. Pas. 1 Car. I, 1625)

In an action of debt, the plaintiff can allege a fictitious place of contracting in order to have a proper venue.

In an action for payment of foreign money, the plaintiff can allege either that the defendant owes and detains or that he detains so much.

BL MS. Add. 35961, f. 3v, pl. 4

John Ward brought a bill of debt against Sir William Kedgewin, as appears in Hil. 22 Jac., rot. 1094, *de placito debito quod reddat £97 12s. 4d. currantem monetam Hamburgense ad valentiam £72 10s. legalis monetae Anglicanae quas ei injuste detinet pro eo quod dictus Williamus 25 Novembris 1615 apud Londinum, viz. in parochia St. Mary de Arcubus in Warda de Cheape Londino*[4] by his bill obligatory acknowledged *se debere dicto Johanni praedicti £97 et solvend.* [. . .] had paid accordingly *ad damnum ipsius Johannis* £20 etc. And Kedgwin demanded oyer of the obligation *in haec verba*. 'Be it known etc. dated at Hamburg'. And upon this, he demurred in law. And two exceptions were taken:

(1) that the bond is dated at Hamburg; and he alleged it to be made in London where it will not be received to vary the place of the date where the

---

[1] *Boroughes v. Taylor* (1596), 4 Coke Rep. 72, 76 E.R. 1043, also Moore K.B. 404, 72 E.R. 657, Gouldsborough 124, 75 E.R. 1039, Cro. Eliz. 462, 78 E.R. 715.

[2] *Regina v. Vaughan* (1591), 9 Coke Rep. 24, 77 E.R. 765, Moore K.B. 297, 72 E.R. 591.

[3] For further proceedings in this case, see below, Nos. 44, 100.

[4] of a plea [in an action of] debt that he render £97 12s. 4d. current money of Hamburg at the value of £72 10s. legal English money which he unjustly detains for this that the said William on the 25th of November 1615 at London, to wit in the parish of St. Mary le Bow in the ward of Cheap in London.

obligation or deed had some date. And this is by the Statute of 6 Ric. II, ca. 2. See Perkins 25; q. pet. Brooks 366; 21 Edw. IV, 26, 74; Coke 6, 47; 31 Hen. VI, Feoffments, 104.[1]

[2.] The second exception was because the action is in the *detinet tantum* where it should have been in the *debet et detinet*, being for money. See F.N.B. 119 h, 120 m,[2] where a difference appears between money and all other chattels because, for money, it must be in the *debet et detinet*, but, if for other chattels, in the *detinet* only.

But for the other part, it was answered, and agreed by the court, as to the first, that he could lay it here in London because there could be such a place as Hamburg, London, in the Ward of Cheap, and the common experience now allows this. And, as to the second, they held that it is good enough be it in the *debet et detinet* or in the *detinet tantum*. In the *detinet tantum* is good because it is not English money nor current here, but of the same nature as plate and bullion, in which case, it is like other chattels. And this is the reason that, in such a case, one will allege ad valentiam, where, if it was money, one will not put the value because of itself it carries the value put upon it and it is *mensura omnium nec de alia re aliqua mensurabilis*,[3] as is 46 Edw. III, 16.[4] And also, in the *debet et detinet* is good also. And this is warranted by many precedents.

And DODDERIDGE cited a notable case to this purpose, 10 Edw. III,[5] in account against a receiver, and he alleged the receipt of so many chrusadoes, a foreign[6] coin, and an exception was taken that it must be named bullion because [it was] not money, and, there, it was resolved that the one and the other are good enough.

And a day was given to show better matter in the principal case. Residuum, placito 9.[7]

---

[1] Stat. 6 Ric. II, stat. 1, c. 2 (*SR*, II, 27); J. Perkins, *A Profitable Book*, sects. 120–122; YB Pas. 21 Edw. IV, f. 26, pl. 19 (1481); YB Hil. 21 Edw. IV, f. 74, pl. 1 (1482); *Richardson v. Dowdale* (1605), 6 Coke Rep. 46, 77 E.R. 323, also Cro. Jac. 55, 79 E.R. 47; Mich. 31 Hen. VI, Fitzherbert, Abr., *Feffements & faits*, pl. 104 (1452).

[2] A. Fitzherbert, *Nouvelle Natura Brevium*.

[3] the amount of all nor of another thing otherwise measurable.

[4] YB Trin. 46 Edw. III, f. 16, pl. 8 (1372).

[5] YB Mich. 6 Edw. III, f. 40, pl. 17 (1366), Fitzherbert, Abr., *Accompt*, pl. 103 (100 florins).

[6] outlandish *MS*.

[7] For further proceedings in this case, see below, No. 9.

5

Hall v. Gerard

(Part 1)
(K.B. Pas. 1 Car. I, 1625)

In this case, the defendant's excuse of self-defense did not prevail against the plaintiff's claim of assault and battery.

BL MS. 35961, f. 3v, pl. 5

Trin. 22 Jac., rot. 1170. Hall brought an action of trespass for assault and battery against Gerard and others. And he alleged a battery in London. The defendant justified because he was possessed of a term *adhuc* running and, so possessed, the plaintiff came upon the land in Camberwell in Kent and the defendant *moliter* put his hands from him to remove him upon which the plaintiff made an assault upon the defendant and the defendant in defense of himself and his possession beat and wounded him and the damage that he had [was] from his own assault, which battery is the same battery, without that that he is guilty at London.

The plaintiff replied *de injuria sua propria* without such cause. And it was moved [by] the plaintiff that this traverse is not well taken because the place is not material, being a personal tort. See 21 Edw. IV, 53; 10 Hen. VII, 27a, the case of waif; 9 Hen. VI, 62b, by Babington.[1]

And it was answered that the justification consists upon the title to the land, which is local, and on account of this, [it is] good. He agreed that, where the trespass is merely personal, the place is not material.

It was moved also for the defendant that the traverse of the plaintiff and his replication was bad (1) because a traverse upon a traverse is not good, 19 Edw. IV, 9; (2) because of his [own] tort is not a [good] plea where the justification consists in the realty, as here it is, *viz.* the maintenance of the title of the term, see Coke, 8, 67,[2] and where it is objected that, here, it is not in the realty and for this, it is not similar to the express case, 2 Hen. VII, 4, and 44 Edw. III, 18, of a ward,[3] proves this; in [an action of] trespass, the defendant justified because the plaintiff was his ward because the ancestor of the defendant held in chivalry; the plaintiff replied *de son tort demesne* without such a cause, and [it was] not good, but he should have traversed the special matter, *viz.* that he did not hold of the

---

[1] YB Mich. 21 Edw. IV, f. 53, pl. 17 (1481); YB Trin. 10 Hen. VII, f. 27, pl. 9 (1495); *Chaworth's Case* (1431), YB Hil. 9 Hen. VI, f. 62, pl. 16.
[2] *Crogate v. Marys* (1608), 8 Coke Rep. 66, 77 E.R. 574, also 1 Brownlow & Goldesborough 197, 123 E.R. 751, 2 Brownlow & Goldesborough 55, 146, 123 E.R. 812, 864.
[3] YB Mich. 2 Hen. VII, ff. 3, 4, pl. 12 (1486); YB Trin. 44 Edw. III, f. 18, pl. 12 (1370).

place and yet the justification by reason of the wardship was not more real that by reason of a lease.

And this same case is put [in] 16 Edw. IV, 4b;[1] and [it was said] there by Bryan, if a defendant in [an action of] trespass justifies by reason of a lease *de son tort demesne*, it is not [a good] plea, and this is for the reason aforesaid.

And the court did not give any opinion, but they adjourned. More of this [at] fo. 19, pl. 30.[2]

6

Pierce v. Atwood

(K.B. Pas. 1 Car. I, 1625)

The plea of ancient demesne can be a good defense to an action of trespass to land.

BL MS. Add. 35961, f. 4, pl. 6

Mich. 22 Jac., rot. 224. Pierce brought [an action of] trespass against Atwood *quare clausum fregit*. The defendant pleaded ancient demesne. And it was now moved, and judgment [was] prayed for the plaintiff because it was said that ancient demesne is not a [good] plea in trespass because it is a personal action, as Alden's case is, Coke 5, 105.[3]

DODDERIDGE: In *ejectione firmae*, in waste, in replevin, in wardship, and the entry actions, ancient demesne [is a good] plea because in those actions *prima facie* the freehold will come into debate or [whether] the plaintiffs are in the realty [rather] than the personalty. And also, in an action of trespass, ancient demesne can be a plea and no plea according to that which afterwards appears because, if the other [party] justifies by reason of his freehold, then it is a [good] plea, otherwise not.

And a further day was given.

7

Marshall v. Allen

(K.B. Pas. 1 Car. I, 1625)

In an action of ejectment, the defendant can plead ancient demesne after an imparlance.

---

[1] YB Pas. 16 Edw. IV, f. 4, pl. 10 (1476).

[2] For later proceedings in this case, see below, No. 75.

[3] *Smith v. Alden* (1601), 5 Coke Rep. 105, 77 E.R. 217, also Cro. Eliz. 826, 78 E.R. 1053, 2 Anderson 178, 123 E.R. 609.

BL MS. Add. 35961, f. 4, pl. 7

Marshall brought [an action of] *ejectione firmae* against Allen as appears in Hilary [term] 22 Jac., rot. 210. And the parties imparled, and, afterwards, the defendant pleaded ancient demesne *et hic paratus est vereficare unde non intendit quod curia cognitionem vult habere et hic paratus est vereficare vel petit judicium si actionem versus eum habere debet.*

And *Sir Thomas Crewe*, king's serjeant, moved for the plaintiff for judgment (1) because, after an imparlance, ancient demesne is not a [good] plea; (2) because he concluded judgment *si actionem*, and the court must give judgment upon the conclusion of the plea.

But it was ruled by the court (1) that, after an imparlance, ancient demesne is a [good] plea and [2] the other is not a conclusion but *nugatio* and surplusage and the other is the conclusion, but, if he had said *actio non* and concluded *unde petit judicium si actionem etc.* and then, upon this conclusion, he will have judgment against him.

And afterwards upon this opinion, by consent, they waived the demurrer and joined issue whether [it was] a frank fee or not.

[Other reports of this case: Cro. Car. 9, 79 E.R. 613; Latch 83, 82 E.R. 286, HLS MS. 1235, f. 20; Palmer 406, 81 E.R. 1145; BL MS. Hargr. 38, f. 17v; CUL MS. Hh.2.1, f. 184v; CUL MS. Ll.3.13, f. 63v.]

8

Bowry v. Wallington

(K.B. Pas. 1 Car. I, 1625)

After a writ of prohibition and a writ of consultation, if there is an appeal in the ecclesiastical court, the appellant there cannot have a writ of prohibition.

BL MS. Add. 35961, f. 4, pl. 8

Note: Between Bowry and Wallington upon the Statute of 50 Edw. III, ca. 4,[1] it was taken by the court that, if a suit be in an ecclesiastical court and [a writ of] prohibition [is] awarded and afterwards [a writ of] consultation [is] granted, that, upon the same libel, no prohibition will be granted again, but, if, there, it be appealed, in this case, then, a prohibition can be granted, but with this difference, if he who appeals prays for the prohibition, there, he will not have it because then there will be suits deferred *in infinitum* in the ecclesiastical courts if the prohibition and consultation were upon the body of the matter and the substance of it because, otherwise, one will be put oftentimes to try the same matter, which is full of vexation.

---

[1] Stat. 50 Edw. III, c. 4 (*SR*, I, 398).

And the case was moved again and argued by *Noy*. And it was thus. Wallington libelled in the ecclesiastical court against Bowry for tithes of wool and lambs. And Bowry, upon a suggestion of a *modus decimandi, viz.* to pay so much money annually, on account of this, obtained a prohibition and had an attachment and declared this, and they were at issue upon the *modus*. And the issue was found for the defendant. And a consultation [was] granted, and, upon this, judgment [was] given against Bowry in the ecclesiastical court, upon which Bowry appealed and then prayed for a new prohibition. And he had it. And now *Noy* moved for a consultation because a prohibition and attachment upon it is but a suit for the contempt of the party in bringing his suit in another court and to translate it [to] the court of the king. And when it is once tried for the defendant, the same thing will not be tried again in vexation. And as to the Statute of 50 Edw. III, 4, upon the misunderstanding of which the question arose, he confessed that the printed books and also the extract of the Parliaments of a roll remaining in the Tower [of London] is 'the same judge' but the Parliament roll itself and the petition is '*liceatque judici ecclesiastico*' without '*eidem*' or '*huiusmodi*'. And the answer of the petition is in these words 'a consultation granted suffices in this cause'. And the Parliament roll itself was brought into court and viewed. But he said that, if it was in the printed book and the extract, yet the same judge will not be intended [to be] the same personal judge but the same judge for having the same jurisdiction and cause because, otherwise, if another commissary be made, as the bishop can when he will, his successor can be newly prohibited, and also a thing could be infinitely tried because, in several places, the suit begins in the court of the archdeacon and, from him, an appeal can be to the bishop and, from him, to the [court of] arches and, from this, to the prerogative [court] and, then, to the [court of] delegates. And, if, upon each appeal, a prohibition could be newly granted, a thing will be infinitely tried. And on account of this, the same judge will here be taken [to mean] the same judge of the cause of the cognizance and jurisdiction. And also, the court Christian is all one same court, as it is in 5 Ric. II, *Triall*, 54.[1] Therefore, all these upon the matter [are] but one judge. By the Statute of 27 Eliz., ca. 8,[2] upon an erroneous judgment given in the king's bench, it is given that the party plaintiff or defendant can have a writ of error and yet the executor can have error in it because he is the plaintiff in this cause and the person interested, though not the personal plaintiff. Thus, if a tenant by a statute merchant be disseised, he can have an assize by the Statute which gives that the [*blank*] because he is the conusee interested, even though [he is not] the personal tenant. Thus here, even though he not be the personal judge to whom the prohibition was directed before, yet it is for the same cause and cognisance and ecclesiastical jurisdiction action.

---

[1] Mich. 5 Ric. II, Fitzherbert, Abr., *Triall*, pl. 54 (1381).
[2] Stat. 27 Eliz. I, c. 8 (*SR*, IV, 714).

And the judges rose up and went to the exchequer chamber and interrupted him and gave a day until the next term.

[Other reports of this case: Benloe 148, 150, 73 E.R. 1016, 1018, CUL MS. Gg.2.30, ff. 47v, 49; Latch 6, 75, 82 E.R. 246, 282, HLS MS. 1235, f. 14; Noy 81, 74 E.R. 1048; Palmer 418, 81 E.R. 1150; Popham 159, 79 E.R. 1257; 1 Eagle & Younge 337; BL MS. Hargr. 38, f. 17v, pl. 2; BL MS. Lansd. 1092, f. 41v; CUL MS. Hh.2.1, f. 188.]

9

Ward v. Kedgewin

(Part 2)
(K.B. Pas. 1 Car. I, 1625)

BL MS. Add. 35961, f. 4v, pl. 9

And now[1] Serjeant *Bridgman* came and said, as the deed is dated at Hamburg, this is intended to be a town because when a thing is alleged to be done *apud* D. or S., it will be intended *prima facie* a town, then, if thus now there can be a town of such a name within Cheapside, but if it be [that] it is of necessity to be elsewhere, then the action must be brought there and not here. And as [is] 3 Hen. IV, 4,[2] [an action of] debt brought in Middlesex upon an obligation dated at London, this was not good because [it is] out of the proper county according to the Statute of 6 Ric. II, 2.[3]

And as to the other point, of *detinet*, he did not speak because the court had given [its] opinion before.

But notwithstanding judgment [was] given for the plaintiff because the court said that, when a thing in a pleading is alleged to be at Dale, there, Dale is intended a town but not so in a deed because it could be dated at a known place.

And as to the other point, DODDERIDGE said that the true difference of the book is that, if a deed be dated and, by the same deed, it does not appear that the place at which it is [is] outside of the realm, it will not be intended to be outside, but, if, by the deed, it appears to be made *in partibus transmarinis*, then an action cannot be brought here. And on account of this, if a deed be dated at Hamburg or Bordeaux, an action can be here by supposition that they are in England because it does not appear judicially to the judges but that they are such places thus known here. And in London, there is a place called Little Britain[4] and another called Scotland. But, if it is expressly in Hamburg *in partibus transmarinis*, then [it is] otherwise. And this is the difference of the books. And the common experience is here thus.

---

[1] For earlier proceedings in this case, see above, No. 4.

[2] YB Mich. 3 Hen. IV, f. 4, pl. 20 (1402).

[3] Stat. 6 Ric. II, stat. 1, c. 2 (*SR*, II, 27).

[4] As in Brittany in northwest France.

And for the *debet et detinet*, he said that it is good in the *detinet* solely because, of nothing but of current money, will the writ be in the *debet et detinet*, as for a horse or wheat. See 9 Edw. IV, 49, and 34 Hen. VI, 12,[1] and the case he cited before to be 10 Edw. III, he said that he had looked at his books and it is 6 Edw. III, F. *Accompt*, 103.[2]

And the judgment was [given] for the plaintiff.

[Other reports of this case: Benloe 149, 73 E.R. 1017, CUL MS. 2.30, f. 48v; W. Jones 69, 82 E.R. 36, BL MS. Hargr. 317, f. 94; Latch 77, 82 E.R. 283; Palmer 407, 81 E.R. 1145; BL MS. Hargr. 38, f. 18, pl. 2; BL MS. Hargr. 30, f. 212 (Turnour's reports); BL MS. Lansd. 1092, ff. 43, 56v; CUL MS. Hh.2.1, f. 185; CUL MS. Ll.3.13, ff. 46, 64.]

10

Powell v. Plunket

(K.B. Pas. 1 Car. I, 1625)

When there is a demurrer to part of a pleading and an issue pleaded to another part, judgment can be given before the issue is tried or the issue can be first tried.

BL MS. Add. 35961, f. 4v, pl. 10

Between Powell and Plunket in action upon the case of words, for part, the defendant justified and, for the rest, pleaded *non culpabilis*. And for the insufficiency of the justification, there was a demurrer. And judgment [was] prayed for the plaintiff by Serjeant *Crewe*.

DODDERIDGE: Before the issue [is] tried for the other part, you cannot have judgment.

Crewe: The books are cross and various in the point. But in the time of Sir Edward Coke, it was, upon solemn argument and great deliberation, adjudged that, when there is a demurrer for part [and] at issue for part, that the judgment can be given before the issue [is] tried or the issue can be first tried, and both ways are good enough.[3]

Upon which, day was given to the other [side] to maintain the justification or judgment will be given before the issue [is] tried. 39 Hen. VI, 50, b.[4]

[Other reports of this case: Cro. Car. 52, 79 E.R. 649; BL MS. Hargr. 38, f. 18, pl. 1.]

---

[1] *Copley v. Davers* (1470), YB Hil. 9 Edw. IV, f. 49, pl. 6; YB Mich. 34 Hen. VI, f. 12, pl. 23 (1455).

[2] YB Mich. 6 Edw. III, f. 40, pl. 17 (1366), Fitzherbert, Abr., *Accompt*, pl. 103 (100 florins).

[3] *Wood v. Metcalfe* (1614), 11 Coke Rep. 38, 77 E.R. 1193, Cro. Jac. 356, 79 E.R. 305, Godbolt 258, 78 E.R. 151, 1 Rolle Rep. 84, 81 E.R. 345.

[4] YB Hil. 39 Hen. VI, f. 50, pl. 15 (1461).

11

Anonymous

(K.B. Pas. 1 Car. I, 1625)

A sheriff can return that a rescue was made out of the custody of a bailiff.

BL MS. Add. 35961, f. 4v, pl. 11

The sheriff returned a rescue and returned it as done to his bailiff. And an exception to it [was] taken because there cannot be a rescue out of the custody of the bailiff because he was in the custody of the sheriff. And they cited Dy. 241[1] and said that, in the [court of] common pleas, it is ordinary to quash a return of a rescue for this exception.

But it was said [by] the court and the clerks that these returns are ordinary in the king's bench and have been always allowed. And though the usage in the common pleas is contrary, yet the usage of each court is law. And on account of this, the exception was not allowed.

Query: If the sheriff brought an action upon the case against the rescuers and alleged a rescue done to his bailiff, whether it will be good as in a return.

[Other reports of this case: Latch 184, 82 E.R. 337.]

12

Cornwallis v. Hamond

(K.B. Pas. 1 Car. I, 1625)

A lord of a manor can declare a forfeiture and enter for acts done in the lifetime of his ancestor.

BL MS. Add. 35961, f. 4v, pl. 12

Cornewallies brought [an action of] *ejectione firmae* against Hamond [entered Trin. 22 Jac., rot. 191], and he pleaded a lease for years by Anthony Hubard. And upon *non culpabilis* pleaded, they were at issue. And a special verdict [was] found to this effect, that James Hubard was seised of the manor of Hales Hall in Norfolk in his demesne as of fee in which these nine acres in which the ejectment was supposed were part and demised and demisable from the time of which memory [does not run to the contrary] by copy of court roll and that the said James so seised by copy devised these nine acres to Hamond in fee *secundum consuetudinem*, by which the said Hamond was seised in fee *secundum etc.*, and so seised committed waste. And they found that James Hamond died (but did not [say] that he died seised of the manor), and that Anthony Hubard was his heir,

---

[1] *Anonymous* (1565), 2 Dyer 241, 73 E.R. 533, also Jenkins 231, 145 E.R. 161.

and that he entered into the manor (but did not say as son and heir), and he was seised in fee and, so seised, entered upon the said Hamond for the waste done and the forfeiture, and he leased to Cornewallies, the plaintiff, upon whom the defendant entered. *Et petunt advisamentum etc.*

And it was argued for the plaintiff that the lord [of the manor] will take advantage of this forfeiture made in the lifetime of his father, first, because it was a right of entry and this will descend to the heir. And he said, if a right of action will descend, *a fortiori*, a right of entry, as, if the father loses by a false verdict, the son and heir will have an attaint. F.N.B. 108.[1] If more dower be assigned than need [be] in the time of my ancestor, the heir will have [an action of] admeasurement. F.N.B. 149. Thus, if the father has a right of action for charters and dies, the heir will have it. 19 Edw. IV, 9, and 19 Edw. IV, 5.[2] If land escheats in the lifetime of the ancestor, the heir will have a writ of escheat, 46 Edw. III, 4; 11 Ric. II, *Escheate*, 13; F.N.B. 144;[3] so that if a right of action will descend from the father to the son, *a fortiori*, a right of entry.

The second reason [is] because it is frequent that rights of entry descend, and, not taken in advantage by the father, the heir will take advantage. And he cited 39 Edw. III, 38, that if [there are] a lord and tenant and the tenant alienates in mortmain and the lord dies, the heir of the lord can enter for the alienation [made] in the lifetime of his father. If a tenant for life alienates in fee and the reversioner dies, his heir can enter for the forfeiture. 27 Ass. 32, by Shardelow;[4] and the judgment there by him intends [it]. 10 Ass. 20.[5] And thus, if in these cases, the right of entry descends to the heir, why not in our case? And by 8 Eliz., in Harper's reports,[6] the case was a copyholder committed a forfeiture and the lord leased the manor, [and] whether the lessee will take advantage of the former forfeiture was the doubt. But there, it was held for clear law that the heir could.

And on the other side, it was said that it is a forfeiture, but at the will of the lord. He said it is not an absolute forfeiture. And thus it differs from all those cases.

But he said that, inasmuch as the verdict is insufficient, he would not argue this because (1) it was found that James Hubard was seised, but it was not found that he died seised, and this will not be inferred unless it be precisely found; (2) it was found that Anthony was his heir and entered, but it was not found that he

---

[1] A. Fitzherbert, *Nouvelle Natura Brevium*.

[2] YB Pas. 10 Edw. IV, f. 9, pl. 23, 47 Selden Soc. 79 (1470); YB Hil. 19 Edw. IV, f. 5, pl. 2 (1480).

[3] YB Hil. 46 Edw. III, f. 4, pl. 7 (1372); YB Hil. 11 Edw. II, Selden Soc., vol. 61, p. 182, pl. 4 (1317), Fitzherbert, Abr., *Escheate*, pl. 13; A. Fitzherbert, *Nouvelle Natura Brevium*.

[4] YB 27 Edw. III, Lib. Ass., p. 136, pl. 32 (1353).

[5] YB 10 Edw. III, Lib. Ass., p. 26, pl. 20 (1336).

[6] *Anonymous* (1566), BL MS. Hargr. 374, f. 49v, pl. 34.

entered as heir. And he could be his heir and he entered after his death and still be a purchaser, in which case, it is clear that he will not take advantage of the forfeiture done before. And he said that it was immediate. It was so because James Hubard had covenanted to stand seised to his own use for life, the remainder in tail to Anthony. And this was the cause, as he said, that the jury did not find neither the continuance of the fee in James until his death nor Anthony entered *ut filius et heres.*

Justice DODDERIDGE: The case in itself is of great consequence and concerns the whole kingdom. This is the first time that it has been moved, and, on account of this, we will advise. The cases put where the heir will have a right of action and a right of entry are not to the reason of this case and, of this kind, infinite could be put in each king's reign. But, here, the forfeiture is not before the lord would thus do it and at the will of the lord to take advantage of it. If, at common law, a tenant has done waste, which was the reason that, the person in reversion dying, the heir could not have an action, and yet a statute was made that he will have [one].[1]

Hitcham, granting because it was a personal action and more in the personalty than realty and the damages the principal, and it was never accounted for a statute.

DODDERIDGE: Could the lord here enter before presentment by the homage?

Hitcham: The presentment is but to give notice to the lord and not to entitle him. And the lord could take notice if he wished.

DODDERIDGE: If the tenant permits waste and afterwards repairs, could the lord enter?

Hitcham: It was once a forfeiture and, on account of this, it remains. And it is not similar to waste by the common law because, there, if the waste be repaired before the jury has a view, it is good enough. And, if a condition was that the tenant will not make waste and he repairs, still the reversioner can enter.

Justice JONES: It is a mischievous case if the lord will be permitted to rake up old forfeitures long time past by many descents.

And [it was] adjudged it is not reasonable that lords will be abridged of their right. *Et adjornatur.*

[Other reports of this case: Benloe 148, 73 E.R. 1016, CUL MS. Gg.2.30, f. 47v; Latch 226, 82 E.R. 358; Palmer 416, 81 E.R. 1149; BL MS. Hargr. 38, f. 21v; BL MS. Hargr. 30, f. 211 (Turnour's reports); BL MS. Lansd. 1092, f. 49v; CUL MS. Hh.2.1, f. 187v.]

---

[1] See Rastell, *Les Termes de la Ley*, 'waste' 7; Statute of Waste, 20 Edw. I (*SR*, I, 109–110).

13

Anonymous v. Lady Molineux

(K.B. Pas. 1 Car. I, 1625)

A protection expires upon the death of the king.

BL MS. Add. 35961, f. 5v, pl. 13

In an action against the Lady Molineux, *Sir Henry Finch*, king's serjeant, moved to have a further day to plead because she had a protection granted by the late King James for her and her heirs and she had not now taken to plead, she being in Yorkshire.

And the court answered that the protection was ended by the demise of the king even though it was for her and her heirs.

[Other reports of this case: Latch 58, 82 E.R. 273.]

14

Clarke v. Login

(K.B. Pas. 1 Car. I, 1625)

Words imputing scandal that harm a person's reputation are defamatory.

BL MS. Add. 35961, f. 5v, pl. 14

Sir Symon Clarke brought an action upon the case against one Login for scandalous words, *viz.* 'Sir Symon Clarke lodged one Faukener, a Jesuit, knowing him to be a Jesuit.' And exceptions were taken that the words were not actionable, first, because he did not say when the lodging was and whether this was before the Statute of 27 Eliz.,[1] thus it is not a felony nor does it draw upon him any penalty; second, because he did not say that Fawkner was an Englishman, and, by this Statute, it is not a felony to lodge and entertain a Jesuit if he be not an Englishman.

But it was adjudged by the court that the words were actionable because, though the crime laid to his charge be not a felony, yet it was a great scandal. And though he had not been an Englishman, yet to lodge Suares[2] or Gregory de Valentia, they being Jesuits, is a great scandal and hurt to good fame and estimation.

[Other reports of this case: W. Jones 68, 82 E.R. 35, BL MS. Hargr. 317, f. 93; Latch 1, 83, 82 E.R. 244, 286; Palmer 410, 81 E.R. 1147; BL MS. Hargr. 30, f. 211v (Turnour's reports); CUL MS. Hh.2.1, f. 186; CUL MS. Ll.3.13, f. 54v.]

---

[1] Stat. 27 Eliz. I, c. 2 (*SR*, IV, 706–708).

[2] Francisco Suarez (1548–1617).

15

Blackston v. Martin

(Part 1)
(K.B. Pas. 1 Car. I, 1625)

A judgment lien attaches to the land held by the judgment debtor at the time of the execution of the judgment and subsequent purchasers hold subject to it.

In a scire facias *in the nature of an* audita querela *to vacate an execution on his land, the plaintiff-grantee need not allege himself to have been the owner of the land at the time of the execution of the judgment against the grantor.*

BL MS. Add. 35961, f. 5v, pl. 15

Between Blackston and Martin [entered Trin. 1 Car. I, rot. 773], the case was [thus]. A statute was acknowledged, and the conusor sold part of his lands to divers men, and the conusee sued execution upon the purchasers, leaving out some. And he brought *audita querela*, and they were at issue in chancery whether the conusor will have other lands than those extended the day the recognizance [was] given or ever afterwards and the lands lying in Durham by which the *mittimus* of the issue to be tried was to Durham which was tried and remanded in[to] the king's bench.

And it was adjudged void and that the record came in without a warrant because, when an issue is joined in the chancery, the chancellor with his own hands must deliver the record into the king's bench and, there, it is to be tried and execution [is] to be awarded from there if needed.[1]

16

Jerome v. Stiffe

(K.B. Pas. 1 Car. I, 1625)

A confession of judgment can contain a defeasance.

BL MS. Add. 35961, f. 5v, pl. 16

Stiffe confessed a judgment to Jerome. And Jerome sued execution and had it. And now, Stiffe comes and moves for a *supersedeas* because this judgment was confessed by agreement and that there will be a defeasance of it made. And upon an examination by oath, it was found true, and a *supersedeas* [was] awarded.

---

[1] For further proceedings in this case, see below, No. 39.

17

Note

(K.B. Pas. 1 Car. I, 1625)

A judgment is dated as of the first day of the term that it was rendered.

BL MS. Add. 35961, f. 5v, pl. 17

Note: [It was said] by the court, if a judgment be given at the end of the term, yet it will have relation to the first day of the term. And this is the essoin day that is always before the first day of the term as it is in the *callendis*.

18

Hall v. Huggen

(K.B. Pas. 1 Car. I, 1625)

A statute governing court costs applies to actions pending but not finished when the statute was enacted.

BL MS. Add. 35961, f. 5v, pl. 18

Between Hall and Huggen upon the new Statute of 22 Jac.,[1] which gives that one will not have more costs than damages, it was adjudged that, if a suit was begun before this Parliament and prosecuted afterwards, that it is within the Statute because the words are 'commenced or prosecuted after'.

[Other reports of this case: Latch 58, 82 E.R. 273, CUL MS. Ll.3.13, f. 10.]

19

Note

(K.B. Trin. and Mich. 1 Car. I, 1625)

BL MS. Add. 35961, f. 5v, pl. [19]

The greater part of Trinity term this year [1625] was adjourned by proclamation because of the grave plague in London and Westminster. And similarly, for the same cause, Michaelmas term was adjourned to Reading.

---

[1] Stat. 21 Jac. I, c. 16, s. 6 (*SR*, IV, 1223).

20

Smith v. Cranshaw

(K.B. Hil. 1 Car. I, 1626)

An action for conspiracy to indict lies even though no indictment was made.

BL MS. Add. 35961, f. 6, pl. 1

Note that the case between Cranshaw and Smyth, which was often debated in the king's bench, *viz.* the action upon the case by Smyth against Cranshaw and Sproll for conspiring maliciously and falsely to indict him for treason for the speaking of treasonable words was the last term at Reading adjudged, as I heard credibly, to be maintainable. And yet, there, *ignoramus* upon the indictment was found. See the action upon the case where, in felony, *ignoramus* was found. Trin. 3 Jac., rot. 246; 6 Jac., 921; 19 Jac., 133.

[Other reports of this case: Benloe 152, 73 E.R. 1019, CUL MS. Gg.2.30, f. 51v; Cro. Car. 15, 79 E.R. 618; Gilbert Cas. 179, 93 E.R. 298; W. Jones 93, 82 E.R. 48, BL MS. Hargr. 317, f. 127; Latch 79, 82 E.R. 284, HLS MS. 1235, f. 15v; Palmer 315, 81 E.R. 1100; 2 Rolle Rep. 258, 81 E.R. 785; BL MS. Hargr. 38, f. 19; BL MS. Lansd. 1092, f. 45; CUL MS. Ll.3.13, f. 48v.]

[The reports of this case by Croke and Palmer were cited in Earl of Macclesfield, *qui tam* v. Starkey (1685), Dodd 295, 325.]

21

Browne v. Dixe

(K.B. Hil. 1 Car. I, 1626)

A case will be removed from an ecclesiastical court upon a writ of prohibition where that court refuses to admit a defense of plene administravit.

BL MS. Add. 35961, f. 6, pl. 2

It was admitted by the bar and bench, if a legatee sue in a court Christian for a legacy and the executor pleads *plene administravit* and this is refused, that a [writ of] prohibition will be awarded. But, if the judge does not refuse the plea, he has the power to try it there because the principal [question] is of his jurisdiction, as the book of 1 Ric. III, 4,[1] is. And upon this, it is not sufficient to allege and surmise for a prohibition that the defendant in a court Christian has pleaded *plene administravit*, but it must be further said what plea the judge there refused to admit.

---

[1] YB Mich. 1 Ric. III, f. 4, pl. 7 (1483).

And see Pas. 22 Jac., common bench, 3; this motion [was] denied to Serjeant Hetley because the court there said that such a suggestion is still the office and duty of the judge and, on account of this, [it is] not receivable.

[Other reports of this case: Benloe 163, 170, 73 E.R. 1027, 1032, CUL MS. Gg.2.30, f. 56v; 3 Bulstrode 314, 81 E.R. 261; Noy 77, 74 E.R. 1045; Palmer 422, 81 E.R. 1152; CUL MS. Hh.2.1, f. 189v.]

22

Note

(K.B. Hil. 1 Car. I, 1626)

A writ of prohibition that is not served upon the defendant expires upon the demise of the king.

BL MS. Add. 35961, f. 6, pl. 3

[It was held] by Justice JONES and so he said that one of his brothers of the [court of] common bench said to him that the opinion and rule there was that, if a [writ of] prohibition be awarded and nothing upon it is done, *viz.* [there is] no attachment upon it, that, by the demise of the king, it is gone; [it is] otherwise if it be a bare prohibition but it is proceeded to attachment etc., to which the other justices agreed.

23

Note

(K.B. Hil. 1 Car. I, 1626)

Depositions to perpetuate testimony taken in the court of the marches of Wales are not admissible in common law courts.

BL MS. Add. 35961, f. 6, pl. 4

[It was said] by him [Justice JONES] also [that] examinations of witnesses *in perpetuam rei memoriam* in the [court of the] marches of Wales are never allowed to be given in evidence in any court of common law.

24

Methold v. Peck

(K.B. Hil. 1 Car. I, 1626)

In an action of assumpsit, a demand for payment must be alleged specifically, but in an action of debt, it can be alleged generally.

BL MS. Add. 35961, f. 6, pl. 5

Between Methold and Peck in an action upon the case upon *assumpsit*, the plaintiff alleged that the plaintiff was in debt to the defendant in a certain sum by an obligation and that at the day of payment, the defendant assumed to himself to deliver to the plaintiff his obligation upon the request, the money being paid, and that the defendant *licet saepius requisitus* has not delivered to him the obligation.

And the opinion of the court was strongly that he must have specially and certainly laid the request in time and place because it is traversable and part of the *assumpsit* and not to be done but upon request.

And Justice JONES remembered divers precedents in the point.

And a day was given, for the plaintiff's satisfaction, to show precedents for and against. But in [an action of] debt, *licet saepius requisitus* is sufficient because [it is] not material and traversable because the bringing of the action [against] the defendant, which is a *praecipe*, is a sufficient demand.

And afterwards, at another day, the court continued of my opinion, by which the parties brought their action etc.

[Other reports of this case: Benloe 157, 162, 73 E.R. 1023, 1027, CUL MS. Gg.2.30, ff. 54, 56v; 3 Bulstrode 297, 81 E.R. 247; Hutton 73, 123 E.R. 1110; W. Jones 85, 82 E.R. 45, BL MS. Hargr. 317, f. 117; Popham 160, 79 E.R. 1258; 2 Rolle Rep. 476, 81 E.R. 926; Winch 112, 124 E.R. 94; BL MS. Hargr. 30, f. 213, pl. 1 (Turnour's reports); BL MS. Hargr. 38, f. 30.]

25

Anonymous

(K.B. Hil. 1 Car. I, 1626)

Tithes are not payable for wood used in the house or used as hedgebote.

BL MS. Add. 35961, f. 6, pl. 6

One prayed for [a writ of] prohibition, and the suggestion was that the parson had libelled in the spiritual court for tithes of wood which the parishioner had in his house and used in hedgebote. And it was granted without difficulty. And thus is the common experience in this case.

26

Bowyer v. Rivet

(K.B. Hil. 1 Car. I, 1626)

Where an heir denies that he has inherited land and it is found against him in an action for the debts of his ancestor, the plaintiff-creditor can have execution only against the defendant's lands that were inherited from the debtor-ancestor.

BL MS. Add. 35961, f. 6, pl. 7

Between Bowyer and Rivet, the case, as it appears [*blank*] was thus. Sir William Bowyer recovered in 12 Jac. against Sir Thomas Rivet in an action of debt. And he died and made his wife executor, who died and made Bowyer her executor. Sir Thomas Rivet died. Thomas Rivet, his heir, against whom Bowyer brought *scire facias* to have execution against Thomas as heir apparent of the land descended to him from Sir Thomas, pleaded *riens per descent* from Sir Thomas. And [it was] found [by the jury] that he had two acres and a half by descent, upon which it was prayed that judgment will be given against Rivet generally, by *Gouldsmith*, because, he said, that this false plea will charge him for his own lands, similarly to the case where the executor pleads *ne unques administrator*. And he put many cases where falsity and covin are abhorred and punished by the law and will subject one's [own] land to the charge, as where one will be amerced *pro falso clamore* and which charges one's [own] land with the amercement. And also he urged Davy and Pepys's case, C. 440,[1] where, in [an action of] debt against the heir, he, for his false plea, made all of his other land liable, between which and our case, he did not put a difference. He urged also Sir William Harbert's case, Coke 3, 11b,[2] where he said that the case was upon a *scire facias* against the heir, as our [case] here is, and a general judgment [was] given against the heir.

But on the other side, it was argued by *Sir Thomas Richardson*, king's serjeant, and *Bankes*, and by all of the justices, *viz.* Chief Justice CREWE, DODDERIDGE, JONES, and WHITELOCKE that execution will be awarded in no other manner against the heir than it would be against the ancestor himself [. . .] other purpose of the moiety of this which he had by descent because, in this case, he cannot be to this intent charged as heir but must be charged as terre tenant and as a purchaser and a purchaser himself by his false plea will never be hurt or will it extend the execution against himself.

And *Bankes* argued that, here, the heir must be charged as a terre tenant and not otherwise. And a false plea by the purchaser will not charge him as will be he

---

[1] *Davy v. Pepys* (1573), 2 Plowden 438, 75 E.R. 658.
[2] *Harbert's Case* (1584), 3 Coke Rep. 11, 76 E.R. 647, also Moore K.B. 169, 72 E.R. 510.

who is charged as heir, as 33 Edw. III, *Execution*, 162, and 6 Edw. III, 15,[1] are. And that he is here charged as terre tenant he proved by three reasons.

1. [An action of] debt here would not lie against the heir as it would where he is bound as heir, but execution is to be sued against him as against another terre tenant, as Dyer 271 is and Coke, 3, 15, in Harbert's case, and in 27 Hen. VI, *Execution*, 135.[2] And Coke, 3, 12b, is express that, in a judgment in debt or a recognizance, the heir is charged and execution will be against him as terre tenant.

2. He is not any place as heir because the judgment does not mention the heir; therefore, he cannot be charged if he not be expressly bound. And, in the record of the recovery, it does not appear that the first will well bind the heir because he acknowledged that he himself [was] bound etc., and he did not bind himself and his heirs.

3. If the heir was named in the obligation so that once he was bound as heir, still the judgment ends the specialty so that, now, he is not bound because the obligation has lost its force and, in the judgment, the heir is not mentioned, similarly to the case of 10 Hen. IV, 21, 24. If an abbot contracts for the use of the house without the assent of the convent and dies, this will bind his successor, being to the benefit of the house. But, if he takes the obligation of the abbot and then he dies, this will not bind the house because the contract is delivery by the obligation. And this was the reason that, in the time of Edward II and Edward III, upon a recovery in debt, the obligation was cancelled because it was taken [to have been] ended and altered in[to] another nature. Thus here, being ended, it will not bind the heir as heir.

4. Here, he cannot be charged as heir because it appears of record that his father is living because it is brought against the heir as heir apparent which he cannot be but during the lifetime of the father. And on account of this it is brought against him as terre tenant.

And as to the objection that, here, he will have his age and, on account of this, he will be charged as heir, this does not follow because, if execution be sued against the heir of a purchaser, he will have his age and yet he is not the heir nor can he be charged as heir of the conusor, but because it is a rule in law that the heir who has by descent will not answer where his inheritance cannot be charged during his nonage.

Justice WHITELOCKE argued to the same intent and for the same reason, *viz.* because, here, the heir is not charged as heir but as terre tenant and as another purchaser will be, in which case, by his false plea, it will not charge him more

---

[1] Mich. 33 Edw. III, Fitzherbert, Abr., *Execucion*, pl. 162 (1359); YB Pas. 6 Edw. III, f. 15, pl. 14 (1332).

[2] *Anonymous* (1568), 3 Dyer 271, 73 E.R. 602; *Harbert's Case* (1584), *ut supra*; Mich. 27 Hen. VI, Fitzherbert, Abr., *Execucion*, pl. 135 (1448).

than otherwise. And also, because the *scire facias* is to have execution of lands descended to him and not to have others than he demanded.

Justice JONES to the same intent [said], here, in this case, I will consider three things: (1) what lien of the ancestor will bind the heir; (2) how the heir will behave himself in pleading; (3) our point in question.

For the first, there are two things necessary to bind one as heir: (1) an express lien because, if one binds himself and uses the name of his heir, this does not bind the heir in any case; (2) descent of inheritance because, without descent of inheritance to him, he is not bound by the act of his ancestor and he is not bound longer than he had the assets descended because if he alienates before the purchase of the writ, the lien is gone, and also, when the heir pleads *riens per descent*, the other [party] can elect to traverse this or to pray for judgment and to take execution when he has assets descended and this descent and lien binds all manner of heirs, in gavelkind, borough English, etc.

For the second thing, he should behave himself truly and plead truly and confess the assets descended to him when [an action of] debt is brought against him as heir, otherwise he will be charged of his other lands for the debt, as Pepys's case in the *Commentaries*. But where, there, in Pepys's case, it is said that, upon a *nihil dicit* or a *non sum informatus* etc., if the judgment passes upon these, that it will be general, I be not of this opinion because the common experience of the [court of] common bench is that such a judgment will not be given against the heir unless upon a false plea pleaded. Luson's case, Dyer 81, and Hemingham's case, Dyer 344,[1] where the judgment passed by a *nihil dicit* so that the holding in C. 441b that, be the heir condemned in debt whatever way, if he does not confess the assets etc., that it will be his own debt is not now taken [for good] law.

And also, I hold for my own opinion that, if the heir pleads falsely and more assets are found, that yet it is in the election of the plaintiff to charge him and to take execution of the assets solely or to take [a writ of] *elegit* of all of his land and he is not bound to take an *elegit* of his land in this case because, otherwise, this inconvenience could arise, if the heir had one hundred acres by descent and two by purchase, if, upon the false plea of the heir, the plaintiff could not have other execution but *elegit* of the moiety of his lands, then on account of this, he is prejudiced because, otherwise, he could have all of the assets by descent in execution. And thus the heir, by this means, will take advantage of his false plea.

(But note: If it not be as Jones said here that, upon a *nihil dicit*, the judgment will not be but of that which he has by descent, it is by this means in the election of the defendant whether the plaintiff will have all of the land descended or the moiety of all that he had according to this which is of greater advantage to the defendant because, if the greater part of his lands is descended, then he would

---

[1] *Luson's Case* (1553), 1 Dyer 81, 73 E.R. 174; *Henningham's Case* (1575), 3 Dyer 344, 73 E.R. 774.

suffer judgment by *nihil dicit*, but, if of his purchase be greater, then he would confess the assets truly.)

For the third consideration, whether the heir in our case will be prejudiced by his false plea, he held as before and that, on account of this, the execution will not be extended further, and [this] for the same reasons as Whitelocke held.

DODDERIDGE: How the heir will be charged for the act of his father is worthy to be considered, upon which, *prima facie*, the books seem to be [in] disaccord. But, being well considered, they accord with an excellent harmony. I have considered of this case, which was moved in Reading. And because my notes are not here, I will speak the more briefly. I will consider how the heir will be charged upon the obligation; second, how upon a recognizance; third, how upon a judgment; fourth, how upon a warranty.

For the first, in [an action of] debt against the heir, he is charged as an heir. And thus, at this day, it is taken as his own debt and, on account of this, in [an action of] debt against the heir, the writ is *debet et detinet*, but against the executors [it is] in the *detinet tantum*. Thus the heir [is] charged as deeply as upon his own contract. But, in former times, from 18 Edw. II until 7 Hen. IV, if executors had assets, the heir was not chargeable. But in 7 Hen. IV, there, the law changed in this point because, now, it is accounted his own debt and [an action of] debt will lie against his executor, as is put in the *Commentaries*, and thus against the heir of the heir to several generations, though of this, Plowden was [in] doubt. And his plea is that he had *riens per descent* the day the writ [was] purchased nor ever afterwards because, if he had alienated the assets, he is discharged of the debt because he is not bound to attend the action of the obligee but he can make his [. . .] of the land.

For the second, in the recognizance, the heir is charged not as heir, but as terre tenant because he is not bound in the recognizance, but the conusor only grants *quod super terras et tenementa levetur*, and it is not against his heirs. But here, he is not merely as terre tenant because he will not have contribution against other terre tenants, but only against those who are heirs, as he himself is. But, to all other intents, he is a terre tenant. And so he is charged, as 32 Edw. III and 27 Hen. VI are.

For the third thing, *viz.* a judgment, which is our case and the point, the heir will be charged as terre tenant and not otherwise for the same cause [as] in a recognizance because he is not bound expressly. And, as I conceive, the book which has been cited at the bar and bench of 33 Edw. III, *Execution*, 162, is expressly in the point; the broken ones of Fitzherbert are obscurely reported, but, upon a comparison with other cases, it would appear to be our case expressly for the charging of the heir by the warranty of his ancestor, though it be upon another learning, yet, there, he being charged as heir, yet, upon his false plea, execution will not be but of the assets. And thus, it seems to me, in the principal case, that the judgment will be special, and, as it seems, it is a plain case.

Chief Justice CREWE agreed and for the same reasons as before. And, in his argument, he affirmed the holding of Jones that the common experience is that a general judgment will not be given against the heir if he does not plead falsely his assets and it is not upon a *nihil dicit* etc.

And thus judgment was given that the plaintiff will have execution of the moiety of the lands descended to the defendant.

Thus, note the diversity of [an action of] debt against the heir and a *scire facias* against the heir.

[Other reports of this case: Benloe 162, 73 E.R. 1026, CUL MS. Gg.2.30, f. 56; 3 Bulstrode 317, 81 E.R. 264; W. Jones 87, 82 E.R. 45, BL MS. Hargr. 317, f. 118; Palmer 419, 81 E.R. 1151; Popham 153, 79 E.R. 1252; BL MS. Hargr. 30, f. 213v (Turnour's reports); CUL MS. Hh.2.1, f. 188v.]

27

Dickenson v. Greenehaw

(K.B. Hil. 1 Car. 1, 1626)

The issue in this case was whether the land in question was discharged of the payment of tithes.

BL MS. Add. 35961, f. 7, pl. 8

Between Dickenson and Greenehaw in an attachment upon a prohibition and entered Hil. 18 Jac., rot. 189, the plaintiff declared that where Robert, the last abbot of Cokersand in Lancashire, was seised in fee of three acres of land, part of the monastery, and that the abbot and his co-monks and all of his predecessors of the abbot were from the time [of which the memory of man runneth not to the contrary] discharged of the payment of tithes, of the order and rule of the Premonstratensians, and that the order of Premonstratensians and all of the monks of it were of time etc. discharged of the payment of tithes for their lands and tenements *quamdiu propriis manibus excolebat* and that the said abbot and all of his predecessors from the time etc. had held the said three acres discharged of the payment of tithes *quamdiu* etc. and thus held until the dissolution of the monastery, and he showed the surrender to Henry VIII and the Statute of 31 Hen. VIII,[1] by the force of which, Henry VIII was seised and held it discharged of the payment of tithes *quamdiu* etc. and, from him, it derived to Edward VI and from Edward VI to Queen Mary and from her to Queen Elizabeth and from her, *viz.* [in the] forty-second [year] of her reign, to Wagstaffe and from him by mesne conveyances to Dickenson, the plaintiff, *quorum praetextu*, he was seised *et gavisus fuit in propria manurantia*. And he showed the Statute of 20 Edw. II,

---

[1] Stat. 31 Hen. VIII, c. 13 (*SR*, III, 733–739).

ca. 15,[1] by which it is enacted that tithes will be paid as usually they were etc., *quorum praetextu* the plaintiff held the three acres discharged of tithes and that, notwithstanding and against the prohibition of the king, the defendant drew him into a plea for them in the court Christian and the judge of it held the plea and the defendant, there, prosecuted him in contempt of the king and to the disinheritance of his crown etc., upon which the defendant demurred and prayed a [writ of] consultation.

And *Sir John Davies*, king's serjeant, for the defendant, thought that a consultation should be granted because his matter of discharge is double: first, his privilege; second, the prescription. And if any of them will not save him, then he must be charged for the privilege. He takes that the Premonstratensians never had such a privilege because it is a maxim in law that all persons will pay tithes and all lands are charged with them of common right. But also there are divers discharges of them allowed by our law (as is manifest by the three orders of the Templars, Hospitalers, and Cistercians, which discharges our law allows). And those are (1) by prescription, (2) by real compositions, (3) by a privilege obtained. And this is by two ways, either by a bull of the pope because taking upon himself to be the great dispenser and steward of the revenues of the church, he took upon himself to discharge them. But this he could not, as it is held by the common law, absolutely do, but he could divert them from one clergyman to another or grant [. . .] by way of retainer. And this must be to the clergy also or second [?] by a general council because some orders were discharged by general councils. Thus some obtained the privilege by a bull of the pope, which are like his patents, some by councils, which are like the statutes, and his decrees were like his judgments. But yet none of them ever had any force in our law nor bind us of England, more than they were received voluntarily and approved by usage and custom so that the privileges that were obtained, unless they were approved here, will not bind because, as was said [in] 11 Hen. IV,[2] the pope cannot alter the law of England. And this is evident because, in all cases where the bulls or constitutions of the pope cross the law of the land, they have always been rejected, as for instance in his bulls, which are of four sorts: first, of provision; second, of citation; third, of exemption; fourth, of excommunication. For those of excommunication, it appears that it was treason at common law and that the treasurer will kneel to Edward II for one who brought them in, and in the perpetual course of the books after, they have always [been] disallowed in pleas so that bulls of citation before the Statute of Provisions[3] was a heinous offense; thus his bulls of provision and of exemption. For his canons that, where they were against the law, they were neglected appears by the canon *quod nullum capias beneficium a laico*. And yet notwithstanding the long time, it continues for benefices and still continues for

---

[1] Stat. 2 & 3 Edw. VI, c. 13 (*SR*, IV, 55–58).
[2] *Rex v. Bishop of Salisbury* (1410), YB Trin. 11 Hen. IV, f. 76, pl. 18.
[3] Stat. 25 Edw. III, stat. 4 (*SR*, I, 316–318).

bishoprics that the clergy hold them of the king. And of lay land,[1] there is also a canon for an exemption of clerks from the temporal jurisdiction. But yet, as Bryan said, 10 Hen. VII, 18,[2] it was never observed here. Thus, the canon said that the time of a lapse will be accounted *per septimanas*, but our law, not regarding this, says that it will be accounted *per menses in kalenda[. . .]*, as is expressly adjudged in 5 Edw. III, rot. 100, in the close roll in the Tower [of London]. And there is a great reason for this because, as it is in 29 Hen. III, membr. 5, in the Tower, the bishops of England need not go to the general councils; thus, as in Parliaments, those who do not send knights are not bound by statutes. And the Council of Lyon, *de bigamis*, is expounded by a statute. Though it will be taken so that, if they had a privilege, as in truth they have by bulls of the pope, if it was not allowed within England, they are not of force to privilege them against the common law of the land of payment of tithes. But this was never allowed here.

And now for the prescription, this cannot aid them because monks are not of the evangelical priesthood or capable of tithes in pernancy, but merely laymen. And then, as the bishop of Winchester's case[3] is, they cannot prescribe *in non decimando*. And Bede says of them that they are mere *laici*. Thus, if their privilege was not allowed, their prescription will not aid him. The privilege of the Premonstratensians [was] made by the general council under Innocent III to discharge those large liberties as the Cistercians, but they never put it into practice. And it seems that they were one of those nineteen abbots and abbeys and yet their privilege is not mentioned in all of the books, as is the Cistercians etc.

Second, they complained to Gregory IX that they were not allowed to put them into practice and notwithstanding this complaint and the command of the pope to the clergy to allow them this privilege, yet, in 54 Hen. III a complaint was against them in Parliament for claiming these privileges. 54 Hen. III, close roll, 9. But the Statute of 2 Hen. IV, ca. 4,[4] put it beyond doubt because this put the Cistercians in *praemunire* for purchasing and putting into execution bulls of exception of their lands purchased afterwards. Now, if the Premonstratensians had had the same privileges, they would not have been omitted out of the Statute. And then came the Statute of 7 Hen. IV, 6,[5] that terrified all to put in execution bulls not put in execution before, upon which it is not to be presumed that after[wards] it was put in execution.

But admitting that the Premonstratensians had this privilege, I say that the plaintiff has not applied the privilege to himself because he has not averred *de facto* that, at the time etc., *propriis manibus excolebat nec ad formam dimittebat*, and

---

[1] mayne *MS*.

[2] YB Hil. 10 Hen. VII, ff. 17, 18, pl. 17 (1495).

[3] *Wright v. Wright* (1596), 2 Coke Rep. 38, 76 E.R. 501, also Moore K.B. 425, 72 E.R. 672, Cro. Eliz. 475, 511, 78 E.R. 726, 760.

[4] Stat. 2 Hen. IV, c. 4 (*SR*, II, 121–122).

[5] Stat. 7 Hen. IV, c. 6 (*SR*, II, 152).

this he must have done if he would take advantage of the privilege, as in Dickenson's case in the *New Book of Entries*, 542;[1] there it is expressly alleged in a similar case as ours here and where the same privilege as here is claimed, that *manibus propriis excolebat*. And the truth is that he said that, after the feoffment to him, he was seised *et gavisus fuit in propria manurantia*, but he did not say that, at the time the tithes [were] due, *gavisus fuit propria manurantia*, and this he must have expressly done; otherwise, he has not applied the privilege to himself. And this is proved by similar cases, the reason of which come to our case. If one prescribe to have a common in arable land when the corn is reaped or in a meadow when the hay is carried and justify by reason of it, he must aver that the corn was carried and the hay when he puts in his cattle; thus he goes into the place where etc., as 17 Ass. 7.[2] Thus, if the king pardons all but those who adhere to M., he who pleads this must aver that he does not adhere to M. Thus, here, the privilege is *quamdiu in propriis manibus* etc. And on account of this, at the time, he must aver that he had it *in propriis manibus* and also where upon the surrender to Henry VIII and the Statute.

They concluded that the king held it discharged; it cannot be in such manner as the abbot held it discharged but it was *quamdiu* etc., and the king cannot be bound to such a beseeming condition. And on account of this, he will not hold discharged, similarly to the case where the abbot had a presentation and another the nomination and the abbot surrendered to him who had the nomination, he will have all because the king does not present for him, [it] being a thing in descent for his Majesty. Thus, for all of these reasons, I conclude that the prohibition was not well awarded. And on account of this, the defendant prayed a [writ of] consultation.

Bankes, contra: And I conceive that no consultation will be granted because, first, I conceive that there is [good] cause for the prohibition; second, that this cause is well applied to us.

For the first, I conceive that the order of the Premonstratensians is discharged of tithes and that this has been allowed here by the law; second, that the prescription to be discharged is good though they have not been discharged by their order and that they are persons able to prescribe in such a privilege; third, that it is not now to be argued whether they have such a privilege or not and whether it was allowed or not; fourth, that though the form fails in the prohibition, yet, if there be matter of substance, it is sufficient to ground a prohibition, upon which a consultation will not be granted.

For the first, that the order of Premonstratensians have this privilege, it is confessed by the other party that, at one time, they had it and this by the bulls of the pope and that it was allowed here and taken notice of and it proves that this

---

[1] *Dickonson, qui tam v. Watter* (1607), E. Coke, *A Booke of Entries* (1614), 'Prohibition', pl. 3, f. 450.
[2] YB 17 Edw. III, Lib. Ass., p. 49, pl. 7 (1343).

bull was confirmed by King John in the fourteenth year of his reign, the charter of whom said that he had under seal. And 22 Edw. I, *membrana* 5; there were twenty-six abbeys of this order and the king took all of them into his protection with all of their immunities. And in 22 Ric. II, John of Gaunt, having *jura regalia* in Lancashire, where this abbey was, confirmed to them the said bull. And also, this had been divers times allowed. And this privilege [was] decreed to them in courts Christian for suits of tithes, as in the case of the Abbey of Bigham, which was of the same order, which he cited etc.

And as to that which was objected, that, if the Premonstratensians had such privileges as the Cistercians in 2 Hen. IV, that the same provision would have been against them, to this I answer that such provision was not against the Templars nor the Hospitalers and yet they had the same privileges.

Second, it could be that they did not strive to enlarge their privilege beyond largely, and thus [there was] no cause of restraint.

Third, there, it was against all religious persons which could include the Premonstratensians also. And by the Statute of 7 Hen. IV, our privilege was not then new. And it was afterward allowed in 22 Ric. II. And further, I conceive that, if the abbot was discharged at the time of the Dissolution, though not *de jure*, yet it is a sufficient discharge within the Statute of 31 Hen. VIII, as in Pridle and Napper's case, Coke, 11, 14;[1] unity was not discharged *de jure*, but yet, if the unity had been from the time [of which memory runneth not] etc., it was a sufficient discharge within this law.

Second, that he could prescribe to be discharged of tithes, I so conceive because they are spiritual persons and capable of cure of souls and also they are capable of tithes in pernancy as if an appropriation is made to them. And as to the doubleness, it is not a defect but an abundance and by the demurrer, as 36 Hen. VI, 7,[2] is etc.

And for the third, that it is not now to argue whether they have such privileges, it is so because they have demurred and this is a confession of all matters of fact, as the rule is in *Commentaries* 55,[3] and it is as strong as if it had been found by a verdict because a demurrer confesses all matters of fact, but not all matters of law.

For the fourth, I conceive that, if it be a matter of substance to ground the prohibition, this will serve, and a consultation will not be granted for the default of form, for which see Dyer 170, 171, and Coke 11, 10.[4]

---

[1] *Priddle, qui tam v. Napper* (1612), 11 Coke Rep. 8, 77 E.R. 1155, also 2 Brownlow & Goldesborough 25, 123 E.R. 794, 1 Gwillim 236, 1 Eagle & Younge 205.

[2] YB 36 Hen. VI, ff. 6, 7, pl. 3 (1457 x 1458) or YB 36 Hen. VI, f. 7, pl. 4 (1457 x 1458).

[3] *Wimbish v. Tailbois* (1550), 1 Plowden 63, 55, 75 E.R. 63, 89.

[4] *Pelles v. Saunderson* (1559), 2 Dyer 170, 73 E.R. 374, 1 Gwillim 130, 1 Eagle & Younge 57, also Jenkins 218, 145 E.R. 150; *Priddle, qui tam v. Napper* (1612), *ut supra*.

And as to the privilege, it is well applied, and it is shown at one time to be in his seisin and manurance. And on account of this, it will be thus intended to continue. And for not showing how he [is] discharged, there is no need because, first, it is an infinite thing, and for this [is] 22 Edw. IV, 4, and 51 Edw. IV, 8.[1] The undersheriff will plead a discharge generally but show how for the infiniteness. Also, the discharges are before the time of memory and, on account of this, not pleadable, as it is in 20 Hen. IV, 15, and in 29 Hen. VI, 75.[2] There, the deed relied upon the prescription and not upon the deed of grant of the annuity where it was beyond the time of memory.

Thus, I conceive and pray that the prohibition will stand and that no consultation will be granted.

[This report is printed at 1 Eagle & Younge 334.]

[Other reports of this case: Benloe 163, 73 E.R. 1027, CUL MS. Gg.2.30, f. 57; Popham 156, 79 E.R. 1254; 2 Rolle Rep. 479, 81 E.R. 928; 1 Gwillim 401; 1 Eagle & Younge 332.]

28

Rex v. Beverley

(K.B. Hil. 1 Car. I, 1626)

An indictment for forcible entry lies where the detaining was with force even though the entry was not with force.

There can be a forcible entry in a moiety of a manor by the owner of the other moiety.

BL MS. Add. 35961, f. 8v, pl. 8[a]

Beverley was indicted for the forcible entry in the moiety of a manor. And an exception was taken to it, first, because the entry was not alleged to be *manu forti* and, on account of this, it cannot be against the Statute of 8 Hen. VI.[3]

But it was ruled by the court, and thus are many authorities in the books, that the entry need not be alleged with force if the *extra tenuit* be with force because, if the entry or the detaining be with force, it is against the Statute. And in the indictment here, the detaining of the possession is laid to be *manu forti*, and this suffices.

---

[1] YB Pas. 22 Edw. IV, f. 4, pl. 14 (1482); YB Mich. 5 Edw. IV, ff. 7, 8, pl. 19 (1465) or YB Mich. 5 Edw. IV, f. 8, pl. 22 (1465) or *Dubray v. Prior of Southwark* (1465), YB Pas. 5 Edw. IV, Long Quinto, ff. 6, 8.

[2] YB Mich. 20 Edw. IV, ff. 13, 15, pl. 17 (1480); YB Trin. 19 Hen. VI, f. 75, pl. 3 (1441).

[3] Stat. 8 Hen. VI, c. 9 (*SR*, II, 244–246).

The second exception was because the entry was alleged to be *in medietatem manerii* and one cannot enter in the moiety of a manor, but his entry will be in the whole because his entry in an entire thing cannot be apportioned, as it was said.

But JONES said that one can enter in the moiety of a manor as well and his entry in it will not be an entry in the other moiety, as, if the king be a tenant in common with another of a manor and one enters in the manor, here, his entry will be but *in medietatem manerii* because, in the other part which is in the king, one cannot enter. But he granted that, if partitioners make a partition of the manor and one enters upon one of them, that, here, it is not an entry in the moiety of the manor because, after the partition, it is one manor.

But DODDERIDGE said that, before the partition, one coparcener has *dimidium manerii*, but, after the partition, he has *medietatem manerii* because *dimidium* is of a thing before it is divided, as among tenants in common and joint tenants; there, they have *dimidium*, each of them, but not *medietatem*. And *medietas* is the half part divided and separate. And thus, he said, it is the difference taken in the *Commentaries*.[1] And yet, as to all privileges of a manor, it is one manor and not the moiety of a manor after partition. And still it can be well alleged in such a case that the entry was in the moiety of the manor because this manor, which is one manor, is but the moiety of an ancient manor.

By which, it was held and agreed by the court that this exception also was not of any force.

[Other reports of this case: Latch 98, 224, 82 E.R. 293, 357.]

29

Whitton v. Weston

(Part 1)
(K.B. Hil. 1 Car. I, 1626)

The issue in this case was whether land formerly owned by the Hospitalers was discharged from the payment of tithes.

BL MS. Add. 35961, f. 8v, pl. 9

Whitton brought an action of debt upon the Statute of 2 Edw. VI, ca. 13,[2] against Weston (*et intratur* Trin. 1 Car., rot. 810) for the not setting forth of tithes of certain corn growing in such land within his parish before the carrying of the corn. And the corn was wheat, by which an action accrued to him to demand so much money, being the treble value of the tithes not set forth, etc.

---

[1] *Bracebridge v. Cook* (1572), 2 Plowden 416, 424, 75 E.R. 626, 639.
[2] Stat. 2 & 3 Edw. VI, c. 13 (*SR*, IV, 55–58).

The defendant said in bar that the prior of St. John of Jerusalem etc. was seised of this land, out of which etc., and that he and all of his predecessors from the time of which memory [runneth not to the contrary] held their land discharged of tithes *quamdiu propriis manibus aut sumptibus excolebant* and so held until the dissolution of this Hospital. And he showed the Statute of 31 Hen. VIII, ca. 13,[1] by which is enacted the discharge of tithes for the patentees and the king of the lands of the monasteries dissolved by it and also the Statute of 32 Hen. VIII, ca. 24,[2] of the dissolution of the said Hospital and also the branch of the Statute of 2 Edw. VI, ca. 13, which enacts that no one will be sued for tithes who should not pay for [?] what he had a discharge by prescription or etc. And he conveys[3] the lands of the prior to Henry VIII and from him to Weston, his ancestor. And he said that Weston, his father, was seised of the said land and died seised and that he, as son and heir, entered and was seised and *adhuc seisitus existit*. And he did not show when his father died and that all this in the year of 21 Jac. (because the corn was alleged to be growing [in] 21 Jac.) he *habuit et gavisus fuit praedictam terram in propria sua manurantia et cultu.* And thus he concluded that the plaintiff did not have title to the tithes and, on account of this, no action of debt accrued to him to demand the said sum for the not setting forth of the said tithes.

And *Noy* for the plaintiff [said] it seems to me that the plaintiff should recover and that the bar of the defendant is not sufficient for two causes:

(1) Because he thought that the purchasers of the lands of those of St. John of Jerusalem do not have the same privilege as the Hospitalers themselves had;

(2) If they had the same privilege, he has not well applied it to himself.

For the first, the point is whether the purchasers of the lands of the Hospitalers will have the privileges as to tithes that the Hospitalers themselves had. And this rests upon the question, *viz.* whether the Hospital of St. John be within the Statute of 31 Hen. VIII, ca. 13, because, if so, then the branch of discharge within it would extend to it, otherwise not. And I conceive, under favor, that it is not within this Statute of 31 Hen. VIII because, first, it is not named within the Statute of 31 [Hen. VIII] because, there, there are specified only 'monasteries, abbacies, nunneries, hospitals, priories, and all other ecclesiastical and religious houses' so that, if it be within the word 'hospitals', it must be ecclesiastical and religious, as many hospitals in England were, and not only religious, as is this of St. John was because these word[s] 'other ecclesiastical and religious' demonstrate that the houses named before were [intended] solely to be ecclesiastical and religious and not only such of those houses that were only ecclesiastical or only religious, as, there, is also specified colleges, and yet no college was dissolved by this except it was ecclesiastical and religious also. And, on account of this, as is said

---

[1] Stat. 31 Hen. VIII, c. 13 (*SR*, III, 733–739).

[2] Stat. 32 Hen. VIII, c. 24 (*SR*, III, 778–781).

[3] I.e. alleged the conveyance.

[in] Coke, 2, 49,[1] no house was dissolved before the Statute of 31 [Hen. VIII] but religious and ecclesiastical [ones]. And yet the Statute recites that hospitals have been surrendered, by which it is manifest that such hospitals as were both religious and ecclesiastical, and not solely religious, were dissolved and within this Statute.

Second, it cannot be within the words 'or any other means as to the king's highness' if it was admitted that it was religious and ecclesiastical, because the coming by Parliament was not brought [?] to be within those general words, being the most high means of coming to it etc. See this reason urged [in] Coke, 2, 46b.

The third reason is because the Act which gives the Hospital of St. John enacts that it will be in the king by force of this Act, which, being after 31 [Hen. VIII], takes it away if it had been included in the Act of 31 [Hen. VIII], as in the Archbishop of Canterbury's case, Coke, 2, 46,[2] which see [it] urged there.

And for the purpose of the second reason, a notable case was adjudged in the [court of] common bench [in] 18 Jac. [1620 x 1621] and it was Wright's case,[3] and it was thus. Certain land of an abbey dissolved by the Statute of 27 Hen. VIII[4] was given to another abbey which was afterwards dissolved by [the Statute of] 31 [Hen. VIII], and, afterwards, the land was granted over to a patentee, and, here, it was adjudged, first, that houses dissolved by 27 [Hen. VIII] were not within the Statute of 31 [Hen. VIII] because it was by Parliament; second, that this union of the land and parsonage in the hands of the second abbey was not discharged because it was not perpetual because the land came to the abbot, who was the parson after the time of memory.

And, as I have said before, the Hospitalers were not ecclesiastical but only religious and also they were not fully this because, by their order, they professed only two of the three vows, *viz.* obedience and chastity, but, for poverty, it was not any [part] of their rule, and yet they were accounted religious etc., but, as ecclesiastical, they were never accounted so because their inception was to be knights and soldiers to conduct pilgrims on their pilgrimages to the Holy Land and, afterwards, [they] professed to defend Jerusalem, so that they were laymen and their profession was to be *in strepitu et secularibus negotiis*, as one canonist said of them. And for their law, *viz.* the canons, they were never capable of any privilege of the clergy. And on account of this, there, they were within the canon prohibiting to lay [?] violent hands upon a clerk. Never was anyone punishable for this upon this canon, but their remedy was to cite the offender before

---

[1] *Green v. Balser* (1596), 2 Coke Rep. 46, 76 E.R. 519, 1 Gwillim 189, 1 Eagle & Younge 113.

[2] *Green v. Balser* (1596), *ut supra*.

[3] *Wright v. Gerrard* (1618), Cro. Jac. 607, 79 E.R. 518, Hobart 306, 80 E.R. 449, W. Jones 2, 82 E.R. 2, 1 Gwillim 375, 1 Eagle & Younge 289.

[4] Stat. 27 Hen. VIII, c. 28 (*SR*, III, 575–578).

the conservators of their liberties. For this, see Westminster II, ca. 47, in the last printing and 43 in the old *Magna Charta* printed in 1556,[1] so that, by the canons, they were not accounted [as] of the clergy. And [see] a case of 31 Edw. I, *Tryall*, Fitz. 99 and 98,[2] by which it appears that it was written to a bishop to certify whether one was professed in the order of St. John of Jerusalem, but this does not prove them [to be] but religious because a bishop can certify profession though not ecclesiastical also, which is not within the Statute of 31 [Hen. VIII]. This [is] proved [by] the preambles because, in cases of religious and ecclesiastical houses, it recites the abominable deeds and acts of them, but, in the Statute of 32 [Hen. VIII], it is recited only that the Hospitalers adhered to the supremacy of the pope. And also, before the dissolution of the abbeys, a commission [was] pleaded to enquire of the abominations of them, and this was returned into the exchequer and remains there of record that at the visitation, the commissioners found that, in such an abbey, such monks kept six, seven, and ten concubines and, in such a nunnery, such [. . .] *sexies peperit, alia quinquies, alia septies.* But, upon this commission, the Hospital of St. John was not visited, by which it appears that it was not then intended to be dissolved by 31 Hen. VIII because the same commissioners did not deal with them, who dealt with the other religious houses.

But as an express authority, the case of Dyer 277[3] could be urged against me because, there, it is admitted that the purchasers of the lands of the Hospitalers were discharged. But the question there was upon that [land] which was in lease before the dissolution and, at the time of the dissolution, was not discharged, but charged, because it was in the hands of lessees. But, to this case, I say that they did not consider there of the principal point, *viz.* whether such lands were discharged by the Statute. But admitting of this suddenly and taking their greater consideration of the collateral point, that, if they have done and considered of the principal, they would not have admitted it, as, there, they have done.

And to conclude this point, in Hilary [term] 44 Eliz., in the common bench, rot. 994, Bell and Quarles against Spurling,[4] upon a special verdict, it was found that the lands out of which tithes were demanded belonged to the Templars and it found the Statute of Edw. II[5] which gave all of the lands of the Templars to the Hospitalers and that the Hospitalers were discharged [from] the time of which etc. of the payment of tithes in their hands of the land being *quamdiu propriis manibus aut sumptibus excolebant*, and it found also the Statute of 31 Hen. VIII and that the plaintiff was *proprietarius* of the land and manured it at the time etc.,

---

[1] Stat. 13 Edw. I, Stat. of Westminster II, c. 43 (*SR*, I, 92–93).

[2] Mich. 31 Edw. I, Fitzherbert, Abr., *Triall*, pl. 99 and pl. 98 (1303).

[3] *Stathome's Case* (1568), 3 Dyer 277, 73 E.R. 621, 1 Gwillim 132, 1 Eagle & Younge 59.

[4] *Quarles v. Spurling* (1602), Moore K.B. 913, 72 E.R. 993, *sub nom. Cornwallis v. Spurling*, Cro. Jac. 57, 79 E.R. 48, 1 Gwillim 224, 1 Eagle & Younge 157.

[5] Stat. 17 Edw. II, stat. 2 (*SR*, I, 194–196).

and yet [it was] adjudged against the plaintiff in the [action] of prohibition and [a writ of] consultation [was] awarded. And it was upon great debate and argument. And it is in this point an express authority and conclusion.

For the second point, whether he has applied this privilege to himself, he thought not because he said that his father was seised and died seised and that he entered and was and *adhuc est seisitus et habuit et adhuc habet in propria sua manurantia*, and he did not show that his father died so, which could be that he died after the tithes accrued to be due, and thus it could be true that he was seised at all times and manured the land at all times after the death of his father and yet not manured it at the time the tithes [were] due. Also where he said that he manured the land the whole year of 21 Jac. [1623], in which year, the subtraction of the tithes is alleged, this is not sufficient became the grain was wheat, which, as everyone knows, is sown before Christmas in 20 Jac. [1622] and the year of 21 Jac. [1623] begins the 24th of March afterwards so that, even though it was in his manurance in reaping time, yet it does not appear so as the time of the sowing of it. And in the hands of the Hospitalers, it was requisite that they will be at the charge of the sowing, W[eston] sowed it *propriis manibus* because, as it is often put in the canon laws, if they lease their lands at halves, there, tithes will be paid.

And I conceive, if one demise them and sow the land and they re-enter and reap it, tithes will be paid because it is not [*in*] *propriis manibus nec sumptibus.* Thus, if one of the alienees [?] will sow their lands for them because it is requisite and the consideration of the discharge was that they themselves labor in it or it will be at the cost upon poor laborers in their land and where they were not at neither, there, they will not have a discharge. And also, they have not had the manurance of the land to continue in him at the time of the reaping, and it should or, otherwise, it will not be intended to continue, as in 7 Hen. VII, 3;[1] a use will not be intended to continue, and a manurance [is] more transitory than a use etc. so that, upon all, I conclude for the plaintiff in this action and pray judgment for him.

Residuum postea, pl. 11; f. 47b, pl. 92.[2]

30

Shury v. Browne

(K.B. Hil. 1 Car. I, 1626)

A rent reserved to an assignee survives the death of the lessor-assignor.

---

[1] YB Mich. 7 Hen. VII, f. 3, pl. 3 (1491).
[2] For later proceedings in this case, see below, Nos. 31, 225, 280.

BL MS. Add. 35961, f. 10, pl. 10

Between Shury, plaintiff, and Browne, defendant, which is entered Hil. 20 Jac., rot. 177, the case was thus. One made a lease for years, *reddendo et solvendo inde annuatim praedicto* the lessor *et assignatis suis durante termino praedicto* the sum etc. And it was of a common and other lands to which the common was appendant. And whether the rent had a continuance after the lifetime of the lessor was also another question.

The defendant, in the [plea in] bar, showed the assignment and did not show the place of it. And whether it will be intended upon the land or if it will not be intended upon the land, whether the showing of it in the rejoinder will be sufficiently good. And that the plaintiff, by his demurrer upon it, does not foreclose himself of this help was the other question.

And Serjeant *Bridgman* [argued] for the plaintiff. For the first point, he argued that the rent will have a continuance after the death of the lessor because it appears by his own reservation that his intent will be that the rent will remain after his death because it is reserved payable *annuatim et durante termino*. Thus, according to his reservation, which he could make in any manner, he will have the rent. And this differs clearly from Dyer's case, fo. 45,[1] where the lessor reserved the rent to himself; there, it is not but for his own life because he did not lease it to him generally; there, the law intends his meaning to be so far as his words extend. But here, the general intention to restrain it to himself is expressly altered by the words because he manifested his intent to be that, 'during the term' and 'to his assignees', it will be paid. And for express authority, he cited 27 Hen. VIII, 19,[2] where it is put that, if it be reserved to him during the term or to him and his successors or heirs, that it is the same, but, if the reservation had been merely to the lessor, then it will not go after his death because, then, as Moyle said [in] 10 Edw. IV, 18b,[3] it is the same as if he had said reserving rent to me during my life. And, with this, C. 171[4] agrees because the words will not be extended beyond themselves. Thus [is] 11 Edw. III, Ass. 6, and tit. *Ass.*, 86, cited there for 10 Edw. III;[5] if there be a lease of two acres reserving to him a rent for one and to himself and his heirs for the other, there, the first reservation is but for life. But here, in these cases, [there is] nothing to correct the general intention of the words, of which themselves import a reservation, except only to himself.

But in our case, it could not be so intended because he had himself expressed it his intent that he will be paid during the term. And upon this case and reason

---

[1] *Anonymous* (1539), 1 Dyer 45, 73 E.R. 97.

[2] *Dokeray's Case* (1535), YB Mich. 27 Hen. VIII, ff. 14, 19, pl. 6.

[3] YB Mich. 10 Edw. IV, 49 Hen. VI, f. 18, pl. 22, 47 Selden Soc. 160 (1470 x 1471).

[4] *Hill v. Grange* (1557), 1 Plowden 164, 75 E.R. 253.

[5] YB 11 Edw. III, Lib. Ass., p. 29, pl. 6 (1337), Fitzherbert, Abr., *Assise*, pl. 86.

is the resolution in Mallory's case, Coke, 5, 112,[1] which, in our case, is express authority and judgment. And with this, he concluded for the plaintiff.

On the other side, it was argued that the reservation extends only to the lessor himself, and it is not aided by the words *durante termino praedicto*. And for this, it was cited adjudged in the point [in] Butcher and Richman's case, Hil. 33 Eliz., rot. 1316, in replevin;[2] the heir justified by reason of a lease made by his father reserving a rent to himself, his executors, and assigns *annuatim durante termino praedicto*, and there, judgment was for the plaintiff because the rent in this case was not reputed to continue after the death of the lessor, and yet, there, it spoke of executors and his intent was apparent by it, but it will not alter the general intention of the preceding words. And also another [case] was cited to this purpose, *viz.* Hill and Hill, Pas. 4 Jac. 112, in the common bench, and, for the assignment not being alleged in any place, it was said that it will be intended to be upon the land. And he resembled it to the case of 5 Hen. VII, of attornment, and of 21 Hen. VII, 23,[3] of tender of homage.

And, if it will not be thus intended, still, he said, if issue on it be joined, it comes in sufficient time in the rejoinder. And there, it was agreed that all of the rent reserved here issues out of the land and not out of the common.

And the judges showed their opinions briefly, but not to be bound by it, but they took time to advise further.

WHITELOCKE: The rent is the recompense and the consideration for the land and, on account of this, *prima facie*, it is intended to last as long as the lease and rise with the reservation of it. And on account of this and upon this reason, if the party leases it with the reservation of the law, it would give it to him and his heirs and thus will give to each the rent according to the estate with which he departs, as in the case of two joint tenants and to the heir of one of them and they lease etc., but if he would not lease it with the disposition of the law, then, there, the law intends that his meaning is to have his own limitation followed, and, on account of this, it will not extend beyond the words themselves. And this is the reason of Dyer 45; C. 171; 10 Edw. IV, 18; and 11 Edw. III, 45, or that had [in] 14 Hen. VI, 26.[4] But [it is] otherwise, if he did not restrain the reservation expressly; there, the law would not implicitly extend the recompense to the time of

---

[1] *Mallory v. Payn* (1601), 5 Coke Rep. 111, 77 E.R. 228, also Cro. Eliz. 805, 832, 78 E.R. 1033, 1058.

[2] *Richmond v. Butcher* (1591), 2 Leonard 214, 74 E.R. 488, Cro. Eliz. 217, 78 E.R. 473, 1 Anderson 261, 123 E.R. 462.

[3] YB Hil. 21 Hen. VII, ff. 22, 23, pl. [14] (1506).

[4] *Anonymous* (1539), 1 Dyer 45, 73 E.R. 97; *Hill v. Grange* (1556), 1 Plowden 164, 171, 75 E.R. 253, 264, also 2 Dyer 130, 73 E.R. 284; YB Mich. 10 Edw. IV, 49 Hen. VI, f. 18, pl. 22, 47 Selden Soc. 160 (1470 x 1471); *Killam v. T.* (1435 x 1436), YB 14 Hen. VI, f. 26, pl. 77.

the [. . .].[1] And on account of this, in C. 171,[2] the lease was made at midsummer, reserving a rent to the Annunciation and Michaelmas, and yet the first day of payment was resolved to be Michaelmas, though it was not first named, or, otherwise, the lessee would enjoy the land a half year paying nothing. And this is also the reason of Lofield's case, C. 10.[3]

But here in our case, the party has not leased it at the disposition and ordering of the law, but he has specially restrained it to himself and his assigns. And, if he had not gone further, it would have been for his own life. But, here, he declared his intent by the subsequent words, that it will be during the term so that it carries the intention of the reservation. And it shows his intent that his intent will be here pursued, as, in all other cases of reservation, it will be. And this is to have continuance after the death of the lessor if the term continues so long. Thus as now adjudged, the assignee here will have the rent, be the lessor dead or not. And, as it seems to me, Mallory's case is express in the point.

JONES agreed. And he said that the difference between an express and an implied reservation was not ever adjudged. The first case of it is this of 11 Edw. III, and, there, he said that this could be good law for the apparent difference of reservations in the same deed; thus, there, it expressly appears that he did not intend to have them the same. Then came 14 Hen. VI, and, there, it is put without contradiction by two that, though the reservation be to the lessor himself, yet it will go to the heir with the reversion. Then, 10 Edw. IV came expressly contrary to it. And after this, 27 Hen. VIII and fo. 19 against 28.[4] Then [in] Dyer 45, the difference was expressly put, but, there, one judge and two serjeants said that it is a narrow difference. But [in] C. 171 the difference [was] taken by one of the counsellors in the case, and thus, as I confess, is the opinion at this day, and to this intent they applied the case of 6 Edw. II, of warrants, vouched. Dyer 45, and this opinion and the reason of it, I hold for good law.

But our case is proved more plainly by the reason of this case because, here, the intent of him, by the limitation for the payment to endure for the term, is not to be or to have it constrained[5] by the first words, 'to him'. And we must take all of the words together. And I ground this upon the transposition of the terms in Hill and Grange's case, C. 171. And thus, the intent of it must be or, otherwise, two judgments, *viz.* Mallory's case and Whitelock's case, are expressly crossed by it. And for the judgment cited of 33 Eliz., the copy of which was shown here, I do not know the reason of it and upon what they grounded themselves, whether upon the matter in law or upon the pleading.

---

[1] elese *MS.*

[2] *Hill v. Grange* (1557), *ut supra.*

[3] *Young v. Milton* (1612), 10 Coke Rep. 106, 77 E.R. 1086, also 1 Brownlow & Goldesborough 61, 123 E.R. 665.

[4] *Dokeray's Case* (1535), YB Mich. 27 Hen. VIII, ff. 14, 19, pl. 6; f. 28, pl. 16.

[5] distreyne *MS.*

And for the bar, here, the not showing of the place is faulty because, first, it will not be intended to be done upon the land because one can lease in London land which lies in York. And if it will not be so as it will not be, then also it will be too late to show it in the rejoinder because, though the old books are thus, yet the course is now altered and generally received [as] otherwise. Thus, as now advised, I agree with Brother Whitelocke.

DODDERIDGE delivered no opinion, but he seemed to incline against the two last. He said that, if the party would not allow the law to dispose of the rent, then it will be according to his reservation.

In this, there are three things to be considered: (1) the rent reserved, (2) the persons to whom, so that they are privies, (3) the time of payment, how long it endures and when it will begin. And, in all of these cases, the reservation being the act of the party, he can frame it in what manner he wishes because, for the first, he can reserve no rent, he can reserve a rent for part of the term and for part not, and, for part, he can reserve a rose and, for another part, money, so that, in this part, it will be according as he will limit.

This second, for the person, it will be also as he limits it, so that there be privity, as he can limit it solely to his heirs or solely to his assigns or solely to himself. And two joint tenants, if they lease, they can reserve the rent to one of them, so that the reservation is the creature of the lessor, and, what shape he will put upon it, this it will be. Thus, in our case, the reservation is to him and his assigns during the term, by which his intent appears, as it seems to me, to be that the rent will be paid but for his life, *viz.* to him if he survives the term and to his assignee if the assignee and the assignor survive the term. And this, as it seems to me, does not hurt Mallory's case nor Whitelock's in any manner.

The third thing considerable in a reservation is the time during which the rent will be paid and this, if it is not limited, is during the term, and, if he limits it during the term, then, it goes to the heir with the reversion as incident [to it] if there not be any restraint of the person. But here in our case, the assignee could have [it], but not the heir by any means because it is not reserved to him.

Thus, this I have said to inform myself of the reasons of the case. And, if the precedents are as they were vouched, it is well to follow them. And on account of this, it is fit that the counsel attend us with them.

Chief Justice CREWE: As advised, I agree with my brothers Jones and Whitelocke and for the same reasons. And I also think [that], here, the heir cannot have the advantage of the reservation because he is not mentioned. And this was the reason of the case in [the year] 33 of the queen because I heard it. And there, the heir brought an action for the rent, and not the assignee, as here, and, there, I remember it was said that, if the assignee, which is our case, had distrained, he could well avow. Thus, this precedent is not by way of our case nor does it conclude but that the rent here lasts after the life of the lessor.

And afterwards, at another day, Dodderidge [being] absent, the final resolution of the court was requested; they said that they continued of the same opinion.

[Other reports of this case: Benloe 159, 73 E.R. 1024, CUL MS. Gg.2.30, f. 55; 3 Bulstrode 328, 81 E.R. 272; Latch 99, 82 E.R. 294, HLS MS. 1235, f. 37v; BL MS. Hargr. 38, f. 36, pl. 3; BL MS. Lansd. 1092, f. 74v; CUL MS. Ll.3.13, f. 88v.]

[Related cases: Coles v. Shury (1626), below, Nos. 68, 168.]

31

Whitton v. Weston

(Part 2)
(K.B. Hil. 1 Car. I, 1626)

BL MS. Add. 35961, f. 11, pl. 11

Serjeant *Bridgman* [argued] for the defendant briefly.[1] As to the objection that it does not appear that the defendant, as to the time of the sowing and tilling manure, it is, notwithstanding, good enough because it appears by the showing of the plaintiff in his declaration that he, at this time, manured it [and] that, in such cases, the Hospitalers will pay tithes.

But for the main point, here, I hold, first, that the king and his patentees have this privilege; second, that the clause of discharge in 31 Hen. VIII[2] reaches to these lands of the Templars.

For the first, it is plain by the words of 32 [Hen. VIII],[3] which dissolved this hospital, which enacts that all the privileges of the Hospitalers will belong to the king. And this was one of the privileges. And this appears by another branch also, which takes away the privilege of sanctuary from those lands, so that, if the former clause of giving to the king the privilege had given this of tithes to the king as well [?] as it would have done the sanctuary, and, where it can be said that, if the intent was that they will be discharged, there could have been such a clause in the Statute of 32 [Hen. VIII] as is in the Statute of 31 [Hen. VIII], I answer that it was there for two reasons:

(1) For the inducing of purchasers and of notification of it; that, without this express clause, the law would have operated;

(2) For the reason of the infinite means and divers ways they have to discharge, which dissolves them by 31 [Hen. VIII], but, here, those of the Hospitalers have but one means of discharge and this is by bulls of the pope and allowance here all times.

And also, it was but one house dissolved by 32 [Hen. VIII]. Thus, the notification to the purchasers by expressing it by a clause [was] not so necessary.

---

[1] For other proceedings in this case, see, Nos. 29, 225, 280.

[2] Stat. 31 Hen. VIII, c. 13 (*SR*, III, 733–739).

[3] Stat. 32 Hen. VIII, c. 24 (*SR*, III, 778–781).

For the second, I hold that the clause of discharge in 31 [Hen. VIII] reaches to this house dissolved by 32 [Hen. VIII] because it is within the words 'other means' as 'to his Majesty's hands'. And I deny the reason given in C. 2, the Archbishop's case,[1] that a house dissolved by Parliament is not within those words because, as to the case put there, that bishops are not within the words of 13 Eliz. 'or others having spiritual promotions', there is no need because they were provided for before by a Statute of 13 Eliz.[2] And this was a reason by the law which I deny utterly.

And the case in Dyer 277[3] is express in the point, and, there, [it was] resolved by four judges, excepting the lord keeper, who was then Sir Nicholas Bacon, an erudite man. And for the case cited of 44 Eliz., Spurling's case,[4] I confess that it was thus adjudged by three against one, *viz.* Sir Thomas Gawdy was mainly against it. And afterwards, Pas. 11 Jac., between Oare and Bowyer, in the common bench,[5] the question came again, and, there, two justices were against two and *sic pendet*; so that, upon all, I conclude for the defendant and pray judgment for him.

More, [*blank*].[6]

32

Bellow v. Griffin

(K.B. Hil. 1 Car. I, 1626)

A case can be removed out of the court of admiralty where the defendant there is not given a copy of the plaintiff's pleading.

BL MS. Add. 35961, f. 11v, pl. 12

Between Bellow and Gryffin, one of the parties sued the other in the [court of] admiralty and that other demanded the libel [in order] to have a copy of it. It was denied, upon which it was moved for a [writ] of prohibition. And, upon an affidavit of this matter, it was granted. And thus it was in another case of the

---

[1] *Green v. Balser* (1596), 2 Coke Rep. 46, 76 E.R. 519, 1 Gwillim 189, 1 Eagle & Younge 113.

[2] Stat. 13 Eliz. I, c. 10 (*SR*, III, 544–545).

[3] *Stathome's Case* (1568), 3 Dyer 277, 73 E.R. 621, 1 Gwillim 132, 1 Eagle & Younge 59.

[4] *Quarles v. Spurling* (1602), Moore K.B. 913, 72 E.R. 993, *sub nom. Cornwallis v. Spurling*, Cro. Jac. 57, 79 E.R. 48, 1 Gwillim 224, 1 Eagle & Younge 157.

[5] *Urrey v. Bowyer* (1611), 2 Brownlow & Goldesborough 20, 123 E.R. 791, 1 Gwillim 250, 1 Eagle & Younge 214, BL MS. Hargr. 385, f. 80 (Calthorpe's reports).

[6] For other proceedings in this case, see, Nos. 29, 225, 280.

same nature in this same term for the fault of the copy of the libel. See *Old Entries* 491, for a precedent in this case.

33

Lisle v. Budden

(K.B. Hil. 1 Car. I, 1626)

A person cannot sue for a tort that was done to land before he had title to it.

BL MS. Add. 35961, f. 11v, pl. 13

Between Lisle and Budden, the plaintiff alleged a trespass done 20 April in the year 20 Jac. [1622]. The defendant said that *diu ante praedictam* time *quo, viz. 29 die Aprilis anno* 20 [Jac.], the plaintiff made to him a lease of the said land *habendum* of the date of the deed by force of which he entered etc. And it was here held by the court that the *viz.* was void if there had not been more in the case, but inasmuch as the *habendum* made it manifest that the title to the land did not exist at the time of the trespass because the commencement of the lease was pleaded to be after the trespass was [done], thus [there was] no title.

34

Rex v. Bradbery

(K.B. Hil. 1 Car. I, 1626)

An indictment that is technically defective will be quashed.

BL MS. Add. 35961, f. 11v, pl. 14

Bradbery was indicted for forcible entry in certain land *existens liberum tenementum* etc. And it did not say *ad tunc existens liberum* etc. And upon a motion for this, it was presently quashed. And for the same exception, another indictment at another day was quashed. And this is a common exception.

35

Rex v. Barchy

(K.B. Hil. 1 Car. I, 1626)

An indictment that is technically defective will be quashed.

BL MS. Add. 35961, f. 11v, pl. 15

Another indictment was quashed, and this was of Barchy. And it was because he was presented *per sacramentum* and it did not say *per bonum et legalem hominem*, as it should etc.

36

Anonymous

(K.B. Hil. 1 Car. I, 1626)

A right of way can be obstructed, but it cannot be removed.

BL MS. Add. 35961, f. 11v, pl. 16

One was indicted because, where the king from the time [from which the memory of man runneth not] for him and his people had a [right of] way in such a place, the party indicted had removed this way *ad nocumentum* etc. And this was held impossible because he could divert the way by the stopping of the ancient way but he could not remove the way. And on account of this, the indictment was quashed.

37

Mountford v. Sydley

(K.B. Hil. 1 Car. I, 1626)

A distress against a parishioner cannot be taken upon tithes set out but not yet taken up by the parson.

BL MS. Add. 35961, f. 11v, pl. 17

Munford brought an action of trespass against Sydley (*ut patet* Hil. 22 Jac., rot. 312). And it was for the taking of three loads of oats.

The defendant justified because the place where the taking was supposed was part of the manor of S. And he held it by copy of the court roll and [it was] demised and demiseable at all times by copy and that one J.S., lord of the manor, granted it by copy to J.N., who leased to the defendant and, for damage feasant, the defendant took the oats.

The plaintiff replied that he is the parson of D. And that the place where etc. is within the parish and that the said J.N. leased the said land to the defendant for one year and that he sowed and reaped the land and set out the tithes and, afterwards, he took them back, and thus etc.

The defendant rejoined and fortified his bar and traversed *absque hoc quod* J.S. leased to him for one year.

And upon this, the plaintiff demurred.

And it was adjudged here for the plaintiff that the traverse was not material because had the defendant an estate for one year or for several or at will, so that there is possession of a term with land, his dividing of the tithes was good and the parson can also take [them], but, if one who has nothing to do [with it] comes into my land and divides the ninth part from the tenth, there, the parson cannot take them so that, here, the traverse is of a thing not material and also it is but a conveyance of the title to the tithes and, on account of this, not traversable. Also, when here, the parson comes by way of replication and shows that he [the defendant] cannot take for damage feasant because they were his tithes, here, the defendant should have shown how long the tithes were left upon the land so that the court could adjudge whether he [could have] carried them [away] in a convenient time because, if he did not do it, then the defendant could distrain them for damage feasant, but the parson will have a convenient time, as 12 Edw. IV, 6, is.[1] One could have traversed the being within the parish or that the plaintiff is the parson or that they were not his tithes. Any of these ways, he could have, if they would, if it would have saved him truly. But the traverse here is not material if it was found for the defendant. By which it was adjudged for the plaintiff.

Note that, in this case, it was agreed by all of the justices and the others that, in this case, if the parson left the corn too long upon the land, that the defendant could distrain it damage feasant or he could have an action upon the case against the parson, as it was adjudged in Wiseman and Donnan's case[2] for not fetching away tithe cheese, by which the house of the plaintiff was encumbered, and Stuckley's case, in the [court of] common bench, for not taking away tithe hay etc.

[Other reports of this case: 3 Bulstrode 336, 81 E.R. 279; W. Jones 89, 82 E.R. 47, BL MS. Hargr. 317, f. 123; 1 Gwillim 424; 1 Eagle & Younge 351; BL MS. Hargr. 30, f. 217, pl. 2 (Turnour's reports).]

[Affirmed on appeal: Cro. Car. 63, 79 E.R. 658.]

38

Johnson's Case

(K.B. Hil. 1 Car. I, 1626)

A suit for the repair of a chapel is not within the jurisdiction of the court of high commission.

---

[1] YB Pas. 12 Edw. IV, f. 6, pl. 16, 1 Eagle & Younge 46 (1472).

[2] *Wiseman v. Denham* (1623), Godbolt 329, 78 E.R. 194, Ley 69, 80 E.R. 637, 2 Rolle Rep. 328, 81 E.R. 831, Palmer 340, 381, 81 E.R. 1114, 1133, 1 Eagle & Younge 328.

BL MS. Add. 35961, f. 12, pl. 18

A suit was in the high commission court, and it was for the reparation of a chapel. And, even though it was a spiritual thing and of the spiritual jurisdiction, as was granted by all, yet [a writ of] prohibition was awarded because the commission of this court is of transcendent and erroneous crimes and not small matters of ecclesiastical jurisdiction nor of the interest between parties. And on account of this, as Justice JONES said, in the [court of] common pleas, prohibition was awarded to them where the suit was for alimony or for a pension etc. and there, JONES rehearsed how, in the case of a minister indicted for manslaughter and [it was] found and afterwards pardoned and those of the high commission would deprive him, they were prohibited.

[Other reports of this case: Latch 10, 82 E.R. 249.]

39

Blackston v. Martin

(Part 2)
(K.B. Hil. 1 Car. I, 1626)

BL MS. Add. 35961, f. 12, pl. 19

Between Blackston and Martin[1] in [a writ of] *scire facias* in the nature of an *audita querela* to avoid an extent of the land in a statute acknowledged by Sir William Blackston because Sir William had other lands at the time of the statute acknowledged, issue was joined upon this. And [it was] found that he had other lands. And now, it was moved in arrest of judgment that the plaintiff in the *scire facias* has not averred himself to be the tenant of the land at the time of the suing of the execution.

And it was said that the *scire facias* here must be as certain as a declaration. As in 32 Hen. VI, 14,[2] in *scire facias* upon a recognizance to appear etc., the condition must be expressed and the certainty of it. Thus [is] Dyer 197;[3] a *scire facias* to revoke letters patent must express the case certainly and the former grant, and it will not be taken here by implication who was the tenant etc. because, he said, it has grave damage that [one] could imply who was a tenant or, otherwise, the land was not extended *ad damnum* of him any more than a declaration will be taken by implication, as Com. 202 and 206, in waste;[4] the plaintiff declared on a grant to

---

[1] For earlier proceedings in this case, see above, No. 15.
[2] YB Mich. 32 Hen. VI, f. 14, pl. 22 (1453).
[3] *Rex v. Blage* (1561), 2 Dyer 197, 73 E.R. 436.
[4] *Stradling v. Morgan* (1560), 1 Plowden 199, 75 E.R. 305.

himself of a reversion, and it did not appear whether the [waste] was before or after the grant, and, there, it was not good, and yet, there, he concluded that it was
to his disheritance, which strongly implied that it was a grant before the waste
was [done] etc., but a declaration must contain truth and certainty, as is said in
Stradling's case, and so must the *scire facias* which is in the place of it here.

And here, if he was not the tenant at the time of the suing of the execution,
even though the land was tortiously charged, yet he will hold it thus as a feoffor
holds. And he cited 15 Edw. IV, 24,[1] where the feoffee will not have [a prosecution for] forgery for a forgery in the time of his feoffor, and Penruddock's case,
Coke, 5, and F.N.B. 149,[2] that a feoffee will not have admeasurement of dower
but he will take in the same plight as the feoffor held.

And it was urged on this side by *Bankes*.

And *Calthorpe* here said that it is alleged that Blackston was seised in fee at
the time of the recognizance and it will be intended to continue and, on account
of this, if it be not shown, it cannot be intended that the plaintiff was seised at
the time of the suing of the execution. And he cited for express authority that
the plaintiff should aver himself to be the tenant at the time of the execution, 17
Edw. III, 27, by Seton, and 35, by Thorpe, and 43a, which see,[3] upon which on
this side, it was concluded that the *scire facias* was bad and the judgment [was] to
be stayed.

On the other side, it was said that the *scire facias* is a writ and the nature of
it is to be brief. And on account of this, it will be construed[4] similarly to where a
writ was brought to distrain beasts of the plough and it did not aver that he did
not have other cattle, but, inasmuch as it is said *contra formam statuti*, it implies as
much. And divers precedents were cited where the *scire facias* was as it is here, as
Trin. 6 Hen. IV, rot. 505 and 101, in the common bench, and Mich. 16 & 17 Eliz.,
[rot.] 1313, and Trin. 34 Eliz., [rot.] 327, and divers others in the Petty Bag.

And of this opinion was the court except DODDERIDGE, who said that he
had not advised upon the case and, on account of this, he would not deliver his
resolute opinion. But after the other three justices agreed for the plaintiff, he also
agreed, and judgment was given for him.

WHITELOCKE said that, here, if he who brings an *audita querela* was not the
tenant *tempore* etc., it must have been shown on the other side and not come in on
the side of the plaintiff because the *scire facias* is to know what he can say that the
extent will not be defeated and, if there be a cause on his part, to show it.

---

[1] YB Pas. 15 Edw. IV, f. 24, pl. 5 (1475).

[2] *Clark v. Penruddock* (1598), 5 Coke Rep. 100, 77 E.R. 210, also Cro. Eliz. 234, 78
E.R. 490, Jenkins 260, 145 E.R. 185; A. Fitzherbert, *Nouvelle Natura Brevium*.

[3] YB Pas. 17 Edw. III, f. 27, pl. 24 (1343); YB Pas. 17 Edw. III, ff. 34, 35, pl. 46
(1343); YB Trin. 17 Edw. III, f. 43, pl. 32 (1343).

[4] prise per intendment *MS*.

Justice JONES agreed that, if the plaintiff was not the tenant at the time of the suing of the execution, that he could not have this action because he will hold as his feoffor held it. And to this intent, he said that it had been adjudged that, if an inquisition be found of my lands, that my feoffee will not traverse it. But he took a difference because, if an extent be sued for land and, before the *liberate* be sued, a feoffment is made, there, the feoffee will avoid it because he is the party aggrieved for it; otherwise, if he came in after the *liberate*. And he said, if, after the *liberate*, the feoffment be made of part to one and of part to another, that the one will not have contribution against the other, and, also, if a purchaser had a cause for contribution and made a feoffment, his feoffee will not have it. And, in the case at bar, he said that it was in the nature of a chancery suit and, on account of this, so express certainty is not required in it. And he said that he had enquired of the clerks of the chancery, who informed him that the constant form of the chancery was not to aver himself the tenant. By which, he concluded for the plaintiff.

DODDERIDGE, as above.

Chief Justice CREWE: The objections are strong and colorable. And the precedents from ancient times until 35 Eliz. [1592 x 1593] always express that the plaintiff was tenant at the time of the execution. And I have seen many of them upon a command to search for such precedents. But after this time, the constant form is, as this writ in our case is, [in] all the time of King James, by which to overthrow all precedents, I were not now advised, by which etc.

And thus judgment was given for the plaintiff.

[Other reports of this case: Benloe 161, 73 E.R. 1026, CUL MS. Gg.2.30, f. 55v; 3 Bulstrode 305, 81 E.R. 253; W. Jones 82, 90, 82 E.R. 44, 47; Latch 3, 112, 274, 82 E.R. 245, 300, 383, HLS MS. 1235, f. 42; Palmer 410, 81 E.R. 1147; BL MS. Hargr. 38, f. 46; BL MS. Lansd. 1092, f. 85v; CUL MS. Hh.2.1, f. 186; CUL MS. Ll.3.13, f. 102v.]

40

Rex v. Taylor

(K.B. Hil. 1 Car. I, 1626)

In this case, the indictment for barretry was adjudged to be good and sufficient.

BL MS. Add. 35961, f. 12v, pl. 20

One Taylor was indicted for barretry, and exceptions were taken:

(1) Because it did not conclude *contra pacem* etc. But this was disallowed because it was contained in the indictment *quod est gravis perturbatio pacis* etc. and it is necessarily *contra pacem*.

(2) Because it said that he was, and it did not say *adhuc* is, a barretor. And this also was disallowed because, if he was, though he did not continue, yet he could be indicted for it.

(3) Because it concluded *contra formam statuti* where it should be *diversarum statutorum*. But this was not allowed because this clause is not but surplusage because one could have been indicted for this at common law.

41

Anonymous

(K.B. Hil. 1 Car. I, 1626)

A judgment creditor can orally tell a sheriff to release the judgment debtor.

BL MS. Add. 35961, f. 12v, pl. 21

It was said *per curiam* for clear law that, if one be in execution and the party to that suit says to the sheriff by parol that he discharged the party of all executions [and] that he would that he leave him at large etc., that this is a good warrant for the sheriff though it be by parol and the execution a thing of record.

[See] below, f. 47, pl. 91; f. 140, pl. 5.[1]

42

Martin's Case

(K.B. Hil. 1 Car. I, 1626)

In this case, a plaintiff who falsely sued and caused the arrest of a defendant was himself arrested and imprisoned.

BL MS. Add. 35961, f. 12v, pl. 22

One Martin, a man of value etc., who had been the mayor of Northampton, coming to London, was arrested upon a feigned action merely to disgrace him, being a tradesman. And the party would not accept a good bail offered to him, but he would have him at the Counter [Prison]. And upon this [being] proved, the party who thus arrested him was committed to prison.

---

[1] *Smith v. Man* (1626), below, No. 223; *Wheatly v. Escort* (1628), BL MS. Add. 35961, f. 146, BL MS. Lansd. 1083, f. 229v, LI MS. Maynard 21, f. 374v.

43

Anonymous

(K.B. Hil. 1 Car. I, 1626)

An attorney of the court who gets a parliamentary protection to avoid being sued will be struck off the roll of the court.

BL MS. Add. 35961, f. 12v, pl. 23

Justice JONES showed to his brothers that an attorney of this court [of king's bench], intending to avoid a suit against himself, in the last Parliament, was in the protection of one of the lower house and, now, at this Parliament, is in the protection of one of the lords of the higher house so that it made much mischief. And he said that he had known in the [court of] common bench upon information of the same cause that such [an] attorney had been put out of the rolls. And thus, it was agreed that the attorney here will be.

44

Warner v. Harding

(Part 2)
(K.B. Hil. 1 Car. I, 1626)

BL MS. Add. 35961, f. 12v, pl. 24

The case before, fo. 1b, pl. 3, between Hardwyine and Warner[1] was argued again by *Noy* for the plaintiff and Serjeant *Hitcham* for the defendant, but Hitcham was not provided for it, as he himself said, and what he spoke was out of an old memory of that which he had spoken of it in the [court of] common bench, where the same case was in question.

Noy made two questions here: (1) whether the condition be given to the queen; (2) if it be given, whether it be performed.

For the first, he argued that the condition was inseparable from the person of Shelley and, on account of this, it was not given to the crown, neither by the Statute of 33 Hen. VIII,[2] nor by the private act of attainder by the words 'of all of his inheritances', and conditions [that are] but inseparable conditions and which cannot [be] performed by an attorney, as here it cannot be, it cannot by this word be given to the queen. But it could be objected that, by such a construction, a means is given for traitors to convey their land and to shield it from forfeiture and thus treason [would be] favored. To this, I answer that this does not make any mischief in the law because the common law does not favor the transferring

---

[1] For other proceedings in this case, see Nos. 3, 100.
[2] Stat. 33 Hen. VIII, c. 20, s. 4 (*SR*, III, 857).

of the conditions, and, on account of this, if there be not a sufficient provision against it, the fault is in the statute. And also, there are other means here [as] easy as this to avoid the forfeitures, *viz.* the duke of Norfolk's case, etc.[1] And the common law was wary in the transferring of conditions so that, at common law, the extent had been upon the statute acknowledged and, there, a reversion had been granted, the grantee could not have tendered the money and redeemed the land until 10 Edw. III when it was enacted that he could. And this statute was put here in this court by a *mittimus* and here it is of record, and it is not extant in any other case. And on account of this, it being a personal and individual action, it cannot be transferred. And it is similar to an attornment which one cannot do in the person of [?] the attorney, as 2 Hen. VII, 27, and 32 Hen. VI, 22, are.[2] But, where a plea is pleaded afterwards that the defendant cannot attorn, there, in *quid juris* or *per quod servitia*, the tenant can make attorn[ment], and also it was part of the ceremony that he then declares the intent, and this was necessary, similar to the case of 10 Hen. II, 9,[3] by Keble; if a letter of attorney be to make a feoffment in English and he made [it] in Latin, it is void. And there is a tenure in Suffolk where one holds by coming on a certain day into the hall of[4] the lord and there *facere saltum suslatum et babutum* and, there, without question, if he does not observe the postures of his body limited, it is not performance of the service. Thus here, the declaration of Shelley himself is material and it makes the condition not performable by any other or by an attorney. And also, none would doubt but that, the attainder notwithstanding, that Shelley could have done it himself because it is an act of his natural body and that a monk or other incapable person could do similarly. Where one makes a lease for so many years as J.S. will name and, afterwards, J.S. is attainted or professes [religious vows], yet he has not lost this power because it is a natural act that anyone can do. And then, he having power to do it, it is not transferred to another. And, under favor, I do not see any difference between this and the case of the duke of Norfolk in Englefield's case.[5] And also, this very case was twice adjudged in the common bench: the first upon the pleading, but the other [was] upon the matter in law.

(But it is to be remembered that, in the argument before, it, the judgment aforesaid, was shown without the seal of the common bench, but, then, aspersion was cast upon it by the counsel of the other party, who said that they forbore to render the reason of the judgment and prayed the judges to enquire of it from

---

[1] *Duke of Norfolk's Case*, 7 Coke Rep. 13, 77 E.R. 43.

[2] YB Trin. 1 Hen. VII, ff. 26, 27, pl. 2 (1486); *Bishop of Ely v. Elverton* (1454), YB Hil. 32 Hen. VI, f. 22, pl. 4.

[3] YB Mich. 10 Hen. VII, f. 9, pl. 20 (1494).

[4] daver sale *MS.*

[5] *Regina v. Englefield* (1591), 7 Coke Rep. 11, 13, 77 E.R. 428, 431, also Moore K.B. 303, 72 E.R. 595, 4 Leonard 135, 169, 74 E.R. 779, 800, Popham 18, 79 E.R. 1139, 1 Anderson 293, 123 E.R. 480.

those of the common bench. And thus, now later, *Hitcham* gave an answer to the judgment being now cited.)

For the second, whether the condition (admitting it forfeited) was performed. And *Noy* held not because it is alleged that a gold ring was tendered but it did not say of what value and the words are that, if he tender a gold ring or pair of gloves of 12d. or 1s. in money etc. so that the price of 1s. refers to the ring as well as the gloves, similar to the case if I covenant in consideration of £5 paid to me by J.S. to give to him a cow or a horse of £10, here, without question, if he gave to him a cow of 40s., it is not performance of the contract because, there, without question, the subsequent words of £5 goes to both; thus here, because *magis et minus non variant speciem*. And it is a rule that a generality that follows particulars or that goes before particulars will have relation to all of the particulars as if a lease for life be a remainder for life rendering rent, here, rendering rent goes to both estates, as 19 Edw. II, in tit. *Avowry*, it is thus, if there be a lease for life, the remainder for life, without impeachment of waste, the last clause, 'without impeachment of waste', goes to both estates. And to this purpose, there was a case in the common bench, Trin. 3 Jac., rot. 1619, between Brakenbury and Brakenbury, where there was a covenant that the defendant within two years will convey such land to the plaintiff or will become bound in an obligation, here, the precedent clause will have relation to the particulars following so that it was sufficient for the defendant to be bound within the two years. Thus [is] Dyer 347;[1] one was bound before such a day to make a lease for 31 years if A. will assent and, if not, for 21 years; there, if A. will not assent, the lease for 21 years is to be made before the day because this refers to both. Thus in 5 Edw. IV, 127,[2] the condition was, if the defendant appear before the justices of gaol delivery or before the justices of peace *rationabile praemunitione inde habita*, there, he must have notice as well to appear before the justices of peace as otherwise because *praemunitione* goes to both. Thus, in our case, the price of 1s. will go as well to the gold ring as to the gloves. And on account of this, it not being alleged to be of this price, the condition was not sufficiently performed.

And also, the certificate is that he tendered to the heir apparent, that he could not be an heir during the lifetime of the ancestor and the proviso is that if he tender to the feoffee or his heir and, here, the tender was to the heir apparent. And for this, [see] Pas. 35 Eliz., rot. 242; Audley brought [an action of] debt against Nudegate, as heir apparent to the ancestor, and he recovered in the common bench, and, here, it was reversed by [a writ of] error because, by his own showing, he was not then heir to the ancestor because he was heir apparent, in the [court of] common pleas, during the lifetime of the ancestor.

And thus, he concluded for the plaintiff.

---

[1] *Gage v. Fourthe* (1576), 3 Dyer 347, 73 E.R. 780, also 1 Anderson 49, 123 E.R. 347, Benloe 276, 123 E.R. 194.

[2] YB Mich. 5 Edw. IV, Long Quinto, f. 127 (1465).

Hitcham [argued] for the defendant, and he reduced the whole question to this point: whether the condition be given to the queen because, for the performance notwithstanding, the objection is good perform[ance] and according to the word of the proviso and for the condition being given to the queen, he said that the declaration is incident to the tender and that, there, the law, without his speaking, would have implied [it]. And on account of this, the expressing of it is not material, but it will be as much as if he had not expressed this clause, and then, clearly, it will be given to the queen, as [is] 37 Eliz., Arrow and Smith's case;[1] a lease was for life upon a condition that the lessee will make no lease but with a proviso that they will terminate upon his death, and he made a lease without this proviso, and yet [there was] no forfeiture because this clause was no more than the law says. Thus, in our case, the law implies the declaration. And on account of this, it is not material to express it. And a stronger case than Englefield's case, there cannot be on our side.

And thus he briefly concluded for the defendant.

More [at] fo. [*blank*], pl. 8.[2]

45

Frampton v. Haughton

(K.B. Pas. 2 Car. I, 1626)

A plea objecting to venue cannot be made after a defendant has demurred.

A judgment must recite that it was made upon the consideration of the court.

BL MS. Add. 35961, f. 13v, pl. 1

Between Frampton and Haughton in a writ of error [entered Mich. 1 Car. I] upon a judgment given in an action upon the case in the court of Bridgnorth before the bailiffs there, the plaintiff in the court paravail alleged that where the defendant was his acquaintance, that he, in consideration that the plaintiff would be bound with him in an obligation to J.S., he would discharge and guard indemnified the plaintiff and that afterwards, the plaintiff was forced to pay the money for the defendant and that the defendant, in consideration that the plaintiff forbear to sue him upon the said *assumpsit*, assumed at such a place within the jurisdiction of the court of Bridgnorth to pay to him the money within forty days. And the defendant demurred. The plaintiff imparled and, afterwards, joined with him in the demurrer. And the bailiffs gave judgment for the plaintiff. And it was thus entered *et ideo videtur curiae etc.* and it did not give judgment *in*

---

[1] *Haddon v. Arrowsmith* (1596), Cro. Eliz. 461, 78 E.R. 699, Owen 72, 74 E.R. 910, Popham 105, 79 E.R. 1214.

[2] For other proceedings in this case, see Nos. 3, 100.

facto ideo consideratum est. And after a writ to enquire of damages [was] awarded and executed, they gave judgment *ideo consideratum est.*

And here, three errors were moved, first, that a place where the first *assumpsit* was laid was not expressed by which it could appear whether it was within the jurisdiction of the court or not and also whether issue had been joined upon it there had not been a place of the venue and the first *assumpsit* was the ground of the second.

And it was not allowed because DODDERIDGE said that the second *assumpsit* was the ground of the action and, if this was in the jurisdiction, it is good, and also that the first *assumpsit* is not traversable here, and, if it was, still, by the demurrer, it was confessed. And the exception for the default of the venue [was] saved by the demurrer.

And JONES said here that it is the same as a count upon *indebitatus assumpsit* where it is not traversable whether he was indebted or not nor will the place be put in certain.

Another exception was that the plea was discontinued, which, in the case of a demurrer, is not aided, even though, in the case of a verdict, it may be. And this was because the title of the court was *placita tenta in curia domini regis coram J.S. et J.D., balivis etc.*, and the judgment was given by J.N. and J.G., bailiffs, and it did not show the removal of the old bailiffs, which is the common course in all pleas before annual officers.

But the court did not speak to this.

The third [exception] was in the judgment itself because it was not an express judgment, but only [that] the bailiffs gave their opinions, and, on account of this, the first judgment being void, the following judgment of damages was also void. And on account of this, the judgment was reversed.

46

Anonymous

(K.B. Pas. 2 Car. I, 1626)

The issue in this case centered upon bail upon an audita querela.

BL MS. Add. 35961, f. 13v, pl. 2

One brought *audita querela* because, being voluntarily let at large by the sheriff, he was taken again in execution. And he prayed that this be allowed. And in this case, it was said that the plaintiff must be bailed in open court, or before two justices at least, to have sufficient bail, to which, DODDERIDGE said that the course of the court is, if the *audita querela* be upon a matter of fact, as it is here, it is true, but, if the plaintiff, upon a prayer of allowance of it, shows a release, then there is not need of such good bail.

47

Hudson v. Barman

(K.B. Pas. 2 Car. I, 1626)

It is not defamation to call one who is not a merchant a bankrupt.

BL MS. Add. 35961, f. 13v, pl. 3

Between Hudson and Barman, the plaintiff, in the action of case, declared that, where he was honest and of good fame, the defendant had said of him 'he is a base, broken rascal; he has [gone] broke twice, and I will make him break the third time.' And in arrest of judgment, it was moved that those words are not actionable, first, because the plaintiff has not alleged himself to be a merchant nor to make his living by buying and selling, in which case, if the words had been plainly that he was a bankrupt, an action upon the case would not lie because otherwise he is not damaged[1] by it; thus, he should declare that he is a merchant or etc. And thus [is] Coke 4, 19, a, b;[2] the cases are of a merchant. To which, the court agreed.

The second reason [was] because, admitting that these words were spoken of a merchant, yet, they are not actionable because it is a strained construction to construe [?] 'broken' by 'bankrupt'. But the court did not speak to this.

And there, it was said by DODDERIDGE and agreed by JONES that to say that such a merchant, naming him, 'has been twice bankrupt' is not actionable because it does not impair his credit and many merchants have [gone] broke and afterwards become great, rich men.

[Other reports of this case: *sub nom. Hutton v. Bourman*, Benloe 170, 73 E.R. 1032, CUL MS. Gg.2.30, f. 61; *sub nom. Hill's Case*, Latch 114, 82 E.R. 301; *sub nom. Marshall v. Allen*, Noy 77, 74 E.R. 1044; BL MS. Hargr. 38, f. 70, pl. 2.]

48

Note

(K.B. Pas. 2 Car. I, 1626)

In an action of trover or detinue, the defendant is not liable if he is not in possession of the goods.

In an action of trover or detinue, the plaintiff is not entitled to the possession of the goods before a final judgment is rendered in his favor.

---

[1] indemnified *MS.*

[2] *Brittridge's Case* (1602), 4 Coke Rep. 18, 76 E.R. 905.

BL MS. Add. 35961, f. 13v, pl. 4

In an action upon trover and conversion or a detinue, it is well pleaded for the defendant to say that he found the goods and lost them again because he is, in such a case, chargeable only in regard that they are in his possession. And also, he can detain them until the plaintiff proves them to be his goods. [It was said] by DODDERIDGE.

49

Watkins's Case

(K.B. Pas. 2 Car. I, 1626)

A writ of prohibition that is not served upon the defendant expires upon the death of the king.

BL MS. Add. 35961, f. 14, pl. 5

Serjeant *Athow* argued that [a writ of] prohibition where there is not any appearance nor declaration, but a bare prohibition, will not abate by the demise of the king by the Statute of 1 Edw. VI,[1] by which it is enacted that no action, suit, bill, or plaint which pends or will pend will abate by the death of the king. And here, the prohibition is within the word 'suit', and it pends because there is no need of a return. And it is not similar to a prohibition in the chancery because this is returnable [in] another court and it does not pend before it. But here, before an appearance, it pends. And he could appear and nonsuit the plaintiff. And it is not similar to an information because, there, the king recovers something. Thus, he does not here. But, if the information be by an original writ of debt, there, all will stand; in the other, it is before; all will abate but the information itself. And, as to this, that the conclusion is in contempt of *domini regis nunc, quod non competit* to another king, thus is *scandalum magnatum*, and yet it is not discontinued for this, and yet this is *tam pro domino rege quam etc.* But inasmuch as the king does not recover anything, this is the reason that the form[ality] to make him a party will not abate the same by the demise of the king.

CREWE and DODDERIDGE agreed.

JONES: The difference has been commonly taken where there was a bare prohibition and where there has been an appearance or other proceedings upon it. There, it will not abate; [it is] otherwise if [it is] a nude prohibition. And thus, I have taken the law and the rule of the court to be.

WHITELOCKE agreed.

---

[1] Stat. 1 Edw. VI, c. 7 (*SR*, IV, 12–13).

And JONES said that there is a difference between a prohibition in the king's bench and the common bench because, there, it is grounded upon a precedent information and there is a different power in prohibitions.

DODDERIDGE agreed and said that thus it was certified in the great case of prohibitions[1] in the time of King James. And on account of this, the prohibition in the common bench is in the nature of a judicial process issuing out of the rolls and grounded upon the precedent information and, on account of this, it will not abate there.

And afterwards, DODDERIDGE changed [his] opinion and agreed with Jones. And the court advised the serjeant to sue a new [writ of] prohibition.

[Other reports of this case: Latch 114, 82 E.R. 301.]

50

Anonymous

(K.B. Pas. 2 Car. I, 1626)

For a tender of a settlement of a tort to be valid, it must be for a sum certain.

BL MS. Add. 35961, f. 14, pl. 6

Note: In [an action of] trespass, it was admitted by the counsel of the defendant and the court [that], if the defendant tender to the plaintiff and show to him money and say to him 'please yourself for the trespass and, if here be not enough, ask [for] more and you shall have it', that this is not within the new Statute[2] because he did not tender a certain amends.

51

Carleton v. Hutton

(K.B. Pas. 2 Car. I, 1626)

The courts of common law, not the ecclesiastical courts, have the jurisdiction to determine the rights to a seat or a pew in a church.

The ecclesiastical courts have the jurisdiction to prevent disturbances in churches.

BL MS. Add. 35961, f. 14, pl. 7

In a prohibition between Carelton and Hutton, it was admitted by the counsel and taken for clear law by the court and said that thus it has often been adjudged that, if one prescribe that he and all those who have been tenants of one

---

[1] *Langdale's Case* (1608), 12 Coke Rep. 58, 77 E.R. 1338.
[2] Stat. 21 Jac. I, c. 16, s. 5 (*SR*, IV, 1223).

such house have used from time [of which memory runneth not to the contrary] etc. to have the first seat in such a long seat in a church or to have such a pew, that, there, it belongs to the temporal court and not to the spiritual [court] and it is decidable by an action upon the case. But, if strife be in the church for this, the ordinary can inhibit him who did not have the possession to disturb the other for the quiet of the church, but he cannot inhibit him who has the possession because he cannot alter the possession in such a case.

After, 125, pl. 8.[1]

[Other reports of this case: Latch 116, 82 E.R. 302; Noy 78, 74 E.R. 1045; Palmer 424, 81 E.R. 1153; BL MS. Hargr. 38, f. 64v, pl. 1; CUL MS. Hh.2.1, f. 190.]

52

Daniel v. Upley

(Part 1)
(K.B. Pas. 2 Car. I, 1626)

A devise will be construed according to the intent of the testator.

In this case, the devise in issue granted a widow a power of appointment, not a fee simple.

A power can be exercised by a married woman.

BL MS. Add. 35961, f. 14, pl. 8

Between Danyell, plaintiff, and Upley, defendant, in [an action of] *ejectione firmae* (*intratur* Hil. 22 Jac., rot. 945 or 745 or 720) upon a special verdict, the case was thus. John Upley, the ancestor, seised in fee etc. devised in these words, 'Item: I will and bequeath to Agnes, my wife, my house and all the lands to it belonging to dispose of at her will and pleasure and to give it unto which of my sons she will.' And he died. The wife entered, and she took for a husband one John Sheires. And, being married, she made a feoffment to William Upley, the youngest son, in fee and made a livery accordingly. John Upley, the son, released to him with warranty in the lifetime of the mother. And afterwards Sheires, the husband, the wife having levied a fine as a *feme sole* to William Upley, released to him all demands. And afterwards, he entered and leased to the plaintiff etc. And this case was argued [in] Michaelmas [term] 22 Jac. [1624].

And afterward, by the default of a special verdict, it was abandoned and brought about again and argued this term. And the counsel of the plaintiff made in this case but one point, *viz.* whether, by the words of the devise, the wife had

---

[1] *Twisden v. Sidley* (K.B. 1628), BL MS. Add. 35961, f. 131, pl. 8; BL MS. Lansd. 1083, f. 212v, pl. 8.

a fee or not. Four points, as he said, have been moved here: (1) whether the wife had a fee; (2) admitting that she had, whether, here, there be a condition annexed to it which compelled her to give [it] or not; (3) how this enures, she being a married woman when she made the feoffment; (4) upon the Statute of 4 Hen. VII,[1] whether the husband be barred by the fine.

But he said that all depended upon the first. And on account of this, it seemed to him that the wife had an absolute fee here clogged with no condition. First, if the words had not gone further but had been only 'I give to dispose at her will and pleasure,' then it had been clear that nothing but the fee simple absolute had been [given] here because his intent was joint, as the case of Littleton, if one devises *in perpetuum*, it is a fee simple, even though some have made a distinction where the devise was to him *in perpetuum* and where to him and his assigns *in perpetuum*. See Littleton 586; Perkins 557; and *Devise*, F. 20; *Devise*, B. 33;[2] because the intent will declare the will and no precise form of the words is required. And *Devise*, B. 39,[3] is express in this. If the words had not been further, then the subsequent words do not alter it. And if they are still less, it is a fee and they make it a conditional estate to the plaintiff. But the subsequent words are not a condition because a condition is compulsory and, here, it is left to her will and free election because she is to give and a gift is free and to give to which of the sons as [she] thinks good and thought is free, thus, at her free election and will without compulsion and, on account of this, without a condition. And also that the following words do not alter the precedent if they are transposed is made evident because, if it was 'to give unto which of my sons she will and to dispose of at her will and pleasure', then, clearly, it had been an absolute fee in her, and, by consequence, her feoffment during the marriage [was] bad. And thus, the title of the defendant is not good.

Serjeant *Henden* for the defendant divided the case into these questions: (1) whether the wife had here an authority[4] only or an estate; (2) if she had an estate, whether it be not bound with a condition to give and a power to dispose to which of the sons she would; (3) whether this power be taken away by the coverture so that she could not execute it; (4) whether the release of the husband barring him from his entry does not bar him to avoid the fine levied by the wife.

First, he argued that, if the devise had been to dispose at her will etc. only, then, it had been a fee simple absolute, according to the book. And it has been adjudged that a devise that J.S. will be heir is a fee simple. But here, it is not but

---

[1] Stat. 4 Hen. VII, c. 24 (*SR*, II, 547–548).

[2] T. Littleton, *Tenures*, sect. 586; J. Perkins, *A Profitable Book*, sect. 557; YB Mich. 22 Edw. III, f. 16, pl. 59 (1348), Fitzherbert, Abr., *Devise*, pl. 20; Brooke, Abr., *Devise*, pl. 33.

[3] 7 Edw. VI, Brooke, Abr., *Devise*, pl. 39 (1553).

[4] I.e. a power.

an authority, similar to B., *Devise*, 48, and Dyer 323,[1] where [there was] a devise that his feoffees would make an estate; and [it is] similar to Trin. 41 Eliz., Pigot and Garvye's case,[2] where one devised land in tail to the son and that J. and B., his overseers, would have the letting and setting of the lands and the receiving of the profits for the education of his son, there, it was adjudged that the overseers did not have an interest nor could they lease in their own names but [they had] only an authority. Thus here.

And if the devise gave to Agnes an estate, yet she had authority to sell and to give to the son, which cannot be taken away by the coverture because an authority, as this is here, cannot be extinct. And on account of this, if a devise be to executors to sell, it, notwithstanding, descends to the heir where [there is] other matter they could sell. See Kell. 40b,[3] with which agrees 39 Ass. 17; 40 Edw. III, 16.[4] And the reason is because the power that they have is collateral to their estate. And for this is 13 Hen. VII, 11.[5] If one devises that his feoffees will sell and they make a feoffment, yet, against their feoffment, their power to sell remains. Thus here, the power to give to his son is collateral to his estate in the fee, and, on account of this, it is not destroyed by the coverture and that, where one has authority to do a thing, it is not hindered by coverture, as a married woman can name how many years a lessee will have. And 20 Hen. VII, 19;[6] where a devise was to the wife to sell, she can sell to her husband, therefore, during the coverture. And *Cui in vita*, 19,[7] agrees that, if a wife, a devisee to sell, takes a husband, yet she can sell because the authority [is] collateral to her estate.

For the release with warranty of John, the oldest brother, it has been admitted. And it is without question that it bars the future right.

He agreed with Littleton, with which agrees 24 Edw. III, 70; 22 Edw. III, 24; 17 Edw. III, 67,[8] because, in those days, a warranty being a common assurance, it was taken to give a right.

For the fourth [point], he took it [to be] clear that the release of the husband has barred him to defeat the fine because, by the release of the demands, he is barred of his entry which solely is the means to avoid the fine because, as are

---

[1] 29 Hen. VIII, Brooke, Abr., *Devise*, pl. 48 (1537 x 1538); *Lingen's Case* (1573), 3 Dyer 323, 73 E.R. 731.

[2] *Pigot v. Garnish* (1599), Cro. Eliz. 678, 734, 78 E.R. 915, 966.

[3] *Anonymous* (1501), Keilwey 40, 72 E.R. 198, 116 Selden Soc. 387.

[4] YB 39 Edw. III, Lib. Ass., p. 236, pl. 17 (1365); YB Pas. 49 Edw. III, f. 16, pl. 10 (1375).

[5] *Anonymous* (1501), Keilwey 40, 72 E.R. 198, 116 Selden Soc. 387.

[6] YB Pas. 10 Hen. VII, f. 20, pl. 9 (1495).

[7] Hil. 34 Edw. III, Fitzherbert, Abr., *Cui in vita*, pl. 19 (1360).

[8] YB Mich. 24 Edw. III, f. 70, pl. 80 (1350); *Favacourt v. B.* (1343), YB Mich. 17 Edw. III, f. 67, pl. 85.

Coke 7, fo. 8b, and 17 Ass. 17,[1] if a married woman levies a fine, that this bars her unless the husband enters; but, if he enters, he avoids it, by which, for all the matter, he concluded for the defendant.

DODDERIDGE said here that, if it had been to give to J.S., a certain person, then it had been a condition, but, being general to give to which of the sons she pleased, it is a question. And also, here, it is not a condition because, then, the oldest brother will have [it] for non-performance, which was not the intent of the testator.

And JONES said that it could be construed that she will have an estate for life and, thus, to give at her will and pleasure to which of her sons she wished so that she had authority to dispose of the reversion.

And a day was appointed by the justices to show their resolution, which see, below, Tr. 2, pl. 12.[2]

53

Bellamy v. Alden

(K.B. Pas. 2 Car. I, 1626)

A writ of prohibition lies to an ecclesiastical court where a party there cannot prove his case because of the two-witness rule.

BL MS. Add. 35961, f. 15, pl. 9

[In a case] between Belamy and Alden, a prohibition was awarded to the spiritual court upon this suggestion, that an executor or administrator brought in his account and, among other things, of so much money paid to one upon a bond and, for this, by the testimony of the obligee and also the showing of the bond and an acknowledged bond also, in which the testator was bound to his surety to save him harmless, and yet this proof was not admitted.

And Justice WHITELOCKE said that one hundred [writs of] prohibition have been awarded where the spiritual court would not allow proof that is good in our law,[3] as *singularis testis*, which in their law, is not proof.

[Other reports of this case: Benloe 171, 73 E.R. 1033, CUL MS. Gg.2.30, f. 61; Latch 117, 82 E.R. 303, HLS MS. 1235, f. 46; Noy 78, 74 E.R. 1045; CUL MS. Hh.2.1, f. 191v; CUL MS. Ll.3.13, f. 108.]

---

[1] *Earl of Bedford's Case* (1586), 7 Coke Rep. 7, 8, 77 E.R. 421, 423; YB 17 Edw. III, Lib. Ass., f. 51, pl. 17 (1343).

[2] For later proceedings in this case, see below, No. 104.

[3] I.e. the common law.

54

Bird v. Robinson

(K.B. Pas. 2 Car. I, 1626)

The issue in this case was the breach of a condition of a grant to use the land for the benefit of the poor.

BL MS. Add. 35961, f. 15, pl. 10

Bird brought [an action of] *ejectione firmae* against Robinson and declared of a lease made to him by the mayor and commonalty of the City of Oxford. And upon the general issue, it was given for him in evidence that the mayor and commonalty leased to him and made letters of attorney to one to deliver the deed and possession, which was done, and that he was ejected. And for title to the commonalty and mayor, it was given in evidence that Henry, earl of Huntington, 4 Eliz. [1561 x 1562], gave it to certain feoffees to the use of them and their heirs and, by another deed delivered at the same time, it was declared to be to the intent that they will employ it to the use of the poor and that, if they convert it to another use, that it will be lawful to him to re-enter and that the feoffees died and the heir of the survivor gave it to the mayor and commonalty to the aforesaid intent, (and to prove this deed, one of the commonalty was admitted to give [it] in evidence, *quod nota*) and that thus [the lands] were employed until 22 Eliz. [1579 x 1580], at which time, Henry, earl of Huntington, made this feoffment and letter of attorney to make a livery to Brasenose College and disseised them. And the possession continued with the College for forty-five years.

And on the other side, it was labored to be proved to the jury that there was a misemployment (and, upon this point, the matter rested in the end) and that, upon this, the earl made the feoffment and letter of attorney, as is said before, to the College, under which the defendant claimed. But the College could not prove that a livery was made to a sufficient attorney deputed by them to receive it because the estate and seisin was upon the back of the feoffment delivered April 15. Thus, if livery was made, it [was] made to the attorney of the College who, at the time, did not have authority but by parol. (But as Serjeant *Crewe* said, if it could be proved it was made and delivered before the date, it will not estop the jury, as Goddard's case, Coke, 2, 4,[1] was adjudged.) Thus, upon this point, no title was proved to the College.

Then, on the other side, it was urged that, still, even though the College did not have a right, yet, if the misemployment be found, then, the title is in the earl and, then, [there is] no tort nor title in the City, by which it was urged by the other party that it admits the misemployment, yet, until the entry to the earl, it

---

[1] *Goddard v. Denton* (1584), 2 Coke Rep. 4, 76 E.R. 396, also 3 Leonard 100, 74 E.R. 566.

was not re-vested in him. And on account of this, they urged, first, that where one had a right[1] of entry, as here, the letter of attorney with a feoffment is not valid. Otherwise, if one had a right of entry and, on account of this, if a disseisee makes a feoffment and letter of attorney to make a livery, it is good. [It is] otherwise, as is said, where one has a title of entry.

Second, they urged that the authority of the attorney was to enter and deliver seisin and, on account of this, to this intent only and, therefore, if he enter and do not make livery or [make] a void livery, that it does not reduce the land to his [. . .] because it was not his authority. And thus, the title in the City still remains, by which, to deliver [to] the court, a former letter of attorney was produced, by which a deed authorized the entry to the use of the earl, by which it was said to the jury that the point rests solely whether there was a misemployment or not.

[Other reports of this case: Benloe 171, 73 E.R. 1033, CUL MS. Gg.2.30, f. 61v.]

55

Ramsey v. Michell

(Part 1)
(K.B. Pas. 2 Car. I, 1626)

An original writ from the chancery can be issued out of term time, but a judicial writ, such as a capias, *cannot be.*

A general appearance cures the lack of process.

BL MS. Add. 35961, f. 15, pl. 11

Between Ramsey and Michell in a writ of error (Hil. 22 Jac., rot. 1017), it was assigned for error that the first *capias* bore the date July 21, which was out of every term, and it was returnable July 10, which was in term, and that the *alias* and *pluries* bearing dates in term, thus, [it was] upon the matter of an *alias* and *pluries* without an original *capias*. And it was moved by *Bankes* that it was erroneous because each process and judicial writ must bear a date and be purchased in term because, if the day of the *teste* be not a *dies juridicus*, it is erroneous. And on account of this, a writ bearing a date upon the Sabbath day is erroneous because [it is] not a *dies juridicus*, as in the commentaries of Fitzherbert and Brooke, the case of 12 Edw. IV, and 2 Eliz. Dyer are.[2]

And it was said by the court that the terms of Easter and Trinity are moveable terms and are guided by the change of the moon. And on account of this, if

---

[1] title *MS.*

[2] *Prior of Lantony's Case* (1472), YB Pas. 12 Edw. IV, f. 8, pl. 22; *Fish v. Broket* (1560), 2 Dyer 181, 73 E.R. 400, 401.

it be not averred that the *teste* was out of the term, the judges are not held to take notice of it judicially, but it was so averred in the assignment of error.

And DODDERIDGE and JONES said that the original [writ] can bear a date out of term, and the reason is because it goes out of the chancery, which it is never closed, as are the other courts. And the chancellor can, if he wishes, sit out of term. And this is the reason of the difference.

But DODDERIDGE moved that, if the plaintiff in error appeared upon this *capias*, he has made it good and it is saved by the appearance.

Et adjornatur. Residuum, pl. 19.[1]

56

Godfrey v. Abrahall

(K.B. Pas. 2 Car. I, 1626)

A contract that is made on the high seas is a maritime contract that is in the jurisdiction of the court of admiralty.

BL MS. Add. 35961, f. 15v, pl. 12

[It was said] by the Court, if a contract is finished *super altum mare* it is an admiralty case, as, if the owner of a ship comes to one in London and says to him that, if he brings in such things to victual the ship, that he would give and pay to him as then they agree, this is a marine contract.

[Other reports of this case: Latch 11, 82 E.R. 249, HLS MS. 1235, f. 37; BL MS. Hargr. 38, f. 33v, pl. 2.]

57

Rex v. Jones

(Part 1)
(K.B. Pas. 2 Car. I, 1626)

An indictment for murder can be removed into the court of king's bench so that it can be tried in another county by impartial jurors where it is not possible to get an impartial jury in the county where the offense was committed.

The court of king's bench has the power to bail anyone imprisoned for any cause.

Bail is appropriate where a speedy trial cannot be had because a foreign jury is needed.

---

[1] For further proceedings in this case, see below, No. 64.

BL MS. Add. 35961, f. 15v, pl. 13

It was moved [in a case] between Herbert and Vaughan to have [a writ of] *certiorari* to remove an indictment for murder into the king's bench to the intent to send it to be tried in an indifferent county because it was impossible in respect of the power of both parties to have twelve sufficient indifferent jurors. And in was granted in this case of necessity according to other precedents of the same nature.[1]

58

Constable v. Clobury

(Part 1)
(K.B. Pas. 2 Car. I, 1626)

Where the obligations of a contract are joint and several, a co-obligee can sue any obligor individually. Also the obligee need not allege non-performance by the other obligors.

BL MS. Add. 35961, f. 15v, pl. 14

Between Constable and Colbury, in an action of covenant (entered Hil. 1 Car., rot. 425 [or 435]), the case was [thus]. The plaintiff alleged a charter party of the plaintiff and another of one part and the defendant and another of the other part. And he showed it to the court. And it was entered *in haec verba*, and the indenture was between the plaintiff and another of one part and the defendant and two others of the other part, and he showed that, by the same indentures, the plaintiff covenanted and let to freight to the defendant and the two others one such ship called *D*. and covenanted to make a voyage to depart with it the next fair wind to Pharo in Spain and afterward,[2] if it be appointed, to go to such place etc. and that the defendants covenanted each by himself separately and the defendant by himself to pay his part of the freight and also of the primage, average,[3] and petty lodinage. And he assigned the breach for non-payment of the freight and primage etc.

The defendant traversed the setting forth with the first fair wind. And there was a demurrer upon this.

And it was argued that the traverse was idle and immaterial:

(1) Because, here, it was not a conditional contract, *viz.* that, if the plaintiff set out with the next fair wind and arrived etc., in which case, the condition being precedent, the performance of it was colorably transferable, but they are distinct covenants and a covenant against a covenant upon which there is a

---

[1] For later proceedings in this case, see below, No. 186.

[2] dilonque *MS*.

[3] overage *MS*.

reciprocal remedy given to both parties. And on account of this, one is not a bar to the other. And thus it was adjudged in 48 Edw. III, 3 and 4, Sir Ralph Poole's case,[1] where one covenanted with another to serve him in his wars and the other to give to him so much money *per annum*, here, in [an action of] annuity or debt, he need not allege that he had served him because they are separate covenants by which they have equal remedies and not consideration or condition precedent, and on account of this, the alleging of it in the count at bar was not necessary. And on account of this, [it is] not traversable.

(2) If, here, it be a condition precedent or consideration of the setting forth with the next wind, it was not the substance nor matter but the effecting of the voyage, and he could miss the next fair wind without his default because, at this time, there could be a leak in the ship or [. . .] sick or, as DODDERIDGE [said], the next fair wind could blow for an hour and cease so that it was not possible to be done. Thus, for these causes, the traverse is not material to the point, and, always, the traverse must fasten upon a material allegation, as in 15 Edw. IV, 2,[2] in [an action of] trespass, the defendant said that J.S. was seised and died seised and his heir entered and enfeoffed the defendant's father who died and it descended to him by which he entered, there, the first death was not material, therefore, not traversable, but solely the second, upon which ground, see 19 Hen. VIII, 7; 32 Hen. VI, 16; and 2 Hen. V, 2;[3] the writ itself, by which etc.

On the other side, it was said that he would not maintain the traverse. But he took three exceptions to the declaration:

(1) Because he alleged the indenture between him and another of one part and the defendant and another of the other part and showed an indenture between the defendant and two others of the other part; thus, it was not the same indenture upon which he pleaded, and thus he has not shown the document upon which he pleaded.

(2) He showed that the defendant and others covenanted to make the freight and average and he alleged that the defendant had not paid it where, if the others had paid it, it is sufficient, and on account of this, he must have alleged that the defendant nor none of the others have defrayed it.

(3) Because they have not expounded the words of art of average, primage, and petty lodinage.

To the two first, the court thought them not material because each covenanted for himself and, as Mathewson's case[4] is, it is as separate deeds, and on account of this, there is no need to recite the other parties of the other part except

---

[1] *Pole v. Tochess* (1374), YB Hil. 48 Edw. III, f. 2, pl. 6.

[2] YB Mich. 15 Edw. IV, f. 2, pl. 3 (1475).

[3] YB Pas. 19 Hen. VIII, f. 7, pl. 7 (1528); YB Mich. 32 Hen. VI, f. 15, pl. 23 (1453); YB Pas. 2 Hen. V, f. 2, pl. 6 (1414).

[4] *Mathewson v. Lydiate* (1597), 5 Coke Rep. 22, 77 E.R. 84, Cro. Eliz. 408, 470, 546, 78 E.R. 652, 708, 792.

the defendant himself and, for the same cause, it is not to be intended that the parties undertook one for the other, but each for himself. Thus, the first and second [were] disallowed.

And the third [was disallowed] also because, though the words are not known to the judges, yet they are to the parties, being merchants etc.

Et adjornatur. See more, pl. 44.[1]

59

Millen v. Faudry

(K.B. Pas. 2 Car. I, 1626)

One can use self help to drive off cattle belonging to another person out of one's own land, and this can be done with the assistance of a dog.

An action of trespass does not lie where a dog comes onto one's land.

BL MS. Add. 35961, f. 16, pl. 15

Millen brought [an action of] trespass against Faudry, *et intratur* Hil. 22 Jac., rot. 1079. And he alleged the chasing with a dog of his sheep in a place called Bessels. The defendant pleaded in bar that the place where etc. is next adjacent to Green Close, being the freehold of the defendant, and that they are not separated by any fence and that he found the sheep pastured in his garden [upon] which he with a small dog chased them and the dog pursued them into the place called Bessill and chased them there by a small time and that the defendant, as soon as he saw it, *increpavit, Anglice* rated him, *et desistere fecit.* Upon which, the plaintiff demurred.

And it was argued that, even though the law allows one to chase cattle out of one's land with a little dog, as Tiringham's case, Coke 4, and Crogat's case, Coke 8,[2] are, yet it does not allow him to chase them further because, by the same reason that he can chase them into the next land, by the same reason a league distant and thus *in infinitum.* And here, he has not alleged that it, the dog, immediately pursued but *ut vidit,* as soon as he saw or perceived, and he could have been willfully blind a long time. See 7 Hen. VII, 2; 20 Hen. VII, 20; 15 Hen. VII;[3] where, in [an action of] trespass for cattle, it is a good plea that he immediately pursued

---

[1] For further proceedings in this case, see below, No. 88.

[2] *Phesant v. Salmon* (1584), 4 Coke Rep. 36, 76 E.R. 973; *Crogate v. Marys* (1608), 8 Coke Rep. 66, 77 E.R. 574, also 1 Brownlow & Goldesborough 197, 123 E.R. 751, 2 Brownlow & Goldesborough 55, 146, 123 E.R. 812, 864.

[3] YB Mich. 7 Hen. VII, f. 16, [1], pl. 1 (1491); YB Mich. 15 Hen. VII, f. 17, pl. 13 (1499).

them and drove them again out etc. And thus, if he exceeds here the authority that the law gives to him, he is a tortfeasor.

Of the other side, it was argued by the counsel, and the court adjudged it that it is a good justification because:

(1) It is certain that one can chase cattle out of one's land and is not bound to allow them to continue doing damage and take himself to his action or distress, as the books cited are clear. Thus, as he can do this with a dog, of necessity, it follows that he will not be punished for the following of the dog into other land after the sheep because it is not to be intended by the law that one will have such command of a dog to make him stay when he would. And on account of this being a thing of necessity following a lawful act, there, the law will not punish it. And on account of this, in such cases, when one in the doing of a lawful thing does to his neighbor a tort which he could not [a]void by any means, the law will not punish it. In 21 Edw. IV, 64,[1] if one drives his cattle [upon] the highway and they escape into the lands of a stranger and he immediately pursues them and drives [them] out, he will not be a trespasser by this. Thus in 22 Edw. IV, 8;[2] where one, plowing, turns his plow upon the land of his neighbor and the horses, being unruly, subvert part of the land and the other horse snatch a mouthful of grass, it is a good excuse because it was against his will. 43 Edw. III, 8;[3] one pursued wild beasts with hounds which were in the chase and being recalled do not desist, but follow and kill the deer in the chase or forest, this is not punishable because it was not in his power to hinder them. In 21 Hen. VII, 28,[4] and so also it was adjudged [in] 21 Jac. [1623 x 1624] between Jenins and Maydston,[5] if one had sheep to be among his sheep, he can drive them home to separate them and depart. And there is a great difference in the intention of the law between dogs and other cattle because the law intends of the other cattle that one has more government and rule of them than of a dog. And on account of this, without question, one cannot have [an action of] trespass against one because his dog comes upon his land.

Chief Justice CREWE cited the case of 38 Edw. III,[6] where one flew a falcon at a pheasant in his own land and the falcon seized the pheasant in another's land, there [as said] by Knyvet, he could not justify the coming upon the land and the taking of the hawk and the pheasant in the other's land. And he said that it was not similar to our case because, there, the inception of the act was his pleasure and, on account of this, for pleasure, the law does not respect [it].

---

[1] YB Mich. 21 Edw. IV, f. 64, pl. 37 (1481).

[2] YB Pas. 22 Edw. IV, f. 8, pl. 24 (1482).

[3] YB Hil. 43 Edw. III, f. 8, pl. 23 (1369).

[4] YB Trin. 21 Hen. VII, ff. 27, 28, pl. 5 (1506).

[5] *Jennings v. Playstowe* (1620), Cro. Jac. 568, 79 E.R. 486, 2 Rolle Rep. 161, 163, 81 E.R. 725, 726.

[6] YB Pas. 38 Edw. III, f. 10b, pl. [16] (1364).

And 6 Edw. IV;[1] if one tops wood and it falls into another's land, there, if he had pleaded that he did all that was in him to hinder it, it had been good, but, there, it was not so.

DODDERIDGE: It is a clear and trivial case, and, without question, the action will not lie. In 12 Hen. VIII,[2] there is a difference taken, if my beasts stray into another's land, the owner can drive them out, but a stranger cannot. Thus [it is] clear that one can chase cattle out of his own land. 8 Edw. IV;[3] if one drives cattle by a vill and they run into a house, as is common in London here to have an ox run into a shop, the driver is not a tortfeasor for it because, in every tort, there must be *injuria et damnum*. And always *injuria est voluntaria et damnum absque injuria* where, in *injuria absque damnum*, there is no tort. And here, there could be *damnum*, but it is not *injuria vel potius neque injuria neque damnum* because he has not alleged that his cattle were impaired and the other has not shown that it was against his will. And all this is confessed by the demurrer.

And he said that he had seen many precedents before the justices of the forest where one had taken a deer that he found in his purlieu or lands outside of the purlieu and chased it into the forest but that he had blown his horn, which was to the intent to recall his dogs, and this excused him and also because the blowing of his horn gave notice to the forester that a wild beast was pursued with dogs in the forest. And, in the time of Lord Popham, it was adjudged upon great deliberation that, if one found a fox in his land, that he could follow and pursue [it] with hounds in whatever land it will be followed because it is a nuisance animal and for the good of the public to destroy it; thus of a wolf. And this is the reason of Bracton, where he says that an outlaw *caput gerit lupinum*[4] because it is permitted to men to pursue him as a wolf or other hurtful beast.

(But note it seems to me [Paynell] this does not justify the hunting of vermin unless he who hunts them finds them in his own land or in another's land where he can enter by license because the common hunters are as hurtful to the country as the vermin themselves. And for this here, I heard that, in 12 Jac. [1614 x 1615], it was adjudged [to be] no justification of a trespass to say that the common knowledge was that a fox kennelled in the land of the plaintiff by which he went there to kill it etc.)

Also, he cited 12 Hen. VIII and 9 Edw. IV,[5] that, if wood falls into another's land or a fruit tree hangs over another's land and fruit falls from it, I can justify the going in to take it without doing other damage.

---

[1] YB Mich. 6 Edw. IV, f. 7, pl. 18 (1466).

[2] YB Mich. 12 Hen. VIII, f. 9, pl. 2, 119 Selden Soc. 42 (1520).

[3] *Godfrey v. Godfrey* (1470), YB Pas. 10 Edw. IV, f. 7, pl. 19, 47 Selden Soc. 67.

[4] *Bracton on the Laws and Customs of England* (S. E. Thorne, ed., 1968), vol. 2, pp. 354, 362.

[5] YB Mich. 6 Edw. IV, f. 7, pl. 18 (1466).

Justice JONES said that the case is clear and all of the books have been cited that are to the matter, by which it needs no discussion. But he said that, if the defendant had not prohibited his dog when it was out of his land, but incited it further, and it had been averred by the other side, it had made him a tortfeasor. And, upon the aforesaid reasons, he took a difference between a chase with a dog and by himself because, if a dog chased them further than the land of its master, it is not a tort because he could not command it as he would; [it is] otherwise when he chases them himself etc. Thus, he said, if a dog chases them into another's land than the owner of the sheep, it is not a tort. But, if the defendant himself had chased them into another's land than of the owner etc., it is a tort because it is permitted to me to drive the sheep of J.S. into the lands of J.S. out of my lands, but not into the lands of J.D. Thus, he agreed that, because it was the following of necessity of a lawful act, which act, there, the law says for necessity is to be done and the exceeding of his authority was involuntary and without damage, judgment was given for the defendant.

[Other reports of this case: Benloe 171, 73 E.R. 1033, CUL MS. Gg.2.30, f. 61v; W. Jones 131, 82 E.R. 70, BL MS. Hargr. 317, f. 131; Latch 13, 119, 82 E.R. 250, 304, HLS MS. 1235, f. 46v; Popham 161, 79 E.R. 1259; BL MS. Hargr. 38, f. 48; BL MS. Lansd. 1092, f. 87; CUL MS. Hh.2.1, f. 192v; CUL MS. Ll.3.13, f. 110.]

60

Newman v. Marsh

(K.B. Pas. 2 Car. I, 1626)

When the seisin of a dean and chapter is pleaded, what estate they had must be alleged.

Where a person claims under a will, the will must be alleged in the pleading.

BL MS. Add. 35961, f. 16v, pl. 16

[In an action] between Newman and Maistre in replevin (entered Trin. 22 Jac., rot. 922), the defendant avowed as bailiff to Lady Wade. And he pleaded that the dean and chapter of etc. were seised of the place where the taking in etc. *in jure collegii* and made a lease of it to [*blank*], of which the plaintiff claimed the land for eighty years and conveyed the reversion to Sir William Wade. And he showed that, in his time, the rent was in arrears and that he devised the reversion to Lady Wade with [. . .][1] and that, after his death, the rent was also in arrears and for the rent due to the testator as executrix and for rent in her own time in arrears in her own right and Marsh, as bailiff to her, avowed the taking etc.

And upon this, the plaintiff demurred. And by his counsel, three exceptions were taken to the avowry:

---

[1] subayly *MS.*

(1) Because he had not shown of what estate the dean and chapter were seised because they could have an estate *pur auter vie* and then the lease for years could be ended by anything that is showed if the *cestui* at whose life be dead. And on account of this, according to all of the precedents, he must have pleaded that he was seised *in domenico ut de feodo ut in jure ecclesiae*. And always, when one pleads a seisin, he pleads also of what estate the seisin is, as Littleton says, *in domenico suo ut de feodo vel de feodo talliato*,[1] with which agrees 8 Edw. III, 56a.[2] And there is a difference in the limitation of the estate to the dean and chapter because, there, if the lands are given to them without a limit, the estate will be a fee, as 11 Hen. VII and 11 Hen. IV[3] are; otherwise if to the abbot or parson or other corporation sole. But, if one pleads that a dean and chapter are seised, this will be intended seised in fee if it be not so pleaded, and the reason is because it could be otherwise intended. In the *Commentaries* in Fulmerston's case,[4] if it be pleaded that an abbot was seised *in domenico ut de feodo*, this will be intended *in jure domus* because he could not be otherwise seised. But to plead such of a dean and chapter is not good because they could be seised in another manner. And because, here, they could be seised in another manner than in fee, it will not be so intended.

And with this, the justices agreed. And they said that, clearly, the pleading of it in this manner was not to be aided and it was against reason and all of the precedents. And upon this, judgment was given against the avowant.

[2] The second exception was because he did not show the letters testamentary to enable her as executrix.

And to this, it was answered that, here, it is not to recover anything but in the defendant only, and on account of this, according to 36 Hen. VI, 16,[5] where it is to recover nothing or it is in the possession, he will not show the testament. See Com. 52a.[6]

But the court held that he must show the testament because the avowant is the actor and will recover, and not merely a defendant, but he makes a title, and the ground of it is the testament and because it is within the rule where an executor entitles himself to goods and sues them etc.

[3] The third exception was because he did not show when Sir William died, so it did not appear for what in his time he avowed. But inasmuch as she had title to both rents, though in divers manners, the court did not allow it. But for the others, judgment [was] given.

---

[1] T. Littleton, *Tenures*, sects. 10, 18.

[2] YB Mich. 8 Edw. III, f. 55, pl. 7 (1334).

[3] YB Mich. 11 Hen. VII, f. 12, pl. 36 (1495) or YB Hil. 21 Hen. VII, f. 7, pl. 6 (1506); *Abbot of Battle v. Neel* (1410), YB Trin. 11 Hen. IV, f. 84, pl. 34.

[4] *Fulmerston v. Steward* (1554), 1 Plowden 102, 75 E.R. 160, also 1 Dyer 102, 73 E.R. 225.

[5] YB 36 Hen. VI, f. 16, pl. 11 (1457 x 1458).

[6] *Wimbish v. Tailbois* (1550), 1 Plowden 38, 52, 75 E.R. 63, 83.

[Other reports of this case: Latch 14, 121, 82 E.R. 251, 305; Popham 163, 79 E.R. 1261; CUL MS. Hh.2.1, f. 194v; CUL MS. Ll.3.13, f. 112.]

61

Gray v. Fox

(K.B. Pas. 2 Car. I, 1626)

The issue in this case was whether the mere failure to pay a rent, as opposed to a denial to pay, will result in the forfeiture of a copyhold.

BL MS. Add. 35961, f. 17, pl. 17

In the case of Ulysses Fox, it was said by Serjeant *Crewe*, of counsel, against the copyholder that [if] the copyholder by rent or other service be required to pay the rent or to do his services and he did not deny to do it or confess that he must do [it], but makes continual excuses and the rent is and remains unpaid, that it is a forfeiture and it will be taken for a denial. And this appears [in] 42 Edw. III, 25,[1] where the jury found that the tenant by copy would not do his services, by which the prior seized. And Willowe's case in the *New Entries*, where the lord demanded and the tenant said to him that he was not at this instant provided and prayed for time and the lord appointed him to pay it such a day or the sale of the manor and it was not and it was adjudged here (1) that it was a forfeiture upon the second default and not upon the first because, otherwise, there, he could be infinitely delayed; (2) that if he had appointed him a place outside of the manor, he was not bound to attend there.

And on the other side, it was said by *Ashley* and *Bramston*, serjeants, that such a delay was not a forfeiture. Also, because it was doubted whether the service was due or not, it could not be a forfeiture. And for this, Vernons and Higgins case, 26 Eliz., was cited, where the lord demanded the rent and the tenant said to him that, if it be due, he would pay, otherwise not, and that, until it be proved to be due, he would not pay, and [it was] adjudged no forfeiture because, otherwise, the tenant did not have a means to make it clear what was doubtful and it is not reasonable that one will forfeit his land for nonfeasance of it which *non constat* if it is due to be done or not.

[Other reports of this case: Latch 122, 82 E.R. 305, HLS MS. 1235, f. 47v; BL MS. Hargr. 38, f. 50; BL MS. Lansd. 1092, f. 90; CUL MS. Hh.2.1, f. 195; CUL MS. Ll.3.13, f. 113.]

---

[1] YB Mich. 42 Edw. III, f. 25, pl. 9 (1368).

62

Rex v. Matchet

(K.B. Pas. 2 Car. I, 1626)

The issue in this case was whether treason is a bailable offense.

BL MS. Add. 35961, f. 17, pl. 18

One Matchet was indicted for extolling the jurisdiction of the pope and [saying] that he had supreme power within this realm. And he was let to bail, *quod nota*, because, in treason, one is not bailable and this is of itself by the common law treason. But I [Paynell] saw the indictment and, there, it was not '*proditorie*' nor any word of the same intent. And also, by the Statute of 5 Eliz., 1,[1] this offense is made *praemunire* the first time and the second treason. See the Statute, and note that it is in the affirmative that, for the first time, he will incur the pain of *praemunire*. Therefore, query if it takes away the common law and if he could not be indicted the first time as a traitor. But this Statute gives power for the first time to deal with him in the gentler way. And on account of this, it seems that the treason is bailable.

[Other reports of this case: Palmer 426, 81 E.R. 1154; CUL MS. Hh.2.1, f. 195v.]

63

Kelley v. Reynell

(Part 1)
(K.B. Pas. 2 Car. I, 1626)

Where a declaration lays the cause of action in a different county than the original writ does, this is error, but it is cured by the Statute of Jeofails.

BL MS. Add. 35961, f. 17v, pl. 19

Between Kelley and Rennells in a writ of error [entered Trin. 22 Jac., rot. 503] upon a judgment in the common bench upon an action upon the case, upon a diminution alleged, the original was certified in the County of Devon and the declaration was in another county. And this was assigned for error inasmuch as now, upon the matter, he had a faulty original and, where there is no original, it is aided by the Statute.[2] But a material variance of the county is a faulty original, this is not aided. See Coke 5, 74b, an affirmation of a judgment; it was said that, upon this point assigned for error, the court of common bench took an admeasurement and it was argued there. And here, a case in 18 Jac., one Brown's

---

[1] Stat. 5 Eliz. I, c. 1, s. 1 (*SR*, IV, 402–403).
[2] Stat. 18 Eliz. I, c. 14 (*SR*, IV, 625).

case, was cited, and, there, the declaration was in Middlesex and, upon a diminution alleged, it was certified in Surrey; on the other side, diminution was alleged and another original was certified in Middlesex agreeing with the declaration, and the judgment, upon debate, [was] affirmed. And another case [was] 20 Jac., where the bill in the court here was in one county and the declaration in another county.

DODDERIDGE: There is a great difference between the case of 18 Jac. and this because, there, two originals were certified and, on account of this, it will be intended that he declared upon the [correct] original. But a false original is not aided.

JONES: This case was not adjudged in my time in the common bench, but, when I was there, the greater opinion was upon the difference between two originals and where but one and it varied, as here. And the reason urged there against was because, *non constat* if the declaration was upon this original, it could be the cause of their judgment. But here, it is certified and of record which concludes all that was upon such original. And on account of this, even though they in the common bench do not have a ground to take the declaration upon this writ, yet we, here, are to ascertain it by the record and certification.

CREWE agreed and cited one Pollard and Whit's case,[1] to be adjudged 14 Jac. accordingly, and he commanded the roll of it to be searched for, as it was adjudged upon debate.

Et adjornatur. Residuum, pl. 26; f. 47, pl. 86.[2]

64

Ramsey v. Michell

(Part 2)
(K.B. Pas. 2 Car. I, 1626)

BL MS. Add. 35961, f. 17v, pl. 20

In the case, *supra*, pl. 11,[3] it was now ruled by the court, *viz.* DODDERIDGE and JONES, that the appearance upon the exigent saved the mispurchasing of the judicial process because all discontinuances and miscontinuances are aided by an appearance. And there is no difference where he appeared upon the exigent and where upon the other processes, as here, he made [it] upon the *capias utlagatum.*

---

[1] *Holland v. Blite*, 14 Jac. I, rot. 340, *sub nom. Pollard v. Blight* (1618), Cro. Jac. 479, 79 E.R. 408.

[2] For further proceedings in this case, see below, Nos. 70, 218.

[3] For earlier proceedings in this case, see above, No. 55.

And note that, here, the judgment was upon *non sum informatus* and not upon a verdict because, then, it had been aided by the Statute.[1] But here, it is left to the common law and aided by it. See *Discontinuance of process*, B., 11 and 14.[2]

[Other reports of this case: Latch 11, 118, 82 E.R. 249, 303, HLS MS. 1235, f. 46v; BL MS. Hargr. 38, f. 69, pl. 1; CUL MS. Ll.3.13, f. 109.]

65

Hodges v. Moore

(Part 1)
(K.B. Pas. 2 Car. I, 1626)

An obligee, suing upon a contract, must allege that he has fully performed all of the conditions of the contract.

BL MS. Add. 35961, f. 17v, pl. 21

Hodges brought an action upon the case against Mare. And he alleged how that the defendant promised £1500 if he would marry one such and that he had married accordingly and requested of the defendant the £1500. And it was moved in arrest of judgment because the plaintiff had not declared that, at the time of the request of the money, he gave to him notice that he had married etc.

And the opinion of DODDERIDGE and JONES was that he must give notice and the request for the money without giving notice was not sufficient. And DODDERIDGE said that there have been three or four of these cases here now recently.

But a day was given further. See more, pl. 27.[3]

66

Anonymous

(K.B. Pas. 2 Car. I, 1626)

A writ of outlawry to enforce a judgment cannot be quashed on the motion of the judgment creditor.

---

[1] Stat. 18 Eliz. I, c. 14 (*SR*, IV, 625).

[2] YB Hil. 12 Hen. IV, f. 17, pl. 15 (1411), Brooke, Abr., *Discontinuans de proces*, pl. 11; YB Pas. 9 Hen. V, f. 3, pl. 8 (1421), Brooke, Abr., *Discontinuans de proces*, pl. 14.

[3] For further proceedings in this case, see below, No. 71.

BL MS. Add. 35961, f. 17v, pl. 22

A recovery in [an action of] debt was had. And the defendant [was] outlawed upon it. And, after the outlawry, the party [was] satisfied, and he had his acquittance. And yet the outlawry was returned. And it was moved to stay the filing of it, but it was not granted because, now, the king has the interest for the outlawry which the party cannot dispense with.

67

Reynell v. Elworthy

(Part 1)
(K.B. Pas. 2 Car. I, 1626)

A jailer can take a bond from his prisoner to secure his custody, but not for the ease of the prisoner.

BL MS. Add. 35961, f. 17v, pl. 23

Sir George Reynells brought an action of debt against Elworthy upon an obligation. The defendant pleaded that it was upon a condition to be a true prisoner and that it was made for the ease etc., and he showed the Statute of 23 Hen. VI.[1] And there was an issue upon this. And [it was] found that it was not for ease. And now, it was moved in arrest of judgment that such an obligation to a jailer upon such a condition was against the Statute of 23 Hen. VI. And it was divers times moved, and the justices labored for an end because it touched so much the prison of the king's bench and it was of great consequence. But Elworthy desired [a ruling on the] law. And on account of this, a day was given to hear counsel.

But upon the motion now, DODDERIDGE said that a jailer is not precisely limited within the Statute to the words of the obligation. But the intent of the Statute was to take away from the sheriffs and jailers their security by which they presumed and they were saved harmless when they allowed the prisoners to go at their liberty. And here, it is to be considered that the court of king's bench abounding with business, the prison of it was so strait that it could not contain the prisoners. And on account of this, anciently, by the rules of the court, it was allowed to the jailer to keep them in a certain house adjacent there[to]. And this is called 'the rule' because, by the rule of the court, they are permitted to keep [prisoners] there. Now, this is not as strong as the prison itself. And on account of this, if, for his security and not for ease, he took such a bond, it is not against the Statute. And here, it was found that it was not for his ease. Nay, he said, in [an action of] debt against a prisoner, it is not sufficient to him to show, as before, if he does not aver, that it was for ease.

---

[1] Stat. 23 Hen. VI, c. 9 (*SR*, II, 334–336).

To which, Justice JONES agreed.

See Dive's case, Com. 62;[1] such an averment, which was for the deliverance of the plaintiff. Trin. 2, pl. 2.[2]

68

Coles v. Shury

(Part 1)

(K.B. Pas. 2 Car. I, 1626)

The question in this case was whether the rent in issue continued after the death of the first lessor.

BL MS. Add. 35961, f. 18, pl. 24

[The case] between Shurry and Coles was the same case as before, f. [*blank*], pl. 10.[3] And the judgment there was cited and urged here. And it was said that a writ of dower was brought [upon] this judgment.

And DODDERIDGE was *valde iratus* because he said that it was not adjudged. And he said to the attorney that because, when the court differ in opinion, as he said they are in this case, and he enters a judgment, he will go to prison.

But note, as it appears before, the court was divers times moved in this and, afterwards, Dodderidge [being] absent, their opinions being demanded, they answered that they continued in their same opinion and it was, peradventure, taken for a judgment. And thus I [Paynell] then took it.

After Trin. 2 Car., the case was argued by those who argued Brown's case, before, and their arguments were the same as then. And on account of this, I omitted them in a report of this term. The entry of Coles' case is Pas. 22 Jac., rot. 62.

69

Shury v. Pigot

(Part 1)

(K.B. Pas. 2 Car. I, 1626)

Riparian rights are not extinguished by any unity of possession.

---

[1] *Dive v. Maningham* (1550), 1 Plowden 60, 75 E.R. 96.

[2] For later proceedings in this case, see below, No. 94.

[3] *Shury v. Browne* (1626), above, No. 30; for later proceedings in this case, see below, No. 168.

BL MS. Add. 35961, f. 18, pl. 25

Shury brought an action upon the case against Pigot. And he alleged how that he had in such a place a watering place for cattle and of such place in the land of the defendant flowed a stream to the said watering place and that the defendant had stopped the stream.

The defendant pleaded that the place where the watering place is is a rectory and that King Henry VIII was seised of it and also of a manor in that place by which the stream flowed etc. and thus, for the unity of possession, he intended that it was extinct.

And it was argued to the contrary by *Dorrell*. And he cited the case of a warren,[1] that it is not extinct by unity, and of 11 Hen. VII,[2] where one had a gutter between two houses and he made a feoffment of one [and] the gutter remained.

And of the other side, it was argued that it was extinct because it was a profit *a prendre* in another's soil similar to the common in Tirringham's case, Coke 4.[3] And he cited 22 Edw. II, B., *Extinguishment*, 11,[4] of an extinguishment of a way by unity, and the query in Dyer 295b[5] that said it was adjudged in 36 & 37 Eliz. in Harrison's case that the charge to keep the fence was not revived after unity. And he took also an exception to the declaration because the prescription was general where he should have prescribed specially, *viz.*, that until such time, *viz.*, of the unity, the tenants of the rectory have used to have the stream flowing by the land of the defendant and that at all times afterwards, similar to the special prescription of C. 4, 38a, at the top of the folio.[6]

Et adjornatur. More, f. 38, pl. 21; f. 41b, pl. 43.[7]

---

[1] *Peche's Case* (1457), YB Pas. 35 Hen. VI, f. 55, pl. 1; *Anonymous* (1573), 3 Dyer 326, 73 E.R. 738.

[2] YB Trin. 11 Hen. VII, f. 25, pl. 6 (1496).

[3] *Phesant v. Salmon* (1584), 4 Coke Rep. 36, 76 E.R. 973.

[4] YB Mich. 11 Hen. IV, f. 5, pl. 12 (1409), Brooke, Abr., *Extinguishment*, pl. 11.

[5] *Anonymous* (1570), 3 Dyer 295, 73 E.R. 663.

[6] *Phesant v. Salmon* (1584), *ut supra*.

[7] For later proceedings in this case, see below, Nos. 151, 174.

70

Kelley v. Reynell

(Part 2)
(K.B. Pas. 2 Car. I, 1626)

BL MS. Add. 35961, f. 18, pl. 26

The case before, pl. 19,[1] was moved again by Serjeant *Crewe* to have an affirmance of the judgment.

And CREWE and WHITELOCKE, justices, were of opinion to affirm it upon the grounds, *viz.*, that, here, upon the matter of the [de]fault of the original writ, it is as much as if there had been some writ.

But DODDERIDGE and JONES [were] resolutely against this because here, by the certificate of the *custos brevium*, it is certified that the declaration is upon the writ and so the court is bound by the certificate, and, on account of this, it is not as if [there were] no writ, but it is a writ truly in the matter of substance. And in this case, peradventure, the [court of] common place cannot give judgment otherwise because it cannot judicially appear to them that the declaration was upon this writ and, on account of this, it will adjudge as if it was upon no writ. But it appears to us here judicially by the certificate of the *custos* etc. that there is a writ upon which they proceeded. And, on account of this, we are bound. And, if the certificate be false, he can have an action upon the case against the *custos*. And they took the same differences as before.

Et sic pendet.

71

Hodges v. Moore

(Part 2)
(K.B. Pas. 2 Car. I, 1626)

BL MS. Add. 35961, f. 18, pl. 27

At another day, in the case, *supra* 21,[2] *Noy*, argued that he must have given notice because it was not sufficient to come and demand the money without showing for what he demands it and it is a rule, if an act is to be done precedent to another and it is not to be done neither by the plaintiff nor by the defendant, there, there is no need for notice because it will be intended that one did not have as good notice of it as the other. And on account of this [if] A. is bound to B. to perform the award of C., A. must take notice of it at his peril. But, if he is bound

---

[1] For other proceedings in this case, see Nos. 63, 218.
[2] For earlier proceedings in this case, see above, No. 65.

to B. to stand to the award of B., he is bound to give notice to him because the act was to be done by himself who is the party etc. This was the case of one Garney,[1] that one granted the reversion that he had upon a lease for years to another for years to begin after the termination, forfeiture, or surrender of the lease upon condition that, if the rent be in arrears, that he will enter, the lessee surrendered to the lessor, he waived the possession and the rent day occurs, and [it was] adjudged that the lessor cannot enter because the grantee of the reversion must here have notice of the surrender made to the lessor, otherwise he will not forfeit his interest for non-payment of the rent where he did not have notice that his term [had] begun. Also a bargainee of a reversion without an attornment will take the rent, but he will not have advantage of the condition broken before notice to him made of the change of the reversion; thus, here, the act being done by one of the parties, he must have given notice.

And of this opinion was the court, that, here, he must give notice that he had married, and not to make a bare request, as if one be bound to me to pay £10 at my return from Rome, when I demand it, I must notify him that I have been to Rome and require him to pay.

And DODDERIDGE said that it has been divers times resolved as it now is. And on account of this, it was said to the counsel to look in the record [to see] whether a notice does not sufficiently lie [there]. And it was shown to them that the request made lay and *adhuc requisitus* which related to all of the premises before and it is as much to say that being requested to pay the money for the marriage and according to the agreement.

Et adjornatur.

And afterwards, *Noy* relinquished this exception, and judgment was given against the defendant. By which, query of the notice *supra*.

[Other reports of this case: Benloe 184, 73 E.R. 1043, CUL MS. Gg.2.30, f. 67v; Cro. Car. 90, 79 E.R. 679; Latch 15, 48, 150, 82 E.R. 251, 268, 320, HLS MS. 1235, f. 66; Popham 164, 79 E.R. 1262; BL MS. Hargr. 38, f. 68, pl. 4; BL MS. Lansd. 1092, f. 126v; CUL MS. Hh.2.1, f. 213v; CUL MS. Ll.3.13, f. 157.]

72

Walden v. Vessy

(Part 1)
(K.B. Pas. 2 Car. I, 1626)

Where fees are payable at a rate up to a certain amount and at a lesser rate above, where the amount upon which the fees are based is above that amount, the fees are payable at the first rate up to that amount and at the second rate thereabove.

---

[1] *Gurney v. Saer* (1584), 3 Leonard 95, 74 E.R. 563.

BL MS. Add. 35961, f. 18v, pl. 28

In an action of debt by Walden and Jesson against Vessy (*et intratur* Hil. 1 Car., rot. 710) upon the Statute of 29 Eliz., ca. 4, of fees of a sheriff,[1] he alleged that the defendant had recovered in [an action of] debt against one such and had execution etc. delivered to them, being sheriffs of Sarum, and execution was for £180, by which they demanded £7 according to the Statute.

And upon this, there was a demurrer. And two points [were] moved upon the words of the Statute:

(1) Upon these words, 'which shall be lawful to be had and taken that is to say 12d. of and for every 20s. where the sum extends not £100 and 6d. of and for every 20s. being over and above the said sum of £100' etc., whether the Statute intends by these words that the sheriff will have only 6d. in the pound when the sum exceeds £100 [or] that, for each pound under £100, he will have 12d. and 6d. for each pound above was the first question.

(2) Upon the exception of corporations and executions 'to be had or done in any city or town corporate', whether they are of the same Statute for executions sent from a high court and executed there or only executions of judgments given within the corporation.

And it was argued and shown for the plaintiff the cases of Gore and Gore, 5 Jac., and 14 Jac., rot. 531, between Ludley and Michell,[2] for the first point expressly that an action was brought for fees, as here, and he demanded 12d. for each pound not beyond £100 and 6d. for each above and he recovered.

And the court showed their opinions but with this protestation that they would not be bound by their opinions given extemporaneously.

Chief Justice CREWE took the intent of the Statute was that, if the execution was of £100 or under, to provide sufficient rewards for the execution of it and their care, danger, and trouble about it, but this intended that, when the sum exceeded £100, that then, the sum being so great, 6d. per pound thereout was sufficient. For the second [point], he took [it] that, if the execution was of a judgment out of a superior court, then it was not within the exception even though it be executed in an incorporated town because the care and trouble is as much as if he had executed it elsewhere. But, if the execution be of a judgment given in the court of the corporation, there, the trouble is not much because, there, it will not be carried outside of the corporation, but the prison[er] is taken at the place of the taking. And also, when it is upon an action in their court, he must be taken in their jurisdiction, which is not much labor to find him.

DODDERIDGE: Upon the first, whether there could be two interpretations of these words and none of them [be] against the letter, as has been said, and by

---

[1] Stat. 29 Eliz. I, c. 4 (*SR*, IV, 769).

[2] *Probey v. Michell* (1616), Moore K.B. 853, 72 E.R. 950, 1 Rolle Rep. 404, 81 E.R. 567.

this, this interpretation will be taken that more agrees with reason; it is not to be thought that the sense before taken was the intent of the Statute because by this means, if the execution be of £200, he will not have more for the executing of it than he will have for £100 because, if he will not have but 6d. in the pound when the sum exceeds £100, when the sum is £200, he will have but £5 and as much he will have if it was but of £100, nay, that he is worse by the Statute, if the sum be £100 for the execution of it, he will have £5 and, if the sum be £101, by this exposition, he will have 50s. and 6d. Thus, by this exposition, he will have more for the executing of the lesser sum than he will have for executing the greater. And on account of this, the other sense is to be taken, *viz.*, that, for each pound where the sum does not exceed £100, he will have 1s., and, where the sum exceeds this, that he will have 6d. for each pound beyond this. And this is with reason and admits of no absurdity.

For the second point, he agreed with Crewe upon the same difference.

JONES agreed with Dodderidge in all. He said that he had known three questions come in judgment upon this Statute:

(1) Whether, upon this Statute, a sheriff can maintain [an action of] debt for his fees, and [it was] often ruled that he can. And upon this ground, where a sum is given to someone by the Statute and no means is limited for him to come to it, the [common] law gives him an action of debt. And upon this ground also, it was resolved that where in common experience that upon the Statute of Edw. VI, of tithes,[1] [an action of] debt lies for the not setting of them out, it appears thus it was resolved in this case that [an action of] debt lies by force of the words 'shall be lawful to be had and taken'. And Silliard's case,[2] when I was a student, a presentment after the Statute.

[2] The second question has been upon the person who will take the fees and upon this has been two questions, (1) when a bailiff of a liberty makes an execution by a warrant of the sheriff, whether the sheriff or the bailiff will have the poundage; (2) upon execution of a statute, when one makes the extent and the other makes the *liberate*, but I do not remember now how these have been ruled.

[3] The third question is this now before us. And this was not a new question made in my time in the [court of] common bench. And I was of the opinion as I now be. And I agree as my brother Dodderidge has taken the law. And thus, for the first and second points, he agreed with Dodderidge.

And thus was WHITELOCKE.

More, f. 47, pl. 85.[3]

---

[1] Stat. 2 & 3 Edw. VI, c. 13 (*SR*, IV, 55–58).

[2] *Suliard v. Stamp* (1597), Moore K.B. 468, 72 E.R. 701.

[3] For later proceedings in this case, see below, No. 217.

73

Hayward v. Fulcher

(Part 1)
(K.B. Pas. 2 Car. I, 1626)

*The issues in this case were whether there was a misnomer of the grantor-corporation,
whether a corporation can exist without assets, and whether an exception of woods in a
lease of land can be valid.*

BL MS. Add. 35961, f. 19, pl. 29

In an action of trespass between Hayward and Fulsher upon a special verdict
found, the case was thus. The dean and chapter of Norwich, being translated by
Henry VIII from the prior and convent *in decanum et capitulum ecclesiae cathedralis
Sanctae Trinitatae Norwici*, [in] 2 Edw. VI, by a deed enrolled, surrendered their
church and all of their possessions to Edward VI, and, afterwards, in the same
year, the same king constituted, ordained, and newly incorporated them *per nomen decani et capituli ecclesiae cathedralis Sancti et Individuae Trinitatae Norwici ex
fundatione Regis Edwardi Sexti*. And afterwards, he regranted to them all their
possessions by the name of *decani et capituli etc.* omitting *ex fundatione* Edward
VI. And it found the Statute of 1 Edw. VI, 8,[1] of the confirmation of their patents made by Edward VI. And afterwards, the dean and chapter made a lease
of the manor of Taverham, part of their possessions, by the name of *decanus et
capitulum ecclesiae cathedralis Sanctae Trinitatae Norwici*, being the name of the
incorporation before the surrender and differing from the new name only by the
omission of *'Individuae'* and *'ex fundatione Edwardi Sexti'*, of all woods and underwoods growing upon the said manor, excepting the woods and underwoods
growing in a place *vocat* Taverham Wood and upon the ditches and banks of the
same and the timber trees and oaks, ashes, and elms growing within the said
manor with egress and regress [to] cut and carry and provided that, if the lessee shall hinder or disturb the dean and chapter or etc. to cut and carry etc. the
said woods and underwoods, that then [. . .][2] to reenter. The dean and chapter
topped timber in the manor outside of Taverham Wood and, being disturbed to
carry, made a lease of it to one of the parties to the action and put their common
seal to it and the letter of attorney to one to enter upon the land in their name
and take possession and then to deliver the lease to the lessee as their deed upon
the land. And whether this lease was good was the question.

And in maintenance of this last lease, it was argued by *Thomas Beddingfield*
of Gray's Inn (1) that the first lease was void by reason of the misnomer of the

---

[1] Stat. 1 Edw. VI, c. 8 (*SR*, IV, 13–14).

[2] lirra *MS.*

corporation; (2) admitting it [to be] good, that still, to enter for the condition broken, title was given. And for the second lease, the first avoided.

For the first, he said that there are three misnomers of the corporation:

(1) By the addition to the name of the corporation;

(2) The transposition of the name, not reciting it in the very order;

(3) Omission of some part of their name.

For the first and second, they do not vitiate a grant made by or to them because *utile per inutile non vitiatur*.[1] And on account of this, the addition does not vitiate it, as in Dr. Ayres' case, Coke 11, 20,[2] where the name of the corporation was *praepositus et* scholars *aulae reginae* of Oxford and the confirmation was *per nomen praepositi, sociorum, et scholarium aulae vel collegii reginae in universitate de Oxoniense* where the addition was of *sociorum* and *collegii in universitate*, and yet notwithstanding these three additions, the misnomer, it was good.

Thus in Com. 437, Croft and Howell's case,[3] there, the name of the corporation made had the words 'wardens and Croft', and yet, if there had not been another variance, it had been good, but yet, if the addition be in the name of the foundation, then in such a case, the addition would vitiate the grant, as in 30 El., in the Dean of Windsor's case,[4] where the name of the corporation was the *Collegium Regis* of Windsor and the grant was by the name of *Collegium Regis et Reginae* because the grant was in the time of Queen Mary, being married to Philip of Spain, and on account of this addition being in the name of the founder, the grant was void.

For the omission, if it be a matter of circumstance, it will not avoid the grant, but, if it be of substance, yet, if it be implied in the matter before or subsequent, it is good enough notwithstanding. And on account of this, in our case, I grant that the omission of the words '*individuae*' is not material because it is implied in the word 'Trinity'. And thus, in the book, Dyer 278,[5] [it is] ruled. And thus, the name of the Corporation of Lynn in Norfolk is the Mayor and Burgesses *Burgi Domini Regis de Lynn Regis* and the grant to them was to the Mayor and Burgesses *de Lynn Regis* omitting '*burgi domini regis*'. And [it is] still good because that Lynn is a borough is implied in '*Burgensis*' and that it is *Burgus Regis* is implied by the addition of *Regis* to Lynn. And this was adjudged [in] C. 10, 124.[6]

---

[1] *Attorney General v. Dowtie* (1584), 3 Coke Rep. 9, 10, 76 E.R. 643, 644. Cf. Ulpian in *Digest* 45.1.1.5; *Black's Law Dictionary* (1933), p. 1792.

[2] *Alcock v. Ayray* (1614), 11 Coke Rep. 18, 77 E.R. 1168, also Lane 15, 33, 145 E.R. 261, 276.

[3] *Croft v. Howel* (1578), 2 Plowden 530, 75 E.R. 783.

[4] *Dean of Windsor's Case* (1587 x 1588), cited in *Mayor of King's Lynn v. Payn* (1612), 10 Coke Rep. 120, 124, 77 E.R. 1108, 1113–1114.

[5] *Dean of Carlisle's Case* (1568), 3 Dyer 278, 73 E.R. 622.

[6] *Mayor of King's Lynn v. Payn* (1612), 10 Coke Rep. 120, 77 E.R. 1108.

But, where the omission is substantial and not implied, there, it is material, and it will avoid the grant, as the omission [of] *scolarium* in the Merton College Case, Coke 10, 125,[1] and infinite other cases serve to prove, so that, in this case, the omission of the name of the founder being material, it vitiates the grant and makes it void.

But it could be objected that, by the surrender of the old corporation's possessions, the corporation is not extinguished but continues.[2] And on account of this, it can grant by the old name if it wishes. But to this, I answer that, by the surrender, the corporation is destroyed. [For] persons to be corporate, possessions are necessary to the corporation because they must be named of some place. And as to the case that, if the possessions of the abbot are recovered, that the corporation remains, this does not hurt in our case because, there, of necessity, it must continue; otherwise, they are disabled to bring their [writs of] error. But yet they are incorporated there. But to this purpose before, they have recovered again their possessions, and, on account of this, there is a difference between a recovery against them of their possessions and surrenders of their possessions. And that the corporation of the dean and chapter are dissolved by the surrender of their possessions is expressly adjudged [in] Dyer 282b, the Dean of St. Patrick's case.[3]

For the second point, he argued first that the exception of the woods and underwoods here was good even though it was an exception of a thing before demised. And on account of this, he took a difference where one excepts a thing expressly demised because, there, such an exception is void, as if one leases two acres [of land] except one, it is void for the repugnancy. And, where a thing is demised but implicitly, as if one leases a manor, there, all the lands pass, but implicitly. And on account of this, an exception of one acre there is good, as is put [by] Com. 361a.[4] Thus, for the same reason, a lease of a mill reserving the profits of it is a good reservation, as it is in Com. 524.[5]

Thus, in our lease of the manor except the woods and the lands, the exception is good. And with this accords Herlakenden's Case in C. 4, 61,[6] and divers cases in addition.

But it could be objected that, here, the woods and underwoods are expressly named and leased and, on account of this, it accords with the rule taken, it cannot be excepted. To this, he answered that the expression of them was idle and it will have passed and be implied by the law. And on account of this, the expression

  [1] *Fisher v. Bois* (1588), 10 Coke Rep. 125, 77 E.R. 1115, also Moore K.B. 266, 72 E.R. 571, 1 Anderson 196, 123 E.R. 427.
  [2] demur *MS*.
  [3] *Archbishop of Dublin v. Bruerton* (1569), 3 Dyer 282, 73 E.R. 633.
  [4] *Stowel v. Lord Zouch* (1562), 1 Plowden 353, 361, 75 E.R. 536, 548.
  [5] *Welcden v. Elkington* (1578), 2 Plowden 516, 524, 75 E.R. 763, 775.
  [6] *Ivy v. Herlakenden* (1589), 4 Coke Rep. 62, 76 E.R. 1025.

of them *nihil operatur*, as in Bourough's [case], C. 4, and Davenport's case, C. 8, 149,[1] which he put. Upon this rule, he took another difference, where one excepts all which he had demised before and where but part or but part of the time; there, the expression is good even though they be of things expressly demised before, as Dyer 264b;[2] a husband leased a house and shop excepting and reserving to himself the shop; here, the exception of the shop before expressly demised is good because [it was] not for all of the time. Thus [is] the case before cited, Com. 324, a lease of a mill except the profits for life [was a] good exception etc. And yet, in any case, the exception of a thing that passes but implicitly is not good, but it is in the case of inseparable incidents, as in Dyer 288,[3] a lease of a manor except the perquisites of the court [is] void for the inseparable incidents. Thus, in our case, all not being excepted, the exception remains good.

Then, he argued that, if the trees are excepted, by consequence, the tops of them also because they are of the same nature (and he cited Dyer 29; 22 Edw. III, 8; and 14 Hen. VIII, 1)[4] and, on account of this being good except the tops by the general exception and being hindered to carry them, the condition was broken.

Then, it is to see whether the entry by the attorney to deliver the deed be good or not. And he argued that it was and that, he having authority to enter, that it will be taken first an entry to revest the estate and then to deliver the lease because it is a rule [that] when one has a right to enter, there, his entry cannot be tortious, as in 17 Edw. III, 11; 21 Edw. IV, 9; 9 Hen. VI, 29 and 30.[5] And as to this, that all is here done in one instant, this can be because the law will make the order that the possession upon the entry will be first revested before the lease [be] delivered, as if the lessee for life and the reversioner made a feoffment; here, there will be first a surrender before the feoffment. Thus [is] Com. 540b;[6] a disseisor leased for years and, afterwards, he joined with the disseisor and then of the disseisee. Thus here, when the attorney entered, it will be first a reducing of the estate and then a delivery of the deed.

And thus, by all, he concluded for the defendant [upon the] second lease.

Calthorpe, contra: And he argued first that the lease by their old name of the corporation was good because, he said, that the patent of their new corporation was void because the corporation remained notwithstanding their surrender of

---

[1] *Boroughes v. Taylor* (1596), 4 Coke Rep. 72, 76 E.R. 1043, also Cro. Eliz. 462, 78 E.R. 715, Moore K.B. 404, 72 E.R. 657, Gouldsborough 124, 75 E.R. 1039; *Bradshaw v. Davenport* (1610), 8 Coke Rep. 144, 77 E.R. 693.

[2] *Horneby v. Clifton* (1567), 3 Dyer 264, 73 E.R. 586.

[3] *Acton's Case* (1570), 3 Dyer 288, 73 E.R. 647.

[4] *Earl of Pembroke's Case* (1348), YB Trin. 22 Edw. III, f. 8, pl. 15; *Bishop of London v. Nevell* (1522), YB Mich. 14 Hen. VIII, f. 1, pl. 1, 119 Selden Soc. 88.

[5] YB Trin. 9 Hen. VI, f. 29, pl. 34 (1431).

[6] *Paramour v. Yardley* (1579), 2 Plowden 539, 540, 75 E.R. 794, 796.

their possessions, as the books of C. 3, 75; Coke 10, 28;[1] and Pet. Bro. 170 are clear that the king, intending to make a corporation *de novo* where the old corporation remains in effect, was deceived and, on account of this, his grant [was] void, similar to the case where he, thinking that he had possession of the land, grants the land; this will not pass the reversion. Kel. 18; C. 4, 35; and Dyer 197;[2] where he, thinking that an office was not void, grants the reversion of it.

Second, if the patent is good, yet it is in the affirmative and does not exclude, but that they can use their old name because it is granted to them that they can plead and be impleaded *per nomen etc.* But it does not say *et non per aliud nomen.* [It is] similar to the case where a statute is in the affirmative, it does not take away a former power, as [in] Dyer 50 and C. 113,[3] the rule is put. And for this [is] Dyer 232; C. 11, 64;[4] the Statute provides that a lease under the augmentations seal will be good, but this does not take away the force of the great seal for the same lands. And on account of this, in the incorporation of Lynn *de novo*, C. 10, 124,[5] it is aided *et non per aliud nomen.* Thus notwithstanding this, they can use one name or the other, as where a man is named by two names, it is a good plea that he is known by the one name and the other, as it is in Pet. Bro. 73 and in 1 Edw. IV, 7, and 5 Edw. IV, 5 and 20.[6] There is a difference where one grants by his false name, this binds him, but he cannot take by a false name. And thus [is] the difference.

Third, admitting these against him, yet the variance here in this is not material, nor will it subvert the grant because, first, here, there is sufficient certainty of description to grant and *quando de persona constat nihil fuit error nominis.*[7] Second, the name of the founder is not of the essence of the corporation. There are four causes[8] of a corporation: (1) the efficient, and this is in the grant of the king or prescription; (2) the formal, and this is the place of their corporation, but even though it must be named of some place, yet it is not necessary that they are

---

[1] *Case of the Dean and Chapter of Norwich* (1598), 3 Coke Rep. 73, 76 E.R. 793, also 2 Anderson 120, 165, 123 E.R. 577, 601; *Baxter v. Sutton* (1612), 10 Coke Rep. 1, 28, 77 E.R. 937, 966, also Jenkins 270, 145 E.R. 194.

[2] *Lord Willoughby de Broke v. Lord Latimer* (1497), Keilwey 4, 72 E.R. 156, 115 Selden Soc. 304, also YB Mich. 12 Hen. VII, f. 8, pl. 5; *Hunt v. Coffin* (1561), 2 Dyer 197, 73 E.R. 435 or *Rex v. Blage* (1561), 2 Dyer 197, 73 E.R. 436.

[3] *Earl of Southampton's Case* (1541), 1 Dyer 50, 73 E.R. 109; *Townsend's Case* (1554), 1 Plowden 111, 113, 75 E.R. 173, 176, also 1 Dyer 106, 73 E.R. 233.

[4] *Case of Leases of the Duchy of Lancaster* (1564), 2 Dyer 232, 73 E.R. 512; *Shoyle, qui tam v. Foster* (1614), 11 Coke Rep. 56, 64, 77 E.R. 1222, 1232, also 1 Rolle Rep. 88, 81 E.R. 349, 2 Bulstrode 324, 80 E.R. 1158.

[5] *Mayor of King's Lynn v. Payn* (1612), 10 Coke Rep. 120, 77 E.R. 1108.

[6] *Abbot of Ramsey's Case* (1461), YB Mich. 1 Edw. IV, ff. 6, 7, pl. 15; YB Trin. 5 Edw. IV, f. 5, pl. 20 (1465); YB Pas. 5 Edw. IV, Long Quinto, f. 20 (1465).

[7] Cf. *Black's Law Dictionary* (1933), p. 678.

[8] Sic in MS.

[. . .] and place; (3) the material cause, of the men who are the corporation; (4) the final cause. And of these four, two only are necessary: the material and the formal; the efficient and final, even though they are necessary to the making, they are not necessary to be expressed in their name. And on account of this, the omission here of the founder was not a material omission. But, if the name given to them be sufficient to distinguish them from all others, the proper use of the name is sufficient. And for this, [see] Pas. 8 Jac., Sir Ralph Evers' case,[1] where a grant [was] made to Sir Ralph Evers, lord Evers, and he was not a knight at this time, and yet the grant was good and yet, as the books are, knight is part of the name but *constabat de persona etc.* And this is the reason of the case in 26 Edw. III, 66 and 67, the Prior of Coventry's case, and 27 Edw. III, 32,[2] where the saint in the name of the corporation was omitted and yet [it was] good. And he confessed that this point is left at large in the three reports because, there, it was resolved upon the assistance of the Statute. But he said that he heard the Lord Coke, in arguing Ayres' case, cite a case where they made a lease as here by the same name and the lease [was] adjudged good. Thus, upon this, he concluded this first point.

For the second, he agreed that the exception of the trees and woods etc. were good and also that, by the exception of the trees, the tops also were excepted. But he argued that the condition did not extend to the trees nor to the hindrance to carry away and cut the trees outside of Taverham Wood. And this is plain by the words of the deed because they excepted first all the 'woods and underwoods growing in Taverham Wood and all the trees growing' etc.; then came the condition, and this provided that, if he disturbed him to 'cut and carry the said underwoods or woods', that then etc. Now, this cannot extend if it hinders him in the trees because he has expressly limited the condition to the said woods and underwoods, and the word 'said' enforces it the more and more fully shows to what the intent extends the condition. And a condition being to defeat an estate will be taken strictly and it limiting who would enter for a disturbance in Taverham Wood excludes his intent to enter for a disturbance of the trees outside of the wood because *qui de uno expresso dicit de alio negare videtur.* Thus, here, as in Goodal's case, Coke 5, 96;[3] [if[the condition be that he will pay to him and his heirs, there, the enumeration excludes the executors. Thus [is] Trin. 38 El., Ewer's case, rot. 539;[4] one having land in Norfolk and a house and also lands and a house in Suffolk devised to one his lands and house in Norfolk and all his

---

[1] *Lord Ever's Case* (1610), 1 Bulstrode 21, 80 E.R. 726.

[2] *The Queen v. Prior of Coventry* (1352), YB Trin. 26 Edw. III, f. 12, pl. 13; YB Mich. 27 Edw. III, f. 12, pl. 57 (1353).

[3] *Goodall v. Wyat* (1597), 5 Coke Rep. 95, 77 E.R. 202, also Jenkins 261, 145 E.R. 187, *sub nom. Goodale v. Wyat*, Gouldsborough 176, 75 E.R. 1076, Moore K.B. 708, 72 E.R. 855, Cro. Eliz. 383, 78 E.R. 629, Popham 99, 79 E.R. 1209.

[4] *Ewer v. Haydon* (1596–1599), Cro. Eliz. 476, 658, 78 E.R. 727, 897.

other lands and tenements in Suffolk, it will not pass because, then, it would have made the same form of the devise of the one as of the other. Thus, by reserving the woods and underwoods in one place of the manor and of the trees of timber in the other part, his intent appears there to have only the timber trees. And the expressing of the entry for the disturbance of the taking 'of the said woods and underwoods' shows his intent was not to enter for the disturbance of trees.

Lastly, he agreed that, if one had title of entry, there, he could make a deed of lease and a letter of attorney to deliver it upon the land even though it be in one instant. And this is Bragg's case [cited] in Butler and Baker's case, C. 3.[1] But the matter that he moved here, that the lease by the sealing of the dean and chapter without any delivery of it was their deed inasmuch as a corporation cannot deliver a deed no more than they can deliver seisin. And, on account of this, of necessity in this case, the deed is a deed without delivery. And thus, it is a deed and lease before the delivery by an attorney. His delivery was void, as Bragg's case is, and a lease made before he had possession of the land. And thus, upon this point, the second lease [is] void. And thus, he concluded against the second lease.

More, f. 41, p. 44.[2]

74

Anonymous

(K.B. Pas. 2 Car. I, 1626)

A case can be removed out of an ecclesiastical court where the defendant cannot prove his case there because of the two-witness rule.

BL MS. Add. 35961, f. 20v, pl. 30

It was moved for a [writ of] prohibition to the spiritual court. And the suggestion was that the plaintiff was sued there for tithes and he pleaded a composition with the parson and proved it by one witness, and it was not allowed. And the court granted the prohibition.

---

[1] *Jennings v. Bragg* (1595), Cro. Eliz. 447, 78 E.R. 687, also cited in *Butler v. Baker* (1591), 3 Coke Rep. 25, 35, 76 E.R. 684, 707.

[2] For later proceedings in this case, see below, Nos. 175, 271.

75

Hall v. Gerard

(Part 2)
(K.B. Pas. 2 Car. I, 1626)

BL MS. Add. 36961, f. 20v, pl. 31

The case before, fo. 2, pl. 5, of Hall and Gerard,[1] was moved again by *Noy*. And he argued that judgment will be given for the plaintiff. It has been objected that the traverse *de injuria sua propria* is not good where the justification is by reason of a freehold or lease for years, but, notwithstanding, for three causes, the plaintiff will have judgment:

(1) Because, here, the justification is not merely in the realty but [is] mixed with the personalty and, where it is mixed with the personalty, *de injuria sua propria* is a good traverse and there is no need to traverse the title, as the defendant pretends. For this, see 8 Hen. VI, 34.[2] And also, the justification is not, here, upon the lease, but upon the assault upon him by putting his hands gently upon him to remove him from his possession so that the realty is but an inducement to the justification.

(2) Their title is neither certain nor traversable by reason of the uncertainty because he has not justified by reason of the lease for a term *diversorum annorum* and this uncertainty we cannot traverse if he has not shown a certain term.

(3) By his demurrer, he has confessed our plea and that it was *de injuria sua propria* and that it was *de son tort [demesne]*, thus even though the issue was not a well tendered one, by the demurrer having confessed the tort, judgment must be given according to the right of the cause according to the Statute of 27 Eliz., ca. 5.[3] And thus, this [is] helped by this Statute.

By which, he concluded for the plaintiff.

And the other side was not ready, and on account of this, a day was given to them. See the *Book of Entries*, tit. *Assault*, pl. 17. And afterwards, judgment was given for the plaintiff.

[Other reports of this case: Latch 20, 128, 221, 273, 82 E.R. 254, 308, 355, 382, HLS MS. 1235, ff. 17v, 50; BL MS. Hargr. 38, ff. 22, 67; BL MS. Lansd. 1092, f. 56v; CUL MS. Ll.3.13, ff. 55v, 119v.]

---

[1] For earlier proceedings in this case, see above, No. 5.

[2] YB Hil. 8 Hen. VI, f. 34, pl. 37 (1430).

[3] Stat. 27 Eliz. I, c. 5 (*SR*, IV, 712).

76

Goodwin v. Willoughby

(K.B. Pas. 2 Car. I, 1626)

The issue in this case was whether any valuable consideration was pleaded for a contract not to sue.

BL MS. Add. 35961, f. 21, pl. 32

Between Goodwin and Willoughby, executrix of her husband, in an action upon the case, the plaintiff alleged how the husband of the defendant was indebted to him upon an account between himself and the husband in such a sum, and he died, and that the defendant, fearing to be sued for it and in consideration that the plaintiff forebear to sue her until such a time, [promised] that she would pay the money etc.

And upon [a plea of] *non assumpsit* and a verdict against her, it was moved in arrest of judgment by *Stone* that, here, [there was a] failure[1] of consideration in two things: (1) because he has not shown certainly how the debt accrued upon the account, which he should have done so that a traverse could have been taken to it because it is traversable because, if [there was] no debt, [there was] no consideration for the promise. And on account of this, for the non-certainty lying to it, this is the first fault. (2) Here, he has not shown that the wife was executrix or administratrix or executor *de son tort* or another cause for which she will be chargeable to the debt of the husband, and, if she is not chargeable, then [there was] no consideration for this promise, but [it is a] *nudum pactum* and no more than if I promise one £20 if he would not sue me where he had no cause of suit.

For the first, it seemed to the court that it was good, this notwithstanding, because it is certain enough and he will not be compelled to plead all the circumstance of the account, which will be too tedious. And thus, he could have taken well enough.

For the second exception, Chief Justice CREWE thought [it] good notwithstanding, inasmuch as it is a good consideration to be free of a suit.

But DODDERIDGE [was] *contra* for the reason before alleged.

Justice JONES doubted and delivered no opinion because he remembered Withipole's case,[2] where Withipol, an infant, promised in consideration of certain silks and velvets to pay such a sum and he died; his wife, his executrix, in consideration that the creditor forbear himself, promised to pay it at such a day, and this was a good promise; and yet, here, he did not have any right to recover anything against her. And also, he said that he remembered a judgment given

---

[1] fault *MS.*

[2] *Stone v. Wythipol* (1593), Cro. Eliz. 126, 78 E.R. 383, Owen 94, 74 E.R. 924, 1 Leonard 113, 74 E.R. 106, Latch 21, 82 E.R. 254.

expressly in this point that is here, but he did not remember [for] which side. And on account of this, he would not deliver any opinion until he had viewed his notes.

DODDERIDGE: In that case, there was color to sue the wife, but not here.

Stone: There, the promise by the infant was voidable and not void, and on account of this, it could be good etc.

JONES and DODDERIDGE: The promise of an infant is absolutely void, and [to] this, he can plead *non assumpsit*. And there is a difference between this and [a plea of] *non est factum* because, there, it is by delivery [?] of his hand, and on account of this, it is not void. But an oral lease is void, and he can plead *non dimisit*. And a lessee is a disseisor if he enters. And thus, here, by the same reason, *non assumpsit* is a good plea by an infant.

Query whether he can give in evidence his nonage or that he must show his infancy and conclude thus *non est factum*. Query how they intended their holding because many marvelled at it.

[Other reports of this case: Latch 141, 82 E.R. 315, HLS MS. 1235, f. 62; Noy 81, 74 E.R. 1048; Palmer 441, 81 E.R. 1162; Popham 177, 79 E.R. 1273; BL MS. Hargr. 38, f. 66; BL MS. Lansd. 1092, f. 119v; CUL MS. Hh.2.1, f. 209v; CUL MS. Ll.3.13, f. 147v.]

77

Mulsor v. Note

(Part 1)
(K.B. Pas. 2 Car. I, 1626)

A judgment creditor has priority over a bond creditor.

BL MS. Add. 35961, f. 21, pl. 33

Between Mulsor and Note, [a writ of] *scire facias* [was] sued against an executrix upon a judgment. She pleaded that her husband was bound in a statute staple [and] further that she did not have goods. And judgment was given against her according to Pemberton and Barram's case, C. 4, 59b.[1]

See more, pl. 47.[2]

---

[1] *Pemberton v. Barham* (1590), 4 Coke Rep. 59b, 76 E.R. 1022.

[2] For later proceedings in this case, see below, No. 91.

78

Jermin v. Randall

(K.B. Pas. 2 Car. I, 1626)

One is estopped to deny that which one has admitted in a written contract.

BL MS. Add. 35961, f. 20, pl. 34

Hil. 1 Car., rot. 445, Randall's case. The defendant was bound to the su-
pervisors of the parish of Topcroft in Norfolk in an obligation upon a condition
'that whereas it is ordered by J.S. and J.C., two justices of peace, that the defendant will pay 2s. a week to them for the maintenance of his base child, that he
shall perform their award'. The defendant pleaded that they did not make such
an award. And [there was a] demurrer upon this.

And [it was] judged no plea because, by his deed, he is estopped to say that
there was not such an award, as if one be bound to be nonsuited in formedon,
there, it is not a [good] plea to say that he had no formedon pending because it is
against his deed, but, otherwise, where he is bound to be nonsuited in all actions
by him pending, there, it is [a good] plea to say that he had no action. And for
this, 22 Edw. IV and 3 El., Dyer,[1] were cited.

[Other reports of this case: Latch 125, 82 E.R. 307; Noy 79, 74 E.R. 1046; CUL MS.
Ll.3.13, f. 117v.]

79

Covert v. Wilcocks

(K.B. Pas. 2 Car. I, 1626)

A release of a claim can only be made upon a written deed or payment of satisfaction.

BL MS. Add. 35961, f. 21, pl. 35

Between Covert and Wilcocks, the plaintiff in an action upon the case alleged how the defendant in consideration that the plaintiff will cure one such of
his wounds promised to give to the plaintiff as much as he will deserve. And he
alleged how he had cured him and he deserved £10 and he had requested it of
him and he [the defendant] had not paid him.

The defendant said that the plaintiff *ex spontanea voluntate relaxavit* the defendant from his promise, upon which, the plaintiff demurred.

And it was argued for the plaintiff that the declaration was good because,
here, there was good consideration even though there was not a benefit to the

---

[1] YB Pas. 22 Edw. IV, f. 1, pl. 5 (1482) or YB Mich. 22 Edw. IV, ff. 37, 38, pl. 22
(1482); *Rainsford v. Smith* (1561), 2 Dyer 196, 73 E.R. 432.

defendant but it was a charge and trouble to the plaintiff. And thus [. . .]. And also, here, there is sufficient certainty of the sum even though he refers to the uncertainty because afterward it could be certain.

Second, he argued that the bar of the defendant was not good because, first, there could not be a release because it was not by a deed and it cannot be an accord because it is not alleged to be upon satisfaction, but it is alleged to be *spontanea voluntate*; thus, [there was] no satisfaction to make it an accord.

And no one on the other side was ready [to argue]; therefore, it was adjourned. And at the other day, it was moved again and adjudged accordingly.

[Other reports of this case: BL MS. Hargr. 38, f. 67, pl. 1.]

80

Audley v. Joy

(K.B. Pas. 2 Car. I, 1626)

The court of king's bench has the power to supervise municipal government.

BL MS. Add. 35961, f. 21v, pl. 36

Memorandum that this term a writ [was] issued to the Corporation of Bedford to admit Audley to the office of town clerk there, the reversion of which they had granted to him in the lifetime of the old town clerk. And it was according to divers precedents that the court then remembered.

And DODDERIDGE said that this power was an ancient and particular flower of this court. And the reason for it is that they are the chief conservators of the peace, and, on account of this, when there is a faction in a corporation by the removal of the officers, it belonged to them to see to it and to prevent the mischief that accompanies it. And this in divers times has been used, as Bagg's case, Coke 11, and Middleton's case, 16 El., Dyer 333,[1] for the enfranchisement of a disfranchisee.

And also, he remembered another precedent in 43 Eliz., with which he said that he was of counsel, and, there, the writ was by the warrant of Justice Fenner. Also, the case of Middlecote, town clerk of Boston, was remembered, and a writ of restitution of an alderman in Coventry.[2] And the writs in those causes were to restore *vel causam nobis significes*, and, upon the return, the case will be adjudged.

And here, as DODDERIDGE said, the return is not traversable, but, if it be false, the party aggrieved should have his action upon the case against those who made the return.

---

[1] *Bagg's Case* (1615), 11 Coke Rep. 93, 77 E.R. 1271; *Middleton's Case* (1574), 3 Dyer 332, 73 E.R. 752.

[2] *Warren's Case* (1619), Cro. Jac. 540, 79 E.R. 463, 2 Rolle Rep. 112, 81 E.R. 693.

JONES said that he had known such a writ to restore a clerk to his place in a corporation.

And WHITELOCKE said that there was such a writ was to restore a constable to his office, who was duly elected and put out by the bailiff of the liberty of lord Wentworth.[1]

Noy said that there are divers precedents in divers cases of such a writ in the time of Edward III and all times afterward. And he said that he had seen a writ to restore a recorder of a city to his place.

DODDERIDGE said that, in the time of Mountague, in Norwich, the mayor was restored by such a writ.

And on account of this, here, by award, the writ [was] issued. And a day [was] given to the next term to make their return.

[Other reports of this case: Latch 123, 82 E.R. 306; Noy 78, 74 E.R. 1045; Popham 176, 79 E.R. 1272; BL MS. Hargr. 38, f. 67v; BL MS. Lansd. 1092, f. 93v; CUL MS. Ll.3.13, f. 116v.]

81

Dawberne v. Martin

(K.B. Pas. 2 Car. I, 1626)

In this case, the reproachful words spoken against the plaintiff were not defamatory.

BL MS. Add. 35961, f. 21v, pl. 37

Dawberne, an attorney, brought an action of slander against Martin for these words, 'he is a knave of record and a forgoing knave'. But he did not say that it was in parlance of his office or that there was a former communication of it in his declaration.

And the opinion of the court was that they were not actionable because they are words of reproach but not of slander. And it was not a communication of his office.

And [it was said] by the counsel at the bar, if one says of a judge, not speaking of his office, that he is a corrupt man, it is not actionable, [it is] otherwise if he says that he is a corrupt judge because, there, the corruption is alleged in his office. And Sir William Brunkard's case[2] was where one said of him that he was a cozener and lived by cozening, and no action [lay]. And 'forgery' is too general because smiths forge and do honest forging.

And JONES said that it was the case of Justice Fenner against his brother where his brother said that he had forged his father's will to cozen him. And it

---

[1] *Constable of Stepney's Case* (1611), 1 Bulstrode 174, 80 E.R. 864.
[2] *Brunkard v. Segar* (1617), Cro. Jac. 427, 79 E.R. 365.

was doubted by the court whether they were actionable, and he never had judgment upon it.

And afterwards, in this principal case, judgment was arrested.

See f. 95, pl. 14,[1] by Jones [. . .] case adjudged actionable.

[Other reports of this case: Latch 20, 38, 82 E.R. 254, 263, HLS MS. 1235, f. 62; Palmer 441, 81 E.R. 1161; Popham 177, 79 E.R. 1272; BL MS. Hargr. 38, f. 66v; CUL MS. Hh.2.1, f. 209v.]

82

Baker's Case

(K.B. Pas. 2 Car. I, 1626)

In this case, the plea of the defendant was good and thus issue was properly joined, and judgment was entered on the verdict in favor of the plaintiff.

BL MS. Add. 35961, f. 21v, pl. 38

In [an action of] debt against George Baker as executor of Thomas Baker (*intratur* Trin. 1 Car., rot. 280), the defendant came etc. and *dicit quod onerari non debet qui dicit quod factum praedictum non est factum suum.*[2] And it was found against him.

And in arrest of judgment, *Henden* moved this, that it should be *non est factum testatoris* and that the one had relation to the next three persons who went before and thus the plea is *quod non est factum* of the executor and, thus, issue [was] joined upon a non-material thing.

But the court held that '*suum*' will have relation to anything going before, and on account of this, it will be referred to that to which it could reasonably relate to make the plea good, as in 7 Hen. VII,[3] a husband and wife bringing [an action of] trespass for the goods of the wife and the writ was '*quare cepit sua*' and the exception [was] because '*sua*' related to both and the wife did not have goods, and it was ruled that '*sua*' related to the husband only

And on account of this, here, the exception *non allocatur.*

[Other reports of this case: Latch 125, 82 E.R. 307; CUL MS. Hh.2.1, f. 220v.]

---

[1] *Riall v. Radford* (K.B. 1627), BL MS. Add. 35961, f. 101, pl. 14; BL MS. Lansd. 1083, f. 171, pl. 14.

[2] "He said that he should not be bound who says that the aforesaid deed is not his deed."

[3] YB Mich. 7 Hen. VII, f. 2, pl. 2 (1486).

83

Bayly v. Bugs

(Part 1)
(K.B. Pas. 2 Car. I, 1626)

Where a lessee of land is liable to pay rabbits to the lessor weekly as shall be requested, the lessor cannot demand all of the rabbits that are due to be given at one time at the end of the period.

BL MS. Add. 35961, f. 22, pl. 39

In the case of one Baggs, there was a lease of a warren, reserving annually 100 couples of rabbits to be paid between Midsummer and Christmas by so many a week as the lessor shall appoint. Whether now, for the default of appointment, the rabbits are discharged was the question and also whether the lessor could appoint all the number to be paid in one week.

And [it was said] by the court upon the motion it was a duty etc. in the nature of a rent. And on account of this, it will not be discharged. And in a case that there had been a reservation of £40 to be paid as he weekly required, a default of request will not prejudice him, clearly.

And for this second [point], he could not appoint them to be appointed[1] all in a week because he had reserved it *septimanatim*.

And DODDERIDGE resembled it to the case of estovers granted to be taken annually; he cannot omit one or two years and take all the third year, according to 27 Hen. VI, 10.[2]

Residuum afterwards, 45.[3]

84

Barneloe v. Glarsedge

(K.B. Pas. 2 Car. I, 1626)

In an appeal of murder, the jury can find the defendant guilty of homicide.

A person acting in conjunction with others can be found guilty even though one of the others struck the blow.

---

[1] Sic in MS.

[2] YB Trin. 27 Hen. VI, f. 10, pl. 5 (1449).

[3] For later proceedings in this case, see below, No. 89.

BL MS. Add. 35961, f. 22, pl. 40

In an appeal by Bainabow against Gossage of murder, it was said by the counsel of the appellee to the jury that, if they did not find him guilty of murder, that they must find him not guilty generally and not enquire of manslaughter because this is not the issue and also that, if they do not find that the appellee struck the decedent, that, even though he was in the company, it was not anything.

But the court [was] *contra*. And, for the last point, it was clearly against the law because it will be [deemed] the stroke of each. For the first [point], they said that it had been resolved divers times contrary, *viz.* that upon an appeal of murder, he can be found guilty of homicide. And thus they said it was done two times within the four years, *viz.* in the appeal against Sir Charles Blunt[1] and the appeal against Rolfe, where they were acquitted of murder and found guilty of homicide. And upon this debate of the court, see C. 4, 40a, Wetherall's case,[2] agreeing. And the reason of it is, as DODDERIDGE said, because an appeal of murder contains an appeal of homicide and one can have an appeal of homicide only.

[Other reports of this case: Benloe 171, 172, 73 E.R. 1033, 1034, CUL MS. Gg.2.30, ff. 61, 61v; Latch 126, 82 E.R. 307.]

85

Note

(K.B. Pas. 2 Car. I, 1626)

The extent of the responsibility of a bail.

BL MS. Add. 35961, f. 22, pl. 41

It was said by *Browne*, clerk, to the chief justice that, if one be a bail for another, that anyone, during the same term, can declare upon the same bail.

And the chief justice [CREWE] asked him whether such bail will be responsible for all other actions. And he said not, but that he will be as a common bail and it will serve only to declare upon as to all other actions.

---

[1] *Clement v. Blunt* (1624), 2 Rolle Rep. 461, 81 E.R. 916, Benloe 142, 73 E.R. 998.

[2] *Wetherel v. Darly* (1583), 4 Coke Rep. 40, 76 E.R. 983, also Cro. Eliz. 296, 78 E.R. 549.

86

Lucas v. Warren

(K.B. Pas. 2 Car. I, 1626)

In a sale of land, the seller can make the conveyance in any form that he wishes.

BL MS. Add. 35961, f. 22, pl. 42

Between Lewcas and Lewarren, in [an action of] debt upon an obligation, the condition of which was that the defendant will make a conveyance in fee simple to the plaintiff, the defendant said that the plaintiff did not notify him what manner of conveyance the plaintiff would have.

And [it was] adjudged no [good] plea because, in such a case, it is not at the election of the obligee to make the estate, but the obligor can make what manner of conveyance he wishes. And on account of this, [it is] no [good] plea. See Coke 5, 226,[1] agreeing.

[Other reports of this case: Latch 126, 82 E.R. 307; CUL MS. Hh.2.1, f. 197v; CUL MS. Ll.3.13, f. 118v.]

87

Drope v. Thaire

(K.B. Pas. 2 Car. I, 1626)

An innkeeper is liable for goods left in his custody even though the owner of them does not lodge at the inn.

An innkeeper is liable to the owner of goods stolen from the inn where the owner's servant entrusted them to the innkeeper.

BL MS. Add. 35961, f. 22, pl. 43

Drope brought an action upon the case against Thayer [entered Trin. 1 Car. I, rot. 115] and alleged that, where, *secundum legem et consuetudinem Angliae*, a hostler who holds common inns *ad hospitandum hospites per partes ubi huiusmodi hospitia tenentur transeuntes*[2] must keep the goods of their guests so that no damage will accrue [?] to their said guests, that one Rowley, servant of the plaintiff, having divers goods etc. of the plaintiff in his custody, came to the house of the defendant, a common inn, *et ibidem hospitavit* and that the goods were stolen by

---

[1] Perhaps *Countess of Rutland v. Earl of Rutland* (1604), 5 Coke Rep. 25, 26, 77 E.R. 89, also Moore K.B. 723, 72 E.R. 864, Cro. Jac. 29, 79 E.R. 23.

[2] for lodging guests by the duty where such lodging is made for transients.

the default of the hostler *ad damnum etc.* And upon the issue, it was found for the plaintiff.

And it was moved in arrest of judgment by *Bulstrode*, first, because he did not show that the servant lodged there and it is not sufficient to make one a guest to come into an inn and put his goods there if he is not a *hospitatus, viz.*, lie and eat there. And on account of this, he must lay in his declaration that he lay there. And thus, he said, it was adjudged in Kelley and Clark's case, Mich. 5 Jac., which was entered Pas. 4 Jac., rot. 244,[1] and, there, one Sands's case[2] was cited to be adjudged that the leaving of the goods in the inn was not sufficient to make him a guest and, unless [he is] a guest, then he is not within the custom of the land. But upon a reading of the record, this exception fell off because it was alleged that he lay there with his goods and that, in the night, his goods were stolen.

But DODDERIDGE said that, if one comes to his inn and puts in his goods and then goes back and returning seeing his goods stolen, that he can have this action even though he did not lie there because, peradventure, seeing it, it made him to lie elsewhere.

The second exception was because the custom, as it is alleged, does not extend to others than to guests, *ita quod damnum non eveniat hospitibus pro defectu etc.*[3] And in the beginning of the writ, it is *in eisdem hospitantes eorum bona et catalla infra etc. custodire*[4] so that, on account of the custom, no one can have this benefit nor an action for it but the guest only. And there are divers parts of the land considerable. And on account of this, upon the words of the writ, if it not be a common inn, the custom does not extend to it. Thus, the guests must be *transeuntes et non vicines etc.* Thus here, the hostler is only charged with the goods of the guest and for his guest. And if, in truth, the custom is more large, then it is his fault because he has not laid it so. And for this [is the case of] Trin. 7 Jac., rot. 1535;[5] there, the master brought an action as here and he laid specially that the custom was *quod communes hospitatores etc. bona et catalla eorum necnon bona et catalla omnium in legitima custodia hospitis existens*[6] and concluded the writ specially also, *ita quod damnum non eveniat hospitibus aut aliquibus aliis etc.*[7] And thus he should have done here. And even though this is the common law and it is not a necessary recital, a misrecital of it will not bind, as in many other cases

---

[1] *Gelley v. Clerk* (1607), Cro. Jac. 188, 79 E.R. 164, Noy 126, 74 E.R. 1090.

[2] *Sands's Case* (1603 x 1604), cited in *Watbroke v. Griffith* (1609), Moore K.B. 876, 877, 72 E.R. 968.

[3] so that the loss did not result to the guests through the fault etc.

[4] to the same guests to keep their goods and chattels under etc.

[5] *Beedle v. Morris* (1609), Cro. Jac. 224, 79 E.R. 194.

[6] that common innkeepers etc. their goods and chattels also the goods and chattels of all being in the lawful custody of the guest.

[7] so that the loss did not result to the guests or any others etc.

etc. See the *New Entries* 345 for such an action by the master where the servant was robbed in the inn.

To this, it was answered by the court that the master in such a case can have the action.

And JONES said that it had been often times adjudged in the common bench that the master can have an action against the hundred upon the Statute of Winchester[1] for a robbery done to his servant and yet this is a stronger case than it is here because, there, by the Statute of 27 Eliz.,[2] he who will take advantage of the Statute must swear that he did not know who robbed him and yet the master will bring the action and the servant will make the oath; thus, by the same reason in this case.

DODDERIDGE: Here, the master or the servant can have the action, and the one who brings it first will recover and will prevent the action of the other, as in a case where a servant is robbed, the master can have an appeal of robbery and the servant can have an appeal of robbery. Thus [is], 18 Edw. II, tit. *Coron*, 2; merchants, joint tenants, and one is robbed of their common goods, both can join in the action and both in the appeal; thus here. And because it is said that the writ contains the writ of the common law, it is not so because, there, it is *transeuntes* and yet, without question, if one be robbed at the end of his journey, he can have this action, and yet he is not *transeuntes* by this place but intends to return.

And [it was said] by him and JONES, if one comes to the inn and boards there as agreed for his meat and lodging for a quarter of a year or a month, that he is not a guest in this sense. But if he comes to London and stays in an inn for all the term or for half a year without such an agreement, he is a guest.

And [it was said] by the court this allegation of the custom is not necessary, it being the common law. And on account of this, the misrecital of it will not hurt. And thus, notwithstanding the exceptions, judgment was given for the plaintiff.

[Other reports of this case: Benloe 173, 73 E.R. 1034, CUL MS. Gg.2.30, f. 62; Latch 126, 82 E.R. 307, HLS MS. 1235, f. 50; Noy 79, 74 E.R. 1046; Popham 178, 79 E.R. 1274; BL MS. Hargr. 38, f. 65; BL MS. Lansd. 1092, f. 95; CUL MS. Hh.2.1, f. 197v; CUL MS. Ll.3.13, f. 118v.]

---

[1] Stat. 13 Edw. I (*SR*, I, 96–98).
[2] Stat. 27 Eliz. I, c. 13, s. 9 (*SR*, IV, 722).

88

Constable v. Clobury

(Part 2)
(K.B. Pas. 2 Car. I, 1626)

BL MS. Add. 35961, f. 22v, pl. 44

And now the case *supra*, pl. 14,[1] was moved again by Serjeant *Davenport*. And he strongly urged the two exceptions put before. And yet [it was] ruled as before because the court said that, if an obligation be [made] by two jointly and severally to pay £20, it is good if the plaintiff counts in debt against one that he has not paid without saying *nec eorum alter*, which *Davenport* conceded. And thus it is the same as this case.

The other exception that he took [was] because the plaintiff counted *quod cum per indenturam etc. quod* the plaintiff will go with the next fair wind etc. and that the defendant *convenisset* to pay the freight etc. so that he had here left out *testatum est* or other words so that now it is an imperfect sentence without sense because *cum* did not have any verb to govern, and it cannot be understood because it is the gist of the action and upon this verb depends the action of covenant.

But the court said that, inasmuch as the indenture is entered *in haec verba*, that this exception is not valid because, now, the recital of the indenture is tolled by the entry *in haec verba*.

And on account of this, judgment was given for the plaintiff.

[Other reports of this case: Benloe 146, 73 E.R. 1015, CUL MS. Gg.2.30, f. 47; Latch 12, 49; 82 E.R. 249, 269, HLS MS. 1235, f. 1; Noy 75, 74 E.R. 1042; Palmer 397, 81 E.R. 1141; Popham 161, 79 E.R. 1259; BL MS. Hargr. 38, f. 60v, pl. 2; BL MS. Lansd. 1092, f. 3; CUL MS. Ll.3.13, f. 1; HLS MS. 1197, f. 1.]

89

Bayly v. Bugs

(Part 2)
(K.B. Pas. 2 Car. I, 1626)

BL MS. Add. 35961, f. 23, pl. 45

The case which was touched, *supra* 39,[2] was thus. The plaintiff brought an action in London and alleged a lease of a warren in [. . .] etc. reserving a rent and 100 pairs of coneys to be paid [. . .] weekly by such number as the plaintiff

---

[1] For earlier proceedings in this case, see above, No. 58.
[2] For other proceedings in this case, see No. 83.

will appoint and that the term was assigned to the defendant, and, for 96 pairs of coneys [in] arrears etc., he brought his action etc.

And now [it was] resolved by the court that, without an appointment, he need not pay them because the request here is part of the reservation and part of the contract, as [if] he promised to pay upon request an obligation to pay between Midsummer and Michaelmas so much money upon request.

There, [it was said] by CREWE, without a request, it is gone forever.

And [it was said] by JONES, here, it is in the nature of a rent. And [it was said] by him, if one reserves £40 rent to be annually paid between Midsummer and Michaelmas by such sums weekly as the party will require, there, he does not lose his rent. But he took a difference where the thing reserved can without a demand to the lessee be paid at one time as well as at another, as, in the case put before, there, the rent, if it is not required weekly, can be laid up until the last, and things that cannot thus be reserved. And for this, he put this case; if one lease a dairy reserving 100 pounds of butter payable between May Day and Holymas by such quantities weekly etc., here, he will not be compelled to pay all the last week. Thus, he put this case; if it was reserving 100 couples of woodcocks payable between etc. and the last week is after the time of their departure overseas, there, he is not bound to pay all in the last week; thus of a reservation of roses between Midsummer and Christmas.

But JONES moved an exception because the plaintiff had brought his action in London where the lease was made and, after that, the term was assigned over and this action against the assignee [. . .][1] as he said, should have been laid in the county where the warren is because, where the action is maintainable only upon the real contract and not upon the personal [contract], as here, there, it must be brought where the land is. And for this, he cited Trehern's case,[2] which, he said, was adjudged in the common bench (the term and roll[3] of which he promised the counsel on the other side to show to him upon attendance at his chamber), which was such a one in London made a lease of land in Surrey rendering rent, and he demised the reversion and died; the devisee brought [an action of] debt for the rent in London, and [it was] adjudged not good because, now, he could not maintain the action but upon the realty, and, on account of this, he should have brought his action where the land is.

And the court advised further. See 74a.

[Other reports of this case: Latch 128, 271, 82 E.R. 308, 381; BL MS. Lansd. 1092, f. 96; CUL MS. Hh.2.1, f. 198; CUL MS. Ll.3.13, f. 120.]

----

[1] enquise *MS.*

[2] *Treherne v. Claybrook* (1624), Hutton 68, 123 E.R. 1106, Winch 26, 69, 124 E.R. 23, 58.

[3] [In margin:] See Treherne's case, Mich. 17 Jac., rot. 600, in the common bench, [in] Waller's office, as JONES said the next day in court.

90

Anonymous

(K.B. Pas. 2 Car. I, 1626)

An action to quash a false bond to keep the peace is triable by the court and not by a jury.

BL MS. Add. 35961, f. 23, pl. 46

Upon the new Statute of [*blank*][1] touching binding to good behavior by which it is enacted, if he who is bound can falsify the articles exhibited, that the other at whose suit etc. will pay costs, there was a question by the justices how this falsification will be tried because it is the first putting of it in operation. And it was agreed that it will be by examination in court, and, then, if they find the suggestions false, they will award costs.

91

Mulsor v. Note

(Part 2)
(K.B. Pas. 2 Car. I, 1626)

BL MS. Add. 35961, f. 23, pl. 47

The case before, 33,[2] was now moved on the other side. And it was put by him to be thus, that, in a *scire facias* against an executrix for a judgment in [an action of] debt against the testator, the executrix pleaded that the testator was bound in a statute and that the conusee had sued execution etc.

And it was said by the court that, if it had been upon a recognizance in which a *scire facias* lies against the executrix so that they have a day to plead the judgment, there, clearly, it is not a [good] plea that the conusee had sued execution because it was her folly that she did not plead the judgment if she did not have goods otherwise, as she is held to do, because she must take notice of it and satisfy this before the statute. But in our case, the doubt is because she never had a day to plead it. But yet they held that, upon this special matter, the executrix can have an *audita querela* and have the goods back. And on account of this, even though she did not have a day to plead it, she will be charged with the judgment. And thus, the judgment remained as it was before.

---

[1] Stat. 21 Jac. I, c. 8 (*SR*, IV, 1217–1218).
[2] For earlier proceedings in this case, see above, No. 77.

92

Anonymous

(K.B. Pas. 2 Car. I, 1626)

The ecclesiastical courts have the jurisdiction to determine an issue concerning a pension payable out of the land of a parsonage.

BL MS. Add. 35961, f. 23v, pl. 48

Whitwell moved for [a writ of] prohibition to the spiritual court because they held a plea of a pension granted out etc. And it was denied because even though, upon a pension, a writ of annuity can be maintained and though it issues out of the land of the parsonage, still, it can be sued in a spiritual court. And thus, it was adjudged in the common bench, as DODDERIDGE said, when he was a serjeant.[1]

93

Luther v. Holland

(Part 1)
(K.B. Trin. 2 Car. I, 1626)

An action for perjury under the Statute of 5 Eliz. I, c. 9, does not lie for a false affidavit before the masters in chancery.

BL MS. Add. 35961, f. 23v, pl. 1

One brought an action of debt upon the Statute of 5 Eliz.[2] for perjury. And he assigned the perjury in an affidavit made before the masters of the chancery. And it was ruled by the whole court upon a question that such perjury is not within the Statute. And also, they said that, in the star chamber in such cases, they proceed against them at common law and not upon the Statute.

Serjeant *Towse* moved this at the rising of the court, and it was in the case between Luter and Holland, of which, more, pl. 14.[3]

---

[1] I.e. 1604, 1607–1612. J. H. Baker, *The Order of Serjeants at Law* (1984), p. 509.

[2] Stat. 5 Eliz. I, c. 9 (*SR*, IV, 436–438).

[3] For further proceedings in this case, see below, No. 106.

94

Reynell v. Elworthy

(Part 2)

(K.B. Trin. 2 Car. I, 1626)

BL MS. Add. 35961, f. 23v, pl. 2

And now, it was argued by Serjeant *Hetley* that, in the case *supra*, f. 16v, pl. 23,[1] judgment will be arrested because he thought the obligation [was] void. And he said that he saw no difference between our case and the case of Dive and Maningham's case in the Commentaries, 62,[2] etc. because the mischief is equal if the marshal had this liberty as if the sheriff. And on account of this, there is not any difference between them, but that that is the case of a sheriff; in this case, it is of the marshal. And if the sheriff is bound by it, *a fortiori*, the marshal is because the sheriff is *saepe* to carry his prisoners to the court here in Westminster. And because it could be a good argument that they could take security for their indemnity not having abroad so good a means to guard them as if they were [at] all times in the prison or near to it, as the marshal is. But the marshal is not put to this hazard. And on account of this, [he is] less to be favored than him. But I conceive that, here, he is within the letter of the law and, if not, yet within the equity of that which is within the letter. The words of the Statute[3] are in the preamble: 'The king considering the great extortion and oppression which be and have been by his sheriffs, under-sheriffs, etc., keepers of prisons' and, in the proviso that he will not take bonds, enacted that 'no sheriff nor any of his officers or ministers aforesaid shall take etc. any bond' etc.

And, here, Sir George Reynell is a keeper of the prison who had the custody of the prisons and, on account of this, [is] expressly within the letter of the act. But, if he was not in the letter, yet he is within the intent because the intent of the law was to remedy two mischiefs. One, that when prisoners were under the custody of the sheriffs, for their gain and other reasons of extortion, they would put them in harsh guard to enter into bonds or otherwise they would not allow them any liberty but inflict upon them the strict custody that the law required and, by such means, extort from them sums or obligations for sums, to prevent this was a cause of the statute and the remedy that it thought convenient was to make all obligations to him void but such that the statute limited and thus cut off his extortion by this means.

Another mischief was that, having an obligation for being a true prisoner, then he was secure and had the prisoners bound stronger with bonds of paper than they could be with bonds of iron and [it was] more safe for the jailer. And

---

[1] For earlier proceedings in this case, see above, No. 67.

[2] *Dive v. Maningham* (1550), 1 Plowden 60, 75 E.R. 96.

[3] Stat. 23 Hen. VI, c. 9 (*SR*, II, 334–336).

by such means, he did not regard whether they went at large or not. And thus debtors who the law intended to save *in salva et arcta custodia* having hardship to the intent to force them to pay the sooner have their liberty and never think of payment. And thus execution which is the end and effect of the law is frustrated. And to this mischief also is a branch of the statute appropriate by taking away the effect and force of all obligations than these prescribed by the statute. Now, these mischiefs could be in the marshal. And on account of this being so grievous and of great consequence, it is not convenient to leave him to his will in this. And also, the warden of the Palace of Westminster and the warden of the Fleet [Prison] are excepted, which shows that all keepers of prisons, except these [who] are excepted, are within this law.

Thus, he concluded for the defendant that judgment should be arrested.

Serjeant *Davenport contra*: The question here is not solely whether the marshal can take such bonds, as here he has done, but also whether it being found, as it is here, to be not for ease or favor whether it be within the words of the statute, to which I say first that such a bond as here, merely for the security of the jailer, and not for the cause of ease or for favor, is not against the statute, but that a sheriff, marshal, or other jailer can take it. Second, though sheriffs and other jailers cannot take such a bond, yet the marshal can so that it be not for ease and favor.

For the first, the condition is in this case to do a legal act, *viz.* to be a true prisoner, and on account of this, it is a lawful condition. Thus, [it is] out of the case of 2 Hen. IV,[1] where a sheriff took an obligation to save harmless for the deliverance of withernam because the delivery of it was unlawful. And thus, it was here if it was to save harmless for all escapes, and, as it is to do a lawful act, thus this lawful act was not made the means for an unlawful act because it is found that it was to a lawful intent. And on account of this, the condition being to a lawful intent and lawful of itself, it is not prohibited by the statute because it is not the intent of the statute to prohibit all bonds to sheriffs but only those that are for ease etc. and *colore officii*. And on account of this, if one indebted to a sheriff be his prisoner and, being in prison, gives to him his bond for his debt, this, without question, is good and not within the Statute. And for this, he cited Hil. 17 Jac., rot. 1276, between Sir George Key and Skinner, where Skinner, being his prisoner, made a bond to him and he had judgment (but note [that] no judgment was entered upon the roll); and Hil. 20 Jac., rot. 706, the same plaintiff against Dayly upon a single bill; and 28 Hen. VI, 4;[2] there, [an action of] debt was brought by the lieutenant of the Tower [of London] for a debt due for victuals for his prisoners.

But for the second, if any sheriff cannot take such a bond, yet the marshal can because he has a greater charge and more to guard and the true prison is not sufficient for his prisoners and, on account of this, he is forced to keep them

---

[1] YB Mich. 2 Hen. IV, f. 9, pl. 44 (1400).

[2] *Bodulgate's Case* (1449), YB Mich. 28 Hen. VI, f. 4, pl. 21.

within the Rule, which is a weak place and yet [it is] allowed by divers rules anciently of the court, and, on account of this, there is a reason to allow him a security for his indemnity. And this is not a new case because our very express case was adjudged [in] Hil. 14 Jac. 1202, between the same plaintiff and Sir Thomas Perient, our case to all purposes. And thus, he concluded for the plaintiff.

And another argued to the same intent and cited Costo's case, 21 Hen. VII,[1] that where all fees are taken away by this same statute, those same that the statute allows, yet there, this seems standing with reason and good conscience, as the book there says, it is not within the general purview. Thus here, it stands with reason and good conscience here that Sir George can take security from his prisoners for the reason given. Therefore, it is not [with]in the statute.

And another day was given to hear more argument in the case.

[Other reports of this case: Latch 23, 143, 82 E.R. 255, 316, HLS MS. 1235, f. 63v; Popham 165, 79 E.R. 1263; BL MS. Hargr. 38, f. 82, pl. 2; BL MS. Lansd. 1092, f. 121; CUL MS. Hh.2.1, f. 210v; CUL MS. Ll.3.13, f. 150v.]

95

Rex v. Davy

(Part 1)
(K.B. Trin. 2 Car. I, 1626)

An executive pardon is a private and special pardon, and it must be sued out ad hoc; however, a legislative pardon is general, and it can be pleaded without more.

BL MS. Add. 35961, f. 24, pl. 3

One Davy was indicted for usury at Windsor for taking 2s. for the loan of 20s. from the 20th of June to the 20th of July of the same year. And it was removed into the king's bench. And there, the defendant pleaded the General Pardon of the Coronation, by which all usuries and usurious contracts are pardoned, which were made before such a day. And now, he was attainted before the Pardon. And he showed the Pardon under the seal and prayed to be discharged. And it was urged for him that this Pardon had relation to take away the offense inasmuch as it pardoned all usuries made such a day. And on account of this, having pardoned the usury, it has pardoned the judgment which followed upon it. And he cited Coke 6, 13,[2] that a general pardon that comes after an attainder in burglary pardons it, and Burton's case, Dyer 135,[3] where adultery be sentenced, by the pardon afterwards, it was pardoned.

---

[1] *Coste's Case* (1506), YB Hil. 21 Hen. VII, f. 16, pl. 28.

[2] *Cases of Pardons* (1587), 6 Coke Rep. 13, 77 E.R. 272.

[3] *Burton's Case* (1578), 110 Selden Soc. 364, Latch 22, 82 E.R. 255, 6 Coke Rep. 13, 77 E.R. 273.

But the court said that the Pardon of the Coronation is but a special pardon and it must be sued out by each who would have the advantage of it under the seal. And on account of this, [it is] but as an ordinary pardon. And, if a private pardon after the attainder pardons a felony, it is not good; otherwise of a general pardon by Parliament, and thus the difference. See [in] accord C. 6, 14a,[1] the end of the case, and 36 Hen. VI, 24, Quartermayne's case.[2]

But a day was given further. More, pl. 17.[3]

96

Barry v. Styles

(K.B. Trin. 2 Car. I, 1626)

The issue in this case was the validity of a rent payable to the grantee of the lessor where the grant was made during the term of the lease.

BL MS. Add. 35961, f. 24v, pl. 4

One sued in the court of requests against a lessee for years for a rent for life granted by the lessor before the lease. And he suggested that he had lost his deed of rent. And upon this, the court there decreed that the lessee will pay him the rent during his life, *viz.* the life of the grantee. And upon this, it was moved for [a writ of] prohibition, it being against reason to charge the termor after the term.

And Justice DODDERIDGE said that the decree will be intended as the grant of such rent by such lessee and as it was not good but during the term because, if the lessee for years granted a rent for life, this will charge him as a rent only during the term. See Coke 7, Butt's case.[4] And the decree so intends; it is good.

JONES said that the supposal of the loss of the deed is but to give jurisdiction to them,[5] and on account of this, upon this, he will have a prohibition because it is not fit that a court of equity will relieve one against the principles of the [common] law and it is a principle of the law that the deed of the grant made his estate in this case.

But DODDERIDGE said we should consider the time, and it has been a long time in chancery to have seisin of a rent seck devised to him; he would have been dismissed.

But JONES said that Lord Ellesmere compelled one to attorn upon a grant of a reversion.

[Other reports of this case: Latch 24, 82 E.R. 256.]

---

[1] *Burton's Case* (1587), *ut supra.*

[2] *Quatermain's Case* (1457 x 1458), YB 36 Hen. VI, f. 24, pl. 21.

[3] For further proceedings in this case, see below, No. 109.

[4] *Butt's Case* (1600), 7 Coke Rep. 23, 77 E.R. 445.

[5] I.e. the court of requests.

97

Chelely's Case

(K.B. Trin. 2 Car. I, 1626)

A return in a writ of restitution to a franchise cannot be traversed, but a false return can be a ground for an action upon the case.

BL MS. Add. 35961, f. 24v, pl. 5

WHITELOCKE, in the case of Chelely, said that, if the return in a writ of restitution to a franchise be false, he can traverse it because otherwise he could not be restored.

But CREWE, DODDERIDGE, and JONES [were] clearly to the contrary and [said] that he is put to his action upon the case and he will recover damages but never traverse the return, and thus is Bagg's case.[1]

98

Hungerford v. Haviland

(K.B. Trin. 2 Car. I, 1626)

In this case, the custom of paying a certain relief upon each descent and alienation of certain copyhold land was held to be valid.

BL MS. Add. 35961, f. 24v, pl. 6

[In] Hilary 22 Jac., rot. 194, Hungerford brought an action upon his case against Haverland. And he declared that he was seised of the manor etc., that there is a custom that, from the time of which memory [runneth not to the contrary] etc., the tenants, upon each descent and alienation, have used to pay to the lord so much, *viz.* the value of the land for a year, for relief and that one Smith held a house etc. by service of fealty, rent, suit to the court, and relief *secundum consuetudinem manerii* and that the said Smith aliened to Haviland and Haviland devised it to Haviland, the defendant, and that the plaintiff showed to the defendant that 20s. for arrearages of rent and £5 for two reliefs were due to him and that he would sue him for this debt *legis cursu* and that the defendant assumed upon himself, in consideration that he forbear to sue him if the plaintiff could make [it] appear to two such [persons] in the country that the rent and relief are due, to pay him. And he alleged that he had made it appear to the said two that the rent was in arrears for the presentment of homage and that the reliefs were due by *rotulos curiae*, and yet the defendant has not paid him according to his promise etc.

---

[1] *Bagg's Case* (1615), 11 Coke Rep. 93, 77 E.R. 1271.

And upon this declaration, the defendant did not respond but judgment [was] given by *nihil dicit*, and a writ of enquiry of damages [was] returned. And in arrest of the final judgment, four exceptions have been moved at the Reading term[1] and, there, disallowed, but one, which now this term was also, upon open argument, disallowed by the court.

The exceptions disallowed at Reading were now recited. And the first, I did not hear. The second was that he has alleged that, by custom, he should have a relief upon each alienation that this cannot extend to a devise that is an alienation within the time of memory and, on account of this, not within the custom; third, that the promise is here if he made it to appear to J.S. and J.D. that it was due and this is intended to be by the verdict and the better proof. But these were overruled.

And to the third, it was now said by JONES that the difference is where one is bound to do a thing appears to a private man and where to a judge, according to 10 Edw. IV.[2]

And *Calthorpe* urged that his exception was that he had pleaded that he made it appear *per rotulos* and did not show to the court the rolls for them to adjudge whether, upon them, it could appear to the said J.S. and J.D. And he urged the case of 22 Edw. IV, 40,[3] where one was bound to tender a sufficient release and he pleaded that he had tendered a sufficient release but he did not show it to the court, that they should adjudge whether it was sufficient.

But JONES answered that this will not do here for the infiniteness because it will be infinite to show the rolls by which, peradventure, he made it appear to J.S. and J.D., as whether an under sheriff is bound to discharge the sheriff, there, it is sufficient to say that he has discharged without saying in particular how. But the exception that now was insisted upon and in which the court showed their resolution was that he has here shown a relief by a custom and he has not shown a custom to maintain a distress for it and, without a custom in such a case, he cannot distrain, as in Godfrye's case, Coke 11, 42.[4] And, if he cannot distrain, he is without a remedy for it. And thus, [it is] not due. And then, the consideration that he would forbear to sue him was void and thus the *assumpsit*. It is true that it was argued [to] the court and disallowed and judgment [was] given for the plaintiff. And a doubt arose upon the obscure pleading of it because, first, he alleged that the tenants of the manor have used upon each alienation and descent to pay so much for a relief and, then, he showed that Smith held of him by fealty etc. and relief *secundum consuetudinem*. And the court here thought it to be pleaded as a tenure and not as a custom and that *secundum consuetudinem* referred to show the

---

[1] See above, No. 19.

[2] *Alblaster v. Bendisch* (1470), YB Trin. 10 Edw. IV, f. 11, pl. 5, 47 Selden Soc. 96.

[3] *Lord Lisle's Case* (1483), YB Hil. 22 Edw. IV, f. 40, pl. 2.

[4] *Bullen v. Godfrey* (1614), 11 Coke Rep. 42, 77 E.R. 1199, also 1 Rolle Rep. 32, 73, 81 E.R. 306, 337.

certainty of the relief. And thus, if it be a relief by a tenure, distress is incident to it of common right.

WHITELOCKE: There are two kinds of reliefs, one properly a relief, and this is always upon a descent and incident to each tenure even though it is not part of the tenure. And this kind of relief [is] ancient; we can read of it in the Assize of Clarendon[1] in the time of Henry II and in Glanvill, book 9, ca. 4,[2] where he pleads it, and he says that the fee of a knight is 100s. and of socage of the annual value, with which Littleton agreed.[3] But the baronies were not certain, as he says. But the Statute of Magna Carta[4] put it in certainty. And this relief is incident of common right, as in *Reliefe*, 13,[5] given to hold by fealty and rent *pro omnibus demandis*, yet the relief [is] due. And [it is said] by Littleton[6] one can distrain for it, and yet it is not part of the tenure but a fruit of it, and yet it savors of the tenure because one cannot have an action of debt for it nor can the executors of the lord. See C. 3, Pennant's case.[7]

The other kind of relief, which is not a proper relief, is by a custom or reservation of the party. And this is not properly a relief, but a service. And for this, [see] Edw. III, 13, by Herle,[8] and 31 Ass. 11; it is said that this is not a relief. And here in our case, the relief is laid to be [an] improper relief by reservation in the nature of a service. But if it had been by a custom, it had not been distrainable and thus remediless. But here [it is] by reservation and, on account of this, [it is] distrainable etc.

JONES: A relief [is] properly no part of the tenure, but [is a] fruit of it, as a wardship, and it is properly upon a descent and not upon a succession of the abbot, dean, etc., and it is the doubling of the rent of the socage. And distress is incident to it. But, if it is altered out of its proper course and is payable other[wise] than upon a descent, as upon an alienation or death of the predecessor or if it is not the annual value of the land, but a certain sum, then, it is either by prescription and is properly a service or by custom. And then, if he has [not] a usage to distrain for it, he does not have a remedy for it. And yet these last species are abusively and promiscuously called in the books reliefs also, as in Mantell and Redsole's case,[9] where 5s. upon an alienation [is] called a relief. And, in my country

---

[1] C. Stephenson & F. G. Marcham, edd., *Sources of English Constitutional History* (1972), vol. 1, pp. 76–80.

[2] *Glanvill* (G. D. G. Hall, ed., 1965), pp. 107–109.

[3] T. Littleton, *Tenures*, sects. 112, 126.

[4] Stat. 25 Edw. I, c. 2 (*SR*, I, 114).

[5] Fitzherbert, Abr., *Relief*, pl. 13 (temp. Edw. I).

[6] T. Littleton, *Tenures*, sect. 127.

[7] *Harvey v. Oswald* (1596), 3 Coke Rep. 64, 76 E.R. 775, also Moore K.B. 456, 72 E.R. 692, Cro. Eliz. 553, 572, 78 E.R. 798, 816.

[8] *Prior of Preston's Case* (1329), YB Pas. 3 Edw. III, f. 13, pl. 8.

[9] *Woodland v. Mantel* (1553), 1 Plowden 94, 75 E.R. 148.

of North Wales, it is a custom to pay 10s. for a relief upon a descent and not more
or less. And such a custom is said in 14 Hen. IV[1] to be in Cornwall. And this being certain, it is not a relief but by a custom only. And if there be not a custom to
distrain for it, he has no remedy etc.

DODDERIDGE: A relief is properly this which is [due] after the death of the
ancestor and not upon succession because, there, [it is] no debt unless by custom.
But the other thing that is paid upon an alienation is properly a fine for the alienation, and not a relief. And if it be reserved upon the creation of the tenures, as
it could before the Statute of *Quia emptores*,[2] then it is a service and [is] distrainable. But if, by a custom, it is not distrainable, he is remediless. And the true
and proper relief Bracton speaks of in book 2, f. 83, is *praestatio ab heredibus etc.*
And of others improper are the books of 18 Edw. III, 16, which Fitzherbert has
more largely [in] tit. *Avowry*, 99, and 16 Hen. I, and B., *Releife*, 13, out of the old
Natura Brevium.[3] And yet it is a relief that is properly a relief that can by custom
be due upon a succession, as [are] the books of *Releife*, 14; and 3 Edw. III, 13; 5
Edw. IV, 72, 20;[4] which three are manifest. But a true relief is not part of the tenure. And on account of this, the executors of the lord have [a remedy] for it. And
in this are *Avowry*, 233; 7 Hen. VI, 13; B., *Debt*, 194; Coke 3, 60.[5] But if it be by
a custom, he should have also a custom to maintain the distress or, otherwise, it
is not good, as in Godfrye's case, which is good law. And [there is] no difference
between the reason of this and our [case] if it be a relief by custom.

And thus, judgment was given for the plaintiff.

[Other reports of this case: Benloe 180, 73 E.R. 1040, CUL MS. Gg.2.30, f. 66; 3 Bulstrode 323, 81 E.R. 268; W. Jones 132, 82 E.R. 70, BL MS. Hargr. 317, f. 132; Latch 37,
94, 129, 82 E.R. 263, 291, 309, HLS MS. 1235, ff. 35v, 53; 2 Rolle Rep. 370, 81 E.R.
858; BL MS. Hargr. 38, ff. 30v, 79; BL MS. Lansd. 1092, ff. 70, 97; CUL MS. Hh.2.1,
f. 199; CUL MS. Ll.3.13, ff. 81v, 122.]

---

[1] *Finch's Case* (1412), YB Mich. 14 Hen. IV, f. 2, pl. [5], or YB Mich. 14 Hen. IV,
ff. 2, 8, pl. 6 (1412).

[2] Stat. 18 Edw. I, stat. 1 (*SR*, I, 106).

[3] YB Trin. 18 Edw. III, f. 26, pl. [18] (1344), Fitzherbert, Abr., *Avowrie*, pl. 99;
Brooke, Abr., *Releife*, pl. 13.

[4] *Baldry v. Bernyngham* (1385), YB Hil. 8 Ric. II, Ames Found., vol. 4, p. 233, pl.
22, Fitzherbert, Abr., *Relief*, pl. 14; *Prior of Preston's Case* (1329), *ut supra*; YB Mich. 5
Edw. IV, Long Quinto, ff. 70, 72 (1465); perhaps YB Pas. 5 Edw. IV, f. 2, pl. 20 (1465).

[5] Mich. 34 Edw. I, Fitzherbert, Abr., *Avowrie*, pl. 233 (1306); *Prior of Montague's
Case* (1428), YB Mich. 7 Hen. VI, ff. 12, 13, pl. 17; YB Pas. 21 Edw. III, f. 9, pl. 28
(1347), Brooke, Abr., *Dett*, pl. 194; *Harvey v. Oswald* (1596), *ut supra*.

99

Anonymous

(K.B. Trin. 2 Car. I, 1626)

An ecclesiastical court does not have the jurisdiction to determine the boundaries of parishes.

BL MS. Add. 35961, f. 25v, pl. 7

One parson sued another for tithes in the spiritual court. The defendant there pleaded that the place was in another parish. And for this, *Littleton* prayed [for a writ of] prohibition because it does not belong to them to try to boundaries of parishes and that this prohibition is warranted by 39 Edw. III and that it is common experience.

And the court said that it was common experience and granted it.

100

Warner v. Harding

(Part 3)
(K.B. Trin. 2 Car. I, 1626)

BL MS. Add. 35961, f. 25v, pl. 8

And now, the justices showed their judgment in Warner and Hardwin's case, of which, see above, ff. 1b, 2a, pl. 3, f. 11b, pl. 24.[1]

And WHITELOCKE began. And, after a recital of the case, he said, in this case, there is not but one point, and it is whether this condition here given[2] to the queen, by which the choses are forfeited by the attainder of treason, will be infinite and the more inasmuch as forfeitures are now greatly enlarged over the common law by statutes and especially by the Statute of 33 Hen. VIII.[3] This point in general is well settled by the authorities of Englefield and Marys, of Winch's case, of Dowtye's case,[4] and they are all upon this law of 33 [Hen. VIII] so that, by these, it is clear that the conditions are given to the queen upon the attainder by this Statute.

---

[1] For earlier proceedings in this case, see above, Nos. 3, 44.

[2] est done *MS*.

[3] Stat. 33 Hen. VIII, c. 20, s. 4 (*SR*, III, 857).

[4] *Regina v. Englefield* (1591), 7 Coke Rep. 11, 77 E.R. 428, also Moore K.B. 303, 72 E.R. 595, 4 Leonard 135, 169, 74 E.R. 779, 800, Popham 18, 79 E.R. 1139, 1 Anderson 293, 123 E.R. 480; *Attorney General v. Dowtie* (1584), 3 Coke Rep. 9, 76 E.R. 643, 1 Leonard 21, 74 E.R. 19.

But the point now in particular is whether this condition here be forfeited and if it be so inseparably annexed to the person of William Shelley to make the declaration that another cannot perform it and thus the forfeiture prevented by it because, if it be tied to the person of William Shelley, it is not forfeited because a forfeiture is *foris facere* and, if one cannot *facere* this *foris*, it gives[1] it to the other; it cannot be forfeited. And on account of this, a wardship of an heir cannot be forfeited because it cannot be transferred to another, thus others [?] *pro consilio impendendo*, as [is] Dyer, f. 2, and Dyer 377.[2] And on account of this, the point and pinch of the case here is whether the declaration is annexed to the person of the tenderer and not to William Shelley. But the declaring is a clause that, there, the law imposes.

For the maintenance of my conclusion, I ground myself first upon the rule of the law that when the law imposes a thing to be done and the party imposes it also, the imposition of the party is void and it will be said the act of the law *qui expressio eorum quod ius mandat inutilis*. And on account of this, thus, the law will be as not expressed.

And thus, without question, the condition has been given to the queen. And here, the declaration of the intent is a necessary thing and required by the law upon each tender. And without his expression that he will make a declaration, there, the law would have commanded because the bar holds [that] without a declaration of the intent of the tender, it had not been sufficient to divest the uses. And the tender is the act of the body and the declaration the soul of this act and thus implied by the law. And thus, it has no express operation but is vain, as the expression upon the reservation of a rent that he [can] distrain, as Littleton says. Nay, add to this case any particular circumstance, as that, if he be in arrears by twenty days, that he could distrain, yet it is void, as in the former case. And the particularity of the circumstance does not make it good. Thus, if there be a condition upon a feoffment and the proviso is afterwards for the condition broken, this proviso is idle, as Littleton also said. And if, there, the condition was that he enter signifying that he enter for the breach of the condition, this would not alter the case. It is commonly put in the cases that, if the rent be in arrears being lawfully demanded, he will not re-enter, there, if it be lawfully demanded are surplusage because, there, the law so says. And, if it was limited to be demanded by the person of the lessor, this does not alter the case. Thus, in our case, there, the law implies the declaration upon the tender. And on account of this, the expressing of it is not material.

My second reason here is that the tender of the ring here is a corporal act. And it had two effects, one proper, the other improper. The proper effect is the transmutation of the ownership of the ring because, by the gift, the ownership is

---

[1] est done *MS*.

[2] *Oliver v. Emsonne* (1514), 1 Dyer 1, 73 E.R. 4; *Gage v. Fourthe* (1576), 3 Dyer 347, 73 E.R. 780, also 1 Anderson 49, 123 E.R. 347, Benloe 276, 123 E.R. 194.

altered. And this is the natural effect. The improper effect here is the transmutation of the use from the one to the other. And the divesting of it from him is what was before. And this is the improper effect because it does not have such an effect naturally, but *ex pacto et provisione partia*. Now, when a corporal act as here is inured with an improper operation, the declaration of it must be that it is to such an improper intent. Bracton, lib. 2, fo. 17 or cap. 17, has these words to this intent that, where there is such a corporal act, that it has in it three things: (1) *corporis actus*, (2) *affectus animi*, (3) *adminiculum juris*, which is thus intended that when such a corporal act is done to make it to operate otherwise than naturally, it must be declared *affectus animi*.

Third, by *adminiculum juris*, by the exposition of the law, it will have such an operation, otherwise not. And Bracton exemplifies this by an entry in lands because he says, when one enters, that, there, there is an *actus corporis* and the proper effect of it is *naturalis possessio*.

And on account of this, without the expression of the *affectus animi*, the intent will not have *per adminiculum juris* an improper effect, *id est* to gain legal possession. And on account of this, there, it must be expressed for what he enters. And on account of this, there, he said, if one enters as in hunting or hawking, it is not an entry to gain the possession. Thus is the Parson of Honylane's case in the *Commentaries*[1] that, because his intent was not to reduce the possession, there, it did not have this effect. Thus, 43 Edw. III, *Feoffments*, 51;[2] if one bail a charter of feoffment upon the land, this will not have [any] other effect than its proper [one], to be the delivery of the deed and not to be a livery [of seisin] because this is improper. But, if he declares that it will be in the name of livery, then it will have this improper effect, but without such a declaration, not. And with this agrees Sharp's case, C. 6, and Thorogood's case, C. 9, 135.[3] Thus here, in our case, the proper effect of the tender of the ring will not be altered without expressing such an intention, therefore, to this declaration incident by the law.

My third reason is because this case is within the general case of notice because, if the law enjoins a declaration without this, the party does not have notice. And, if he does not have notice, he cannot be a party to it because he cannot consent without notice nor disassent to take because *ubi non est noticia, ibi non est consensus*. And for this is Dyer 354;[4] there was a proviso that, if a tender be made at the font stone in Sarum Church, that the use will be void, and, there, for lack of notice of the tender, it was held void by three justices by reason of the uncertainty. And, if there [it was void] for the uncertainty, here *a fortiori* because, here,

---

[1] *Panel v. Moor* (1553), 1 Plowden 91, 75 E.R. 145.

[2] Pas. 43 Edw. III, Fitzherbert, Abr., *Feffements & faits*, pl. 51 (1369).

[3] *Sharp v. Swan* (1600), 6 Coke Rep. 26, 77 E.R. 292, also Cro. Eliz. 482, 78 E.R. 734, Moore K.B. 458, 72 E.R. 693; *Thoroughgood's Case* (1612), 9 Coke Rep. 136, 77 E.R. 925.

[4] *Barrough's Case* (1576), 3 Dyer 354, 73 E.R. 793.

[there is] more uncertainty because he could tender divers things and when he would and to what person he would. Thus [it is] uncertain in the thing tendered, in the times, and in the persons to whom. Thus [is] Co. 8, Frauncis' case;[1] without notice of the purchase of the reversion by bargain and sale, the bargainee will not take advantage of the condition of entry for non-payment of the rent, and yet the bargain was of record. Thus [is] Pennant's case, C. 2;[2] without notice of the alienation, the acceptance by the reversioner of the rent does not bar him from entry.

Thus, here, the tender to the feoffee will not divest the use without a declaration because, without it, he cannot have notice of the intent of it and also, where there are a tender and declaration, they are in the nature of the principal and accessory, and *accessorium sequitur principale.*[3] And on account of this, the tender being given to the queen, the declaration is accessory to it. It cannot be but given also. If a feoffment be made upon a condition that, if the feoffor pay etc., yet he can pay *per alterum* and also, if he dies, the heir can pay. And he put it as expressly you would, yet he can do it *per alterum*, as if it was limited that, if he pay in person, because *quod potest facere per seipsum potest facere per alium et quod facit per alium per seipsum facit.*[4] And this rule is intended of civil actions, not natural [ones], because a demand of rent, payment of money, and civil actions are not restrained to the person. Thus [is] Coke 9, Combe's case;[5] a copyholder can surrender by an attorney. And on account of this, we see where conditions are tied to the person. And it is but in two cases, (1) where the act is an act of the mind; (2) where the act of the body. Both of these appear in Englefield's case[6] because, there, if his seeming had been after the proviso, there, it had been otherwise; if it had been upon a condition that, if it seemed to him vicious and, upon this, he tender the ring, there, his discourse and intellect cannot be transferred because [it is the] operation of the soul and the most inseparable act that can be.

Thus for the second, if it be limited to the act of the body, this also is untransferable. And for this is the Duke of Norfolk's case,[7] there, it [re]cites where

---

    [1] *Milner v. Fraunces* (1609), 8 Coke Rep. 89, 77 E.R. 609, also 2 Brownlow & Goldesborough 277, 123 E.R. 940.

    [2] *Harvey v. Oswald* (1596), 3 Coke Rep. 64, 76 E.R. 775, also Moore K.B. 456, 72 E.R. 692, Cro. Eliz. 553, 572, 78 E.R. 798, 816.

    [3] *Black's Law Dictionary* (1933), p. 22.

    [4] what one can do by oneself he can do by another and what one does by another he does by himself.

    [5] *Atlee v. Banks* (1613), 9 Coke Rep. 75, 77 E.R. 843.

    [6] *Regina v. Englefield* (1591), 7 Coke Rep. 11, 77 E.R. 428, also Moore K.B. 303, 72 E.R. 595, 4 Leonard 135, 169, 74 E.R. 779, 800, Popham 18, 79 E.R. 1139, 1 Anderson 293, 123 E.R. 480.

    [7] *Duke of Norfolk's Case*, 7 Coke Rep. 13, 77 E.R. 431.

the proviso was that, if he revokes it with his own hand, there, it cannot be performed by another; thus, [it is] not given to the king.

And thus by these reasons, here, the condition is given to the queen and by consequence etc.

JONES [held] to the same intent. There is but one point in the case, whether the queen had here but an estate for the life of Shelley or a fee by the performance of the condition. There have been two questions at the bar, (1) whether the condition [be] given to the queen; (2) whether there was a performance. But the last was waived, and, on account of this, I will not speak to it, but only [say] that the condition was performed upon the return of Fortescue because he had tendered to the heir apparent of Hungerford. And this cannot be but when Hungerford was dead because, before, he is not the heir apparent and, then, he appears to be the heir and then truly heir apparent.[1] And on account of this, the remainder to the heir apparent of J.S. is a remainder in abeyance. And, if the return of the commission had not been good to himself, the verdict in finding that he had tendered it to the heir of Hungerford had not aided it because the performance of the condition must stand of record. But this was waived by the counsel, and, on account of this, I waive it also.

And because it is said that the price of the ring is not averred and, on account of this, it could be of no value, second, I say that the price of 12d. refers to all. And yet, [it is] good because it is senseless to take a ring of gold to be of less value.

Now for the point whether the condition be given to the queen, and it is not upon the two statutes of 28 Eliz. and 33 Hen. VIII.[2] The nature of the condition is for non-performance to reduce the estate to what is annexed. And by the common law, it is not transferrable to strangers. But by the Statute of 32 Hen. VIII, ca. 34,[3] the grantors of a reversion are enabled to have the advantage of them to say which conditions are given by the Statute of 33 [Hen. VIII]. It is to know that all conditions are to be forfeited by them for treason except those that are annexed to the person of the feoffee himself or performable by a stranger or that lie in a contingency or such that induce the nature of them to the possession of conditions annexed to the person. It is clear for[4] these performable by a stranger and in contingency. The reason of these is because they are not in my power and that which is not in my power, I cannot forfeit. [It is] similar to Malory's case, Coke 5;[5] where a conusee of a reversion bargained, there, because no attornment

---

[1] Sic in MS.

[2] Stat. 29 Eliz. I, c. 1 (*SR*, IV, 766–767); Stat. 33 Hen. VIII, c. 20, s. 4 (*SR*, III, 857).

[3] Stat. 32 Hen. VIII, c. 34 (*SR*, III, 788–789).

[4] per *MS*.

[5] *Mallory v. Payn* (1601), 5 Coke Rep. 111, 77 E.R. 228, also Cro. Eliz. 805, 832, 78 E.R. 1033, 1058.

was [made] to the conusee, he could not transfer the benefits that he himself did not have. Thus, if the condition be that, if the chief justice do, as it is put in Englefield's case, another but he could not perform it, but, if he performed, the king will have the advantage of the performance. Thus, as it has been said, if it is tied to the mind or a personal act as to the handwriting etc. and, peradventure, if it had expressly been provided that, if William Shelley tender in person, there, this alters the case because it is more than the law says, but I do not affirm it. Thus a condition to accrue is not given by this statute because it is against nature to accrue to increase but upon the original estate.

There have been three objections:

(1) That in the tender, there are two acts, the tender and the declaration and that another cannot declare. To this, I answer that, if the condition had not been other but that if he tender, that the uses had been void, then it had been without question but another could have done it, then the declaration is implied in the tender. And in Combe's case, Coke 9, if one covenants to stand seised to the use of one with a power to make leases, there, he cannot make a lease by an attorney, but the reason there is because, in such a case, the estates of the lessees arise out of a privy covenant and his lease is but a declaration of the use, which he cannot make by an attorney. But, if one makes a lease for life with such a power for[1] livery, there, he can make such a lease by an attorney. And thus it is to be intended, and thus, in the case, there, [it is] to be intended.

[2] The second objection [is] that William Shelley, here, can tender even though he be attainted, therefore, [it is] individual and not separated by the attainder. I answer thus can the queen tender also, each for his interest, similar to Littleton's case. A feoffee and his wife can tender each for his interest. And this I say by admittance. But I say that William Shelley, being attainted, cannot tender. But, if it had been a personal action, then, he could have performed it and no other, as if it had been if he go to Rome. But, because it is given to the queen, William Shelley cannot perform it.

[3] The third objection [is] because, here, the declaration of his intent is individual to William Shelley himself, in which the answer of Brother Whitelocke is the sole reason that can be given (and on account of this, if I use it, it is this which in former times judges have done without scruple because often you find them to argue to the same intent and almost in the same words) and this is that the declaration is implied by law and, on account of this, it is not material nor has operation that a declaration is incident to the tender. And Gresham's case in Dyer[2] in a case cited by my brother Whitelocke is good law even though it does not cite authority for it but it was adjudged [in] 3 Jac. in the exchequer in the case

---

[1] per *MS.*
[2] *Gresham's Case* (1580), 3 Dyer 372, 73 E.R. 835, 110 Selden Soc. 383.

of Christ Church in Oxford that, where the abbot of Strata Marcella[1] had made a lease rendering rent with a condition that, if it be lawfully demanded and [in] arrears after the day, that he will enter [and] the abbey was dissolved and the reversion came to the king, there, it was resolved that the demand was incident by law and, on account of this, the king [was] not bound with it. And it was not taken for the reason that the king was not bound to demand because, if the abbot had been bound otherwise than by act of the law, *viz.* by a special agreement, there, the king is bound to demand or otherwise the condition does not go to the king. To this purpose also is the case of 16 Eliz.,[2] where one devised legacies and the residue to his executors to pay his debts, the devise to his executors [was] void because the law says as much. But, in our case, peradventure, if he had made general conditions and sentences had been otherwise and, on account of this, if there had been a proviso that, if William Shelley tender a ring and 'then William Shelley shall declare his intent' etc. and even though the Statute of 33 [Hen. VIII] had been taken strictly, yet, of late, it has been begun to be enlarged. And I learned this in the late great case of Lord Sheffield in the [court of] exchequer chamber,[3] where it was resolved that a right of action involved with a right and estate was forfeited by this and, in account of this, by this, I was encouraged in this case to extend the Statute also. And, if this condition is not given to the king, no condition will be given because it is an ordinary condition for the paying of money and conditions more in privity have been given. And on account of this, the king in the right of his ward entered by the common law for a condition broken.

And 16 Eliz., a chantry priest made a lease for life upon a condition;[4] there, the king can have the condition. And he had the privilege of the Cistercians, which is more personal than this here.

For the two judgments objected, one in the exchequer, the other in the common bench, for that in the exchequer, it is the confession of the attorney of the king that can also easily pass being, as here, the case is of little prejudice to the king, having passed the inheritance to the other and, on account of this, he cannot gain but some few leases. For the judgment of the common bench, I reverence this, and thus I was bound also to reverence Englefield's judgment. And everyone is to judge upon his own conscience. And it seems to me that Englefield's case [is] more strong than ours here.

---

[1] *Regina v. Vaughan* (1591), 9 Coke Rep. 24, 77 E.R. 765, Moore K.B. 297, 72 E.R. 591.

[2] *Hunks v. Alborough* (1574), 3 Dyer 331, 73 E.R. 748, Moore K.B. 98, 72 E.R. 466, Benloe 219, 123 E.R. 154, 1 Anderson 22, 123 E.R. 332.

[3] *Lord Sheffield v. Ratcliffe* (1625), 2 Rolle Rep. 374, 501, 81 E.R. 860, 943, W. Jones 69, 82 E.R. 36, Hobart 334, 80 E.R. 475, CUL MS. Ll.3.15, BL MS. Hargr. 38, f. 10v, Godbolt 300, 78 E.R. 176, Palmer 351, 81 E.R. 1119.

[4] *Anonymous* (1574), 3 Dyer 337, 73 E.R. 761.

And thus he concluded etc.

DODDERIDGE, *contra*: This is not a new case. It has been in all the courts of Westminster and adjudged in them except this court. And I reverence their judgments. And I have seen the records of them and found them full of excellent reason. And on account of this, I follow them and conceive that the condition was not given to the queen. And I will agree with all the cases put by my brothers. I will not deny any. The reasons upon which I ground are three:

(1) The nature of the proviso, and, there, the principal act is the declaration of his intent and the tender of the ring where etc. but a ceremony and circumstance and the declaration required is not a general declaration but a special [one] appropriated to the person of William Shelley because it is provided that he will do this because it is said '*ipso tunc expressante declarante*'. What can be more personal than that? And I hold that, if another tender the ring here and William Shelley make the declaration, that it is good enough because it is but accessory. And this is not, as has been said, a declaration that the law requires because it is more, that, here, it is required that William Shelley will make the declaration with his tongue. And I do not see more difference between this and the Duke of Norfolk's case, than the tongue and the pen, because the declaration was required by the pen of the duke and, here, by the tongue of Shelley, which cannot be transferred.

The differences taken in Englesfield's case are allowed and agreed by me, that personal conditions are saved and that it was more personal than, here, this was.

I was fearful, I confess, upon the Statute of 33 Hen. VIII and the case of Sheffield lately adjudged that, by the extent of it, it was enlarged to rights of action clothed with possessions. And our case is not similar to Englefield's because, there, it is provided that, if Frances or any other person tender, which was a clear difference.

My brother Jones granted, if it had been a separate act and the condition had been 'and if he declare' etc., that this had been otherwise. And I say that the words '*ipso tunc declarante et expressante*' are the same as if he had said '*et ipse expressaverit et declaraverit*', and, by the rules of good grammar, the participle of the presentence can be varied by the subjunctive, as it is to be seen in 27 Hen. VIII, Dockwraye's case,[1] in the cases put by Audley, where he says that, if I lease a house upon condition that my wife, being a widow, if she would have this, that the lease will cease, there, this is as much as if it had said, if my wife as were a widow, there put [at] fo. 19 at the end. And no words could be more personal than '*ille ipse*'. And the declaration of the intent of the tender the law requires because, otherwise, it had been a dumb show to tender the money without more. But that Shelley will make a declaration the law does not require. They are acts that are individual. In Combe's case, a copyholder can surrender in court by an

---

[1] YB Mich. 27 Hen. VIII, f. 14, pl. 6 (1535).

attorney but, if it had been outside of the court, he could not do it by an attorney. *Annuity*, 51;[1] a prior granted an annuity until he promoted the grantee to a benefice; there, another cannot promote him.

My second reason is upon the nature of the election. It was said that this proviso was a very uncertain proviso and [this] because he needed a certain notice etc. It is true it is totally uncertain, and yet the uncertainty can be reduced to a certainty by an election. And it is here at his election when he would tender during his lifetime; second, to whom he would tender to the feoffees, to the heirs of some of the feoffees, to one of them, or to all. Third, it is in election that he would tender a gold ring, 12d. in money, a pair of gloves, etc. And that to do these things is in his election no one would deny. Thus, we see the distinction of the election. And this you will find [in] 10 El. Dyer 281;[2] in a case of election, there, it is a defense to be *interna, libera, et spontanea separatio unius rei ab altera sine compulsione consistens in anima et voluntate*. It has been granted that nothing is more personal and inseparable from the person than the mind and intent. And it was truly granted, and it cannot be denied so that it can be more personal than an election that is *interna spontanea consistens in mente et voluntate*. And if so, then certainly it cannot be transferred. And though this condition be not given to the crown, yet there are enough conditions that could pass. And on account of this, never have I read nor heard of an election transferred from a person. It is a thing so personal. And this is the reason of Bullock's case, Dyer 281, before cited, that the heir cannot elect when the father dies before an election. And on account of this, if I give to one Whiteacre and Blackacre, the one for life, the other in fee, and he is attainted, will it now be the king's election which he will have for life? Never. (Query, if he dies not being attainted, whether the heir [may] elect.) It is more personal than a writ of error (which still is not forfeitable) because, there, the heir can have it and, in some cases, the feoffee, as Dyer, fo. 16 or 1b.[3] And [it is] more personal than a corody which belongs to a foundership. B., *Corody*, 6.[4] But put the case further, and then he can transfer it from himself and forfeit it, but always to a privy, never to a stranger. And on account of this, if he makes a feoffment of both of the acres, then the feoffee will not make an election, but the first feoffor; thus, it passes to the privy.

And I conceive that it is a more personal condition here than in the duke of Norfolk's case and the stronger case. For the case of the Cistercians, where the privilege to be acquitted of tithes was given to the king even though it was *quamdiu propriis manibus excolebat*, this was not against me because it is given by a Statute. And, if the words of it had not been large enough, it had been lost, as the

---

[1] Hil. 33 Edw. I, Fitzherbert, *Abr., Annuitie*, pl. 51 (1359).

[2] *Bullock v. Burdett* (1568), 3 Dyer 280, 73 E.R. 630, also Moore K.B. 81, 72 E.R. 455, 1 Anderson 11, 123 E.R. 326, Benloe 148, 123 E.R. 113.

[3] Note (1512), 1 Dyer 1, 73 E.R. 2.

[4] YB 14 Hen. VI, f. 11, pl. 43 (1435 x 1436), Brooke, *Abr., Corodies & Pencions*, pl. 6.

tenure in frankalmoign was upon the translation [of lands] from the Templars
to the Hospitalers because the words of this Statute of 17 Edw. II,[1] by which it
was done, is not as long as the Statute of the Dissolution of the Monasteries[2]
was because it gives to the king and his patentees 'all privileges in as large and
ample manner as the abbots etc. enjoyed them'. And on account of this, it does
not touch our case.

The third reason upon which I insist are the former judgments in this case:
first, in the exchequer upon the *monstrans de droit*; second, in the common bench.
I have enquired of those who were living and judges in the time of these judgments, and I heard that it did not go upon such scandalous grounds as were in-
timated and insinuated at the bar, even though it was not fully said so, yet, by
their dubious speeches, aspersions were cast upon them, first, for that in the exchequer, it was said that it was upon the confession of the attorney general and
that it was an easy matter to get, naming the reversion of the inheritance being
granted to him who brought the *monstrans de droit* and, by this, the king to lose
or gain nothing by this unfaithfulness. If you believe that the court of exchequer
would allow the attorney general to confess what thing he would, you would
suppose it a simple[minded] court naming what is in a thing that binds the right
forever, as a *monstrans de droit* does, and, though it does not concern the king in
profit by this case, yet it concerns him greatly to have such a point adjudged. And
on account of this, we must not presume that they would allow such a confession
against the law how little soever it concerns the king in particular. And thus, the
judges of the common bench have adjudged Corbet's case in the First Reports.[3]
And yet it was a feigned case to try the opinions of the judges and not to venture
so great an inheritance as Mildmay's, which was not receded from when the true
case of Mildmay[4] came before them, but it confirmed their former resolutions,
even though the former action was feigned. And, in the point of gain or loss, it
does not concern the parties. And we know who was the attorney [general] at
the time of this confession; he was a learned man and an honest man, and, if the
right had not been so, he would not have confessed it. (By Davies and Richardson, he meant Hobart.)[5]

And for the judgment of the common bench, my brother Hutton, who solely
survives those who adjudged it, said that it was often debated and adjudged upon
mature deliberation and [that] by a learned and honest bench as ever was, when

---

[1] Stat. 17 Edw. II, stat. 2 (*SR*, I, 194–196).

[2] Stat. 31 Hen. VIII, c. 13, s. 1 (*SR*, III, 733).

[3] *Corbet v. Corbet* (1599–1600), 1 Coke Rep. 77, 76 E.R. 178, also Moore K.B. 601,
72 E.R. 785, 2 Anderson 134, 123 E.R. 585.

[4] *Hethersall v. Mildmay* (1605), 6 Coke Rep. 40, 77 E.R. 311, also Moore K.B. 632,
72 E.R. 805.

[5] Henry Hobart was attorney general from 1606 to 1613. J. Sainty, *A List of English
Law Officers* (1987), p. 45.

a case came to judgment, that we used in this our best endeavor and learning to discover the truth and honestly judge accordingly. And, on account of this, we leave our reverence and regard former sages as we desire to have our judgments respected and reverenced when we are dead and gone. And on account of this, for these reasons and the reverence to former judgments that I always will give to my judgments, I will go with the plaintiff.

Chief Justice CREWE agreed with Dodderidge. And he argued very briefly and much to the intent of Dodderidge. He said that the case of Englefield had a very large preamble but, when it came to the purview, there, it was too short. And he compared it to the case of 4 & 5 Phil. & Mar., ca. 8,[1] which he said that he had seen the Statute adjudged there and the preamble recited that women having in their hands sums of money and their portions were often times varied and, on account of this, it enacted that it will not be legal to convey away any woman under sixteen years of age, yet if one conveyed away a woman who did not have her portion nor anything but possibilities, this is within the Statute because the purview is larger than the preamble, but contrary. In Englefield's case, the preamble is larger than the purview, but, there, if it had, in the proviso, restrained the tender and the declaration to himself, it had been otherwise. And on account of this, he said here that the form [to] prescribe was *forma quae dat esse rei*[2] and that, as Dodderidge said, it does not differ from the duke of Norfolk's case but as the tongue and pen differ. And, thus, he agreed with Dodderidge for the plaintiff.

And, thus, the court divided two against two.

[Other reports of this case: Benloe 139, 73 E.R. 995, CUL MS. Gg.2.30, f. 31; W. Jones 134, 82 E.R. 71, BL MS. Hargr. 317, f. 134; Latch 24, 69, 102, 82 E.R. 256, 279, 295, HLS MS. 1235, ff. 7v, 38v, 54; Noy 79, 74 E.R. 1046; Palmer 429, 81 E.R. 1155; 2 Rolle Rep. 393, 81 E.R. 873; BL MS. Hargr. 38, ff. 9, 39, 61v, 71, 169; BL MS. Lansd. 1092, ff. 22, 78, 100v; BL MS. Add. 35961, f. 119 (Widdrington's reports); CUL MS. Hh.2.1, f. 200v; CUL MS. Ll.3.13, ff. 24, 92, 125v; HLS MS. 1196, f. 1; Trinity College Dublin MS. 718, part 1.]

101

Evans v. Askwith

(Part 1)

(K.B. Trin. 2 Car. I, 1626)

The issue in this case was the validity of the permission of the lessor to hold a deanery in commendam *with a bishopric.*

---

[1] Stat. 4 & 5 Phil. & Mar., c. 8 (*SR*, IV, 329–330).

[2] Cf. *Black's Law Dictionary* (1933), p. 804.

BL MS. Add. 35961, f. 28, pl. 9

Evans brought an action of trespass against W. Askwith (*et intratur* Hil. 22 Jac., rot. 1164) for entering into a house called the Parsonage House and a close in Gilbert and Sutton and taking away three loads of corn etc. Upon *non culpabilis* pleaded, the jury found that Dr. [John] Thornborough, dean of York, was elected bishop of Limerick in Ireland, and, before confirmation, he obtained letters patent which recited that the bishopric of Limerick was not competent and sufficient to maintain the state and carriage of the bishop and, on account of this, for his further maintenance, granted to him power *retinere in commenda dignitatem decanatus et omnia emolumenta proventus et in proprios usus convertere ad sustentationem etc. ac si esset in titulo*[1] with a clause of non-residence and dispensation of performing his office in the deanery. And afterwards, he was consecrated bishop. And further, they found that Matthew [Hutton], archbishop of York, made a lease of the place where etc. to Dorothy Askwith to begin on the day etc. for twenty-one years according to the Statute and that, after Thornborough was postulate, that it was confirmed for Thornborough to be bishop of Bristol. And the king assented. And before confirmation, he purchased other patents *retinere decanatus de* York *in commenda*, and then it was confirmed. And then they found that Matthew, the archbishop, made another lease of the same tenements, which was a concurrent lease, which was confirmed by Thornborough. Matthew died, and Toby [Matthew], archbishop of York, made a lease of the place where etc. to Askwith, the first lessee, to commence etc., the former lease then not fully expired, which lease was confirmed by Thornborough, the dean, and the chapter, under which lease the defendant claimed. And the plaintiff sued the concurrent lease.

And it was argued by *Bankes* for the plaintiff. And he said that, here, there was first a good lease by the bishop and it is not questioned. Then, it is to prove that the confirmation was good and that the dispensation came in time so that Thornborough was sufficiently dean to make the confirmation. And yet he agreed that, it being a concurrent lease, if it had not been confirmed by the dean, it had not been good, according to Fox's case[2] cited in the Bishop of Sarum's case, Coke 10.[3] He also agreed that the taking of the bishopric in Ireland was an avoidance of his deanery in England if the dispensation had not come in time. And this appears by *Triall*, 57 and 54, in Fitzherbert's *Abridgment*.[4] And it is an avoidance not by the common law but by the canons of the church, being a general constitution.

---

[1] to retain *in commendam* the office of dean both all arising emoluments and, for his own use, to direct for sustenance etc. and whether it be in title.

[2] *Fox v. Collier* (1579), Moore K.B. 107, 72 E.R. 472, 1 Anderson 65, 123 E.R. 356.

[3] *Stanton v. Green* (1613), 10 Coke Rep. 58, 60, 77 E.R. 1013, 1018; also cited in *Bishop of Chichester v. Freeland* (1625 x 1626), J. Bridgman 29, 30, 123 E.R. 1177.

[4] YB Pas. 19 Edw. III, Rolls Ser. 31b, vol. 13, p. 76, pl. 27 (1345), Fitzherbert, Abr., *Triall*, pl. 57; Mich. 5 Ric. II, Fitzherbert, Abr., *Triall*, pl. 54 (1381).

And with this agrees 10 Edw. III, 1, by Parninge, and 5 Edw. III, 9.[1] And yet, if a parson or dean etc. be made a titulary bishop, such as were called *nullatenses* and utopian bishops, as are the four patriarchs of the pope, of Jerusalem, Constantinople etc. and they are bare titles without office and *beneficia*, this does not make an avoidance, but only such that have possessions and a living etc.

And, for the point of the confirmation, [it is] good because the dispensation is good for four reasons:

(1) Here, there is a person able to dispense, the king. If respite be had at common or statute law, by the Statute, it is clear. And for the common law, it is said in *Ayde*, 103,[2] *reges sacro oleo uncti sunt spiritualis jurisdictionis capaces*; therefore, he can dispense here with the bishop to hold the deanery. And 11 Hen. VII, 12;[3] the king can dispense with a priest to have two benefices and with a bastard to be a priest. Thus, here, there is a person able to dispense.

(2) The dispensation came in sufficient time before the consecration because, before consecration, he is not a bishop. And thus, until this, his benefice becomes void. And thus his dispensation *retinere* comes soon enough. 38 Edw. III, 29;[4] a bishop before consecration is similar to an infant *en ventre sa mere*, not in being, but he can be vouched as such an infant in respect of an apparent expectancy, but he cannot be summoned *ad warrantizandum* because he is not in being before he has his temporalities. And as, F.N.B. 2,[5] a writ of right can be directed to a bishop elect's bailiffs, and Coke 8, 96,[6] and F.N.B. 62, he can certify an excommunication, this is not against us because, before he has his temporalities, he is not a bishop but only for ministerial acts of necessity in the service of the court of the king. And he is not similar to the parson because he, by institution, is a full parson, but a bishop not until consecration.

(3) Here, the bishop is an absolute dean and in the deanery by virtue of the former title and his ancient installation so that this dispensation is a confirmation and anticipates the avoidance, which the taking of the bishopric would have operated. And thus [he is] dean in the same manner as he was before the taking of the bishopric. And upon this reason are the cases adjudged [in] 41 Edw. III, 5, and 11 Hen. IV, 37, etc. and Dyer 222b, Parkhirse's case;[7] there, it was adjudged that he

---

[1] *Rex v. Bishop of Norwich* (1336), YB Hil. 10 Edw. III, ff. 42, 1, pl. 3; *Rex v. Bishop of Bath and Wells* (1331), YB Hil. 5 Edw. III, f. 9, pl. 29.

[2] Hil. 33 Edw. III, Fitzherbert, Abr., *Ayd de roy*, pl. 103 (1359).

[3] YB Mich. 11 Hen. VII, ff. 11, 12, pl. 35 (1495).

[4] YB Mich. 38 Edw. III, f. 29b (1364).

[5] A. Fitzherbert, *Nouvelle Natura Brevium*.

[6] *Richeson v. Trollop* (1608), 8 Coke Rep. 68, 77 E.R. 577, also Cro. Jac. 213, 79 E.R. 185.

[7] *Rex v. Bishop of Salisbury* (1367), YB Mich. 41 Edw. III, f. 5, pl. 13; *Rex v. Bishop of Salisbury* (1409), YB Mich. 11 Hen. IV, f. 37, pl. 67; *Parkchust's Case* (1564), 2 Dyer 233, 73 E.R. 515.

remains parson by virtue of the *commenda* and he does not have it by a new gift and he could resign etc. And see F.N.B. 49; institution [?] by the bishop of London *parsona ecclesiae* of E. etc. And this is where it was *per commendam*, and there, in the writ, [he was] named parson. And F.N.B. 36; he can have [an action of] spoliation which proves him [to be a] parson. It is also thus always where the *commendam* is *recipere* because, there, he is not dean nor parson, and, thus, of such a *commendam* is the book to be understood. 27 Hen. VIII, 15,[1] where it is said that the cardinal[2] [was] made *commendatarius Sancti Albani* and he was not the abbot because, in such a case, he is similar to the deputy dean in 11 Hen. IV, 84.[3]

But it could be objected that, even though the dispensation came soon enough in the creation of him [as] bishop, yet it came late in the translation because, by the election there, he is an absolute bishop without doing more because consecration will not be but once and, on account of this coming after the election, it came late.

And to this, I answer that this is the general case of *commendam*s upon translations and the common form and manner. And on account of this, two [things are] to be regarded in point of right in ease of translation. The translation is not perfected nor is he an absolute bishop until confirmation, which is an act after the election and this is with the king [as] the metropolitan. And for express authority [is] the book above cited of 38 Edw. III, 29;[4] there, the traverse was *absque hoc quod* the bishopric [was] void by translation. Thus, until he [was] fully translated, he was not bishop and this is not before consecration.

Also, it could be objected that, in this case, the *commendam* is not to *retinere* the deanery but *dignitatem decanatus*; thus, he is not full dean.

To this, I answer that he had granted to him *dignitatem* and, afterwards, he granted to him the profits and, thus, in particular, all things that pertain to it. And this is as much an amount as he had granted them in the gross name because *partes simul sumptae aequant totum*. And on account of this, if the king grants to J.S. the demesne of such a manor and the services and royalties and advowsons etc., it is the same as if he had granted to him the manor by the name of the manor. Thus here, he has granted all things that belong to the deanery and, on account of this, it is as good as [if] he had granted the deanery itself.

And thus he concluded for the plaintiff.

Noy for the defendant [argued] against. The question is whether the confirmation here be good because, otherwise, being a concurrent without a good confirmation for the dean, it is not good. It is not denied but that the taking of a bishopric in any place is an avoidance of the deanery even though it be in another kingdom. And the reason of it is because a bishopric is a prelature and a

---

[1] *Dokeray's Case* (1535), YB Mich. 27 Hen. VIII, ff. 14, 15, pl. 6.

[2] conditional *MS.*

[3] *Abbot of Battle v. Neel* (1410), YB Trin. 11 Hen. IV, f. 84, pl. 34.

[4] YB Mich. 38 Edw. III, f. 29 (1364).

different character from a priest and an incompatible character. And this is the reason, and not for the cause of subordination, as if a parson takes a bishopric of the same diocese, or a remembrancer of the exchequer be made a baron of it, or a judge of the common bench [be made a judge] of the king's bench, but for the reason of the incompatibility of the characters. See 24 Edw. III, 76, and 19 Edw. III, *Triall*, 57,[1] and the record of this case in Pas. 19 Edw. III, rot. 324, in the common bench. And, there, it was that he was translated to the bishopric of Utrecht, and [it is] not certain as the book is.

The questions that are to the form of it are three:

(1) When a bishop holds his deanery *per commendam*, whether he be in by his ancient title and an incumbent as he was before or not.

And I hold not. And there is a difference where the dispensation is to retain it *per vim prioris tituli* and where *in commendam* because, in the first case, he remains in by the former installation, otherwise in F.N.B. 49, where the bishop of London brought [an action of] *juris utrum* and it was in the name of the parson; it was objected that this proves him the parson notwithstanding his *commendam*. I say that this book is fully mistaken because it is to be intended there that he was a parson imparsonee and not *in commendam*. And this appears where he put the same case of an abbot and dean, fo. 50, see 49 Hen. VI, 16; 12 Edw. IV, 20,[2] because I have never read nor heard that a commendatory can maintain a real action. And the reason was because he was not a parson nor etc., but only he had it committed to him. See 32 Hen. VI;[3] a brother of St. John of Jerusalem had a *commendam*, and he brought an action; there he must name himself *commendatarius*.

It could be objected out of F.N.B. 36, that a commendatory can have [an action of] spoliation. This I well grant because it is the nature of a personal action which he can maintain, but a real action, no one but the true parson can have. And, as for the difference of a *commendam retinere* and *recipere*, I deny this because they are entirely to one [same] purpose.

But admit that a *commendam retinere* continues him a dean as he was before, the second question is whether this commendam, being only *retinere dignitatem decanatus*, will continue him dean to this purpose in a deanery his three things, the office, the jurisdiction, and the profit. And here, he is dispensed only to retain the jurisdiction and the profits, but not the office. And on account of this, he is not a plenary dean. And thus, he cannot confirm. His office consists in the administration of the sacraments and the saying of divine services and in his counsel in the confirmation of the grants of the bishop. And it does not give to

---

[1] *Rex v. Bishop of Worcester* (1350), YB Trin. 24 Edw. III, f. 29. pl. 21; YB Pas. 19 Edw. III, Rolls Ser. 31b, vol. 13, p. 76, pl. 27 (1345), Fitzherbert, Abr., *Triall*, pl. 57.

[2] *Abbot of Colchester v. Dory* (1470 x 1471), YB Mich. 10 Edw. IV, 49 Hen. VI, f. 16, pl. 20, 47 Selden Soc. 147; *Prior of Burton's Case* (1411), YB Pas. 12 Hen. IV, f. 20, pl. 6.

[3] Perhaps *Prior of Ely's Case* (1454), YB Trin. 32 Hen. VI, f. 5, pl. 6.

him to retain but the profits and dignity only. Now, the dignity is only jurisdiction, and it is jurisdiction which makes the dignity. And on account of this, these which they have [are] solely an office of administration, as a parson not named of the dignity. But those who have jurisdiction are dignities and their dignity consists in this. See 3 Edw. III, 9,[1] where it is said that one cannot hold a promotion and dignity also in the church; where they are distinguished, 11 Hen. IV, 40; Bro. 800; 7 Hen. VI, 27; 27 Hen. VI, 5; see Coke 3, 75,[2] a deanery remains even though all of the possessions are gone. But for express authority, he cited one Morlye's case in the chancery for the parsonage of Stalburge,[3] which he said was well known to the judges; there, the bishop of Gloucester was translated to Bristol, and he took a *commendam* to hold his bishopric of Gloucester with Bristol and, afterwards, the archbishop confirmed a grant made by the parson and patron and the bishop of Gloucester, and [it was] ruled good; yet, if he had been the bishop of Gloucester and the ordinary, there, the supra-ordinary could not have confirmed. See 50 Edw. III [*blank*]; 61 Ass., fo. 31, where there are two deans and chapters to one bishop and one confirms, it is not good; thus of a deputy dean. 11 Hen. IV, 84.

The third question is whether the bishopric of Limerick be void by the postulation and assent of the king before the confirmation. And I hold that it is. And thus, the *commendam* comes late, by which the postulation and assent are void. He cited *Summa Rosella* and Panormitanus.[4] And he said that there was a difference of election of one who did not have a canonical impediment; there, he should have a consecration; where there be a continual impediment, there, only the assent of him and the superior [?] is requisite. But there is a difference of *postulatione solemnis*, where the bishop who was consecrated was elected, and *minus solemnis*, where a monk, there, by the assent of the monk. And an abbot is not a bishop without a consecration. And here, the consent of the king can be oral because to his consent in an ecclesiastical thing, the same solemnity is not required, as in a temporal [thing]. And on account of this, he can present orally.

Then he took three exceptions to the verdict: one because it did not find that the corn belonged to the plaintiff, and on account of this, forged no title to the plaintiff; second, it did not find in what parish the corn grew; third, it has found that Askwith entered and leased to the defendant and it did not show a re-entry by the plaintiff and, without a re-entry, he could not have a trespass but, when he had re-entered, then, by relation, he could have [an action of] trespass.

---

[1] *Rex v. Bishop of Bath and Wells* (1331), YB Hil. 5 Edw. III, f. 9, pl. 29.

[2] YB Hil. 11 Hen. IV, f. 40, pl. 3 (1410); *Abbot of Fontneis v. France* (1429), YB Pas. 7 Hen. VI, f. 27, pl. 18; *Rex v. Kemp* (1448), YB Mich. 27 Hen. VI, f. 5, pl. 35; *Case of the Dean and Chapter of Norwich* (1598), 3 Coke Rep. 73, 76 E.R. 793, also 2 Anderson 120, 165, 123 E.R. 577, 601.

[3] I.e. Stalbridge, Dorset.

[4] Antonius de Rosellis (d. 1466); Nicholaus de Tudeschis (d. 1445).

Et adjornatur. More, fo. 36, pl. 5; f. 48b, pl. 93; f. 51, pl. 6.[1]

102

Markham v. Cobb

(Part 1)

(K.B. Trin. 2 Car. I, 1626)

The issue in this case was whether a private person can sue a tortfeasor after he has been prosecuted in criminal proceedings for the same act.

BL MS. Add. 35961, f. 29v, pl. 10

Markham brought an action of trespass against Cobb. And he alleged a breaking of his house and the taking away of £3000 in money. The defendant pleaded that he was by the procurement of the plaintiff indicted of burglary and taking away of the said money and that he was acquitted of the burglary and found guilty of the felony and took him to charge etc. and that the same burglary and this trespass were the same. And whether this was a bar to the action was the question.

And it was argued by *Calthorpe* that this will bar him, first, because when he indicted him, there, *agitur criminaliter* and, on account of this, he cannot resort to the inferior kind of suit, and *agere civiliter*, any more than a plaintiff [can] resort to an action of a higher nature to the action of the inferior. And to this purpose, he cited Coke 4, 43, Hudson's appeal.[2]

And he applied this, second, that *nemo bis vexari debet pro uno delicto*.[3] And he cited Coke 4, 39, that, upon this reason, *autrefoits acquit* [is a] good plea, and Coke 4, 40, Dorleye's case.[4]

Third, because, by the common law, upon an indictment of felony, there was no means to recover the goods before the Statute of 21 Hen. VIII, 11;[5] if one had been robbed, he had no remedy for the goods unless he immediately pursued him and, in an appeal at his own suit, attainted him. And this was to force a man to pursue felons and put them in the hands of the justices. *Corone*, 460; Stamford,

---

[1] For later proceedings in this case, see below, Nos. 135, 226, 257.

[2] *Hudson v. Lee* (1589), 4 Coke Rep. 43, 76 E.R. 989, also Moore K.B. 268, 72 E.R. 573, 1 Leonard 318, 74 E.R. 290.

[3] No one should be vexed twice for one offense.

[4] *Vaux v. Brook* (1586), 4 Coke Rep. 39, 76 E.R. 982, also 2 Leonard 83, 74 E.R. 377; *Wetherel v. Darly* (1583), 4 Coke Rep. 40, 76 E.R. 983, also Cro. Eliz. 296, 78 E.R. 549.

[5] Stat. 21 Hen. VIII, c. 11 (*SR*, III, 291).

167; see 8 Edw. III, 11;[1] if one takes my goods feloniously, the ownership is altered by it. But see 13 Edw. IV, 3; Stanford, 60, *contra*.[2] And he said that he never saw or heard of such an action brought before and that there is not in any book express authority in the point one way or the other.

And Justice JONES said that it was a good case because on the other side, if the indictment prevents me, one could as a tortfeasor take my goods and be indicted and, on account of this, I [be] without a remedy. See 6 Edw. IV, 4, etc.,[3] a case which, as it seems to me, proves the case fully, which was not cited.

Residuum, f. 38, pl. 22.[4]

103

Blage v. Lamb

(K.B. Trin. 2 Car. I, 1626)

The issue in this case was whether a right of way is extinguished when the owner of the dominant estate purchases the servient estate.

BL MS. Add. 35961, f. 29v, pl. 11

Blage brought [an action of] trespass against Lamb, and [it is] entered 17 Jac., rot. 295. And the question was, if one has a way over the land of another and afterwards purchases the land, if it be by a feoffment of the land in which the way is, [is it] extinct.

And this term it was argued by *Philip Jermyn* that it is extinct. And he cited Davies [*blank*]; *Admeasurement*, 8; *Chemin*, 2; 11 Hen. IV, 5, by Hankford; 11 Hen. VII, 21; Dyer 295; and 8 Hen. VII, 5,[5] that, by a feoffment of the land in which he had a warren, that it is extinct.

And Justice JONES said that there has been a difference taken between things that remain after the unity, as a warren and liberties and ways, and these are not extinct by the unity. But things that do not remain, as a rent, common, etc., these continue extinct.

---

[1] Hil. 22 Edw. III, Fitzherbert, Abr., *Corone*, pl. 460 (1348); W. Stanford, *Les Plees del Coron* (1557), f. 167; YB Hil. 8 Edw. III, f. 10, pl. 30 (1334).

[2] YB Mich. 13 Edw. IV, f. 3, pl. 7 (1473); W. Stanford, *Les Plees del Coron* (1557), f. 60.

[3] YB Mich. 6 Edw. IV, f. 4, pl. 11 (1466).

[4] For later proceedings in this case, see below, Nos. 152, 185.

[5] *Rex v. Forth* (1604), Davis 1, 80 E.R. 491; YB Trin. 20 Edw. III, Rolls Ser. 31b, vol. 15, p. 62, pl. 51 (1346), Fitzherbert, Abr., *Admeasurement*, pl. 8; Fitzherbert, Abr., *Chemin*, pl. 3; YB Mich. 11 Hen. IV, f. 5, pl. 12 (1409); *Copie's Case* (1495), YB Trin. 11 Hen. VII, f. 25, pl. 6; *Anonymous* (1570), 3 Dyer 295, 73 E.R. 663; YB Trin. 8 Hen. VII, ff. 1, 5, pl. 1 (1492).

And another difference he said has been held, where one makes a feoffment of such land because it is by livery of all that he has in the land and where by another conveyance.[1]

Et adjornatur.

And afterwards, judgment was given against the plaintiff because he prescribed *quod omnes occupatores* of such land have used to have the way over.

104

Daniel v. Upley

(Part 2)

(K.B. Trin. 2 Car. I, 1626)

BL MS. Add. 35961, f. 30, pl. 12

And now, the case between Danyell and Ubley, above 7b,[2] was argued by the justices. And by them, *una voce*, judgment was given for the defendant.

WHITELOCKE: Many things have been moved in the case, but I conceive but one point in the case. And this is what is operated by this devise because it is found that, after the feoffment of the wife to William Ubley, that they, both the husband and wife, continued at all times [in] possession. Thus, if, upon this feoffment, the right of the land was in him, the points upon the releases of the elder brother and the husband are over, and the point of the fine also. Here, there are two parts of the word considerable: the first, 'I give to my wife the house to dispose of at her will and pleasure' second, 'and to give to which of my sons whom she think best'. By the first words, she had an estate for life, and by the second part of them, she had an authority to give to which of the sons she wished. And the general and true rule that devises will be construed according to the intent of the devisor and will have *benignam interpretationem* in the one [?] which, as Dyer says in Scholastica's case,[3] is *inops consilii*. And on account of this, there, he compared it to an act of Parliament in that the intent, not the words, are to be observed. And on account of this, there, the law would so marshal the words disordered for want of counsel as he would have done if it had been upon sound advice.

And here, I so marshal the words that they will carry to the wife an estate for life by the first words and no more because it is controlled by the subsequent words. And examples of this kind of marshaling agreeing with the intent, we find in our books, as Dyer 357,[4] where a devise was to the wife in fee, the remainder to

---

[1] conveniency *MS*.

[2] For earlier proceedings in this case, see above, No. 52.

[3] *Newis v. Lark* (1571), 2 Plowden 403, 75 E.R. 609, Benloe 196, 123 E.R. 138, IT MS. Petyt 511, vol. 13, f. 53v.

[4] *Chycke's Case* (1577), 3 Dyer 357, 73 E.R. 801.

her son; there, the wife had for life, the remainder for life to the son, remainder in fee to the wife. And he cited the cases that you can see [in] Com. 523.[1]

And, if we examine the words here, there are two *verba cardinalis, disponere* and *dare*. If he had not gone further than the first clause, then, it had been a fee simple to her. But *dare* controls it and shows his intent that she will not have the inheritance. *Dispono* of its nature signifies more the ordering of the form than of the substance. And *dare* signifies the gift itself and the substance of the gift. Thus, the disposition is the manner, and *dare* the matter because *disponere est collatio rerum in ordine*. And thus it is taken in the law, as appears by Dyer 266,[2] where one devised that another will have the 'disposing, setting, letting, and ordering'; there, no interest passed to the vendor. Thus was adjudged, 41 Eliz., in Pigot and Garnon's case,[3] agreeing. And even though they are not words as are required in a grant, it will bind well. *Devise*, B., 38 and 39, and Perkins;[4] a devise to one and his assignees in fee; thus here because the last words of inheritance are disposed by it, by the first sense, it disposed my estate for life, by the ordinary words, she had a power to give it to any of her sons, but she could not give it to a stranger. And it is here a limitation, as 29 Ass. 17,[5] where the devise was to one for life and that he will be her chaplain and pray for her soul. And it is similar to the case of paying in Boreston's case[6] so that, even though a married woman, she can make the gift to any of her sons according to the limitation, as appears by 28 Hen. VII, 20, and *Cui in vita*, 19,[7] inasmuch as it is an authority that she has to perform, coverture is not a disability, by which etc.

Justice JONES: Here, there is but one point for the reasons aforesaid. And it was reduced to this point in lord Leye's time, being then argued upon a verdict which, afterwards for a default, was discontinued, and, now, it is cured as [. . .]. And I conceive that the intent here is that the wife will have [it] for her life and a power to dispose of the reversion. And thus it appears it was conceived *in pais* by the parties to all of the conveyances in the case. But their construction does not matter, but what the law says. And I hold that the law upon other words would thus also construe and, because the devisor is intended to be *inops consilii*, on account of this, there, the law will aid him in the manner of the limitation and supply it. But, in the matter, it never aids him to make his bad intent to stay for the construing of the intents of wills. First, it must be gathered out of the matter

---

[1] *Welcden v. Elkington* (1578), 2 Plowden 516, 523, 75 E.R. 763, 772–774.

[2] *Anonymous* (1537), 1 Dyer 26, 73 E.R. 59.

[3] *Pigot v. Garnish* (1599), Cro. Eliz. 678, 734, 78 E.R. 915, 966.

[4] 7 Edw. VI, Brooke, Abr., *Devise*, pl. 38 and pl. 39 (1553); J. Perkins, *A Profitable Book*, sect. 557.

[5] YB 29 Edw. III, Lib. Ass., p. 159, pl. 17 (1355).

[6] *Hynde v. Ambrye* (1587), 3 Coke Rep. 16, 76 E.R. 664.

[7] Perhaps YB Pas. 21 Hen. VII, f. 20, pl. 1 (1506); Hil. 34 Edw. III, Fitzherbert, Abr., *Cui in vita*, pl. 19 (1360).

within the will, and not of matter outside, as, [in] Cheynye's case, Co. 68,[1] the rule is given. Second, there, there must be a stronger intention one way than the other because, if one devise to the other by words the intent of which are sufficiently strong to carry such an estate as if they were in a grant, there, they will be expounded as they will be in a grant, as in 22 Edw. III, 16;[2] a devise to one without limiting of any estate, there, it will be but for life as it is in a grant because it stands indifferent and the intention is not stronger one way than the other. But a devise to one *in perpetuum* is a fee [simple] because, there, there is a strong presumption that he intended to give a fee [simple] by the words *in perpetuum*. Thus, if one devise to one paying so much, there, he has a fee because, there, the law intends that this is a valuable consideration for the fee. And thus is Collyer's case, Co. 6, and C. 3, 21, and Mary Portington's case.[3] It is similar to the case of a bargain and sale before the Statute of Uses.[4] Thus [is] the case of 4 Edw. VI, B., *Devise*;[5] a devise to one to dispose and sell, there, by reason of the word 'sell', he will have a fee because this implies his intent. Thus, it is otherwise where the intent is equal on both sides, as in one Erasmus Cook's case, 28 Eliz., [there were] two coparceners, and one devised her property to a stranger and did not say more; there, the devisee did not have an estate but for life because 'property' does not signify but her part of the land, but it can also signify her part of the estate. But because, here, it stands indifferent, therefore, it was not but for life.

Thus was Dixon and Marshe's case,[6] where one devised her land to her two sons 'equally to be divided'; there, it was adjudged that it was but a devise for life and that, here, the younger will have [it] but for life in the moiety. And yet, it was objected against this construction, first, that, by the will, that it was the intent that it will be equally between the brothers; second, that then the devise, by this construction, to the elder will be void because his estate for life can merge in the reversion. And, upon this reason and difference, was Coke 6, 17, Wilde's case,[7] adjudged.

---

[1] *Lord Cheyney's Case* (1591), 5 Coke Rep. 68, 77 E.R. 158, also Moore K.B. 727, 72 E.R. 867.

[2] YB Mich. 22 Edw. III, f. 16, pl. 59 (1348).

[3] *Collier v. Walker* (1595), 6 Coke Rep. 16, 77 E.R. 276, also Cro. Eliz. 379, 78 E.R. 625; *Hynde v. Ambrye* (1587), 3 Coke Rep. 16, 76 E.R. 664; *Portington v. Rogers* (1613), 10 Coke Rep. 35, 77 E.R. 976, 2 Brownlow & Goldesborough 65, 138, 123 E.R. 817, 860.

[4] Stat. 27 Hen. VIII, c. 10 (*SR*, III, 539–542).

[5] 7 Edw. VI, Brooke, Abr., *Devise*, pl. 39 (1553).

[6] *Dickons v. Marsh* (1594), Gouldsborough 182, 75 E.R. 1080, *sub nom. Dickens v. Marshall*, Cro. Eliz. 330, 78 E.R. 579, *sub nom. Deacon v. Marsh*, Moore K.B. 594, 72 E.R. 780.

[7] *Richardson v. Yardley* (1599), 6 Coke Rep. 16, 77 E.R. 277, also Moore K.B. 397, 72 E.R. 652, Gouldsborough 139, 75 E.R. 1050.

Thus, in our case, if the first words had been of themselves without the last, *viz.* 'I give to my wife to dispose of at her will and pleasure', these words alone had not carried but an estate for life. There, there is not a stronger intention to alter them in the nature of a grant. And this is warranted by the case where one devised to another the 'dispensing, setting, and letting' of his land. But, put the case further 'and to sell', as it is in 4 Edw. VI, then, it will be a fee.

Then, he came to the point of the case. The addition 'and to give to which of my sons whom she please' does not go to her estate for life because it is given to her freely. And on account of this, the words are a devise to the wife for her life, the reversion to the one of the sons to whom she would give. And it is as if he had said expressly 'I give to my wife during her life to dispose of at her will and pleasure and to give it to which' etc. And this, I take to be the intent of the will upon the words and scope of the will. And the construction of every will must be gathered out of the will itself. And in such a case, no case is a brother to another. And then, if it be thus, the wife had an authority to dispose of the reversion, which the coverture did not hinder her of because a wife can be an attorney to another or can revoke uses, as it is put in Portinton's case, though there be coverture. And the book of 34 Edw. III, *Cui in vita* 19, is the express authority for it.

But admit that it is a fee in the wife (as it can be) because I find a like case to it and this is in a note written with Justice Warburton's own hand, where it is said 'Note that, [in] 14 Hen. VIII, it was adjudged that a devise to one "and his to do there with his will" makes a fee simple.' Yet he can convey it because, then, it is not an absolute fee, but conditional, and an estate upon a condition, a wife can dispose, as [in] 34 Edw. III, aforesaid, it was adjudged. And, if in time, she did not dispose, it is forfeited, as 38 Ass. and Littleton are.[1] And thus, here, that she will dispose generally; then, it had not been a condition because it is not limited to a certain person to whom it will dispose, but, being limited here to one of the sons, it is otherwise.

An infant cannot dispose because the law intends that he does not have the wit, and a married woman because she does not have the will. But where the estate of an infant is bound with a condition to make a feoffment, there, the making is not a prejudice to him. And on account of this, there, the intendment of the law vanishes. And thus it was where a married woman etc. because, there, she is compelled and her making is not a prejudice to her husband. Thus it was ruled upon this ground [in] 15 Jac., Button and Inghan's case, where the gift was in tail, the remainder in it upon condition that the tenant in tail will grant a rent charge in fee, there, this binds the remainder.

But it could be objected that here the intent of the devise taking effect, she was unmarried and she could have thus done, and, on account of this, her taking of a husband afterwards disabled her, similar to the case of a disseisin during the

---

[1] YB 38 Edw. III, Lib. Ass., f. 222, pl. 7 (1364); T. Littleton, *Tenures*, sects. 355–360.

time that the wife was unmarried and a descent during the coverture, otherwise where, after the disseisin, the wife be imprisoned because it is not her act. To this, he answered that he dare not ground upon this difference because he found a book expressly where the condition was when she was unmarried and took a husband afterwards, yet it did not disable her. And this is the book cited by all hands, 34 Edw. III, *Cui in vita*, 15, aforesaid. Thus, *quacumque via data*, he concluded for the defendant.

At another day, DODDERIDGE, upon all of the matter, [said] I agree for the defendant. Divers questions have been moved, but, in fact, there is but one. And this is what estate Agnes had by the devise, whether she had an absolute estate in fee or a conditional or whether an estate for life with a power to dispose of the reversion or whether an absolute estate in fee with this limit that she could not dispose of it but to one of her sons. But be it one or the other, it is the same for the defendant.

I will divide my argument into two branches: first, I will consider the estate of Agnes and her power; second, the execution of it. She has duly executed it. It is a general rule, and a vulgar [one], but yet the great rule for the exposition of wills [is] that a last will will be construed according to the intent of the devisor. In each grant and deed, there, the law looks to the intent of the parties. But in a will in a special manner, there, it is the chief guide of their exposition. And for this, there are divers notable reasons from the etymology of the word because *testamentum est testatio mentis*, as is said [in] Com. 343 and 279.[1] Then, if thus it will be expounded according to the mind and, of this, some have notably and wittily observed that words in law that have their ending in 'ment', as Parliament, arbitrement, testament, will be expounded according to this which by reason will be collected to be their intent.

Second, of the definition of will, *testamentum est justa sententia de rebus nostris de eo quod quis post mortem suam fieri voluit.*[2] And, if thus, then the intent will be here the principal verb which rules the sentence solely. Bracton calls it *testatio ex causa mentis*; and he says that it is to be expounded according to the intent *qua vivere desist et de mortuis nil nisi bonum praesumendum*.

The third reason [is] because, if the words in a will are sufficient to demonstrate what his intent was, that it will be taken, and not the literal or legal construction of the law. This is because, at the making of it, one is intended to be *inops consilii* taken up with thoughts of his last departure and his great accounts. And, if the law interprets the grants of the king favorably for him inasmuch as it supposes [him] to be incumbered with *ardua regni*, *a fortiori quantum* he has

---

[1] *Brett v. Rigden* (1568), 1 Plowden 340, 343, 75 E.R. 516, 521; *Graysbrook v. Fox* (1565), 1 Plowden 275, 279, 75 E.R. 419, 425.

[2] *Testamentum est voluntatis nostrae iusta sententia de eo quod quis post mortem suam fieri velit.* A will is a lawful expression of our wishes as to what someone wishes to be done after his death: *Digesta*, 28.1.1.

received the sentence 'dispose of thy house and set it in order for thou must die'.[1] And also, he has the violence of sickness to encounter with. The words there will not be taken literally, as will be his deed etc. *Suprema voluntas quod mandat fieriquejubet parcere necesse est.* Thus, being *in extremis* and also *inops consilii*, as Bracton, li. 6, ca. [*blank*], fo. 18, says, *nihil est equitati magis conveniens etc.*[2] And this reason was much insisted and urged in Scolastic's case.

But yet, this rule is not so large but that it has some restraints. Every intent will not be performed, as if the intent be repugnant in itself, as it was in Germyn and Ascot's case, Coke, 1, 85,[3] or against the law, as it was in Bret and Ridgen's case, in the *Commentaries*,[4] where, without question, his intent was that the heir will have the land, but it was against the law that he will take it in the nature of a descent where nothing was in the ancestor. Thus, if his intent be uncertain, then, it is void, as in Cheyne's case, C. 5. Thus, no intent will be taken but that which is taken and extracted out of the words, as also appears in Cheyne's case. And in this case, I remember that Chief Baron Manwood, who drafted the will, offered to depose that it was the intent of the devisor to restrain the elder son as the others, but, there [it was] agreed that no foreign averment will be taken outside of the will. And other exceptions are outside of this rule. But I do not intend to make a reading on wills, but come to the particular.

A will will be taken by the intention in each part of it, as can be shown in examples upon all of the parts of the will. But I restrain myself to the intention of the estate in a will. And this will be always taken according to the intent. A gift to one *in perpetuum* is not but an estate for life in a grant, but, in a devise, it is a fee simple. 18 Hen. VIII, fo. 9; 34 Hen. VI, 2, thus to one and his assigns; 34 Hen. VI, 7, a gift to one and his heirs male is a fee simple, but such devises an estate tail; 27 Hen. VIII, p. 27.[5] Thus, a gift to two and *heredibus* is not good even though they are with a warranty to their heirs. But a devise to two and *heredibus* with a warranty to their heirs in fee simple is good. A grant of the manor of D. in which I had nothing at the time of the grant [is] good, but a devise thus with purchase afterwards is good. 39 Hen. VI, 18, and Chapman's case in the *Commentaries*.[6] A devise to one after the death of the wife of the devisor, there, nothing is expressly devised to the wife, yet, because his intent

---

[1] II Kings, chap. 20, v. 1.

[2] *Bracton on the Laws and Customs of England* (S. E. Thorne, ed., 1968), vol. 2, p. 67.

[3] *Germin v. Arscot* (1595), in *Corbet v. Corbet* (1599–1600), 1 Coke Rep. 85, 76 E.R. 191, also Moore K.B. 364, 72 E.R. 631, 1 Anderson 186, 123 E.R. 422, 2 Anderson 7, 123 E.R. 517.

[4] *Brett v. Rigden* (1568), 1 Plowden 340, 75 E.R. 516.

[5] YB Trin. 19 Hen. VIII, f. 9, pl. 4 (1527); YB Mich. 34 Hen. VI, ff. 5, 7, pl. 16 (1455); YB Mich. 27 Hen. VIII, f. 27, pl. 11 (1535).

[6] YB Mich. 39 Hen. VI, f. 18, pl. 23 (1460); *Chapman v. Dalton* (1565), 1 Plowden 284, 75 E.R. 434.

appears, she will have [it] for her life. And here, the law has a nimble eye to spy his intent. And this is the book of 13 Hen. VII, 13, *Devise*, 52 and 48, B.[1] A devise to one for life, the remainder over, there, if the particular tenant refuses, yet the remainder will stand, otherwise in a grant. 37 Hen. VI, 37; Com. 114, 344; and Scolaster's case.[2] A donee to him and the heirs male of his body had issue, a daughter, who had a son; there, the son will not have [it] because it was not conveyed by heirs male, but, upon such a devise, the son will have [it]. 28 Hen. VI, *Devise*, F., 18; 11 Hen. VI, 12, *Devise*, B., 32.[3] Thus, a devise to the Church of St. Andrew's of Holborn is good to the parson and his successors, 21 Ric. II; *Devise*, 7, F.,[4] but such a grant [would be] void. Thus, a multitude of cases could be cited where the intent in the limitation of the estate will make the estate, and not the words taken legally.

And thus, in this part, the intent [is] taken, and not the legal interpretation. But these few cases I have gleaned out of a multitude and heap of other cases so that the intent, if it be not absurd, impossible, or repugnant in itself or to the law, will be taken.

Now, for the particular case in question, in this, there are, as was said, two clauses: the first, 'I give etc. to dispose at her will and pleasure'. Here, if these words had been alone, it had been a fee, and yet the word 'dispose' does not import property but the order, guide, and direction of the thing because one can have the disposing of things that are [the property of] other men, as [is] the case in Dyer 27,[5] cited. Before the Statute of Ric. III,[6] a *cestui que use* had nothing in the land; he could not give or sell or lease it; and yet he had the disposing of it. There is a notable case for the exposition of this word 'disposing', and [it was] adjudged two times in the point: 4 Edw. IV, *Waste*, F. 11; 17 Edw. III, 7.[7] One leased to a privy and granted to him that he could dispose and use the house to his best advantage, yet he could not pull down the house and sell the timber, but he had such disposition that he could have without a disheritance to the lessor and such disposing as belonged to such estate.

---

[1] YB Hil. 13 Hen. VII, f. 17, pl. 22 (1498), Brooke, Abr., *Devise*, pl. 52; 29 Hen. VIII, Brooke, Abr., *Devise*, pl. 48 (1537 x 1538).

[2] *Townsend's Case* (1554), 1 Plowden 111, 75 E.R. 173; *Brett v. Rigden* (1568), 1 Plowden 340, 75 E.R. 516; *Newis v. Lark* (1571), 2 Plowden 403, 75 E.R. 609, Benloe 196, 123 E.R. 138, IT MS. Petyt 511, vol. 13, f. 53v.

[3] Trin. 28 Hen. VI, Fitzherbert, Abr., *Devise*, pl. 18 (1450); *Faringdon v. Darel* (1432), YB Mich. 11 Hen. VI, ff. 12, 13, pl. 28, Brooke, Abr., *Devise*, pl. 32.

[4] YB Hil. 49 Edw. III, f. 3, pl. 7 (1375), Fitzherbert, Abr., *Devise*, pl. 7.

[5] *Anonymous* (1537), 1 Dyer 26, 73 E.R. 59.

[6] Stat. 1 Ric. III, c. 1 (*SR*, II, 477–478).

[7] YB Trin. 4 Edw. II, Selden Soc., vol. 42, p. 150, pl. 37, YB Trin. 4 Edw. II, f. 114 (1311), Fitzherbert, Abr., *Wast*, pl. 11; YB Hil. 17 Edw. III, f. 7, pl. 21 (1343).

But here, in our case, 'dispose' is knitted with the word 'give'. And on account of this, there will be such a disposition as he had to which the thing was given because *dare*, as Bracton said, *est rem accipientis facere cum effectu*. Li. 2, ca. 5, f. 11.[1] *Et rem transfert ad alium.*[2]

Thus, if there had been no more, these first words, without question, had been a fee simple. And this agrees with B., *Devise*, 7 Edw. VI. But the warbling is upon the two words, and yet, all agree in the main for the defendant 'and to give it to which of her sons she thinks best'.

Here, two questions were moved: first, if this be a condition that she will give to one of the sons or an authority. First, if it be an authority, whether the interest does not surround it. For the first, it is not a condition because a condition is compulsory to do or not to do something upon a penalty. But here, she is not bound to dispose, but she can leave it to descend. And, if she would dispose of it, then, it will be to one of her sons. But here, it is an authority annexed to an interest. And yet, for the second authority, it can in the case of a will stand with the interest. And it will not be drowned in it, but it will be intended that the feoffment or other act that she makes, this [is] by force of the authority.

But it is otherwise in a case other than a will, as if one made a feoffment to the use of his last will and devised his lands, not having relation nor reference to the feoffment; there, this passes according to his general interest, and not according to the authority created by the feoffment to the uses of the will. Thus an office found by an escheator will be generally intended *virtute officii et non virtute brevis*.

Thus here, she had an authority to sell, and she did it as servant to the testator, and the devisee will be in by the devisor. And thus is 19 Hen. VI, 23;[3] and there, it is put, if one devise that his executors convey by a fine, this is good even though there is no estate in the executors. And the true difference is where there is a devise to the executors to sell; there, they have an interest joined with the authority. [It is] otherwise where it is that the executors will sell; there, they have but an authority only. And the difference appears in all of the books where the case is mentioned, as 21 Hen. VI, 12; 21 Edw. IV, 24; 9 Hen. VI, 24;[4] and twenty others more, so that the clearest way to avoid a difference of opinions is to say that she had a fee simple and an authority to dispose it. And then, it will not be pressed with an imagination of a reversion.

But it is not material how this falls for the main point. Now, for the second part of my argument to consider her execution of her authority. And it is found that it was by a feoffment. And, whether this was good was the question. An

---

[1] *Bracton on the Laws and Customs of England* (S. E. Thorne, ed., 1968), vol. 2, p. 49.

[2] It is to make a thing the recipient's effectively and transfer the thing to another.

[3] YB Mich. 19 Hen. VI, f. 23, pl. 47 (1440).

[4] YB Pas. 21 Edw. IV, f. 24, pl. 10 (1481); *Farington's Case* (1431), YB Trin. 9 Hen. VI, ff. 23, 24, pl. 19.

infant, out of imbecility of nature, [and] a married woman, in respect that she has submitted herself to her husband and all her will, cannot regularly make a grant, and, if a feoffee of them or a lessee enter, he will be a disseisor because they are void acts. 13 Hen. VII; 18 Edw. IV; 3 Hen. VII. But here, the feoffment is good in two cases: a wife or an infant can convey, first, if they have an authority; second, if [they are] compelled by a condition. And in these cases, they can prejudice the husband and the heir. For the first, [see] 10 Hen. VII, 2,[1] *per curiam expresse*, such a wife can sell to her husband because she did it by an authority and as the servant to another, and not in her own right, but in another capacity, being an attorney to another and representing him. Perkins [*blank*],[2] in the case of feoffments, put a notable case to this purpose, where one made a feoffment to J.S. and a letter of attorney to one to make livery, that this is good, thus, conversely, where the husband makes livery to his wife. Thus, if the grant of the wife be to her advantage, it will bind her, as 45 Edw. III,[3] a feoffment to the husband and wife rendering rent; there, the rent enured by way of grant and yet it bound the wife because it was to her advantage to have the land rendering this rent.

For the second, that the wife, being compelled with a condition, she can make the feoffment, the often cited book of 34 Edw. III adjudged it so if the feoffment be good.

The other points follow of themselves because, then, the possession that she had with her father and mother was her possession, and, thus, the release and fine [were] also good because the husband, by her release, is barred to defeat the fine.

And thus, [he held] for the defendant.

Justice CREWE [held] to the same intent. It [is to be] considered first what estate she had. By the first words, she had an estate in fee. But the question is whether the second [clause] does not control it. But the best construction is that she had an estate for life with a power to dispose of the reversion. Then here, her feoffment is a good execution of her authority and it will not be taken nor can it operate in the nature of a feoffment because, then, it would carry her estate for life, which was not intended but that to keep [it] to herself. But it will be as a nomination by her which [son] will have the reversion. And it is a fee though she can do [it]. And he put the case of lady Russell, where lady Russell made a feoffment to the use of herself and her husband and reserved[4] a power to give any part of her land to any of her kindred, and, afterwards, she married and made a feoffment to one of her kindred of part, and [it was] good because, there, there was an authority to name, and the feoffee took by force of the estate of the first feoffees, and her feoffment [was] but a nomination of one to whose use it will stand.

---

[1] YB Pas. 10 Hen. VII, f. 20, pl. 9 (1495).

[2] J. Perkins, *A Profitable Book*, sect. 196.

[3] YB Mich. 45 Edw. III, f. 11, pl. 7 (1371).

[4] resumed *MS*.

And he cited the case of one Butler and Bensey, which, as he said, he had cause to know, where Butler made a feoffment to the use of lord Lisle and reserved a power to assign notwithstanding any part to his wife, and, afterwards, by a sealed deed, he gave part to the wife, and it [was] good, and yet the husband could not enfeoff his wife, but it was not a nomination, and the estate of the wife arises out of the estate of the recoverors.

And thus, he concluded for the defendant. And judgment was entered accordingly.

[Other reports of this case: Benlow 189, 73 E.R. 1038, CUL MS. Gg.2.30, f. 64v; W. Jones 137, 82 E.R. 73, BL MS. Hargr. 317, f. 139; Latch 9, 31, 134, 82 E.R. 248, 264, 312, HLS MS. 1235, f. 59; Noy 80, 74 E.R. 1047; BL MS. Hargr. 38, ff. 54v, 85; BL MS. Lansd. 1092, f. 112v; CUL MS. Hh.2.1, f. 206; CUL MS. Ll.3.13, f. 139.]

105

Rex v. Bell

(K.B. Trin. 2 Car. I, 1626)

In this case, an incomplete indictment for perjury was quashed.

BL MS. Add. 35961, f. 32, pl. 13

Bull was indicted for perjury because, being examined before Sir Robert Rich, a master of the chancery, upon interrogatories, he had forsworn himself. And it was not shown in the indictment what authority Sir Robert had to administer the oath. And for this cause, it was quashed.

[Other reports of this case: 3 Bulstrode 322, 81 E.R. 268.]

106

Luther v. Holland

(Part 2)
(K.B. Trin. 2 Car. I, 1626)

BL MS. Add. 35961, f. 32, pl. 14

The case before, pl. 1,[1] was moved again. And it was ruled by the court, and judgment [was] given *quod querens nihil capiat per billam* because he did not show what authority the master of the chancery had to administer an oath.

And it was said by Serjeant *Bramston* that, where the authority is by a patent, that the plaintiff is not privy to [it] and, on account of this, cannot plead it.

---

[1] For earlier proceedings in this case, see above, No. 93.

And there, DODDERIDGE said that the masters of the chancery are but clerks. And, in Bracton, they are called *clerici primae formae*, and, even though they will be with the lord chancellor, yet they are not assistants to them, and they are what they are intended in the Statute[1] which says *quotienscunque evenerit etc. concordant clerici de cancellaria de breve faciendo.*[2] And there are three kinds of clerks in the chancery: *clerici magistrales* and, of these, Bracton speaks *sunt quaedam brevia magistralia et saepe variantur secundum varietatem casuum factorum et querelarum,*[3] and these are actions upon the case, and they are called *actiones informatus,* and these belong to the clerks of the first form. Second are the *cursitorii,* and these are those who sign[4] *brevia de cursu,* which have a certain form in the Register, and, on account of this, they are called *actiones formatus,* and, of these, Bracton says they are *quaedam brevia formata super certis casibus de cursu quae nullatenus mutari possunt.*[5]

And JONES said that, by this, it was intended a clerk of the petty bag.

And WHITELOCKE said that the clerks of the chancery were in former times clergymen and thus they are called *magistri,* not for the authority that they have in the court. And this was the reason that the chancellor had the gift of all of the benefices of the king under twenty marks *per annum* to advance the masters of the chancery with. And, until the Statute, they could not marry any more than others of the clergy. See 14 Hen. VIII, ca. 8, the Statute that the six clerks could marry.[6]

[Other reports of this case: Latch 132, 82 E.R. 311, HLS MS. 1235, f. 58v; Noy 80, 74 E.R. 1047; BL MS. Hargr. 38, f. 99v, pl. 2; BL MS. Lansd. 1092, f. 111; CUL MS. Hh.2.1, f. 205v; CUL MS. Ll.3.13, f. 137.]

107

Anonymous v. Browning

(K.B. Trin. 2 Car. I, 1626)

A case will be removed out of an ecclesiastical court where that court is attempting to apply to a layman a canon which has not been received and allowed by the common law.

---

[1] Stat. 13 Edw. I, Stat. of Westminster II, c. 24 (*SR*, I, 83–84).

[2] however often it may happen etc. the clerks of the chancery agree as to making a writ.

[3] They are certain magistral writs and they are often changed according to the variety of the cases made and the complaints.

[4] esonont *MS.*

[5] Some writs are formed upon specific cases [and are matters] of course, which can in no way be changed. *Bracton on the Laws and Customs of England* (S. E. Thorne, ed., 1977), vol. 4, p. 285.

[6] Stat. 14 & 15 Hen. VIII, c. 8 (*SR*, III, 216).

BL MS. Add. 35961, f. 32v, pl. 15

Browning libelled against one in the ecclesiastical court for the irreverent speaking of him, being a minister and clergyman, for saying of him that he drank so much that he fell under the table and was said to be carried away and that at another time he was where good beer was and looked out at the window and called in company and they never left till they had drunk out a barrel of beer.

And yet [a writ of] prohibition was awarded because their canons do not bind the laity unless they are received and allowed by the law.

108

Button v. Anonymous

(Part 1)
(K.B. Trin. 2 Car. I, 1626)

The issue in this case was what are the proper allegations necessary for a justice of the peace who was accused of official malfeasance to make out a case of defamation.

BL MS. Add. 35961, f. 32v, pl. 16

Sir William Button brought an action upon the case against one for these words, 'Sir William had two servants who were indicted for the stealing of sheep from me, and Sir William dealt with me not to prosecute them.' And he alleged that he was a justice of the peace. And it was adjudged that the action lay, JONES and WHITELOCKE being there solely.

After, [pl.] 23.[1]

109

Rex v. Davy

(Part 2)
(K.B. Trin. 2 Car. I, 1626)

BL MS. Add. 35961, f. 32v, pl. 17

And now, the case before, pl. 3,[2] was moved again, and Davy was present. And it was adjudged that the pardon in this case did not free him. And on account of this, Davy was committed for his fine etc.

[Other reports of this case: Latch 141, 82 E.R. 315, HLS MS. 1235, f. 63; BL MS. Hargr. 38, f. 82, pl. 1; CUL MS. Ll.3.13, f. 149v.]

---

[1] For later proceedings in this case, see below, No. 115.

[2] For earlier proceedings in this case, see above, No. 95.

110

Randall v. Bray

(K.B. Trin. 2 Car. I, 1626)

A person other than the victim of the crime cannot arrest one upon a suspicion of felony unless there be communis fama.

BL MS. Add. 35961, f. 32v, pl. 18

An action upon the case was brought. And the plaintiff alleged that the defendant had charged him with a felony for the stealing of a ploughshare and the defendant had him arrested and brought before a justice of the peace and, afterwards, indicted him of it.

The defendant justified because his [plough]share was taken away and he suspected the plaintiff, and he complained of this to the justice, and he was bound by the justice to prosecute, without that that he maliciously indicted.

And exceptions were taken, first that it is not a justification to charge and accuse of a felony upon a suspicion. And he cited the books of 7 Edw. IV and 27 Hen. VIII, 25, and Dyer 23b,[1] that one cannot arrest one upon a suspicion unless there be *communis fama* when he does it. Second, he did not answer to the arrest. Third, he did not traverse that he maliciously arrested and charged him, but solely that he did not maliciously indict him.

And Justice JONES said here that there is a difference between an arrest and to accuse or to charge because one cannot arrest one upon a suspicion of felony unless there be *communis fama*. Also, there is a difference between the party to whom the robbery or felony was done and a stranger because the party can arrest anyone whom he suspects in regard of his interest and accuse him without the suspicions or fame of others.

And I [Paynell] take [it] that this was between Randall and Bray, *quod intratur* Trin. 1 Car., rot. 1097.

111

Delavall v. Clare

(Part 1)
(K.B. Trin. 2 Car. I, 1626)

An action of assumpsit *lies against an infant for necessaries. The plaintiff can allege in the replication that the goods bought were necessaries.*

---

[1] YB Mich. 7 Edw. IV, f. 20, pl. 19 (1467); YB Trin. 27 Hen. VIII, f. 22, pl. 17 (1535); *Anonymous* (1565), 2 Dyer 236, 73 E.R. 522.

BL MS. Add. 35961, f. 32v, pl. 19

Delavall, a tailor, brought an action upon the case against Clare. And he alleged that the defendant, in consideration that the plaintiff will buy for him so much satin and taffeta etc. that will make him a suit, that he would pay him for it and also for the shaping of them.

The defendant said that, at the time etc., he was under age and under the governance and wardship of one such and that his guardian bespoke the clothes etc. and promised payment *absque hoc quod* he assumed and promised. And upon this, the plaintiff demurred. And it was entered Pas. 2 Car. [I, rot.] 521.

And the opinion of the court was against the plaintiff, first, because an action upon the case would not in this case lie against an infant to bind him to his promise even though it was for necessaries. And the reason is because, then, he will be taken from waging his law, which an infant will not be, inasmuch as it is not supposed in him so much discretion to provide for sufficient proof as one of age will be presumed.

Second, because, here, it appears that the contract was for satin and taffeta and it does not have that he was of the estate and quality agreeable to have them [as] necessary.

Third, the plaintiff has here demurred generally and does not show the cause, and, thus, he will not take advantage of the matter of form. And here, the plea, which amounts to the general issue, is a good plea in substance, but not in form because he must for brevity and, as Baldwin said [in] 28 Hen. VIII,[1] to spare parchment take the general issue. And on account of this, it being good in substance, a demurrer for form must have been express, as C. 10, Dr. Leyfield's case, and *Novell Entries*, fo. 14.[2] And here was cited Hil. 20 Jac. to be adjudged between Stanely and Holby by Dodderidge and Haughton, that an action upon the case against an infant upon [an action of] *insimul computaverit* for necessaries does not lie for the reasons aforesaid.

See more, Mich. 2 [Car. I], pl. 72.[3]

112

Stileman v. Cremer

(K.B. Trin. 2 Car. I, 1626)

If two parsons jointly have the tithes of one place, the parishioner is not bound to lay the tithes out in moieties, but the parsons will divide them themselves.

---

[1] *Draper v. Capper* (1536), 1 Dyer 18, 19, 73 E.R. 39, 40.

[2] *Layfield v. Hillary* (1611), 10 Coke Rep. 88, 77 E.R. 1057, also Cro. Jac. 317, 79 E.R. 272, 1 Bulstrode 154, 80 E.R. 846; *Semayne v. Gresham* (1602), E. Coke, *A Booke of Entries* (1614), 'Action sur le case', No. 11, ff. 12, 14.

[3] For later proceedings in this case, see below, No. 203.

BL MS. Add. 35961, f. 33, pl. 20

Between Stileman and Cremer in an action of debt upon the Statute of 2 Edw. VI,[1] for not setting out of tithes, it was adjudged without difficulty that, if two parsons have the tithes of one place between them, that, if the party set out the tithes, it is sufficient. And he is not bound to lay them out in moieties, but the parsons will divide [them] themselves.

[Other reports of this case: Latch 8, 24, 228, 82 E.R. 247, 255, 359, HLS MS. 1235, f. 65; 1 Eagle & Younge 351, 354; BL MS. Hargr. 38, f. 83v; CUL MS. Hh.2.1, f. 212v; CUL MS. Ll.3.13, f. 155.]

113

Stileman v. Cremer

(K.B. Trin. 2 Car. I, 1626)

The question in this case was whether a plaintiff can have a judgment after a verdict and a continuance entered as of the first term.

BL MS. Add. 35961, f. 33, pl. 21

In another action between Stileman and Cremer, the plaintiff had a verdict found for him, and, afterwards, it was continued divers terms by the rules of the court. And after the first term, the plaintiff released, and the continuance was not entered upon the roll. And now, the plaintiff would enter his judgment as of the first term, and not of this term that judgment was given. And if he could was the question because, then, the defendant could not have a day to plead his release, but is put to his *audita querela*.

And it was appointed to see precedents. But, if the plaintiff had entered the first continuance, then, it had been a good plea *puis le darrein continuance*.

[Other reports of this case: BL MS. Hargr. 38, f. 104.]

114

Anonymous

(K.B. Trin. 2 Car. I, 1626)

A joint obligor who is the administrator of the creditor cannot, as administrator, sue his co-obligor for the debt.

---

[1] Stat. 2 & 3 Edw. VI, c. 13 (*SR*, IV, 55–58).

BL MS. Add. 35961, f. 33, pl. 22

[There were] two obligors, and one had the administration of the obligee committed to him. And he brought [an action of] debt against his companion as administrator, and he recovered. And he brought an *audita querela*, and he prayed to have it allowed. And thus it was, and he left out execution to bail.

115

Button v. Anonymous

(Part 2)
(K.B. Trin. 2 Car. I, 1626)

BL MS. Add. 35961, f. 33, pl. 23

The case before, 16,[1] was rehearsed again, and the record [was] viewed in full court. And now the words were 'Sir William Button had two servants which were prosecuted for stealing sheep and Sir William spake to me not to prosecute.' And first, because it was not shown that they were stolen cattle and thus, if it was falsely prosecuted, it was not bad to speak to him to desist. Second, he did not show that the sheep belonged to the prosecutor. Third, because he did not show in what county they were prosecuted because it could be in another county than where Sir William was a justice and thus not against his office. And for these reasons, the words were held not sufficient, as they were laid, to bring an action.

And here, these cases were cited by Serjeant *Crewe*: 31 El., rot. 803, Norwell and Avery for saying that the plaintiff was couped up for forgery because he could be couped for it and still [be] honest; and Sir John Hollis, now earl of Clare, his case, Hen. IV [*blank*] 719,[2] where it was said of him that he kept a company of thieves and traitors and gave them nothing but base blue liveries, and [it was] adjudged against him by his consent, the court being divided, and he brought [a writ of] error upon this, and [it was] affirmed. Thus [is] Ball's and Huano's case, 36 El.,[3] where he said of the plaintiff that he was a cunning knave and that there was not a purse cut within twenty miles of Wellingford but he had his share, and, because he did not aver that he had cut a purse within twenty miles etc., he could not have judgment.

And on account of this, he discontinued his action. And he brought a new [action], and he so averred, and he recovered.

[Other reports of this case: Latch 49, 82 E.R. 269; Popham 180, 79 E.R. 1275; BL MS. Hargr. 38, f. 104.]

---

[1] For earlier proceedings in this case, see above, No. 108.

[2] *Hollis v. Briscow* (1605), Cro. Jac. 58, 79 E.R. 49, Yelverton 64, 80 E.R. 45.

[3] *Ball v. Roane* (1593), Cro. Eliz. 308, 342, 78 E.R. 559, 591.

116

Evans v. Binion

(K.B. Trin. 2 Car. I, 1626)

Audita querela *is not available to correct a pleading filed by an attorney in bad faith, but the attorney should be sued for malpractice.*

BL MS. Add. 35961, f. 33, pl. 24

See Pas. 2 Car., rot. 107, between Evans and Binion, an *audita querela* [was filed] because the attorney of the defendant, contrary to instructions and by covin, pleaded another plea, which was found against him, and, there, he did not proceed. And, there, [it was said] by the court, upon the first motion without question, it does not lie, but he is put to an action upon the case against the attorney if the matter be thus.

117

Griffin v. Ewer

(K.B. Trin. 2 Car. I, 1626)

A writ of error that is dated before the judgment of the lower court was given is not valid.

BL MS. Add. 35961, f. 33, pl. 25

In [a writ of] error between Griffin and Ewer of a judgment given in the court of great sessions in Wales, the writ of error bore a date before the judgment [was] given. And afterwards, the judgment was given. And it was sent to the [court of] king's bench. And it was moved that it was not well removed for this cause and because the court cannot proceed to the examination of the errors. See for this 1 Ric. III, 4; 22 Hen. VI, 7; B., *Error*, 76, and B., 417; and C. 11, Metcalfe's case.[1] And afterwards, a new writ of error was brought of this *quia coram vobis residet*, and it was allowed.

Query of this writ *quod coram vobis* etc. because, if it is not well removed by the first writ, I [Paynell] do not understand how the record will be said *residere coram etc.*

Et intratur Hil. 1 Car., rot. 619.

---

[1] YB Mich. 1 Ric. III, f. 4, pl. 8 (1483); *Pomeray v. Abbot of Buckfast* (1443), YB Mich. 22 Hen. VI, f. 5, pl. 7, Brooke, Abr., *Errour*, pl. 76; *Metcalfe v. Wood* (1614), 11 Coke Rep. 38, 77 E.R. 1193, also 1 Rolle Rep. 84, 81 E.R. 345, Cro. Jac. 356, 79 E.R. 305.

118

Saul v. Clarke

(K.B. Trin. 2 Car. I, 1626)

The issues in this case were whether an heiress is such a privy to her grantor-father that she will be foreclosed of the rights in the same land that she inherited from her uncle and whether the non-claim of her uncle for five years after the death of his brother without male issue had barred him or whether he could have another five years after the death of the tenant for life.

BL MS. Add. 35961, f. 33v, pl. 26

Thomas Saule brought [an action of] *ejectione firmae* against Nicholas Clarke, *et intratur* Hil. 20 Jac., rot. 450 [or 460]. And he alleged a demise of lands in Hardington in the County of Somerset. And upon [a plea of] the general issue, the special verdict afforded this case. John Sydenham, seised of the said lands in fee, [in] 23 Hen. VIII, gave them to Alexander, his younger son, and to the heirs male of his body, and [in] 37 Hen. VIII, he levied a fine to the said Alexander and his heirs to the use of him and the heirs male of his body engendered. John died. John Sydenham, the elder son, [was] his heir. Alexander, [in] 5 Edw. VI, devised the lands to Archer and Maude, his wife, for their lives, the remainder to Joan, their daughter, for her life with a warranty. [In] 16 Eliz., Alexander levied a fine to Middleton with a warranty to the use of Taylor and his heirs, who, [in] 20 Eliz., bargained and sold to Mallet. And thus, by mesne assignments, they came to the lessor of Clarke, the defendant. Alexander had issue, Elizabeth, his daughter, and he died without male issue. Elizabeth was married to Poynes, by whom she had issue, the lessor of the plaintiff. [In] 37 Eliz., John, the elder brother, died, Elizabeth being his heir. [In] 17 Jac., the tenant for life died, and Robert Poynes, the lessor, entered. And whether the entry here was lawful was the question.

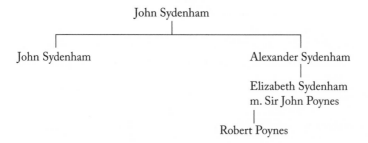

Briefly, the case is a tenant in tail to him and his heirs male of his body, the reversion being to his elder brother, [who] made a lease for life, the remainder for life, which is a discontinuance, and he levied a fine of the reversion with a warranty, and he died without male issue, having issue, a daughter. Five years passed. The tenant died. Elizabeth, both his heir [and] tenant for life, died. And the heir of Elizabeth entered.

And it was argued Pas. 1 Car. by Browne for the plaintiff and by Mason for the defendant. But I did not then attend the case, and, on account of this, I did not attend their argument as well. And now this term,[1] it was argued by Noy for the plaintiff and by Glanvill for the defendant.

And the case was divided into two parts: first, upon the fine of 16 [Eliz.]; second, upon the warranty upon the fine. The points were, first, whether Elizabeth be such a privy to Alexander, to whom she was heir, and she will be foreclosed of the reversion which she claimed of John, her uncle; second, whether the non-claim of John for five years after the death of Alexander without male issue had barred him or whether he could have another five years after the death of the tenant for life. Two points arise upon the warranty: first, whether the grant of the reversion with a warranty in this case, being a reversion in fee, be a discontinuance before the grant executed in the life of the tenant in tail; second, whether the warranty could have barred her in reversion *viz.* Joan, and if yet not being ever barred on account of this, whether Elizabeth, his heir, will be barred by it to claim an estate to descend to her after the warranty.

Noy: Another question has been moved, *viz.* to whose use the reversion upon the fine levied to Alexander will be. But of this, there is no doubt but that the reversion is to the conusor. It was objected that, if one grant a reversion, even though it be without consideration, yet it will be to the use of the grantee because a grant in a deed implies consideration. But this I deny because deliberation only was implied, not consideration. And on account of this, even though there was a grant by a fine, yet it will not be to the use of the grantee without express consideration, see 14 Hen. VIII, 10,[2] because implied consideration is not of force to raise a use as a feoffment with a warranty. And yet a warranty implies consideration inasmuch as it binds to give in recompense. And, if it was true that the implicit consideration carried the use, then every fine upon which no use is limited will be to the use of the conusee because, in every fine, the conusee pays the silver of the king and the chirograph entered is that *pro hac recognitione* the conusee *dat* to the conusor so much money etc. But this is the common course and, on account of this, no more than in the case of a recovery commonly suffered, will it be to the use of the recoveror. Also, here, the fine will pursue the precedent agreement, and it will be taken to such uses as the precedent conveyance of 23 Hen. VIII was. And he cited Dyer 237; *Estoppel*, F., 211; 8 Ass. 33.[3]

---

[1] Trin. 2 Car. I, 1626.

[2] *Gervys v. Cooke* (1522), YB Mich. 14 Hen. VIII, ff. 4, 10, pl. 5, 119 Selden Soc. 108, 121.

[3] *Bromeley v. Bennet* (1565), 2 Dyer 237, 73 E.R. 525; *Anonymous v. Garnon* (1382), YB Mich. 6 Ric. II, Ames Found., vol. 2, p. 47, pl. 34, Fitzherbert, Abr., *Estoppell*, pl.

But, for the first point, whether, here, the daughter, being the heir and privy in blood to him who levied the fine, be barred by it because, by the Act,[1] all parties and privies are barred and, here, she is a privy in blood, but yet, inasmuch as he did not claim the estate for her, she will not be barred by his fine. And he cited the case of 19 Hen. VIII, 7, by Englefield, and Dyer 3, and C. 3, 79a,[2] because, where one does not claim as heir to him who levies the fine, he will not be barred by it. And he cited Mackwilliams' case,[3] where, if a tenant for life of the father levies a fine and dies, it is not [to] his brother and yet it was entailed to him and his brother [was] heir to him.

But it is objected that, here, she could not make herself heir to her uncle but through his father. And on account of this, it is similar to the case of 20 Hen. VI, 4,[4] where the heir of the wife cannot have an appeal because he conveyed himself by a wife. But this is merely upon the estate. And it is not similar to our case. And, here, even though she must make her resort to the father, yet she does not convey herself by the father. And for this, it was adjudged in Hobbie's case[5] in the exchequer, where there were two brothers and one had a daughter and the father of the son was attainted, yet the daughter could inherit [from] her uncle because, even though the blood of the father was corrupt, yet she did not convey by him, but it was solely resorted to to induce the consanguinity. And thus, the common law expounds parties and privies in a similar manner also. And in this point, he cited Trin. 32 Eliz., 944, Smy and June's case,[6] where Sir Robert Cotton, tenant for life, the remainder to his elder son in tail, levied a fine, there, [it was] adjudged that the heir was not barred because he did not claim an estate by him and also that he could enter and he was not bound to five years because his father was not bound. See 2 El. and 7 El., Dalison's reports, pl. 3 and 11.[7]

For the second point, he argued that John, here, and thus his heir, had an election to enter after the death of Alexander without male issue or to omit it and enter after the estate for life. And thus, he had two five-year [periods] similar as if a tenant for life levied a fine, there, the reversioner can enter and avoid the

211; YB 8 Edw. III, Lib. Ass., p. 19, pl. 33 (1334).

[1] Stat. 4 Hen. VII, c. 24 (SR, II, 547–548).

[2] YB Pas. 19 Hen. VIII, f. 7, pl. 8 (1528); *Anonymous* (1528), 1 Dyer 2, 3, 73 E.R. 7; *Fermor v. Smith* (1602), 3 Coke Rep. 77, 76 E.R. 800, also 2 Anderson 176, 123 E.R. 607, Jenkins 253, 145 E.R. 180.

[3] Either *Godfrey v. Paston* (1615), cited in *Croker v. Kelly* (1625), 2 Rolle Rep. 490, 81 E.R. 935, Benloe 143, 73 E.R. 1013, Cro. Jac. 689, 79 E.R. 598, or *Godfrey v. Wade* (1623), W. Jones 31, 82 E.R. 17, Winch 41, 124 E.R. 35.

[4] YB Trin. 20 Hen. VI, f. 43, pl. 25 (1442).

[5] *Hobbie's Case* (1598 x 1599), cited in *Godfrey v. Dixon* (1619), 2 Rolle Rep. 93, 81 E.R. 680.

[6] *Cotton's Case* (1590), 1 Leonard 211, 74 E.R. 194, Cro. Eliz. 219, 78 E.R. 476, CUL MS. Dd.11.64, f. 169.

[7] *Anonymous* (1559 x 1560), Dalison 26, 123 E.R. 245.

fine, but, if he omits [to do so for] five years, then his title of entry for forfeiture is gone.

But yet he had another title by which he could enter and void the fine. And this is after the death of the tenant for life and, on account of this, he will have another five years after his death. And he cited Coke 3, 78b, and Com. 373 and 367.[1]

For the third point, he argued that the grant of the reversion with a warranty did not make a discontinuance, first, because, at first, it was not a discontinuance inasmuch as the warranty descended upon the daughter, Elizabeth, and the land went to his brother, and on account of this, it not being a discontinuance at the beginning to John, it will not be a discontinuance to his heir and the warranty was a warranty in gross and the title descends after the warranty. But, if the warranty had descended after the title, it had been otherwise.

Second, because a grant of a reversion upon a discontinuance for life is not of itself a discontinuance even though it be with a warranty. And he cited 36 Ass. 8 and 21 Hen. VIII, 53, *postem* [?], expressly in the point.[2]

And it could be that the tenant in tail be disseised and release with a warranty that the warranty there makes a discontinuance, and, on account of this, the whole fee is turned in right. And on account of this, our case differs from L. 601 and 706,[3] where he put the case that, if a tenant in tail be disseised and the son release with a warranty, his son will be bound because the tenant in fee is found in a right. But it is not thus here.

For the fourth point, whether, by this warranty, he in reversion be barred, he argued not because the Statute of Westminster II[4] excludes it because the mischief there provided for is the non-reverter to the donor as [?] the non-descender to the issue. And this, in the case of issue, has been always expounded to make the warranty void unless he had assets. And on account of this being in the same mischief to the donor, as is rehearsed there, it will be also thus expounded against him. And he cited 43 Ass. 42; *Garranty,* 16; *Garranty,* 77; 6 Edw. III, 17; 7 Edw. III, 44 and 48; *Garranty,* 27, 42, 44, 28, 53.[5]

---

[1] *Fermor v. Smith* (1602), *ut supra*; *Stowel v. Lord Zouch* (1562), 1 Plowden 353, 75 E.R. 536.

[2] YB 36 Edw. III, Lib. Ass., p. 215, f. 8 (1362); YB Trin. 21 Hen. VI, ff. 52, 53, pl. 8 (1443).

[3] T. Littleton, *Tenures*, sects. 601, 706.

[4] Stat. 13 Edw. I, c. 1 (*SR*, I, 71–72).

[5] YB 43 Edw. III, Lib. Ass., p. 277, f. 42 (1369); Pas. 41 Edw. III, Fitzherbert, Abr., *Garrantie*, pl. 16 (1367); Hil. 23 Edw. III, Fitzherbert, Abr., *Garrantie*, pl. 77 (1349); *Witefild's Case* (1332), YB Mich. 6 Edw. III, f. 57, pl. 66; YB Mich. 7 Edw. III, f. 44, pl. 3 (1333); YB Mich. 7 Edw. III, ff. 47, 48, pl. 17 (1333); *Ros v. Graa* (1341), YB Mich. 15 Edw. III, Rolls Ser. 31b, vol. 6, p. 388, pl. 55, Fitzherbert, Abr., *Garrantie*, pl. 27; Mich. 27 Edw. III, Fitzherbert, Abr., *Garrantie*, pl. 42 (1353); YB Trin. 7 Edw. III, f. 34, pl. 34 (1333), Fitzherbert, Abr., *Garrantie*, pl. 44; Mich. 31 Edw. III, Fitzherbert, Abr., *Gar-*

And thus, he concluded for the plaintiff.

Against this, it was argued by *Glanvill*. And he began with the points upon the warranty first. And he argued, first, that the grant of this reversion with a warranty depending upon the estate for life, that it made a discontinuance. It made it now an absolute discontinuance. And on account of this, he took for a ground that, where the warranty is annexed to the fee, if where another estate that would make a discontinuance, that, there, the warranty of itself made the discontinuance. And on account of this, it differs from the case where he had the reversion in tail and granted it in fee with a warranty because, there, nothing passes but for his life and for the annexed warranty, but to the estate, which does not make a discontinuance. And this is the reason that a release with a warranty to the disseisor makes a discontinuance, because [it is] annexed to the fee, as L. 601 and 602 puts the case and 746.[1] And this difference appears [in] Coke 10, 97; and with this 45 Edw. III, 21, agrees and 21 Hen. VII, 11, by Frowick.[2] And this also appears [in] Coke 3, 51,[3] where a feoffment and a release with a warranty are marshalled to be equivalent.

Thus here, having a reversion in fee, the grant of it with a warranty makes it an absolute discontinuance. And if thus, then, it suffices by us because, then, the entry was not lawful, but he is put to [an action of] formedon. And thus, the entry back again upon his lessee [is] null and an ejectment.

But further, he argued, first, that this warranty for the reversion is absolutely a bar because, by the common law, all warranties were bars. And on account of this, if this warranty is not aided by any statute, it will be a bar. There are three statutes that have color to bar in this case because, as Littleton, 711,[4] says, a lineal warranty is a bar to demand a fee simple unless it be restrained by some statute. And here, the warranty is lineal because there is a possibility to derive his title by Alexander, nay, an impossibility to do otherwise. The statutes that have color are, first, the Statute of Chester,[5] but this restrains but tenants by the curtesy and bars seisin in the right of their wives. And on account of this, it was not proved contrary. The second is the Statute of 11 Hen. VII, of jointures.[6] But this restrains the jointuresses from discontinuances by feoffment or warranty. And on account

---

rantie, pl. 28 (1357); *Anonymous v. Graa* (1336), YB Hil. 10 Edw. III, f. 14, pl. 34, Fitzherbert, Abr., *Garrantie*, pl. 53.

    [1] T. Littleton, *Tenures*, sects. 601, 602, 746.

    [2] *Heywood, ex dem. Seymor v. Smith* (1612), 10 Coke Rep. 95, 77 E.R. 1070, also 1 Bulstrode 162, 80 E.R. 853; YB Trin. 45 Edw. III, f. 21, pl. 24 (1371); YB Hil. 21 Hen. VII, f. 11, pl. 12 (1506).

    [3] *Linch, ex dem. Brown v. Spencer* (1594), 3 Coke Rep. 50, 76 E.R. 749, also Cro. Eliz. 513, 78 E.R. 762, Moore K.B. 455, 72 E.R. 691, 2 Anderson 44, 123 E.R. 537.

    [4] T. Littleton, *Tenures*, sect. 711.

    [5] Stat. 6 Edw. I, Stat. of Gloucester, c. 3 (*SR*, I, 47).

    [6] Stat. 11 Hen. VII, c. 20 (*SR*, II, 583).

of this, it is nothing also. The third [is] the Statute *de donis*,[1] and, upon this, the question arises because, by this, it is provided that the donee *non habeat potestatem alienandi* which includes warranties. But, by this, it is to be thought what made the mischief for which the Statute provided. And this appears fully, that it was for the disinheritance of issues, and not the reversioners. And this is plain because, in the first part of the Statute, it recites the conditional estates which, now, are estates tail. And it says *durum videbatur etc. in omnibus enim praedictis casibus post prolem suscitatam . . . habuerunt . . . potestatem alienandi . . . et exheredandi . . . exitum illorum.*[2] Thus, it was this that *durum videbatur* the law did not provide for him in the reversion. And it was a rare case to have the donor heir of the donee, and, there, the law did not provide for rareties but for mischiefs that could often enure. And with this agrees 6 Edw. III, 56, 57,[3] where it agrees that, if the reversion had not been in the crown, that it had been bound with the warranty; and 7 Edw. III, 58, *Counterple de voucher*, 57; 27 Edw. III, 83, *Garranty*, F., 42,[4] but, there, the plaintiff will not have[5] a demurrer; and 41 Edw. III, *Garranty*, 16. And even though John Sydenham, of whom she claimed the fee, was not barred, yet it was not for her because it was her laches to allow the discontinuance to remain unpurged, as if a tenant for life makes a feoffment with a warranty, if he in reversion does not avoid it during his lifetime, he will be barred. And even though it was not at first a discontinuance, yet, if she defers her entry until the estate and the warranty [is] conjoined, then, it will be a bar. See 35 Hen. VI, 53; and *Garranty*, 9.[6]

And for the objection that the estate descended after the warranty, this objection could be made against all collateral warranties because they, for the most part, descend in gross and the estate [is] barred afterwards. And the case of Littleton, 706,[7] is a case applicable to all of the points of our case, and it is not so easily avoidable, as a show of this has been made.

Third, he argued upon the fine, first, that Elizabeth was such a privy within the Statute who is bound by the fine of Alexander by the purview, without question, she is included. Therefore, if not excepted, she is bound by the first proviso except the second saving is of present rights, so that they are pursued within the five years. And, without question, it is not within it, and, within the saving of

---

[1] Stat. 13 Edw. I, c. 1 (*SR*, I, 71–72).

[2] it seemed harsh etc. in all the cases aforesaid, after issue begotten, they should have the power of alienating and disheriting their issue. Stat. 13 Edw. I, c. 1 (*SR*, I, 71).

[3] YB Mich. 6 Edw. III, ff. 56, 57, pl. 65 (1332).

[4] YB Mich. 7 Edw. III, f. 54, pl. 35 (1334), Fitzherbert, Abr., *Counterple de vouche*, pl. 57; Mich. 27 Edw. III, Fitzherbert, Abr., *Garrantie*, pl. 42 (1353).

[5] nessa *MS*.

[6] YB Trin. 21 Hen. VI, ff. 52, 53, pl. 8 (1443); Mich. 38 Edw. III, Fitzherbert, Abr., *Garrantie*, pl. 9 (1364).

[7] T. Littleton, *Tenures*, sect. 706.

future rights, it is not because she is privy to him who levied the fine. And a privy here must be intended a privy in blood because the heir is excluded by the word 'party' before. And on account of this, privy must have this meaning. And he said that, in this point, it would be to judge by the book before cited, of Dyer 3,[1] because, there, our case is put in effect, that the ancestor being disseised by the father, the father levied the fine, this barred the issue of the father even though he died in the lifetime of the ancestor.

Fourth, he argued that, here, he will not have but one five-year [period]. And he took a difference between this and Tooker's case, Coke 3, in Farmor's case,[2] because, there, he was not bound to take advantage of the forfeiture and the forfeiture did not make the lease void. But, here, the lease for life to Archer made against him in the remainder [was] void, and, on account of this, his title was but one for which he will not have but one five years. And this Statute is a statute for the repose of purchasers and a statute of peace. And on account of this, it must have a peculiar construction. And he cited Saffin's case, an interest for years is within the Statute and a copyholder. Coke 9, 104.[3]

And thus, he concluded for the defendant.

See more Michaelmas 4 *Caroli regis*, in the king's bench, p. 27, fo. 215.[4]

[Other reports of this case: Benloe 174, 73 E.R. 1035, CUL MS. Gg.2.30, f. 63; W. Jones 208, 82 E.R. 111; Latch 64, 72, 82 E.R. 276, 280, HLS MS. 1235, ff. 5v, 12v; BL MS. Hargr. 38, ff. 5v, 15, 90v, 242v, 267; BL MS. Lansd. 1092, ff. 13, 37v; CUL MS. Ll.3.13, ff. 17, 39v; HLS MS. 1063, f. 56.]

119

Morgan v. Moore

(K.B. Trin. 2 Car. I, 1626)

A local custom must appear in the record of the lower court and not first appear in the pleadings on appeal.

BL MS. Add. 35961, f. 35, pl. 27

In a writ of error between Morgan and Moore upon a judgment in [an action of] debt upon *concessit solvere* given in Bristol, where the custom was to bring [actions of] debt upon a *concessit solvere*, the parties joined in error. And, now, the

---

[1] *Anonymous* (1527), 1 Dyer 2, 73 E.R. 7.

[2] *Laune v. Toker* (1591), cited in *Fermor v. Smith* (1602), 3 Coke Rep. 78, 76 E.R. 805, also Cro. Eliz. 254, 78 E.R. 509.

[3] *Saffyn v. Adams* (1605), 5 Coke Rep. 123, 77 E.R. 248, also Cro. Jac. 60, 79 E.R. 50.

[4] For further proceedings in this case, see *Saule v. Clerke* (1628), BL MS. Add. 35961, f. 220, pl. 28; BL MS. Lansd. 1083, f. 316, pl. 28 (Widdrington's reports).

question was whether, after the joinder in error, a plea *ad informandum conscientias* could be had where the custom will be aided.

And it was held by the court not because, then, there will be no certainty in the errors assigned.

But JONES said that, after *in nullo est erratum* [be] pleaded, it is late but, before, the defendant can allege the custom and conclude thus *in nullo erratum*.

But DODDERIDGE said that the custom must appear in the first record and not upon the pleadings in error though one will lose the advantage of the custom by affirming his judgment. 2 Ric. III, fo. 9b.[1]

[Other reports of this case: Latch 134, 82 E.R. 311; CUL MS. Hh.2.1, f. 206; CUL MS. Ll.3.13, f. 138v; HLS MS. 1235, f. 59.]

120

Charles v. Jenkins

(K.B. Trin. 2 Car. I, 1626)

A judgment must state that it is based upon a consideration of the case.

BL MS. Add. 35961, f. 35, pl. 28

In [a writ of] error between Charles and Jenkins entered Mich. 22 Jac., rot. 229, the judgment was reversed because it was entered *ideo concessum est* where it should be *ideo consideratum est*.

121

Anonymous

(K.B. Trin. 2 Car. I, 1626)

The privilege of Parliament can be asserted only by a special writ.

BL MS. Add. 35961, f. 35, pl. 29

PER CURIAM: The court should not surcease against one of Parliament unless a special writ of Parliament be brought to them. And, in every action, they must have a special writ because the judges are not bound to take notice but by matter of record, but the parties who prosecute are in danger.

And it was said by *Noy* that Mich. 12 Edw. IV, in the pleas in the exchequer, is an excellent plea for this learning of the privilege of Parliament, and it is Marshe's case.

---

[1] YB Mich. 2 Ric. III, f. 9, pl. 21 (1484).

122

Lyon v. Grise

(K.B. Trin. 2 Car. I, 1626)

A general appearance cures discontinuances and miscontinuances.

BL MS. Add. 35961, f. 35, pl. 30

In [a writ of] error between Lyon and Grise, entered rot. 388, Hil. 1 Car., it was assigned that the sheriff returned *cepi corpus* and, afterwards for three terms, there was not any continuance and, afterwards, he appeared *gratis* and, on account of this, he did not have a day. It was alleged for error, but *non allocatur* because the appearance aids it because the purpose of process is an appearance and this helps all discontinuances and miscontinuances.

123

Anonymous

(K.B. Trin. 2 Car. I, 1626)

An action upon the case does not lie for usury money.

BL MS. Add. 35961, f. 35, pl. 31

PER CURIAM: An action upon the case for usury money is not maintainable because it is illegal and thus branded by the common law, Parliaments, and all other writers, which [is a] difference between it and an obligation.

124

Clempson v. Poule

(K.B. Trin. 2 Car. I, 1626)

The issues in this case were whether a person had been denied a right of entry to a house as contracted for and whether this issue was properly pleaded.

BL MS. Add. 35961, f. 35, pl. 32

In [an action of] debt between Clempson and Poule, entered Trin. 1 Car., rot. 643, the defendant demanded oyer of the condition of the obligation which was that, whereas the plaintiff had leased a house to the defendant reserving the parlor and the parlor chamber, that, if the defendant allowed the plaintiff at all times to have free egress and regress to them etc.

The defendant pleaded that he had allowed him to have egress and regress *secundum formam conditionis*.

The plaintiff replied that the defendant *clausit et oppressulavit exteriores januas domus praedicti et sic oppressulatas et clausas*[1] continued from such a day to such a day, being a half a year *custodivit per quod* he could not have ingress etc.

And upon this, the defendant demurred. And it was divers times moved, and the court was loath to give their resolution, and they would have put the parties to re-do[2] it, but one party would not assent.

And, afterwards, upon advice and more motions, it was found for clear law that, without an assent after a demurrer, the parties could not replead and [they] allowed the law to be so, according to Ridgewaye's case, Coke 3,[3] but, afterwards, the court is to adjudge upon the whole matter. And thus, the law [is] clear. And with this agrees Turnor and Bonham's case, Coke 8.[4] And on account of this, the court delivered their opinions.

And WHITELOCKE argued that the bar was bad because the condition was that he will have free egress and he pleaded that he had egress without *libero* and thus, the bar being bad, the plaintiff will have judgment, be the replication good or not, unless it is contrary to the count and be repugnant to it.

JONES, for the defendant [held] *contra*. The bond [is] in a great sum of £200, and for this, upon a slip or for keeping him out an hour, it is harsh to recover so much. But it is to see what the law is. And I hold that the bar is good and the replication [is] bad, and thus for the defendant because, first, that he did not plead that he allowed him to have free egress, this is not necessary because egress implies as much because, if he be bound to allow one to have egress and regress, there, the law intends that it will be free. And also, there, he has pleaded that he had egress etc. *secundum formam conditionis*.

For the replication, it is not good because it does not show a breach, but, by the meaning [of it], it is not necessary to leave the doors open at all times but it is lawful in day and night to shut them, but, when the plaintiff knocks and requires to enter, then, he must open. But here, which is another fault, he has not shown a request to enter. And also, there could be other ways than *per exteriores januas*, and he did not plead that there were not.

DODDERIDGE, *contra*: The bar [is] bad because he must have said that he had free egress etc. but, even though he had ingress, if he be hindered of the common [way] and another way is not free, thus if he draw a ditch about the house, and even though the law allows him to keep his house shut, as is Seyman's case, Coke

---

[1] closed and shut the exterior doors of the aforesaid house and thus the shutting and closing.

[2] reserer *MS*.

[3] *Grils v. Rigeway* (1594), 3 Coke Rep. 52, 76 E.R. 753, also Popham 41, 79 E.R. 1159, Moore K.B. 660, 72 E.R. 822, Gouldsborough 180, 75 E.R. 1078, Cro. Eliz. 318, 439, 78 E.R. 568, 679.

[4] *Turnor v. Lawrence* (1610), 8 Coke Rep. 132, 77 E.R. 673; *Bonham v. Turnor* (1610), 8 Coke Rep. 107, 77 E.R. 638, also 2 Brownlow & Goldesborough 255, 123 E.R. 928.

5,[1] yet, by his own covenant, he could be bound to leave it open at seasonable times because it will have a reasonable construction, *viz.* that he will have egress and ingress at seasonable times, *viz.* in the day, when the law allows people to be walking, and not in the night because night-walkers are punishable. And on account of this, he is not bound by the covenant to keep it unshut in the night. But yet, there, if the plaintiff demands entry in the night, he must open to him. If one is bound to allow another to have a way over his land, if he lock the gate, there is a forfeiture without an entry demanded because it is not free and he will not be bound to go about out of his way to demand the key. Thus, the bar [is] faulty.

And the replication [is] good because *clausit exteriores januas* will be intended *omnes* because *indefinitae universalis praepositio aequipollet generali.* And on account of this, a request to enter is not necessary.

Thus, upon the whole matter, the plaintiff will have judgment.

And afterwards, it was moved for the opinion of the chief justice to make the court divide or to end it. And JONES was, as he said, confirmed in his opinion. But it was afterwards referred to arbitration.

[Other reports of this case: Benlow 172, 73 E.R. 1034, CUL MS. 2.30, f. 62; Latch 47, 146, 82 E.R. 268, 318; BL MS. Hargr. 38, f. 102v; BL MS. Lansd. 1092, ff. 124v, 127; CUL MS. Hh.2.1, ff. 212v, 213v; CUL MS. Ll.3.13, ff. 154v, 157v; HLS MS. 1235, ff. 64, 66.]

125

Hawkes v. Blackaller

(K.B. Trin. 2 Car. I, 1626)

The issue in this case was whether, when a plaintiff joins issue on a void plea, rather than demurring, the verdict will be set aside or is cured by the statute of jeofails.

BL MS. Add. 35961, f. 35v, pl. 33

Blackaller brought [an action of] trespass against Hawkes in an inferior court for an entry into a house and the taking of wool. The defendant pleaded that he did it by license of the plaintiff, to which the plaintiff replied *de injuria sua propria.* And upon this, [they were] at issue.

And the jury gave their verdict thus, that *quoad captionem et asportationem lanae etc. defendens est culpabilis, et quoad residuum transgressionis non culpabilis.*[2] And upon this, judgment was given for the plaintiff. And in [a writ of] error, entered Hil. 1 Car., rot. 721, it was often moved that, because such issue upon the license

---

[1] *Semayne v. Gresham* (1604), 5 Coke Rep. 91, 77 E.R. 194, also Moore K.B. 668, 72 E.R. 828, Cro. Eliz. 908, 78 E.R. 1131, Yelverton 29, 80 E.R. 21.

[2] as to the taking and carrying away of the wool etc., the defendant is guilty, and as to the rest of the [alleged] tort [he is] not guilty.

of the party was a void issue because an issue taken upon a void plea is void, that the judgment itself found upon it was erroneous. See 12 Edw. IV, 10, and Coke 8, 67, for such an issue.[1]

And it was answered that, if he had demurred upon the plea, then, it had not been good. But here, the issue being joined upon an affirmative and a negative and the verdict [was] found, it is aided by the Statute of Jeofails,[2] as Nichol's case, Coke 5, 43.[3]

And the court was taken to deliver their opinion. And another error was moved [that was] not moved before. And on account of this, the court did not speak to the first error.

The second error was the finding of the jury which found him guilty. And on account of this, the judgment was reversed. But the reason was not given at the bar nor the bench.

Query whether it was because they did not find according to the issue because they found not guilty where it was not in issue, but whether *de injuria etc.* and so they found this which was not in the charge and they did not find nor respond to the question asked, or whether it was because they found him guilty for taking away the wool, which was a trespass and thus *vi et armis*, and, afterwards, they found *quoad residuum vi et armis* and thus [to the] contrary.

[Other reports of this case: BL MS. Hargr. 38, f. 102.]

126

Hoarde v. More

(K.B. Trin. 2 Car. I, 1626)

An ecclesiastical court does not have the jurisdiction to determine the ownership of a patronage.

BL MS. Add. 35961, f. 36, pl. 34

Between Hoarde and More, *Noy* moved for [a writ of] prohibition to the court Christian because, after institution and induction, it held a plea of the title of the patronage and the suit was to remove the incumbent. And it was granted. And [it was] said by the court that it had been done so divers times.

---

[1] *Crogate v. Marys* (1608), 8 Coke Rep. 66, 77 E.R. 574, also 1 Brownlow & Goldesborough 197, 123 E.R. 751, 2 Brownlow & Goldesborough 55, 146, 123 E.R. 812, 864.

[2] Stat. 32 Hen. VIII, c. 30 (*SR*, III, 786–787); Stat. 18 Eliz. I, c. 14 (*SR*, IV, 625).

[3] *Chamberlain v. Nichols* (1595), 5 Coke Rep. 43, 77 E.R. 121, also Cro. Eliz. 455, 78 E.R. 694, Moore K.B. 692, 72 E.R. 844, Jenkins 257, 145 E.R. 183.

127

Felton v. Weaver

(Part 1)

(K.B. Trin. 2 Car. I, 1626)

An appellee cannot allege an incomplete record on appeal after he has joined in the writ of error.

A writ of certiorari *can be sent to a lower court on the motion of the higher court in order to reverse a judgment.*

BL MS. Add. 35961, f. 36, pl. 35

In [a writ of] error between Felton and Weaver, entered Hil. 1 Car., rot. 647, the case was [thus]. [An action of] debt was brought against an executor at Bridgnorth. The Defendant said *plene administravit* at Shrewsbury, and the venue was at Bridgnorth. And [it was] tried, and judgment [was] given, and [a writ of] error [was] brought. Errors were assigned, and the parties joined in [a plea of] *in nullo est erratum*. And afterwards, the plaintiff [was] granted a certificate to certify the [writ of] *venire facias* that was returned.

And now, the question was whether the court could refuse it or admit [it] at their discretion because it was agreed by both [sides] at the bar.

And [it was said] by JONES and WHITELOCKE and CREWE and DODDERIDGE that, after a joinder in error, the party cannot allege a diminution because, by his joinder, he has admitted this full record. But yet, the court by their discretion can award a certificate. But yet, they never do it except to affirm the judgment, *nunquam* to reverse. It was also agreed by all, if, upon such a certificate, matter appears to reverse the judgment, if the certificate be entered upon the roll (as it was not here, but upon a rider that was not received in court), then they should reverse it. But the question was now whether they could refuse to receive the certificate.

And JONES said that a certificate upon a diminution must not issue without a motion in court, and that, in Bishop's case, Coke 5,[1] there, it was moved to have a certificate to affirm the judgment and, when they came and it was entered, they made another use of it and reversed the judgment. And, because it was a full case to this purpose, the court demanded to see the roll of Bishop's case, but it was not shown this term. And the Bishop of Rochester and Young's case[2] was cited, where a certificate will issue to reverse the judgment, 14 Jac., but the court remembered this case, and they said that it was by consent.

See more, fo. 38, pl. 20.[3]

---

[1] *Bishop v. Harecourt* (1592), 5 Coke Rep. 37, 77 E.R. 110, also Cro. Eliz. 210, 78 E.R. 466, 1 Anderson 240, 123 E.R. 451, 1 Leonard 210, 74 E.R. 194.

[2] *Young v. Bishop of Rochester* (1616), 3 Bulstrode 224, 81 E.R. 189, 1 Rolle Rep. 432, 81 E.R. 588.

[3] For further proceedings in this case, see below, No. 150.

128

Cary v. Anonymous

(K.B. Trin. 2 Car. I, 1626)

In this case, the words spoken of a lawyer were held to be defamatory.

BL MS. Add. 35961, f. 36, pl. 36

In the case of Corye of Gray's Inn (where these words were adjudged action-able 'You, a counsellor, a fool, an ass, a hangman, a counsellor of the law, a fool in your profession.'), it was said by Justice JONES that it is not sufficient to say that he was *eruditus in lege* but he must say that he was *homo conciliarius.* And he said that in [an action of] maintenance against Broughton[1] coming into question upon the evidence to the jury whether one who is not a barrister can give counsel and it was ruled not even though he had letters patent to enable him in all manner as if he had been called [to the bar], and it was there said to be Auditor Fleetwood's case,[2] where these words 'You, the king's receiver, you are his deceiver are you not?' [were spoken].

[Other copies of this report: Popham 207, 79 E.R. 1297.]

129

Rex v. Savile

(K.B. Trin. 2 Car. I, 1626)

The punishment for an assault in the royal palace is the loss of the aggressor's right hand.

BL MS. Add. 35961, f. 36, pl. 37

Sir Thomas Savile was indicted for a breach of the peace in the palace, *viz.* for an assault of one Wortley, knight, and he pleaded his pardon.

And there DODDERIDGE [said] that to strike in the palace was the loss of the right hand by the law.[3] And, in this point, our law agrees with the laws of France, Spain, and of all other nations because, as the person of the king, so his palace and courts of justice are here sacred that such a contempt and affront is adjudged to merit such a punishment. And he said that the book is, which he said to the students to take notice of, that, where one came armed into the palace and be-ing brought to the bar in his complete armor, the cause was demanded and he answered that it was in his defense, being in the power of a great man then in

---

[1] *Broughton v. Prince* (1590), 3 Leonard 237, 74 E.R. 656.

[2] *Fleetwood v. Curle* (1620), Cro. Jac. 557, 79 E.R. 478, Hobart 267, 80 E.R. 413, Palmer 69, 81 E.R. 982.

[3] E.g. *Davis's Case* (1461), 2 Dyer 188, 73 E.R. 415.

the court, and he was committed to prison by the court during the pleasure of the king, and his lands [were] forfeited during his life. And he said this was 21 Edw. III.

[Other copies of this report: Popham 207, 79 E.R. 1297.]

[Related cases: Wortley v. Savile (1629), Littleton 278, 124 E.R. 245, Hetley 142, 124 E.R. 408, W. Jones 239, 82 E.R. 126, Cro. Car. 205, 79 E.R. 780.]

130

Anonymous

(K.B. Trin. 2 Car. I, 1626)

No fine is payable for the filing of a declaration in an action of trover.

BL MS. Add. 35961, f. 36v, pl. 38

It was said by *Browne* in an action upon the case for trover and conversion that the fine for the declaration was so much.

JONES: Is any fine paid for trover and conversion?

Browne: Yes, Sir, and it has always been here.

JONES: In the [court of] common bench, he does not pay any.

And afterwards, all of the justices said that a fine for this should not be paid, contrary to all of the clerks. *Quaere rationem.*

131

Rex v. Town of Maidstone

(K.B. Mich. 2 Car. I, 1626)

The question in this case was whether the filing of a roll can be stayed after judgment and execution.

BL MS. Add. 35961, f. 36v, pl. 1

In the *quo warranto* against the Town of Maidstone, judgment was entered in a roll not filed, but a writ of execution to seize the liberty was awarded to the sheriff. And now, it was moved by Serjeant *Finch*, recorder, to stay the filing of the roll and that a plea can be received in respect of divers causes. And whether, in any case after the judgment entered upon the roll and execution awarded, whether the judges can stay the affixing of the roll was the question.

And Serjeant *Henden* and *Noy* [said] that they cannot because the king's bench, when a judgment is given, cannot, though it be the same term, reverse it without a writ of error. And if in another term, it is not reversible by them at all.

F.N.B. 211.[1] And he cited 15 Edw. IV, 7,[2] that, if a judgment [be] given in the eyres, it cannot be reversed there after the eyre ends.

But DODDERIDGE and JONES said that of this that their powers were then ended. And DODDERIDGE said that, after the eyre ends, they do not have the custody of their own records, but some were sent to Kent and some to the common pleas. And he cited Chamberlin's case and Sir John Webb's case, where, in such a case as here, the roll, without assent, cannot be rejected. And in John Webb's case, the king's attorney would not consent.

And a day was given further to speak to this point or to the king's attorney to consent because he took advice.

[Other reports of this case: Popham 180, 79 E.R. 1275; *sub nom.* Tufton and Ashley's Case, Cro. Car. 144, 79 E.R. 727.]

132

Anonymous

(K.B. Mich. 2 Car. I, 1626)

The issue in this case was whether court costs for abandoning an appeal can be pardoned.

BL MS. Add. 35961, f. 36v, pl. 2

Serjeant *Richardson* moved for a [writ of] consultation. And the case was in a suit in a spiritual court *ad instant[iam] partis.* The plaintiff recovered and [received] costs also, and then he appealed, and then came the General Pardon.[3] And upon the appeal [being] deserted, costs [were] taxed so that they were not taxed upon the body of the matter but for the deserting of the appeal. And he said that it was so ruled in Parker and Sport's case that, in such a case notwithstanding the Pardon, if the appellant deserts his appeal, that the costs were well taxed because the cause is remanded to the inferior court again to affirm the former sentence.

133

Attorney General v. Lane

(K.B. Mich. 2 Car. I, 1626)

A recusant convict can sell his land if it be done bona fide.

---

[1] A. Fitzherbert, *Nouvelle Natura Brevium.*

[2] YB Mich. 15 Edw. IV, ff. 6, 7, pl. 12 (1475).

[3] Stat. 21 Jac. I, c. 35 (*SR*, IV, 1269–1275).

BL MS. Add. 35961, f. 36v, pl. 3

Note: In a motion, *Heath*, attorney general, admitted as clear law that a recusant convict can sell his land if it be *bona fide*, and on account of this, the king [is] ousted from the profits, as in a case of outlawry. But if it be not without slander, it is within the Statute of Fraudulent Conveyances.[1]

[Other reports of this case: Popham 180, 79 E.R. 1275.]

134

Hollet v. Parker

(K.B. Mich. 2 Car. I, 1626)

In this case, the consideration for a contract for the sale of goods was properly pleaded.

BL MS. Add. 35961, f. 36v, pl. 4

[In a case] between Hollet and Parker, *Hitcham* moved in arrest of judgment because the declaration was that the plaintiff had sold to the defendant all the barley such a day and that the defendant, *postea* and in consideration that he had sold to him, the same day, promised to pay to him so much for it. And he moved that it should have been *tunc et ibidem* promised because, here, the consideration was for a thing executed.

But DODDERIDGE, JONES, and the court held it was good enough.

135

Evans v. Askwith

(Part 2)
(K.B. Mich. 2 Car. I, 1626)

BL MS. Add. 35961, f. 37, pl. 5

And now the case of Evans and Askwith was to be argued by the civilians, but they prayed for a further day. But now, the court opened the points to them in which they desired to be informed. And the principal [point] was whether, when a bishop be elected bishop of another place, if he, after the assent of the superior, who is now the king by Statute,[2] and by his own assent, ceases to be the bishop of the former place before confirmation because, if [he is] a plenary bishop before confirmation, the *commendam* comes too late.

And now at this time upon the moment, Dr. *Duck* said that, in the case of a translation, there are four acts considerable: (1) election; (2) consent of him and

---

[1] Stat. 13 Eliz. I, c. 5 (*SR*, IV, 537–538).

[2] Stat. 1 Eliz. I, c. 1 (*SR*, IV, 350–355).

the superior; (3) confirmation; (4) possession. Whether possession be necessary to the confirmation of the translation has been the question and [it has been] disputed. But the opinion of Panormitanus[1] is that it is not necessary. And upon this point, the bishop of Speyer, being elected archbishop of T[rier] and not being received at the archbishopric, would have gone back to Speyer, but he could not because, without possession of [*blank*], he was fully discharged. And also he cited the bishop of Florence's case, where he was made a cardinal by the pope but he had not assented, and [there was] a dispute whether he ceased to be bishop without his consent, and it was ruled with this distinction, *viz.* if he was removed by the pope *propter utilitatem ecclesiae*, there, it does not need his assent, but if *propter meritum personae*, there, the consent [is] necessary, and, in all consents, they are *propter meritum personae*.

More, fo. 48b, pl. 93.[2]

136

Galthorp v. Reynell

(K.B. Mich. 2 Car. I, 1626)

A court can stay execution of its own judgments if good cause be shown.

BL MS. Add. 35961, f. 37, pl. 6

Galthorp brought an action of debt upon an escape against Sir George Reynell because, where one Culpeper was in execution for £300 damages to him, he let him escape. And the case was thus. A [writ of] *habeas corpus* was directed by the higher house of Parliament, and Sir George certified the cause and he was taken within such a day that was within the time of the privilege of Parliament, he being a servant to lord Cromwell, where in truth, as it was pretended, he was taken out of the time of privilege, upon which he was dismissed. And upon this, the [action for] escape [was] brought. And he recovered by a verdict. And it was moved to stay the judgment and to go to a new trial because the return of Sir George was erased by the servant and it was not returned false by him.

And DODDERIDGE said that he cannot without consent.

And then, the plaintiff would not consent.

DODDERIDGE: Nay, then know that we can do [it] though judgment be given. If cause appears to us, we can stay execution, as in 11 Hen. IV.

---

[1] Nicholaus de Tudeschis (d. 1445).

[2] For other proceedings in this case, see Nos. 101, 226, 257.

And Jones remembered the case of 7 Hen. IV,[1] where it was said that he will not have execution until Gabriel blows his horn.[2]

137

Rex v. Wheelehouse

(K.B. Mich. 2 Car. I, 1626)

In this case, an insufficient indictment for nightwalking and frequenting a house of prostitution was quashed.

BL MS. Add. 35961, f. 37, pl. 7

One Wheelehowse was indicted at Northampton because he was a *noctivagus* and he was a haunter of a house suspected of prostitution.[3]

And Serjeant *Crawley* moved to quash it. And he took three exceptions: (1) because it was for haunting a house suspected of prostitution, and it did not say that, in fact, it was a bawdy house; (2) because the indictment was taken *coram justiciariis pacis infra villam* Northampton, and the house of prostitution is laid to be *infra libertates villae* Northampton, and it did not say *infra jurisdictionem huius curiae* according to Long's case, C.;[4] (3) it did not say that it was knowing it to be a bawdy house.

And the court seemed to allow these exceptions. But, because a charge in the indictment, *viz. noctivagus*, was not good, day was given to the other party to maintain the indictment. And afterwards, it was quashed.

[Other reports of this case: Benloe 199, 73 E.R. 1056, CUL MS. Gg.2.30, f. 77; Popham 208, 79 E.R. 1297.]

138

Edsol v. Bengor

(K.B. Mich. 2 Car. I, 1626)

In an action of trespass for a battery, the plaintiff must allege where the battery was done.

---

[1] YB Trin. 7 Hen. IV, f. 19, pl. 26 (1406).

[2] The archangel Gabriel will blow his trumpet on the day of judgment at the end of time: Revelation, chap. 10, verse 7, and chap. 11, verse 15.

[3] Bawdry *MS.*

[4] *Long's Case* (1604), 5 Coke Rep. 120, 77 E.R. 243.

BL MS. Add. 35961, f. 37, pl. 8

Edsall brought [an action of] trespass against Benger, *quod intratur* Hil. 1 Car., rot. 527, for a battery, which [was] found for the plaintiff. And [it was] moved in arrest of judgment that there was no place where the battery [was] done. And on account of this, the judgment [was] arrested.

[Other reports of this case: Latch 273, 82 E.R. 382.]

139

Hamond v. White

(Part 1)
(K.B. Mich. 2 Car. I, 1626)

Tenants in common must join as co-plaintiffs in actions to recover for torts done to their common property, such as plowing up a common appendant.

BL MS. Add. 35961, f. 37v, pl. 9

[In a case] between Hammond and White, *quod intratur* Trin. 2 Car., rot. 158, [where] two tenants in common of land to which a common is appendant and the land in which they have the common is plowed up, one of them brought an action upon the case. And upon [a plea of] *non culpabilis*, it was found for the plaintiff.

And now *Whistler* moved in arrest of judgment because they must join in this action because [it is a] personal action, according to the rule of Littleton.[1] And he cited 13 Hen. VII, 26,[2] where a prior brought an action upon the case for the corrupting of the water of a river, and, there, Keble took an exception because the prior had nothing in the river but in common etc., and, there, [it was said] by Bryan, if [there are] two tenants in common of a water and the water is corrupted to the nuisance of the house of one of them, he will have an action sole who is not a tenant in common of the house, by which it was admitted by him that, if he had been a tenant in common of the house, he could not have [it] sole. And he cited also 35 Hen. VI, 56, by Moyle,[3] the same case; if two joint tenants of land to which a common [is] appendant and pits be dug in the common, one sole will not have [an action of] trespass. And he said that there is not any difference as to this purpose between a general writ of trespass and trespass upon the case.

Et adjornatur. More fo. 39b, pl. 32.[4]

---

[1] T. Littleton, *Tenures*, sects. 315, 316.
[2] YB Trin. 13 Hen. VII, f. 26, pl. 4 (1498).
[3] *Peche v. Anonymous* (1457), YB Pas. 35 Hen. VI, ff. 55, 56, pl. 1.
[4] For later proceedings in this case, see below, No. 163.

140

Sharp v. Rolt

(K.B. Mich. 2 Car. I, 1626)

In an action on a contract for non-payment of the purchase price, the plaintiff need not allege to whom the price was to be paid but it will be inferred to be the obligee.

BL MS. Add. 35961, f. 37v, pl. 10

Between Sharpe and Rolt in an action upon the case upon *assumpsit*, in consideration that the plaintiff will deliver to such certain clothes that the plaintiff had made for him, the defendant assumed to pay for them, and he did not say to whom he would pay, and it [was] moved in arrest of judgment.

And now *Wooldrich*, notwithstanding, moved for judgment because the precedent communication and agreement will put this in certainty, *viz.* that he will pay to the plaintiff, with whom the agreement [was] made. And he said that the precedent communication would reduce the uncertainty of time [and] of estate [and] of person, as in our case. For time, he cited the case of Perkins, 797,[1] where, if one [is] bound in an obligation upon a condition that, if the obligee enfeoff him of Blackacre, that he will pay £10, there, no time limited the grant, but it will be now after the feoffment. For the estate, in P. [*blank*] case, C. 8,[2] one devised that one will be his steward of his manors during his life, and he devised to him a rent of etc., and he did not limit what estate in the rent; it will be taken [as] such an estate as in the office, which was for life. For the thing, Dyer 42,[3] one enfeoffed one of an acre of land, and he was bound upon a condition that, where he had enfeoffed the plaintiff of such acre, that he will warrant to him, and he did not say what thing he will warrant; yet, it [was] intended that he warranted the acre of which the former communication was. For the person, where this will be put in certain by a former agreement and communication, he cited Dyer 126; 4 Edw. III, 4; Co. 168.[4] A gift to one in the premises *habendum* to him and Alice St. in frank marriage [was] good by reason of a precedent agreement. Thus, [where there was a] feoffment to J.S. and his heirs with a warranty and it did not say to what the warranty [was], it will be as the precedent estate. 22 Edw. IV,

---

[1] J. Perkins, *A Profitable Book*, sect. 797.

[2] *Pexhall's Case* (1609), 8 Coke Rep. 83, 77 E.R. 601.

[3] *Executors of Grenelife v. W.* (1530), 1 Dyer 42, 73 E.R. 91.

[4] *Throgmorton v. Tracey* (1555), 2 Dyer 124, 126, 73 E.R. 272, 274–275; YB Hil. 4 Edw. III, f. 4, pl. 7 (1330); *Fulmerston v. Steward* (1554), 1 Plowden 101, 108, 75 E.R. 160, 170.

16; *Voucher*, 258 (or 268) and 262.[1] And in Co. 8,[2] it is said that the reservation of a rent upon a lease was [. . .][3] to reserve it to no person, but it leaves it to the reservation of the law. 14 Hen. VII;[4] a devise that land will be sold to pay debts and it did not say who will be the executors, it will be as the communication of the debts shows it. Thus [is] 4 Edw. II, *Obligation*, 16, and 40 Edw. III, 5.[5] One bound himself to A., and in the deed was also *et ad maiorem huius[modi] rei securitatem inveni A. et B. fideiussores qui se in totum et in solidum obligaverunt*,[6] and it did not say to whom they bound themselves, yet [it was] good. Thus [is] 2 Edw. IV, 22;[7] one covenanted to deliver to the other barley and, to perform it, he was bound in 100s., and it did not say to whom; there, it [was] held that it will be intended according to the former agreement. And C. 140;[8] it was ruled that an agreement will be taken according to the intent of the parties and a set form of the words is not necessary.

And of this opinion was the court for the same reasons, by which a rule was given that he will have judgment if cause not be shown [to the contrary] on Saturday.

But Serjeant *Hetley* came, and he showed cause, but it was not allowed, by which judgment was given.

[Other reports of this case: Cro. Car. 77, 79 E.R. 668; Latch 151, 272, 82 E.R. 320, 382; Noy 83, 74 E.R. 1050; Popham 181, 79 E.R. 1276; BL MS. Hargr. 38, f. 125v; CUL MS. Hh.2.1, f. 215; CUL MS. Ll.3.13, f. 161; HLS MS. 1235, f. 69.]

141

Busher v. Earl of Tullibardine

(Part 1)
(K.B. Mich. 2 Car. I, 1626)

A protection must be put in by a plea and must be accompanied by security to answer.

---

[1] YB Trin. 22 Edw. IV, f. 15, pl. 41 (1482); YB Hil. 6 Edw. II, Selden Soc., vol. 43, p. 15, pl. 15, YB Hil. 6 Edw. II, f. 187 (1313), Fitzherbert, Abr., *Voucher*, pl. 258; YB Mich. 12 Edw. II, Selden Soc., vol. 65, p. 145, pl. 62, YB Mich. 12 Edw. II, f. 363 (1318), Fitzherbert, Abr., *Voucher*, pl. 262.

[2] *Chappel v. Whitlock* (1609), 8 Coke Rep. 69, 77 E.R. 580, also 1 Brownlow & Goldesborough 169, 123 E.R. 734.

[3] surest *MS.*

[4] YB Hil. 14 Hen. VII, f. 14, pl. 4 (1499).

[5] YB Trin. 4 Edw. II, Selden Soc., vol. 42, p. 166, pl. 24 (1310), Fitzherbert, Abr., *Obligacion*, pl. 16; YB Hil. 40 Edw. III, f. 5, pl. 11 (1366).

[6] and for the greater security of such thing, I have gotten A. and B., sureties, who have bound themselves jointly and severally.

[7] YB Mich. 2 Edw. IV, f. 22, pl. 19 (1462).

[8] *Browning v. Beston* (1552), 1 Plowden 131, 140, 75 E.R. 202, 216.

BL MS. Add. 35961, f. 38, pl. 11

The earl of Tyllybarne in Scotland[1] prayed for the allowance of the protection. And [it was held] by the court he must come in by a plea. He must plead it. And, if it be allowed, still, he must find bail to answer at the end of the year before [being] released at large.[2]

142

Bevin v. Coolmer

(K.B. Mich. 2 Car. I, 1626)

A promise not to sue upon a bond in consideration for a promise to pay the debt is an enforceable contract.

BL MS. Add. 35961, f. 38, pl. 12

Between Bevin and Coolmer, in an action upon the case, the plaintiff alleged that, where the defendant was in debt to him by an obligation and the plaintiff intended to sue him upon it, the defendant in consideration that the plaintiff will forebear (and he did not say how long nor *per rationabile tempus*) to sue the defendant upon the said bond, the defendant assumed to pay the debt etc. and he had not paid etc. And upon [a plea of] *non assumpsit*, [it was] found with the plaintiff.

And now, *Littleton*, moved in arrest of judgment that, here, [there was a] fault of consideration of the promise because it was not said how long he will forebear and, on account of this, he could sue him within an hour if he wished to and, on account of this, [there was] no advantage to the defendant nor consideration that he will pay. And in Mich. 12 Jac., Keble's case was adjudged, where one, in consideration that the other will make to him a lease at will, promised; [it was] held it was no consideration because it could [be] made and terminated with one breath. And he said it was adjudged [in] Trin. 28 Eliz., rot. 523, between Smith and Smith, where the consideration was as here *quod non implacitaret* generally, [it was held] that it was not good. And this was, as I understand it, in the common bench.

And DODDERIDGE said that it has been adjudged that in consideration that one forebear *per paululum tempus* is not good but *per rationabile tempus* is good because the court will adjudge upon the reasonableness.

But the court held the consideration [to be] good because the court took that, by this promise not to sue him upon the bond indefinitely, he had subjected

---

[1] William Murray, second earl of Tullibardine (d. 1627): G.E.C., *The Complete Peerage*, vol. 12, part 2, pp. 64–65 (G. H. White, ed., 1959).

[2] For later proceedings in this case, see below, No. 260.

himself to the action upon the case if anyone sued the bond and it is as much as if he had agreed that he will sue the bond at some time and thus he had barred himself of his best assurance and he has taken the word of the defendant and thus [there was] good consideration. Thus, his exception [was] not allowed.

[Other reports of this case: Popham 183, 79 E.R. 1277.]

143

Petty v. Hobson

(K.B. Mich. 2 Car. I, 1626)

A record can be amended upon an appeal.

BL MS. Add. 35961, f. 38, pl. 13

Bankes moved for the amendment of a record. And the case was [thus]. A *postea* was returned by Francis Harvy, knight, where, in fact, he was not a knight at the time. And judgment [was] given upon it in the [court of] common bench. And [a writ of] error [was] brought in the [court of] king's bench. And there, [it was] assigned for error that there was not such a justice of assize as Francis Harvy, knight, and he moved that it will now be amended and 'knight' put out [of the record].

And the justices were of opinion that it will be inasmuch as it is assigned for error and it was not the fault of the clerk.

And *Bankes* urged that it is [to be] amended in the common bench.

But JONES said that, in former times, before the rolls grew to this magnitude, upon [a writ of] error brought, they used to deliver with their hands the record itself. But now, for the difficulty to sever it from the others, he sends the transcript. But yet this which he sends, in law, is the record. And this which remains with them but a *vacat*. And on account of this, the amendment of it [is] not material.

[Other reports of this case: Latch 161, 82 E.R. 326, HLS MS. 1235, ff. 72, 73; Noy 86, 74 E.R. 1053; BL MS. Lansd. 1092, f. 137v; CUL MS. Hh.2.1, f. 219v; CUL MS. Ll.3.13, ff. 171v, 173v.]

[Related cases: Petty v. Robinson (1626), below, No. 197.]

144

Rideout's Case

(K.B. Mich. 2 Car. I, 1626)

A sheriff can return that a rescue was made out of the custody of a bailiff.

BL MS. Add. 35961, f. 38, pl. 14

A rescue was returned against Rydeoute. And it was moved by *Ashley* for an exception that it was *a custodia ballivorum* where it should be *a custodia vicecomitis*. And yet [it was] ruled good by the court. And either way [is] good enough. Before, pl. 11, f. 3.[1]

145

Arnold v. Dichton

(Part 1)
(K.B. Mich. 2 Car. I, 1626)

The issue in this contract case was whether the plaintiff had alleged a breach.

BL MS. Add. 35961, f. 38, pl. 15

Between Zachary and Pitkin in an action upon the case, the plaintiff declared that the defendant, in consideration that the plaintiff marry the daughter of the defendant, promised to provide for him and his wife sufficient esculents and piculents for two years and also to give to him etc. and that the plaintiff married etc. and he did not keep his promise, upon which the plaintiff intended to sue the defendant, upon which, in consideration that the plaintiff will not sue the defendant, the defendant promised that the plaintiff *haberet tam bonam et rationabilem portionem quam daret alicui alio* of his children. And he showed that he did not sue and also that the defendant *dedit* to such a one of his children land to the value of £20 *per annum* where he had not given to him but 30s. And upon this, he brought his action. And the action was brought against the executor.

And upon [a plea of] *non assumpsit*, [it was] found for the plaintiff.

And *Noy* moved in arrest of judgment that, here, there is not laid any breach because the *assumpsit* by the testator of the defendant was *quod haberet tam bonam etc. quam daret etc.*, and the plaintiff laid the breach *quod dedit* to one of his children £20 *per annum* and not *dedit alicui* more than 30s.; now *daret* will have relation to the time after the promise, and it is not material [what] he had given before the promise to any of his children because he will not be bound to give to the plaintiff so much, but *tantum quantum daret* that is and it relates to the future time. Thus, if the plaintiff not having laid a time when the gift to the other of £20 *per annum* was, it will be intended before the promise because, being indifferent, it will be taken more strongly against the plaintiff and, thus, though he had not given to the defendant *tantum*, it is not a breach.

The second exception was because he said *quod non dedit* to him etc. and the *assumpsit* was *quod haberet*; thus, if he did not give or procure it to be done, it is

---

[1] *Anonymous* (K.B. 1625), see above, No. 11.

the same. And on account of this, he should have said that *non haberet* because the promise is laid *quod haberet*.

More, pl. 36.[1]

146

Barker v. Ringrose

(K.B. Mich. 2 Car. I, 1626)

It is not defamation to call a tradesman a bankrupt.

BL MS. Add. 35961, f. 38, pl. 16

Barker brought an action upon the case against Ringrose. And he declared that, where he was of the trade of woolwinders [. . .] the defendant had spoken these words of him that he was a 'bankrupt rogue'. And it was moved in arrest of judgment that the trade of woolwinder is a laboring trade and does not consist of buying and selling [and] the plaintiff has not laid that he used to buy and sell. And on account of this, such words of such a tradesman [are] not actionable.

And of such opinion was the court, that for calling a laborer a bankrupt is not actionable. And a woolwinder is but a laborer within the Statute of the Staple of 27 Edw. III.[2] And for such words of a comber or a shearman or a mason or a plowman, which are laboring occupations, no action lies. But it has been adjudged that, to call a shoemaker a bankrupt, this is actionable because, as Dodderidge said, he buys his leather before he works it and he sells it again wrought.

[Other reports of this case: Popham 185, 79 E.R. 1279.]

147

Jobson's Case

(K.B. Mich. 2 Car. I, 1626)

Writs of habeas corpus *can be sent into the county palatine of Durham.*

BL MS. Add. 35961, f. 38v, pl. 17

Note: This term, a [writ of] *habeas corpus* [was] awarded to Durham though [it is a] county palatine. And it is ordinary to remove things from there by [writs of] *certiorari*, as the court now said.

---

[1] For later proceedings in this case, see below, Nos. 167, 249.

[2] Stat. 27 Edw. III, stat. 2 (*SR*, I, 332–343).

And *Noy* said that, [in] the grant of the county palatine, the law reserved to the king writs of error and *habeas corpus*, by which he is to have an account of the liberty of his subject restrained in any part of the realm.

And DODDERIDGE said that there was a famous case in the beginning [of the reign] of King James where [a writ of] *habeas corpus* was directed to the [Town of] Berwick,[1] and, there, they pleaded the privileges granted to them by Edward I that they will be governed by the law of Alexander III of Scotland. And yet the *habeas corpus* [was] awarded. And thus have been [writs of] *habeas corpus* directed to Calais and Bordeaux, when [they were] in the hands of the kings of England.

And Justice JONES said that *habeas corpus* lies in Wales at common law, and yet it [is] more severed from the realm than the counties palatine.

[Other reports of this case: Latch 160, 82 E.R. 325.]

148

Powell v. Noy

(K.B. Mich. 2 Car. I, 1626)

The question in this case was how a constable-defendant could recover the statutory double court costs after a discontinuance.

BL MS. Add. 35961, f. 38v, pl. 18

[In a case] between Powell and Noye, it was moved upon the Statute of 21 Jac., cap. 12,[2] that [an action for] trespass of assault and battery was brought against the defendant and discontinued. And it was moved that the defendant was a constable, and, on account of this, by the Statute, he should have double costs upon this discontinuance. But though it will be made apparent at court that he was a constable and that it is brought for an action done by him as a constable, inasmuch as it does not appear by the record, it was the question because, if they would not admit proof here by an affidavit, the proviso of the Statute as to this breach of discontinuance [would be] idle.

Justice JONES said that he could have an action of debt for the double costs, as upon the Statute of Edw. VI,[3] which gives costs where a surmise for a [writ of] prohibition [is] not proved. But this way could not hold because he cannot have [an action of] debt for costs before they are taxed by the court, and they [are] not taxed before [it is] ascertained that [he is] a constable etc. But, if a verdict pass for the defendant in such a case, the usage in the Guildhall is as [. . .]

---

[1] Perhaps *Browley's Case* (1601), cited in *Bourn's Case* (1619), Cro. Jac. 543, 79 E.R. 465.

[2] Stat. 21 Jac. I, c. 12, s. 3 (*SR*, IV, 1220–1221).

[3] Stat. 2 & 3 Edw. VI, c. 13, s. 14 (*SR*, IV, 57).

chief justice said to pray that it will be shown upon the dorse of the *postea* that he was a constable and this [is] good. And an attorney moved there that he could [*blank*] the defendant plead by protestation that he is a constable etc. and by a plea of not guilty.

And DODDERIDGE allowed of this way.

But it was said that a protestation [is] not traversable nor could it for this be ascertained.

And it was said that, in this case at the bar, now, there was no help, and JONES said, nor hereafter because he thought this breach of the Statute [was] idle.

149

Calfe v. Bingley

(K.B. Mich. 2 Car. I, 1626)

Where one defense is pursuant to another defense, it is not an improper double plea.

If a judgment debtor dies before an unsuccessful execution, his bail is discharged.

BL MS. Add. 35961, f. 38v, pl. 19

Joshua Calfe and Benjamin Calfe brought a *scire facias* against Bingly, the bail of one Hall, *quare executione habere non debeat* against him, inasmuch as Hall had not satisfied the judgment nor rendered himself to prison. (And this is entered Hil. 22 Jac., rot. [*blank*].)

The defendant pleaded that, after the judgment, he brought a writ of error and, pending it, the principal [debtor] took himself to prison *in executione manucaptorum* and that he died before the return of the *scire facias*, upon which, the plaintiff demurred specially. And he showed for cause that the bar [was] double, second, that he pleaded the render to prison and [it is] merely [?] upon the record.

And *Calthorpe* argued [for] the plaintiff now (because it was divers times moved before but, before, he did not fully understand the case), and he moved that the bar is treble because, first, he pleaded that he brought a writ of error; second, that he rendered him to prison; third, the death of the principal [debtor] before the *scire facias* [was] returned, and even though, as he confessed, none of them is material because of the death, yet inasmuch as they have the color of a plea and mislead the court, it will be said [to be a] double plea, as is 4 Edw. IV;[1] one pleaded two feoffments of separate ancestors, though none of them [were] material, yet because it encumbered the court, it was a double plea. Thus is 21 Hen. VII, 10;[2] the assets solely [was] material, yet inasmuch as he did not rely upon the assets, it was double etc.

---

[1] YB Pas. 4 Edw. IV, ff. 3, 4, pl. 4 (1464).

[2] YB Hil. 21 Hen. VII, ff. 9, 10, pl. 11 (1506).

DODDERIDGE agreed, that, in a case that two immaterial pleas or one plea not material and another [that is] good be pleaded, one with double, these mislead and encumber the court. But here, he said that it is not because one matter is pursuant to the other.

The second exception that he moved, that he pleaded one plea here, *viz.* render to prison, [is] solely triable by the record and he did not conclude upon the record but he averred *et paratus est verificare.* And he cited Kel. 180, where an appearance [was] pleaded, and Dyer 27, where he said *quantum* pleaded a record where it was said he concluded upon this; with which agrees 6 Edw. IV, 11.[1]

The third thing was for the insufficiency of the matter because, by him, the death here does not discharge the manucaptors because, presently, upon the judgment given and the *capias* returned against the principal *non est inventus*, the bail, by the rigor of law, were chargeable; and, though the course is to award a second *scire facias* against the bail before they are charged and, if he brings in the body upon any of them, to discharge him, yet this is *ex gratia curiae* because the recognizance that the bail enters is that the principal will satisfy the judgment or render his body, which, in strictness, is forfeited if he does not come in upon the *capias*. But, if the principal dies before the emanation of the first *scire facias* and the return of *non est inventus*, there, the bail is charged, *quod omnes* agree because, there, he cannot ever be brought in. And he cited Justice Williams' case against Vaughan, 3 Jac.,[2] in which he said that, first, it was resolved that, as in our case, it was sufficient to declare that he had not brought in the body nor satisfied the judgment; second, that [if] the death [was] after the *capias* [was] returned, the bail could not be discharged.

And Justice JONES said that, in the common bench, in Style and Sougates's case, it was doubted whether, by the judgment upon a *capias* against the principal, he was liable. But there, it was ruled, if, before the *capias* [be] returned, the principal dies, the bail [is] discharged. And thus it was adjudged in Hobbs and Tadcaster's case, in *audita querela*,[3] the same question [was] resolved.

But here, in this case, it was agreed PER CURIAM. And upon this point, judgment [was] given against the plaintiff because he had not shown that a *capias* was awarded etc.; it should have come in in the replication because, if he had replied what the verity was etc. and that the *capias* was returned *non est inventus* before his death, then, the defendant had been overthrown.

[Other reports of this case: Benloe 184, 73 E.R. 1043, CUL MS. Gg.2.30, f. 67v; 3 Bulstrode 331, 81 E.R. 275; W. Jones 138, 82 E.R. 74, BL MS. Hargr. 317, f. 141; Latch

---

[1] *Anonymous* (1515), Keilwey 180, 72 E.R. 356, 116 Selden Soc. 678; *Abbot of Westminster v. Executors of Clerke* (1537), 1 Dyer 26, 73 E.R. 59; YB Mich. 6 Edw. IV, f. 1, pl. 4 (1466).

[2] *Williams v. Vaughan* (1605), Moore K.B. 775, 72 E.R. 899, Cro. Jac. 97, 79 E.R. 83.

[3] *Hobbs v. Tadcaster* (1598 x 1601), Gouldsborough 174, 75 E.R. 1074, Moore K.B. 432, 72 E.R. 677, Cro. Eliz. 597, 78 E.R. 839.

149, 82 E.R. 319, HLS MS. 1235, f. 65v; Noy 82, 74 E.R. 1049; Popham 185, 79 E.R. 1279; BL MS. Hargr. 38, ff. 42v, 115; BL MS. Lansd. 1092, f. 124v; CUL MS. Hh.2.1, f. 213.]

150

Felton v. Weaver

(Part 2)

(K.B. Mich. 2 Car. I, 1626)

BL MS. Add. 35961, f. 39, pl. 20

And now, the case between Felton and Weaver, before f. 35, pl. 35,[1] was moved again. And the question was whether the return that now was in a rider and not affixed to the record will be received or not. And it was argued that it will be. And it was granted that, when he has joined in error, then, the defendant cannot pray for a [writ of] *certiorari*. And he cited 7 Edw. IV, 2; 28 Hen. VI, 10; 9 Edw. IV, 32; *Error*, 44; and 22 Edw. IV, 45.[2] But yet the court cannot grant the *certiorari ex officio ad informandam conscientiam*. And for the most part, it is to affirm the judgment. But, if the certificate be for the reversal of the judgment and it be entered, then the judges should reverse it. And he cited divers cases where, upon the certificate, the judgment was reversed: Hooke and Sir William Fountaine's case, *quod intratur* Trin. 14 Jac.; and *Novel Entries*, fol. 254, 267, and 268; and Gage's case, C. 5, *quod intratur* Mich. 39 & 40 [Eliz.]; and Bishop's [case], C. 5, upon which he principally relied, *quod intratur* Pas. 33 Eliz., rot. 361; and the Bishop of Rochester's case and Younge, entered Trin. 13, rot. 52.[3]

And afterwards, upon the view of the record of Bishop's case, it was awarded that the roll will not be received because [in] Bishop's case, as it appeared by the roll, the *certificare* was not after the joinder in error, but, there, the defendant said nothing, upon which *nihil dicit* was entered, and, afterward, the court, upon the

---

[1] For earlier proceedings in this case, see above, No. 127.

[2] YB Mich. 7 Edw. IV, f. 22, pl. 27 (1467); YB Trin. 28 Hen. VI, f. 10, pl. 19 (1450); YB Mich. 9 Edw. IV, f. 32, pl. 5 (1469); YB Hil. 8 Edw. IV, f. 23, pl. 1 (1469), YB Hil. 7 Edw. IV, f. 25, pl. 1 (1468), Fitzherbert, Abr., *Errour*, pl. 44; YB Hil. 22 Edw. IV, f. 45, pl. 11 (1483).

[3] *Hows v. Fountaine* (1616), 1 Rolle 381, 81 E.R. 549, 3 Bulstrode 202, 81 E.R. 170; *Downehale v. Catesby* (1594), E. Coke, *A Booke of Entries* (1614), 'Error', pl. 10, ff. 252, 254; *Low v. Bishop of London* (1604), E. Coke, *A Booke of Entries* (1614), 'Error', pl. 14, ff. 264, 267, also *sub nom. Boswel's Case*, 6 Coke Rep. 48, 77 E.R. 326, Cro. Jac. 92, 79 E.R. 79, Jenkins 281, 145 E.R. 202; *Gage v. Tawyer* (1599), 5 Coke Rep. 45, 77 E.R. 124, also Moore K.B. 571, 72 E.R. 765, Noy 171, 74 E.R. 1130, Jenkins 258, 145 E.R. 184; *Bishop v. Harecourt* (1592), 5 Coke Rep. 37, 77 E.R. 110, also Cro. Eliz. 210, 78 E.R. 466, 1 Anderson 240, 123 E.R. 451, 1 Leonard 210, 74 E.R. 194; *Young v. Bishop of Rochester* (1616), 3 Bulstrode 224, 81 E.R. 189, 1 Rolle Rep. 432, 81 E.R. 588.

prayer of the party, awarded [a writ of] *certiorari*, and, upon this return, reversed the judgment.

But, in the principal case, in the roll which was refused to be received, it was after *in nullo erratum* joined [was] entered and *super hoc* the plaintiff *venit* and assigned new error and, upon this, he prayed for a *certiorari*, which the court here held that they could award a *certiorari ex officio*, as well to reverse as to affirm the judgment. But [they] agreed that, after *in nullo erratum* joined, the plaintiff cannot pray for the *certiorari*.

And for this, Justice JONES observed divers cases in which the judgment was reversed upon the *certiorari* but yet it was not entered as required by the plaintiff, but as awarded by the court for their information, as *Novel Entries*, 254 D [*blank*], there, the entry [was] *et quia videtur curiae expeditionis* etc.; Jo. granted *certiorari*; thus *ibidem* 242, the Marquess of Winchester's case;[1] and *ibidem* 266. And on account of this, the record here of Bishop's case does not warrant, but falsifies, the report that the *certificare* was after *in nullo erratum*, where [it was] upon *nient dedire*, and which was at the prayer of the plaintiff where it does not thus appear to the court by the record.

And Chief Justice CREWE said that, after [a writ of] *scire facias ad audiendum errores*, the plaintiff cannot allege a diminution, nor the defendant, after a joinder in error.

And Justice JONES said that he thought before the consideration of the precedents that the *certiorari ex officio* could not have been [issued] except to affirm the judgment.

And DODDERIDGE said that thus is the law without question.

And here, there was awarded in the principal case a *certiorari ex officio curiae* and the return of that which [was] not in the prayer of the plaintiff [was] refused. And the new *certiorari* was returned also this term. And the judgment [was] reversed.

[Other reports of this case: W. Jones 139, 82 E.R. 75; Latch 152, 82 E.R. 321; Noy 83, 74 E.R. 1050; BL MS. Hargr. 38, f. 116; CUL MS. Hh.2.1, f. 215.]

---

[1] *Bishop of Winchester v. Norreis* (1576), E. Coke, *A Booke of Entries* (1614), 'Error', pl. 5, ff. 240, 242, also *sub nom. Regina v. Marquess of Winchester*, 3 Coke Rep. 1, 76 E.R. 621, Moore K.B. 125, 72 E.R. 483, 1 Leonard 270, 74 E.R. 246.

151

Shury v. Pigot

(Part 2)

(K.B. Mich. 2 Car. I, 1626)

BL MS. Add. 35961, f. 39, pl. 21

The case between Shury and Pigot was now moved again (which see before, f. 17a, pl. 25, *et intratur* Hil. 1 *Caroli*, rot. 124).[1] And it was argued for the plaintiff that the watercourse, for the unity of possession of the place *a quo* and of the place *ad quem* the land upon which the watercourse [is], is not extinct, [i.e.] the watercourse. And the case of a common, Teringham's case, C. 4, and 14 Hen. IV, *recordare longum*; and 21 Edw. III, 2, of a way; and 35 Hen. VI, 55, of a warren; and Dyer 326, 295; and 11 Hen. VII, 25, [were] cited.[2] And a difference [was] taken between profits *a prendre*, which always is by unity [?], and things which had an existence notwithstanding the unity [?], as a warren etc. And some exceptions [were] taken to the pleadings, which the court did not regard.

And on the other side, it was argued that it will be extinct. And he resembled it to the case of a way. And he put the said cases upon it. And he took exceptions to the declaration, which were not regarded.

But DODDERIDGE said that there was a great difference between a watercourse and a way because the one is of necessity and the other not. And he said that his opinion was that it was not extinct.

And thus, at this time, it seemed to the court.

Et adjornatur. See Davis 5b.[3]

---

[1] For other proceedings in this case, see Nos. 69, 174.

[2] *Phesant v. Salmon* (1584), 4 Coke Rep. 36, 76 E.R. 973; YB Mich. 14 Hen. IV, f. 2, pl. 6 (1412); YB Hil. 21 Edw. III, f. 2, pl. 5 (1347); *Peche's Case* (1457), YB Pas. 35 Hen. VI, f. 55, pl. 1; *Anonymous* (1573), 3 Dyer 326, 73 E.R. 738; *Anonymous* (1570), 3 Dyer 295, 73 E.R. 663; *Copie's Case* (1496), YB Trin. 11 Hen. VII, f. 25, pl. 6.

[3] *Rex v. Forth* (1604), Davis 1, 5, 80 E.R. 491, 495.

152

Markham v. Cobb

(Part 2)

(K.B. Mich. 2 Car. I, 1626)

BL MS. Add. 35961, f. 39, pl. 22

The case before, fo. 15, pl. 10, of Markham and Cob, *quod intratur* Pas. 1 [Car. I], rot. 112 [or 92],[1] was now argued again by *Bankes* for the plaintiff. And he took exceptions to the bar of the defendant inasmuch as he showed that the plaintiff procured [him] to be indicted and he did not say that he procured; thus, he has not pleaded that the plaintiff procured the defendant to be indicted.

The second exception [was] that he did not plead that the plaintiff gave in evidence against him or procured another to do it because the Statute of 21 Hen. VIII[2] does not give restitution unless he be convicted upon evidence given by the party or by his procurement; thus, he has not shown that the plaintiff here could have restitution upon this Statute.

The third exception [was that], without an averment that the taking, for which he was indicted, and this taking, for which the [action of] trespass [was] brought, are the same taking, there is not color to bar the plaintiff by the indictment. But here, the averment is faulty because he has averred that the offence, for which he was indicted, and the offense, for which [the action of] trespass was brought, are the same offense, which is impossible, [i.e.] that burglary can be a trespass for the matter in law. He argued how the plaintiff could have restitution upon the Statute of 21 Hen. VIII, yet he could waive it and take the benefit that the [common] law gives to him, *viz.* by [an action of] trespass, because one is not bound to take the benefit of a statute, as 3 Edw. IV, 12, and Dyer 304;[3] an alien can waive the trial *per medietatem* given by the Statute.[4] Thus, if upon the Statute of Bankrupts,[5] one can choose to come in and to be satisfied of his debt by this way. And at common law, he was not barred of his action by the indictment. Thus, the Statute here does not take away the common law, as C. 207;[6] the Statute[7] that gives that actions can be brought in Wales does not take away the jurisdiction of another court. And at common law, if he was indicted and

---

[1] For other proceedings in this case, see Nos. 102, 185.

[2] Stat. 21 Hen. VIII, c. 11 (*SR*, III, 291).

[3] *Gray's Case* (1463), YB Mich. 3 Edw. IV, f. 11, pl. 3; *Anonymous* (1571), 3 Dyer 304, 73 E.R. 683, also Jenkins 239, 145 E.R. 167.

[4] Stat. 27 Edw. III, stat. 2, c. 8 (*SR*, I, 336); Stat. 28 Edw. III, c. 13 (*SR*, I, 348); Stat. 8 Hen. VI, c. 29 (*SR*, II, 261–262).

[5] Stat. 1 Jac. I, c. 15 (*SR*, IV, 1031–1034).

[6] *Stradling v. Morgan* (1560), 1 Plowden 199, 207, 75 E.R. 305, 317.

[7] Stat. 34 & 35 Hen. VIII, c. 26 (*SR*, III, 926–937).

attainted and afterwards pardoned so that, at one time, by the attainder, the action was suspended, yet, by the pardon, it was revived. See 6 Edw. IV, 4, and Dy. 124 agreeing.[1]

Calthorpe, contra: To the first exception, [he said], upon all [of the matter] of the bar, it appears to the court that he was the person indicted.

To the second, the plaintiff did not give evidence nor procure it. The defendant has pleaded that, by his procurement, he was indicted and convicted, which conviction will be intended by a verdict. And thus, it does not necessarily follow that the evidence [was] by his procurement also.

To the third, burglary includes trespass. And on account of this, the same offense can be both a trespass and a burglary.

For the matter in law, he took a diversity. And he said that, before an indictment and before it appears to the court to be a felony, one can bring [an action of] trespass for a felony done, but not afterwards, because the felony drowns the tort. And for this [is] Dy. 50;[2] where murder was made treason by Parliament,[3] now, [on account] of this, an appeal of murder does not lie because it is drowned in the major [offense]. Thus [is] Dy. 235;[4] where a petit treason [was] pardoned, this pardoned the murder. Thus [in] 3 Hen. VII, 10,[5] an accessory to him who counterfeited money could not be indicted as an accessory to the felony which was merged into the treason. 11 Hen. VII, 22;[6] an indictment of rape in a leet [court] as a trespass [is] void because it is more than a trespass and this name[7] merges it into the felony.

The second reason [was] he could elect to have [an action of] trespass [rather than] to indict and to have, thus, restitution. And, here, by his indictment, he has made his election that he will not go to the other course now.

Third, it was not ever known that one [could] bring such an action or that this way was reasonable [for] these goods. And he took a difference where, after a pardon of felony, a stranger is restored to his action, as 7 Hen. IV; 9 Hen. IV; and 11 Hen. IV are.[8] But he said that, by the same offense, there was not any way that a party, after an attainder, [can] bring [an action of] trespass.

Et adjornatur. See more, f. 43, pl. 54.[9]

---

[1] YB Mich. 6 Edw. IV, f. 4, pl. 11 (1466); *Carewe's Case* (1555), 2 Dyer 124, 73 E.R. 271.

[2] *Rex v. Saccombe* (1541), 1 Dyer 50, 73 E.R. 110.

[3] Stat. 22 Hen. VIII, c. 9 (*SR*, III, 326).

[4] *Anonymous* (1564), 2 Dyer 235, 73 E.R. 519.

[5] YB Trin. 3 Hen. VII, f. 10, pl. 2 (1488).

[6] YB Pas. 11 Hen. VII, f. 22, pl. 11 (1496).

[7] I.e. rape.

[8] Perhaps YB Pas. 7 Hen. IV, f. 39, pl. 4 (1406); YB Mich. 9 Hen. IV, f. 7, pl. 21 (1407); YB Trin. 11 Hen. IV, f. 94, pl. 57 (1410).

[9] For other proceedings in this case, see Nos. 102, 185.

153

Keymor v. Hallet

(Part 1)

(K.B. Mich. 2 Car. I, 1626)

In this case, the words spoken were held to be defamatory and actionable.

BL MS. Add. 35961, f. 39v, pl. 22

Keymor brought an action upon the case against Hollett. And he alleged that the defendant spoke of him these words: 'Mr. Keymor is a base fellow and has had four or five children by Agnes, his maid, and has murdered them or caused them to be murdered', *ubi re vera*, he was *nunquam* incontinent.

And it was moved in arrest of judgment by *Philip Jermyn* that the words are not actionable. First to say that he had children by his maid is not slander because he could have married her and then had children by her. Second, for the other words, that he had murdered etc., he had [*blank*] the plaintiff, of his own showing, showed this to be impossible because he has averred that he was *nunquam* incontinent and thus, if he did not have children by Agnes, he could not murder them who were not, as in Snagg's case, 4, 16,[1] the plaintiff alleged that the defendant had a wife and, here, [if] and the defendant said that the plaintiff had killed his wife, here, of his showing, it appeared to be no slander.

Residuum, pl. 34.[2]

154

Vigors v. Wood

(K.B. Mich. 2 Car. I, 1626)

The issue in this case was whether an incomplete pleading of nonage was cured by the judgment according to the Statute of Jeofails.

BL MS. Add. 35961, f. 39v, pl. 23

Between Vigors and Wood, in an action upon the case against an executor *durante minore aetate*, *Noy*, moved in arrest of judgment, against the plaintiff, because he had not declared nor averred the nonage of the infant.

Justice JONES: It is aided by the Statute.[3]

Noy: By the Statute, an averment of lives is aided, but not the averment of nonage.

---

[1] *Snag v. Gee* (1597), 4 Coke Rep. 16, 76 E.R. 896.

[2] For later proceedings in this case, see below, No. 165.

[3] Stat. 18 Eliz. I, c. 14 (*SR*, IV, 625).

The other exception he took [was] because he declared that he had assets *tempore impetrationis huius billae* and he did not show when the *impetrationis* was. And he cited Sir Anthony Ashley's case, which he said was adjudged lately, where, in [an action of] trespass, the plaintiff alleged a *continuando usque impetratione huius billae* and he did not say *scilicet* such a day nor show when the bill [was] purchased, and the jury there found for the plaintiff and assessed damages, and, because it did not appear of record for what time the damages [were] assessed, the judgment [was] arrested.

155

Lewis v. Whitney

(K.B. Mich. 2 Car. I, 1626)

A pardon does not apply to a conviction in an ecclesiastical court in a private prosecution. However, if a pardon comes after a conviction and before court costs are taxed, it is not clear whether the court costs are pardoned.

BL MS. Add. 35961, f. 39v, pl. 24

Between Lewis and Whitney in a suit in the spiritual court, the case was [thus]. The plaintiff there sued the other for these words: 'Lewis is a pander but W. his pander'[1] etc., and he recovered. And a sentence [was] given for costs, but they were not taxed. The defendant appealed, and, pending the appeal, there came the Pardon of 21 Jac.[2] Then, the defendant deserted his appeal. And upon this, £5 costs [were] given against him, and the cause [was] remitted to serve[3] the sentence. And for the £5 costs upon the abandoning of the appeal, the plaintiff sued. And the other prayed for [a writ of] prohibition because, now, the Pardon had pardoned the offense, and, on account of this, he could not have costs upon the principal. And he said that thus it was ruled in Deverell and Adams' case and also upon the body of the matter because the spiritual court cannot find a plea of these words because [they were] words of anger. And as the common law would not find a plea of it, yet it will not allow the spiritual court to. And he cited Cadorg [?] and Thomas' case, Mich. 6 Jac., where [a writ of] prohibition [was] granted upon a suit in a spiritual court for calling [one a] whore's son and here though a pander is known, the meaning of it, yet the law does not take notice of the signification of it, as of a bawd, which is presentable in leet [courts]. And he said that the origin of the word was Pandarus of Troy, of whom Chaucer spoke.[4]

---

[1] Sic in MS.

[2] Stat. 21 Jac. I, c. 35 (*SR*, IV, 1269–1275).

[3] estre *MS*.

[4] G. Chaucer, *Troilus and Criseyde*.

And on the other side, it was said by *Richardson* that it was ruled in Porter and Spowle's case, two terms past, that, for the costs for the deserting of the appeal, the court could proceed. And thus, he said that in the records of the time of Henry VI, 'knave' is a good addition.

But the court here thought contrary to Serjeant Richardson because, when the pardon came, he was in the process of prosecuting[1] the appeal and thus, on account of this, he will not be punished.

And here, it was said by DODDERIDGE and JONES that actions in spiritual courts are civil or criminal, civil as a suit for legacies, tithes, etc. and these are solely for the interest of the plaintiff, and, on account of this, there, if a pardon comes, either before or after costs [are] taxed, it does not matter nor wipe them away. Criminal suits are twofold: *ad instanciam* or *ex officio*. If it be *ex officio*, if a pardon comes before or after the judgment, all is pardoned because it is solely for the interest of the king. If it be *ad instanciam*, there, if it does not come before the sentence, the interest of the party is not pardoned.

And here, JONES said that he doubted, though it was admitted by Richardson against himself, whether the pardon, coming after the sentence and before costs [are] taxed, wipes them away. And here, Justice JONES said it was adjudged in the [court of] common bench in Calthrop's case that the spiritual court cannot punish one for calling another a drunkard, and the question was taken that one cannot sue another for such a slander in the spiritual court, as the spiritual [court] cannot punish nor hold a plea of the principal. And there, it was held that the spiritual court cannot punish drunkenness because, though it be a spiritual offense and against the Decalogue, yet they cannot punish all spiritual offenses.

[Other reports of this case: Benloe 186, 73 E.R. 1044, CUL MS. Gg.2.30, f. 69; Latch 155, 82 E.R. 322, HLS MS. 1235, f. 70; Noy 85, 74 E.R. 1051; BL MS. Hargr. 38, f. 119v; BL MS. Lansd. 1092, f. 133; CUL MS. Hh.2.1, f. 216v; CUL MS. Ll.3.13, f. 165v.]

156

Hall v. Dow

(K.B. Mich. 2 Car. I, 1626)

A lessor who sues for the rent due need not allege the date of the enrollment of the sale of the reversion to a third party.

Where a lessor, during the term of a lease, sells the reversion to a third party, the lessor will have the rent incurred before the enrollment of the deed of sale of the reversion.

---

[1] en veigne de prosecute *MS.*

BL MS. Add. 35961, f. 40, pl. 25

Between Hall and Dew, *quod intratur* Trin. 2 Car., rot. 1420, the plaintiff brought [an action of] debt. And he declared that J.S. was seised in fee of tenements etc. and he leased them to the defendant the 25th of March *anno habendum ab inde pro termino unius anni* rendering *pro anno* such a sum *ad festum Michaelis et Annunciationis* by equal portions, by which he was possessed, the reversion to J.S., and that after the first of November, upon a bargain, he sold[1] the reversion to the plaintiff by a deed enrolled within six months. And for the rent due for the last half year, he brought [an action of] debt. And upon [a plea of] *nihil debet*, [it was] found for the plaintiff.

And it was moved in arrest of judgment, first, that there was not any rent to be paid after the Michaelmas [29 September] payment and thus *nihil* [was] due to the plaintiff by his [own] showing because he showed that the lease was made upon the day of the Annunciation [25 March] to commence *ab inde* for one year rendering etc. to Michaelmas and the Annunciation *per equales portiones*. Now, the first payment will be made upon the day of the lease because, otherwise, he could not pay it at Michaelmas and the Annunciation during the term because the term will be ended the next year upon Lady [Day] Eve [24 March]. And even though Michaelmas be named first, yet the law will order it as it should be. And thus it is in Hill and Grange's case in C.,[2] where a lease was made in August rendering rent at the Annunciation and Michaelmas by equal portions; there, the first payment will be at Michaelmas, though [it was] named last.

The second exception [was] because he will not have entitled himself to the rent because he has shown a grant of a reversion by a deed enrolled the first of November, enrolled within six months, and it could be yet enrolled after the Annunciation, in which case nothing is due to the bargainee, but the bargainor will have the rent.

To the first [exception], JONES said, as the plaintiff pleaded that the lease was made upon the 25th of March *pro uno anno ab inde*, the lease will end upon the next 25th day of March, and thus the rent will be paid and *ab inde* will be taken *a confectione* and exclusive of the day 25. And, if it was made at noon, the term will end next year at noon.

But DODDERIDGE said that there will not be a fraction of a day, but, if it be made at noon of the 25th day, it will end the night of the next 25th day because the lease was *pro uno anno* and, on account of this, it will not end the night before, and, thus, the lessee will lose the half day. There will not be a fraction of the day. And thus, he will hold for a half day after his lease ends.

---

[1] the first of November J.S. bargained and sold: BL MS. Lansd. 1083, f. 52.

[2] *Hill v. Grange* (1556), 1 Plowden 164, 75 E.R. 253, also 2 Dyer 130, 73 E.R. 284.

To the second exception, DODDERIDGE and JONES held, first, that there is no need to allege the day of the enrollment, but, if it be material, it will come in from the other party, as Hynde's case, C. 4.[1]

Second, they said that, if the bargainee will not have the rent incurred before the enrollment, it will make a foul stir because the law has taken [it to be] thus. And he said it was that thus it was adjudged upon solemn argument in 5 Jac. in Alsop's case.[2]

[Other reports of this case: Benloe 187, 73 E.R. 1045, CUL MS. 2.30, f. 69v; Latch 157, 82 E.R. 323, HLS MS. 1235, f. 71; BL MS. Hargr. 38, f. 210; CUL MS. Hh.2.1, f. 218; CUL MS. Ll.3.13, f. 168.]

157

Henderson v. Codner

(K.B. Mich. 2 Car. I, 1626)

Pending an appeal, a bail can render the principal debtor in executione manucapto-rum *but not* in executione judicii.

BL MS. Add. 35961, f. 40, pl. 26

In the opening of the record of Hinderson and Codner's case[3] by *Noy*, it was said to him by JONES and DODDERIDGE that it was agreed by them in the case before, of Calfe and Bingley,[4] that pending a writ of error, the bail can render the principal [debtor] *in executione manucaptorum* but not *in executione judicii*. And on account of this, it was said that he could spare his labor in this point.

158

Ratcliffe v. Buck

(Part 1)
(K.B. Mich. 2 Car. I, 1626)

A plea in abatement that the plaintiff does not have standing to sue cannot be made af-ter an imparlance.

---

[1] *Libb v. Hynde* (1591), 4 Coke Rep. 68, 76 E.R. 1037, also 1 Anderson 285, 123 E.R. 475.

[2] *Bellingham v. Alsop* (1604), Cro. Jac. 52, 79 E.R. 44.

[3] Note *Cadner v. Anderson* (Hil. 20 Jac. 1 [1623]), cited in Latch 149, 82 E.R. 319.

[4] *Calfe v. Bingley* (K.B. 1626), above, No. 149.

Following an unsuccessful plea of the plaintiff's disability, it depends upon the conclusion of the plea as to whether the defendant can answer over or whether the plaintiff will be given a judgment.

BL MS. Add. 35961, f. 40, pl. 27

In an action brought by Ratcliffe against Bincke, *intratur* Trin. 2 [Car. I], rot. 894, the defendant pleaded after an imparlance that the plaintiff was a recusant convict and he demanded judgment upon the action.

And by the conclusion of the plea, which was solely in disability of the person, as excommunication, by the statutes and also because, after an imparlance, a plea to the person is not pleadable, *Bankes* demurred. And he had judgment. See afterwards, f. 49, p. 3.[1]

159

Wingfield v. Leith

(K.B. Mich. 2 Car. I, 1626)

When a person is sued by a bill of Middlesex in the court of king's bench, the omission of an addition in the defendant's name is not a material error.

BL MS. Add. 35961, f. 40, pl. 28

Wingfield brought [an action of] debt against Leithe in the [court of] king's bench. And it was moved by *Hitcham* in arrest of judgment after a verdict that, here, there was no addition to the defendant's [name].

But it was ruled [to be] no exception because the declaration is against him *in custodia marescalli*, thus no proceed[ing]. Outlawry does not lie here as if it were by a writ. And on account of this, it is not within the Statute of Hen. V, for additions.[2]

And though *Hitcham* said that *in custodia marescalli* was a fiction, DODDE-RIDGE said that this fiction upholds their court because, without it, they cannot hold pleas but in [actions of] trespass *vi et armis* and in appeals of pleas between party and party.

[Other reports of this case: Benloe 188, 73 E.R. 1046, CUL MS. Gg.2.30, 69v; BL MS. Hargr. 38, f. 120.]

---

[1] For later proceedings in this case, see below, Nos. 229, 235.

[2] Stat. 1 Hen. V, c. 5 (*SR*, II, 171).

160

Rex v. Lamb

(Part 1)
(K.B. Mich. 2 Car. I, 1626)

In this case, a defective indictment for witchcraft was quashed.

BL MS. Add. 35961, f. 40, pl. 29

In Lambe's indictment for witchcraft, *Athow* took these exceptions:

First, because it was presented that he exercised *quasdam malas et diabolicas artes, Anglice* witchcraft. Here, he said that the *Anglice* could make the precedent words signify otherwise than in fact they signify and thus he is not indicted of witchcraft.

But to this, the chief justice [CREWE] said that it is the common form of all indictments of witchcraft and, if it be bad, they are all bad.

Second, he excepted because [it is said] such a day he exercised etc. by force of which *diversis diebus postea et antea languebat*, which is impossible that, by force of an act done, he languished before it [was] done.

Third, it is said *die et anno supradictis*, and, before, there were two days and years mentioned. Thus the relation [is] uncertain.

Fourth, it is said that *supradicto die 15 Decembris annis supradictis*. Now, a day cannot be in two years, one and the same day.

Fifth, because it is not shown in what part of the body the lord of Windsor was debilitated by the bewitching of which he was indicted, where the Statute[1] says 'if it be at death or weakenings of the body or any part of it'. And it is not said that he had debilitated his body nor any particular part.

But the court gave a day to the king's attorney to consider of the indictment.

And now, the court examined how Lamb came to the copy of the indictment because it is not grantable without a special warrant of the court.

And here, it was said by JONES and CREWE that the Statute has two branches and, by the first branch, the very familiarity with a wicked spirit is a felony without any consequence of it.

See more, pl. 61.[2]

---

[1] Stat. 1 Jac. I, c. 12 (*SR*, IV, 1028–1029).

[2] For later proceedings in this case, see below, No. 192.

161

Chapman v. Chapman

(K.B. Mich. 2 Car. I, 1626)

In this case, the lessee had contracted to pay the rent due, and, therefore, no demand for its payment was required.

BL MS. Add. 35961, f. 40v, pl. 30

[In a case] between Chapman and Chapman, in [an action of] debt, *quod intratur* Trin. 20 [Jac. I], rot. 483, the defendant demanded oyer of the condition of the obligation, which was to perform all of the covenants in certain indentures, by which the defendant was the lessee of the plaintiff. And there, he covenanted to pay the rent; *quibus auditis*, he pleaded performance of the covenants.

The plaintiff assigned a breach inasmuch as he had not paid the rent, upon which the defendant demurred.

The cause of the demurrer was shown by *Bankes*, because he has not alleged in the replication that he demanded the rent. And for this, he cited 14 Edw. IV, 4; 20 Edw. IV, 18; 21 Edw. IV, 22; pB 428; and 22 Hen. VI, 57,[1] where this difference appears, that, if a lessee for years be rendering rent and he covenants to pay the rent and then binds himself to perform all of the covenants, there, if the rent not be demanded, the obligation is not forfeited. But, if he binds himself to pay the rent, there is no need of a demand.

But, *inspecto recordo*, the condition of the obligation was 'If the obligee shall pay, observe, and keep the rents, covenants, and agreements' etc., so that the obligation was to pay the rent etc., by which by his own argument, he had not cause to demand, for which, a day [was] given to show a better cause for the demurrer or judgment will be given.

See C. 7, 28, Maunde's case.[2] See after, f. 92, pl. 5.[3]

[Affirmed on appeal: Cro. Car. 76, 79 E.R. 667; Hutton 90, 123 E.R. 1122; BL MS. Hargr. 38, f. 121.]

---

[1] YB Pas. 14 Edw. IV, f. 4, pl. 3 (1474); YB Hil. 20 Edw. IV, f. 18, pl. 7 (1481); YB Mich. 21 Edw. IV, ff. [38], 42, pl. 4 (1481); YB Trin. 22 Hen. VI, f. 57, pl. 7 (1444).

[2] *Maund v. Gregory* (1601), 7 Coke Rep. 28, 77 E.R. 454.

[3] *Powlson v. Warren* (1627), BL MS. Add. 35961, f. 98v, pl. 5.

162

Jegon v. Purkas

(K.B. Mich. 2 Car. I, 1626)

An obligation payable on an impossible date or on no specified date is payable immediately.

BL MS. Add. 35961, f. 40v, pl. 31

Between Jegon and Purkas in [an action of] debt upon an obligation upon a condition to pay £200 upon the 32nd of September, the defendant pleaded *solvit ad diem*. And upon this, [they were] at issue. And [it was] found for the plaintiff. And it was moved in arrest of judgment that, here, there was no issue joined because there was not anything doubtful, but [it was] impossible that it would be found otherwise than it was because it is impossible to pay upon the 31st of September because there is not such a day in September. Thus, the issue [was] joined upon a thing [that was] not doubtful. And whether an obligation be made payable at an impossible day or *sine die* is payable presently, [see] 21 Edw. IV, 36.[1] And it was said it is not similar to Nicolls' case, C. 5,[2] because, there, there was an issue, but not a legal issue.

But it was ruled here to be good notwithstanding the exception because the issue was *solvit ad diem*. And now, if there was not a day, it was payable presently and thus [on the] day in law. And on account of this, whether *solvit* at the day that he should pay was the issue.

And afterwards, at another day, *Finch*, the recorder, moved this again.

JONES: All that you said was said before and overruled, and you do not speak more unless it be that it be out of a better mouth.

And afterwards, *Noy* moved [that] it [was] yet adjudged.

[Other reports of this case: W. Jones 140, 82 E.R. 75, BL MS. Hargr. 317, f. 143; Latch 158, 82 E.R. 324; Noy 85, 74 E.R. 1052; BL MS. Hargr. 38, f. 121v; CUL MS. Hh.2.1, f. 218.]

[Affirmed on appeal: Cro. Car. 78, 79 E.R. 669.]

---

[1] YB Pas. 21 Edw. IV, f. 36, pl. 30 (1481).

[2] *Chamberlain v. Nichols* (1595), 5 Coke Rep. 43, 77 E.R. 121, also Moore K.B. 692, 72 E.R. 844, Cro. Eliz. 455, 78 E.R. 694, Jenkins 257, 145 E.R. 183.

163

Hamond v. White

(Part 2)

(K.B. Mich. 2 Car. I, 1626)

BL MS. Add. 35961, f. 40v, pl. 32

The case before, 29, p. 9,[1] was moved again. And now, [it was] ruled by the court that the action upon the case by a tenant in common was not good. And they took the difference where the tort was equally wrong to both; there they must join. But, if the wrong be particular, as the chasing of the cattle of one [of them], there, he will have the action solely. And they cited the case of 1 Hen. V,[2] where one tenant in common brought an action for removing the boundary against a stranger, and it was not allowed, and 47 Edw. III,[3] where [there was an action of] trespass for hurting a dovecote and a warren by a tenant in common.

[Other reports of this case: W. Jones 142, 82 E.R. 76; Latch 152, 82 E.R. 321; Noy 84, 74 E.R. 1050; BL MS. Hargr. 38, f. 122; CUL MS. Hh.2.1, f. 215v.]

164

Barker v. Beckham

(K.B. Mich. 2 Car. I, 1626)

In this case, consideration for a promise not to sue was sufficiently pleaded.

BL MS. Add. 35961, f. 40v, pl. 33

Barker brought an action of case against Beckham. And he declared that, where divers combes of barley, divers capons, and divers sums of money were unpaid to him by the defendant, the defendant, in consideration that the plaintiff forbore himself to sue at common law, promised to pay to him so much as S.K. set down in writing to be owed according to the account of arrearages for fifteen years and that S.K. had set down that 3s. *per annum* was due. And thus, for so much, being the sum accordingly of 38s. for twenty-five years not paid, he brought [an action of] *assumpsit*. And [the jury] found for him.

And it was moved in arrest of judgment:

First, that there was not consideration here for the promise because, first, he has not shown that any rent was due to him, but he said only that so much was unpaid and thus it could be still not due and also it could be unpaid to him as a

---

[1] For earlier proceedings in this case, see above, No. 139.

[2] YB Hil. 1 Hen. V, f. 1, pl. 1 (1414).

[3] YB Mich. 47 Edw. III, f. 22, pl. 54 (1373).

receiver of the king or a common person, and thus the promise to him in consideration of the forbearance created no [cause of] action.

Second, because he has alleged that he intended to sue him and in consideration etc., and, upon the intent, an action is not foundable. 17 Edw. IV, 3, by Choke.[1] Also he has not said for what time he would forbear, but indefinitely that he forbore, and thus he could sue him in an hour afterwards. Also, he could forbear to sue him and still he could distrain. And on account of this, the consideration [is] not valuable.

But this exception was not now moved because, the other day when it was first moved for this, no answer [was] given to this second exception because the promise was to pay so much as S.K. set down to be due for fifteen years and he had not set down but what was due for one year. But these exceptions were not allowed because, first, it will be intended to be due to the plaintiff and it is a foreign intendment that he will be a bailiff or receiver.

Second, it has been divers times ruled that, upon an *intendisset implacitare*, it is well satisfied.

Third, that the promise generally to forbear will be taken [to be] during his life. And thus it was ruled, as JONES said, four hours since, and if, he sues him during his lifetime, he will have an action upon the case.

For the last exception, the record [makes] it clear because it appears by it that both parties were agreed the arrearages of fifteen years to be the arrears but that the rent *per annum* [. . .] was the was the matter referred to S.K.

Thus judgment [was] given for the plaintiff.

165

Keymor v. Hallet

(Part 2)
(K.B. Mich. 2 Car. I, 1626)

BL MS Add. 35961, f. 40v, pl. 34

The case of Keymor and Hally, before, f. 38b, pl. 22,[2] was ruled now.

Lecto recordo, it appeared for the first exception that Agnes, at the time of the words, was the wife of one J.S. Thus, it could not be intended that she will have lawful issue by him.[3]

And for the second, the court did not think [there was] any contrariety between the count and the words. But peradventure, if he had said that he did not have any children by her in truth, JONES doubted that it had been contradictory.

---

[1] *Browne v. Hawkins* (1477), YB Trin. 17 Edw. IV, f. 3, pl. 2.

[2] For earlier proceedings in this case, see above, No. 153.

[3] I.e. the plaintiff.

And, for the words 'has killed' *ex causa dicendi et antecedentibus* that the words were intended *in malam partem*, thus it is not to be intended a lawful killing or an accidental killing, as *per infortunium*.

And thus judgment [was] given for the plaintiff.

[Other reports of this case: W. Jones 141, 82 E.R. 75, BL MS. Hargr. 317, f. 144; Latch 159, 82 E.R. 324; Popham 187, 79 E.R. 1281; BL MS. Hargr. 38, f. 122v; CUL MS. Hh.2.1, f. 218v.]

166

Palmer v. Litherland

(Part 1)
(K.B. Mich. 2 Car. I, 1626)

An administrator of a decedent's estate who commits waste and then renounces the administration is liable for the waste.

BL MS. Add. 35961, f. 41, pl. 35

Between Palmer and Litherland, *quod intratur* Trin. 2 [Car. I], rot. 1416, [an action of] debt was brought against one as administrator. He pleaded that, before the writ [was] brought, he renounced the administration and the ordinary received it. The plaintiff replied that, before the renunciation, he had administered and that the renunciation was by fraud. The defendant rejoined by protestation that [it was] without fraud for the plea, as before, that he had renounced etc., upon which, he demurred.

And it was now agreed by the court that the administrator can here renounce and the ordinary can accept it after administration, but he is not bound to accept it and also to show he should not accept it, and also that, if the ordinary commits a new administration, that it ends the first, but the first could not be charged by it as executor *de son tort* with the administration [that] was lawful, nor as administrator because it is ended. And thus, it was argued among the court, if an administrator releases and then refuses, what [is the] remedy for the creditor[1] of the intestate.

And Justice JONES said that, before his coming from the [court of] common pleas, there was this case of an administrator *durante minore aetate* [who] wasted and the executor came of full age and it was doubted that [he had a] remedy here. And some said that he was chargeable as for his [own] tort, but some [said] that he will be charged upon the special matter.

Thus, at last here, it was upon the moment[2] agreed that he could not be charged in a case of waste of the goods but upon the special matter which will be

---

[1] dettee *MS.*
[2] sur sodayne *MS.*

otherwise a mischievous case, otherwise none will ever have an action against an administration but that he refuses, having wasted. And [. . .] the next etc. See Packman's case, C. 6.[1]

More, pl. 75.[2]

167

Arnold v. Dichton

(Part 2)
(K.B. Mich. 2 Car. I, 1626)

BL MS. Add. 35961, f. 41, pl. 36

In the case of Alnut and Ritken, before at f. 37a, p. 15,[3] the exception was allowed and the judgment [was] arrested by DODDERIDGE and JONES, WHITE-LOCKE *contra*, because the promise extended to the future time, that he will give afterwards, and not that he had now given, and, even though it could be that he will give nothing to the other children, yet it is good, [as said] by DODDERIDGE and JONES.

After, 34, p. 22.[4]

168

Coles v. Shury

(Part 2)
(K.B. Mich. 2 Car. I, 1626)

BL MS. Add. 35961, f. 41, pl. 37

Coles brought [an action of] replevin against Shury (*quod intratur* Pas. 22 Jac., rot. 62, of which, see before, fo. 9, pl. 10, f. 17, pl. 24)[5]. The defendant avowed because, a long time before, one was seised in fee and gave to Edmund Shury and the heirs male of his body the remainder over, the remainder to the right heirs of Edward. And the tenant in tail made a lease for years reserving a rent yearly during the term to the lessor and his assigns of £7, both at Lady [Day] and Michaelmas by equal portions, and that, afterwards, the tenant in tail levied

[1] *Wilson v. Packman* (1595), 6 Coke Rep. 18, 77 E.R. 281, also Moore K.B. 396, 72 E.R. 651, Cro. Eliz. 459, 78 E.R. 698.

[2] For later proceedings in this case, see below, No. 206.

[3] For other proceedings in this case, see Nos. 145, 249.

[4] For other proceedings in this case, see Nos. 145, 249.

[5] For earlier proceedings in this case, see above, No. 68; see also *Shury v. Brown* (1626), above, No. 30.

a fine to Yateman, but he did not say to what use, and that, afterwards, Yateman suffered a recovery, in which the tenant in tail was vouched and it was to the use of Yateman in fee, who granted to the avowant, who, for rent [in] arrears, avowed, and he did not aver the life of Shury, the first lessor.

And upon this, he demurred. And whether the rent in this case will have a continuance after the death of the first lessor was the question which now and before [. . .] was argued.

And for the plaintiff, it was argued that, by the death, the rent is gone and, consequently, the non-averring of the life in this case is fatal. Dy. 15;[1] it is said that it is a rule that conditions and agreements are private laws between the parties and, on account of this, similar to a private act of Parliament between them and, on account of this, if, by their agreement, they have not sufficiently provided for themselves, the law would not help them. And to each reservation, there are five things to be considered: (1) the thing reserved; (2) the place of payment; (3) the continuance of the payment; (4) the persons to whom; (5) the terms of the payment. And for all of these, the law provides, unless there be a provision made by the party, and, if he provides and does not follow the law, with this, the law would not extend his reservation beyond his words. And for this [is] 21 Hen. VII, 25;[2] if a rent be generally reserved, it will go with the reversioner, and, if no time of payment be limited, it will go payable at the end of the year. And [in] C. 8, 71, in Whitlock's case,[3] it is said that the better reservation is general and, for the lessor, it [has] the operation of law. Thus, [if] one leases two manors rendering rent, the law reserves it out of both, but the party, by his particular reservation, can make a separate reservation. And with this agrees Dy. 308; C. 5, 55.[4]

For the person of the lessor, if he leases it, at law, it will be with the reversion. 14 Hen. VI, 26.[5] But yet he cannot reserve contrary to the law, as it will be in our case. And on account of this, if a gift be in tail *tenendum de capitalibus dominis*, this is a void *tenendum*. 2 Edw. IV, 5.[6] Thus [is] 17 Edw. III, 69;[7] a gift by a husband *tenendum* of him and the wife [is] void as to the wife. Thus, he could reserve it to other persons than the law limits, but not to the contrary and out of depravity.

---

[1] *Bold v. Molineux* (1536), 1 Dyer 14, 15, 73 E.R. 31, 33, also Benloe 13, 123 E.R. 10, 1 Anderson 1, 123 E.R. 320.

[2] YB Trin. 21 Hen. VII, f. 25, pl. 2 (1506).

[3] *Chappel v. Whitlock* (1609), 8 Coke Rep. 69, 77 E.R. 580, also 1 Brownlow & Goldesborough 169, 123 E.R. 734.

[4] *Winter's Case* (1572), 3 Dyer 308, 73 E.R. 697; *Knight v. Breech* (1588), 5 Coke Rep. 54, 77 E.R. 137, also Moore K.B. 199, 72 E.R. 530, 3 Leonard 124, 74 E.R. 582, 1 Anderson 173, 123 E.R. 414, Gouldsborough 15, 75 E.R. 965.

[5] *Killam v. T.* (1435 x 1436), YB 14 Hen. VI, f. 26, pl. 77.

[6] YB Pas. 2 Edw. IV, f. 5, pl. 10 (1462).

[7] YB Mich. 17 Edw. III, ff. 68, 69, pl. 94 (1343).

For the place, this, if it is not expressed, is the land. But the reservation of a party can alter it also, as C. 4, 75;[1] the reservation can be payable out of the land. Thus, *Avowry*, 258;[2] a gift in tail, remainder in tail, rendering rent, this will issue out of the whole estate. But, as I heard Justice Haughton take the difference, if the reservation intervenes between the remainders, it will charge only the first remainder.

And for the person to whom the reservation is made, which is the principal question here, he cited 10 Edw. IV, 18; *Ass.* 86; 27 Hen. VIII, 19; Dy. 45; and Mallories's case.[3] And also, he argued that the reservation will be taken against the reservor, as C. 10, 127;[4] rendering rent payable at the usual feasts or twenty days after, the twentieth day is the day of payment. Thus [is] C. 10, 108;[5] two tenants in common reserved a horse; they will have but one. But if they grant one horse annually, he will have two horses. Thus of a heriot; one heriot will not be multiplied except by a feoffment of part. And, for the case in 5 Edw. IV, 4a,[6] if two joint tenants reserve a rent to one upon a lease for years or life, this is a reservation to both of them because it will follow the reversion. But, if they make a feoffment in fee, reserving a rent to one, this is good to one solely because, there, it is not annexed to the reversion.

And *Jermyn* now cited Wotton and Edwin's case, Trin. 5 Jac., rot. 3777, common bench,[7] where the reservation was to him, his executors, and assigns, but not *durante termino*, and [it was] adjudged it ended by his death and the executors [were] not bound to have it; and Hil. 33 Eliz., rot. 1316, in the common bench,[8] where the reservation was to him, his executors, and assigns during the term, and, there also, [it was] adjudged that by the death, it is gone; and Pas. 4 Jac., Hill and Hill's case, rot. 112,[9] where one, seised of land of custom of a freehold, made a lease reserving a rent during the life of himself and his wife during

---

[1] *Boroughes v. Taylor* (1596), 4 Coke Rep. 72, 76 E.R. 1043, also Moore K.B. 404, 72 E.R. 657, Gouldsborough 124, 75 E.R. 1039, Cro. Eliz. 462, 78 E.R. 715.

[2] Hil. 34 Edw. III, Fitzherbert, Abr., *Avowrie*, pl. 258 (1360).

[3] YB Mich. 10 Edw. IV, 49 Hen. VI, f. 18, pl. 22, 47 Selden Soc. 160 (1470 x 1471); YB Pas. 11 Edw. III, Rolls Ser. 31b, vol. 1, p. 46 (1337), Fitzherbert, Abr., *Assise*, pl. 86; *Dokeray's Case* (1535), YB Mich. 27 Hen. VIII, ff. 14, 19, pl. 6; *Anonymous* (1539), 1 Dyer 45, 73 E.R. 97; *Mallory v. Payn* (1601), 5 Coke Rep. 111, 77 E.R. 228, also Cro. Eliz. 805, 832, 78 E.R. 1033, 1058.

[4] *Clun v. Archer* (1613), 10 Coke Rep. 127, 77 E.R. 1117, also 4 Leonard 247, 74 E.R. 851, Cro. Jac. 309, 79 E.R. 265.

[5] *Young v. Milton* (1610), 10 Coke Rep. 106, 108, 77 E.R. 1086, 1089, also 1 Brownlow & Goldesborough 61, 123 E.R. 665.

[6] YB Trin. 5 Edw. IV, f. 4, pl. 7 (1465).

[7] *Wooton v. Edwin* (1607), 12 Coke Rep. 36, 77 E.R. 1317, Latch 274, 82 E.R. 383.

[8] *Richmond v. Butcher* (1591), Owen 9, 74 E.R. 861, 2 Leonard 214, 74 E.R. 488, Cro. Eliz. 217, 78 E.R. 473, 1 Anderson 261, 123 E.R. 462.

[9] *Hills v. Hills*, Moore K.B. 876, 72 E.R. 967.

the term, and, there, [it was] adjudged that, by the death of the husband, the rent was not ended, but then Coke and Warburton [spoke] against the other three that it will be ended and they took an exception to the pleadings of the fine because it was not pleaded to whose use and thus the use resulted to the conusor, and this, he said, he solely moved to the consideration of the court.

On the other side, both deeds [were] argued by *Barksdale* that the rent continued, and he insisted upon the words *durante termino* which, as he said, will be taken during the whole term. And thus they were taken [in] P. 23,[1] where the condition was if he would *intrabit* during the term and that [was] during the whole term. And, in some cases, the law binds the words to the intent of the party. And here, it appears that his intent was that the rent will be paid during the term. And on account of this, the law will supply his words, as in 3 Jac. Warnor and Aggas' case;[2] the lessee granted his term to the lessor, rendering rent during the term with a clause of distress if he be in arrears during the term; there, it expounded arrears during the time and space of the years.

Another reason why the words 'during the term' precede and, by the court, will be altered by the subsequent words [is] because *expressum facit cessare tacitum* but *expressum non facit cessare prius expressum.*[3] And for this is pB 140; a lease for life to three *habendum successive*, the *habendum* is void, but a lease to three *habendum successive* [is] good because, here, by the premises, the estate for life is but implied and, on account of this, it could be contradicted by the subsequent words. And with this [agrees] Dy. 361a and *Feffments*, 94.[4] It is a rule given, if the words [be] doubtful, the law will [not] regard the second words. And on account of this, there, a gift in frank marriage *habendum* in fee, the *habendum* is void because the mind of a man is more intent at the beginning of his speech than at the end and more regards it than the end in that his intention languishes. And this is the reason of P. 164,[5] where a rent was reserved in August during the term payable at [the Feasts of] the Annunciation and Michaelmas; there, the first payment will be at Michaelmas; otherwise, it could not be paid during the term.

And this is also the reason of Malory's [case] C. 5, 112,[6] that otherwise, if the rent is not payable to the successor, it will not be paid the whole term. And for a direct printed authority in the point is the saying [?] of Audley, 27 Hen. VIII,

---

[1] *Colthirst v. Bejushin* (1550), 1 Plowden 21, 75 E.R. 33.

[2] *Warner v. Agus* (1604), Noy 109, 74 E.R. 1075.

[3] Cf. *Black's Law Dictionary* (1933), pp. 727–728.

[4] *Anonymous* (1577), 3 Dyer 361, 73 E.R. 809; *Blaunket v. Simonson* (1308), YB Hil. 2 Edw. II, Selden Soc., vol. 17, p. 126, pl. 61, YB Hil. 2 Edw. II, f. 29, Fitzherbert, Abr., *Feffements & faits*, pl. 94.

[5] *Hill v. Grange* (1556), 1 Plowden 164, 75 E.R. 253, also 2 Dyer 130, 73 E.R. 284.

[6] *Mallory v. Payn* (1601), 5 Coke Rep. 111, 77 E.R. 228, also Cro. Eliz. 805, 832, 78 E.R. 1033, 1058.

19;[1] if the reservation be to the lessor and it does not say during the term to him, he will not have [it], by which it shows that, if he said 'during the term' that the heir will have [it] notwithstanding the particular reservation. And as to Richman's case, 33 Eliz.,[2] there, there is a reservation to the executors expressly and this, being particular, excludes all others particulars, as an heir. But here 'assign' is a general word, and, on account of this, it will not exclude the executors nor the heirs because a special will exclude another special, but not a general a special. And by C. 5, 97,[3] a condition that he will pay to the heir, this excludes the executor, but a condition that he pay to the assignee does not exclude the executor and, as there, the executor [is] excluded by a reservation to the heir, thus, here, by the reservation to the executors.

Second, there, the avowry was by the heir, and it appears that the ancestor [was] dead, not here; it stands indifferent whether he be or not. And this is the answer that I give to Richman's [case].

Further, he argued that, though it is not averred here that the lessor [is] alive, yet it will be intended that he is because it is an avowry by the assignee, *ut pro reditu [blank] existent insolute*. Thus if, after the death of the lessor, it is not due, it will be taken that the lessor is alive because he averred that the rent was due to him; therefore, this implies all necessary circumstances. And thus it was ruled [in] 12 Jac. in Arundell's case;[4] where the heir avowed and did not aver the death of the [ancestor], but inasmuch as he averred [that] the rent was in arrears and unpaid to him, this inferred[5] the prior death; otherwise, nothing was due to him. Thus [is] C. 10, 59;[6] the life of a bishop was well [averred by] *per praedictum nuper episcopum*.

Second, though the death is to be averred, yet here [it is] not, because it is a natural thing and, on account of this, without a showing, [it is] presumed to continue, as Dy. 329;[7] the condition of the obligation to pay so much yearly toward the educating of A.B., and, in [an action of] debt, the plaintiff, first, did not aver the life of A.B., and yet [it was] good. Thus [is] 38 Hen. VI, 27;[8] the lessee of so

---

[1] *Dokeray's Case* (1535), YB Mich. 27 Hen. VIII, ff. 14, 19, pl. 6.

[2] *Richmond v. Butcher* (1591), Owen 9, 74 E.R. 861, 2 Leonard 214, 74 E.R. 488, Cro. Eliz. 217, 78 E.R. 473, 1 Anderson 261, 123 E.R. 462.

[3] *Goodall v. Wyat* (1597), 5 Coke Rep. 95, 97, 77 E.R. 202, 205, also Jenkins 261, 145 E.R. 187, *sub nom. Goodale v. Wyat*, Gouldsborough 176, 75 E.R. 1076, Moore K.B. 708, 72 E.R. 855, Cro. Eliz. 383, 78 E.R. 629, Popham 99, 79 E.R. 1209.

[4] *Arundell's Case* (1614 x 1615), cited in *Arundell v. Meade* (1621), Palmer 267, 81 E.R. 1076.

[5] ceo enforce que *MS.*

[6] *Stanton v. Green* (1613), 10 Coke Rep. 58, 77 E.R. 1013.

[7] *Anonymous* (1537), 3 Dyer 329, 73 E.R. 744.

[8] YB Pas. 38 Hen. VI, f. 27, pl. 8 (1460).

much *pur autre vie* brought [an action of] trespass, and he did not aver the life of the lessor, and yet [it was] good.

And no one would affirm in the pleading of a grant of a reversion and attornment that it will be averred the parties to be living. And thus is 10 Edw. IV, 18, 24, 30;[1] the defendant avowed for damages in the right of the lessee of a husband and wife and he did not aver the life of the wife, and yet [it was] ruled good because avowry is a bar as to any purpose. The avowant is the actor because, as one of the defendants, he defends the [tort] and force.

As to the exception to the pleading of the fine and not saying to whose use, he said that by the common law, the use was to the conusee, as the estate made. And the common law does not take notice of uses. And on account of this, the pleading, according to the common law, is good. Also in the *New Entries* 344[2] and C. 2, 88, there, the fine was pleaded without saying to whose use. And P. 477;[3] three feoffments were pleaded and not whose use. But as to this, there is a difference if one pleads a feoffment or fine and a lease is limited to another [person] than the conusee or feoffee; there, he must plead it. But if it be limited to the conusee, there is no need because it [is] intended by the common law.

And thus, he concluded [for] the avowant.

And now Justice JONES said, for the fine, admitting that the use resulted, yet it was not for the plaintiff because, then, the case is a tenant in tail levied a fine to his [own] use and then the conusee, who has nothing in the land, suffered a recovery, in which the tenant in tail and now the tenant in fee is vouched, and a recovery had, this will bind the issue because, by the fine, the entail was barred and, by the recovery, the tenant in fee cannot falsify to say *quod partes finis nihil habuerunt.*[4]

And he said that the law favors reservations. And he cited it to be adjudged [in] 27 Eliz.; an administrator of a term for forty years made a lease for twenty, rendering rent, and he died intestate; the second administrator averred the rent.

DODDERIDGE: Dyer denied [it] and marvelled that it was.

JONES: Yes, faith, it was so adjudged.

And he said also that this case was adjudged: a tenant in fee made a fraudulent conveyance and, afterwards, made a lease for years, rendering rent, now this, notwithstanding the reservation, [was] good and the lessee [was] held to pay it.

Which DODDERIDGE granted.

---

[1] YB Mich. 10 Edw. IV, 49 Hen. VI, f. 18, pl. 22, 47 Selden Soc. 160 (1470 x 1471).

[2] *Eggerton v. Deane* (1603), E. Coke, *A Booke of Entries* (1614), 'Formedon', pl. 19, ff. 342, 344.

[3] *Nichols v. Nichols* (1575), 2 Plowden 477, 75 E.R. 711, also Benloe 245, 123 E.R. 173.

[4] Cf. *Black's Law Dictionary* (1933), p. 1328.

JONES: Do you think, if one devise land to one for years, rendering rent, and devise the reversion to another, is this good?

DODDERIDGE granted it good.

And then JONES said it has been adjudged.

And yet [there is] no privity between the lessee and him in the reversion in those cases because DODDERIDGE [said] that it is an infallible and undeniable ground that a rent cannot be reserved to a stranger. And on account of this, in Cofeeld's case,[1] the reservation to him who will have the reversion is void.

And the justices took a day to advise.

More, f. 72, pl. 31.[2]

[Other reports of this case: Benloe 182, 188, 73 E.R. 1041, 1046, CUL MS. Gg.2.30, ff. 66v, 69v; Latch 44, 255, 264, 82 E.R. 266, 373, 378, HLS MS. 1235, f. 110; Noy 96, 74 E.R. 1062; Palmer 481, 81 E.R. 1181; BL MS. Hargr. 38, ff. 100, 123; BL MS. Lansd. 1092, f. 218v; CUL MS. Ll.3.13, f. 264.]

169

Apsley v. Knowles

(K.B. Mich. 2 Car. I, 1626)

The failure of a declaration in an action of trespass to allege that the defendant's act was contra pacem *is cured by the entry of the judgment.*

BL MS. Add. 35961, f. 41v, pl. 38

Between Apsley and Knowles in [an action of] trespass, the plaintiff alleged a trespass in the time of King James with a *continuando* until in the time of King Charles. And upon [a plea of the] general issue, a verdict [was] found for the plaintiff, and judgment was entered contrary to the rule of court. And now, it was moved in arrest of judgment where worse than a bad judgment[3] [was] entered. And 2 Edw. IV, 24, and 1 Edw. III, 2, and Wimbish and Talboys' case[4] [were] cited, and the Lord Leithe's [case], that he should allege *contra pacem* of both kings, and *N. Entries*, 565. And it was urged that thus lately it has been ruled in the [court of] common bench, and, upon this exception, judgment [was] arrested.

---

[1] *Young v. Milton* (1612), 10 Coke Rep. 106, 77 E.R. 1086, 1 Brownlow & Goldesborough 61, 123 E.R. 665.

[2] For other proceedings in this case, see above, No. 68; BL MS. Add. 35961, f. 78, pl. 31, BL MS. Lansd. 1083, f. 137v, pl. 31 (Widdrington's reports).

[3] ou potius dun dole judgment *MS*.

[4] YB Mich. 2 Edw. IV, f. 24, pl. 23 (1462); YB Hil. 1 Edw. III, f. 2, pl. 10 (1327); *Wimbish v. Tailbois* (1550), 1 Plowden 63, 55, 75 E.R. 63, 89.

But JONES said that, upon a demurrer, this is a good exception, but not after a verdict.

And it was said that this exception at the Reading term[1] made in one Jarvys's case [was] overruled after a verdict. But because judgment was entered, though against the rule of court, and this exception [was] doubtful, it stood.

And JONES said thus it should.

After, f. 73, p. 34.[2]

[Other reports of this case: BL MS. Hargr. 38, f. 45v; CUL MS. Ll.3.13, f. 101v.]

170

Harvey v. Reynell

(Part 1)
(K.B. Mich. 2 Car. I, 1626)

In an action of debt against a jailer for an escape, it is not a good defense that the prisoner was recaptured after the action was begun.

BL MS. Add. 35961, f. 42, pl. 39

In [an action of] debt by Harvy against Sir George Reynell upon an escape, *quod intratur* Trin. 2 [Car. I], rot. 1179, [the plaintiff] alleged an escape in London. The defendant said that [on] such a day, the party escaped to Surrey and *quod antea, scilicet 8 Maii secundo Caroli*, he retook him.

And upon this, he demurred, first, because the plaintiff alleged an escape in London and the defendant confessed and avoided an escape in Surrey. Thus, he did not respond to the escape which the plaintiff alleged but, here, he should have traversed *absque hoc*, as if one alleged a battery at S., which is a transitory action (as it is here and, here, he could allege an escape in any county where the prisoner went) and the defendant justified at T., he should traverse the battery at S.

The second exception [was] because he said that *ante, scilicet* and the day is after the filing of the bill and the action brought because the record is *memorandum quod alius, scilicet Hilario primo [Caroli], protulit billa etc.*, and this was before 8 May 2 Car., and, after the action [was] brought, the retaking could not serve [him].

And of this opinion was the court, though he retook him before he pleaded with the plaintiff.

---

[1] Because of a virulent outbreak of the plague in London in the summer of 1625, Trinity and Michaelmas terms, 1625, were adjourned to Reading; see above, Note, No. 19.

[2] *Langley v. Stoke* (1627), BL MS. Add. 35961, f. 79, pl. 34, BL MS. Lansd. 1083, f. 139v, pl. 34 (Widdrington's reports), also Godbolt 399, 78 E.R. 235, Latch 260, 82 E.R. 376, Noy 97, 74 E.R. 1063.

And as to this that was said on the other side, that the *scilicet* is idle and, on account of this, it will be intended before the bringing of the bill, JONES said that, if the *scilicet* be of an impossible day, as 31 September or 30 February, there, it will be void, but not where it is only repugnant in itself.

More, f. 41, pl. 56; f. 44b, pl. 62.[1]

171

Greene v. Iwyn

(K.B. Mich. 2 Car. I, 1626)

An attorney can make an appearance for a dead party.

BL MS. Add. 35961, f. 42, pl. 40

Between Greene and Iwyn, in [a writ of] error, *quod intratur* Trin. 1 [Car. I, rot.] 1237, it was assigned for error that one of the parties was dead before the verdict [was] given. And, upon this, the defendant in error joined *in nullo erratum*. And it was moved that this error was contrary to the record because it was entered after the verdict [was] given *ad quem diem venerunt partes praedicti per attornatos suos*.

But it was not allowed because, if it was that he appeared in his proper person, it had been contrary to the record, but one could appear as an attorney though the party be dead, and that he was. Thus the joinder *in nullo erratum* has confessed that [he was an] infant because, otherwise, he could have taken issue upon it.

And on account of this, the judgment was reversed.

172

Ashfield v. Ashfield

(Part 1)
(K.B. Mich. 2 Car. I, 1626)

The question in this case was whether a lease made without license by an infant copyholder was void or merely voidable.

BL MS. Add. 35961, f. 42, pl. 41

In [an action of] trespass by Ashfield against Ashfield *quod intratur* Trin. 2 [Car. I], rot. 911 [or 913]), the case was [thus]. An infant copyholder made a lease for years, without a license, rendering rent. And at full age, he was admitted by

---

[1] For later proceedings in this case, see below, Nos. 187, 193, 265.

the lord [of the manor], and he accepted the rent of the lessee.[1] Whether he now will avoid the lease or not was the demurrer.

And it was argued that he will not avoid the lease. And first, it was argued that this lease by the infant was not a forfeiture. And on account of this, he took a difference between a condition in a deed and in law. If an infant breaks a condition in a deed, it is gone. 31 Ass. 17; *Coverture*, B., 17, 48, 46.[2] But if it be a condition in law, then, there is also a difference whether it be with a confidence, as a parkership etc., or without a confidence. And on account of this, if a tenant for life alienates, being an infant, or in mortmain, in these cases, he will avoid them at full age. And this appears in C. 8 above.[3] But if an infant levy a fine, being a tenant for life, and does not reverse it during his nonage, it is a perpetual forfeiture because, at full age, he cannot avoid it. *Fines*, 120.[4]

Second, he argued that, if it be a forfeiture, then, by the lease, he has made a disseisin to the lord and gained to himself the freehold in reversion because, if a tenant at will makes a lease for years, it is a disseisin, as it is in 21 Hen. VII, 36, and 10 Edw. IV, and 21 Edw. IV.[5]

Third, he argued that, admitting him a disseisor, that still, by the admittance of the lord, it is not converted to the copyholder again. And thus it comes back to the droitural estate. 19 Hen. VI, 22, by Portington;[6] a remainderman disseised a lessee for life who died; now, the estate of the remainderman became droitural. But this is where he had a droitural inheritance, and a tortious [*blank*]. But where the droitural estate that after [*blank*] is the less, there, it will not convert to the droitural. And for this [is] 7 Edw. VI, Clifford's case, Dy. [. . .];[7] the lessee entered before the day; after the day, he continued [as a] disseisor. And thus it was adjudged [in] 37 Eliz., Alexander and Latrell's case. Also, when the droitural estate that comes to the tortious is not senior to the tortious, it does not alter it. And for this [is] 12 Edw. IV, F., *Discontinuance*;[8] a lessee for life released to the disseisor; this did not alter the estate of the disseisor because it makes it droitural for any part. Thus [is] 39 Hen. VI, 26;[9] a disseisor took the wife of the

---

[1] lessor *MS*.

[2] YB 31 Edw. III, Lib. Ass., p. 188, pl. 17 (1357), Brooke, Abr., *Coverture & Infancie*, pl. 71; YB Trin. 11 Edw. IV, f. 1, pl. 1 (1471), Brooke, Abr., *Coverture & Infancie*, pl. 48; YB Pas. 9 Hen. VII, f. 24, pl. 7 (1494), Brooke, Abr., *Coverture & Infancie*, pl. 46.

[3] *Whittingham's Case* (1603), 8 Coke Rep. 42, 77 E.R. 537.

[4] YB Mich. 18 Edw. II, p. 568 (1324), Fitzherbert, Abr., *Fynes*, pl. 120.

[5] YB Trin. 21 Hen. VII, f. 26, pl. 3 (1506); YB Mich. 10 Edw. IV, 49 Hen. VI, f. 18, pl. 22, 47 Selden Soc. 160 (1470 x 1471); YB Mich. 12 Edw. IV, f. 12, pl. 5 (1472).

[6] YB Mich. 19 Hen. VI, ff. 21, 22, pl. 43 (1440).

[7] *Clifford v. Warrener* (1553), 1 Dyer 89, 96, 73 E.R. 192, 210.

[8] YB Pas. 12 Edw. IV, f. 11, pl. [30] (1472), Fitzherbert, Abr., *Discontinuance divers*, pl. 29.

[9] *Scot v. Dogge* (1460), YB Mich. 39 Hen. VI, f. 26, pl. 37.

disseisee as a wife; this does not alter because the droitural title is junior. Thus here, the right that the heir has by admittance is junior to the disseisin. And on account of this, he remains a disseisor.

But admit that his tortious estate is gone, yet though the estate out of which it is [is] gone, the estate remains because it is a ground that the same person will not avoid his [own] act. And for this [is] *Entre congeable*, 21;[1] a father disseised the ancestor and made a feoffment, and the ancestor died; the father, against his own feoffment, cannot enter. Thus [is] L. 112 and 21 Hen. VI, 4;[2] a disseisee released to the disseisor; the disseisor will not have a rent granted by himself. And he cited to this purpose C. 7, 14, Arderne's case; 11 Hen. VII, 21, Edrictus' case; Dy. 51, by Baldwyn; and Co. 8, Swain's case; and 39 Hen. VI, cited there.[3]

Then, he concluded that, if an infant makes a lease for years, rendering rent, that whether it be void or voidable is not a question because he said that, [in] many books, it is voidable only, as 7 Edw. IV[4] and P. 445, and thus, by the acceptance of the rent, to be made good.

More, 26, pl. 58.[5]

173

Piburne v. Anonymous

(K.B. Mich. 2 Car. I, 1626)

The court will give effect to the clear intent of a testator, as where he used the word feoffee rather than devisee.

BL MS. Add. 35961, f. 42, pl. 42

In [an action of] *ejectione firmae* between Piburne and another for the great Inn of the Garter in Windsor, the sole question in law was, and [it was] ruled by the whole court, if one devise his land to J.S. and his heirs to the use of divers [persons] for life and, afterwards, he devises that his feoffee, after the death of them, will stand seised to the use of one in fee, that this is good because, though *de facto* he does not have any feoffees, yet it appears that the intent was that J.D.

---

[1] Trin. 15 Edw. IV, Fitzherbert, Abr., *Entre congeable*, pl. 21 (1475).

[2] T. Littleton, *Tenures*, sect. 477; *Mill v. Clifford* (1443), YB Pas. 21 Hen. VI, f. 41, pl. 12.

[3] *Arden's Case*, cited in *Regina v. Englefield* (1591), 7 Coke Rep. 11, 14, 77 E.R. 428, 433, Moore K.B. 303, 325, 72 E.R. 595, 607; *Eriche's Case* (1496), YB Pas. 11 Hen. VII, f. 21, pl. 10; *Reade v. Bullocke* (1543), 1 Dyer 56, 57, 73 E.R. 125; *Swayne v. Becket* (1608), 8 Coke Rep. 63, 77 E.R. 568, also Moore K.B. 811, 72 E.R. 921, 1 Brownlow & Goldesborough 231, 123 E.R. 772; YB Mich. 39 Hen. VI, f. 13, pl. 17 (1460).

[4] YB Pas. 7 Edw. IV, f. 5, pl. 16 (1467).

[5] For later proceedings in this case, see below, Nos. 189, 287.

will have the land in fee. And they relied upon B., *Devise*, 48, and Dy. 323, Lingin's case.[1]

[Other reports of this case: *sub nom.* Bushfield v. Kiarsborough, Benloe 184, 73 E.R. 1046, CUL MS. Gg.2.30, f. 69v.]

174

Shury v. Pigot

(Part 3)
(K.B. Mich. 2 Car. I, 1626)

BL MS. Add. 35961, f. 42v, pl. 43

And now, the justices showed their opinion in the case of Shury and Pigott, of which see before, fol. 38, p. 21.[2] And they all agreed that by the unity of possession the watercourse is not extinct. They also agreed that the declaration and the bar, for the form of them, were well enough pleaded, but, for the matter of the bar, which was the unity, that this was insufficient. The exceptions to which the court spoke were these:

First, that the plaintiff had declared that, such a day, *decurrebat et currere solebat* of such place etc., and he pleaded it by way of prescription, as to say that such person and all whose estate etc. and thus he bound it to the certain person which, in the pleading of the prescription, is not by way of a custom, as to say that, in such place, there has been such a custom that etc. Thus, he has not pleaded it by way of prescription nor of custom. But it was answered by the court that this pleading in a case of a watercourse is the usual pleading and a sufficient allegation of the custom because it is said that *currere solebat a tempore cuius etc.*

Another exception was because the plaintiff had prescribed that the water had used to run to the parsonage and he did not say that the parsonage was an ancient rectory, as [in] the case in Dy. of Ilbrewer's Park.[3] But the court answered that this is not necessary because the law presumes rectories to be ancient and as ancient as the introduction of Christianity. And this which the law intends, there is no need to aver.

Another exception [was] because the plaintiff did not declare that the defendant *vi et armis* stopped the [water]course because, even though an action upon the case is not *vi et armis*, yet, as it is said [in] C. 9, 50b,[4] it is *causa causans et causa*

---

[1] 29 Hen. VIII, Brooke, Abr., *Devise*, pl. 48 (1537 x 1538); *Lingen's Case* (1573), 3 Dyer 323, 73 E.R. 731, also Jenkins 239, 145 E.R. 167.

[2] For earlier proceedings in this case, see above, Nos. 69, 151.

[3] *Withers v. Iseham* (1552), 1 Dyer 70, 73 E.R. 148.

[4] *Earl of Shrewsbury's Case* (1610), 9 Coke Rep. 42, 50, 77 E.R. 793, 806. Cf. *Black's Law Dictionary* (1933), p. 291.

causata; the first could be *vi et armis*; the other not. But it was ruled no exception because, here, it was impossible that the *causa causans*, *viz.* the stopping of the water, will be *vi et armis* because it was upon his own land, where he cannot do a thing *vi et armis*. And on account of this, a difference was taken, *viz.* if one make a nuisance to me which is a trespass to another for which the other can have [an action of] trespass *vi et armis*, there, in an action upon the case, I can allege the action *vi et armis*, otherwise not, as if one dig in my [right of] way or common, there, I can have an action upon the case *quare vi* etc. he dug by which I lose my common or be hindered in the way. But, if the action of the land does it, then he will not have such a writ because no [action of] trespass lies against him; as appears [in] 12 Hen. VIII.[1]

For the matter in law, they all agreed that the unity did not extinguish it and that this case differs from all other cases of a way, common, etc. because, these, one cannot have in his own land because one in his own land has liberty to go as well in one part as in another, and, for a common, one who has all of the profits cannot be said to have part, so that those by the unity do not have any existence. But the course of water has existence.

And he urged, notwithstanding the unity, [that] another reason was because this is a thing that nature begun and it did not begin by a grant or prescription and the acts of nature cannot be suspended or extinguished. Also, there is not any interest that the plaintiff claims here in the land such as Bracton calls [at] fo. 221[2] [*blank*] as *ius fodendi eundi* and [*blank*], but it is only to have the benefit of nature and of a natural course of it.

But the main reason was because the plaintiff showed that he was barred of necessity from his house to water his cattle and to brew etc. and as well as one can bereave one from the water as well he can of another element. He agreed because both seem necessary. And for this, it was cited to be Popham's opinion in 37 Eliz. in the argument of Harrison's case, that a [right of] way to the market and to the church will not be extinguished by the unity of possession because they are of simple necessity. And they all relied upon the book of 11 Hen. VII, 25, the case of the gutter.[3]

And thus judgment was given for the plaintiff. And here, it was agreed by all. And thus, CREWE said, it was adjudged in Drake and Day's case, 3 Jac.,[4] that by the unity of the thing [. . .] that another must do [it] without that that it is extinguished according to the dubious opinion in Dy. 295b.[5]

---

[1] *Harcourt v. Spicer* (1520), YB Trin. 12 Hen. VIII, f. 2, pl. 2, 119 Selden Soc. 7.

[2] *Bracton on the Laws and Customs of England* (S. E. Thorne, ed., 1977), vol. 3, p. 164.

[3] *Copie's Case* (1496), YB Trin. 11 Hen. VII, f. 25, pl. 6.

[4] *Drake v. Doylye* (1604), Noy 14, 74 E.R. 985.

[5] *Anonymous* (1570), 3 Dyer 295, 73 E.R. 663.

[Other reports of this case: Benloe 188, 73 E.R. 1046, CUL MS. Gg.2.30, f. 70; 3 Bulstrode 339, 81 E.R. 280; W. Jones 145, 82 E.R. 77, BL MS. Hargr. 317, f. 149; Latch 153, 82 E.R. 321; Noy 84, 74 E.R. 1051; Palmer 444, 81 E.R. 1163; Popham 166, 79 E.R. 1263; BL MS. Hargr. 38, f. 111v; BL MS. Lansd. 1092, f. 130v; CUL MS. Hh.2.1, f. 215v; CUL MS. Ll.3.13, f. 162v.]

175

Hayward v. Fulcher

(Part 2)

(K.B. Mich. 2 Car. I, 1626)

BL MS. Add. 35961, f. 42v, pl. 44

And now in the case before, fo. 10, p. 29,[1] between Hayward and Fulcher, *quod intratur* Trin. 21 Jac., rot. 662, it was argued for the plaintiff by *Noy*. And he argued, first, that the lease made by the dean and chapter to the assignee of Sotherton was bad; second, admitting it good, still that, for the condition broken, it was gone.

First, he argued that, for the misnomer of the corporation, the lease made by them was void. And to this which was said that it is harsh for the corporation to dispute this point upon which they have all of their possessions, because it could be said, if this be here a misnomer, then it is also a misnomer in the grant to them of their possessions by Edward VI because it is the same name that is there, to this, he answered that, in the case of the grant of the king to them, it is helped by the statutes of 25 Eliz., c. 3, and 1 Edw. VI, ca. 8,[2] and thus this does not prove but that they are misnamed. And thus, a grant made by them by such a false name [is] bad. He confessed that much of this point is argued in the case of the Dean and Chapter of Norwich, C. 3, 73, etc.[3] And, there, there is an opinion that the old corporation of the dean and chapter made by the transfer of the Benedictines remained not dissolved. But still, he conceived to the contrary because there were not any of the resolutions there, but only an opinion because, first, here, there are apt words of surrender of their corporation and to dissolve it because, by their surrender, they surrendered to Edward VI their cathedral church with all their possessions, lands, tenements, and *jura, franchesia, et privilegia* and, as the corporation began by the patent of the king, so it could be dissolved by a surrender. And now, they surrendered *ecclesiam cathedralem* and this cannot be intended of the material church [*blank*], but the church in the abstract and the congregation and their right to be such a spiritual corporation and

---

[1] For other proceedings in this case, see Nos. 73, 271.

[2] Stat. 23 Eliz. I, c. 3 (*SR*, IV, 661–663); Stat. 1 Edw. VI, c. 8 (*SR*, IV, 13–14).

[3] *Case of the Dean and Chapter of Norwich* (1598), 3 Coke Rep. 73, 76 E.R. 793, also 2 Anderson 120, 165, 123 E.R. 577, 601.

though a church in law has the signification of the material church, as *Register* 45,[1] a [writ of] consultation to proceed *super emendatione corporis ecclesiae*; thus, in the Statute of *Circumspecte Agatis Ecclesiae Discooperta*.[2] Yet, the more usual acceptation is for the corporation and congregation, as in 18 Edw. II, *Trespass*, 237,[3] a trespass for coming to the abbey etc. and *ad deteriorationem ecclesiae suae praedictae*, where it did not speak of the church before but of an abbey, and this could not be to the deterioration of the material church. Thus [is] Reg., 155, and F.N.B., 55d;[4] [a writ of] waste against a tenant in dower *ad exhereditationem ecclesiae suae* by an abbot, which could not be of a material church; and Reg., 237; [in a writ of] *juris utrum*, it is said *jus ecclesiae*, and for a master of a hospital, *jus domus*, which is not intended but of a corporation. Thus *ecclesia* is an apt word to surrender the corporation.

And as to this [is] 29 Ass. 33; a grant of a rent *percipiendum de abathia*; and Dy. 233;[5] *si fuerit absens a collegio*; where they are taken for the site of the abbey and college. There, it is restrained to the place and cannot have another meaning.

Another reason for which the surrender of the church surrendered their corporation is because the material church was not ever theirs, but the bishop's, and, on account of this, what they do not have, they cannot surrender. And by 18 Edw. III, it appears that the soil of the cathedral church belongs to the bishop.

Also, if, by these words, the corporation was not dissolved, a great inconvenience would ensue because, then, by the Statute of 21 Hen. VIII, 31,[6] notwithstanding them, the monasteries and their corporations remained during the lifetime of the monks because they do not have other words in their surrender than are here, nor than in the statutes as was done of certain persons beyond the seas; these but pretend to be succeeded [?] of the Abbey of Westminster, but they were [. . .][7] a corporation in name only and not in verity. Also, when Queen Mary made Westminster an abbey again, she refounded it *de novo* so that it appears that then it takes [. . .][8] of the possessions of the dissolved corporation. And thus, in fact, they were upon each surrender of the monastery, the monks were placed in others which remained for their sustenance.

Also, if the old corporation was not dissolved, then the bishop will have two deans and two chapters, which was not the intent, and, in one chapter, he will have six prebends and *nihil unde praeberetur*. And he said that a prebend *dicitur a*

---

[1] *Registrum Brevium.*

[2] Stat. 12 Edw. I (*SR*, I, 101–102).

[3] *Abbot of Glastonbury v. Parson of Schilmerle* (1324), YB Mich. 18 Edw. II, p. 573, Fitzherbert, Abr., *Trespas*, pl. 237.

[4] *Registrum Brevium*; A. Fitzherbert, *Nouvelle Natura Brevium.*

[5] *Case of the College of Windsor* (1565), 2 Dyer 233, 73 E.R. 516.

[6] Stat. 31 Hen. VIII, c. 13 (*SR*, III, 733–739).

[7] aera *MS*.

[8] que parle perd *MS*.

praebendo quod praebetur to him not *a praebendo quod praebet* for of the dividend and portion *quod sibi praebetur et quod vocatur* some [*blank*] *praebendurus*. But if the word *ecclesiae* would not serve, still the word *franchesiae* would because to be a corporation is a franchise. And for this [is] *N. Entre*, in *quo warranto*, they claimed to be a *corpus incorporatum*, f. 577.[1] Thus, if it be a privilege and a franchise to be a corporation, by the surrender of them, the corporation was surrendered.

And, as to the triple objection in C. 3, 75,[2] that the corporation must remain of necessity: (1) to counsel the bishop; (2) to aid him to decide controversies; (3) to confirm his grants, he gave a response that to have a dean and chapter is not necessary:

First, because, before there were any chapter, the clergy of the diocese was the chapter and his assistants in these affairs. But afterwards, the bishop, who did not desire overmuch counsel, by their means, this power was reduced to the few whom he fed *ad mensam* and ruled [. . .] to please him. And, at this day, divers bishoprics do not have chapters, as Meath in Ireland and others which were remembered. Thus, if the old corporation be dissolved, then the grant here by the name of the old corporation is not good because it is gone.

Then, it is to see if the variance of the new name be such a misnomer that vitiates the grant of it. There are several cases in the Mayor of Lynn's case and Dr. Ayrys' case,[3] with which he will not trouble the court. But there, there is a rule put that such a misnomer as would abate a writ would not avoid a grant because one can have a new writ, but not a new grant, as he would. But this is not universally true because the reason that the writ abates is because there is not any such corporation as is denoted by this name. And thus, the same reason holds in a grant if there not be such a corporation thus called. But this is not of [trifling], but of material, variances because the name makes the corporation and is the corporation and [is] of the essence of the corporation. And here, the omission of *ex fundatione* Edward VI is material because, by this, it is distinguished from all others and [it is] part of the name. And he cited Fish and Boys' case, C. 10, and 35 Hen. VI, 6;[4] the omission of the name of the saint, and Wingat's case, Dy., where it was named *capella regis et reginae* of Windsor,[5] because such additions are not for a memorial, but part of the name.

---

[1] *Attorney General v. Helden* (1610), E. Coke, *A Booke of Entries* (1614), 'Quo Warranto', pl. 1, f. 527.

[2] *Case of the Dean and Chapter of Norwich* (1598), *ut supra*.

[3] *Mayor of King's Lynn v. Payn* (1612), 10 Coke Rep. 120, 77 E.R. 1108; *Alcock v. Ayray* (1614), 11 Coke Rep. 18, 77 E.R. 1168, also Lane 15, 33, 145 E.R. 261, 276.

[4] *Fisher v. Bois* (1588), 10 Coke Rep. 125, 77 E.R. 1115, also Moore K.B. 266, 72 E.R. 571, 1 Anderson 196, 123 E.R. 427; *Abbot of Strafford's Case* (1456), YB Mich. 35 Hen. VI, f. 6, pl. 10.

[5] *Dean of Windsor's Case* (1587 x 1588), cited in *Mayor of King's Lynn v. Payn* (1612), 10 Coke Rep. 120, 124, 77 E.R. 1108, 1113–1114.

For the second part of the argument, upon the condition, he argued that it was broken and that the condition included the trees as well as the other woods. And, first, that for the exception of the woods and underwoods and trees, first, that the tops of the trees are excepted, he would not argue this because though in 27 Ass. 29,[1] where the woods are excepted *proviso* that he does not cut it between May and Michaelmas, it was doubted if he will have the hawks there [*blank*] because he could not have the trees during this time. Yet 14 Hen. VIII[2] and 16 Edw. IV are express that, by the exception of the trees, all of the profits of [them] are excepted and the lessor will have the hawks etc.

But the question here is whether the condition extends to the timber trees outside of the woods because the exception was of woods and underwoods to grow or growing in a wood called Taverham Wood and of all trees of oak and elsewhere [it] provided that, if the lessee hindered to carry the said woods and underwoods, the disturbance was found in the trees out of the woods. And he argued that the word woods includes trees. And he cited 22 Edw. III, 8;[3] where by the name of woods, all trees [were] excepted. And this, he said, was the meaning of the parties because the lessor provided liberty to cut and carry and, as trees are cut, then, more properly, wood, *lignum* [*blank*]. Thus, when he has made the trees woods, then he provides for the hindrance.

It could be here argued that the carrying away of the tops by the lessee (because thus it was found) is not a hindrance or disturbance to him to carry it within the words of the condition, but I will not argue this because [there is] no question because a disturbance by way of prevention is as strong a disturbance as an actual [one]. *Covenant*, 29;[4] it was ruled, if a lessee promises to leave the house in repair at the end of the term and, before it,[5] he breaks it, the promise is not broken because he can rebuild it, but if [there be] promise to leave a wood in as good a plight and he cuts it, it is broken presently because he cannot save it during the term. Thus here, the taking away of the wood was a present breach because he cannot purge this act afterwards. And in Sir Anthony Mayn's case, C. 5, 21,[6] the lessor promised to accept the surrender of the lessee and he alienated the reversion, this present prevention [was a] breach of the covenant. Thus, if a feoffee upon a condition to re-enfeoff makes a lease, this prevents him to do it [and is a] forfeiture.

---

[1] YB 27 Edw. III, Lib. Ass., p. 136, pl. 29 (1353).

[2] *Bishop of London v. Nevell* (1522), YB Mich. 14 Hen. VIII, f. 1, pl. 1, 119 Selden Soc. 88.

[3] *Earl of Pembroke v. A.* (1348), YB Trin. 22 Edw. III, f. 8, pl. 15.

[4] Fitzherbert, Abr., *Covenant*, pl. 29 (temp. Edw. I).

[5] I.e. the end of the term.

[6] *Main v. Scot* (1596), 5 Coke Rep. 20, 77 E.R. 80, also Moore K.B. 452, 72 E.R. 689, Cro. Eliz. 449, 479, 78 E.R. 689, 731, Popham 109, 79 E.R. 1217, 2 Anderson 18, 123 E.R. 523, Jenkins 256, 145 E.R. 182.

Another thing has been moved, *viz.* that, inasmuch as the dean and chapter, upon the breach of the condition, had made a lease under the common seal and made a letter of attorney to deliver it as their deed upon the land, that this was not good inasmuch as it was a deed before and, on account of this, the delivery upon the land [was] void, to this, I do not see a difference between this and Jennings' case, C. 3, 35,[1] because, here, there is no impediment of person, for which the first delivery will not be good, but only of estate, which, by the entry of the attorney, is avoided by the second delivery.

And thus, he concluded for the plaintiff.

Bankes, contra, for the defendant: And he argued that it is agreed with me that it was a good corporation [*blank*] of the dean and chapter and also that this lease was made by its ancient name. Thus, if it was not a corporation, it was not dissolved, and they have two names; the grant by either of them is good. Beside the resolution of the court in the book of C. 3, 75, that the old corporation remains, reason also enforces it so that there is no need to insist upon this. But this resolution has been opposed by divers reasons:

First, that the surrender of the church cannot be intended of the water and soil, but of the corporation. I deny this because the soil of the church belongs to the bishop and the corporation [was] extracted out of the bishop. And on account of this, it is not in their power to surrender the corporation, as [in] 25 Ass. 8 and 18 Edw. III, 27.[2] It is said also that, by the surrender of the franchises, that the corporation is gone. But this cannot be because the franchises and privileges are incidents to the corporation and appendants. And I have heard that, by a grant of the principal, the appendants would pass, but never that, by a grant of the appendants, the principal will pass.

It was objected also that otherwise the bishop will have two chapters and two deans. The response [is], first, it is not novel to have two deans, as in Dy. 282,[3] St. Patrick's has two deans; second, here, there are not two deans because the new corporation is not good but the patent of them [is] void because the king intended a new erection where the first was not dissolved and thus [he was] deceived where he intended an act of creation and it was but of confirmation. I will not wander in the ground of the land; where he intended to build anew, if the old foundation was not gone, the grant was void. 9 Edw. IV, 6, and 9 Edw. IV, 11b;[4] if the king grants the office of [*blank*] etc. with the accustomed fee where there was not such an office before, it is void because he thought that there was

[1] *Jennings v. Bragg* (1595), Cro. Eliz. 447, 78 E.R. 687, also cited in *Butler v. Baker* (1591), 3 Coke Rep. 25, 35, 76 E.R. 684, 707.

[2] YB 25 Edw. III, Lib. Ass., p. 116, pl. 8 (1351); YB Trin. 18 Edw. III, f. 27, pl. 24 (1344).

[3] *Archbishop of Dublin v. Bruerton* (1569), 3 Dyer 282, 73 E.R. 633.

[4] YB Trin. 9 Edw. IV, ff. [6], 11, pl. 3 (1469).

such an office before. And this also is the reason of 46 Edw. III, *Peticion*, 28,[1] and 27 Edw. III, 59; if a manor escheats to the king, which was held of a common person, and he grants it reserving tenure immediately of himself, this will make a repeal of it. It was also adjudged in the Parliament, because the use in such a case has been always to reserve to the lord who was before and because he did not now so do, it will be intended that he conceived that the manor came to him immediately and, being deceived, it is void. And upon this reason also is the case of Terrington Fair, C. 1, 49,[2] because, there, the queen intended to erect a new fair where there was another before. Thus [in] C. 11, 3 and 4,[3] it was resolved that, if the office of auditor be granted to two and the king recites this grant of it to another in reversion, because a refusal voids the grant of it, it is void. And this grant is not enabled by the Statute of 1 Edw. VI[4] because it enables grants of manors and possessions but not to enable a void grant where the king was deceived. And this appears [in] C. 10, 110,[5] upon the Statute of 18 Eliz.,[6] which has as large words and more than this Statute. Also, it enables letters patent of grants to corporations but not of incorporations, *viz.* those by which incorporations are made. Thus, it appears that the corporation [was] thus not dissolved, *viz.* the court of the dean and chapter.

And thus, if they have two names, admitting the second to be good, still the grant [is] good because they could grant by either name. *Breve*, 458, and 11 Hen. VII, 27, and 21 Edw. IV, 70;[7] a corporation can be impleaded by one name and grant by another. Thus, upon all this matter, there is not any misnomer because the reasons before do not prove any dissolution of the old corporation. And also 20 Hen. VI, 8, and B., *Corporations*, 78, and C. 10, the case of Sutton's Hospital,[8] are expressly that, in such a case, it is not dissolved.

But admit, which I deny, that the second incorporation be good, yet, if the first continues, it can grant by either name, as I have said.

But for the second part of the case, admitting the lease good, then I say first that there is not a condition. Second, if it be, yet it does not extend to the trees

[1] Hil. 46 Edw. III, Fitzherbert, *Abr.*, *Peticion*, pl. 18 (1372).

[2] *Basset v. Corporation of Torrington* (1568), cited in *Attorney General v. Bushopp* (1595–1600), 1 Coke Rep. 26, 49, 76 E.R. 64, 111, also 2 Anderson 154, 156, 123 E.R. 596, 597, also 3 Dyer 276, 73 E.R. 617.

[3] *Auditor Curle's Case* (1610), 11 Coke Rep. 2, 77 E.R. 1147.

[4] Stat. 1 Edw. VI, c. 8 (*SR*, IV, 13–14).

[5] *Legat v. Cockle* (1612), 10 Coke Rep. 108, 77 E.R. 1090.

[6] Stat. 18 Eliz. I, c. 2 (*SR*, IV, 608–610).

[7] YB Hil. 21 Edw. IV, f. 78, pl. 14 (1482), Brooke, *Abr.*, *Brief*, pl. 458; YB Trin. 11 Hen. VII, ff. 26, 27, pl. 10 (1496) or YB Trin. 11 Hen. VII, f. 27, pl. 12 (1496); YB Mich. 21 Edw. IV, ff. 67, 70, pl. 53 (1481).

[8] YB Mich. 20 Hen. VI, ff. 7, 8, pl. 17 (1441); YB Mich. 20 Hen. VI, f. 7, pl. 17 (1441), Brooke, *Abr.*, *Corporations*, pl. 78; *Baxter v. Sutton* (1612), 10 Coke Rep. 1, 28, 77 E.R. 937, 966, also Jenkins 270, 145 E.R. 194.

out of the wood. Third, if it does, yet there is not any breach here found. Fourth, if it be, yet there was not a sufficient lease made to the plaintiff.

For the first, the words are that the lessor promised to stand to the arbitration of the lessor to etc. and to allow the lessor to cut and carry the said woods and underwoods and, if he does not, that it will well lie to the lessor to reenter. And I conceive that this is no condition, first, because they are of the words of the lessee only; second, it comes between other promises in the bundle; third, because the words are not indifferent to be spoken by the lessor or lessee, nor are they the words of the lessor *tantum*.

For the first, Dy. 60a;[1] the lessee promised, if he alienated, that the feoffor will enter; there, this was not a condition. In P., Browning's case,[2] this point was moved, but it was not resolved. But [in] Dy. 79,[3] there, the words are indifferent, to be spoken by one or the other, and, on account of this, it was a condition. For the second and third [points], pB. 295; a proviso among other promises will not make a condition. And C. 270;[4] to the condition are requisite the third condition and quality aforesaid.

For the second, I conceive that the words extend only to the woods because it is a double exception, one of woods, the other of trees. And the words are that he not disturb in the woods, thus being two distinct of entire difference, trees and woods, because 14 Hen. VIII, 1, and C. 5, 11;[5] by an exception of the woods, the soil [is] excepted; but not by the exception of trees no more in the ground which will serve the tree by the nourishment of the vegetable soul of it. C. 11, 49,[6] agrees.

Second, if the lease be of a manor except the woods, in a *praecipe* for it, there must be a saving clause, otherwise, if the exception [is] of the trees, as C. 11, 49, it is agreed by law. Also, a condition that is penal and goes in defeasance will be taken strictly and not extended beyond the express words. And this is the reason of 27 Hen. VIII, 6;[7] the condition *mandare feffavi* was performed by a making of

---

[1] *Anonymous* (1551), 1 Dyer 69, 70, 73 E.R. 147.

[2] *Browning v. Beston* (1552), 1 Plowden 131, 140, 75 E.R. 202, 216.

[3] *Chickeley's Case* (1553), 1 Dyer 79, 73 E.R. 169.

[4] *Lord Cromwel v. Andrews* (1601), 2 Coke Rep. 69, 70, 76 E.R. 574, 577, also 1 Anderson 17, 230, 123 E.R. 330, 445, 2 Anderson 69, 123 E.R. 550, Jenkins 252, 145 E.R. 178, Cro. Eliz. 15, 891, 78 E.R. 281, 1115, Moore K.B. 105, 471, 72 E.R. 470, 703, Gouldsborough 116, 75 E.R. 1034, Yelverton 3, 7, 80 E.R. 3, 5, Savile 115, 123 E.R. 1044, 3 Dyer 311, 354, 73 E.R. 704, 796, Noy 44, 74 E.R. 1013, Benloe 201, 123 E.R. 141.

[5] *Bishop of London v. Nevell* (1522), YB Mich. 14 Hen. VIII, f. 1, pl. 1, 119 Selden Soc. 88; *Ive v. Sammes,* (1597), 5 Coke Rep. 11, 77 E.R. 64, also Cro. Eliz. 521, 78 E.R. 770, 2 Anderson 51, 123 E.R. 541.

[6] *Stamp v. Clinton* (1614), 11 Coke Rep. 46, 49, 77 E.R. 1206, 1211, also 1 Rolle Rep. 95, 81 E.R. 354.

[7] YB Pas. 27 Hen. VIII, f. 6, pl. 18 (1535).

deeds. And Dy. 343;[1] a lease of a manor upon condition that he not alienate any part; a voluntary grant of a copyhold is not a forfeiture because a penal condition and a penal statute are in the same degree. 18 Edw. IV, 16,[2] upon the Statute of Westminster II, for age;[3] and Dy. 123;[4] a lease by an abbot rendering rent and a release of the rent [is] not within the Statute of 31 Hen. VIII.[5]

For the fourth, here, there was not found any breach because it was found that the dean and chapter cut down a top of an ash and that the lessee carried away part of the bough, which could be the leaves, because they [are] part of the bough, and yet [it was] no hindrance to carry the wood, and a verdict will not be supplied by an inference to defeat an estate. C. 8, 89.[6]

For the fourth, the lessee of the dean has not entitled himself [in the pleading], it was found that, after this supposed breach, the dean and chapter made a lease to the plaintiff and sealed it and made a letter of attorney to deliver it upon the land as their deed. And this, under favor, was not good because, by the affixing of the common seal without more, it becomes the deed of the corporation and their lease, at this time, that they do not have but a right of entry which could not be leased because one who does not have but a right cannot attorn, 21 Hen. VI, 8,[7] and a right of goods is not grantable, 6 Hen. VII, 8.[8] And thus, according to the rule of Mowbray, 30 Edw. III, 31b,[9] if the first deed be void, the letter of attorney to make possession upon it is also void. And also, if the first delivery was good as his deed, he cannot have a second delivery, but the way has to be, upon the breach of the condition, to have made a letter of attorney for entry and then to have made a lease or to have made an escrow of the lease and a letter of attorney to affix the seal upon the land in delivering possession to the lessee. But as it was done, it is not good.

Thus upon all, he concluded for the defendant.

More, 41, pl. 21.[10]

---

[1] *Earl of Arundel's Case* (1575), 3 Dyer 342, 73 E.R. 771, also Jenkins 242, 145 E.R. 170.

[2] YB Mich. 18 Edw. IV, f. 16, pl. 18 (1478).

[3] Stat. 13 Edw. I, of Westminster, c. 40 (*SR*, I, 91).

[4] *Granado v. Dyer* (1555), 2 Dyer 123, 73 E.R. 269.

[5] Stat. 31 Hen. VIII, c. 13 (*SR*, III, 733–739).

[6] *Milner v. Fraunces* (1609), 8 Coke Rep. 89, 77 E.R. 609, also 2 Brownlow & Goldesborough 940.

[7] Perhaps *Pilkinton's Case* (1441), YB Mich. 20 Hen. VI, f. 8, pl. 17.

[8] *Broker's Case* (1490), YB Mich. 6 Hen. VII, f. 7, pl. 4.

[9] YB Mich. 30 Edw. III, f. 31 (1356).

[10] For other proceedings in this case, see Nos. 73, 271.

176

Rose v. Harvey

(K.B. Mich. 2 Car. I, 1626)

A plea of tender need not allege the place and the time of the tender.

BL MS. Add. 35961, f. 44, pl. 45

Between Rose and Harvey in [an action of] covenant, *quod intratur* Trin. 2 Car., rot. 1480, the plaintiff showed how the defendant had promised to pay to J.S. such a sum of money to the use of the daughter of the plaintiff upon her marriage or to give to J.S. sufficient security for it before such a day and that he has not done it etc.

The defendant pleaded that he offered to J.S. sufficient security for the money before the day *post confectionem* of the said indentures, upon which the plaintiff demurred generally. And for the cause of the demurrer, it was shown:

First, that the bar is vicious in form, and this for three causes:

(1) He has pleaded that he offered sufficient assurance and he did not show what manner of assurance, which he should have done [so] that the court can adjudge upon it whether it be sufficient. And thus is 35 Hen. VI, 10, and 22 Edw. IV, 40.[1] If one be held to discharge one of etc. and he pleads that he has discharged, he must show how.

(2) He has not alleged the place of the tender of the security so that, if he has an issue to be made upon it, there could be a venue, and this is the reason for alleging the place, as is said [in] C. 231; thus [is] 6 Edw. IV, 2; 11 Hen. VII, 23;[2] and 10 Hen. VII, 26.

(3) He has not alleged the time of the offer of the security because this is of the substance of the plea here and, though he is not to make it at the day certain, yet, if he alleges performance, he must show the certain time. And express authority in this is C. 27b,[3] by Morgan, in [an action of] debt upon an obligation conditioned to pay so much before such a day, the defendant said that he had paid it before the day, this without putting a day in certain, and, there, they said it was not. And thus is 7 Hen. VII, 5,[4] in [an action of] trespass, the defendant justified his entry within the year for mortmain without showing the day of his entry; it was not good. And, there, it is put also to be adjudged [that] the lessee brought [an action of] covenant upon a promise that he will not eject during the

---

[1] YB Mich. 35 Hen. VI, f. 10, pl. 16 (1456); *Lord Lisle's Case* (1483), YB Hil. 22 Edw. IV, f. 40, pl. 2.

[2] *Willion v. Berkley* (1560 x 1561), 1 Plowden 223, 231, 75 E.R. 339, 351; YB Mich. 6 Edw. IV, ff. 1, 2, pl. 4 (1466); YB Trin. 11 Hen. VII, f. 23, pl. 1 (1496).

[3] *Colthirst v. Bejushin* (1550), 1 Plowden 21, 27, 75 E.R. 33, 44.

[4] *Eliot v. Count* (1491), YB Mich. 7 Hen. VII, f. 5, pl. 6.

term, and he showed that he was ejected during the term without showing the day; it was not good.

Also, he moved that, by the indentures, the defendant promised to pay to J.S. so much or to give him sufficient security before such a day *post datum praesentium* and the defendant pleaded that, before the day *post confectionem praesentium*, which could be the same day because *confectio*, as Claybon's case is, includes the day of the making and a date excluded, thus, it could be that he paid the same day which was not the contract, but *quod post datum praesentium* before such day etc.

The second cause of the demurrer was upon the matter because he took the law to be that, by this contract, he has undertaken that J.S. will accept the money or assurance and, on account of this, the refusal of the offer by J.S. is not a good matter in bar. In the case of an obligation to pay so much to a stranger, it is clear [that], if the stranger refuses, the obligation is forfeited. 2 Edw. II; 4 Hen. IV, 4; 36 Hen. VI, 8 and 9.[1] And he took the case of a contract to be as strong. And for express authority, thus, it was adjudged in a case of covenant, 33 Hen. VI, 19, and C. 5, 23;[2] one [was] bound to pay so much as the ecclesiastical judge will order; there, the obligor undertook anything that the judge will order; Lambe's case, by which etc.

And the court said that, upon the general demurrer, the exception of place and time will not aid, but fall off.

And DODDERIDGE said that there is not a difficulty in this case.

And a day was given to the other party to answer or judgment peremptory [will be entered] and the box paid.

177

Sacheverell v. Dale

(Part 1)
(K.B. Mich. 2 Car. I, 1626)

The issue in this case was what interest in trees a life tenant without impeachment of waste can pass to a lessee.

BL MS. Add. 35961, f. 44, pl. 46

Between Sacheverell [and Dale] in [an action of] trespass, *quod intratur* Pas. 2 [Car. I], rot. 75, the case was opened to be thus. A tenant for life without impeachment of waste with liberty to cut, carry, etc. and to make leases for twenty-one years or three lives made a lease for life excepting the woods and underwoods growing and to grow excepting sufficient to keep in repair the rail and

---

[1] YB 36 Hen. VI, f. 8, pl. 5 (1457 x 1458).
[2] *Lamb v. Brownwent* (1599), 5 Coke Rep. 23, 77 E.R. 85, also Cro. Eliz. 716, 78 E.R. 950.

pale of the park and fifty trees yearly to uphold the houses in the park and the tops of all the trees. And afterward, the lessor cut wood upon the ground.

And it was said that the lessee here in this case could reserve the trees because he has an interest in them. And it is not similar to Ive's case and Saunders' case, C. 5,[1] because, there, the lessee for years did not have any interest in the trees, as the lessee for life here has, and, on account of this, it is not similar.

Second, it was said that the second exception was void because it was repugnant to the first exception, similar to the lessee of land reserving the profit or the excepting [of] the thing leased because he leased excepting the wood and underwood excepting the tops of the trees; there, by the exception of the tops of the trees, he has in part frustrated the first exception.

And a day was given to the other party peremptory.

More, f. 45, p. 64.[2]

178

Brown's Case

(K.B. Mich. 2 Car. I, 1626)

Where a person gets a writ of habeas corpus, *it will not be allowed until he has paid the jailer's fees.*

BL MS. Add. 35961, f. 44, pl. 47

One Browne was indebted to the jailer for meat and drink. And he would have removed himself by [a writ of] *habeas corpus* in the [court of] king's bench.

And it was moved by *Henden* that the usage is in such a case not to allow it until the party has satisfied the jailer if the *habeas corpus* be at the suit of the person himself.

And so it was agreed. But, here, because it did not appear whether it was his own suit or [that] of another, it was ordered that he will not be discharged out of the Marshalsea [Prison] before he has satisfied the other.

---

[1] *Ive v. Sammes* (1597), 5 Coke Rep. 11, 77 E.R. 64, also Cro. Eliz. 521, 78 E.R. 770, 2 Anderson 51, 123 E.R. 541.

[2] For later proceedings in this case, see below, No. 195.

179

Attorney General v. Inhabitants of Huntingdonshire

(Part 1)
(K.B. Mich. 2 Car. I, 1626)

The county must keep its bridges in repair unless someone else must do it by prescription or by tenure.

BL MS. Add. 35961, f. 44, pl. 48

In an information by the king against the inhabitants of Huntingdonshire for not repairing the bridge of St. Neots, the issue was whether they should, or solely, repair the bridge. And upon the evidence, it appeared that they should repair but the moiety. And it was ruled that the jury cannot find generally that they should not repair the bridge which in words is true, but they should find the special matter and thus they found a special verdict.

And it was said to the jury by DODDERIDGE, if it [was] found that the inhabitants of Huntingdonshire are not bound to the repair, they should find who is and lay it upon some reason.

And JONES said here that, if the king grants to one to be free of charges toward the reparation of castles and bridges, as Henry II had done to the prior of St. Neots, that it is good unless the prior was to maintain the bridge solely and he will not be contributory with the other inhabitants.

And DODDERIDGE said that, by the common law, the county must repair the bridges if it does not appear that another must by prescription or tenure do it. And this is before the Statute of 22 Hen. VIII, c. 5.[1]

More, f. 47b, pl. 91.[2]

180

Baldock v. Cleyland

(K.B. Mich. 2 Car. I, 1626)

In this case, a verdict was affirmed as good and sufficient.

BL MS. Add. 35961, f. 44v, pl. 49

Baldock brought an action of debt against Dr. Cleyland. And he declared that Cleyland retained him to do all his commands justly and honestly for so much *per annum*, and he averred that he had done *omnia mandata sua justa et licita*. And upon this, he recovered. And the judgment was that he recover the debt

---

[1] Stat. 22 Hen. VIII, c. 5 (*SR*, III, 321–323).

[2] For later proceedings in this case, see below, No. 224.

and his damages without saying *occasione inden[turae]* or similar, but generally *quod recuperet damna*. And upon this, [a writ of] error was brought, *quod intratur* Hil. 22 Jac., rot. 590. And the errors assigned were:

First, that the retainer was to do all his commands legally and honestly and he has averred that he has done all his commands, legal and honest, adjectivally, where the retainer was adverbially. And he could do his legal commands and not [do them] legally.

Second, because the damages are not given *occasionis* etc. And all the precedents are, if it be in debt, *occasione detentionis*; if in *ejectione firmae*, *occasione transgressionis et ejectionis etc.* But here, it is *quod recuperit debita et damna* without more, and it did not say for what the damages are.

But notwithstanding those exceptions, the judgment was affirmed because the court said, if he does not do his commands legally, it is not any doing of the command because he who commands a thing to be done commands also that it will be done honestly [and], for the second, the damages will be intended for the detainment.

Thus, the judgment was affirmed.

[Other reports of this case: Popham 193, 79 E.R. 1285.]

181

Parker v. Newsam

(K.B. Mich. 2 Car. I, 1626)

A right of way can exist only from one's land to a public road or public place or where the owner of the right of way has a right to be.

BL MS. Add. 35961, f. 44v, pl. 50

Between Parker and Newsam in an action upon the case for stopping [up] his [right of] way, the plaintiff declared that he was seised of such a house etc. and that he etc. had used [from the] time of which memory [runneth not to the contrary] to have a [right of] way over the land of the defendant *usque ad talem campum vocatur* Deanfield and that the defendant had stopped [it].

And upon [a plea of] not guilty, the verdict was for the plaintiff. And it was moved in arrest of judgment that the plaintiff had not alleged that he had any estate in Deanfield nor anything to do in it, but, if it was the way to the highway, though he did not have there an estate in the *[terminus] ad quem*, yet, for his general interest, he could have a way to it.

And Justice JONES said that, if he prescribes for a way to his neighbor's house, it is not good. And because it is alleged that he had a way *ad quendam campum*, it was ruled to be good because a *campus* is a large, open place in which divers men have lands. And thus he could aver [it]. But, if it was to have a way to such a close and he did not show that he had any estate in the close, the court said that it will be otherwise.

[Other reports of this case: Latch 160, 82 E.R. 325, HLS MS. 1235, f. 71v; CUL MS. Hh.2.1, f. 218v; CUL MS. Ll.3.13, f. 170.]

182

Wilks v. Gransgrove Churchwardens

(K.B. Mich. 2 Car. I, 1626)

The ecclesiastical courts have jurisdiction over the repairing of a church.

The majority in a parish can bind the minority as to the repair of a church.

BL MS. Add. 35961, f. 44v, pl. 51

The wardens of the church of Gransgrove libelled in the ecclesiastical court against Wilks for taxation for the casting of bells and showed that it was agreed by the major part of them that the bells will be newly founded and that each will be rated toward it.

And [a writ of] prohibition was prayed because this party was not consenting to it and a by-law without a custom will not bind except those who assent. And he cited 44 Edw. III, 19.[1]

But the prohibition was denied because it is an ecclesiastical cognizance for the repairing of a church and the greater part will bind the lesser because the consent of the major part, in law, is the consent of all, otherwise one refractory fellow in a parish will hinder a public good.

[Other reports of this case: Popham 197, 79 E.R. 1288.]

183

Ewins v. Pound

(K.B. Mich. 2 Car. I, 1626)

Where a person is sued on a debt on a judgment in a court baron, he can wage his law in defense.

BL MS. Add. 35961, f. 44v, pl. 52

Ewins brought [an action of] debt against Pound. And he declared upon a recovery in a court baron. The defendant waged his law. And whether it will be received was demanded of the court.

---

[1] YB Trin. 44 Edw. III, f. 9, pl. 14 (1370).

And it was ruled that in a country [?][1] recovery in such a court which is not a court of record, the defendant can wage his law. And thus, [as said] by DOD-DERIDGE, is 2 Edw. IV, by which he, in this case, waged his law.

Intratur, Trin. 2 [Car. I], rot. 1489.

184

Kinly v. Cobb

(K.B. Mich. 2 Car. I, 1626)

In an action of ejectment, the place of the ejectment must be alleged with specificity.

BL MS. Add. 35961, f. 44v, pl. 53

Between Kinly and Cob in [an action of] *ejectione firmae,* the judgment was arrested for the uncertainty because the declaration was *de uno messuagio sive tenemento.* And thus, it was said, it was the common experience and that this is a common exception.

[Other reports of this case: Popham 197, 79 E.R. 1289.]

185

Markham v. Cobb

(Part 3)
(K.B. Mich. 2 Car. I, 1626)

BL MS. Add. 35961, f. 44v, pl. 54

And now in the case of Markham and Cobb, before, fo. 21, p. 22,[2] the justices showed their opinion. And all agreed for the plaintiff, that he will have judgment upon the insufficiency of the bar and the exceptions before taken.

But, for the matter in law, DODDERIDGE and WHITELOCKE held that the bar was not good.

But JONES, *contra,* argued that it will be unreasonable that the greater offense will be a protection for the lesser and that, when one has done an offense that deserves punishment, that it will be absurd, by the commitment of a greater offense and more heinous [one], that he will find protection. And he cited 6 Edw. IV, 4,[3] where one in execution for damages [that were] recovered in [an action of] redisseisin committed a felony to him, this did not clear him of the damages; and Dy.

---

[1] est contra: BL MS. Lansd. 1083, f. 61v.

[2] For earlier proceedings in this case, see above, Nos. 102, 152.

[3] YB Mich. 6 Edw. IV, f. 4, pl. 11 (1466).

124,[1] where one in debt to the queen committed treason and, afterward, he was pardoned, still the debt was not gone. And he said there was one Trussell's case,[2] who was greatly in debt and he committed a felony to the intent to be pardoned and thus to defeat his creditors, but it was adjudged that he could not. And this case the other justices remembered also.

JONES argued and agreed with the cases put by Dodderidge because they are not of the same thing, but in other actions. And on account of this, if one commits a trespass and afterwards commits a felony, this does not extinguish the trespass because [they are committed] in divers acts. But in the same act, as the case is here, the felony drowns and merges the act. And yet he agreed that, before an indictment of the felony, it is in the election of the party *agere civiliter vel criminaliter*, but, when the party is indicted for the same act, he cannot ever have [an action of] trespass. And this [is] for three reasons:

(1) when it is found by a verdict that the defendant has taken the goods feloniously, the plaintiff is concluded to say that he took them as a trespasser;

(2) if one has committed a felony at common law, there was not any remedy for the party robbed to have his goods back except, at his suit, the [other] party was attainted, and this was to make that inconvenience will not be made to [the prosecution of] felonies, but, if, by this way, he could have a remedy, the prosecution of offenders is gone;

(3) an indictment at the suit of the king was a bar to the appeal of the party, and this was for the folly and negligence of the party, that he did not prosecute the offender before the king, and it will be a foolery, as he said, that an indictment will be a bar to the greater action, and it will not be to the lesser, *viz.*, trespass. And it is plain, if the party had here brought his appeal, he did not bring one that resorted to his action of trespass, which is his inferior action. And this is from the book of 3 Edw. III, *Corone*, 367.[3]

WHITELOCKE, *antea*: And his reason was because, here, the party was but convicted, and not attainted, in which case, he will not forfeit his goods to the king. And thus, the plaintiff cannot have restitution. But he, as Justice Jones said, was quite out because the books have adjudged and resolved that, by the conviction solely, he will forfeit his goods.

But judgment was given for the plaintiff upon the insufficient pleading *una voce*.

And DODDERIDGE said that the case was a good case. And, *ut credo*, he was convinced by the arguments of Jones.

---

[1] *Carewe's Case* (1555), 2 Dyer 124, 73 E.R. 271.

[2] *Banyster v. Trussel* (1596), Cro. Eliz. 516, 78 E.R. 764.

[3] *Anonymous* (1329), Eyre of Northamptonshire, Selden Soc., vol. 97, p. 160, Fitzherbert, Abr., *Corone & plees del corone*, pl. 367.

[Other reports of this case: Benloe 185, 73 E.R. 1046, CUL MS. Gg.2.30, f. 70; W. Jones 147, 82 E.R. 79, BL MS. Hargr. 317, f. 151; Latch 144, 82 E.R. 316, HLS MS. 1235, f. 64; Noy 82, 74 E.R. 1049; BL MS. Hargr. 38, ff. 99v, 116v; BL MS. Lansd. 1092, f. 122; CUL MS. Hh.2.1, f. 211v; CUL MS. Ll.3.13, f. 151v.]

186

Rex v. Jones

(Part 2)

(K.B. Mich. 2 Car. I, 1626)

BL MS. Add. 35961, f. 45, pl. 55

In the case where Griffith Jones [and] three others were indicted for murder for the killing of one in keeping possession against one of the commissioners out of chancery to deliver possession [in] the case between Herbert and Vaughan, the prisoners this term were bailed.

And on account of this, DODDERIDGE said that he thought that it was fitting to show the reason why they were bailed. And he said that, before the Statute of Westminster I, ca. 13,[1] every constable and jailer would have bailed prisoners and, on account of this, by this Statute, it was limited which persons have the power to bail and which could be bailed, but yet notwithstanding this, the high court of the king's bench has the power, by their discretion, to bail any man imprisoned for any cause. And they are not restrained because in them *summa confidentia* is put for matters of the crown. And thus, it was, he said, resolved in Egerton and Morgan's case,[2] where one was bailed in an appeal and afterward, however, he was found guilty. And thus has the king's bench in all ages used this power. And as to them, the Statute is admonitory in which cases to be tender to use their discretion, and not obligatory. And on account of this, he said that he would have the reasons of this bailment known, *viz.*, that the prisoners have been two years now imprisoned for lack of a trial because the jury was to come from Shropshire and they could not be now tried before Easter or Trinity term. Thus, they will be defeated or [*blank*] before it. And also, where the bail were men of £500 *per annum*, ten men [were] sufficient.[3]

[Other reports of this case: Latch 12, 82 E.R. 249; BL MS. Add. 35961, f. 161, pl. 35; BL MS. Lansd. 1083, f. 245v, pl. 35 (Widdrington's reports).]

---

[1] Stat. 3 Edw. I, c. 15 (*SR*, I, 30).

[2] *Egerton v. Morgan* (1610), 1 Bulstrode 69, 80 E.R. 770.

[3] For earlier proceedings in this case, see above, No. 57.

187

Harvey v. Reynell

(Part 2)

(K.B. Mich. 2 Car. I, 1626)

BL MS. Add. 35961, f. 45, pl. 56

In the case of Harvey and Reynell, before, [f.] 23, pl. 39,[1] for the point, it was shown for express authority that the retaking of the prisoner was not soon enough to prevent the plaintiff if it be not before the action [was] brought. And it is not material whether the defendant has pleaded or not because, by the bringing of the action, this liberty of retaking is gone; 34 Edw. I, *Det*, 162; 13 Edw. III, *Bar*, 253; 13 Edw. IV, 9, by Brian; 3 Edw. VI, *Escape*, B., 45 and 43; Rigwaie's case;[2] because, for part of the action, he was at the charge, and, if, after a retaking, he [would] be barred, he will lose the charges of bringing the action.

And as to the exception that the '*viz.* 8 May' will be idle and thus the retaking [was] well laid before the filing of the bill, it was said that it could not be because, if the '*viz.*' be void here, then it was solely pleaded what reverses him before the bringing of the action, and he did not show the day in certain. Thus then, no day [was] pleaded of the retaking.

Post, f. 44b, p. 62; more.[3]

188

Brown v. Stroud

(K.B. Mich. 2 Car. I, 1626)

The issue in this case was whether the contract in dispute was executed or executory.

BL MS. Add. 35961, f. 45, pl. 57

In [an action of] covenant between Sir Robert Browne and Sir Richard Strowde, *quod intratur* Trin. 2 [Car. I], rot. 960, the case was thus in effect. A. covenanted with B. to perform and observe certain articles of agreement between

---

[1] For other proceedings in this case, see Nos. 170, 193, 265.

[2] Mich. 34 Edw. I, Fitzherbert, Abr., *Dette*, pl. 162 (1306); *Abbot of Westminster's Case* (1339), YB Mich. 13 Edw. III, Rolls Ser. 31b, vol. 3, p. 38, pl. 19, Fitzherbert, Abr., *Barre*, pl. 253; *Lord Say's Case* (1473), YB Pas. 13 Edw. IV, ff. 8, 9, pl. 4; 5 Edw. VI, Brooke, Abr., *Escape*, pl. 45 (1551); YB Mich. 9 Hen. IV, f. 24, pl. 3 (1407), Brooke, Abr., *Escape*, pl. 43; *Rigeway's Case* (1594), 3 Coke Rep. 52, 76 E.R. 753, also Gouldsborough 180, 75 E.R. 1078, *sub nom. Grills v. Ridgeway*, Cro. Eliz. 318, 439, 78 E.R. 568, 579, Moore K.B. 660, 72 E.R. 822, Popham 41, 79 E.R. 1159.

[3] For other proceedings in this case, see Nos. 170, 193, 265.

them in which it was awarded that A. will have from B. the manor of D. in exchange for the manor of S. which belonged to A. and that they, each of them, will enter at the following Michaelmas into the manors interchangeably and also that A. will pay to B. £1200, which was the surplus, as the manor of S. was better than the manor of D., for the exchange of the manors. B., before Michaelmas, sold the manor of S. And now the question was whether A. was bound to pay the money.

And it was argued yes because, here, there was a perfect agreement and distinct articles and the bargain [was] executed and, even though there was no date of payment, yet it will be intruded[1] upon a request, *viz.* in a convenient time, and, if the other cannot have the manor of S., he is put to his [action of] covenant. And he cited 37 Hen. VI, 8b.[2]

On the other side, it was said that this agreement was not executed, but executory. And on account of this, the money [is] not payable before the exchange [. . .].[3] And inasmuch as he has disabled himself to execute the exchange, the money is not payable. And that it is executory appears because it is agreed that it will be paid for the exchange. And he cited 9 Edw. IV, 20 and 21,[4] where a composition was made that a prior will have a rent *pro decimis*; there, if he did not have the tithes, the prior will not have the rent; and 15 Edw. IV, 4,[5] where he was held to make a new pale for the old; if he did not have the old, he will not make a new [one]; thus, for our executory agreement. Thus [is] C. 134,[6] an annuity *pro consilio*, and Dy. 75,[7] for twenty marks to have a cake of wax etc. But he relied upon 15 Hen. VII, 10, by Fineux;[8] if one covenants with me to pay £10, and I covenant to serve him, I will have an action though I do not serve him, but if I covenant to pay £10 for the same cause, there, if I do not serve him, I will not have the [action of] covenant.

And the court persuaded them to arbitration because they perceived that it was an unkind suit.

Trin. 3, p. 32.[9]

[Other reports of this case: Popham 198, 79 E.R. 1289; BL MS. Hargr. 38, ff. 160, 183v, 201v; BL MS. Lansd. 1092, f. 293; CUL MS. Ll.3.13, f. 333.]

---

[1] Sic in MS.

[2] YB Mich. 37 Hen. VI, f. 8, pl. 18 (1458).

[3] persited *MS.*

[4] YB Trin. 9 Edw. IV, ff. 19, 20, pl. 22 (1469).

[5] *Prior of St. Faith v. Abbot of Langley* (1475), YB Mich. 15 Edw. IV, ff. 2, 4, pl. 5.

[6] *Browning v. Beston* (1555), 1 Plowden 131, 134, 75 E.R. 202, 207.

[7] *Andrew v. Boughey* (1552), 1 Dyer 75, 73 E.R. 160.

[8] YB Trin. 15 Hen. VII, f. 10, pl. 17 (1500).

[9] *Brown v. Stroud* (1627–1628), BL MS. Add. 35961, ff. 79, 139v, BL MS. Lansd. 1083, ff. 138v, 222 (Widdrington's reports).

189

Ashfield v. Ashfield

(Part 2)

(K.B. Mich. 2 Car. I, 1626)

BL MS. Add. 35961, f. 45v, pl. 58

In the case of Ashfield, before 23, p. 41,[1] it was argued that the lease could not be made good by acceptance. And first, he argued that a lease for years by an infant rendering rent was not only voidable, but void. And he cited 18 Edw. IV, 2 and 4.[2]

But JONES interrupted him and said that it was not a question but that it will be still voidable, by which he argued that a lease of a copyhold by an infant was void though a rent was reserved, first, because it is a wrong to three persons and entirely the act of the infant. What are tortious are void. 2 Ass. 2; 12 Ass. 33;[3] and 3 Hen. IV. A command by an infant to disseise another to his use [is] void because, by this, he will subject himself to the action and he will commit a tort. Thus here, if it is not void, it will be a forfeiture and thus he will prejudice himself. And C. 5, Russel's case;[4] an infant executor cannot release a debt without a satisfaction because it [is a] *devastavit* and an infant will not do a thing that [is] penal to himself. And on account of this, in Hollidaie's case, 5 Jac., it was adjudged, if an infant contracts to pay for his debt so much or, if he fails, the double [value], the contract [is] void for the penalty, as [said] by Dier.[5] Thus [is] 32 Eliz.; an infant promised to pay so much for clothing, yet he could aver that they were not worth so much and thus his promise did not bind him. And that it was a forfeiture if the lease was good appears by Penifather's case, C. 4,[6] where it is said that infants and married women are bound by the custom, and 31 Ass. 17 and Whitingham's case, ca. 8;[7] a reversioner could enter upon an infant for a condition broken. Also, though the lease is not good here, yet even though he had acted against his fealty and as much as it was in him to commit a tort, it will

---

[1] For other proceedings in this case, see Nos. 172, 287.

[2] YB Pas. 18 Edw. IV, ff. 1, 2, pl. 7 (1478).

[3] YB 2 Edw. III, Lib. Ass., p. 3, pl. 2 (1328); YB 12 Edw. III, Lib. Ass., p. 37, pl. 33 (1338).

[4] *Russel v. Prat* (1584), 5 Coke Rep. 27, 77 E.R. 91, also 1 Leonard 193, 74 E.R. 178, 4 Leonard 44, 74 E.R. 718, Moore K.B. 146, 72 E.R. 496, 1 Anderson 177, 123 E.R. 417.

[5] Perhaps *Ayliff v. Archdale* (1603), Cro. Eliz. 920, 78 E.R. 1142.

[6] *Clarke v. Pennifather* (1584), 4 Coke Rep. 23, 76 E.R. 923.

[7] YB 31 Edw. III, Lib. Ass., p. 188, pl. 17 (1357); *Whittingham's Case* (1603), 8 Coke Rep. 42, 77 E.R. 537.

be a forfeiture similar to the case of 30 Ass.[1] cited in C. 1, Brendon's case.[2] And, if the lease be void here, then, the confirmation cannot be for an acceptance, as is C. 3, Penant's case.[3] Also, here, when the son [was] admitted after the lease [was] made, this was a new grant to him and as much as the lord [of the manor] has taken advantage of the forfeiture and regranted it back, and thus he comes in paramount [to] the first lease, and he cannot affirm it.

Afterward, 43, p. 37, p. 3, 37.[4]

190

Saunders v. Mariton

(K.B. Mich. 2 Car. I, 1626)

In this case, a contract was found to have been made and broken.

BL MS. Add. 35961, f. 45v, pl. 59

Between Saunders and Meriton, *quod intratur* Trin. 2 [Car. I], rot. 1077, the case was [thus]. Two covenanted that land is discharged of all incumbrances by them or any other person or persons. And there was a former lease made by one of them. Whether it was an incumbrance within the covenant because [made] but by one [was the question].

And [it was] ruled without argument, clearly, that it was, and on account of this, the covenant [was] broken, and thus judgment [was] given.

More, 92b, f. 123, pl. 16, reversed for error.[5]

[Other reports of this case: Latch 161, 82 E.R. 325; Noy 86, 74 E.R. 1052; Popham 200, 79 E.R. 1291; CUL MS. Hh.2.1, f. 219; CUL MS. Ll.3.13, f. 171.]

191

Anonymous

(K.B. Mich. 2 Car. I, 1626)

The ecclesiastical courts have jurisdiction to determine the payment and the customary non–payment of mortuaries.

---

[1] YB 30 Edw. III, Lib. Ass., f. 181, pl. 47 (1356).

[2] *Gardiner v. Bredon* (1597), 1 Coke Rep. 67, 76 E.R. 161.

[3] *Harvey v. Oswald* (1596), 3 Coke Rep. 64, 76 E.R. 775, also Moore K.B. 456, 72 E.R. 692, Cro. Eliz. 553, 572, 78 E.R. 798, 816.

[4] For other proceedings in this case, see Nos. 172, 287.

[5] *Saunders v. Mariton* (1628), BL MS. Add. 35961, f. 129; BL MS. Lansd. 1083, f. 209; LI MS. Maynard 21, f. 373 (Paynell's exchequer reports).

BL MS. Add. 35961, f. 45v, pl. 60

If a parson [sue] in the spiritual court for a mortuary and the executor pleads that the custom was always to pay none, here, there will not be a [writ of] prohibition because, the principle belonging to the spiritual court, the trial of this custom belongs to them also. See 2 Ric. III.

But JONES said that, if, in the spiritual court, they would allow this by custom which is not, within our law, a custom, there, peradventure, a prohibition lies as if they allow payment for forty years to bind because the Statute of Hen. VIII[1] is that no mortuaries will be paid but where they have been paid by custom, which is intended a custom at common law.

192

Rex v. Lamb

(Part 2)
(K.B. Mich. 2 Car. I, 1626)

BL MS. Add. 35961, f. 45v, pl. 61

And now, the indictment of Lamb, and the exceptions, was moved again; above fo. 39b, pl. 29.[2] And it was quashed principally upon this exception, that it was as *quod exercavit quasdam malas et diabolicas artes, Anglice* witchcraft. Now, all of the justices agreed that, if the words precedent did not signify witchcraft, as they agreed they do not, then the English words do not make the indictment because, by the Statute of 26 Edw. III,[3] all pleas must be in Latin. And here, it fails for that it is not in Latin, but English. But, if it had been the proper Latin word for witchcraft or if there had been such words of which the law takes notice to signify such a thing, it had been good by the *Anglice*. But here, the Latin did not so signify nor in our law is it intended to signify thus. And on account of this, it is void. And this was the main reason for quashing the indictment.

[Other reports of this case: Benloe 185, 73 E.R. 1046, CUL MS. Gg.2.30, f. 70; W. Jones 143, 82 E.R. 76, BL MS. Hargr. 317, f. 145; Latch 156, 82 E.R. 323, HLS MS. 1235, f. 70v; Noy 85, 74 E.R. 1052; BL MS. Hargr. 38, f. 120v; BL MS. Lansd. 1092, f. 134v; CUL MS. Hh.2.1, f. 217v.]

---

[1] Stat. 21 Hen. VIII, c. 6 (*SR*, III, 288–289).

[2] For earlier proceedings in this case, see above, No. 160.

[3] Stat. 36 Edw. III, stat. 1, c. 15 (*SR*, I, 375–376).

193

Harvey v. Reynell

(Part 3)

(K.B. Mich. 2 Car. I, 1626)

BL MS. Add. 35961, f. 45v, pl. 62

Richardson moved the case of Harvey and Rennells. And he argued that the retaking, though it was after the action [was] commenced, was good enough, inasmuch as it was upon a fresh suit because, he said, even though some opinions are against it, if yet it was not ever thus adjudged, it seemed to him that a strong reason is that a retaking after the action [brought] is a good bar. And his reason was that, when the jailer has retaken the prisoner upon a fresh suit, now, the law does not say that there was any escape, but the law says that, now, he was always in custody. Thus, if he was always in custody, he has never escaped. But, when he has retaken him, he will be said always to continue in possession and custody. And to prove this, he cited C. 36, Plat's case,[1] where it was said that the retaking will be said possession with continuance. And thus [is] 13 Hen. VII, 1; 14 Hen. VII, 1; 10 Edw. IV, 10; and the opinion of Brian [in] 13 Edw. IV, 9.[2]

It is intrudable where there was not a fresh suit also. The point of the writ is *permisit ire ad largam quo voluit*, which is not done upon a fresh suit, but flies for [. . .] but he did not have liberty to go where he would. Also when the jailer retook him to that intent, it will be this if he not be in execution for the party because the jailer cannot keep him until he be satisfied, but he will be in execution for the plaintiff, thus as [in] Kel. 3 and 6 Hen. VII, 12, and 10 Hen. VII, 12, and 10 Hen. V;[3] if a prisoner be released and retaken anew, the sheriff will not be fined because, now, by relation there was not any escape.

But he said, be it as he would, still, there is an incurable flaw in the declaration because he declared that [in] 16 Hilary he recovered and Trin. 29 upon an execution and he had a *capias* returnable *mense Michaelis* next, upon which the defendant was arrested 24 July 19 *Jacobi et quod 20 Junii anno decimo praedicto* he was removed by [a writ of] *habeas corpus* to the king's bench and committed to the marshal, who allowed him to escape. Now, if the commitment to the marshal was not good, there was not any escape. And here, the *habeas corpus* was before the arrest; it was 24 July and the *habeas corpus* was 20 *Junii anno decimo*. Thus, by

---

[1] *Platt v. Lock* (1551), 1 Plowden 35, 75 E.R. 57.

[2] YB Mich. 13 Hen. VII, f. 1, pl. 1 (1497); YB Mich. 14 Hen. VII, f. 1, pl. 1 (1498); YB Trin. 10 Edw. IV, f. 10, pl. 4 (1470); *Lord Say v. Lord Nottingham* (1473), YB Pas. 13 Edw. IV, ff. 8, 9, pl. 4.

[3] *Anonymous* (1496), Keilwey 2, 3, 72 E.R. 155; YB Mich. 6 Hen. VII, ff. 11, 12, pl. 9 (1490); YB Trin. 10 Hen. VII, f. 25, pl. 3 (1495); YB Hil. 10 Hen. IV, f. 7, pl. 2 (1409).

force of this *habeas corpus*, he could not be committed in execution for it for that there was not an arrest.

To this, the justices said that, if a *habeas corpus* be sued in the vacation, the *teste* is always the last day of the precedent term, and on account of this, by virtue of the *habeas corpus* dated 20 June, he could be delivered in execution upon an arrest the 24th of July for the necessity in this case. But here, the *habeas corpus* is laid *anno decimo*, thus nine years before. But it was said it was the fault of the clerk because the bill upon the file and the paper book were 19 *praedicto*. And on account of this, [it is] amendable. And a day was given to have the bill and paper book [produced] in court.

And for the matter in law, all of the court agreed that, if the retaking be not before the action [was] commenced, it came too late to bar the plaintiff because, once his action is well brought, it will not [have] been done tortious[ly] and *ex consequenti*, he will answer [for the] costs for the matter *ex post facto*. And they compared it to the case of waste and reparation before an action brought, put [by counsel], 13 Edw. I; 29 Hen. VI; and C. 5, Whelpdale's case.[1] But, when the action once attaches, then [it is] too late.

And JONES said that he knew but two cases where a subsequent act will abate [an] action, first, Wroth and Wigges' case, C. 4,[2] where, pending an appeal, the defendant was convicted upon an indictment; and C. 3, Pursloe's case,[3] where proclamations incurring pending the [*blank*] will bar it. But these are upon particular reasons. But otherwise, no subsequent act pending the action will be a bar.

And for the *scilicet*, if it be void, he doubted. And he referred it to the consideration when the record comes in because, if it be contrary to the matter before alleged sufficiently, it is void.

And JONES said, if it be necessary to allege a day in certain of the retaking and he has alleged it in the *videlicet*, it cannot be void because, then, he has not alleged any day. But, if he need not allege it, then, the *videlicet* could be void, otherwise not. And on account of this, it is not similar to the case now pending, where the defendant avowed for rent as remainderman and showed the death of the tenant for life and *quod postea, scilicet etc.*, which was before the death of the tenant for life. Here, the *scilicet* is void because there is no need to show the day when the rent was in arrears because [it is a] real action. And on account of this, it is void.

---

[1] YB Mich. 39 Hen. VI, f. 32, pl. 45 (1460); *Whelpdale v. Whelpdale* (1604), 5 Coke Rep. 119, 77 E.R. 239.

[2] *Wrote v. Wigges* (1591), 4 Coke Rep. 45, 76 E.R. 994, also Cro. Eliz. 276, 78 E.R. 531.

[3] *Purslow's Case* (1581), cited in *The Case of Fines* (1602), 3 Coke Rep. 84, 90, 76 E.R. 824, 842.

And for the traverse *absque hoc quod* there was another escape, they held it good enough because, if he escaped [on the] 29th of such a month and is not re-taken before the 30th, it is an escape the 29th[1] of the same month.

And also when there is an escape in Surrey, it is an escape in all of the counties of England. And on account of this, the averment of *eadem escapia* is good without a traverse.

More, 38, p. 14.[2]

194

Jenkins v. Vivian

(K.B. Mich. 2 Car. I, 1626)

The issues in this case were the correct method of pleading the use of a common for cattle in a moor.

BL MS. Add. 35961, f. 46, pl. 63

[In a case] between Jenkins and Vivian in [an action of] trespass, *quod intra-tur* Trin. 1 [Car. I], rot. 331, the defendant pleaded that he was seised of a great moor and that the plaintiff was also seised of a great moor, to which the place in which etc. is adjoining and that the plaintiff and *omnes occupatores* of the said close at the moor adjoining have used to enclose against the moor and that the defendant has used and all those whose estate etc. have had a usage to have a common for the cause of vicinage for his cattle *levant et couchant* and that he put in his cattle in his own moor, which went into the close of the plaintiff by the default of the enclosure. And, upon this, he demurred.

And the first exception was because he did not prescribe for the common for the cause of vicinage and allowance. 16 Eliz., Dy.

The second exception [was] because he charged *occupatores* with the enclosure where he should have said the plaintiff and all of the tenants of it and shown of what estate. But of this, it was doubted because he is a stranger to the estate of the plaintiff and it could, in the alleging [?] of it, be easily tried [?] and he will not be chased [?] to know the estate of another.

The third exception [was] because he has prescribed for a common for his cattle *levant et couchant* and he has not averred that they were thus.

And this was allowed by all of the court because, having alleged the custom so strictly, he must pursue it. And judgment was given for the plaintiff.

[Other reports of this case: Latch 161, 82 E.R. 325; Popham 201, 79 E.R. 1292; CUL MS. Hh.2.1, f. 219; CUL MS. Ll.3.13, f. 170v.]

---

[1] 20 *MS.*

[2] For other proceedings in this case, see Nos. 170, 187, 265.

195

Sacheverell v. Dale

(Part 2)
(K.B. Mich. 2 Car. I, 1626)

BL MS. Add. 35961, f. 46, pl. 64

The case before, f. 43a, pl. 46, between Secheverall and Dale[1] was now argued, and it was thus. A tenant in fee levied a fine, and it was to the use of himself for life without impeachment of waste and with a power to cut and sell the
trees, the remainder to another for life the [*blank*] of the manor, the remainder
in fee and with a power to the tenants for life to make leases for twenty-one years
or three lives. The lessee for life made a lease for three lives, excepting all of the
wood growing or to grow, excepting sufficient [wood] to pale the park and fifty
trees for the repairing of the houses in the park and the tops of the trees, excepting for fire boot, to the lessee for three lives. And he died. Then, the remainderman for life entered and cut the trees. And the lessee for lives brought [an action
of] trespass.

In this case, these points were moved, first, whether the reservation of the
trees by the lessee for life here was good or not. And as to this, it was argued that
it was not, first, on account of this, when the lessee for life be without impeachment of waste, he, on account of this, does not have any interest in the trees,
but only an authority to take them during his estate, but no interest. And on account of this, having but an authority, it is determinable with the estate. And on
account of this, as, here, he had made a lease, he cannot except[2] his authority.
And he cited 27 Hen. VI, *Wast*, Statham, [Abr.], 47, that a tenant for life without impeachment and another cuts the trees, the tenant will not have damages
because the property [belongs] to the lessor; and 3 Hen. VI, 45;[3] where a lessor
reserved *quod liceret vendere et succidere*, this was not an interest in the trees, but
an authority, and on account of this, the lessee could, before the lessor, take the
small branches, and this was not an exception of the trees or an interest in them.
And thus [in] 41 & 42 Eliz., Mich., between Lechford and Saunders,[4] it was
ruled, if a lessor excepts[5] *quod liceat succidere et vendere*, it is not an exception of
the trees nor no interest in them. And thus here, the lessee for life did not have
more but a power to cut, which, with the land, is gone, having leased it in[to]
other hands. Thus, his exception [is] void.

---

[1] For earlier proceedings in this case, see above, No. 177.
[2] accept *MS*.
[3] YB Pas. 3 Hen. VI, f. 45, pl. 21 (1425).
[4] *Lecheforde v. Saunders* (1599), 2 Anderson 133, 123 E.R. 585.
[5] accepts *MS*.

Another reason is because the estate of the lessee for three lives is derived out of the fine and [is] paramount to the estate of the lessee for life so that he is not in by him nor his lessee because, otherwise, when the lessee for life dies, the estate of the lessee for three lives is gone, which is not so. And also, otherwise, it will be a use upon a use. And he cited for this C. 1, 134 and 176,[1] where it is said that such a lease is derived out of the first estate, and thus, it cannot be subject to his exception being but by another and not by him.

Another reason was because the privilege here is annexed to the estate of the lessee and, on account of this, when he has granted it, the privilege is gone. 3 Edw. III, 44, de la Jeles' case;[2] a lessee for years without impeachment except[3] confirmation, the estate being gone, to which the privilege [is] gone. 5 Hen. V, and Dy. 10[4] agree and, as to this which was said, if a lessee for life with a proviso, as here, to make leases lease reserving a rent, that [it is] good, he took a diversity where the power was to lease and receive also and where only to lease. In this case, he held that he cannot reserve because paramount, as he has said. And in Lea and Wrothe's case, C. 6, in Fitzwilliam's case,[5] there, the lessee had a power to reserve a rent, but C. 10, in Lovey's case,[6] he had not.

On the other side, it was argued that the exception [was] good because the lessee for life without impeachment has an interest in the trees. And this, he said that he would not argue because it is the resolution is Boules' case, C. 11.[7] And on account of this, having an interest, it is not similar to Sandes and Ives' case, C. 5,[8] of a reservation of trees for the lessee for years.

But the principal point that he conceived was whether the exception of the lops and tops of the trees excepted be a bar and frustration of the first exception. And he argued not because it was repugnant to the first exception and, on account of this, void. And he cited Dyer, where there was a lease reserving the profits, and 34 Ass. 11,[9] by which a grant of a piscary [that] excepted *piscariam meam*

---

[1] *Dillon v. Freine* (1589 x 1595), 1 Coke Rep. 113, 76 E.R. 261, also Popham 70, 79 E.R. 1184, 1 Anderson 309, 123 E.R. 489; *Kingsmill v. Sharrington* (1582 x 1584), 1 Coke Rep. 175, 76 E.R. 379, also Cro. Eliz. 34, 78 E.R. 300, Moore K.B. 144, 72 E.R. 495, Jenkins 247, 145 E.R. 174.

[2] *Idle v. Tieis* (1329), YB Mich. 3 Edw. III, f. 44, pl. 30.

[3] accept *MS*.

[4] *Abbot of Bury v. Bokenham* (1537), 1 Dyer 7, 10, 73 E.R. 19, 23.

[5] *Leaper v. Wroth* (1588), cited in *Fitz-William v. Fitz-William* (1604), 6 Coke Rep. 32, 33, 77 E.R. 300, 301.

[6] *Prowt v. Worthen* (1613), 10 Coke Rep. 78, 77 E.R. 1043, also 2 Brownlow & Goldesborough 103, 123 E.R. 839.

[7] *Bowles v. Bury* (1613), 11 Coke Rep. 79, 77 E.R. 1252, also 1 Rolle Rep. 177, 81 E.R. 413.

[8] *Ive v. Sammes* (1597), 5 Coke Rep. 11, 77 E.R. 64, also Cro. Eliz. 521, 78 E.R. 770, 2 Anderson 51, 123 E.R. 541.

[9] *Abbot of Rivaux's Case* (1360), YB 34 Edw. III, Lib. Ass., p. 207, pl. 11.

[was] a void exception, and 33 Hen. VI, 28,[1] a lease reserving herbage [was] a void reservation; thus here. He reserved the trees except the tops. The exception [was] void because thus the reservation of the trees [is] void. But he said that, here, he excepted the lopping and topping; this does not give to the lessee the tops but only an authority to do the act, as 12 Hen. VII, 25, and 13 Hen. VII, 13; a license to hunt and kill deer does not give the deer; 18 Edw. IV, 14.[2]

And the justices spoke upon the moment[3] to this.

DODDERIDGE: By the [provision] without impeachment of waste, the lessee has an interest in the trees. This [is] clear. But it does not last longer than his estate. When he here made a lease, it went out of all of the estates and will bind them. Thus, when he reserved the trees, this is good because thus it was the intent of the parties. And this is not against the law. And otherwise, it will be an absurdity that the lessee will have the power to cut and sell a tree and to make leases and yet, by the making of the lease, that he cannot reserve his interest. And it is not similar to the exception of the trees by the lessee for life or for years without such an interest where this was a trick devised to oust all of the lessors of an action of waste. But now, when the lessee died, so that the reversion came to the remainderman for life with the same privilege, whether the exception will aid him or if, during this lease for three lives, he cannot cut the trees is the question [. . .],[4] I find, for the exception out of the exception, this ends with the death of the lessor, and the lessee, on account of this, is to have but the ordinary boots of the tenant for life.

JONES agreed that, by [the provision] without impeachment [of waste], he has an interest. But, if he does not execute it during his estate, it is gone because it is concomitant with it. And on account of this, if he grants his estate reserving the trees, it is not good. But, in our case, he has not granted all of the trees to him. And on account of this, [it is a] good reservation because he had the possibility of re-entry after the three lives. And on account of this, if a tenant after a possibility grants his estate, reserving trees, it is void, but, if he leases for life, not [?] reserving, it is good.

For the exception, he said that he did not speak to it. But, for the cutting by the remainderman, he said that this is the question. And he thought the estate of the lessee for three lives operated partly out of the first estate and partly of the estate of the lessor because it will hold the charge as the charges of the lessee for life because he is not a bare nominator, but a grantor also in part.

---

[1] *Abbess of Sion's Case* (1460), YB Trin. 38 Hen. VI, ff. 33, 38, pl. 2.

[2] *Case of the Dean of St. Paul's* (1496), YB Trin. 12 Hen. VII, f. 25, pl. 6; *Earl of Suffolk v. Barney* (1498), YB Hil. 13 Hen. VII, ff. 12, 13, pl. 1, or *Duchess of Norfolk v. Wiseman* (1498), YB Hil. 13 Hen. VII, f. 13, pl. 2; YB Mich. 18 Edw. IV, f. 14, pl. 12 (1478).

[3] sur le sodaine *MS.*

[4] que 41 *MS.*

WHITELOCKE agreed.

DODDERIDGE [said] to Noy, who was to argue next, thus see upon what the case pinches, in what we are agreed, and in what we differ and doubt, and, for this, apply yourself to it.

[Other reports of this case: Latch 163, 268, 82 E.R. 326, 380; Popham 193, 79 E.R. 1285; BL MS. Lansd. 1092, f. 136v; BL MS. Hargr. 38, f. 126v; CUL MS. Hh.2.1, f. 220; CUL MS. Ll.3.13, f. 172v.]

196

Harrison v. Errington

(K.B. Mich. 2 Car. I, 1626)

In this case, the return of the sheriff was defective because it did not show that the execution on the judgment debtor's goods was proper, nor did it show that the execution was properly done.

BL MS. Add. 35961, f. 46v, pl. 65

Harrison was indicted in the county palatine of Durham because, where a judgment was given and execution awarded upon the goods, the sheriff made a warrant to four *conjunctim et divisim* to make execution and it was rescued riotously. And upon this, a writ of error [was] brought upon the judgment given in it. And the prisoner, being removed by [a writ of] *habeas corpus* because he must assign his errors in person, assigned by *Bankes*, first, that it does not appear upon what writ the warrant of the sheriff was grounded that he will lose his goods, as it must, because, upon a *capias*, if the sheriff makes a warrant to deliver goods, it [is] void. Second, the warrant was to the four *conjunctim et divisim*, and three of them did it. And on account of this, the warrant was not pursued and the resistance [was] legal. There is a difference between a ministerial and a judicial court.[1] 14 Hen. IV, 34;[2] a return by a coroner was not good because [it was] judicial, but the taking of the indictment *super visum corporis* was good because [it was] ministerial. Third, the indictment [was] before the justices of gaol delivery, who did not have power of rescue. Fourth, [it was] found that they riotously made the rescue, which one cannot do any more than conspire. 11 Hen. IV, 25;[3] it was said *juratores* presenting, and not the names of the jurors, and it must appear who they were because they could be villeins or outlaws and thus not *legales homines*.

And *Noy* twice moved the same exceptions and the same reasons, by which it was reversed.

---

[1] Sic in MS.

[2] *Clarke v. Wilkes* (1413), YB Hil. 14 Hen. IV, f. 34, pl. 52.

[3] *Canon's Case* (1410), YB Hil. 11 Hen. IV, f. 41, pl. 8.

[Other reports of this case: Benloe 194, 73 E.R. 1052, CUL MS. Gg.2.30, f. 73v; Popham 202, 79 E.R. 1292; BL MS. Hargr. 38, f. 126.]

197

Petty v. Robinson

(K.B. Mich. 2 Car. I, 1626)

Judges can take judicial notice of the death of the king.

A clerical error is amendable.

BL MS. Add. 35961, f. 46v, pl. 66

Between Petty and Robinson, *quod intratur,* Trin. 2 [Car. I], rot. 694, in [a writ of] error in [an action of] replevin in [the court of] common bench, it was moved for error, first, that divers continuances [were] made in the time of the king who was and of the now [king] and [there was] no mention of the demise of the king and yet it was said that the issue was tried *coram justiciariis dicti domini regis,* who will be intended King James, no other king being mentioned.

But it was ruled that *inter dominum regem* was before mentioned generally, that this will have relation to the now king, and *dicti domini regis* having reference to [him], it is good. And the judges are to take [judicial] notice of the demise of the king as they are of each estate concerning him.

The second error was because the commission of *nisi prius* was directed to Francis Harvey, *armiger,* and the justice who held the trial was Francis Harvey, *armiger,* and the *postea* was returned by Francis Harvey, *militem.*

But it was not allowed because the error intended was not sufficiently assigned because this which is here assigned is that he who tried the issue was a gentleman and he who returned it was a knight, which could stand together, because at the return he could be a knight and at the caption *miles*[1] and, on account of this, he must have gone farther and alleged that also the return was *armiger.*

And JONES agreed and also held that this, if it had been well assigned, was amendable because [it was] but an error of the clerk of assizes, who had the commission before him to have directed him in the names of the justices of assize.

And thus, the judgment [was] affirmed.

[Other reports of this case: Benloe 193, 73 E.R. 1052, CUL MS. Gg.2.30, f. 73; Popham 203, 79 E.R. 1293; BL MS. Hargr. 38, f. 133v.]

[Related cases: Petty v. Hobson (1626), above, No. 143.]

---

[1] Sic in MS.

198

Rochester v. Keckhall

(K.B. Mich. 2 Car. I, 1626)

The land from which a plaintiff was ejected must be specifically alleged in the pleadings.

BL MS. Add. 35961, f. 46v, pl. 67

In [the case between] Rochester and Keckhall in an action upon an *ejectione firmae* (*intratur* Trin. 2 [Car. I, rot.] 892), the judgment was reversed for these errors.

First, the declaration was of an ejectment *de uno burgagio sive tenemento*, which [is] uncertain.

Second, the judgment was against the defendant and not *quod capiatur*.

Third, the judgment was *ideo concessum* and, for this last also.

There was another judgment, between Pell and Stranguish, entered Pas. 2 [Car. I, rot.] 234, also reversed.

Before, f. 34, pl. 28.[1]

[Other reports of this case: Noy 86, 74 E.R. 1053; Popham 203, 79 E.R. 1293; HLS MS. 1235, f. 72; CUL MS. Hh.2.1, f. 219; CUL MS. Ll.3.13, f. 171.]

199

Pincent v. Sheiris

(K.B. Mich. 2 Car. I, 1626)

An action of trespass upon the case lies for malicious prosecution.

BL MS. Add. 35961, f. 47, pl. 68

Nota quod, between Pincent and Sheiris, [in] an action upon the case because the plaintiff was bail for one in debt to the defendant and that the principal [debtor] had rendered himself *in exoneratione manucaptorum* and yet the defendant sued a *scire facias* against him, and he had sued this judgment, and he took the plaintiff in execution, and the plaintiff in the action upon the case recovered.

Note [this] because he could have had an *audita querela* and also that [an action of] case lies in any case [for] a false action against one.

---

[1] *Charles v. Jenkins* (1626), above, No. 120.

200

Parson of Orford's Case

(K.B. Mich. 2 Car. I, 1626)

Fish in a pond are not tithable.

BL MS. Add. 35961, f. 47, pl. 69

The parson of Orford in Suffolk libelled for tithes of oysters and other fish that the defendant fed in a water within the parish and caught in the haven of Orford. And [a writ of] prohibition was granted. And the court held that fish in a pond are not tithable.

201

Anonymous

(K.B. Mich. 2 Car. I, 1626)

An action of false imprisonment does not lie against a person who executes in good faith a writ of arrest the day after the king dies and the writ abated thereby.

BL MS. Add. 35961, f. 47, pl. 70

A [writ of] *capias* issued in the time of King James, who died 27 March [1625], and it was executed the 28th of the same month, upon which the other brought [an action of] false imprisonment. And the defendant wished to have an imparlance because the bailiff who made the arrest did not have notice of it.

But it was said to him by the court, if his matter was thus, he could aid himself by a special pleading because, in this short time, the law does not bind him to take notice of it.

And Justice JONES said that, in his circuit, he gave a judgment of death against some after the death above, that he knew of it, and they were hanged, and he could not help it.

202

Thursby v. Warne

(Part 1)
(K.B. Mich. 2 Car. I, 1626)

A commission of sewers ends upon the death of the king, but orders and assessments of the commissioners of sewers survive the death of the king.

BL MS. Add. 35961, f. 47, pl. 71

Between Thursby and Warne, *quod intratur* Trin. 2 [Car. I, rot.] 1033, in [an action of] trespass for the taking of beasts [on] 15 March, 1 Car. [1626]. The defendant justified by force of a commission of sewers of King James. And upon this, he demurred. And [it was] adjudged bad because the commission ended by the demise of the king.

After, 49, p. 1.[1]

203

Delavall v. Clare

(Part 2)
(K.B. Mich. 2 Car. I, 1626)

BL MS. Add. 35961, f. 47, pl. 72

Delavall brought an action upon the case against Clare (*vide* of this, before, fo. 17, pl. 19).[2] And he alleged how the defendant brought to him a piece of satin and requested him to shape it into hose and a doublet for him and [. . .] all things necessary for the making up of it. And he promised to give him *quantum meruit* for the making and to pay for the things that he bought etc. And he showed that he shaped it and deserved 13s. and that he disbursed £16 for taffeta etc. for the making up etc. and he had not paid him *ad damnum*.

The defendant pleaded that, when the promise was made by him, that he was under age and under the governance of one Hilton and that his guardian bespoke the suit *absque hoc quod assumpsit*. And upon this, [the plaintiff] demurred.

And, now, the exception that an action upon the case does not lie against an infant was waived because the court, upon advice, ruled that he could. And thus a precedent was vouched, Trin. 15 Jac., rot. 1374, [in the] king's bench, between Gill and Blakeston, where [*blank*] brought an action upon the case against an infant for beer for his necessary housekeeping.

But it was insisted upon that the plaintiff should have shown that they were necessaries because an infant [can]not [be] charged but for necessaries and, on account of this, the declaration [was] insufficient. And on account of this, the plaintiff [should] not recover though the bar [was] bad, as it was confessed, for the repugnancy and contrariety.

But it was ruled here that it was good enough and that the averment should come in in the replication. But inasmuch as the bar was bad, upon which the plaintiff could demur, it was not good for this averment. Thus it was good because the replication was that the place of this averment was not necessary.

---

[1] For later proceedings in this case, see below, No. 227.

[2] For earlier proceedings in this case, see above, No. 111.

And thus judgment for the plaintiff was given for this averment, See *N. Entres*, 125, 126,[1] and Gillet's case, before cited.

[Other reports of this case: Benloe 186, 73 E.R. 1047, CUL MS. Gg.2.30, f. 70v; Latch 156, 82 E.R. 323, HLS MS. 1235, f. 70v; Noy 85, 74 E.R. 1052; BL MS. Hargr. 38, f. 125v; BL MS. Lansd. 1092, f. 134v; CUL MS. Hh.2.1, f. 217v; CUL MS. Ll.3.13, f. 167; *sub nom.* Vere v. Delavall, W. Jones 146, 82 E.R. 78, BL MS. Hargr. 317, f. 149.]

204

Wood v. Stokley

(K.B. Mich. 2 Car. I, 1626)

In this writ of error, the lower court had proceeded properly according to the common law and the errors alleged were de minimis.

BL MS. Add. 35961, f. 47, pl. 73

Between Wood and Stokley in [a writ of] error upon a judgment given in an inferior court, the errors assigned were:

First, that the style of the court was *placita coron[ae] etc. ibi [. . .] tenta virtute literarum patentium dominae reginae Elizabethae etc.* and the proceedings were *ideo praeceptum est J.S. secundum consuetudinem quod attachiatus fuit etc.*, as thus the process [was] all *secundum consuetudinem*. And thus, it was said, he proceeded in another court than they began because the court was by letters patent and the proceeding [was] by custom.

But *non allocatur* because '*secundum consuetudinem*' is void here because he can make such a process by the common law as incident to a court of record. But, if he had made a process not warrantable but by the custom, and not by the common law, it had been otherwise. And also, where they have jurisdiction, as they have in some places, to proceed in a common law course or [in] a chancery course, if they begin at common law and proceed in a course of chancery, this is error because then he begins in one court and ends in another.

Another exception was because, in the entry of the return of the jury by the bailiff, he [is] named Robert and [in] the entry of the default of the defendant, it is said '*et praedictus Robertus petit quod jurata capiatur per defaltam*', this Robert being lately named and, on account of this, *praedictus* must have relation to him and thus the inquest [was] awarded by default of the prior, of a stranger, who was not the plaintiff nor the attorney for the plaintiff.

But, inasmuch as the plaintiff was named Robert, *non allocatur* because it will have relation to him who could do it, and *ut res magis valeat quam pereat*.[2]

---

[1] *Thompson v. North* (1605), E. Coke, *A Booke of Entries* (1614), 'Det', pl. 8, f. 125.

[2] Cf. *Black's Law Dictionary* (1933), p. 1714.

205

Crab v. Tooker

(K.B. Mich. 2 Car. I, 1626)

A joint power does not survive the death of one of the grantees.

BL MS. Add. 35961, f. 47, pl. 74

Between Crab and Tucker in [an action of] covenant, *quod intratur* Hil. 1 [Car. I, rot.] 315, the case was [thus]. One, in consideration of marriage of his eldest son, with a covenant to find for his son and his wife and the children that they will have good and sufficient board as long as they agree to live together with the father and that, if the son and the said wife 'shall dislike' to cohabit with the father, that then, for their maintenance, he covenanted to give to them Four Best Gates within his ground etc. The son died. The wife disagreed to cohabit. Whether now he is bound to give to them the Best Gates was the question, *viz.* whether the disagreement here being joined, it could survive because the covenant was, if they disagree, that then.

And it was ruled by the whole court that she could not disagree after the death of the son and that this power will not survive any more than if one devise that his feoffees will sell and one dies, or in Bray's case in Dyer,[1] where a covenant that if they marry where A., B., and C. will appoint and A. dies, because it is a joint act, and with this, agrees C. 5, Brudenell's case.[2] And thus it was ruled now.

[Other reports of this case: Benloe 186, 73 E.R. 1047, CUL MS. Gg.2.30, f. 70v; Latch 162, 82 E.R. 326, HLS MS. 1235, f. 72; Noy 86, 74 E.R. 1053; Popham 204, 79 E.R. 1294; BL MS. Hargr. 38, f. 134; BL MS. Lansd. 1092, f. 136; CUL MS. Hh.2.1, f. 219v; CUL MS. Ll.3.13, f. 172.]

---

[1] *Butler v. Lady Bray* (1560), 2 Dyer 189, 73 E.R. 418, also Benloe 82, 123 E.R. 63, 1 Anderson 5, 123 E.R. 323.

[2] *Brudnel v. Skidmore* (1592), 5 Coke Rep. 9, 77 E.R. 61.

206

Palmer v. Litherland

(Part 2)
(K.B. Mich. 2 Car. I, 1626)

BL MS. Add. 35961, f. 47v, pl. 75

The case before, fo. 40a, p. 35,[1] between Palmer and Litherland was now moved by Serjeant *Crewe* for the plaintiff. And he said that it was a small question in the case because he said that C. 5 is,[2] if administration be granted and the administrator [*blank*] the letters and afterwards committed to another, that he is chargeable. Thus if one makes one an executor for one month and another afterwards, if the first wastes, he [is] chargeable.

And a day was given to the other side peremptory.

[Other reports of this case: Latch 160, 267, 82 E.R. 325, 379, HLS MS. 1235, f. 71v; Noy 86, 74 E.R. 1052; BL MS. Hargr. 38, f. 123; CUL MS. Hh.2.1, f. 219.]

207

Anonymous v. Davis

(K.B. Mich. 2 Car. I, 1626)

In this case, a return of process was quashed because it was insufficient and incomplete.

BL MS. Add. 35961, f. 47v, pl. 76

A rescue was returned *quod feci warrantum* to four such and one of them arrested the party, [and] he was rescued from him. And, because the warrant was *conjunctim* and not *divisim* and the arrest was by one, it was held the return [was] insufficient. Second, it [the return] was that he arrested him at such a place and *quod tunc et ibidem vulneraverunt et maletractaverunt* the bailiff *quod rescusserunt* the prisoner without saying *tunc et ibidem rescussaverunt*. And this was held a good exception because, now, there is not a day nor a place of the rescue.

And this was against Davis and others.

---

[1] For earlier proceedings in this case, see above, No. 166.

[2] *Wilson v. Packman* (1595), 6 Coke Rep. 18, 77 E.R. 281, also Moore K.B. 396, 72 E.R. 651, Cro. Eliz. 459, 78 E.R. 698.

208

Dowse v. Shelly

(K.B. Mich. 2 Car. I, 1626)

A contract will be interpreted according to its clear intent where the erroneous words that were used could have no other meaning.

BL MS. Add. 35961, f. 47v, pl. 76[a]

Between Dowse and Shelly, Trin. 2 [Car. I, rot.] 401, [upon] an obligation made in *decimo secundo libris* for *duodecim libris*. And it was held good by the court because it appears sufficiently what was intended and it could not otherwise be intended nor have another signification.

And JONES said that an obligation in *quadraginta decem libris* for *quinquaginta* has been [held] good.

But he and DODDERIDGE said that it has been also adjudged that an obligation in *centum libris* and *liberis* and *literis* have not been good because these words have another signification which could be intended; *aliter* of *viginti* and seventeen, as is C. 10.[1]

And a day was given peremptory to the other side.

209

Anonymous

(K.B. Mich. 2 Car. I, 1626)

Justices of assize cannot admit one to be a guardian of an infant in another court than where they themselves are justices.

BL MS. Add. 35961, f. 47v, pl. 77

It was admitted that the justices of assize cannot admit one for a guardian of an infant in another court than themselves are justices, as, if a suit be against an infant in the king's bench, a justice of the common bench cannot admit one for his guardian.

But JONES said that he did not see a reason for it because justices of the king's bench can receive cognizance of fines and they of the common bench can receive warrants of attorney in their circuits for the king's bench.

---

[1] *Osborn v. Middleton* (1613), 10 Coke Rep. 130, 133, 77 E.R. 1123, 1129.

210

Foster v. Taylor

(K.B. Mich. 2 Car. I, 1626)

Upon an appeal, a record can be amended to cure a clerical error.

BL MS. Add. 35961, f. 47v, pl. 78

In a writ of error between Foster and Taylor (and *intratur* Mich. 22 Jac., rot. 437) from a judgment given in the common bench in [an action of] *ejectione firmae*, the record, as it appeared by an examination, was erased and *praedicto decimo* [was] made *duodecimo*, by which the judgment was erroneous. And upon this, [a writ of] error was brought and the error [was] assigned. And the point was vicious by the erasure. And now, it was moved to have it amended as it was in the [court of] common place[1] because it was erased for the purpose to make errors. But inasmuch as the error was assigned in the point, whether, now, it could be amended was the doubt.

And in Blackamore's case,[2] it is said that, after errors [are] assigned, the court can [a]mend the record where there is a *vitium clerici*. But it was generally spoken [to]. And it was moved that it was not amendable. And he said that [in] Mich. 11 Jac., [a writ of] error was brought and assigned because a warrant of attorney failed, and it was moved by Yelverton, then solicitor [general],[3] to have it amended, but it could not [be] because it was in the point in which the error [was] assigned. And [in] Pas. 17 Jac., one Abbington's case,[4] there, there was an erasure which made the record erroneous and error [was] assigned, and it was moved by Yelverton also to have it amended, but the court advised, and their reason was because, on account of this, then, the felony will be taken away because no judgment will be reversed for it. And thus it is in our case.

But *Brome*, the secondary, said that, in this case, it was amended.

And thus the court now awarded that it will be amended.

[Other reports of this case: Benloe 186, 73 E.R. 1048, CUL MS. Gg.2.30, f. 70v; Latch 162, 82 E.R. 326, HLS MS. 1235, f. 72; Popham 196, 79 E.R. 1288; BL MS. Hargr. 38, f. 133v; CUL MS. Hh.2.1, f. 219v; CUL MS. Ll.3.13, f. 171v.]

---

[1] lieu *MS.*

[2] *Blackamore's Case* (1610), 8 Coke Rep. 156, 77 E.R. 710.

[3] Henry Yelverton was solicitor general from 1613 to 1617. J. Sainty, *A List of English Law Officers* (1987), p. 62; S. R. Gardiner & L. A. Knafla, 'Yelverton, Sir Henry,' *Oxford Dictionary of National Biography* (2004), vol. 60, pp. 788–790.

[4] Perhaps *Abbington's Case* (1619), 2 Rolle Rep. 112, 81 E.R. 693.

211

Lowly v. Carter

(K.B. Mich. 2 Car. I, 1626)

A lessee who remains in possession after the term of the lease expires is a disseisor.

A conveyance of land after the grantor has been disseised does not pass title.

BL MS. Add. 35961, f. 47v, pl. 79

Between Lowly and Carter in [an action of] *ejectione firmae* for part of the land, *viz.* the manor of Beneham, in the [court of] common bench, which Sir Peter Vanlore purchased of Lord Kellie, who purchased the reversion of them, being in tail to Lord Norris and the heirs male of his body. Upon [a plea of] *non culpabilis*, there was given in evidence for the plaintiff a lease to him of Sir Peter and that, after the lease [was] sealed upon the land, that the cattle of the defendant were upon the land, which the other side said there was not any ejectment because but cattle cannot gain possession. But to remove the scruple, it was proved that, [at] all times since, the defendant had occupied the land.

Then, for the defendant, it was offered to be proved that, before the entry of the defendant, a stranger entered after the lease [was] sealed and then the ejectment must be brought against the other, and not against the second person who entered.[1] But this was not proved; thus, the ejectment was fully proved.

Thus for the title to the lessor, the plaintiff made a show of letters patent of King James to the Lord Kellie, which recited that, where Henry VIII had given etc. to Lord Norris and the heirs male of his body and that Kellie had before purchased from him, *viz.* King James, the reversion upon a condition precedent if he pay 10s. at the receipt of the exchequer (which was common, DODDERIDGE said, [so] that another will not have the grant of the reversion before him), he, in consideration of the service by Lord Kellie and to the intent to remove all scruples whether the land pass or not pass, gave and granted them to him and his heirs, who levied a fine to Sir Peter. And it was pressed for the defendant that the letters patent of the grant of the reversion precedent will be shown or proved because, he said, if there were not any such, then the king [was] induced with color of that which was not [true] and thus the grant [was] void. But there was an erasure.

[It was said] by the court that the former grant was not any consideration for the latter, but others, his good service etc., and the king intended to remove scruples and to make it good if it was not.

But it was pressed by the other side that the intent of the king was to remove all scruples whether anything passed by the first and to make the latter in the nature of a confirmation of the former if there were any patents though [it was]

---

[1] entrer *MS.*

not available but it was not his intent to make the grant unless there were patents before; his intent was to deny the insufficiency, not the defect and absence of patents.

But they were overruled in this for that, then, they have recourse to prove that, after the death of Lord Norris without heirs male of his body and the grant to Lord Kellie, that Kellie had entered upon the defendant (being tenant for three lives to Lord Norris, which lease being ended by his death, he intended to keep because he had paid a great fine for it to Norris a little before his death and also he had surrendered eight years of the old [?] lease because they had not yet expired so that, now, if he will not have the lease for three years, he has lost his fine of £300) and that still the defendant kept the possession and, thus, the possession of Kellie. He levied a fine to Vanlore and thus the lessee, by his continuance, [is a] disseisor. And thus, the fine to Sir Peter extinguished the right. And it made the tortious estate indefeasible and thus, by this way, good, according to the opinion in the end of Buckley's case,[1] which the court held for law.

But they could not prove a clear entry by Lord Kellie, but he proved that some [persons] in his name entered before the fine.

But the other side required proof of the authority of them who entered by him, which the court ruled not to be needful because, by the entry of one without authority or agreement subsequent to the use of him who had the right, the land is not in him. See C. 9, 106a;[2] 16 Hen. VII, 12a.

And this was agreed clearly also, by which it was left to the jury upon the point in fact whether the defendant was a disseisor before the fine because, if so, it was with the defendant.

And it was said, even though the lessee of Lord Norris continued in claiming his term, that this did not make him a disseisor because he will not be a disseisor unless he intended thus, as C., the Parson of Honylamb's case.[3]

But the court responded that, if he continued tortiously, even though he claims but the [term], yet he is a disseisor because it does not apportion his wrong, as was resolved [in] 2 Eliz., Dy., Trapp's case.[4]

Thus, the court [held] against the plaintiff, but yet the jury found for the plaintiff. And the court said that they did not understand the evidence.

---

[1] *Buckler v. Harris* (1597), 2 Coke Rep. 55, 56, 76 E.R. 537, 541, also 2 Anderson 29, 123 E.R. 529, Moore K.B. 423, 72 E.R. 671, Cro. Eliz. 450, 585, 78 E.R. 690, 828.

[2] *Bicknel v. Tucker* (1612), 9 Coke Rep. 104, 106, 77 E.R. 883, 886, also 1 Brownlow & Goldesborough 181, 123 E.R. 741, 2 Brownlow & Goldesborough 134, 153, 123 E.R. 857, 869.

[3] *Panel v. Moor* (1553), 1 Plowden 91, 75 E.R. 145.

[4] *Smith v. Stapleton* (1573), 2 Plowden 426, 75 E.R. 642.

212

Anonymous

(K.B. Mich. 2 Car. I, 1626)

A negative custom of a manor, such as that a copyholder may not make an entail, can be valid.

BL MS. Add. 35961, f. 48, pl. 80

[Upon] evidence to the jury, it was ruled by the court that a custom in a copyhold of a manor that a surrender or grant to one and the heir of his body will be void is a good custom and, even though it be in the negative, because the custom was that surrenders will be made in fee for life or years and not in tail, thus, it is an affirmative mixed with a negative. And on account of this, the surrender here to the use of the heirs of one in tail was void.

213

Locking v. Betts

(K.B. Mich. 2 Car. I, 1626)

A clerical error in the entry of a general verdict can be amended.

BL MS. Add. 35961, f. 48, pl. 81

Between Locking and Betts, in a writ of error upon a judgment given in the common bench in [an action of] replevin, the defendant avowed for rent [in] arrears. And the jury, upon the *postea*, found *pro querente*, and thus was the endorsement of the *postea*. But the clerk, in entering the judgment, entered for the plaintiff *et pro damnis pro non solutione redditus etc.* where it should have been *pro captione et detentione*. And it was moved to be amended.

But Serjeant *Henden* [argued] *contra*, first, because, then, the verdict of the jury will be altered and it will make a new record; second, error was assigned in the point.

But still, it was ruled to be amended because it was the fault of the clerk because, upon the dorse of the *postea*, there is not any more but *pro querente* or *pro defendente*, if it not be a special verdict. And on account of this, the residue is left to the diligence and skill of the clerk, and, if he errs in entering, it will be amended. And thus it was.

214

Anonymous

(K.B. Mich. 2 Car. I, 1626)

An action of debt on a record does not lie where the record is in a superior court.

BL MS. Add. 35961, f. 48, pl. 82

It was moved for [a writ of] prohibition to the stannary court in Cornwall, which holds pleas of all debts and contracts where a party is a tinner, because, there, an action of debt was brought upon a judgment given in the king's bench. And it was granted because [an action of] debt does not lie for a judgment given in a superior court where, if *nul tiel record* is pleaded, there is no means to come to the record.

215

Rex v. Plowden

(K.B. Mich. 2 Car. I, 1626)

An indictment for forcible entry against one's own copyholder need not allege a disseisin.

BL MS. Add. 35961, f. 48, pl. 83

Edmund Plowden was indicted for entering with force upon his copyholder and putting him out of possession, according to the new Statute.[1]

And it was moved by Serjeant *Athow* that it must be *disseisivit* because, even though the frank tenement is [in] the lord, yet, because the Statute gives that, if one be indicted for entering with force upon a copyholder or a lessee for years, that he will have restitution as if it was a frank tenement, but the Statute does not give a new form of the indictment. And on account of this, it retains the form before.

But *non allocatur*. And it was said to him to traverse it.

See below, Mich. 3 [Car. I], f. 110, pl. 47.[2]

[Other reports of this case: Popham 205, 79 E.R. 1295.]

---

[1] Stat. 21 Jac. I, c. 15 (*SR*, IV, 1222).

[2] *Rex v. Fry* (1627), BL MS. Add. 35961, f. 116, pl. 47, BL MS. Lansd. 1083, f. 191v, pl. 47 (Widdrington's reports).

216

Mellhuishe v. Newcot

(K.B. Mich. 2 Car. I, 1626)

The issues in this case were whether the plaintiff pleaded sufficiently the breach of the contract and a formal demand for performance.

BL MS. Add. 35961, f. 48, pl. 84

Between Mellhuishe and Newcot, in [an action of] covenant, which was that the defendant and his son or one of them, upon a request made, will make a jointure to such a woman married to the son. And a breach [was] assigned that they did not make [it], *licet saepius requisitus*. And upon this, [there was a] demurrer. *Et intratur* Mich. 2 [Car. I], rot. [*blank*].

And it was moved, first, that the covenant was 'if they or one of them make' etc. and the breach [was] that they did not make [it] and still it could be that one of them had made [it]; thus, no breach; second, it was to be made upon a request and, on account of this, the request, being the ground and issuable, must have been alleged more certainly. And he cited Methold and Peick's case,[1] [which was] reversed here for want of certainty in the request.

217

Walden v. Vessy

(Part 2)
(K.B. Mich. 2 Car. I, 1626)

BL MS. Add. 35961, f. 48, pl. 85

And now, the case before, f. 17b, p. 28, of Jesson and Walden[2] was moved to have the opinion of the court. And they all agreed that, for the sum about £100, that he will have 1d. for each pound under £100 and 6d. for each above for the reasons above given.

And now JONES said that there was a case pending in the [court of] common bench at his coming from there and it was entered 19 Jac. and between Empson and Batteson,[3] where the defendant was sued for the fees of £100 upon an extent upon a statute and, there, the defendant had entered into an obligation to him made [?] upon condition to pay to him so much, *viz.* £7 for the execution of it, and, upon [an action of] debt brought, the defendant pleaded the Statute of 23

---

[1] *Methold v. Peck* (1626), above, No. 24.

[2] For earlier proceedings in this case, see above, No. 72.

[3] *Empson v. Bathurst* (1620–1622), Hutton 52, 123 E.R. 1095, Winch 20, 50, 124 E.R. 18, 43, Latch 20, 82 E.R. 253.

Hen. VI,[1] which voids the bonds made to the sheriff; the plaintiff replied and showed the Statute of 29 Eliz.,[2] and there were three questions: [first] whether a sheriff could take a penal bond or a bond with a condition for his fees; second, if the fees were due before the *liberate* [was] executed because the extent [is] but part of the execution; third, if he will have more than £4 20s. according to [the rate of] 6d. the pound for the execution; and, upon the third point, as it was there, they were two against two; but afterward, as he said Henden reported to him, judgment was given for the defendant and the third point [was] ruled that he [the sheriff] will have but £4 10s., but, because there were other points upon which the judgment could be maintained, it was not regarded because it was also there agreed, as Henden reported, that the double obligation was void and that, before the *liberate* [was] executed, no fees [were] due. See C.B. 83a, *per curiam*.[3]

[Other reports of this case: Benloe 191, 73 E.R. 1051, CUL MS. Gg.2.30, f. 72v; Latch 17, 51, 82 E.R. 252, 270; Noy 75, 74 E.R. 1043; Palmer 399, 81 E.R. 1142; Popham 173, 79 E.R. 1269; BL MS. Lansd. 1092, f. 3v; HLS MS. 1197, f. 1v; CUL MS. Ll.3.13, f. 2v.]

218

Kelley v. Reynell

(Part 3)

(K.B. Mich. 2 Car. I, 1626)

BL MS. Add. 35961, f. 48, pl. 86

The case before, f. 16b, 17a, p. 19 and 26,[4] was now twice moved. And now, DODDERIDGE was strong in the opinion that, upon the certificate of the *custos brevium*, it could not be taken that the declaration in Exeter was upon the writ in Devonshire because it is contrary to the law, but if he had certified that there was no other writ but this in the negative, then it is otherwise. And thus, *mutavit opinionem*.

But JONES held strongly as before. And he said, if it is not error, there cannot be any error upon the Statute of 6 Ric. II,[5] which gives that, upon a writ in one county, he [can]not declare in another.

To which, DODDERIDGE said yes, certainly, *viz.* where the certificate is that there was not any other writ. By which, it was agreed to award [a writ of] *certiorari ex officio* to certify whether there was any other writ. And [it was] ordered that

---

[1] Stat. 23 Hen. VI, c. 9 (*SR*, II, 334–336).

[2] Stat. 29 Eliz. I, c. 4 (*SR*, IV, 769).

[3] Perhaps *Cooper's Case*, Noy 28, 74 E.R. 998.

[4] For earlier proceedings in this case, see above, Nos. 63, 70.

[5] Stat. 6 Ric. II, stat. 1, c. 2 (*SR*, II, 27).

there will not be any filing *de novo*, as the common case is where a diminution is alleged. And, in truth, the writ was in another county than the declaration, [and it was ordered] to file a new writ of the right county and thus to save the error.

[Other reports of this case: Cro. Jac. 675, 79 E.R. 584; Latch 116, 225, 82 E.R. 302, 357; Palmer 428, 81 E.R. 1155; BL MS. Hargr. 38, f. 69v; BL MS. Lansd. 1092, f. 92v; CUL MS. Hh.2.1, f. 196.]

219

Boulsted v. Anonymous

(K.B. Mich. 2 Car. I, 1626)

Sharp practices not amounting to fraud can be remedied in the court of star chamber, but not in the court of king's bench.

BL MS. Add. 35961, f. 48v, pl. 87

One Boulsted had purchased land and, for security of encumbrances, he exhibited a bill in [the court of] chancery against the vendor, who in the beginning of the term, answered upon his oath that it [the land] was free of all encumbrances. And, on the same day of the presentment, he paid the money and he passed the assurances. And afterwards, he confessed divers judgments upon declarations against him. And it was moved to stay the entry of the judgments until the next term; otherwise for the relation of the lands of the purchaser, for them he will be charged.

But the judgment was entered, and, on account of this, [there is] no remedy but [in the court of] star chamber for his crafty oath because, as it was said, the vendor answered as he was advised by his counsel that he could safely so swear; thus he swore by counsel.

220

Anonymous

(K.B. Mich. 2 Car. I, 1626)

The courts of London can reduce a judgment in the interest of fairness, unless the judgment is for the king.

BL MS. Add. 35961, f. 48v, pl. 88

Note how the mayor of London by custom can mark any judgment given in their courts to moderate it by equity, as 10 Hen. VI[1] is. Yet he cannot mark a judgment upon an information by equity because this [is] the suit of the king in part.

And *Stone*, one of the city counsel, said that he had not ever seen a precedent in a case of an information.

221

Anonymous

(K.B. Mich. 2 Car. I, 1626)

When a case is removed into a higher court, the lower court loses jurisdiction to act further in the matter.

BL MS. Add. 35961, f. 48v, pl. 89

A recognizance for good behavior was removed by [a writ of] *certiorari* into the bench and still the justice of the peace paravail bound him again for the same cause having notice that he was bound in the bench. And it was held a great contempt, and an attachment [was] awarded.

222

Rex v. Featherston

(K.B. Mich. 2 Car. I, 1626)

The issue in this case was whether a nuisance had been sufficiently pleaded.

BL MS. Add. 35961, f. 48v, pl. 90

Fetherston was indicted for stopping *quamdam viam communem ducentem* to divers *messuagiis* in the parish of Fetherstone *usque ad ecclesiam parochialem* of Fetherstone. And the exceptions were, first, that it was said *ad nocumentum ligeorum domini regis* where it was not a general nuisance but a special [one], but the record was *ad nocumentum ligeorum domini [regis] et habitantium* by which [etc.]; second, because he stopped *cum quodam mure lapideo*; but the record was *muro*.[2]

---

[1] YB Mich. 10 Hen. VI, f. 14, pl. 48 (1431).

[2] Fetherston was indicted for stopping 'a certain common way leading' to divers 'messuages' in the parish of Fetherstone 'unto the parish church' of Fetherstone. And the exceptions were, first, that it was said 'to the nuisance of the liege people of the lord king', where it was not a general nuisance but a special [one], but the record was 'to the nuisance

223

Smith v. Man

(K.B. Mich. 2 Car. I, 1626)

Where a plaintiff sues upon a promise to pay where the consideration for the promise was a release, the plaintiff need not allege the details of the release.

BL MS. Add. 35961, f. 48v, pl. 91

Between Smith and Man, in [a writ of] error upon a judgment given at Northampton in an action upon the case and *intratur* Trin. 1 [Car. I], rot. 540, the plaintiff paravail alleged how one such was in execution at his suit and that the defendant, in consideration that the plaintiff *relaxaret et exoneraret* him from execution *ac etiam exoneraret* the sheriff, promised to pay to him so much. And he averred that *relaxavit et exoneravit etc.* And [there was a] judgment for the plaintiff, upon which error [was] assigned because he had averred that *relaxabat etc.*, but he did not show how, which he should have done to the intent that the court will adjudge upon the sufficiency of it because, if it was by parol, it was not a good discharge. And he cited 35 Hen. VI, 9, and 22 Edw. IV, 40 and 43, and Trin. 16 Jac., rot. 322, Rivet's case,[1] where the consideration was that the defendant *exoneraret* the plaintiff of such a debt and the defendant pleaded *exoneravit* and did not show how; and Ross and Harvy's case, above f. 25, p. 45.[2]

But it was answered on the other side and ruled by the court that it was good enough because one in execution can be discharged by parol, as if he comes to the jailer and says 'Let this man out; I discharge him of his execution.' And this, all the court said, was without question. And 27 Hen. VIII, 24, Tatam's case,[3] is express in the point. And there also, as in the case here, it was generally averred *quod relaxabat* from the execution. Thus, [it was] good notwithstanding it.

And JONES said also, if he should have shown how, the defendant will not have an advantage of it upon a special demurrer.

And DODDERIDGE said that there was a diversity where one is bound to assure a discharge etc. of such general acts; there, he must show how, but, where of a release or he confirms, which [are] special acts and but of one kind, there, [it is] sufficient to say that *relaxavit* or *confirmavit*.

And judgment was given for the defendant in the writ of error.

[Other reports of this case: Popham 206, 79 E.R. 1296; CUL MS. Ll.3.13, f. 98.]

---

of the liege people of the lord [king] and the inhabitants' by which [etc.]; second, because he stopped 'with a certain stone wall'; but the record was *'muro'*.

[1] YB Mich. 35 Hen. VI, f. 19, pl. 28 (1456); *Lord Lisle's Case* (1483), YB Hil. 22 Edw. IV, f. 40, pl. 2; *Lorkin v. Collins* (1483), YB Hil. 22 Edw. IV, ff. 42, 43, pl. 3; *Laneret v. Rivet* (1618), Cro. Jac. 503, 79 E.R. 429.

[2] *Rose v. Harvey* (1626), above, No. 176.

[3] YB Mich. 27 Hen. VIII, f. 24, pl. 3 (1535).

224

Attorney General v. Inhabitants of Huntingdonshire

(Part 2)
(K.B. Mich. 2 Car. I, 1626)

BL MS. Add. 35961, f. 48v, pl. 91[a]

In the information against the inhabitants of the County of Huntingdon for not repairing St. Neots Bridge, the issue was whether *debent [vel] solent reparare etc.* And the jury found that part of the said bridge, *viz.* the moiety, is in Huntingdonshire and that the inhabitants *debent reparare.*

And it was moved that the verdict had not found them guilty because the information is for not repairing a bridge in the County of Huntingdon and here it is not a bridge in the County of Huntingdon, but a moiety. Also, the jury had found *quod debent*, which is a matter in law.

But it was answered and ruled [to be] good enough because part of a bridge is a bridge over this part of the water upon which it is. And 43 Ass. 37 and 27 Ass. 8[1] were cited, where these exceptions [were] overruled.

Principium, f. 43, pl. 48.[2]

[Other reports of this case: Benloe 194, 73 E.R. 1053, CUL MS. Gg.2.30, f. 74; Popham 192, 79 E.R. 1285; BL MS. Hargr. 38, f. 134.]

[Related cases: Lucy's Case (1627), Benloe 198, 73 E.R. 1056, CUL MS. Gg.2.30, f. 76v.]

225

Whitton v. Weston

(Part 3)
(K.B. Mich. 2 Car. I, 1626)

BL MS. Add. 35961, f. 48v, pl. 92

More of the case before, fo. 7b, p. 9.[3] Whitton, parson of Marrow, brought an action of debt against Sir William Weston upon the Statute of 2 Edw. VI, ca. 13,[4] for the not setting forth of the tithes etc. And he demanded £173, the double value of the tithes not set forth. The defendant, as to part of the sum, pleaded

---

[1] YB 43 Edw. III, Lib. Ass., p. 275, pl. 37 (1369); YB 27 Edw. III, Lib. Ass., p. 134, pl. 8 (1353).

[2] For earlier proceedings in this case, see above, No. 179.

[3] For other proceedings in this case, see Nos. 29, 31, 280.

[4] Stat. 2 & 3 Edw. VI, c. 13 (*SR*, IV, 55–58).

nihil debet, and, as to the residue, he said that the prior of St. John's of Jerusalem was seised of this land etc. and ([as] before, fo. 4).

And the last term, Serjeant *Davenport* argued for the plaintiff. And he took divers exceptions to the pleading:

First, because the defendant here divided the sum demanded and pleaded one plea to one part and another plea to the other part. When one of the pleas goes to all and always when several pleas are pleaded to several portions[1] and one goes to all, this is a double plea, and it misleads the court. And for this [is] 7 Hen. VI, 29; in [an action of] debt for rent, the defendant pleaded, as here, to part *nihil debet* and, to the residue, an entry in part, and, on account of this, it was not allowed because one goes to all. Thus [is] 7 Edw. IV, 29, Bagot's assize;[2] for part, the defendant pleaded that the plaintiff was an alien and, for part, that *nul tiel office*.

Thus here, in our case, one of the pleas is good for the whole. And peradventure, the issue could be found for one and the plea for the other and thus they [would be] misled.

The second exception [was] because he has pleaded that, by virtue of the statutes etc., the defendant was discharged of the tithes, which is impossible because the person is not discharged but by reason of the land; thus, the pleading is that the land was discharged of the tithes. It is true that, before the Statute of Dissolutions,[3] there, the lands in the hands of the abbots etc. were discharged by reason of the person, but, now, the Statute has that the discharge [is] upon the land. See Dy. 277 and 42 Edw. III, 13.[4]

The third exception [was], in pleading the Statute of 32 [Hen. VIII],[5] he pleaded *quod per actum Parliamenti inceptum etc.* and continued until 30 May next ensuing where it was not continued to 30 May nor begun [in] 32 Hen. VIII, but *anno* 31 [Hen. VIII]. And this has induced a worse error because, afterwards, he pleaded *quod in praedicto Parliamento inactitatus etc.* and that the misrecital of the act, though not necessary to be recited, will be a prejudice. He cited C. 77 and 78 and 7 Edw. III, 26b.[6]

For the matter in law, he argued first that the particular Statute of 32 [Hen. VIII], by which the Hospital was dissolved, did not give this privilege to the king. And his reason was because it was a personal privilege which would not pass by general words, but it must have special and particular words to this effect.

---

[1] persons *MS.*

[2] YB Hil. 7 Edw. IV, f. 29, pl. 17 (1468).

[3] Stat. 31 Hen. VIII, c. 13 (*SR*, III, 733–739).

[4] *Stathome's Case* (1568), 3 Dyer 277, 73 E.R. 621, 1 Gwillim 132, 1 Eagle & Younge 59; YB Pas. 42 Edw. III, ff. 12, 13, pl. 19 (1368).

[5] Stat. 32 Hen. VIII, c. 24 (*SR*, III, 778–781).

[6] *Partridge, qui tam v. Strange* (1553), 1 Plowden 77, 75 E.R. 123, also 1 Dyer 74, 73 E.R. 159; *Tregor v. Walleys* (1333), YB Trin. 7 Edw. III, f. 26, pl. 11, 1 Eagle & Younge 14.

And he cited C. 11, 21,[1] that the tenure in frankalmoigne did not pass to the Hospitalers by the words *tenendum per eadem servicia* that the Templars held, and 3 Edw. III, 11,[2] that the impropriations did not pass, and 35 Hen. VI and C. 11, 13,[3] that a discharge of tithes requires express words. And on account of this, a lease [by a] person rendering rent *pro omnibus exactionibus et demandis* does not preclude tithes.

Another reason [is] because of the Statute of 31 [Hen. VIII];[4] if he did not have the particular discharge of the tithes, they would not have passed by the general words 'in as ample manner and form'.

Also, the Statute of 27 Hen. VIII,[5] which dissolved the lesser monasteries, has as ample words as 32 [Hen. VIII] has, and yet they are not discharged. And also the Statute of Chantries[6] has as large words as 32 [Hen. VIII] has, and yet [there is] no discharge, as appears [in] C. 2, 46 and 49.[7] And on account of this, there, they would have aided it by the Statute of 31 [Hen. VIII].

Secondly, he argued that the Hospital, being dissolved by 32 [Hen. VIII], was not within the words of 31 [Hen. VIII], 'by any other means', because it is to be expounded, as C. 2, 47,[8] of inferior means. And this is one of the resolutions in this case.

Also, 15 Jac., in the common bench, rot. 1510, Wright's case,[9] it was adjudged that the lands that came to the king by the Statute of 27 [Hen. VIII], which dissolved the lesser monasteries, are not within 31 [Hen. VIII] and, on account of this, pay tithes because 'other means' does not extend to equal means. And to say that 31 [Hen. VIII] and 32 [Hen. VIII] were one same Parliament, though different sessions and, on account of this, acts can extend one to the other, this is not a help because C. 79[10] [holds that] separate sessions are as separate

---

[1] *Alcock v. Ayray* (1614), 11 Coke Rep. 18, 21, 77 E.R. 1168, 1172, also Lane 15, 33, 145 E.R. 261, 276.

[2] YB Pas. 3 Edw. III, f. 11, pl. 1 (1329).

[3] *Vicar of D. v. Prior of Pretiwell* (1457), YB Hil. 35 Hen. VI, f. 48, pl. 13, 1 Eagle & Younge 38; *Priddle, qui tam v. Napier* (1612), 11 Coke Rep. 8, 13, 77 E.R. 1155, 1163, also 2 Brownlow & Goldesborough 25, 123 E.R. 794, 1 Gwillim 236, 1 Eagle & Younge 205.

[4] Stat. 31 Hen. VIII, c. 13 (*SR*, III, 733–739).

[5] Stat. 27 Hen. VIII, c. 28 (*SR*, III, 575–578).

[6] Stat. 37 Hen. VIII, c. 4 (*SR*, III, 988–993); Stat. 1 Edw. VI, c. 14 (*SR*, IV, 24–33).

[7] *Green v. Balser* (1596), 2 Coke Rep. 46, 76 E.R. 519, 1 Gwillim 189, 1 Eagle & Younge 113.

[8] *Green v. Balser* (1596), *ut supra*.

[9] *Wright v. Gerrard* (1618), Cro. Jac. 607, 79 E.R. 518, Hobart 306, 80 E.R. 449, W. Jones 2, 82 E.R. 2, 1 Gwillim 375, 1 Eagle & Younge 289.

[10] *Partridge, qui tam v. Strange* (1553), 1 Plowden 77, 79, 75 E.R. 123, 125–126, also 1 Dyer 74, 73 E.R. 159, BL MS. Harley 5141, f. 9v (Dalison's reports).

Parliaments, but this makes for us because, having discharged by express words the monasteries, it will also thus have done for their Hospital if they had intended that it will be discharged.

And for the book of Dy. 277,[1] there, the consideration was only taken upon the Statute of 32 [Hen. VIII] upon a question which, here, does not come in question. And on account of this, it is not against our case and [is] according with our argument. It was adjudged in Sparling and Quarles' case.[2]

And thus, he concluded for the plaintiff.

And this term, Serjeant *Bramston* argued for the defendant. And to the first exception, he answered that it was good enough to divide the plea though one goes to the whole. And thus it was done [in] 37 Hen. VI, 23,[3] because, there, in an assize for the moiety, the tenant pleaded a fine and for the other moiety a re-lease of the ancestor of the demandant in all of the land, and yet this latter plea went to the whole and yet [it was] good. But, if it had not been good, yet, if it was before the Statute of 27 Eliz., he should have demurred specially. And thus is 33 Hen. VI, 6. And now, after the Statute, without question, he will not have an advantage of it upon a general demurrer, which here he has done.

For the second exception, that he must have laid the discharge upon the land and not have concluded *ratione cuius* the person [was] discharged, this was plead-ed as the precedent in the *New Entries* 453, 15 Jac.,[4] was. And on account of this, all of this plea was drawn, and it is the same *mutatis mutandis*.

For the third [exception], that the Statute was misrecited, this is not mate-rial because there is a diversity where it is in the count, as here, and where in the bar because, here, the recital of it was surplusage. And on account of this, the misrecital [in the] first is not hurtful. And this exception was expressly overruled [in] Dy. 95.[5]

For the matter in law, the Statute of 32 [Hen. VIII] only discharges them, and, if not, still, conjoined with 31 [Hen. VIII], [they are] discharged by the Statute of 32 [Hen. VIII]. They are given 'all and singular liberties [and] privi-leges of what nature or quality soever'. Thus, if to be free of tithes be a privilege, it is given because it be of what nature or quality which cannot [. . .][6] because, if it excludes spiritual privileges, then he will not have all privileges of what nature and quality soever. Also, all privileges that [. . .] right of their religion are given, and religion and order in the sense of this Statute are synonymous. And thus,

---

[1] *Stathome's Case* (1568), *ut supra*.

[2] *Quarles v. Spurling* (1602), Moore K.B. 913, 72 E.R. 993, *sub nom. Cornwallis v. Spurling*, Cro. Jac. 57, 79 E.R. 48, 1 Gwillim 224, 1 Eagle & Younge 157.

[3] *Charleton v. J.S.G.* (1459), YB Pas. 37 Hen. VI, f. 23, pl. 12.

[4] *Dickonson, qui tam v. Watter* (1607), E. Coke, *A Booke of Entries* (1614), 'Prohibi-tion', pl. 3, ff. 450v, 453v.

[5] *Whitton, qui tam v. Marine* (1553), 1 Dyer 95, 73 E.R. 207.

[6] que poet ne refiert *MS*.

this privilege also is given. Thus [there is] no way how, without violence to the letter of the Statute, another exception could be made. And also, the intent was accordingly because the intent was to give to the king all of their revenues, and on account of this, consequently, to give to him all of their valuable privileges, as this is here, being the tenth part of their possession.

For the objection that personal privileges are not given except by express words, and 35 Hen. VI and 3 Edw. III, 10, [were] cited for this, for 35 Hen. VI, I answer that the Statute of 17 Edw. II[1] has not as ample words as our Statute and yet there Prisot was of opinion that, by the words *illa et eadem*, the tenure passed. And [in] Pas. 3 Edw. III, it appears that the Templars were dissolved in 4 Edw. II,[2] and, on account of this, the impropriations [were] disappropriated. And on account of this, in 17 Edw. II, it was not the intent to revive them. And this is the given reason of this book.

As to the objection that the Statute of 27 Hen. VIII, nor of 31 [Hen. VIII], [is a] discharge of tithes but 31 [Hen. VIII] by express words, I answer that 27 [Hen. VIII] has not as ample words because it has not the word privileges and 31 [Hen. VIII] has the word privilege. And on account of this, the clause was not needful there but in respect of broken vows [?][3] which those houses were privileged to take away the inconvenience of broken [?][4] searches.

Also divers clauses manifest the intent was to give spiritual privileges because, by express words, the jurisdiction of the ordinary and the privilege of sanctuary was excepted, which otherwise would have passed by the former words. And to conclude with a judgment in the point that, by the word 'privilege', a discharge of tithes passes because, by the Statute of 17 Edw. II, all the lands [and] privileges of the Templars were given to the Hospitalers, and, by reason of this, they always also held the lands discharged, as the Templars held. And thus in Dixon's case, in the *Novell Entries* 453, and, here, there are more ample words than in the Statute of 17 Edw. II.

But, if he is not discharged by 32 [Hen. VIII], still, he is by 31 [Hen. VIII] because it, coming by Parliament, is a means and within these words.

It has been objected that they were not religious and ecclesiastical [persons] and the Statute of 31 [Hen. VIII] intends none but them who are both, and, to prove this, it has been labored out of the canons and antiquities. But it seems to me our books are full to prove that they are because wherever they speak of St. John's, there, it is a proof that they are ecclesiastical and religious. [In] 1 Edw. III, 9,[5] it appears that a writ was awarded to the bishop to certify possession in

---

[1] Stat. 17 Edw. II, stat. 2 (*SR*, I, 194–196).
[2] They were suppressed on 22 March 1312.
[3] Sic in MS; infinite voyes: BL MS. Lansd. 1083, f. 71.
[4] infinite: BL MS. Lansd. 1083, f. 71.
[5] YB Pas. 1 Edw. III, f. 8, pl. 12 (1327).

the order of the Templars, by which it appears that they were dead persons[1] and ecclesiastical. Thus [in] *Tryall*, 98,[2] it appears that one made proofs there. Thus, by the Statute of Westminster II, ca. 43,[3] it appears that they were religious.

It is true that they did not profess poverty, one of the three vows, *viz.* chastity, poverty, and obedience, because they had, as histories report, twenty-nine thousand manors belonging to their order. [In] 27 Hen. VIII, 17,[4] there, it appears that a commander, who was but a member of the Hospital, could not sue in his own name. And [in] *Feffments*, 68,[5] there, a commander avoided a lease made by him because [he was] but a dead person. [In] 32 Hen. VI, 5b, and in 3 Edw. III, 11,[6] it appears that they [were] capable of impropriations, which none but ecclesiastical [persons] are capable of. And, in the Statute of 17 Edw. II, it is mentioned *missarum celebrationibus* with which they could do. [In] 35 Hen. VI, 56,[7] he pleaded that [he was] seised in the right of their church. [In] 42 Edw. III, 22,[8] in [an action of] waste, an exception [was] taken that he did not say *ad exhereditationem ecclesiae*. And Linwood [*Provinciale*], in reciting the ecclesiastical persons, names the Templars [and] Hospitalers, fo. 2.

And to conclude, the book in Dy. 277[9] is full authority, and it cannot be otherwise evaded that, to Dyer, that the judges there misunderstood the law. And for Quarles and Spurling's case, this was not adjudged upon the matter in law, but upon the defects in the pleading. And, in Har and Boyor's case, Pas. 11 Jac.,[10] the court of common bench was divided in opinion; thus it was not yet adjudged against 10 Eliz. in Dy. 277.

And thus, he prayed judgment for the defendant.

And the court now seemed to be of this opinion.

More, 42b.[11]

---

[1] I.e. *civiliter mortui.*

[2] Mich. 31 Edw. I, Fitzherbert, Abr., *Triall*, pl. 98 (1303).

[3] Stat. 13 Edw. I, Stat. Westminster II, c. 43 (*SR*, I, 92–93).

[4] *Dokeray's Case* (1535), YB Mich. 27 Hen. VIII, ff. 14, 17, pl. 6.

[5] YB Mich. 19 Edw. III, Rolls Ser. 31b, vol. 13, p. 353, pl. 27 (1345), Fitzherbert, Abr., *Feffements & faits*, pl. 68.

[6] *Prior of Ely's Case* (1454), YB Trin. 32 Hen. VI, f. 5, pl. 6; YB Pas. 3 Edw. III, f. 11, pl. 1 (1329).

[7] *Bishop of Winchester v. Prior of St. John of Jerusalem* (1457), YB Pas. 35 Hen. VI, f. 56, pl. 2.

[8] *Prior of the Hospital of St. John v. J.* (1368), YB Trin. 42 Edw. III, f. 21, pl. 1.

[9] *Stathome's Case* (1568), *ut supra.*

[10] *Urrey v. Bowyer* (1614), 2 Brownlow & Goldesborough 20, 123 E.R. 791, 1 Gwillim 250, 1 Eagle & Younge 214.

[11] For other proceedings in this case, see Nos. 29, 31, 280.

226

Evans v. Askwith

(Part 3)

(K.B. Mich. 2 Car. I, 1626)

BL MS. Add. 35961, f. 49v, pl. 94

And now, the case of Evans and Askwith, *quod vide* before, fo. 27, p. 9,[1] was argued by the civilians. And it was argued on one side by Dr. Eden, master of Trinity Hall in Cambridge and a master of the chancery, and on the other side by Dr. Duck.

Eden argued that, when a clergyman is promoted to the bishopric to see when his other benefices become void, it is to be considered whether he be a bishop before or not because, if he is not a bishop before, then it is requisite to his creation an election, consecration, confirmation, and enthronement. And in a case that he was not a bishop before, his other benefices are not void before the last act because, before it, he is not a complete bishop. But, if he who is elected was a bishop of another place before, then, to make him a complete bishop, there is required an election, confirmation, and enjoying because, in this case, where one was of the character of a bishop, he will never be again consecrated nor enthroned, any more than to receive ordination two times. But upon which of these acts he will lose his other dignities is the question. And certainly, upon election, he will not because, by this, he is not sure of the other place. First, it is not reasonable to avoid the first by this; then, after an election of him to be a bishop, a mandate goes to the metropolitan to enquire of him and to confirm him if he finds him appropriate. And this is called the royal assent, upon which the archbishop summons the church, and, also, there was a public instrument by which all of the children of the church are commanded to object what they can that this man is not appropriate for the place, and, upon nothing [being] objected, he is confirmed. Thus, until confirmation, he is not sure of the new place. And it is a rule *quod prima vocatio durat usque confirmationem*. And on account of this, if A., a bishop, dies and, afterwards, B. is elected and dies before confirmation, it is *vacat per mortem A. et non per mortem B.* And on account of this, in the case of a provision, when the pope provides one to the bishopric, this provision supplies (in the case where he is chosen from the inferior clergy because, of this, *adhuc* is spoken) the election and consecration. And, in those cases, it is the usage of presentment upon the provision to the bishopric to bestow his other dignities and benefices before confirmation. But this is not according to the law because, of this, the writers of the canon law greatly complain and inveigh, as Hoyeda[2] and

---

[1] For other proceedings in this case, see Nos. 101, 135, 257.

[2] A. Hojeda de Mendoza, *De Beneficiorum.*

Angelus Perusius[1] and others. But, if one of his former dignities was a bishopric, because this is our case, when then will it be void and upon what act because, then, it is not the same case in translation as it is in election. Certainly, this is a hard question, whether, by the very election in the case of a translation, the former bishopric be void or not because an election in the case of a translation is not a form known at common law because, there, there is a rule *quod clericus non potest eligi*. But, in such a case, it is called a postulation because, then, this case is held, the chapter seeing such bishop to be appropriate for their church postulant of the pope, and now of the king,[2] *postulamus et rogamus* is the instrument which will dispense with the other to leave his former bishopric and to come to the other because his former bishop[ric] is his spouse and he cannot take another and relinquish it without a dispensation because it is to marry to it. And this [is] the signification of the *annulus et baculus* anciently given when a bishopric was given by investiture. And upon this postulation comes the royal assent. But before it are one other instrument to the party elect *rogando et postulando* him also to undertake upon himself their bishopric and, if he consents, then comes the consent of the superior, *viz.* the pope when etc. and now the king, and then he is confirmed, and, afterwards, possession follows so that before the dispensation of the pope to recede, there is not any cessation of the first bishopric because, until this, *vinculum matrimonii spiritualis remanet*. But now, since the Statute[3] to abolish the power of the pope, it is more obscure than before because, now, there is not used any dispensation, as before it was used. But, in the place of it, in the royal assent, there is a mandate to the metropolitan bishop in the confirmation to supply all defects. Thus, before the confirmation, now, *vinculum matrimonii* is not dissolved and, by consequence, his bishopric is not void before it because, until the confirmation, this defect of the dispensation is not supplied.

Thus, for the first question, whether he was the dean *in commendam*, he held that he was inasmuch as the *commendam* came before the confirmation and consequently before the avoidance of the first.

For the second question, whether a dean *in commendam* can confirm or not, this is a dubious question *prima facie* in our law. But two or three distinctions would reconcile all. First, *si sit commendatarius perpetuus*, [it is] for life because it is said a perpetual *commendam*. Second, *si ad utilitatem ecclesiae*. Third, *si facere fructos suos*. If there be all of these, it is not a question but he can confirm because such a commendatory, in our law, has *potestatem locandi fructus* [. . .] it is in the common law to make leases, *a fortiori* to confirm leases because such a commendatory has this [. . .] *tituli* Rebuffus, *de Commenda*, paragraphs 61, 62, and 63, and Ludovicus Gomes.[4]

---

[1] Angelus degli Ubaldis de Perusio (d. 1407).
[2] Stat. 24 Hen. VIII, c. 12 (*SR*, III, 427–429).
[3] Stat. 24 Hen. VIII, c. 12 (*SR*, III, 427–429).
[4] P. Rebuffus, *Praxis Beneficiorum*; L. Gomez, *Commentarius*.

The second distinction is of the place because, in some places, a commendatory has such power and [in] another not because, in France and the Dauphiné,
*commendam*s have more strength than in Italy because in France and the Dauphiné they can *locare fructus*, but, as Guido Papa, *In Decisionibus*,[1] upon the decrees[2]
of the Dauphiné, writes, *hoc non observatur apud Italos* because, there, *ecclesia [in]*
commendatoria est ecclesia vacans. And on account of this, there, no prescription
arises against it *quia non contra ecclesiam vacantem*. But our practice of the civil
law in England accords with the practice of France. And on account of this, here,
the law is as there.

The third distinction by which the opinions are to be reconciled, is of time
because, in ancient times, a commendatory was but a depository of the profits
during the vacation and [he was] responsible for them. And on account of this,
the current of the ancients was that *non habet nisi ad alium usum*. But in later
times, they were of more strength, and, as Gomes said, *magis participant de vero*
titulo quam de facere fructus because, in all, there is a clause to take the profits to
their own use. And on account of this, the authorities which are against us are
either antiquated or applicable to the custom of another place than this of which
we take our pattern.

And now, these distinctions, all that can be objected against, can be saved.

Dr. *Duck* [argued] *contra* that this dispensation to hold *in commendam* is void.
And first, all dispensations are odious in law, and, on account of this, [they are]
taken strictly. And on account of this, if a dispensation be granted to a bastard
to have a benefice of such a value, yet, he cannot have one of a lesser value. And
here, this dispensation comes too late. And on account of this, the question is
when the bishopric of Limerick became void. In the case of a translation, there
are four things requisite: (1) election; (2) consent of him who [is] elected; (3) consent of the superior; (4) possession. And which of these acts makes an avoidance
is the question. By the election only, there is not a question that this does not
make an avoidance. And it is also clear that it is void before possession. Thus,
it remains that, upon the assent of the king or upon the assent of the party, the
avoidance will begin. And it is clear that, by the consent of him who is elected,
the avoidance begins. Thus, it is to see whether, here, there appears to be consent.
And certainly there is because the *commendam* is granted *ad petitionem partis et*
non ex mero motu. And upon his receiving of the *commendam*, it is a tacit assent
and a facile assent. It is sufficient to make an avoidance. And on account of this,
if a priest marries, it is an avoidance, or, if he becomes a soldier. Thus, if he stands
by until the pope bestows his benefice to another and does not deny it, thus, by
the consent, the avoidance begins.

But it could be asked when he began to be the bishop of Bristol. This is not
our question because ours is when Limerick became void. But as to this, he was

---

[1] G. Papa, *Decisiones*.

[2] arrests *MS*.

not the bishop of Bristol before possession. And there is a meantime when he is not the bishop of any place.

For the second question, whether a commendatory can confirm, I confess that the practice is that they can make leases. But, by the rule of the common law, they have not such a power.

Commendus began in the year 847, and the first was granted by [Pope] Leo IV. And, in his first institution, he was but a *depositarius*, and he had nothing to his own use. And thus, in such manner, the estimation of commendators continued until the year 1300. And they could not maintain possessory actions as an appellor etc. But after 1300, the writers doubt of the point, and they say *quod materia non est bene clara*. And in fact, though the law was otherwise, it was at this time dangerous to dispute because, now, the brothers and sons of kings and noblemen were cardinals and they had their maintenance by *commendams*. And yet they who [. . .] strong by them said that *habent nisi titulum commendatum* etc. Thus etc.

More, 34, p. 6.[1]

227

Thursby v. Warne

(Part 2)
(K.B. Hil. 2 Car. I, 1627)

BL MS. Add. 35961, f. 50, pl. 1

In the case between Thursby and Warne, *quod vide* above, f. 46, pl. 71,[2] the case was [thus]. The plaintiff brought [an action of] replevin for the taking of his cattle etc. The defendant justified the taking in the time of King Charles by force of a levy taxed for the reparations of sea walls upon the commission of King James, and he did not show the time of the assessment whether the assessment was made in the time of King Charles or James.

And, for this cause, it was adjudged this term to be bad [*blank*] because it was agreed upon the Statute of 23 Hen. VIII, of sewers,[3] that ordinals[4] made by the commissioners and confirmed by the king according to the Statute bind in the time of another king, but, if the assessment be in the time of one king by force of a commission of another king, this is void because the commission is ended, but not the ordinances and assessments before upon the commission and, though, by the Statute, it is provided that there will not be strict pleading

---

[1] For other proceedings in this case, see Nos. 101, 135, 257.
[2] For earlier proceedings in this case, see above, No. 202.
[3] Stat. 23 Hen. VIII, c. 5 (*SR*, III, 368–372).
[4] Sic in MS.

in matters of circumstance for the expedition of the avowant, yet he must plead all material things, without which the court cannot have cognizance to adjudge. And here, it is equally to be intended, whether the assessment was in the time of James or Charles.

And *Athow* said, and many contended, that, in no precedent, is the usage to plead the time of the assessment, to which, the court answered that there is no need in many cases and in few cases near it could the assessment be material. And thus, it was adjudged.

[Other reports of this case: Benloe 193, 199, 73 E.R. 1052, 1056, CUL MS. Gg.2.30, ff. 73v, 76v; Latch 170, 82 E.R. 330, HLS MS. 1235, f. 78; Noy 88, 74 E.R. 1054; BL MS. Hargr. 38, f. 137; BL MS. Lansd. 1092, f. 144; CUL MS. Ll.3.13, f. 183.]

228

Mason v. Dixon

(K.B. Hil. 2 Car. I, 1627)

The issue in this case was whether an action of case sounding in negligence lies against a jailer by an executor of a decedent's estate for an escape in the lifetime of the testator.

BL MS. Add. 35961, f. 50, pl. 2

Lemason brought an action upon the case against Dixon, bailiff of the Liberty of Whitechappel. [Entered Trin. 2 Car., rot. 1365.] And he showed how his testator sued a bill of Middlesex against one J.S. to the intent that, he, being taken upon it and in the Marshalsea [Prison], that he could declare in an action of debt against him, upon which, the defendant took J.S. and allowed him to escape, by which the testator lost his debt. And upon [a plea of] *non culpabilis*, it was found for the plaintiff. And it was moved in arrest of judgment that an action upon the case for an escape does not lie for the executor [for] an escape in the lifetime of the testator because it is a personal action, which does not go to the executors any more than [an action for] trespass, battery, or waste and no more than a personal action which *moritur cum persona*, as an [action for an] escape does not lie against executors, as Whiteacres' case in Dyer[1] is, no more will it lie for him. And in Whiteacres' case, it is called either a trespass or an escape.

But to the contrary, it was said that it is maintainable because the testator has an interest in the body of the debtor and it is like a chattel in him and a gage to answer to the action and that a body of a man can be a chattel, for the taking of which the executor will have an action [for an act] committed *in vita testatoris*. In the book in 7 Hen. IV, 2 and 3,[2] [an action of] ravishment of ward [was]

---

[1] *Whitacres v. Onsley* (1573), 3 Dyer 322, 73 E.R. 729.

[2] YB Mich. 7 Hen. IV, f. 2, pl. 14 (1405).

brought by the executors for a ravishment in the lifetime of the testator. True it is that, at common law, an executor will not have an action for the goods of the testator taken in his lifetime because it was a trespass and a personal tort, but, by the Statute of 4 Edw. III, 7,[1] it is given that they will have *de bonis et catallis asportatis in vita testatoris* within the equity of which they will have [an action of] *ejectione firmae*, as 7 Hen. IV, 6,[2] and [an action of] *quare impedit* of a usurpation in the lifetime of the testator and [an action of] trover and conversion. And thus, for which, not this as here.

And, by another [counsel] on this side, F.N.B. 122a[3] was cited, where an executor had an action upon an escape in the lifetime of the executor where he was in execution, and the reason, as it was said, was because, by the escape, it is become the debt of the jailer and the jailer [is] indebted to him for it. And thus it is said in Platt's case, C. 37.[4] And it was before the Statute of Ric. II[5] because, by the common law, one will have [an action of] debt for an escape. And this appears by 38 Hen. VI, 9; *Dett*, F., 162;[6] and 34 Edw. IV, *Det*.

And thus thought Dodderidge and Whitelocke upon the moment[7] because the intent of the Statute was to aid the executor to grant in the estate of the testator for the payment of the debts and the performance of the will.

But Jones [held] *contra*. And he said that, at the common law, an executor will not have an action for goods taken away etc. because [it is a] personal action etc. But, by the Statute, it is given. And yet, at the common law, an executor could aid himself by [an action of] detinue or replevin, but not by [an action of] trespass because, there, it is to recover damages solely. But, in the others, it is to recover the thing. And on account of this, at common law, he will not have [an action of] *ejectione firmae*, but, after that *ejectione firmae*, the term was recoverable; it lies for executors. But, at common law, he could have [an action of] covenant if the testator [was] ejected. And whether the words of 4 Edw. III will be extended to it here is the question. Whether it be a chattel within the words or the equity has been adjudged [in] 32 & 33 Eliz., in the Bishop of Lichfield's case,[8] that they will have [an action of] *quare impedit* for a usurpation in the lifetime of the testator where he had the next avoidance, and [in] 41 & 42 Eliz., in

---

[1] Stat. 4 Edw. III, c. 7 (*SR*, I, 263).

[2] YB Hil. 7 Hen. IV, f. 6, pl. 1 (1406).

[3] A. Fitzherbert, *Nouvelle Natura Brevium*.

[4] *Platt v. Lock* (1551), 1 Plowden 35, 75 E.R. 57.

[5] Stat. 1 Ric. II, c. 12 (*SR*, II, 4).

[6] YB Pas. 38 Hen. VI, f. 28, pl. 10 (1460); Mich. 34 Edw. I, Fitzherbert, *Abr.*, *Dette*, pl. 162 (1306).

[7] sur le soddaines *MS*.

[8] *Sale v. Bishop of Lichfield* (1590), Owen 99, 74 E.R. 928, 1 Anderson 241, 123 E.R. 451.

the Countess of Rutland's case,[1] upon long debate, [it was] adjudged that they will have [an action of] trover and conversion [for] a finding in the lifetime of the testator, but it was conceived to be in the nature of detinue. Thus, I hardly think that it lies. And, for the mischief, it is also a mischievous case that does not lie against the executors of a jailer, but the case of trover and conversion.

And a day was given further.

See 14 Hen. VII, 17; V.N.B. 123; *Executors*, 106; Russell's case, C. 5, 27,[2] there, trover and conversion for executors for a finding in the lifetime of the testator, and it was said on the side of the defendant that, if one be arrested upon mesne process and the plaintiff dies, the prisoner can be let at large because the process is ended because neither the executor nor the administrator will have a declaration upon the first writ nor another writ for journeys accounts. See 12 Hen. VII, 2, Kelw., and 21 Hen. VII, 23, by Kingsmill. But it was once a cause of action to the testator, and whether it goes to the executors is the question.

More, f. 70, p. 8, f. 133, pl. 18.[3]

[Other reports of this case: Benloe 200, 73 E.R. 1057, CUL MS. Gg.2.30, f. 77; W. Jones 173, 82 E.R. 92, BL MS. Hargr. 317, f. 170; Latch 167, 82 E.R. 328, HLS MS. 1235, f. 78; Noy 87, 74 E.R. 1053; Popham 189, 79 E.R. 1282; BL MS. Hargr. 38, ff. 137v, 200; BL MS. Lansd. 1092, ff. 141, 287v; CUL MS. Ll.3.13, ff. 108, 179, 330v; HLS MS. 1063, ff. 10v, 40v.]

[This case is cited in Hobbs v. Prichard (Ex. 1641–1642), Exch. Cases temp. Car. I, pp. 154, 159.]

229

Ratcliffe v. Buck

(Part 2)
(K.B. Hil. 2 Car. I, 1627)

BL MS. Add. 35961, f. 50v, pl. 3

In the case between Buick and Ratcliffe, *quod vide supra* f. 39, p. 27,[4] Bankes now moved what manner of judgment will be given, whether *respondes ouster* or *quod recuperet*, because he said that, if one pleads in disability of the person

---

[1] *Countess of Rutland v. Countess of Rutland* (1595), Cro. Eliz. 377, 78 E.R. 624.

[2] *Digby's Case* (1499), YB Hil. 14 Hen. VII, f. 17, pl. 7; [Old] *Natura Brevium*; Hil. 17 Edw. III, Fitzherbert, Abr., *Executors*, pl. 106 (1343); *Russel v. Prat* (1584), 5 Coke Rep. 27, 77 E.R. 91, also Moore K.B. 146, 72 E.R. 496, 1 Leonard 193, 74 E.R. 178, 1 Anderson 177, 123 E.R. 417.

[3] *Mason v. Dixon* (1627–1628), BL MS. Add. 35961, ff. 76v, 138v; BL MS. Lansd. 1083, ff. 131, 221 (Widdrington's reports).

[4] For other proceedings in this case, see Nos. 158, 235.

and concludes as he should, if he will be answered there, if it be against the defendant, the judgment will be a *respondes ouster*. But this stands upon this difference, if the plaintiff demurs upon the plea and it be adjudged for him, then, it will be *respondes ouster*, but, in the case that an issue be taken upon the plea and it be found against the defendant, there, the judgment will be peremptory. And this appears by the books of 50 Edw. III, 20; 34 Hen. VI, 8 and 9.[1]

But, here, in our case that makes the question, the defendant has not concluded '*judgment si*' it will be answered, but '*judgment si actio*', and thus he has pleaded a plea in bar what is not a plea in bar. And on account of this, it will be as if there had not been any bar, but *nihil dicit*, and his conclusion has altered the nature of the plea, which in itself was to the person, to a plea in bar. And that a conclusion will alter the nature of the former plea is clear.[2] 22 Hen. VI, 34.[3] If one pleads matter of estoppel and does not conclude upon it, it will not be a plea by way of estoppel, but in bar. Thus, this [is] the reason of 21 Hen. VI, 4.[4] If one pleads a double plea and relies or concludes upon one only, the plea is sufficiently single. And the case in 49 Edw. III etc. does not come fully to this case.

DODDERIDGE: The case is well to be advised upon the Statute. But, for the time, he conceived that the judgment will not be peremptory because this is an ordinary exception in the first and second parts of Edw. III, that the plea is to the action where a plea is pleaded in disability, and yet the judgment is that he will answer. But the reason that, if it be found against the defendant, that it will be peremptory is for the delay and trouble that the defendant put the plaintiff to where, if he knew or could know his plea to be false, but it is well to be advised because this case is upon the Statute.

WHITELOCKE agreed.

Et adjornatur. After, f. 50a, p. 9.[5]

230

Rex v. Anonymous

(K.B. Hil. 2 Car. I, 1627)

A coroner's inquest and investigation must occur at the same time.

A void indictment is the same as no indictment.

---

[1] YB Trin. 50 Edw. III, ff. 19, 20, pl. 13 (1376); *Ashton's Case* (1455), YB Mich. 34 Hen. VI, f. 8, pl. 18.

[2] apport *MS*.

[3] YB Mich. 22 Hen. VI, f. 34, pl. 52 (1443).

[4] YB Mich. 21 Hen. VI, f. 4, pl. 11 (1442).

[5] For other proceedings in this case, see Nos. 158, 235.

BL MS. Add. 35961, f. 50v, pl. 4

Upon an inquisition taken before the coroner in Wales of a murder against fourteen separate persons, it was moved for the quashing of it, first because that it appears it was taken in the time of King Charles and at D. *super visum corporis mortui jacentis apud S.* in the time of King James and, at all times, the inquisition must be *super visum corporis*, as appears by 21 Edw. IV, 70, and 2 Ric. III, 2, Genny's case,[1] which cannot be here because it is not possible at one place and one time to have a view of the body lying dead [at] another day and another time.

Another exception was because the inquest was *de communitate*, where it should be by the four or five towns next adjoining. And this is by the Statutes *de Coronatoribus* and of Rutland and the Statute of Wales,[2] and also with this agrees the precedents of *Novell Entries*, 354,[3] where it is not *de communitate*, but *de villis etc.* And these, *Littleton*, who moved them, took by clear exceptions.

But DODDERIDGE, to the first, to which he solely spoke, thought that the inquisition could be taken at another place and another time than where the body lay if [at] one time, they have had the view similar to the case. The Statute is that the sheriff *accedat ad locum vestatum* and, there, he will make an inquest; yet, the book is that he can, when the view is made, take the inquest at another place. And he said that it was adjudged lately in the case of a great man in the realm that it is not necessary for the coroner to have the view of the body and that it could be enquired without it.

But WHITELOCKE and others at the bar said to him that, in this case, the inquisition was by the grand inquest and not by the coroner, as he took [it], upon which, he seemed to recant. And the case intended was of Lord Norris,[4] as he said first.

And *Littleton* said that it was adjudged [in] Trin. 13 Jac., if one be drowned and the body [is] not to be found, the death cannot be inquired of before the coroner, but the justices of the peace.

And the parties were bound over until Easter term to be newly indicted if it be overthrown because, as DODDERIDGE said, no indictment and a void indictment are the same.

[Other reports of this case: Benloe 202, 73 E.R. 1058, CUL MS. Gg.2.30, f. 77v; Latch 166, 82 E.R. 328; Popham 209, 79 E.R. 1298.]

---

[1] YB Mich. 21 Edw. IV, f. 70, pl. 55 (1481); *Jenney's Case* (1484), YB Mich. 2 Ric. III, f. 2, pl. 5.

[2] Stat. 4 Edw. I (*SR*, I, 40–41); Stat. 12 Edw. I (*SR*, I, 69–70); Stat. 12 Edw. I (*SR*, I, 55–68).

[3] *Anonymous* (1613), E. Coke, *A Booke of Entries* (1614), 'Indictment', pl. 6, f. 354.

[4] Perhaps *Rex v. Lord Norris* (1616), 1 Rolle Rep. 297, 81 E.R. 498.

231

Good v. Laurence

(K.B. Hil. 2 Car. I, 1627)

A judgment of damages in favor of the plaintiff is ad requisitionem.

BL MS. Add. 35961, f. 50v, pl. 5

Between Good and Laurence in [a writ of] error, *quod intratur* Mich. 2 [Car. I], rot. 119, judgment was reversed because damages *de incremento* were adjudged to the plaintiff and not *ad requisitionem* and this, as it was said, has often been ruled an error.

Also, the judgment was *ideo consideratum, adjudicatum, et affectum est etc.* and this is surplusage, and the law has put the form of the judgment.

[Other reports of this case: Benloe 198, 73 E.R. 1056, CUL MS. Gg.2.30, f. 76v; Latch 177, 82 E.R. 333; Noy 89, 74 E.R. 1055; Popham 211, 79 E.R. 1300; BL MS. Hargr. 38, f. 136; BL MS. Lansd. 1092, f. 148; CUL MS. Ll.3.13, f. 189v.]

232

Clapham v. Middleton

(K.B. Hil. 2 Car. I, 1627)

In this case, the judgment was reversed because the plaintiff's declaration was indefinite.

BL MS. Add. 35961, f. 50v, pl. 6

In another case in [a writ of] error, between Middleton and Clappam, it was reversed because the declaration was of the taking of '*diversis testas, anglice* earthen pots' and it did not show the number of them, according to Playtre's case, C. 5, '*quare pisces cepit*'.[1] Mich. 2 [Car. I, rot.] 613.

[Other reports of this case: Benloe 198, 73 E.R. 1055, CUL MS. Gg.2.30, f. 76; Noy 91, 74 E.R. 1057; Palmer 447, 81 E.R. 1164; CUL MS. 3.13, f. 201v; HLS MS. 1235, f. 83v.]

---

[1] *Playter v. Warne* (1583), 5 Coke Rep. 34, 77 E.R. 105.

233

King v. Merrick

(K.B. Hil. 2 Car. I, 1627)

When words are spoken that can have a favorable construction and a defamatory intent does not appear by other words, the words must be construed in mitiori sensu; *however, if subsequent or precedent words show that the intent is defamatory, then an action lies.*

BL MS. Add. 35961, f. 50v, pl. 7

[In a case] between Merrick and King for these words 'I charge thee, King, for felony and charge thee, *viz.* the constable of Newton Flotman in Norfolk, to arrest him' and, laying the words to be spoken in London and it being found for the plaintiff, it was moved in arrest of judgment:

First, that these words were not spoken of the plaintiff, though to the plaintiff. To which, it was answered that they were fully spoken of the plaintiff. And he cited the case in the *Novell Entries*,[1] 'Thou art a bastard and as ill born as mine.'

Second, that, here, there was not any affirmative that he had done a felony or that he has been a felon. And he cited Mich. 11 Jac., Powell and Bull's case: 'I have arrested Powell for [the] stealing of sheep'; and [it was] adjudged not actionable because solely to relate what he had done is not an affirmation that he had done the felony because one can be arrested for a felony that he has not done, to which it was answered that [it was in] 39 Eliz. between Webb and Toole,[2] which words were actionable, 'I will call him in question for poisoning my wife and will prove it', and 38 Eliz., Woodforde's case,[3] 'I did not know Mr. Woodford was your brother but he has forsworn himself in such a court, and I will prove it or bear his charges', and Hil. 44 Eliz., rot. 351, Cox's case,[4] 'This boy did cut my wife's purse and took out of it money and rings, and his father knew of it; therefore, I arrest him of that felony', and, there, it was resolved that the latter words were actionable if they had been of them but inasmuch as the precedent words could be no slander, it mitigated the latter, and on account of this, there, judgment will be given against the plaintiff.

Thus, here, there is a direct affirmative in the principal case, and [it is] is more strong than in the cases put.

Third, it was moved, admit it an affirmative, yet to say generally that one had done a felony is not actionable because it could be intended of a mayhem, which

---

[1] *Derington v. Westwood* (1562), E. Coke, *A Booke of Entries* (1614), 'Action sur le case', pl. 26, f. 29.

[2] *Webb v. Poor* (1597), Cro. Eliz. 569, 78 E.R. 813, Noy 63, 74 E.R. 1031.

[3] *Woodroff v. Vaughan* (1595), Cro. Eliz. 429, 78 E.R. 669.

[4] *Cox v. Humphries* (1602), Cro. Eliz. 877, 889, 78 E.R. 1102, 1113.

is a felony and the indictment [is] *felonice ut felo domini regis*, to which it will be intended, as it is generally intended, a felony by which one will lose his life. And he cited C. 4, Hext's case;[1] 'I doubt not but to arrest her of felony', which proves, as it was answered, that he will have this intention. And it is stronger than the case at the bar. And, if the words are plain and the usual interpretation if they will be taken in a usual sense, it will be an open gap to all slander.

But it was resolved by the court, and judgment [was] given that the action did not lie because, as it was said, a felony could be intended of mayhem.

And JONES took a rule, when words are spoken that can have a favorable construction, there, if, neither by the antecedents nor the consequents, the intent appears, but only the usual acceptation of the words, there, they must be construed *in mitiori sensu*; it will be otherwise if the words, subsequent or precedent, incline the intent otherwise. And this is the reason that to say of one that he has the pox or he has stolen my corn are not actionable without more. But to say that he is a thief for he has stolen my corn, there, the intent appears of such a stealing that it makes him a thief, as it has been adjudged thus to say generally he is forsworn is not actionable. Also, here, in these words, there was not a direct affirmative.

And DODDERIDGE said that Hext's case does not come to this case because, there, it appears that he intended such a felony by which he could be arrested on suspicion, which cannot be applicable to mayhem because, for this felony, one cannot be arrested for a suspicion of [it]. And there, by the adjunct words, the intent appears fully. And he said that actions upon the case vary according to the words and there is as much difference between them as between the faces of men, and they are not to be ruled one by the other, but all by the general rule.

And thus, judgment [was] given for the plaintiff. *Intratur* Pas. 2 Car., or Trin. 2 [Car. I].

[Other reports of this case: Benloe 202, 73 E.R. 1059, CUL MS. Gg.2.30, f. 78; Latch 176, 82 E.R. 333; Popham 210, 79 E.R. 1299; BL MS. Hargr. 38, f. 136v; BL MS. Lansd. 1092, f. 152v; CUL MS. Ll.3.13, f. 188.]

234

Bellamy v. Balthorpe

(K.B. Hil. 2 Car. I, 1627)

Tithes in gross cannot be leased for a year or longer to a stranger to the land except by a written deed. However, tithes can be sold by an oral contract.

---

[1] *Hext v. Yeomans* (1585), 4 Coke Rep. 15, 76 E.R. 893.

BL MS. Add. 35961, f. 51, pl. 8

Between Bellamy and Balthorpe, in [an action of] trover and conversion, of [that] which concerned the title of the earl of Clare to the impropriate parsonage, it was said by DODDERIDGE and JONES for clear law that tithes cannot be leased without a deed for one year any more than for more years. See 19 Hen. VIII, 12; 21 Hen. VII, 22, and 21 Edw. IV, 18b.[1] But yet the parson can sell the tithes of the following year, and this is good without a deed by way of a contract, not by way of a demise. See 21 Hen. VI, 43.[2] Also, the tithes can be leased to another tenant and the owner without a deed because, there, it passes not by way of a grant, but by way of a discharge and retainer. And also, tithes can be leased without a deed conjoined with the rectory because the rectory can pass without a deed. Thus, [there is a] diversity between a lease of tithes in gross and with a rectory and also between a lease of tithes in gross and a sale of them and also between a lease of tithes in gross to a stranger and the terre tenant.

Thus, the counsel was directed to argue not whether tithes can be leased for one year without a deed because, for a demise, the court held that he clearly could not, but, if it had been by way of a contract, it had been otherwise.

And afterwards, judgment was given for the plaintiff for the default of color. See the roll because the pleading is observable.

[Other reports of this case: Benloe 202, 203, 73 E.R. 1058, 1059, CUL MS. Gg.2.30, f. 78; Godbolt 373, 78 E.R. 220; Latch 176, 184, 82 E.R. 333, 337, HLS MS. 1235, ff. 80, 82v; Noy 89, 74 E.R. 1055; 1 Eagle & Younge 355; BL MS. Hargr. 38, f. 135v; BL MS. Lansd. 1092, f. 156v; CUL MS. Ll.3.13, ff. 189, 197v.]

235

Ratcliffe v. Buck
(Part 3)

Cadiman v. Grendon
(K.B. Hil. 2 Car. I, 1627)

BL MS. Add. 35961, f. 51, pl. 9

And now, the case before, f. 49b, p. 3,[3] was moved again, Jones being now present.

And now, DODDERIDGE, *mutata opinione*, thought the judgment will be peremptory because, having commenced his plea *actio non* and he concluded also *judgment si actio*, he has pleaded a plea in bar that is insufficient to bar, but [is]

---

[1] YB Trin. 19 Hen. VIII, f. 12, pl. 9 (1527); YB Pas. 21 Hen. VII, f. 21, pl. 11 (1506); YB Hil. 21 Edw. IV, f. 18, pl. 18 (1482).

[2] *Fitzwilliam v. Parson of Arcsay* (1443), YB Pas. 21 Hen. VI, f. 43, pl. 20.

[3] For earlier proceedings in the case of *Ratcliffe v. Buck*, see above, Nos. 158, 229.

good to the person, and on account of this, as he has not pleaded any plea. And the books cited do not go to this point because this is a middle case. And it is a general rule that, if a plea be pleaded to the person and tried against the defendant, there, it will be peremptory. [It is] otherwise if it be upon a demurrer ruled against the defendant. And the reason is for the delay. But in this also, there is a difference; if the plea be triable by the ordinary, then, it is not peremptory. And it appears by the books. And to plead also to the person, some go also in bar as [in] abatement. And villeinage, outlawry, etc. and in these pleas which go thus in disability which go also in bar, there, if it be ruled against him upon a demurrer, yet it will be peremptory because, in those cases, the conclusion is *judgment si actio*.

And of this opinion also was JONES, upon the moment, because he never heard the case before.

And they said, even though they thought thus, yet they would move it at the table in Serjeants' Inn to have the advice of the others.

And afterwards, at another day, *Calthorpe* moved the case between Dr. Cadiman, plaintiff, and Grendon, defendant, in a writ of battery, in which there was the same plea as in this case, except that, there, he demanded judgment of the bill and also concluded judgment of the bill and also he did not aver his plea by the record *ut debuit*, nor show before which justices Cadiman was convicted of recusancy; and this is entered [in] Trin. 2 [Car. I, rot.] 549. And *Calthorpe* moved to have a peremptory judgment upon the same reasons as in the first case.

And by the occasion of it, the justices delivered their final opinion in both of the cases. And they said they differ and they will have separate judgments: the case of Ratcliffe peremptory and Cadiman's *quod respondes*. And they said that Cadiman's [case] differs apparently from Ratcliffe's because, there, he demanded judgment of the bill, which is in the nature of a judgment of a writ and, on account of this, [it is] similar to a conclusion to the writ, and not to the action.

And DODDERIDGE said that there are several kinds of pleas and each of them has separate conclusions to the jurisdiction and the conclusion *judgment si* the court would acknowledge the person, whether he will respond to the action *si actio*, and also to the writ, judgment of the writ, and, if the plea be to the action of the writ, as where one brings [an action of] *mort d'ancestor* where he must have an assize, there, the conclusion is *judgment si*, by this manner of action, he should maintain. And each plea should have its apt conclusion; otherwise it is not valid.[1] And thus it seemed to him, *ut supra*, that they will have separate judgments.

JONES [held] to the same intent. And he cited 40 Edw. III, 7, in avowry,[2] for an express authority in point because, there, he pleaded as in bar of avowry a plea that only went to the abatement of it and, on account of this, [there was a] peremptory judgment.

And thus, these two cases were ended at one time.

---

[1] avult *MS*.
[2] YB Hil. 40 Edw. III, f. 9, pl. 18 (1366).

[Other reports of Ratcliffe v. Buck: Benloe 194, 73 E.R. 1053, CUL MS. Gg.2.30, f. 75; BL MS. Hargr. 38, f. 134v.]

[Other reports of Cadiman v. Grendon: Benloe 196, 204, 73 E.R. 1054, 1060, CUL MS. Gg.2.30, ff. 75v, 78v; Latch 177, 82 E.R. 334, HLS MS. 1235, f. 80; Noy 89, 74 E.R. 1056; BL MS. Lansd. 1092, f. 148v; CUL MS. Ll.3.13, f. 190.]

236

Alston's Case

(K.B. Hil. 2 Car. I, 1627)

In the court of king's bench, a defendant can crave oyer after an imparlance, but not in the court of common pleas.

BL MS. Add. 35961, f. 51, pl. 10

Woldrich moved that, after an imparlance, oyer cannot be demanded. And he was about to cite divers authorities, but Justice JONES and all of the clerks interrupted and overruled him that the constant course of the [court of] king's bench has [at] all times been diverse from the [court of] common bench in this and that it has before this hour[1] been debated and so ruled, with which, he was not satisfied. But at another day, he moved it again, but he was again overruled.

DODDERIDGE [was] then present, and he cited Wimarke's case,[2] which was from this court. But DODDERIDGE and the clerks said that, in the bench, it was [at] all times so. And the reason of the different custom, as he said, is because, in the king's bench, they can imparl before a declaration because, before this, he [the defendant] does not know for what he is impleaded[3] because the taking[4] being upon [a writ of] *latitat*, which supposes a trespass, the defendant does not know the matter [of the lawsuit], as he can upon a writ. And this is the reason by which, if he will not have oyer after an imparlance, he will not have [it] at any time and it is utterly taken away.

See Wymarke's case; there, the suit was by an original [writ] and thus, being by the same reason, there can be a diversity in the king's bench, where, by an original, the suit begins and where by a bill.

[Other reports of this case: Benloe 201, 73 E.R. 1057, CUL MS. Gg.2.30, f. 77v.]

---

[1] cest houres *MS.*; ceux homes: BL MS. Lansd. 1083, f. 75v.
[2] *Dun, ex dem. Sleford v. Law* (1593), 5 Coke Rep. 74, 77 E.R. 165.
[3] I.e. sued.
[4] I.e. the process.

237

Laycock v. Wiltshire

(K.B. Hil. 2 Car. I, 1627)

The issue in this case was whether, for the non-feasance of an undersheriff, the action should be brought against the high sheriff or the undersheriff.

BL MS. Add. 35961, f. 51v, pl. 11

Between Laycock and Wilshire, an undersheriff, an action upon the case [was brought] against him because the plaintiff delivered to him a [writ of] *latitat* to serve upon one Wilimot, with whom, divers times afterwards, he conversed and could have arrested, and yet he did not do [it], but he returned *non est inventus*. And [it was] found for the plaintiff.

And it was moved in arrest of judgment that this would not lie against him because the law does not take notice of the undersheriff, but the sheriff is chargeable with all escapes and misdemeanors that he does, but solely those for which he [the undersheriff] is to have a corporal punishment.

And of this opinion was the court also, that it [the lawsuit] should be against the high sheriff and not against the undersheriff[1] for the same reason.

But, on the other side, it was urged that this action was directed [. . .] by the court and that there are divers precedents in the point, by which a day was given until the next term.

[Other reports of this case: Latch 187, 82 E.R. 338, HLS MS. 1235, f. 83; Noy 90, 74 E.R. 1057; BL MS. Lansd. 1092, f. 159; CUL MS. Ll.3.13, f. 200.]

238

Wood v. Witherick

(Part 1)
(K.B. Hil. 2 Car. I, 1627)

An action of account lies against an infant for necessaries.

BL MS. Add. 35961, f. 51v, pl. 12

Between Witherick and Wood in [a writ of] error, *quod intratur* Mich. 2 [Car. I, rot.] 1501, upon a recovery in the court of Norwich against an infant in an action upon the case upon *insimul computaverunt* where the infant pleaded in bar the infancy, the plaintiff replied that they were necessaries. And [it was] found so by the jury. And judgment [was] given. And error [was] assigned in the point of the judgment that such an action would not lie against an infant because

---

[1] *judice MS.*

this action, being grounded upon an account between the plaintiff and the defendant, is of such a nature in which an infant easily could be overreached and damaged. And a difference was taken between an action upon the case against an infant upon necessaries, which it was agreed would lie, and this action because, here, in this action, the particulars do not come to be examined again, but the action is founded upon the sum reduced into a certainty by the account between them, but, in the other case, he must declare the particulars so that the court can judge of it. And a case [in] 19 *Jacobi* between Holmy and Sterle was cited to be adjudged in point.

Another error was alleged because the certificate of the record was *placito coram A. et B.*, *nuper vicecomitibus*, thus, it appears to be *coram non judice*.

Another error [was] that the first process was an attachment, where it should be a summons.

Afterward, p. 19.[1]

239

Lindley's Case

(K.B. Hil. 2 Car. I, 1627)

After a nonsuit, a release of one co–defendant by the plaintiff cannot be alleged where that would defeat the other defendant's right to receive court costs.

BL MS. Add. 35961, f. 51v, pl. 13

In the case of one Lindley, it was moved by Serjeant *Davenport* that [an action of] *ejectione firmae* was brought against two [persons] and, at *nisi prius*, the plaintiff was nonsuited, and, afterwards, upon the day in the bench, he would have pleaded a release of one defendant. And he moved that it will not be received and that the nonsuit [will be] pleaded because one defendant cannot bar the other of these costs, according to Ruddock's case, C. 6.[2]

And thus, it was ruled by the court.

240

Sparkes v. Hayly

(K.B. Hil. 2 Car. I, 1627)

Where one is deceived as to the value of a horse that was purchased, the plaintiff must allege a warranty of quality, not a mere affirmation of quality.

---

[1] For later proceedings in this case, see below, No. 245.

[2] *Rasing v. Ruddock* (1599), 6 Coke Rep. 25, 77 E.R. 291, also Cro. Eliz. 648, 78 E.R. 887, Jenkins 271, 145 E.R. 195.

BL MS. Add. 35961, f. 51v, pl. 14

Between Sparkes and Hayly, *quod intratur* Mich. 2 [Car. I, rot.] 612, in [a writ of] error upon a judgment in an action upon the case, where the plaintiff declared how he bought a horse from the defendant and that he affirmed to him that it was worth £7 and fit for a body horse in the cart and divers other good qualities it had so that he, *fidem adhibens*, bought it from the defendant, *ubi revera*, it was not worth but 40s. and it was not serviceable etc. And it was assigned that such an action would not lie unless the defendant warranted the horse to him in such a manner.

And of this opinion was JONES because he said that, then, if one avers he bought something or he is deceived by a horse dealer, he can have an action upon the case.

241

Tindall v. Richards

(K.B. Hil. 2 Car. I, 1627)

There is a difference between a contract to make further assurances and one to make a conveyance as to when an action should be begun.

BL MS. Add. 35961, f. 51v, pl. 15

Between Tindall and Richards in [an action of] covenant, *quod intratur* Trin. 2 [Car. I], rot. 1092, the covenant was that the defendant 'shall do and suffer all acts and things for further assurance as the counsel of the plaintiff shall advise', who advised that he acknowledge a fine and a *dedimus* [*potestatem*] before such, [and he alleged] that he has not done [it] upon a request.

The other said that no writ of covenant was sued forth.

And it was ruled by the court to be a difference where the covenant is to levy a fine because, there, he is not bound before the other has sued out the writ of covenant and where to do all acts etc. and he is advised that he will acknowledge a fine or if the covenant [is] that he will acknowledge a fine, but, there, he is bound to make the conusance and the writ could be sued out afterwards, as the course is. And this diversity [was] held.

[Other reports of this case: Latch 186, 82 E.R. 338; BL MS. Lansd. 1092, f. 158; CUL MS. Ll.3.13, f. 199v.]

242

Spademan v. Jackson

(K.B. Hil. 2 Car. I, 1627)

An action of debt does not lie for a rent reserved by a third person.

BL MS. Add. 35961, f. 51v, pl. 16

Between Spademan and Jackson in [an action of] debt, *quod intratur* Mich. 2 [Car. I], rot. 390, the defendant bound himself to the plaintiff by a deed indented reciting how A.B. had demised to him such land etc. reserving so much rent and, now, he bound himself to the plaintiff to pay to him the same rent at the days of the reservation. And afterwards, he made a default, upon which the plaintiff brought [an action of] debt.

And it was the opinion of the court that [an action of] debt does not lie because it was a thing impossible, to pay to the plaintiff a rent reserved by another, nothing being shown that the reversion is in the plaintiff and the words were that he will pay the same rent, not such a sum as the rent etc.

[Other reports of this case: HLS MS. 1235, f. 82; BL MS. Lansd. 1092, f. 155v; CUL MS. Ll.3.13, f. 196.]

243

Rex v. Gregory

(K.B. Hil. 2 Car. I, 1627)

The Statute of 21 Jac. I against forcible entries applies to copyholders, but not to tenants at will by the custom of a manor.

BL MS. Add. 35961, f. 51v, pl. 17

In the case of one Stacy, *quod intratur*, Hil. 2 [Car. I], because, in the bundle of indictments, one was indicted for forcible entry upon Stacy, being as the words of the indictment *fuerunt tenentes* of such a manor *ad voluntatem domini secundum consuetudinem manerii* and it did not say *per copiam rotulorum*, upon which he was restored by the justices of the peace. And now, a restitution was prayed because the indictment was insufficient and not within the new Statute of 21 Jac.,[1] which gives power to the justices of the peace to restore tenants by copy etc., because there are divers tenants at will *secundum consuetudinem* etc. who are not tenants by copy, as those in Yorkshire who hold by the custom called tenant right and tenants by the verge and tenants in ancient demesne and these are not within this Statute, as was said by the counsel and held by the court, by which he was

---

[1] Stat. 21 Jac. I, c. 15 (*SR*, IV, 1222).

awarded restitution. But three weeks [were] given by an order before the execution of it that the other side provide another abode.

And here, it was said by DODDERIDGE that the wife of a copyholder who had a widow's estate by custom is also a copyholder within this law and yet she does not have the copy of the husband, but the heir [does], but she holds by virtue of the copy granted to the husband.

See afterward 83, p. 47.[1]

[Other reports of this case: Benloe 203, 73 E.R. 1059, CUL MS. Gg.2.30, f. 78v; Latch 182, 82 E.R. 336; CUL MS. Ll.3.13, f. 195v.]

244

Dean v. Steel

(K.B. Hil. 2 Car. I, 1627)

An action for defamation lies for speaking words which insult a person in the trade by which he makes his living.

BL MS. Add. 35961, f. 51v, pl. 18

Between Sterle and Dene in [a writ of] error, *quod intratur,* 2 [Car. I, rot.] 833, the case was [thus]. The plaintiff brought an action upon the case against the defendant in the court of the Borough of Sudbury. And, in the certificate, it was *placita apud Burgum de Sudbury* and *Burgus de Sudbury* in the margin of the record. And he declared that the defendant *apud Sudbury praedictum,* and he did not say *infra jurisdictionem huius curiae* he [the defendant] spoke these words of the plaintiff to be a woolwinder and shifter of wool, 'Thou hast opened my wool and put into it wet wool', by which he disgraced him in his trade etc. And, there, [it was] found for the plaintiff, and damages [were] assessed to the plaintiff [in] 2d., and judgment [was] given *quod recuperet damna per curiam adjudicatur,* at £9 omitting the 2d.

And the errors moved [were]:

(1) That it did not appear that the cause was *infra jurisdictionem curiae;*

(2) That the words were not actionable;

(3) That the damages were assessed by the court and also diminished.

To the first, it was answered that it is as much as amounts to *infra jurisdictionem* because the margin is *Burgus de Sudbury* and the style of the court is *placita curiae Burgi de Sudbury* all etc. and the declaration is *quod fuerunt* spoken *apud Sudbury praedictum.* And he cited Kell. 33, 6a, *Villa de Oxoniae.*[2]

---

[1] *Rex v. Fry* (1627), BL MS. Add. 35961, f. 116, pl. 47; BL MS. Lansd. 1083, f. 171, pl. 47 (Widdrington's reports).

[2] *Rex v. Thornbery* (1496), Pl. 6, Keilwey 33, 72 E.R. 190, 115 Selden Soc. 367.

And, for the third error, he said that they are amendable because [it was] the fault of the clerk in the entry solely.

For the first and last, DODDERIDGE took [them under] advisement.

For the second, the counsel argued, and DODDERIDGE agreed, that the words are actionable because it slanders him in the trade by which he acquires his living.

And DODDERIDGE cited these cases to be adjudged of a tradesman, that he bound by false weights and measures. Thus, he said that, in the [court of] exchequer, there was a case that Bilkdyn put in his dye pin dust by which the silk[1] that he received weighed four more in one pound than before and to say thus of a silk dyer is actionable, and, 24 Eliz., one Samford of Gloucester made excellent cloth that, for the goodness, was much bought up and sought for and he put his mark to [*blank*] and another counterfeited his cloth in show and mark, but they were much worse, and he sold them for Samford's clothes, by which the reputation of Samford's clothes fell, upon which he brought an action upon the case, and [it was] adjudged for him because it was a deceit in slander of him in his trade. Thus he said it was adjudged to say of a fuller that, in fulling his cloth, he makes bracks and fills them up with flocks is actionable; thus here.

But, upon the other points, *adjornatur.*

And afterwards, it was reversed because the judgment was *quod capiatur.*

[Other reports of this case: Godbolt 435, 78 E.R. 255; Latch 188, 82 E.R. 339, HLS MS. 1235, f. 83v; CUL MS. Ll.3.13, f. 201.]

245

Wood v. Witherick

(Part 2)
(K.B. Hil. 2 Car. I, 1627)

BL MS. Add. 35961, f. 52, pl. 19

And now, the last day of the term, the case before, f. 50b, p. 12,[2] was moved again. And, for the first error, it was said, and held by Justice JONES also, [as to] the issue, the finding of the jury had helped it because, though it be admitted that an action upon the case upon *insimul computaverunt* would not lie against an infant because he will not be charged upon his account in that he could be over-reached, yet he is where a demurrer is upon the declaration or if the issue be upon the infancy or another collateral point in which the particulars do not come into evidence to the jury. But, in our case, the issue was whether it was for necessaries so that, now, all of the particulars came into the consideration of a jury and he

---

[1] fish *MS.*

[2] For earlier proceedings in this case, see above. No. 238.

cannot be wronged by his folly in mispleading any more than he will be in an action of debt or upon the case for necessaries which, without question, would lie.

WHITELOCKE [was] of the same opinion.

Chief Justice HYDE *nihil dixit.*

DODDERIDGE *contra, sed hesitanter.*

But afterwards, because the action was brought 15 May and the account [was] alleged 25 May, thus the action [was] brought before he had occasion, it was reversed and none of the other errors [were] moved.

See 10 Hen. VI, 20,[1] that an infant will not avoid an account before auditors.

[Other reports of this case: Benloe 203, 73 E.R. 1060, CUL MS. 2.30, f. 78v; Latch 169, 82 E.R. 330, HLS MS. 1235, f. 78; Noy 87, 74 E.R. 1054; BL MS. Hargr. 38, f. 136; CUL MS. Ll.3.13, f. 182.]

246

Anonymous

(K.B. Hil. 2 Car. I, 1627)

A receiver of the royal customs has the privilege to be sued only in the court of exchequer.

BL MS. Add. 35961, f. 52, pl. 20

Memorandum quod Sotherton, the puisne baron of the exchequer, came into court and demanded to have privilege for a customer, who was sued here. And he showed the Red Book of the exchequer.[2] And it was allowed to him.

247

Anonymous

(K.B. Hil. 2 Car. I, 1627)

An action for defamation for accusing a person of having committed a felony will be tried where the words were spoken, not where the alleged felony was committed.

BL MS. Add. 35961, f. 52, pl. 21

One brought an action upon the case against one in London for speaking words of him that charged him with a felony. The defendant justified because he had done the felony with which etc. in Essex. And he was put to swear to the plea because it changed the [place of] trial.

---

[1] YB Mich. 10 Hen. VI, f. 14, pl. 46 (1431).

[2] PRO E.164/2, f. 36. See also W. H. Bryson, *The Equity Side of the Exchequer* (1975), p. 29.

And JONES said that, if he had justified the words in London by reason of a felony in Essex, in this case, the felony will be tried in London, by which he was ruled to answer his plea.

Clenche, clerk, *contra, vehementer.*

248

Holmes v. Winegreen

(Part 1)
(K.B. Hil. 2 Car. I, 1627)

In an action for taking and detaining charters contained in a box, if the plaintiff proves his right to the charters, his right to the box also is implied.

BL MS. Add. 35961, f. 52, pl. 22

In [a writ of] error between Wingreene and Holmes, *quod intratur* rot. 362, upon a judgment given in an action upon the case for detaining a box of evidence until the plaintiff had made an obligation to the defendant, the defendant pleaded that *non detinuit*. And the verdict found *quod est culpabilis de transgressione in narratione specificata*. And it was moved that this was apparent error, the issue being *non detinuit* and the verdict *quod culpabilis*; thus, the issue [was] not found, but *argumentive*; thus, no verdict [was] given upon the issue.

But DODDERIDGE said that, the issue amounting to the general issue, if the general verdict be given, it is well.

And [it was] adjourned to the next term. Afterwards, f. 71, pl. 16; 58, p. 28.[1]

249

Arnold v. Dichton

(Part 3)
(K.B. Hil. 2 Car. I, 1627)

BL MS. Add. 35961, f. 52, pl. 23

In the case before, f. 37a, pl. 15; f. 40, pl. 36,[2] Serjeant *Bramston* moved that '*daret*' will have relation as well to the time past as future. And he said that, [in] 44 Eliz., it was adjudged, where one brought an action upon the case against one and alleged how the defendant had maimed him and, in consideration that he would not sue him, he promised to give to him *tantam quantum expenderet* in the

---

[1] For later proceedings in this case, see below, No. 278, and BL MS. Add. 35961, f. 77, BL MS. Lansd. 1083, f. 133v (Widdrington's reports).

[2] For earlier proceedings in this case, see above, Nos. 145, 167.

cure of it; and, there, [there was] the same exception as here, that it will have relation to the time after the promise, *et non allocatur.*

But JONES remembered the former opinion of the court, by which *non prevaluit.*

Afterwards, 49, p. 3.[1]

[Other reports of this case: Latch 203, 82 E.R. 347; Popham 183, 79 E.R. 1278; BL MS. Hargr. 38, f. 121.]

250

Note

(K.B. Hil. 2 Car. I, 1627)

A writ of prohibition will lie to remove a case out of a court for the failure of that court to admit evidence that is admissible at common law.

BL MS. Add. 35961, f. 52, pl. 24

If the spiritual court refuses a witness or the son in the case of the father for a witness, where such testimony [is] allowable in our law, it is a good cause [for a writ] of prohibition.

251

Redfern v. Umphry

(K.B. Hil. 2 Car. I, 1627)

A verdict must be based upon the issue that was pleaded.

BL MS. Add. 35961, f. 52, pl. 25

Between Redfurne and Umphry in [a writ of] error upon a judgment in debt given in Bury St. Edmunds in Suffolk, *quod intratur* Trin. 2 [Car. I, rot.] 1553, it was reversed because the issue was upon [a plea of] *non est factum* and the verdict against the defendant [was] *quod debet se* the sum and also it was *misericordia* in the judgment *pro capiatur.*

---

[1] For other proceedings in this case, see, Nos. 145 and 167, and BL MS. Add. 35961, f. 71v, pl. 3, BL MS. Lansd. 1083, f. 119, pl. 3 (Widdrington's reports).

252

Fish v. Wiseman

(K.B. Pas. 3 Car. I, 1627)

The issue in this case was whether and, if so, how execution of a judgment that was affirmed on appeal can be had.

BL MS. Add. 35961, f. 52v, pl. 1

Wiseman recovered in an action of debt in the [court of] common bench against Sir William Fish. And he had execution by a *capias* after the year and a day, upon which Sir William brought [a writ of] error. And, for the same cause, he reversed the execution. But the judgment was affirmed. And upon this, out of the [court of] king's bench, there issued within the year and a day after the judgment [was] affirmed a *capias* against him, upon which he was taken. And he came in by a *cepi corpus*.

And now, he prayed to be dismissed from the execution because, it was said by *Bankes*, that, inasmuch as he was once in execution and delivered out of it, he will not be ever in execution again. And for this, he cited 16 Hen. VII, 2,[1] *per curiam*, that, if one be in execution for a debt recovered in the common bench and it is removed and he [is] let to mainprise, if the judgment be affirmed, he [the judgment creditor] will not have a new execution, but his remedy is against the bail. Thus [is] 2 Edw. IV, 8;[2] if one be condemned in London and he comes at the term for his business and he is taken in execution and let at large by the privilege, he cannot be taken again. And this, he said, was the reason of an escape, who cannot be retaken, 14 Hen. VII, 1,[3] because, once one be in execution, he will not be taken again for the same matter.

Second, he said that, inasmuch as the *capias* is now misawarded, the court can supersede it. And he cited 34 Hen. VI, 45,[4] where such a misaward was superseded.

But the court said to him that he [should] not insist upon the first reason because DODDERIDGE said that all of the books are [good] law, but they prove only where he was once in lawful execution, which here he was not. And he remembered Dyer, Trewinyard's case,[5] where one was delivered by the privilege of Parliament, yet he could have a new action because he was not one who [was] lawfully in execution.

---

[1] YB Mich. 16 Hen. VII, f. 2, pl. 3 (1500).
[2] YB Pas. 2 Edw. IV, f. 8, pl. 19 (1462).
[3] YB Mich. 14 Hen. VII, f. 1, pl. 1 (1498).
[4] YB Trin. 34 Hen. VI, f. 45, pl. 9 (1456).
[5] *Executors of Skewys v. Chamond* (1545), 1 Dyer 59, 73 E.R. 131, 109 Selden Soc. 3.

And JONES here said that the matter was, inasmuch as the process paravail was a *scire facias*, if the judgment here being affirmed whether the same process that, there, should have been awarded not be to be here awarded because he said that in Garnon's case, which [in] C. 5 is reported,[1] there, this very point came in question, and, there, it was the opinion of the court that this court, upon the affirmance of the judgment, should award the same execution that the first must make.

But it was said that the court here is not such, but any time within the year and day after the judgment [is] affirmed to award a *capias*. And it was commanded to search for precedents. And in this case, it was said that, upon a recovery in the king's bench, there, after the year and day, the process is a *capias*. And thus the court said, though the old books are *contra*.

But *Langhorne* said to me that the course was to award a *capias* upon the roll within the year and thus, at any time afterward, he can have an *alias capias*, though past the year. And this stands with the books.

And Sir William was put to his writ of error because the court would not discharge him upon this suggestion and [a writ] of error in process [was] brought to have error in the same court.

[Other reports of this case: Godbolt 371, 78 E.R. 218; Latch 192, 82 E.R. 341; Palmer 447, 81 E.R. 1164; BL MS. Lansd. 1092, f. 162v; CUL MS. Ll.3.13, f. 206.]

253

Evers v. Owen

(K.B. Pas. 3 Car. I, 1627)

A will of chattels need not be in writing.

BL MS. Add. 35961, f. 52v, pl. 2

It was said by DODDERIDGE and JONES in a [writ of] prohibition to the [court of the] marches of Wales that a devise of chattels can be helped with a verbal averment that the intent of the testator was such. And it is not similar to the case of land because, there, the will must be in writing and nothing will be averred but it can be collected out of the writing, as C. 6, Cheyni's case.[2] But a will for chattels can be by parol, and thus it can be supplied by verbal additions if they are proved.

[Other reports of this case: Godbolt 431, 78 E.R. 253; BL MS. Lansd. 1092, f. 185.]

---

[1] *Layton v. Garnon* (1598), 5 Coke Rep. 88, 77 E.R. 188, also Moore K.B. 566, 72 E.R. 762, Cro. Eliz. 706, 78 E.R. 941.

[2] *Lord Cheyney's Case* (1591), 5 Coke Rep. 68, 77 E.R. 158, also Moore K.B. 727, 72 E.R. 867.

254

Gouldsmith v. Bacon

(K.B. Pas. 3 Car. I, 1627)

Equity pleadings and depositions in the court of chancery are not common law records, nor are they chancery records, not being under the seal of the court of chancery.

BL MS. Add. 35961, f. 52v, pl. 3

Gouldsmith brought an action of slander against Benion, Hil. 2 [Car. I], rot. 1020, for saying that he was perjured, who justified because he answered a thing in his answer in the [court of] chancery and deposed contrary in his depositions *prout patet per recordum.* The plaintiff said *nul tiel record.* And at the day, he failed to have them in the court. And the court was moved with this plea and also with the plaintiff who would join issue upon it that he knew it was not a plea, but he should have demurred.

And JONES said that they must replead because, if he will be condemned for not bringing in the record, it will be error because the depositions and the answer are not anything in the chancery in the English court nor are they records as come in under the Great Seal, but he should have averred it *per patriam* and not *per recordum.*

[Other reports of this case: Benloe 204, 73 E.R. 1060, CUL MS. Gg.2.30, f. 79.]

255

Stoke v. Sikes

(K.B. Pas. 3 Car. I, 1627)

A patron of a church can revoke a presentation before the priest is instituted, and the king can revoke before the priest is inducted.

A canon is not binding until it is received by the common law.

BL MS. Add. 35961, f. 52v, pl. 4

[In a case] between Stocke and Sikes, it was moved for a [writ of] prohibition to the court of delegates because the court there, one being presented to a benefice and afterwards another [was], the second [was] admitted, instituted, and inducted, held a plea whether the second will be ousted and also the first presented was son to the latter incumbent and this [is] contrary to the canon[1] that the son [not] succeed the father in his spiritual living. And here, it was said without question that, after institution though before induction, the incumbent

---

[1] W. Lyndwood, *Provinciale* (1929), p. 15.

cannot be removed by a suit in the spiritual court without a [writ of] *quare impedit*, but their hands are closed, be it the presentation of both by the same patron or divers.

And thus, as JONES said, it was ruled in the time of Gawdy, Anderson, and Coke in the common bench because, in the time of each of them, it was a great question. And the civilians stirred it in all of the several times of those chief justices, and, each time, [writs of] prohibition [were] awarded.

And here, it was affirmed by DODDERIDGE and JONES that, by the canon law, a patron cannot repeal his presentation, but *cumulando* as their term is, he can present divers and the ordinary can elect which he would. But in our law, there is no need of this trick because he can directly repeal it before institution, and the king [can] before induction.

For the other point, the court said that this canon was not ever received here and none bind but those that the common law receives, as there is a canon[1] that, if one marry a woman whom he had kept as adulteress, it is not good, but the issue [is a] bastard, but it is not received here.[2]

[Other reports of this case: Latch 191, 253, 82 E.R. 340, 372; Noy 91, 74 E.R. 1057; BL MS. Lansd. 1092, ff. 162, 217; CUL MS. Ll.3.13, ff. 205, 262.]

256

Anonymous

(K.B. Pas. 3 Car. I, 1627)

The issue in this case was whether an ecclesiastical court can appoint an administrator to divide a decedent's estate.

BL MS. Add. 35961, f. 52v, pl. 5

It was moved for a [writ of] prohibition to the spiritual court because it would make one an administrator to divide the estate. And it was said that often it had been granted in the [court of] common bench because they did not have such power.

But the court denied it, and they said they were not of the same opinion. And they said 'go to the common bench for it if they are of opinion to grant it.'

---

[1] *Testa est vis*, X, 4. 17. 6.

[2] Stat. 20 Hen. III, c. 9 (*SR*, I, 4).

257

Evans v. Askwith

(Part 4)
(K.B. Pas. 3 Car. I, 1627)

BL MS. Add. 35961, f. 52v, pl. 6

And now the case of Evans and Aswith was argued again.[1]

Calthorpe, for the plaintiff: The points in the case are four: the first, whether by the election to the bishopric of Limerick before confirmation, whether this makes a cession; second, whether the first *commendam* is good if notwithstanding it be after [he was] translated, whether it be still good; third, whether the second *commendam*, coming between the election and the confirmation to the bishopric of Bristol, be good; the fourth, whether such a dean as he is here can confirm [a lease].

For the first, he agreed the election to the bishopric in Ireland made a cession as well as [if] it was to a bishopric in England and in any place in the world. And thus is 19 Edw. III, *Triall*, 37; 24 Edw. III, 26;[2] and thus was Josua Horne's case, who was made the bishop of Man. And though the law does not take notice of him as a peer of the realm, as appears by *Proces*, 24, and C. 7, Calvin's case,[3] C. 5, yet it takes notice of him as a bishop, as appears by *Briefe*, 800.[4] Thus, this I admit against myself because it has been admitted on my side before.

For the second point, whether the *commendam* to hold *dignitatem decanatus*, whether this made him dean or not, it has been objected that the dignity and the office are different things and, on account of this, the first *commendam* did not give him *decanatum*, but *tantum dignitatem decanatus*, which are different and separate things. And thus, he is not a dean. But this is not so because dean is a name of dignity, as appears [in] l. 5 Edw. IV, 106.[5] And where the dignity goes, there also goes the office. And the civilians have a difference between *diaconus curalis et qui praeest collegio curalis*. He has only *officium* and no dignity. But *qui praeest collegio* has office and dignity also. Thus, wherever the dignity is, there is the officer also.

For the third, whether the election made the deanery void before consecration or confirmation, he argued that it did not because a bishop elect is not a

---

[1] For earlier proceedings in this case, see above, Nos. 101, 135, 226.

[2] YB Pas. 19 Edw. III, Rolls Ser. 31b, vol. 13, p. 76, pl. 27 (1345), Fitzherbert, Abr., *Triall*, pl. 57; *Rex v. Bishop of Worcester* (1350), YB Trin. 24 Edw. III, f. 29, pl. 21.

[3] *Calvin's Case* (1608), 7 Coke Rep. 1, 77 E.R. 377.

[4] *Champion v. Havering* (1311), YB Pas. 5 Edw. II, Selden Soc., vol. 31, p. 27, pl. 7, YB Pas. 5 Edw. II, f. 165, Fitzherbert, Abr., *Briefe*, pl. 800.

[5] YB Mich. 5 Edw. IV, Long Quinto, f. 106 (1465).

bishop but only *nomine*. [In] 38 Edw. III, 30 and 31,[1] it is said that it is *tamquam* [. . .] *emerio [?] in viscere matris*. F.N.B. 3. The writ of right is directed to the bailiff of a bishop elect. But before confirmation, he does not have *potestatem ordinariam*, but, when he is confirmed, then he has. And for this [see] C. 8, 69, Trollop's case;[2] there, the bishop elect could certify an excommunication. But this is to be intended of a bishop elect confirmed. And [see] Dy. 350;[3] there, a bishop elect is the minister to whom the court must write, and he is the minister of the court. But after confirmation, then it goes a step further, and, on account of this, then he can confer *ordines*, and that before confirmation, the law does not consider[4] him a bishop. 4 Hen. IV, 2; 9 Hen. V, 13; 20 Edw. III, *Breve*, 250,[5] make it clear because, until this, the making of him a bishop now abates the writ. And by the books of 41 Edw. III, 36, and 11 Hen. IV, 37, and C. 4, 75, and Davys 76,[6] it appears plainly that a *commendam retinere* [is] not sufficient in time if it comes before confirmation because, before it, there is no avoidance. And with them agrees also Dy. 237 and 7 Jac., Collet and Glover's case,[7] the great exchequer chamber case of *commendam*s. And the case of a translation does not differ from the case of an election because, before a translation be *firma et rata*, there is not any avoidance if the former promotions were below the degree of bishop, but, if the former benefice was a bishopric, then it was held by the civilians that, by the election, it is an avoidance of all of the former, but with this difference, if the promotion of the bishop was *ex assensu*, then, it was not void until an assent. But, if it be *pro utilitate ecclesiae*, then, by an election of the pope or of him who has the supreme power, as now the king has,[8] it was void upon the election. But ours here is not such, but he [was] made by the promotion of the party.

---

[1] YB Mich. 38 Edw. III, ff. 29, 30 (1364).

[2] *Richeson v. Trollop* (1608), 8 Coke Rep. 68, 77 E.R. 577, also Cro. Jac. 213, 79 E.R. 185.

[3] *Anonymous* (1576), 3 Dyer 350, 73 E.R. 785.

[4] eme *MS*.

[5] *Clifford v. J.* (1402), YB Mich. 4 Hen. IV, f. 2, pl. 8; YB Mich. 9 Hen. V, f. 13, pl. 17 (1421); YB Hil. 20 Edw. III, Rolls Ser. 31b, vol. 14, p. 4, pl. 2 (1346), Fitzherbert, Abr., *Briefe*, pl. 250.

[6] *Rex v. Bishop of Salisbury* (1367), YB Mich. 41 Edw. III, f. 5, pl. 13; *Rex v. Bishop of Salisbury* (1409), YB Mich. 11 Hen. IV, f. 37, pl. 67; *Armiger v. Holland* (1597), 4 Coke Rep. 75, 76 E.R. 1047, also Moore K.B. 542, 72 E.R. 746, Cro. Eliz. 601, 78 E.R. 844; *Rex v. Horsefall* (1611), Davis 68, 80 E.R. 552.

[7] *Anonymous* (1565), 2 Dyer 237, 73 E.R. 524; *Colt v. Bishop of Coventry* (1612), Moore K.B. 898, 72 E.R. 982, Hobart 140, 80 E.R. 290, 1 Rolle Rep. 451, 81 E.R. 600, Jenkins 300, 145 E.R. 219, CUL MS. Dd.3.86, part 5, Oxford Bodl. Lib. MS. Eng. hist.c.494, LI MS. Hale 80(g).

[8] Stat. 26 Hen. VIII, c. 1 (*SR*, III, 492).

For the fourth point, whether the dean here be such that he could confirm, he argued that he is. And this he must maintain because otherwise, as he agreed, the concurrent lease was voidable. And this he argued for three reasons:

First, because the commendatory dean here is him to whom the *congé d'eslire* will be directed in the vacancy, and he is the elector of the bishop. And this is clear or otherwise, during this *commendam*, of necessity, there would be a vacancy of the archbishopric and thus the election of Toby, now the archbishop, [would be] void. Then, if he be the elector, he who can elect can be informers of their acts, and thus they should be, as appears by *Graunt*, 104, and 50 Edw. III, Statham, [Abr.], *Assize*, 15; and [in] Dy. 58,[1] there is a query whether the confirmation of one chapter, the other being dissolved, be good. But [in] Dy. 282,[2] there, it is resolved that the confirmation of one, the other being dissolved, is good.

The second reason is because the interest passed from the bishop, but the dean had only but an assent. And this appears [in] Dy. 40b[3] and PB. 601. Then, if nothing passes from him but a bare assent, then a *decanus in facto* can assent, and even though afterwards it is avoided, *viz.* his title to the deanery, yet his confirmation remains good, similarly to the case of acts made by a lord *pro tempore*. [In] Dy. 123,[4] there, it was doubted whether the confirmation of the dean made in the place of Cardinal Pole after the reversal of his attainder, which omitted the election of a second dean, was good or not. But [in] Dy. 273,[5] there, it was resolved that a dean[6] *pro tempore* could make leases, which is more strong. Therefore, *a fortiori*, he can confirm. See 11 Hen. IV, 84; Davys 47; Dy. 145 and 233.[7]

The third reason is because the *commendam* here was *relaxatio juris* and a dispensation with it; the operation of the law is stopped by this *commendam*. And on account of this, it is to be known that this avoidance is made by the law of the church and, before the constitutions made, there was not any avoidance. Then, if the *commendam* here, which is a dispensation, suspends the operation of the constitutions, it is necessary that the acceptance of the bishop not have operation but that, notwithstanding them, he remains as before an incumbent. And that the dispensation of the king will supersede the force of the canons appears [by] *Ayd le roy*, 103.[8] If the king makes an Englishman archbishop of Ireland, he gives

---

[1] *Bishop of Coventry's Case* (temp. Ric. II), Fitzherbert, Abr., *Graunte*, pl. 104; *Anonymous* (1543), 1 Dyer 58, 73 E.R. 128.

[2] *Archbishop of Dublin v. Bruerton* (1569), 3 Dyer 282, 73 E.R. 633.

[3] *Chafyn de Meere's Case* (1538), 1 Dyer 40, 73 E.R. 88.

[4] *Anonymous* (1555), 2 Dyer 123, 73 E.R. 270.

[5] *Walrond v. Pollard* (1568), 3 Dyer 273, 293, 73 E.R. 610, 659.

[6] done *MS*.

[7] *Abbot of Battle v. Neel* (1410), YB Trin. 11 Hen. IV, f. 84, pl. 34; *Case of the Dean and Chapter of Fernes* (1607), Davis 42, 80 E.R. 529; *Bishop of Litchfield v. Fisher* (1557), 2 Dyer 145, 73 E.R. 317; *Parkchust's Case* (1564), 2 Dyer 233, 73 E.R. 515.

[8] Hil. 33 Edw. III, Fitzherbert, Abr., *Ayd de roy*, pl. 103 (1359).

to him also to find the deanery[1] of Pickering there, which he could not do without the dispensation of the king. And that such a dispensation as here continues him an incumbent is plain by Dy. 233,[2] where it was adjudged that he voided the parsonage *per resignationem*, which he could not if Parkhurst was not the incumbent. Thus [is] F.N.B. 36; a parson [was] made a bishop with a dispensation he will have spoliation; therefore, [he was] an incumbent, with which [agrees] 38 Hen. VI, 20, and Register 103 and F.N.B. 49,[3] bishop, a parson can have [a writ of] *juris utrum*; therefore, [he was] an incumbent by the dispensation.

(DODDERIDGE said that it was intended of an impropriation to a bishop, not of a *commendam*.)

And he is thusly an incumbent who can make leases because this was the difference agreed by the greater part of the justices in the argument of Colt and Glover's case, that a commendatory *retinere* was an incumbent and he could lease, but a commendatory *recipere* could not because, there, [he is] but a *custos* and a pure commendatory *non habet in titulo*. And on account of this, he, who is not an incumbent, cannot lease. And in Holland's case, C. 4,[4] though, there, in his report, it does not appear, yet, there, a lease was made by the commendatory, and [it was] held good *qui retinere*, and such a commendatory is an incumbent. Then, if he can lease, *a fortiori*, he can confirm.

And thus he concluded for the plaintiff.

And on the other side, it was argued by *Holborn* for the defendant.

And first, he argued that the dispensation to hold *dignitatem decanatus* was not sufficient to make him dean because, first, he said that the dignity and the office, *decanatus et dignitatem decanatus*, are different things because, in a deanery, there is the spiritual part and the temporal part; the temporal are the possessions, and the spiritual part are counsel and assistance to the bishop. And these different parts appear [by] Dy. 273, 294; 11 Hen. IV, 49; and C. 3,[5] the dean and chapter of Norwich's case. And even though the terms are confounded in common parlance and in some acts of Parliament, yet, in a grant, it cannot pass if it not be the thing denoted by the word of the grant because, by a grant of *dignitatem decanatus* where the deanery itself being another thing, it will not pass. And that they are diverse,

---

[1] demy *MS.*

[2] *Parkhust's Case* (1564), 2 Dyer 233, 73 E.R. 515.

[3] YB Hil. 38 Hen. VI, f. 19, pl. 1 (1460); *Registrum Brevium*; A. Fitzherbert, *Nouvelle Natura Brevium*.

[4] *Armiger v. Holland* (1597), *ut supra*.

[5] *Walrond v. Pollard* (1568), 3 Dyer 273, 293, 73 E.R. 610, 659; YB Hil. 11 Hen. IV, f. 49, pl. 25 (1410); *Case of the Dean and Chapter of Norwich* (1598), 3 Coke Rep. 73, 76 E.R. 793, also 2 Anderson 120, 165, 123 E.R. 577, 601.

he cited *Breve* 800; 11 Hen. IV, 49; 5 Edw. III, 39.[1] And if the queen would have passed the deanery, she would not have given the dignity of the deanery.

The second reason [was] the queen had enumerated here the particulars to the grant to him, *dignitatem decanatus, emolumenta, etc.* Thus, the enumeration of the particulars is an exclusion of those that are not named. Also, there, [there are] no words of the possessions of the deanery.

Another reason [is] because, in the same grant, when the queen granted to him *tenere praebendum* of Fakington, there, it did not say *dignitatem.* Thus, from the difference of the penning, it appears that it did not intend to grant the deanery itself. And in Holland's and Digbi's case, C. 4, and Packhurst's case, Dy.,[2] and the *Book of Entries*, 222, in all of these, the commendam is *retinere rem ipsam.* And certainly, if thus it had been intended, it would have been as the penning of the latter *commendam.*

Also, he did not take it sufficient because she, in it, gave the deanery itself and the pen[ner] of it as the time persuaded, being the first [year of King] James, it was without Coke. Also it was in the dispensation that *retinere et ac si esset in titulo*; thus, he did not hold *in titulo.* And this is the main turning point of the case because, if he be a pure commendatory and he does not hold it *in titulo*, then this curses [?] all of the cases put by the other party because it was argued by the civilians that a pure commendatory does not hold *in titulo.* And thus, clearly, he is not an incumbent because he holds *in titulo.* And if he is not an incumbent, he cannot confirm.

And as to the difference between a *commendam retinere*, that he has *titulum*, and a *commendam recipere*, [who] does not have title, this is not a difference because the purpose of the *commendam* was invented to save the canon that prohibited the having of divers promotions because, on account of this, they could not have divers by title. And on account of this, it was commended, invented, that he could have two, but not *in titulo.* Thus, a commendatory cannot have in title.

And also, [there is] no difference between a perpetual *commendam* and a temporary [one] because *magis et minus non variant speciem*, nor between a *commendam personae* and [one] *curae* because both are made by the same medium, *viz.* dispensation. And for Dy. 233, which seems to pose it, there, it was but the judgment of the jury, and not of the judges, as appears afterwards, 298,[3] which was of an incumbent and he held *in titulo* and thus *vacavit per resignationem.*

[1] *Champion v. Havering* (1311), YB Pas. 5 Edw. II, Selden Soc., vol. 31, p. 27, pl. 7, YB Pas. 5 Edw. II, f. 165, Fitzherbert, Abr., *Briefe*, pl. 800; YB Hil. 11 Hen. IV, f. 49, pl. 25 (1410); YB Mich. 5 Edw. III, f. 38, pl. 24 (1331).

[2] *Robins v. Gerrard* (1599), 4 Coke Rep. 78, 76 E.R. 1054, also Moore K.B. 434, 72 E.R. 678, Gouldsborough 162, 75 E.R. 1066, Jenkins 273, 145 E.R. 197; *Parkchust's Case* (1564), 2 Dyer 233, 73 E.R. 515.

[3] *Parkchust's Case* (1564), 2 Dyer 233, 273, 73 E.R. 515, 612.

For the point of the dispensation after the election, he argued that it came too late because, at the beginning, bishoprics were donative and they could have been given by parol by the king. As well as he could present by parol in place and supply of it, it is now become an election. And on account of this, by the election, he is a bishop to all purposes in the common law, and then the dispensation *retinere* comes too late, the other dignity being void before. And that [he is a] complete bishop by [his] election appears by C. 4, 69. A bishop elect can certify an excommunication. And when he is elected, the power of the guardians of the spiritualities cease. F.N.B. agrees with this, fol. 62, and Dy. 250.[1] He is now the person to whom the court of the king will write. Thus, as to the *spiritualia*, [he is] complete by the election, so as to the *temporalia* because of F.N.B. 1, a writ of right directed to the bailiffs of a bishop elect, and F.N.B. 2 [. . .] to the bailiffs of a bishop elect or to the bailiffs of the king, by which it appears that, before the temporalities [are] delivered to him, the law takes notice of him and his bailiffs because, if the temporalities were delivered to him, the writ could not be as directed to the bailiff of the king. See 4 Edw. IV, 5, and Kel. 185.[2]

Also after election, the bishop is confirmed which proves him a bishop because to confirm presupposes the essence before, otherwise it will be [. . .] because *confirmare est firmum facere*. And that here the Act of Hen. VIII,[3] of election of bishops, which is extended to Ireland, he takes it for granted it is thus. Also it is proved by F.N.B. 169. And the Statute says 'within any of the king's dominions'. And also, ever since the making of this Act, the same order has been observed there, so then, the same order being observed there, there would not be any difference, as the taking of a bishopric will make avoidance.

Also he can be made a bishop and translated without his assent. And this was granted by the other side. Therefore, his assent [is not] material, but, before it, he is a bishop. And [in] 32 Hen. VI, 28,[4] one can be made a bishop in [his] absence. And if assent be necessary, here, there is an implied assent which would serve, as the civilians argue, to divest the bishopric because his acceptance of the *commendam* is an assent to be a bishop.

For the fourth point, he argued that a commendatory dean is a dean as to jurisdiction, but not to confirm and do temporal acts. And he cited 11 Hen. IV, 64; Dy. 144; and Davys 67; *de capitulariter congregatis.*[5]

Also he who confirms must be the dean in title, which a commendatory, as he has argued, is not, but merely a *custos*. And he compared it to C. 5, Prince's

---

[1] A. Fitzherbert, *Nouvelle Natura Brevium*; *Ap Richarde v. Jones* (1566), 2 Dyer 250, 73 E.R. 552.

[2] *Standish's Case* (1515), Keilwey 180, 72 E.R. 357, 116 Selden Soc. 683.

[3] Stat. 31 Hen. VIII, c. 9 (*SR*, III, 728).

[4] YB Hil. 32 Hen. VI, f. 28, pl. 21 (1454).

[5] YB Pas. 11 Hen. IV, f. 64, pl. 16 (1410); *Bishop of Litchfield v. Fisher* (1557), 2 Dyer 145, 73 E.R. 317; *Rex v. Horsefall* (1611), Davis 68, 80 E.R. 552.

case,[1] that an administrator *durante minore aetate* does not have disposing power. And in the case of Colt and Glover, it was agreed that a person *per commendam retinere* is not within the Statute of 23 Edw. III, ca. 7,[2] to plead in bar. And there, in this case, W. Barton cited a case of 32 Eliz. to be adjudged that such a person could not make leases.

Then he took exception to the laying of the action because no entry was found, nor regress, by the plaintiff, and, without a regress, without question, there is not any trespass maintainable.

And thus he concluded for the defendant.

See more, fo. 66, p. 7.[3]

[Other reports of this case: Benloe 187, 73 E.R. 1045, CUL MS. Gg.2.30, f. 69; W. Jones 158, 82 E.R. 84; Latch 31, 233, 82 E.R. 259, 362, HLS MS. 1235, f. 97; Noy 93, 74 E.R. 1060; Palmer 457, 81 E.R. 1169; BL MS. Hargr. 29, f. 115, pl. 1; BL MS. Hargr. 38, ff. 95v, 108v, 148, 150v, 267v; BL MS. Lansd. 1092, f. 190v; CUL MS. Ll.3.13, f. 238v; CUL MS. Mm.4.31, f. 86; HLS MS. 1196, f. 3.]

[Palmer's report of this case is cited in Attorney General v. Crofts (Ex. 1697), Dodd 172.]

258

Herne v. Stuble

(K.B. Pas. 3 Car. I, 1627)

The issues in this case were:

Whether a debt must be alleged in certain when it is pleaded as a defense to an action of detinue;

Whether, in a foreign attachment in London, the custom and the place of the attachment must be alleged in certain;

Whether a debt must be sworn to be a true debt in the pleadings.

BL MS. Add. 35961, f. 53v, pl. 7

Herne brought [an action of] detinue against Stuble, *et intratur* Mich. 2 Car., rot. 601. And he alleged a bailment to be rebailed upon a request and that the defendant, *licet saepius requisitus*, did not rebail back to him.

The defendant pleaded in bar the custom of foreign attachments in London.

---

[1] *Prince v. Simpson* (1599), 5 Coke Rep. 29, 77 E.R. 96, also Cro. Eliz. 718, 78 E.R. 953, 2 Anderson 132, 123 E.R. 584, 3 Leonard 278, 74 E.R. 682.

[2] Stat. 25 Edw. III, stat. 6, c. 7 (*SR*, I, 326).

[3] *Evans v. Askwith* (1627), BL MS. Add. 35961, f. 72v, pl. 7, BL MS. Lansd. 1083, f. 120, pl. 7 (Widdrington's reports).

And divers exceptions were taken to the pleading of it, first, because he had not alleged that the plaintiff was in debt nor did he show how he became indebted but *tantum* that a plaint of debt was levied against the plaintiff, and this he must have shown, how he was in debt. And he cited the cases of 9 Edw. IV, 41, and 5 Hen. VII, 1,[1] where the defendant pleaded that the plaintiff was in debt to him and did not show how, and, there, an exception [was] taken to it and [he was] ruled to show how. And, in the *Book of Entries* 55 and 56, there, it is shown in a pleading of a foreign attachment how the debt accrued.

The second exception was because he had not followed the custom that he had pleaded because he has pleaded the custom to be that, if the bailiff returns that the defendant has nothing by which he can be attached and, being solemnly demanded, makes default, that then etc. and he varied from it in two things because, first, he said that the defendant in the suit there had nothing, but he did not say that the bailiff returned it so, and it must be by the custom to come in by the return of the bailiff or sergeant at mace. Second, he did not allege that the defendant there was solemnly demanded. And all these must have been so pleaded. And that this variance of the custom is material appears by Dy. 196, in the case of a foreign attachment.[2]

The third exception was taken because he did not show the place of the attachment. And it could be out of the jurisdiction of the court. And on account of this, it will be thus intended more strongly against him. And, if one pleads a thing in a particular jurisdiction, he must show that it was *infra jurisdictionem*. And he cited 34 Edw. IV, *Breve*, 789, cited in Spacy's case,[3] that the same action pending in the exchequer was not a plea if it did not show that the exchequer had jurisdiction by the privilege of a party, and Wheelehouse's case, reported before [*blank*],[4] where one was indicted in Northampton for haunting a bawdy house and it did not say *infra jurisdictionem*, and the indictment [was] quashed.

The fourth exception [was that] he has not said here that he swore his debt to be true, but *tantum quod juravit debitum*. And this he must have done, as appears by Dy. 296.[5]

Also this was said by *Ward* for the plaintiff.

And for the defendant, it was answered by *Stone*, for the first, that he need not have alleged how the debt accrued because, here, the debt was pleaded by way of a bar and there is not of record anything; it is not by way of a demand. And for this, he cited 9 Edw. IV, 41, and 5 Hen. VII, 1, aforesaid, where, as he

---

[1] *Hasting's Case* (1469), YB Mich. 9 Edw. IV, f. 41, pl. 27; *Dudley v. Lord Powle* (1489), YB Mich. 5 Hen. VII, f. 1, pl. 1.

[2] *Harwood v. Lee* (1567), 2 Dyer 196, 73 E.R. 433.

[3] Hil. 34 Edw. III, Fitzherbert, Abr., *Briefe*, pl. 789 (1360); *Sparry's Case* (1590), 5 Coke Rep. 61, 77 E.R. 148.

[4] *Rex v. Wheelehouse* (1626), above, No. 137.

[5] *Harwood v. Lee* (1561), 2 Dyer 196, 73 E.R. 433.

said, because he did not plead the debt by way of a demand, it is not necessary; as, there, he is held to plead the certainty of the commencement of it, thus here, he did not plead it but by a bar to him of the other action. And he said that 39 Hen. VI, 19,[1] there, it is our very case. He pleaded the debt and did not allege how, and yet [it was] good.

For the second, when he said *quod juravit debitum*, this cannot have another meaning but *quod juravit fore verum* because it could not be intended as *quod juravit fore falsum* because it [would be] against himself.

For the third objection, that he has not alleged the place of the attachment of the goods and that it could be outside of the jurisdiction, this he compared to 4 Edw. IV, 36,[2] in [an action of] false imprisonment, where it is alleged that the cause arose *infra jurisdictionem* of the [*blank*] and other books, to this, he answered that he had not pleaded the custom to be that the goods attached will be within the jurisdiction, and, on account of this, there is no need to show that they were because the custom that he has alleged warranted the attachment in whatever place.

For the fourth exception, that, here, he had not followed the custom, *viz.* being that it was not returned by the bailiff that he had nothing, he said that it was true, but, here, it is not material because it is an error in the process and during the judgment in force, not reversed, the plaintiff will not have an advantage of it by way of a plea and also because he is a stranger to the first judgment. And for this [is] 21 Edw. IV, 23;[3] a stranger to a plea will not be received to allege a discontinuance. And also, if he was a party to the first judgment and a privy, yet one cannot have an advantage of an error by way of a plea where he can have a writ of error. And, on account of this, if one recovers in an assize, afterwards, in [an action of] redisseisin, it is not a [good] plea that the recovery in the assize was erroneous; thus here etc.

Then, he took an exception to the declaration of the plaintiff because, if it [is] bad, it is not material for the fault[4] of the bar, and this was because it did not lay the time of the request to redeliver, which, as he said, is material here and a part of the contract because he is not bound to redeliver but upon a request. And where it is material and issuable, it must be alleged certainly.

To this, it was answered by the other side that there is a difference in an action upon the case and detinue; as, here, it is in an action upon the case, there, he must allege the request specially, but an [action of] detinue is a *praecipe* and a demand of itself. And on account of this, in [an action of] debt, it is not requisite

---

[1] *Prior of D. v. Lacy* (1460), YB Mich. 39 Hen. VI, f. 19, pl. 26.

[2] *Lawley v. Walwin* (1464), YB Mich. 4 Edw. IV, f. 36, pl. 18.

[3] YB Pas. 21 Edw. IV, ff. 22, 23, pl. 6 (1481).

[4] maleness *MS*.

to allege a request certainly, but he [the debtor] must tender his money [on] the first day if he would save himself from damages.[1]

And with this difference, Justice JONES agreed.

And on the other side, it was also said that there is not any difference where a debt is pleaded in bar and where in demand. And he denied the books to be as was cited, *viz.* 9 Edw. IV and 5 Hen. VII. And he said that in the *Old Entries*, fo. 156, there, the debt was put in issue and that all of the precedents there show the accruing of the debt.

And they adjourned.

[Other reports of this case: Godbolt 400, 78 E.R. 236; Latch 208, 82 E.R. 349; BL MS. Lansd. 1092, f. 189v; HLS MS. 1063, f. 1.]

259

Green v. Moody

(K.B. Pas. 3 Car. I, 1627)

In an action for debt for unpaid rent, the plaintiff need not allege the date of the defendant's entry.

A pleading will not be construed so as to make it allege a falsity.

BL MS. Add. 35961, f. 59, pl. 8

Between Greene and Moody, in an action of debt upon a lease for years, the plaintiff alleged a lease to begin at a day to come, by virtue of which the defendant entered and was possessed. And he did not show the day of his entry.

And it was moved in arrest of judgment because, if he entered before the lease began, it was a disseisin and no rent [was] due, according to Clifford's case, 7 Edw. VI, Dy.[2]

And JONES said that [the words] *virtute cuius* aided it because there could not be a possession by virtue of the lease if there be a disseiser.

But Serjeant *Thynne*, who moved this, urged that so it was in Clifford's case and that a declaration will not be taken by implication.

But JONES and DODDERIDGE said that Clifford's case was of an *ejectione firmae* and, in this case, it is not necessary that there be a possession by virtue of the lease where there could not be an ejectment. But in [an action of] debt, there, the lessee is bound by reason of the contract, which he cannot frustrate by his own act because he cannot surrender nor waive the possession to prejudice the lessor of the rent.

---

[1] I.e. interest.

[2] *Clifford v. Warrener* (1553–1554), 1 Dyer 89, 96, 73 E.R. 192, 210.

Thynne: He can make a feoffment and thus, afterwards, the lessor cannot maintain [an action of] debt against him.

And the court would have advised, but by reason that there was an injunction in the case granted in chancery, judgment was now given against Thynne. And [the court] said to him 'sue a writ of error if you will'.

And afterwards, Hil. 3 Car. [1628], it was affirmed in a writ of error, and the reason was that, by his [own] act, he will not avoid his [own] contract, and also it was here '*virtute cuius*' he entered and this he cannot [do] before the day.

[Other reports of this case: Godbolt 384, 78 E.R. 226; Latch 196, 82 E.R. 343; BL MS. Lansd. 1092, f. 166; CUL MS. Ll.3.13, f. 209v.]

260

Busher v. Earl of Tullibardine

(Part 2)
(K.B. Pas. 3 Car. I, 1627)

BL MS. Add. 35961, f. 59, pl. 9

In a *scire facias* by Busher against Murray, *comes* Tillybarne in Scotland, *quod intratur* Mich. 2 [Car. I, rot.] 194,[1] for having him in execution for debt, he pleaded a protection of the king. And three exceptions were taken to it:

First, because the *teste* of the protection was after the *teste* of the *scire facias*, thus [it was] purchased pending the suit, which is contrary to the books of 11 Hen. IV, 7, and 10 Hen. VI [. . .].[2]

Second, because the cause is not specified in it, *quia moraturus* or *quia profecturus* or similar, and, in all protections, the cause must be expressed. And thus it was ruled [in] 39 Hen. VI, 38 and 39,[3] and thus are all of the protections. F.N.B. 28; V.N.B. 21; and the Register [of Writs].[4] And thus also, it is provided by the Statutes of 13 Ric. II, ca. 16, and 3 Hen. VIII, ca. 4.[5] And the reason is because the cause, if it be false, is traversable, and, if it does not continue, there can be a disallow[ance] of the protection, which will be prevented if it be given[6] without any cause expressed.

---

[1] For earlier proceedings in this case, see above, No. 141.

[2] YB Mich. 11 Hen. IV, f. 7, pl. 17 (1409); YB Mich. 10 Hen. VI, f. 2, pl. 8 (1431).

[3] YB Hil. 39 Hen. VI, f. 38, pl. 3 (1461).

[4] A. Fitzherbert, *Nouvelle Natura Brevium*; [Old] *Natura Brevium*; *Registrum Brevium*.

[5] Stat. 13 Ric. II, stat. 1, c. 16 (*SR*, II, 65–66); Stat. 3 Hen. VIII, c. 4 (*SR*, III, 26–27).

[6] bone *MS.*

Third, it was because, here, there is not a clause that it will be to where *in placitis coram nobis tenendis,* and this court is more high than the justices in eyre, and, there, such a protection is not allowable if it does not have an express clause for the justices itinerant, and not as here, *in omnibus placitis ubicumque etc.*

[Other reports of this case: Godbolt 366, 78 E.R. 215; Latch 197, 82 E.R. 343; BL MS. Lansd. 1092, f. 176; CUL MS. Ll.3.13, ff. 210v, 224.]

261

Taylor v. Tolwin

(Part 1)
(K.B. Pas. 3 Car. I, 1627)

Statutes of jeofails are construed strictly.

An infant need not allege the place where he was underage.

BL MS. Add. 35961, f. 59, pl. 10

Tolwyn brought an action upon the case for words against Taylor in the [court of] common bench. And he recovered by *nihil dicit,* of which Taylor brought [a writ of] error in the [court of] king's bench. And he assigned for error that the defendant was an infant and he appeared by an attorney where it should have been by a guardian and he did not put a place where he was under age of which the venue could come, upon which, issue was taken, and it [was] tried where the first action was laid.

And [it was] found for the defendant in the writ of error.

And now, it was moved that it was mistried because, here, there was not any venue, and, on account of this, the trial [was] void because there was not any venue in the record to warrant the [writ of] *venire facias.* And this is not aided by the Statute of 21 Jac.[1] because [it is] outside of the words of it and statutes of jeofails are taken strictly, never by the equity, as DODDERIDGE said. And on account of this, being out of the words, it is out of the law.

And all this was confessed by Serjeant *Hitcham* of the other side, by which he prayed a repleader.

And here, it was agreed that, after a mistrial, there will not be a repleader as the venue had been of an apt and a due place. But here, the venue was of no place; it was no venue. And on account of this, they awarded a repleader if [good] cause not be shown [to the contrary] at a day certain.

And here, DODDERIDGE said that it is not an issue whether an infant or not at such a time it will be tried by a jury.

---

[1] Stat. of 21 Jac. I, c. 13 (*SR,* IV, 1221).

And it was entered Trin. 2 [Car. I, rot.] 1400, or Hil. 1 [Car. I, rot.] 545. After, f. 58, [pl.] 24.[1]

262

Cremer v. Tookley

(K.B. Pas. 3 Car. I, 1627)

The issues in this case were:

Whether the court of admiralty has jurisdiction over a suit based on a contract for freight to be received in England by a foreign ship and transported abroad where the contract was made abroad;

Whether an attorney-in-fact who sues in the court of admiralty in violation of the statute is as guilty as the principal.

BL MS. Add. 35961, f. 59, pl. 11

[In a case] between Cremor and Tokeley, *quod intratur* Mich. 2 [Car. I, rot.] 423, in an action upon the statutes of 25 Ric. II and 2 Hen. IV[2] for suing in the admiral's court, the plaintiff first showed the statutes and then he showed that the defendant impleaded him against the form of these statutes. And upon [a plea of] *non culpabilis*, it was found that the charter party upon which the contract was grounded was made at Dunkirk *in partibus transmarinis* and that, on account of this, it was agreed between the plaintiff and one Mullibeck, who [was] master of the ship, that the master prepare a ship to sail from Dunkirk to a port etc. named here in England and that, there, he will take her freight and with it will sail to another port which was beyond the sea and that the master will have so much for the freight and that the master made the defendant to be an attorney to sue for it in the admiral's court, which he did accordingly. And [the jury] asked the advice of the court whether he be guilty.

And it was argued for the plaintiff by *Andrews* of Lincoln's Inn.

And first, he argued that, here, in this case, the admiral cannot hold the plea because the plaintiff could have had a remedy by the common law and, then, in such a case, to hold a plea is within the Statute and [is] punishable and that, here, the common law takes cognizance of the case. He said that it is clear because part of the contract is to be performed within the realm, and, where any part is pleadable here, all is, as 48 Edw. III, 2, Sir Raphe Poole's case,[3] where one contracted to do service beyond the sea in a war, because part, *viz.* of the contract, was here, it will be sued at common law. And, because the Statute of 13 Ric. II says that

---

[1] For later proceedings in this case, see below, No. 274.

[2] Stat. 15 Ric. II, c. 3 (*SR*, II, 78–79); Stat. 2 Hen. IV, c. 11 (*SR*, II, 124).

[3] *Pole's Case* (1374), YB Hil. 48 Edw. III, f. 2, pl. 6.

the admiralty will hold a plea of such cases as had been used in the time of King Edward, father of the said king, let us enquire of what things it, by common law, could hold a plea of and what was by the common law in their jurisdiction. [In] 8 Edw. II, *Corone*, 399, by Stanton,[1] it was said that it will not be said the sea, where one can see from one side to the other, but the coroner will have jurisdiction. And [in] 40 Ass. 25,[2] a Norman robbed upon the sea; he was convicted of piracy by the common law. And in 46 Edw. III and 7 Ric. II, Statham, [Abr.], *Trespass*, 38 and 54, there, in [an action of] trespass, there was a justification of an act upon the high seas because, as Belknap said, 6 Ric. II, *Protection*, 46,[3] the sea is of the allegiance of the king. Thus, by the common law, these courts here have jurisdiction upon the sea and of things done upon it. And then, to sue in the admiralty is punishable. And even though the admiral has jurisdiction of flotsam etc., as is C. 5, 106,[4] or of wreck of the sea, he does not have cognizance, as Dy. 326 is.[5] And our case differs from Lacy's case, cited in C. 2 in Bingham's case and C. 5 in Constable's case,[6] because a felony is more local than any other action. And this of necessity must be tried where it was done. *In tempore* Edw. I, *Avowry*, 192;[7] there, it is an [action of] replevin of a ship taken upon the sea; and, there, Berisford said that the king willed the peace be kept upon the sea as well as upon the land. And the Statute of Sel., ca. 5,[8] wills that the admiral have[9] jurisdiction of things done upon the high seas and not within the bodies of the counties, by which it appears that the common law has cognizance of things done upon the sea in any case. And this is where part of the act is to be done within the realm, by which, having here a good remedy at common law, he should not flee to the admiralty.

Second, he argued that the attorney here is such to sue within the Statute against whom the action can lie. And he said that it had not been a question if the party himself here had been the defendant because, though he himself did not prosecute, but his attorney did, yet it is in law his own act and pursuit. And

---

[1] YB 6 & 7 Edw. II, Eyre of Kent, Selden Soc., vol. 24, p. 133 (1313–1314), Fitzherbert, Abr., *Corone*, pl. 399.

[2] YB 40 Edw. III, Lib. Ass., p. 245, pl. 25 (1366).

[3] YB Trin. 6 Ric. II, Ames Found., vol. 2, p. 49, pl. 35 (1382), Fitzherbert, Abr., *Protection*, pl. 46.

[4] *Constable's Case* (1601), 5 Coke Rep. 106, 77 E.R. 218, see also 1 Anderson 86, 123 E.R. 367; BL MS. Lansd. 1088, f. 69; S. A. Moore, *A History of the Foreshore* (1888), pp. 224–241 (Sir John Constable's Case and Sir Henry Constable's Case).

[5] *Anonymous* (1573), 3 Dyer 326, 73 E.R. 737.

[6] *Lacy's Case* (1583), cited in *Stroud v. Horsey* (1589–1600), 2 Coke Rep. 93, 76 E.R. 616, also 1 Leonard 270, 74 E.R. 246, Moore K.B. 121, 72 E.R. 480; *Constable's Case* (1601), *ut supra*.

[7] Fitzherbert, Abr., *Avowrie*, pl. 192 (temp. Edw. I).

[8] Stat. 5 Eliz. I, c. 5, ss. 20, 33 (*SR*, IV, 426, 428).

[9] dit *MS.*

he cited *Bar*, 264,[1] which proves *quod qui per alium fecit per se ipsum facere videtur*[2] and that the act of my attorney is my act. But here, in our case, *est via versa*, whether the act of the attorney will be said his own act. But [as to] attorneys, even though it is the act of the principal,[3] yet, if the act is not lawful, the fault will lie upon them. And the command would not excuse them, but they will see at [their] peril to the lawfulness of it. And on account of this, if an infant makes an attorney to make seisin, he who makes it is by it a disseisor. 9 Hen. VII, 24; C. 10,[4] the case of the Marshalsea; the bailiff was punished for executing the command of the court which did not have jurisdiction; and *Trespass*, 213;[5] a person can beat his villein but, if an attorney does, he is a tortfeasor. Thus, if a bailiff distrains where nothing [be due], it is nothing as he is not the lord. 2 Hen. VIII, 4; 9 Hen. VII, Di. 14; 1 Hen. VI, 6.[6] Also, in [actions of] trespass, all are principals and none are accessories.

And, on account of this, if the master here be guilty, the servant and attorney who aided him is not guiltless. And thus, on account of this point is Ponell's case, Dy. 159,[7] where it is held that either of them was the principal and both [were] suable etc.

Calthorpe, contra: And first, he said that though Mr. Guin in his reading[8] and Mr. Lambert[9] held that the court of admiralty was not ancient, but erected *circa* the days of Edward III, yet he said that it is an ancient court, the beginning of which cannot be known, and [it was] long before the Conquest [1066]. And Dy. 153[10] proves it to be of the time of which memory [runneth not]. And in the Statute of 2 Hen. V, cap. 6,[11] which gives an appeal of acts upon the sea, it is called the ancient custom, which cannot probably intend from the time of Edward III, being at this time but new. And even though in the case from the time of Edward I in [Fitzherbert, Abr.,] *Avowry*, there is no mention of the admiral,

---

[1] Pas. 32 Edw. III, Fitzherbert, Abr., *Barre*, pl. 264 (1358).

[2] *Black's Law Dictionary* (1951), p. 1413.

[3] seignour *MS*.

[4] YB Pas. 9 Hen. VII, f. 24, pl. 7 (1494); *Hall v. Stanley* (1612), 10 Coke Rep. 68, 77 E.R. 1027, also 1 Brownlow & Goldesborough 199, 123 E.R. 753, 2 Brownlow & Goldesborough 124, 123 E.R. 851.

[5] Hil. 33 Edw. III, Fitzherbert, Abr., *Trespas*, pl. 253 (1359).

[6] *Fyloll v. Ashley* (1520), YB Trin. 12 Hen. VIII, ff. 3, 4, pl. 3, 119 Selden Soc. 14; YB Mich. 9 Hen. VII, ff. 12, 14, pl. 8 (1493); *Abbot of Ossney's Case* (1422), YB Mich. 1 Hen. VI, ff. 5, 6, pl. 23.

[7] *Bylota, qui tam v. Pointel* (1558), 2 Dyer 159, 73 E.R. 346, also Benloe 58, 64, 123 E.R. 45, 50, BL MS. Harley 1624, f. 60.

[8] Rice Gwynn's 1607 reading on Magna Carta. J. H. Baker, *Readers and Readings* (2000), p. 94.

[9] W. Lambarde, *Archeion*.

[10] *Hunt v. Ellisdon* (1557), 2 Dyer 152, 73 E.R. 332.

[11] Stat. 2 Hen. V, c. 6 (*SR*, II, 178–181).

yet, in the late notes of Lord Fortescue, there, the case is put at large and judgment asked whether they would take away the jurisdiction of the admiral, and, there, there are records cited from the time of Henry II, Henry III, and King John, which prove the antiquity of this court well enough.

But for the first point, whether, here, the defendant is punishable for this suit in the admiral's court, first, I grant that, if part of the contract was done upon the land, that the common law will have cognizance. But, in this case, here, he is not liable to the danger of this Statute.

My first reason is because, in this case, at the time of the making of this Statute, the law did not take any notice of any ordinary remedy by the common law in this case because, here, the deed upon which this action was grounded, being to go out of the realm, no action was maintainable here upon it. And he cited *Obligacion*, 15, and *Testament*, 6; 6 Edw. III, 16 and 17; 1 Edw. III, 1 and 18; 8 Edw. III, 31; 13 Hen. IV, 5 and 6,[1] which upon a deed to go out of the realm, no remedy here ordinarily [is given], and *ad ea quae frequentius accidunt jura adoptantur*. And for this reason, for such a suit, it was not the intent of the Statute to punish them. And the first books of trials in such cases are 20 Hen. VI, 28 and 29; 21 Edw. IV, 74; 20 Edw. IV, 1.[2] And in these cases, the jurisdiction of the law is maintained by a fiction, *viz.* that the deed was to go to Dunkirk in the Ward of Cheap etc. And on account of this, for such a suit for which the proper court is the admiralty, our law[3] has cognizance but solely by force of a fiction. Such a fictionary[4] remedy will not be said a remedy within this Statute: first being fictionary, second because it was not known at this day and a fiction never will make one to be a tortfeasor, as C. 11, 52.[5] If a disseisor makes a feoffment and disseises between, this does not make the feoffee who comes in by title a trespasser; though between the disseisor and the disseisee, the entry will have relation as if he was always in possession. Thus [is] 18 Hen. VI, 23; and 48 Edw. III, 15.[6] If waste be done before an attornment, the attornment will not have relation to punish him etc.

---

[1] YB Mich. 2 Edw. II, Selden Soc., vol. 17, p. 110, pl. 53, YB Mich. 2 Edw. II, f. 24 (1308), Fitzherbert, Abr., *Obligacion*, pl. 15; Trin. 18 Edw. II, Fitzherbert, Abr., *Testament*, pl. 6 (1324); *Abbot of Croyland v. Prior of Durham* (1332), YB Pas. 6 Edw. III, ff. 17, 18, pl. 29; *Bat v. Abbot of Mermonster* (1334), YB Trin. 8 Edw. III, f. 51, pl. 38; *Pounteney v. Borney* (1411), YB Mich. 13 Hen. IV, ff. 4, 5, pl. 10.

[2] YB Pas. 20 Hen. VI, f. 27, pl. 17 (1442); YB Pas. 20 Hen. VI, f. 28, pl. 21 (1442); YB Hil. 21 Edw. IV, f. 74, pl. 1 (1482); YB Pas. 20 Edw. IV, f. 1, pl. 1 (1480).

[3] I.e. the common law.

[4] Sic in MS.

[5] *Stamp v. Clinton* (1614), 11 Coke Rep. 46, 51, 77 E.R. 1206, 1216, also 1 Rolle Rep. 95, 81 E.R. 354.

[6] YB Mich. 18 Hen. VI, ff. 22, 23, pl. 7 (1439); YB Pas. 48 Edw. III, f. 15, pl. 10 (1374).

Also, as it is said [in] P. 369,[1] the preamble of the Statute is the best key to open the meaning of the makers. And here, the Statute recites that such holding of a plea was to the prejudice of the king and the grievance of the subject. And on account of this, such a suit that is within this Statute must be prejudicial to the king and a grievance to the subject, which our suit, for the causes aforesaid, cannot be accounted.

Also, by the Statute of 32 Hen. VIII, ca. 14,[2] it is provided in a case that the wages, as in our case, be detained contrary to the charter party, that there will be a remedy before the lord admiral, by which he concluded this point that etc.

For the second point, he said that the attorney here who prosecuted for another is not within this law because the words of the Statute are 'a pursuer',[3] which here he is not because here, this which he did was not his own act but [it is] accounted by the law the act of his master. And on account of this, if an attorney does an act in his own name, it is void, as [in] C. 9, 67, Combe's case,[4] it is expressly said, and Dy. 132;[5] a lease made by an attorney in the name of himself [is] void. Thus [is] Dy. 283;[6] a *cestui que use* can make an attorney which will be an [acco]mplishment of the Statute[7] and it will be said a feoffment by himself. C. 7, 75, and Perkins 196 and 199,[8] a husband can be an attorney for the wife to make a livery to him because it is not his own act, but [the act] of the master.

The second reason [is] because the court will not take notice of an attorney or deputy but of him who sets to him [the attorney or deputy] work and, in whose right the act is done, it is him of whom the court will take notice. And he cited the case of Dy. 238 and l. 5 Edw. IV, 5,[9] where the undersheriff is not a person of whom the law takes notice, and of Dy. 238, of a deputy customer, and upon the Statute of 4 Hen. VII, 24,[10] of fines, by suit of a stranger within the five years in the name of the party. Without his privity, he is not a pursuer within this law, but, if it be by his command, then he is. And on account of this, it proves that it is not in such a case the pursuit of the attorney, but of the master. C. 10, 106, and the case of 36 Hen. VI, 29 and 30,[11] where an attorney was within the Statute

---

[1]   *Stowel v. Lord Zouch* (1562), 1 Plowden 353, 369, 75 E.R. 536, 560.

[2]   Stat. 32 Hen. VIII, c. 14, s. 10 (*SR*, III, 763).

[3]   Stat. 2 Hen. IV, c. 11 (*SR*, II, 124).

[4]   *Atlee v. Banks* (1613), 9 Coke Rep. 75, 76, 77 E.R. 843, 844.

[5]   *Greenfield v. Stretch* (1555), 2 Dyer 132, 73 E.R. 288.

[6]   *Anonymous* (1569), 3 Dyer 283, 73 E.R. 635.

[7]   Stat. 1 Ric. III, c. 1 (*SR*, II, 477–478).

[8]   *Atlee v. Banks* (1613), *ut supra*; J. Perkins, *A Profitable Book*, sects. 196, 199.

[9]   YB Pas. 5 Edw. IV, Long Quinto, f. 5 (1465).

[10]   Stat. 4 Hen. VII, c. 24 (*SR*, II, 547–548).

[11]   *Bicknel v. Tucker* (1612), 9 Coke Rep. 104, 106, 77 E.R. 883, 887, also 1 Brownlow & Goldesborough 181, 123 E.R. 741, 2 Brownlow & Goldesborough 134, 153, 123 E.R. 857, 869; YB 36 Hen. VI, ff. 29, 30, pl. 32 (1457 x 1458).

of Praemunire[1] for prosecuting in another's name is not against me by the express letter of this law; 'their counsellors, abettors, attorneys, and proctors' are punishable, but, to the contrary, it being that in this law made in the time of the same king, attorneys are named. It is a strong argument that, if they are intended that they will be within this law, here, it would have named them also.

Then, he took an exception to the verdict because the offense found in it differed from this found in the declaration in place and in persons. And on account of this, it will not be intended the same offense.

Also he moved against the laying of the action here because the information must have been by a writ, and not by a bill, as it is here, because the Statute says that he will have his action by a writ founded upon the case. And for this [is] 42 Ass. 11 and C. 37a.[2] It was held that a bill of debt for an escape does not lie because the Statute[3] says that it will be by a writ. And where the statute appoints a remedy, it must be pursued. And [in] 18 Eliz., ca. 5,[4] it is that no one will be admitted to sue upon a penal statute but by way of an information upon [?] *originavit*, and not otherwise, by which a bill is excluded. And even though Platt's case, Co.,[5] was by bill, yet Plowden took the reason of it to be because no exception was taken to it. And the cases of 2 Ric. III, 17, and 25 Hen. VI,[6] where a bill upon a *praemunire*, is not against it, because the Statutes[7] which give it do not direct the suit to be by a writ specially, as this Statute does.

And thus he concluded for the defendant.

More, 76a.[8]

[Other reports of this case: Godbolt 385, 78 E.R. 227; Latch 188, 82 E.R. 339; BL MS. Hargr. 38, f. 172v; CUL MS. Ll.3.13, f. 202; Folger Library MS. V.b.174, p. 45; HLS MS. 1063, f. 7v.]

---

[1] Stat. 27 Edw. III, c. 1 (*SR*, I, 329); Stat. 38 Edw. III, stat. 2, c. 1 (*SR*, I, 385–386); Stat. 16 Ric. II, c. 5 (*SR*, II, 84–86).

[2] YB 42 Edw. III, Lib. Ass., p. 260, pl. 11 (1368); *Platt v. Lock* (1550), 1 Plowden 35, 37, 75 E.R. 57, 60.

[3] Stat. 13 Edw. I, Stat. Westminster II, c. 11 (*SR*, I, 80–81).

[4] Stat. 18 Eliz. I, c. 5 (*SR*, IV, 615–616).

[5] *Platt v. Lock* (1550), 1 Plowden 35, 75 E.R. 57.

[6] *Peckam's Case* (1484), YB Mich. 2 Ric. III, f. 17, pl. 45; *Rex v. Kemp* (1448), YB Mich. 27 Hen. VI, f. 5, pl. 35.

[7] Stat. 27 Edw. III, c. 1 (*SR*, I, 329); Stat. 38 Edw. III, stat. 2, c. 1 (*SR*, I, 385–386); Stat. 16 Ric. II, c. 5 (*SR*, II, 84–86).

[8] *Cremer v. Tookley* (1627–1628), BL MS. Add. 35961, ff. 106, 223, BL MS. Lansd. 1083, ff. 177, 319v (Widdrington's reports).

263

Anonymous

(K.B. Pas. 3 Car. I, 1627)

The issue in this case was whether, where there are two tenants in common and they are disseised, the re-entry of one is the re-entry for both.

BL MS. Add. 35961, f. 59v, pl. 12

In evidence to the jury, it was contended by Serjeant *Henden* that, if there are two tenants in common and they are disseised, that the re-entry of one is not the re-entry for both. [It was said to be] otherwise by *Athow*, on the same side, for joint tenants and parceners because they must join in an assize; thus, not tenants in common.

But Justice JONES said that the case would be stronger against him than thus because it would be that, [where] one made a lease of part of his land for [a term of] years and did not put the certainty, thus he is a tenant in common for years with him in reversion and a stranger enters[1] in all, whether, by the entry of the lessee, it reverses the reversion for more than his part because, in such a case, without question, by the entry of the lessor, the term will be revested; thus against.

[This] *Henden* denied, and he said that it was this in which he demanded the direction of the court [to the jury].

264

Rex v. Brooker

(K.B. Pas. 3 Car. I, 1627)

The issue in this case was whether anyone other than the heir of a person outlawed for felony can reverse the outlawry.

BL MS. Add. 35961, f. 59v, pl. 13

[In a case] between the lord king and Broker in a writ of error to reverse an outlawry of felony, the case was thus. John Isley, seised in fee of the manor of Sundridge in the County of Kent, had issue, Henry, who, [in] 22 Eliz. [1579 x 1580], was outlawed of felony in the lifetime of the father, John. The father died. Henry devised certain land, part of the said manor of which the father died seised, and he died. And the said land by mesne conveyances came from the said devisee to the protonotary Broker, father of the Broker who now sues to reverse this outlawry, being terre tenant by descent of it from his father. And whether he could was now the question.

---

[1] stronger entre *MS.*

And it was argued against the writ of error by *Holborn* that the terre tenant in this case will not have a writ of error to reverse the outlawry.

And first, he argued that, though this outlawry be reversed, still the terre tenant will not have the land because, even though after a judgment be reversed, it is as if no judgment had been given, as, by 4 Hen. VII, 11, and Dy. 228,[1] it appears where, if a judgment in outlawry be reversed, he can plead *nul tiel record*, yet it is not to all purposes because he who reverses such an erroneous judgment will not have the mesne profits unless it be thus express in the judgment, and, if one recover erroneously and enter in the perquisite of a villein or present to the advowson and, afterwards, it be reversed, still he will retain the perquisite and presentation. 4 Hen. VII, 11.

And he said that [in] 34 Eliz., in one Boulton's case, it was adjudged a jointress of lands suffered a recovery and, afterwards, [it was] reversed for error, yet it remained a forfeiture. See 16 Ass. 16;[2] if a tenant for years suffers a recovery and, afterwards, he reverses it, still the forfeiture is not purged. Thus here, the reversal of the attainder will not have such a relation that the devise of him who was attainted will be good because it is a common law relation. And on account of this, it differs much from the relation by force of a statute because such relations are the most forcible that can be. And upon this, he cited Dy. 24b and *Peticion*, 2, and 3 Hen. I, 55, St. Leger's case, and 11 Hen. VII, 22,[3] upon the relation of the annulling of an act of Parliament of an attainder, and Dy., fo. ult. b,[4] where one presented to two incomparable benefices, the articles do not bind, when he entered upon the two benefices, now, it is thus void by force of the Statute of 13 Eliz.[5] that, now, the first benefice was not ever void by the taking of the second, and thus, upon the relation of the bargain and sale which [was] by force of the statutes. He said that many could be put.

But all these differ from a relation by force of the common law which does not have such a forcible operation. And he put the case of the enrollment of a deed where the remainder is to the king and the king, before enrollment, grants it, which is not good, so that the refusal of the wife, where a joint estate is made to the husband and wife, does not make him by having of the land by relation

---

[1] YB Trin. 4 Hen. VII, ff. 10, 11, pl. 6 (1489); *Palmer, qui tam v. Franklin* (1564), 2 Dyer 227, 228, 73 E.R. 503, 504.

[2] *Earl of Arundel v. Charleton* (1342), YB 16 Edw. III, Lib. Ass., p. 47, pl. 16.

[3] *Danvers v. Bishop of Worcester* (1536), 1 Dyer 24, 73 E.R. 52; YB Trin. 15 Edw. III, Rolls Ser. 31b, vol. 6, p. 228, pl. 25 (1341), Fitzherbert, Abr., *Peticion*, pl. 2; YB Mich. 3 Hen. VII, f. 15, pl. 26 (1487); perhaps YB Hil. 14 Hen. VII, f. 13, pl. 2 (1499).

[4] *Anonymous* (1581), 3 Dyer 377, 73 E.R. 846.

[5] Stat. 13 Eliz. I, c. 12 (*SR*, IV, 546–547).

[one] who can devise it, which are put [in] C. 3, in Butler's case,[1] because these relations are by force of the common law.

But for the point of the terre tenant, here, he cannot reverse this outlawry because he is not privy to him who was outlawed because, put the case the strongest, that admits him who has been the feoffee of the person outlawed, yet he cannot reverse it, *a fortiori*, the feoffee of the feoffee and such and such who comes in from so many conveyances as here he made because he is further from the privity.

And he cited 9 Edw. IV, 13; 22 Edw. IV, 31; 9 Hen. VI, 4b; 6 Ass. 6; and C. 3, Marquess of Winchester's case,[2] that, regularly, no one will have [a writ of] error but him who is privy; and 9 Hen. VII, 24,[3] that if one suffers an erroneous recovery of land of the part of the mother, that the heir of the part of the father [will] have the error of it and not of the part of the mother. And there also, if a younger brother suffers an erroneous recovery after the older brother is dead, he will not have [a writ of] error but the younger [will]. And [he cited] 22 Hen. VI, 28, by Fortescue,[4] that the heir in special tail, nor the heir in borough English, will not have [a writ of] error, but it goes to the heir general because no one is privy but him, and 3 Hen. IV, 29; F.N.B. 21, 1. m; B., *Fauxer de recovery*, 50,[5] where error and attaint will go to the heir general, where [to the] special. Also, he cited one Walters' case of 30 Eliz.[6] to be adjudged that a bail will not have [a writ of] error of a judgment given against the principal though he be aggrieved by it, but he can have advantage of this error by way of a plea. And he said that [in] Marshe's case, cited [in] C. 5, 111a,[7] it was not ever adjudged that an executor will have a writ of error to reverse an attainder by the outlawry of the testator, and yet there is a great privity in estate between them. Also a feoffee of a conusor will not have an *audita querela*. F.N.B. 104; 18 Edw. III, 17; 17 Ass. 44; 12

---

[1] *Butler v. Baker* (1591), 3 Coke Rep. 25, 76 E.R. 684, also Popham 87, 79 E.R. 1199, 1 Anderson 348, 123 E.R. 510, Moore K.B. 254, 72 E.R. 563, Gouldsborough 84, 75 E.R. 1011, 3 Leonard 271, 74 E.R. 678.

[2] YB Trin. 9 Edw. IV, ff. 12, 13, pl. 4 (1469); *Bowser v. Colins* (1482), YB Mich. 22 Edw. IV, ff. 30, 31, pl. 11; YB Mich. 9 Hen. VI, f. 46, pl. 30 (1430); YB 6 Edw. III, Lib. Ass., p. 10, pl. 6 (1332); *Regina v. Marquess of Winchester* (1583), 3 Coke Rep. 1, 76 E.R. 621, also 1 Leonard 270, 74 E.R. 246, Moore K.B. 95, 125, 72 E.R. 464, 483.

[3] YB Pas. 9 Hen. VII, f. 24, pl. 10 (1494).

[4] YB Mich. 22 Hen. VI, f. 28, pl. 42 (1443).

[5] YB Trin. 3 Hen. IV, f. 19, pl. 4 (1425); A. Fitzherbert, *Nouvelle Natura Brevium*; YB Mich. 22 Hen. VI, f. 28, pl. 42 (1443), Brooke, Abr., *Fauxefier de recoverie*, pl. 50.

[6] *Walter v. Pery* (1590), 2 Leonard 101, 74 E.R. 392.

[7] *Marsh's Case* (1591), cited in *Foxley's Case* (1601), 5 Coke Rep. 111, 77 E.R. 228, also Cro. Eliz. 225, 273, 78 E.R. 481, 528, 1 Leonard 325, 74 E.R. 296, Owen 147, 74 E.R. 964.

Ass. 41; 12 Ass. 8; and 20 Ass. 2;[1] and all [were] by [de]fault of privity. Also, he cited Vinny and Mendevill's case,[2] which, as he said, Lord Coke vouched in an argument of a case, which was thus: one seised of land took a wife, and he was attainted of treason, and he made a feoffment; the feoffee levied a fine; five years passed, and, afterwards, the heir reversed the attainder of the father, and [it was] adjudged that the fine did not bar the wife from her dower because she could not reverse the attainder, and, on account of this, during this time, no right was in her and, on account of this, she will have five years after the fine.

And thus, upon all these, he concluded that the terre tenant, because he is not a privy, cannot have a writ of error in this case. Also, he said that, in such a case as here, Kel. 193,[3] there, the heir was caused to carry the writ of error, and not the terre tenant. And also he said that this case cannot be but as it has often times fallen out and, on account of this, if it had been [good] law, without question, before, such a writ of error would have been put in practice. And on account of this, inasmuch as there was not ever any such precedent, he concluded that it was not ever taken for law.

Then he responded to certain books that he said seemed *prima facie* against him. The first was Dy. 2a, b,[4] that a person in reversion or remainder can have a writ of error for a judgment against a tenant for life, but, as to this, he said that the reversion, remainder, and particular estate are one estate, and, on account of this, [there is] enough privity there. Then, the cases there put out of 18 Edw. III, 25, and 17 Edw. III, Assise, 24,[5] that a feoffee of a conusor will have an *audita querela* whether execution be sued against him before the time, to this he said that the reason of it was because the conusor's feoffee [was] made a party to the execution because execution was sued against him and, until execution [was] sued against him, he will not have an *audita querela*, as F.N.B. 104, that it is.

And as to the case of a [writ of] *scire facias* by a grantor of a reversion of a tenant by a statute, as is there also cited out of 32 Edw. III, *Scire facias*, 101 and 134,[6] and 25 Edw. III, 53, he said that, at common law, it was not so, but it was given by a private statute, which is not printed, made *anno* 19 Edw. III, which Statute

---

[1] A. Fitzherbert, *Nouvelle Natura Brevium*; YB Trin. 18 Edw. III, f. 25, pl. 17 (1344); YB 17 Edw. III, Lib. Ass., p. 52, pl. 24 (1343); YB 12 Edw. III, Lib. Ass., p. 38, pl. 41 (1338); YB 12 Edw. III, Lib. Ass., p. 34, pl. 8 (1338); YB 20 Edw. III, Lib. Ass., p. 67, pl. 2 (1346).

[2] Perhaps *Mandevile's Case* (1584 x 1585), cited in *Bartholomew v. Belfield* (1613), Cro. Jac. 332, 79 E.R. 284.

[3] *Kemys v. Regem* (1520), Keilwey 192, 72 E.R. 371, 116 Selden Soc. 717.

[4] Note (1513), 1 Dyer 1, 73 E.R. 2.

[5] YB Trin. 18 Edw. III, f. 25, pl. 17 (1344); YB 17 Edw. III, Lib. Ass., p. 52, pl. 24 (1343).

[6] Pas. 32 Edw. III, Fitzherbert, Abr., *Scire facias*, pl. 101 (1358); 46 Edw. III, Fitzherbert, Abr., *Scire facias*, pl. 134 (1372).

is remembered in the roll of Mich. 22 Edw. III, in the king's bench, rot. [*blank*], which he said that he had seen, but, before, a grantor of a reversion in such a case could not have a writ of *audita querela*, as it is adjudged [in] 6 Edw. III, 53. (See of this Statute, before, 6b.)

And for the case there also, *viz*. Dy. 1,[1] put that an abbot, being the parson impropriate, will have [a writ of] *scire facias*, this was not against it because, there, he is not any stranger, but he comes in privity, *viz*. succession to the parson who recovered the annuity.

And for the case put [of] 12 Hen. VIII, 8,[2] by Pollard, that of a recovery of a parson, the patron will have [a writ of] error, he denied it for [good] law because it stands upon a *fallax* which was the ground and reason of this opinion because the reason there is because the reversion is in the patron.

And B., *Fauxer de recovery*, itself says expressly that this is not [good] law. But admit that it be, still, for the right which remains in the patron, his interest can be that he can maintain it because, as C. 5, Foord's case,[3] it is he has an interest and the person who is party to the writ, even if he is not party to the judgment, can have a writ of error; *Error*, 72;[4] thus, if he be a party to the judgment or verdict, as 44 Edw. III, 6 and 7.[5] But, if he is not in any manner a party, he cannot by any way be admitted to it. See C. 3, 4a.[6] And all this he argued admitting that the terre tenant had been the immediate feoffee to the person attainted. But he said that his case was more strong because he is the feoffee of the feoffee and thus, when one makes a feoffment, he passes all the right that he can have and extinguishes it because as his title was after the title at error in his feoffee, he cannot transfer it, but by his feoffment he will extinguish it because, by the feoffment, the land passed discharged of all of the right which the feoffor had in it. And for this, he cited Sherington and Worsley's case,[7] adjudged 34 Eliz., where one recovered in [an action of] debt against one erroneously and he had execution awarded by [a writ of] *elegit* upon the roll, and, afterwards, the defendant alienated the land; there, the alienee will not have any means to avoid it because,

---

[1] *Anonymous* (1513), 1 Dyer 1, 73 E.R. 3.

[2] *Prior of Huntingdon v. Stanley* (1520), YB Mich. 12 Hen. VIII, f. 7, pl. 1, 119 Selden Soc. 33.

[3] *Bettisford v. Foord* (1595), 5 Coke Rep. 81, 77 E.R. 177, also Cro. Eliz. 447, 472, 78 E.R. 687, 724, 3 Dyer 338, 73 E.R. 763, Benloe 238, 123 E.R. 167, 1 Anderson 47, 123 E.R. 346.

[4] YB Hil. 15 Edw. III, Rolls Ser. 31b, vol. 5, p. 326, pl. 33 (1341), Fitzherbert, Abr., *Errour*, pl. 72.

[5] YB Pas. 44 Edw. III, f. 7, pl. 3 (1370).

[6] *Regina v. Marquess of Winchester* (1583), 3 Coke Rep. 1, 4, 76 E.R. 621, 629, also 1 Leonard 270, 74 E.R. 246, Moore K.B. 95, 125, 72 E.R. 464, 483.

[7] *Charnock v. Worsley* (1588–1592), 1 Leonard 114, 74 E.R. 107, Owen 106, 74 E.R. 934, Moore K.B. 570, 72 E.R. 765, Cro. Eliz. 129, 289, 448, 473, 78 E.R. 386, 543, 688, 725.

as it has been said, when one has title to the writ of error or to the other action to discharge his land, there, if he makes a feoffment or etc. of it, the feoffee will not have the advantage of it.

Thus [is] 32 Eliz.; an erroneous judgment against the ordinary in [an action of] debt was given, and, after he committed the administration, the administrator cannot have [a writ of] error because his title was after the error accrued.

Thus is 7 Jac., Molineux's case;[1] one who had cause to have an *audita querela* made a feoffment; the feoffee cannot have an *audita querela* for the cause aforesaid. And the reason of it is the general rule that rights will not be transferred [in order] to avoid maintenance and other oppressions.

Another reason for which the terre tenant here will not have this action is because this attainder operates upon the blood and not upon the land. And on account of this, it is not such an action that will run with the land, as a writ of error to reverse a judgment can, as in F.N.B., 21, it is held that a tenant in special tail and an heir in borough English can have [a writ of] error of a judgment given against their ancestor because it runs with the land because, if the law is thus, there, the reason is because the judgment there operates upon the land and, on account of this, the reversal of it will run with the land.

But here, the attainder does not operate upon the land. And on account of this, it will not run with it because it operates upon the blood primarily and, by consequent and accident, upon the land because, first, it corrupts the blood and it makes an interruption of the descent and, then, by a necessary consequence, the land must escheat. And on account of this, if he who is attainted dies in the lifetime of his father and without issue, the land that could have descended to him is not touched, but it will descend to other brothers etc. notwithstanding, as appears [in] *Peticion*, 20; *Discent*, 64, b.; 29 Ass. 11; and Dy. 48.[2]

Thus upon all these, he concluded for the defendant in the writ of error.

Bankes, contra, [argued] that the terre tenant, notwithstanding anything that has been said, will maintain this writ of error. And he said that he who argued before had raised those spirits that he could not conjure down, and he made against himself such objections that he cannot answer. And he did not desire it to be adjudged by other cases than by those that he himself has put.

And for the devise by him who was attainted and the validity of it, this is not material because it is not but a conveyance to entitle him to the writ of error. But for the writ of error itself, he conceived that it will run not to the heir general, as an estoppel will, as 35 Hen. VI, Croke's case,[3] of an estoppel, is, but with the land and to the heirs special to whom the land descends. And thus are 3

---

[1] *Dutton v. Molineux* (1609), Cro. Jac. 227, 79 E.R. 196.

[2] Hil. 46 Edw. III, Fitzherbert, Abr., *Peticion*, pl. 20 (1372); YB 3 Edw. II, Brooke, Abr., *Discent*, pl. 64 (1309 x 1310); YB 29 Edw. III, Lib. Ass., p. 158, pl. 11 (1355); *Anonymous* (1540), 1 Dyer 48, 73 E.R. 105.

[3] YB Mich. 35 Hen. VI, f. 32, pl. 41 (1456).

Hen. IV, 9; Dy. 90; pB 337; F.N.B. 21.[1] Only the heir special and him to whom the land goes will have the writ of error. And it is not necessary that he who will have these be privy to the record because a *scire facias* is grounded upon a record and lies more in privity than a writ of error and yet 16 Hen. VII, 9, the Prior of Newark's case,[2] the heir of a purchaser will have a *scire facias* upon a fine by which it was granted by the prior of Newark to find one to sing divine service within the chapel of the manor.

And, under favor, the books of 17 Ass. 24 and 18 Edw. III, 25, are not answered but only endeavored to be answered.

And the report of Sherington's and Worsley's case[3] was misreported because I have the roll of it, and *intratur* Trin. 34 Eliz., rot. 637, king's bench, and it was thus. Sherington recovered in [an action of] debt against Worsley, and a [writ of] *elegit* [was] awarded upon the roll. Then, Worsly alienated to Charnock who, before execution [was] sued against the land, brought a writ of error. And [it was] adjudged that it was maintainable because, where one is aggrieved by an act, be he privy to it or not, the law allows to him a remedy to reverse it. And this is the reason of 21 Hen. VI, 29,[4] that he in reversion or remainder will have [a writ of] error for the loss that he sustained by force of it. But where one is not aggrieved, there, if he be a stranger, then he will not have [a writ of] error. And on account of this, this is the reason that, as 21 Edw. IV, 23,[5] is, that they come not to take advantage by way of [a writ of] error in an escape against him because he is not aggrieved by the error in the record but by his own act in letting the prisoner [go] at large. Thus [is] 21 [Ric.] III, 21;[6] if the principal be arraigned, the accessory will not have avail of the error in his attainder because he is not aggrieved by it, but by his own condemnation.

And for this that it is said that he who devised and under whom we claim was attainted, this is not material because we are now to defeat the attainder itself. And on account of this, we need not rebut by the same thing that we endeavor to disagree [with]. And for this [is] 7 Hen. IV, 40;[7] in [a writ of] error to reverse an outlawry, it is not a [good] plea that the plaintiff was outlawed, though it be in another outlawry than this of which the [writ of] error was brought. 10 Hen. VII, 18;[8] [an action was] brought against one and it did not name [him]

---

    [1] YB Hil. 3 Hen. IV, f. 9, pl. 5 (1402); *Raynolds v. Dignam* (1553), 1 Dyer 89, 90, 73 E.R. 194, 195; A. Fitzherbert, *Nouvelle Natura Brevium*.

    [2] *Prior of Newark's Case* (1500), YB Mich. 16 Hen. VII, f. 9, pl. 2, 115 Selden Soc. 230.

    [3] *Charnock v. Worsley* (1588–1592), *ut supra*.

    [4] *Brokesby's Case* (1443), YB Hil. 21 Hen. VI, ff. 28, 29, pl. 12.

    [5] YB Pas. 21 Edw. IV, ff. 22, 23, pl. 6 (1481).

    [6] YB Mich. 2 Ric. III, f. 21, pl. 50 (1484).

    [7] YB Pas. 7 Hen. IV, f. 39, pl. 4 (1406).

    [8] YB Pas. 10 Hen. VII, f. 18, pl. 5 (1495), see also 115 Selden Soc. 52.

master of the chapel, but, because it was to disprove that he was the master, it was good without him thus named.

And thus [is] 22 Hen. VI, 26, of an abbot;[1] thus [is] 44 Edw. III, 14;[2] in an action for conspiring to cause one to be found a villein, it is not a [good] plea to say that the plaintiff is his villein because it is to disprove it and this [is] the cause of his action.

And 16 Edw. III, *Age*, 45;[3] in a demand of land by [an action of] formedon, it cannot be rebutted by the reversion and assets of the same land descended to him; but, by descent of other land, he could, *Garranty*, 29; 18 Edw. III, 8,[4] by which the attainder here is not to be objected against us.

And also, it was surplusage to show the title because it was sufficient to be a terre tenant as here shown, and a surplusage is not entered nor a bar. 9 Edw. IV, 293; 7 Edw. IV, 19.

Thus, upon all, he concluded for the writ of error.

And the error in the outlawry was because it was against two because *non apparuerunt*, and it did not say *nec eorum alter*, which is a manifest error.

And DODDERIDGE said, here, the matter would be whether any but the heir can reverse it inasmuch as it is an impediment which sticks upon the blood because a personal disability which cannot be redressed but by a personal privity and privity of blood because a personal defect must be removed by a personal privity, as infancy etc.

And JONES said that Marshe's case was not ever adjudged because the executors did not have privity but as to the personal estate.

Et adjornatur. More, 50, p. 5.[5]

[Other reports of this case: Godbolt 376, 78 E.R. 221; BL MS. Hargr. 38, ff. 142, 163, 182v, 253v; HLS MS. 1063, ff. 10, 70.]

---

[1] *Denham v. Chanon* (1443), YB Mich. 22 Hen. VI, ff. 25, 26, pl. 46.

[2] *Abbot of York's Case* (1370), YB Pas. 44 Edw. III, f. 14, pl. 32.

[3] Hil. 16 Edw. III, Fitzherbert, *Abr.*, *Age*, pl. 45 (1342).

[4] Mich. 31 Edw. III, Fitzherbert, *Abr.*, *Garrantie*, pl. 29 (1357); YB Hil. 18 Edw. III, f. 8, pl. 25 (1344).

[5] *Rex v. Broker* (1627), BL MS. Add. 35961, ff. 72, 116v, BL MS. Lansd. 1083, ff. 119v, 192v (Widdrington's reports).

265

Harvey v. Reynell

(Part 4)
K.B. Pas. 3 Car. I, 1627)

BL MS. Add. 35961, f. 60v, pl. 14

And now, the case of Harvy and Rennells, of which [see] above, f. 41, pl. 39, and f. 44, pl. 62,[1] was argued again for one point only because, for all of the others moved before, the court was agreed. And as to this, it was thus. The record is '*memorandum quod alias scilicet de termino Sancti Hilarii anno primo Caroli regis, Harvy protulit hic in curia billam*'[2] against Rennell etc. And then he declared upon an escape.

The defendant said and confessed the escape, but he pleaded that he made a fresh [pur]suit *et quod ante impetrationem huius[modi] billae viz. octavo die Maii secundo Caroli regis,*[3] he re-took him etc. And whether this *viz.* be void or not was now the sole point or whether it will be entirely void and thus the taking have to be taken to be after the filing of the bill.

And it was argued by *Andrews* of Lincoln's Inn that the re-taking will be taken [to be] the day that he has declared and that it will not be a void *viz.* and thus repugnant because, first, if this day of *octavo Maii* does not stand, then he has not shown any day in certain for the re-taking, which, of necessity, he must show, because the day is here material so that, if the *octavi* day here is not the day, then, there is not any date put. And thus, this way, [it is] void, and, if this day stands, then it is repugnant and after the day of the bill, and thus, whichever way. And that here he must show the day precisely and that it is here material appears because the time here makes the matter. And on account of this, it must be precisely shown, as the rule is taken [in] C. 24a,[4] where the time is issuable. And for this [it is] issuable. And for this [is] C. 4, 70;[5] there he did not plead generally that the bargain and sale was enrolled before the fine [was] levied, but it said *viz.* such a day. Thus [is] 8 Hen. VI, 10,[6] in [an action of] waste in the tenant, the defendant said that, before the writ [was] purchased, the plaintiff entered, *viz.* [on] such a day, and thus he should because, before the writ [was] purchased,

---

[1] For earlier proceedings in this case, see above, Nos. 170, 187, 193.

[2] It is to be remembered that, also, to wit in Hilary term in the first year of King Charles [1626], Harvey brought here in court a bill.

[3] and that, before the suing out of such bill, to wit the eighth day of May in the second [year of] King Charles [1626].

[4] *Colthirst v. Bejushin* (1550), 1 Plowden 21, 24, 75 E.R. 33, 38.

[5] *Libb v. Hynde* (1591), 4 Coke Rep. 70, 76 E.R. 1040, also 1 Anderson 285, 123 E.R. 475.

[6] YB Mich. 8 Hen. VI, f. 10, pl. 23 (1429).

generally it is not good. Thus here, *ante impetrationem billae* generally is not good. But it must specify the day certain. And then, as, of necessity, he must show the day, there, the showing of it will not be void. Also, if it was not compellable to show the day, still, if one pleads a thing that he need not, it will guard him well who pleads it sufficiently because, as he need not plead it, still, if he pleads it badly, it will be a prejudice to him, similar to the case of Palmer, C. 4;[1] if the sheriff comes one term and puts the beginning and end, it is certain; and [if] this does not agree with the lease, the sale is void, and yet he could have sold it without naming the beginning.

And thus for these reasons, he concluded etc.

Calthorpe, contra: And [he said] that the *viz.* is void because it was sufficiently certain before, upon which the court could know and judge that the retaking was before the bill [was] exhibited. And on account of this, [it is] surplusage which he was not forced to show, nor will it harm him. And for this, in 40 Eliz., was one Bushop's case; the plaintiff declared for a trespass done [on] 4 May 39 Eliz.; the defendant said that, a long time before the supposed trespass, *viz.* 5 May 39 Eliz., the plaintiff leased to him, and yet [it was] ruled to be good and the *viz.* [was] idle. Thus [is] Pas. 5 Jac., between Bigot and Short,[2] in [an action of] *ejectione firmae*, the plaintiff alleged that he was possessed of a term [on] 20 October 4 Jac. and that the defendant *eodem die Octobris viz. 20 die Octobris anno tertio Jacobi* ejected him, and yet the *viz.* [was] void and the count [was] good notwithstanding it.

And thus he concluded for the defendant.

But the Court resolved that the *viz.* here was not void and idle.

And he took a difference where the time to which the *ante* refers be put in certain and where generally because, if the first time to which the *ante* had relation be general and no day in certain, there, the *ante* is not sufficient, as in the case here, the time to which the *ante* refers is *impetratio huius billae* and [there is] no day in certain and, on account of this, as he said that *ante impetrationem etc.*, there is no certainty of the time. But if, here, the exhibiting of the bill had been laid to be on a day certain and after[wards] he had said generally *ante impetrationem billae etc.*, it had been sufficient without putting the day in certain. And on account of this, the day he has after, there, it will not be material. And, on account of this, it differs from the case put before because, there, the *ante* had reference to the time which was put in certain.

And on account of this, DODDERIDGE said to the other party 'apply yourself but to prove that the exhibiting of the bill will be also necessarily intended to be the first day of the term as if it had been expressly thus set down to be now; if so,

---

[1] *Palmer v. Umphrey* (1597), 4 Coke Rep. 74, 76 E.R. 1045, also Cro. Eliz. 584, 78 E.R. 827, Gouldsborough 172, 75 E.R. 1073, Owen 18, 74 E.R. 868, Moore. K.B. 422, 702, 72 E.R. 670, 851.

[2] *Brigate v. Short* (1607), Cro. Jac. 154, 79 E.R. 135.

the *ante* would have relation to the time certainly set down if the exhibiting of the bill will be necessarily intended to be the first day of the term, being generally alleged to be exhibited Hilary *primo Caroli.'*

And upon this point, a further day was given to speak etc.

[Other reports of this case: Benloe 185, 73 E.R. 1047, CUL MS. Gg.2.30, f. 70; Godbolt 433, 78 E.R. 254; W. Jones 144, 82 E.R. 77, BL MS. Hargr. 317, f. 147; Latch 200, 82 E.R. 345, HLS MS. 1235, f. 93; Noy 93, 74 E.R. 1059; BL MS. Hargr. 38, f. 132v; BL MS. Lansd. 1092, f. 183v; CUL MS. Ll.3.13, f. 230.]

[Connected cases: Randall v. Harvey (1623), 2 Rolle Rep. 390, 81 E.R. 871, Palmer 394, 81 E.R. 1140.]

266

Dunn v. Dean of Carlisle

(K.B. Pas. 3 Car. I, 1627)

A judgment in a lower court can be executed unless the record is removed to a higher court.

BL MS. Add. 35961, f. 60v, pl. 15

Dun recovered against the dean and chapter of Carlisle in the court paravail there, upon which the defendant there brought a writ of error, and it was to remove a plea which is *in curia nostra*. [*Intratur* Hil. 2 Car. [I, rot.] 796.] And they certified the judgment which was given in the time of King James.

And upon this, *Davenport*, the king's serjeant, now moved that they paravail will proceed to execution notwithstanding because the record certified here is not this for which the [writ of] *certiorari* was awarded and thus it is not removed and, if it is not removed, the writ of error *quia coram nobis residet* does not lie. And he cited Dy. 206b, the case of Romney Marsh,[1] which agrees in everything with this.

And JONES said that, if a record is once removed, he will not have execution paravail though it be erroneously removed.

But DODDERIDGE said that there is a difference where a record is not well removed and where it is not removed at all and where it is well removed and *postea* the writ of error abates by the death etc. because, whether it be abated by a death or plea and insufficiency, yet if the record be removed, it will not be remanded nor execution there made. But, where the record is not removed, it is otherwise. And here, the record is not at all removed because the writ of error is of a judgment given *in curia nostra* and they certified a judgment *in curia prioris regis*. Thus, it is not the record of which the error is brought, but a different species.

---

[1] *Anonymous* (1561), 2 Dyer 207, 73 E.R. 456.

But Jones said that there are one hundred precedents of [writs of] error *quod coram nobis* where the record comes without a warrant. And yet he said that it is in the election of the court to dismiss or retain it.

And afterwards, the rule was that they will proceed to execution paravail. See F.N.B. 71d; C. 3, 2a; C. 11, 41b.[1]

[Other reports of this case: Godbolt 375, 78 E.R. 221; Latch 198, 82 E.R. 344; BL MS. Lansd. 1092, ff. 166v, 176; CUL MS. Ll.3.13, ff. 211, 224.]

267

Sutton's Case

(K.B. Pas. 3 Car. I, 1627)

The common law courts will not prohibit an ecclesiastical court to remove a clergyman for incompetence in his office.

BL MS. Add. 35961, f. 61, pl. 16

Dr. Sutton, chancellor of the bishop of Gloucester, was cited in the high commission court to answer why he will not be removed from his office. And [there was an] article against him that the archbishop within his province had the charge of seeing the places under the inferior bishops to be supplied by able men and that the said Sutton was not learned in the canon laws to the discouragement of the students in this law, who see the places bestowed under insufficient [. . .] and the decay of this learning in the realm.

He answered that he has this office by the letters patent of the bishop and confirmed etc. and thus he has a freehold in it and he should enjoy it for his life. And upon this, a [writ of] prohibition was prayed to the [court of] high commission because they hold a plea of freehold and also, before the Statute of 37 Hen. VIII,[2] all such commissaries and chancellors were priests, as Sutton here is, and this enables doctors of canon law, but it does not exclude priests. And also, the Constitutions of 1603,[3] which are called the Canons, which never were confirmed by Parliament, yet if they are in force, it requires only that such officer have sufficient skill etc. and it does not exclude priests. Thus because it is his freehold, which they cannot question, he prayed [a writ of] prohibition.

But the court, *viz.* Dodderidge and Jones, denied it because, here, though it be an office and freehold, yet it is an office of skill, for the want of which, he can

---

[1] A. Fitzherbert, *Nouvelle Natura Brevium*; *Regina v. Marquess of Winchester* (1583), 3 Coke Rep. 1, 76 E.R. 621, also 1 Leonard 270, 74 E.R. 246, Moore K.B. 95, 125, 72 E.R. 464, 483; *Metcalfe v. Wood* (1614), 11 Coke Rep. 38, 77 E.R. 1193, also Cro. Jac. 356, 79 E.R. 305, Godbolt 258, 78 E.R. 151, 1 Rolle Rep. 84, 81 E.R. 345.

[2] Stat. 37 Hen. VIII, c. 17 (*SR*, III, 1009).

[3] *The Anglican Canons 1529–1947* (G. Bray, ed., 1998), pp. 258–453.

be put out, and of this, the court here does not have cognizance nor can it judge whether he has skill in this law. And on account of this, it is apt for them to try it. But if the article had been against him that the grant of the predecessor of the bishop did not bind the successor, then the [writ of] prohibition will issue because they [would] try that which the court cannot try and we have cognizance. But being that the article is for insufficiency, it is good.

And DODDERIDGE said that [writs of] prohibition are always where they proceed against the [common] law, which they do not here. And in such a case, [a writ of] prohibition is grantable though we not have cognizance. Another is when it takes cognizance of such things of which we have the cognizance. And in all [writs of] prohibition, there is this clause '*ut gladius gladium adjuvet.*'[1] But here, if now there will be [a writ of] prohibition, *gladius gladium destruet* because, then, there will be insufficient men in those places to the great detriment of the commonwealth and unjust proceedings in those courts which greatly impact the commonwealth and yet [there would be] no remedy to remove them. And a parson has a freehold and yet they, for cause, can deprive him. And officers in this court and the [court of] common pleas have a freehold and yet we can, for cause of insufficiency, remove them, and the case of a herald, there, the marshal's court took from him his office for his insufficiency, and this court would not prohibit them. And all was because insufficiency was the cause, which is a condition in [common] law to answer to their officers and of which this court does not have cognizance.

And thus, the [writ of] prohibition [was] denied. And here, though the [court of] high commission does not have power in this, which the court would not dispute, yet the archbishop, as archbishop, has power in this cause. See C.B. 77, p. 3, same case in the [court of] common bench.

[Other reports of this case: Cro. Car. 65, 79 E.R. 659; Godbolt 390, 78 E.R. 230; Latch 228, 82 E.R. 359; Littleton 2, 22, 124 E.R. 106, 117; Noy 91, 74 E.R. 1057.]

268

Anonymous

(K.B. Pas. 3 Car. I, 1627)

When a manor is leased but an advowson is reserved to the lessor, after the lease ends, the advowson is remitted and appendant again to the manor, and not perpetually severed.

---

[1] *Bracton on the Laws and Customs of England*, vol. 4 (S.E. Thorne, trans., 1977), p. 327.

BL MS. Add. 35961, f. 61, pl. 17

YELVERTON, a justice of [the court of common] bench, came into [the court of] king's bench to ask their opinion in this case. One, seised of a manor to which an advowson is appendant, made a lease for life of the manor excepting the advowson, and the lessee for life died. Whether the advowson be now remitted and appendant again or whether it be in gross and perpetually severed [was the question].

And DODDERIDGE and JONES, who were then the court, held without question that it is re-appendant and [there is] no perpetual severance.

And of this opinion, as I [Paynell] heard, were all of the court of common pleas, clearly, but, for the satisfaction of the counsel who desired a special verdict upon it and to spare the costs of the party in a special verdict, Yelverton came.

And see 38 Hen. VI, 33, etc., the Abbess of Sion's case,[1] agreeing with these opinions.

269

Ayleworth v. Crompton

(K.B. Pas. 3 Car. I, 1627)

Error in the premises of a declaration is not material and is cured by a judgment.

Error in an outlawry is fatal and reversible.

BL MS. Add. 35961, f. 61, pl. 18

Dr. Ayleworth brought a writ of error against Crompton to reverse a judgment and outlawry in [an action of] debt given against him in the [court of] common bench (*et intratur* Mich. 2 [Car. I, rot.] 348). And he assigned the error, first, for the variance between the writ and the declaration because the writ was simply Ayleworth, clerk, and the declaration was Umfry Ayleworth, clerk, *alias dictus* Umfry Ayleworth, of such a place, etc., and it omitted 'clerk'. Thus, it varies from the declaration. And a variance between a writ and declaration, if it be material, is an error. 20 Hen. VI, 42; 38 Edw. III, 21.[2] And a variance is strictly taken. And a small variance will make faults. 4 Hen. VI, 26; *quatuordecim* and *quatuordecem*.[3]

The second error was in the outlawry because Ayleworth did not have an addition of mystery[4] etc. because *clericus* was omitted in the *alias dictus*. And where

---

[1] *Abbess of Sion's Case* (1460), YB Trin. 38 Hen. VI, f. 33, pl. 2.

[2] YB Trin. 20 Hen. VI, f. 42, pl. 21 (1442); YB Mich. 38 Edw. III, f. 21, pl. [9] (1364).

[3] YB Trin. 4 Hen. VI, f. 26, pl. 6 (1426).

[4] I.e. profession or trade.

process of outlawry lies, it must have an addition. Also, the *capias* is *et capias Ay-leworth ita quod habeas corpora eorum* where it will be *eius*. And thus, [it is an] insufficient *capias*, which is the same as no *capias*.

Another error in the outlawry was because he returned the outlawry *et quod quinto exactus non comparant*, and, there, it was well and particularly to be the day and place, but the four others did not show particularly, but in general, *et sic de hustingo in hustingum* four times before at several hustings. And he cited *Entres*, 312.

And also, the judgment here was given by *nihil dicit*, and thus it is not helped by the statutes of jeofails.[1]

And on the other side, it was said that he will not take advantage of this error which he could have pleaded in abatement of the writ. 18 Edw. IV, 19.[2] And in 44 Edw. III, 42,[3] there, [an action of] debt was brought upon a lease against A. and the lease was to a clerk, as here, and still [it was] good.

But the court said that the *alias dictus* and the omission of clerk there is not material if it be in the premises because, if the omission was in the premises and supplied in the *alias dictus*, still this would not aid it. And on account of this, the *alias dictus* is not material, as appears in Warneford's appeal, Dy.[4] And thus is the current of the other books, *contra* to 5 Edw. IV, 141,[5] by which it will be amended if, upon examination, it appears the fault of the clerk.

But for the *quinto exactus etc. sic etc.*, they said that this was erroneous.

But *Keeling*, a clerk, said that all of the old entries are thus, as the later rehearse particularly the place and time, upon which they advised further.

But for the *corpora eorum*, they held this manifest error [and] incurable.

270

Rex v. Mayor of Oxford

(K.B. Pas. 3 Car. I, 1627)

The court of king's bench has the power to supervise municipal corporations and to order the restoration of a person to a municipal office.

BL MS. Add. 35961, f. 62v, pl. 20

In the case of one Harris, a writ was directed to the mayor and commonalty of Oxford commanding them to restore Harris to the place of alderman, from which they had deposed him, etc. They returned by protestation that the writ is not such

---

[1] Stat. 32 Hen. VIII, c. 30 (*SR*, III, 786–787); Stat. 18 Eliz. I, c. 14 (*SR*, IV, 625).

[2] *Prior of St. Andrew of York v. Prior of Christ Church* (1478), YB Mich. 18 Edw. IV, ff. 18, 19, pl. 28.

[3] *Prior of Bradestock's Case* (1370), YB Mich. 44 Edw. III, f. 42, pl. 46.

[4] *Warneford's Case* (1541), 1 Dyer 50, 73 E.R. 111.

[5] Perhaps YB Pas. 4 Edw. IV, f. 14, pl. 23 (1464).

to which [they] need to make a return for the cause shown, that the Borough of Oxford is an ancient borough and so continued until 38 Hen. VIII [1546] and then it was made a city and incorporated anew and [there is] a mayor, four aldermen, two chamberlains, and a common council, and that the aldermen are there elected during life if they so long continue of good behavior and that the mayor has the regiment of the said city and that, there, from the time of which [memory runneth not to the contrary], when it was a borough and, afterwards, since it has been a city, that it has been a custom that, if a freeman behaved himself amiss in the disgracing of the government or laying ignominy upon the mayor etc., that they have used to convene such delinquent and upon examination and the guilt[1] to remove from him any franchise or to fine according to their discretion. And then [they] showed that the said Harris was made a freeman and that, at the time of the making thus, he swore and took an oath to be obedient to the mayor etc. and that, afterwards, he was chosen to be an alderman and that, then also, he was sworn. And then [they] showed that one Dean was elected to be mayor and sworn in the exchequer at Westminster and that a writ was directed to the City of Oxford commanding them to obey the said mayor etc. and that the said Harris acknowledging it in a place called The Mile Bench in Oxford, a place where the mayor and aldermen used to meet to go in solemnity to the church, divers being assembled and their officers with their with their ensigns of magistracy, the said Harris, there, had a communication from the said mayor and he said of him that he was a base fellow and a base companion and, being admonished that he will not speak thus, he repeated the words again, and, being the second time admonished, he repeated them the third time, that the mayor was a base fellow and that 'you are a base fellow' *innuendo* him who admonished him and that this was to the common damage of the city and a reproach of the magistracy and overthrow of the government there. And then, [they] showed that they summoned a common council and that Harris being there present and being there charged with the words and found guilty of them and that afterwards at another council, being required to absent himself until they consulted what will be done with him, he refused, by which they calling to mind that, before this time, he being etc. made a false return of a burgess to Parliament and also that he was before disfranchised [for] words to the lord of Wallingford, they [removed] him from being an alderman, and, in his place, they elected one such, by which they cannot now restore him to his place again etc.

And to this return, there were divers exceptions taken, first, that their custom was that the mayor, aldermen, and common council will disfranchise and they returned that he was disfranchised *per consilium civitatis* and this could be their counsel at law; second, it did not show that the mayor etc. were present at the judgment of disfranchisement given nor at the time of the hearing, which it must have done, because, if he did not hear the cause, he could not judge of it,

---

[1] culptione *MS*.

and this was an exception in Bag's case, 11.[1] The third exception was because it was said that the disfranchisement was *per consilium burgi praedicti* where, in truth, it should be *burgorum* etc. because there cannot be a counsel to the city or borough but to the citizens and burgesses, and this also was an exception in Bagge's case and Dy. 160;[2] one cannot be the [. . .] to the court of admiralty because the court cannot have a deputy. Fourth, they said that the mayor, aldermen, and common council used to disfranchise and they said that the mayor, aldermen, chamberlains, and common council had done it; thus, the chamberlains joined, and this [was] without warrant, and such an exception is also [in] C. 11, 96.[3] The fifth exception was to the council itself because it was said that the custom to disfranchise for words was not a good custom because, for the franchise, it was a freehold of which, for words, one will not be disfranchised because disfranchisement will not be done upon an easy and little matter, as appears [in] Dy. 333 and 14 Hen. IV, 25 and 26, and Trin. 17 Jac.,[4] a custom to remove *ad libitum* was adjudged bad.

Then, for the causes of the false return of a burgess, this is not any cause of disfranchisement. And also it is not here said in the return that Harris was summoned to answer for himself, but that it was objected against him, [he] being present, where he must have had a legal summons.

Then for the exception in the return, taken to the writ because it did not show for Harris that he had any benefit by the place of alderman nor that he had lost any franchise, free customs, or privileges by it and, thus, it has complained of him of a thing without a profit and a mere burden and to be restored to a name and dignity and office of trouble, to this he said that it appears to the court of itself, that, being an alderman has a privilege by it. And on account of this, it need not be averred. And also thus are all of the precedents, *viz.* Bagg's case and the precedent of Hen. VI cited [in] Dy. 333,[5] where they do not show any privileges brought by reason of the franchise. And thus also is a writ of restitution of 6 Edw. III, close roll, Mich. 8, in the Tower [of London], where the writ was to Bristol, and it recites that 'whereas *abjudicatis* etc. such a liberty', it commands them to restore him, and it does not recite any particular prejudice that he had by the disfranchisement.

And thus *Littleton* concluded for the alderman.

Noy, contra [argued] that, here, he should not be restored because this case differs from all of the cases that have been put of a restitution to a franchise

---

[1] *Bagg's Case* (1615), 11 Coke Rep. 93, 77 E.R. 1271.

[2] *Bylota, qui tam v. Pointel* (1558), 2 Dyer 159, 73 E.R. 346, also Benloe 58, 64, 123 E.R. 45, 50, BL MS. Harley 1624, f. 60.

[3] *Bagg's Case* (1615), *ut supra.*

[4] *Middleton's Case* (1574), 3 Dyer 332, 73 E.R, 752; YB Hil. 14 Hen. IV, ff. 25, 26, pl. 33 (1413); *Warren's Case* (1619), 2 Rolle Rep. 112, 81 E.R. 693, Cro. Jac. 540, 79 E.R. 463.

[5] *Anable's Case* (temp. Hen. VI), 3 Dyer 333, 73 E.R. 753.

because they are [to] restore him to the freedom of the town, but this here is not to this purpose, but to restore him to the office and place. And on account of this, the protestation is good because it does not appear to the court that he had any benefit by the place of an alderman, but the place of a freeman implies a privilege of itself. And here, he is not removed from the liberty of the city, but from this place. And on account of this, it must show that he had a benefit by it. And in the writ of 6 Edw. II, there, they recite a particular wrong, that he lost the freedoms and free customs of the place by it, as appears by it, as was truly vouched by the year [book] and roll on the other side. Thus also is a writ to this purpose, 33 Hen. VI, in the bundle of bills in equity, and this also recites that, on account of this, he lost[1] free customs etc. And this is upon the intent, as he conceived, in Dy. 333 because another writ he never saw of the same nature in the time of Henry VI. But there, it is said to be to London but this writ of 33 [Hen. VI] is to Bristol.

(Note: In Dyer, it is said that a precedent from the [court of] king's bench was found from the time of Henry VI thus thought to be entered [in] those records.)

And this is the reason that he will show some prejudice because one will not be for an office of charge and incumbrance and of no benefit, as [is] 8 Edw. IV, 7;[2] if I grant my ward to one to marry, I cannot retake him, but, if I put him at a school, I can retake him as I will please because the other does not have but a charge and trouble by it. Thus, [one] committed [by] the king to be a surveyor of his houses will not have an assize for this office because he does not have a profit by it, as 27 Hen. VIII, 28,[3] is. Thus [is] 31 Hen. VIII, b., *Grants*, 134.[4] If one be ousted from an office of which he does not have a profit, he does not have any remedy; thus here, for all that appears to the court, if it not be had nor it appear that there is any profit to be an alderman because the law does not take notice what an alderman is because, in some places, he is the chief officer of the borough; in some, as here, one of the assistants of the mayor. And alderman of itself does not signify but one of the ancient men. And Hovenden 346[5] says that an alderman is one of the elder and wiser men of the corporation. Thus, then, he was to be one of the wiser and elder men, and this is all. And this he can be notwithstanding all that they can do because they could not take from him the age nor wisdom that he has.

Then, for the exception that the false return was a cause, it is not a sufficient cause. He said that this is not recited as a cause of his removal nor as a motive and it [was] added to it because they said that, calling to mind etc., that he made this false return, they removed for the cause of the words.

---

[1] leese *MS*.

[2] YB Mich. 8 Edw. IV, f. 7, pl. 2 (1467).

[3] YB Mich. 27 Hen. VIII, f. 28, pl. 13 (1535).

[4] 31 Hen. VIII, Brooke, Abr., *Grantes*, pl. 134 (1539 x 1540).

[5] Roger of Hoveden, *Chronica*.

For the exception that they said that he was removed *per consilium* and did not show who this counsel was, he said that it must not be, because, when one pleads a thing that is infinite, he will not be forced to show the particulars, as if one pleads an election by the greater number, he will not name them in particular because it will be prolix and tedious. Thus, if one be bound to collect the green-wax [payments], he will not show particularly of what he has collected it. And also, when he said the counsel indefinitely, this intends all the counsel because *indefinitu propositio aequipollet universali*. And for this is 6 Hen. VII;[1] counsel *dedit advisamentum*. It is not true if all of the council did not give it.

For the exception that he was not summoned, he said, if he appeared *gratis* without process, it is good enough because the summons is not this [which] the law regards, but that the party has his answer. And on account of this, if he was there present at the time, it had been a superfluous thing to summon him.

For the exception of *consilium burgi* or *civitatis*, this is better than *consilium civium et maioris*, as the other side would have it, because the walls and houses do not make the city, but the inhabitants and citizens. And for this [is] 10 Hen. VII, 20;[2] the presidents and scholars make the college; and L. 5 Edw. IV, 7;[3] the monks and abbot are the monastery, not the walls of the house. And it is [a] good authority '*quod tota civitas exiit obviam Jesu*'.[4]

Then, as to that which is said that a custom to disfranchise for words is unreasonable, to this, it is said that, if it be a custom, as it is because London had such a custom, both Oxford and London *eodem utabatur lege et consuetudine*, as they claim in divers eyres. Thus, it is reasonable because a custom is always *usitata et approbata per communem consensum*, and this to which there is a general consent is equal and just. And if it not be a custom, it is necessary to be made a custom because, otherwise, by words, all government could be subverted and the magistracy there disgraced, which tends to the overthrow of the city and of everyone's estate where this *paresia* and liberty of speech traductive of governors and government is tolerated. And on account of this, it is not reason but that such words will be a cause of disfranchisement, tending to the overthrow of the city. And how severe[ly] our law has avenged words spoken against public officers appears by these following cases.

In 33 Edw. I, the lord Bruce was sued in account in the exchequer by his mother, and, there, judgment [was] given against him, with which the lord being moved, he said to the then chief baron, '*rogere, rogere, iam habes a me quod diu petisti*'. The chief baron asked him wherein; he said '*habes damnum et dedecus meum*.' And for those words being nothing more, he was committed by the king's council

---

[1] YB Trin. 6 Hen. VII, f. 4, pl. 3 (1491).

[2] YB Pas. 10 Hen. VII, ff. 19, 20, pl. 7 (1495).

[3] *Dubray v. Prior of Southwark* (1465), YB Pas. 5 Edw. IV, Long Quinto, ff. 6, 7.

[4] Matthew, chap. 8, verse 34.

to the Tower [of London] and made to go bare-headed in his doublet and hose to all of the courts of Westminster and to ask for pardon for his speeches.

Thus, in 23 Edw. III, in the [court of] common bench, an attorney having prosecuted against one a lawful course, he conceived against him displeasure and threatened him to beat him when he went out of town and he did it and it being found, he was condemned in 200 marks damages to the attorney's great damage at this day and committed to prison. And the reason of the judgment was because, as it is entered and said in the roll, *quantum in ipso fuit non permisit regnum regnare*. Thus words and acts against governors and the government are the taking of the royal scepter from the hand of the king and the overthrow of the crown.

And thus he concluded against the alderman.

Littleton: For the difference in the writ of restitution to the franchise and to the place of office as alderman, this is not a difference because thus is Bagge's case because, there, he was restored to the place of chief burgess and yet he did not show a particular prejudice.

DODDERIDGE: *Consilium civitatis* is well [said] because the Parliament is called *consilium regni, non regis et populi*.

JONES: Both writ and statutes are good, but by way of a purchase, as gives *civitati Oxoniae*, it is not.

DODDERIDGE: To say that, for words, one will not be disfranchised is not true because it is as the words are because, if they are spoken *in actu ordinario* and not in reference nor upon occasion of his office, it is not material. Thus, the *causa dicendi* is material. And he cited the case of Lumly and Winter, where Winter was disfranchised because he and Lumly having sold scarlets, Lumley said that his scarlets were better than Winter's and he debased Winter's, upon which Winter wrote to him and said in the letter that, if he said thus, he was a knave; on account of Lumly's being an alderman, Winter was disfranchised, and upon this, [a writ of] error [was] brought to St. Martin's before Dodderidge and Winch, commissioners, and it was there taken [to be] no cause because it was not spoken in reference to his authority, but *actu ordinario*, but, afterwards, it was compounded [out of court] and no judgment [was] given.

And JONES said that he had counselled in the cause, but he did not remember how it ended.

Thus, DODDERIDGE said, the mayor of a town being at the tables and, observing his play, the other said, 'Did you ever see such a fool! You have lost your game for your foolish play.' And for those words, the mayor imprisoned him, and the other brought [an action of] false imprisonment, and [it was] adjudged that it would lie because, *ex causa dicendi*, those words were not punishable, but words that scandalize government and bring it into contempt are without question a cause for disfranchisement.[1]

Thus, it was here said that, if the occasion of these words and the precedent communication had been returned thus, it would have been here.

To which JONES and DODDERIDGE said they will be ordered to make their return upon oath, as it had been before done, and, if they do not return the due circumstances, he can have an action upon the case or an indictment of perjury upon their oath.

And JONES said that he could be indicted, *viz.* the mayor, for perjury upon his general oath, that there will not be false returns. But of this, query, because it is said to the contrary in Bag's case, C. 11, 98a.

And JONES said that, in the case of Warren,[2] who was an alderman of Bristol, the putting in upon oath was an end of all.

And here, *Noy* said that it is against the ancient course, next after the writ of restitution, to award [a writ of] attachment [or] indictment, but he used to have an *alias* [and] *pluries* etc.

But JONES said that the course is ancient and the difference is, when the writ of restitution is out of the chancery returnable here, there, the use [is] to have an *alias* and *pluries*, but, when it issues out of this court originally, the first process is [a writ of] attachment.

[Other reports of this case: Benloe 202, 73 E.R. 1059, CUL MS. Gg.2.30, f. 78; Latch 229, 82 E.R. 360; Noy 92; 74 E.R. 1058; Palmer 451, 81 E.R. 1166; BL MS. Hargr. 38, f. 143v; BL MS. Lansd. 1092, f. 178v.]

271

Hayward v. Fulcher

(Part 3)
(K.B. Pas. 3 Car. I, 1627)

BL MS. Add. 35961, f. 63v, pl. 21

Now, the case between Hayward and Fulcher, before, 24, p. 44,[3] was argued again by Serjeant *Davenport* for the plaintiff. And he made three questions and points in the case, which he argued.

First, whether, by the grant to King Edward VI of all their possessions etc., the old corporation was dissolved or not so that there was no dean and chapter in

---

[1] Perhaps *Simmons v. Sweete* (1587), Cro. Eliz. 78, 78 E.R. 338, also cited by Dodderidge in *Stampe v. Jenkin* (1623), 2 Rolle Rep. 273, 81 E.R. 794.

[2] *Warren's Case* (1619), 2 Rolle Rep. 112, 81 E.R. 693, Cro. Jac. 540, 79 E.R. 463 (Alderman of Coventry).

[3] For earlier proceedings in this case, see above, Nos. 73, 175.

existence before the new erection, and, for this, he said that the words of the surrender are considerable and it is to be known that, though, at the beginning, the dean and chapter were a spiritual corporation and not spiritual as Walrond and Pollard's case, Dy.,[1] is, yet, now, they consist of temporalities also and thus, at the beginning, a bishop was more spiritual without any possessions, but, now, it is not so, but the temporalities are appendant. And [in] 28 Ass. 8,[2] it is said that the possessions of the dean and of the bishop were engrossed and, afterwards, he divided [them] between the bishop and the dean. And on account of this, now, if the possessions are gone, the corporation is destroyed. And here, for as much as the temporalities enured not by the grant to Edward VI, they passed in the way of interest, but the spiritual part of it passed by way of extinguishment and surrender, which can be a surrender as well to the inferior ordinary as to the superior, which the king is. And here, when they have surrendered the mutual church, there is not a church in which to exercise their spiritual function. And on account of this, it is not similar to the cases of other corporations because they can remain, notwithstanding all of their possessions are gone.

And he cited and applied the cases of 15 Assize 8; *Extinguishment*, B., 35; *Corporation*, b., 78; and 20 Hen. VI, 7 and 8, by Paston.[3] And that, by the taking of all of the possessions, the corporation is destroyed appears by the judgment of Parliament because thus it is recited by the Statute of Dissolutions,[4] [by] which, by the surrender of etc. into the hands of the king, the [monastic] houses were dissolved. And yet, there, there are not as strong words [to] dissolve as in our case. And on account of this, [I] will come to the cases that strike near to our case. And for this [is] Dy. 294;[5] there, by the resignation of the *prebendam* of Curry, the corporation and deanery was extinguished.

(But there, he surrendered the *hereditamenta tam spiritualia quam temporalia*.)

And Dy. 273, there, it is put, and there was no question but that the deanery of Curry (because, there, they came to our very case of a dean) was dissolved [by] the surrender of the dean. Thus [is] Dy. 282b;[6] the dean and chapter of Christ Church in Ireland surrendered their possessions, and, on account of this, it extinguished the corporation because, there, it was newly erected, and it was moved, the book says, expressly without the assent of the bishop, and yet [it was] good. Also [is] Dy. 280;[7] in the case of this same dean and chapter here and upon

---

[1] *Walrond v. Pollard* (1568–1570), 3 Dyer 273, 293, 73 E.R. 610, 659.

[2] YB 25 Edw. III, Lib. Ass., p. 116, pl. 8 (1351).

[3] YB 15 Edw. III, Lib. Ass., p. 43, pl. 8 (1341); YB Mich. 20 Hen. VI, f. 7, pl. 17 (1441), Brooke, Abr., *Extinguishment*, pl. 35; Brooke, Abr., *Corporations*, pl. 78; YB Mich. 20 Hen. VI, ff. 7, 8, pl. 17 (1441).

[4] Stat. 31 Hen. VIII, c. 13 (*SR*, III, 733–739).

[5] *Walrond v. Pollard* (1568–1570), *ut supra*.

[6] *Archbishop of Dublin v. Bruerton* (1569), 3 Dyer 282, 73 E.R. 633.

[7] *Corbet's Case* (1568), 3 Dyer 279, 73 E.R. 627.

the same patent, it is said that the old corporation was dissolved and a new [one] erected. And this agrees with the opinions of the time because thus it appears to be the opinions of this time because, without question, the sages of the law that then were were of counsel in those conveyances, being concerning so great possessions. And in the patent of the new erection, there are divers clauses that show their opinions to be that they are an absolute[1] dissolution and extinguishment of the corporation. And this point is not resolved in the three reports and the case there of the dean and chapter.

And the second point that he argued was whether the omission of *ex fundatione Edwardi sexti* was a material misnomer. And this he argued briefly. And he put but two cases upon it to prove that it was. Dy. 150. He cited also C. 10, 124a, and the case of the dean of Windsor, there also 124b.[2]

And also, he said that, there, there is a difference between ancient and new corporations, as this is because ancient corporation could be thus by divers names, but not new [ones].

The third point was whether the exception extended to the trees as well as to the other woods because it excepts all the woods and underwoods in Taverham Wood and also all great trees of oak, ash, and elm growing out of the premises and, afterwards, comes the condition that, if he does not allow to cut and carry any part of the woods and underwoods before excepted that then, and this point, he said, the explanation of it will make the argument of it. And thus, in brief, he concluded it.

And also, all the case on the other side at another day was argued by Serjeant *Bramston*. And he argued the three points aforesaid, and two others he spoke to briefly, and he took two exceptions *de novo* to the special verdict.

But first, he answered some objections. And first for Corbet's case, Dy. 280, which is the main case against us, it is plain that, there, the matter in fact solely is related and not any opinion in the case for the law in the point. And thus, it is not made against us. For the case of Dy. 282,[3] where a dean and chapter [were] dissolved, this does not match our case because, there, there were two chapters; and on account of this, there was not such a necessity as in our case because, notwithstanding this, the bishop did not lack his chapter, which he will in our case if it be a dissolution, but he lacks its assistance. Thus, these are not against us.

Then, to begin with the reasons that enforce our side (and, there, he began with the resolution of the Dean and Chapter's case, C. 3, 74)[4] because, there, our

---

[1] absent *MS*.

[2] *Eaton College Case* (1556), 2 Dyer 150, 73 E.R. 327; *Mayor of King's Lynn v. Payn* (1612), 10 Coke Rep. 120, 77 E.R. 1108; *Dean of Windsor's Case* (1587 x 1588), cited in *Mayor of King's Lynn v. Payn* (1612), 10 Coke Rep. 120, 124, 77 E.R. 1108, 1113–1114.

[3] *Archbishop of Dublin v. Bruerton* (1569), *ut supra*.

[4] *Case of the Dean and Chapter of Norwich* (1598), 3 Coke Rep. 73, 76 E.R. 793, also 2 Anderson 120, 165, 123 E.R. 577, 601.

very point is one, of two, that was resolved by the two chief justices and the lord chancellor, that the surrender of the old corporation did not destroy [it], but it remained notwithstanding, and, if it had not been dissolved, as, there, it was, yet it is confirmed by divers authorities and reason because consider the words that must make the extinguishment of the corporation because, first, they surrendered their jurisdictions, privileges, rights, [and] franchises. And none of these words would [destroy] the corporation because, on account of this, they give it that they had but not given themselves by those [words]. Then, they granted all of their lands, tenements, and hereditaments, and none of them would pass the corporation because [of] 15 Ass. 8;[1] by the recovery of the possessions of the prebend, this does not extinguish the prebend, but he can have [a writ of] error and remain a corporation notwithstanding.

And here, he cited Dy. 10 Eliz., the Dean of Wells' case,[2] and other cases before cited. And he cited C. 9, 26,[3] where it is said that the corporation existed before any possessions; and, on account of this, it could exist without possessions now. And it is not of the essence of a corporation to have possessions.

Then, if any words serve, it must be the word *ecclesiam*. And this, here, will not serve because, by the grant of their church, the corporation did not pass because the corporation was not surrendered by express words and the word church will not be taken [as] other than the fabric of the cathedral church, for the material church. And this is proved because, in the regrant, the king granted to them *ecclesiam praedictam*, therefore the 'aforesaid church' was not their spiritual corporation. And each abbacy [exists] in itself and is a church, as appears [in] *Trespass*, 237;[4] and each hospital is a house, as [is] 42 Edw. III, 22;[5] and each prebend is a church also and [is] seised *in jure ecclesiae*. And yet, by the grant of the abbey, the corporation is not dissolved, as appears [in] C. 3 and the cases of Petit Brooke, before [cited]. And of a hospital, no one would say that, by the surrender of the house, the hospital is destroyed, and so of a prebend, because [in] Dy. 293,[6] by a grant *de prebenda*, the spiritual part of it does not pass if it does not have the word *spiritualia*. And there then [is] that reason, that, here, by the grant *de ecclesia*, that the corporation of dean etc. will pass.

---

[1] YB 15 Edw. III, Lib. Ass., p. 43, pl. 8 (1341).

[2] *Walrond v. Pollard* (1568–1570), *ut supra*.

[3] *Regina v. Vaughan* (1591), 9 Coke Rep. 24, 26, 77 E.R. 765, 769, also Moore K.B. 297, 72 E.R. 591.

[4] *Abbot of Glastonbury v. Parson of Schilmerle* (1324), YB Mich. 18 Edw. II, p. 573, Fitzherbert, Abr., *Trespas*, p. 237.

[5] YB Mich. 42 Edw. III, ff. 21, 22, pl. 1 (1368).

[6] *Walrond v. Pollard* (1568–1570), *ut supra*.

And for the case of 10 Eliz., Dy., this was, as the book said, confirmed by Parliament,[1] which makes for our case.

Then, if all of these words separately would not operate to extinguish the corporation, certainly, they cannot all conjoined. And this first point is the principal [one] because, if it be good for us and the corporation remains, the lease is good by the old name of the corporation.

And the other point is not material. But admitting it, the second point is whether the omission of *ex fundatione Edwardi sexti* be such a misnomer that etc. And he argued that it is not because it is not a material nor substantial omission. And only omissions of substance are vicious, as appears [in] Dy. 278.[2] Then, it is to see what will be said [to be] part of the substance, and that is a large field. But upon this, he took a ground that such an omission is only of substance that omits such a part of a name that distinguishes the corporation from all others because names exist to distinguish. And, if they have such a name by which they can be known from all others, the name is good. And here, he cited the difference of several. And he cited C. 10, 124.[3]

But to come to our case, he said that he cannot compare the omission of the name of the founder to the better case, that of the omission of the name of the saint, in which, of ancient times, they were taken. And yet it did not vitiate their grant. And here, he cited 26 Edw. III, 66; 17 Edw. III, 32; 4 Edw. IV, 4; and 8 Ass. 24.[4]

And for the objection that this here is a new corporation and, on account of this, it cannot be known by another name than the true [one], he said that it is old enough to gain a name of reputation which would serve because, to this, time of memory is not required, as appears [in] 21 Hen. VI, 4.[5]

And to conclude this point, the principal case of the Mayor of Lynn, in the 10th report,[6] is more strong than here because, there, it omitted *regis*, who is twice named in their corporation and the name of the founder also, and yet [it was] good.

For the third point, he first argued that this is not a condition because it goes in this manner. They 'covenanted and agreed that the said etc. the lessee shall not stand to the award of the dean and chapter for things concerning the said lands etc. and that, if the lessee shall hinder the dean and chapter and their servants to carry any part of the said woods or underwoods before excepted if, then, it

---

[1] *Landewibrevye College Case* (1567), 3 Dyer 267, 73 E.R. 593; Stat. 1 Edw. VI, c. 14 (*SR*, IV, 24–33).

[2] *Case of the Corporation of the Cathedral of Carlisle* (1568), 3 Dyer 278, 73 E.R. 622.

[3] *Mayor of King's Lynn v. Payn* (1612), 10 Coke Rep. 120, 77 E.R. 1108.

[4] *The Queen v. Prior of Coventry* (1352), YB Trin. 26 Edw. III, f. 12, pl. 13; YB Mich. 27 Edw. III, f. 12, pl. 57 (1353); YB 8 Edw. III, Lib. Ass., p. 17, pl. 24 (1334).

[5] YB Mich. 21 Hen. VI, f. 4, pl. 8 (1442).

[6] *Mayor of King's Lynn v. Payn* (1612), 10 Coke Rep. 120, 77 E.R. 1108.

shall be lawful to re-enter.' And this, he said, was not a condition but a covenant because, first, it is spoken in the words of the lessee and this is unresolved in Browning's case, in the C.[1] But, if, there, it be a condition, yet it differs from our case because, there, the covenant was that, if he did not make etc., the lease will be void. And on account of this, it is more reason to be a condition there because, if it be a covenant, he did not have another remedy because he could not have a covenant there upon an act which lies in the operation of the law. But here, there is not such a necessity, but he can have [an action of] covenant if he would not allow him to enter.

Also, even though a condition can come between covenants, yet it was never seen that the same sentence will be [taken] for part a covenant and for part a condition. See Dy. 6.[2] And on account of this, it differs from Cromwell's case, C. 2.[3]

But admit this a condition, still it does not extend to the trees because the party himself, by the words, has put an apparent difference between the trees and the woods and underwoods, and he has applied the condition, if it be one, solely to the woods and underwoods and, beyond the limitation of the party, the law will not extend the words. And it is not thus absurd, as it has been objected, that they will have the care of the underwoods and will make such a provision for it and, for the great timber, left [?] it at large because, if there had been a proviso to restrain the lessee from cutting the woods, it had been a colorable objection. But here, it is by way of a reservation to the lessor. And on account of this, it is likely that the lessor, who reserves to himself a power to cut and carry wood, was more careful not to be disturbed in the underwoods, which was an annual profit, than in the timber *sparsim* growing, which, being a spiritual corporation, he could not have taken for his private profit without danger of [making] delapidations and deprivation.

Also, here, the words of the exception will not be pressed according to the literal sense of the words, but in this sense in which the lessor intended them. And the intent of the party was that it was as is aforesaid. But, if the intent not be apparent, but doubtful, then, *in re dubia*, the stronger will be taken to maintain the estate of the lessee and *contra* to the condition.

Another point he said he put, he remembered and only touched because it is not much denied on the other side, and this is that, by the sealing of the lease by the dean and chapter, this is their deed (*viz.* the lease to Hayward, the plaintiff), and thus the case is not except such a one, having title to enter, made a lease to

---

[1] *Browning v. Beston* (1552), 1 Plowden 131, 140, 75 E.R. 202, 216.

[2] *Anonymous* (1537), 1 Dyer 6, 73 E.R. 15.

[3] *Lord Cromwel v. Andrews* (1601), 2 Coke Rep. 69, 76 E.R. 574, also 1 Anderson 17, 230, 123 E.R. 330, 445, 2 Anderson 69, 123 E.R. 550, Jenkins 252, 145 E.R. 178, Cro. Eliz. 15, 891, 78 E.R. 281, 1115, Moore K.B. 105, 471, 72 E.R. 470, 703, Gouldsborough 116, 75 E.R. 1034, Yelverton 3, 7, 80 E.R. 3, 5, Savile 115, 123 E.R. 1044, 3 Dyer 311, 354, 73 E.R. 704, 796, Noy 44, 74 E.R. 1013, Benloe 201, 123 E.R. 141.

B. of the entry and delivered it as his deed and he made a letter of attorney to one to deliver it upon the ground, having entered into the possession of the land. This is not good according to Bragg's case, C. 3, 39.[1] And here, the sealing of the corporation made it an absolute deed without more ceremony. And then, without question, the lease cannot be good before a re-entry.

Then, he took two exceptions to the pleading and the finding of the special verdict, first, because the verdict found that the dean and chapter made an indenture for carrying a demise and it did not say to whom the demise was. And then, it found the indenture *in haec verba*, 'this indenture made etc. between the dean etc. of one part and Hayward of the other part'; thus, it does not appear, nor can it be necessarily implied, that the lessee in the indenture and the plaintiff are one and the same person. And thus, no title [was] found for the plaintiff. And, if this had been in the pleading as it is here in the special verdict, it had been clearly bad because, in pleading, to say *quid quidam* J.S. etc., it will not be intended J.S. before spoken, as Dy. 70 and C. 8, 57,[2] are. And even though a special verdict will not have as much certainty, yet it must have a convenient certainty [so] that it can by other circumstances appear to be the same man. See C. 4, 65a.[3] And he cited the pleading of Adam and Lambert's case,[4] in which he said the same exception was taken and long insisted upon and often argued, though it was not reported by the Lord Coke, where the lessee sued that the ejectment [that] was brought was laid to be by Snelling and Butler and the jury found *quid quidam* Butler and Snelling were seised and leased to the plaintiff, and thus it was to be entered to be the same persons; it was much debated. And at the last, because of divers circumstances, as the lessees of the same town, beginning and end, it was agreed as necessary a lease [?] given [?] by the same persons. But it was agreed that, if there had not been such circumstances, it had not been good.

Also he cited a case of Trin. 39 El. 46, 3k, where one brought [an action of] trover and conversion of certain goods, a silver skillet, a silver dish, etc. and the jury found that the plaintiff was possessed of a silver skillet and a silver dish etc. and lost them and they came to the hands of the defendant etc. and did not say the silver skillet etc. mentioned in the count or to such effect, and the plaintiff recovered, but it was reversed in the exchequer chamber for no other cause but that

---

[1] *Jennings v. Bragg* (1595), Cro. Eliz. 447, 78 E.R. 687, also cited in *Butler v. Baker* (1591), 3 Coke Rep. 25, 35, 76 E.R. 684, 707.

[2] *Withers v. Iseham* (1552), 1 Dyer 70, 73 E.R. 148; *Earl of Rutland v. Earl of Shrewsbury* (1608), 8 Coke Rep. 55, 57, 77 E.R. 555, 559, also Jenkins 283, 145 E.R. 205, 2 Brownlow & Goldesborough 229, 123 E.R. 913, 1 Bulstrode 4, 80 E.R. 710.

[3] *Cartwright v. Roberts* (1591), 4 Coke Rep. 64, 76 E.R. 1031.

[4] *Adams v. Lambert* (1602), 4 Coke Rep. 96, 76 E.R. 1079, Moore K.B. 648, 72 E.R. 815.

it did not appear but that the goods in the verdict and in the declaration could be diverse. And this reversal was Mich. 43 & 44 Eliz., rot. 418.[1]

The second exception here was because it does not appear that the trees in which the disturbance was laid were growing or great trees at the time of the demise because, otherwise, the exception does not extend to them because the exception is of 'all the woods and underwoods and Taverham Wood and also all great trees of oak, ash, and elm growing upon the said manor'. Now, the jury found that the trees etc. were growing upon the baron's part of the manor, but it did not say that, there, they were growing at the time of the demise and, if they were not, then, they are not excepted and, by consequence, the lessee could disturb the cutting of them.

And thus, upon all, he concluded for the defendant.

And here, JONES said that the first exception he himself had noted in the margin of the book for an exception.

And a day was given to the next term for the other side to speak to these exceptions only.

More, 74a, Mich. 3 *Caroli regis*, king's bench, p. 16, fo. 95.[2]

[Other reports of this case: W. Jones 166, 82 E.R. 88, BL MS. Hargr. 317, f. 162; Palmer 491, 81 E.R. 1186; BL MS. Hargr. 38, ff. 50v, 144v, 187, 189v, 267; BL MS. Lansd. 1092, f. 263v; HLS MS. 1063, ff. 4, 29.]

272

Anonymous

(K.B. Pas. 3 Car. I, 1627)

A very small error is sufficient to reverse an outlawry.

BL MS. Add. 35961, f. 64v, pl. 22

An outlawry was reversed because it appeared that the county court was held thirty days after the other. Thus, [there was] more than one month between county [court] and county [court]. Thus, all acts then were void.

Justice JONES said a light matter would serve to reverse an outlawry.

---

[1] *Bateman v. Elman* (1601), Cro. Eliz. 866, 78 E.R. 1093.

[2] *Hayward v. Fulcher* (1627–1628), BL MS. Add. 35961, ff. 101, 132, BL MS. Lansd. 1083, ff. 171, 211 (Widdrington's reports).

273

Rex v. Barrell

(K.B. Pas. 3 Car. I, 1627)

One will not be convicted of perjury in giving false evidence unless the perjury led to a false verdict and the perjury was malicious.

BL MS. Add. 35961, f. 64v, pl. 23

One Barrell was indicted for perjury in [giving] evidence upon an indictment of murder because he swore that the party did it etc. And it was quashed, first, because it did not show that, by reason of his oath, he was found guilty because the perjury, upon which one will be indicted, must be such that leads the jury also [to] perjury upon an indictment. It is not within the Statute of 5 Eliz.,[1] upon which the indictment here is framed. Also it was not found that it was perjury *malitiose*.

274

Taylor v. Tolwin

(Part 2)
(K.B. Pas. 3 Car. I, 1627)

BL MS. Add. 35961, f. 64v, pl. 24

And afterwards, in the case before, f. 53, p. 10,[2] *Hitcham* showed that the plaintiff had repleaded and that he had pleaded that he was under age at such place. And *Hitcham* moved to have it put out of the book because he must assign for error generally that he was under age and it will come in on the side of the defendant to say that [he was] at full age at such place. Thus, the trial will come where the full age is laid, and it will be intricate to traverse *absque hoc quod* he was under age at such place.

And JONES said that, if an obligation was sued against one and the plaintiff alleged that the defendant being of full age at such place became indebted and bound etc., the defendant could say that he was under age at the other place without a traverse of the full age because it was surplusage in the count and out of course. Thus here, for the plaintiff to show where he was under age is surplusage.

But the serjeant [*Hitcham*] desired to have it for plainness put out.

And so it was ruled.

---

[1] Stat. 5 Eliz. I, c. 9 (*SR*, IV, 436–438).

[2] For earlier proceedings in this case, see above, No. 261.

[Other reports of this case: Godbolt 382, 444, 78 E.R. 225, 261; Latch 194, 218, 82 E.R. 342, 354; BL MS. Lansd. 1092, ff. 164, 227v; CUL MS. Ll.3.13, ff. 208, 273v, 302.]

275

Marget v. Harvey

(K.B. Pas. 3 Car. I, 1627)

A general appearance cures all defects in the process.

BL MS. Add. 35961, f. 64v, pl. 25

Between Margete and Harvy in [a writ of] error upon a judgment in an inferior court (*quod intratur* Trin. 2 [Car. I, rot.] 1478), it was assigned that a *capias* was the first process in an action upon the case, second, that the *capias* was *ita quod habeas corpus ad proximam curiam* and it did not say in certain at what day and the court could be held long after and one will not be in custody and not have a day certain for appearance.

But afterward, it appeared by the record that the party appeared, thus, all the faults of the process [were] saved by the appearance. 9 Edw. IV, 18; 12 Hen IV, 17.[1] Thus, the judgment was affirmed.

So it was [held] also between Sampson and Gatefield, Trin. 2 [Car. I, rot.] 1180,[2] where the appearance saved the mis-awarding of the *capias*.

[Other reports of this case: Latch 193, 82 E.R. 342; Palmer 449, 81 E.R. 1165.]

276

Rex v. Man

(K.B. Pas. 3 Car. I, 1627)

An indictment must allege the place where the offense was committed.

BL MS. Add. 35961, f. 64v, pl. 26

Two separate indictments of barretry were quashed because they did not show the place where he was *communis barrectator*. And yet one of them in the *per quod jurgia* etc. had a place, but [it was] not in the premises.

[Other reports of this case: Godbolt 383, 78 E.R. 226; Latch 194, 82 E.R. 342; Palmer 450, 81 E.R. 1165.]

---

[1] YB Trin. 9 Edw. IV, f. 18, pl. 20 (1479); YB Hil. 12 Hen. IV, f. 17, pl. 15 (1411).

[2] *Samson v. Gatefield* (1627), Godbolt 400, 78 E.R. 236.

277

Lickfield v. Melhurst

(K.B. Pas. 3 Car. I, 1627)

In an action brought by a husband and wife for a tort done to the wife, a judgment in favor of both the husband and wife is not erroneous.

BL MS. Add. 35961, f. 64v, pl. 27

Lickfield was the plaintiff in [a writ of] error against Melhurst in two separate actions, one of a judgment given against him in an action upon the case by Melhurst and his wife for words spoken of the wife (*et intratur* Hil. 2 [Car. I], rot. 253), the other of battery brought by the same parties for a battery done to the wife. And the error assigned in both was because the judgment was that the husband and wife will recover damages, where it was said that the wife will not recover damages. But yet, notwithstanding this, the judgment was affirmed. And the other record was Hil. 2 [Car. I], rot. 236. Thus both [were] affirmed.

[Other reports of this case: Godbolt 369, 78 E.R. 217.]

278

Holmes v. Winegreen

(Part 2)
(K.B. Pas. 3 Car. I, 1627)

BL MS. Add. 35961, f. 64v, pl. 28

The case before, f. 51a, p. 22,[1] was moved divers times this term and the error aforesaid. And the court was of the same opinion as Dodderidge then was for the same reason.

And still *Calthorpe* cited one Alsop's case[2] to be such that, upon the issue of *non assumpsit*, the jury found that, for non performance of the promise, the plaintiff had sustained damages etc. And [it was] adjudged a void verdict and that he will not have the issue [taken] by implication.

But DODDERIDGE asked where the record of this case was. And he said that he did not credit his unwritten verities.

Another error was that the action was for the taking of the box with the charters and detaining *quosque* etc. and he did not show that the box was his box nor that it was sealed nor closed so that the charters drew it with them, and yet

---

[1] For earlier proceedings in this case, see above, No. 248.

[2] Perhaps *Alsope v. Sytwell* (1602), Yelverton 18, 80 E.R. 13, or *Shelley v. Alsop* (1605), Yelverton 77, 80 E.R. 54.

damages were assessed entirely for both and that it must be sealed or locked or otherwise it does not go with the charters. [This] appears by 36 Hen. VI, 27; C. 323; 3 Hen. VII, 15.[1]

But DODDERIDGE said that it was well notwithstanding this because the charters draw the box with them, be it closed or not, because what if it were tried with [. . .], as he said, and not sealed or locked, and it has been adjudged that trespass *de una bago cum centum libris* taken and [. . .] that the bag was *saca* nor that [it was] sealed but that the money was his and yet [it is] good as entire damages.

Then, it was moved that the verdict was '*et juratores super sacramentum suorum dixerunt*' where it will be *dicunt* and also that the judgment '*est consideratio fuit pro est*'. And these two were thought material.

And a day [was] given to the next term to defend them. [See] after f. 71, pl. 16.[2]

[Other reports of this case: Godbolt 370, 78 E.R. 218; Latch 195, 82 E.R. 342, HLS MS. 1235, f. 85v; BL MS. Lansd. 1092, f. 164v; CUL MS. Ll.3.13, f. 208v.]

279

Mulleyn v. Dole

(K.B. Pas. 3 Car. I, 1627)

A written obligation sued upon must be proffered in the pleadings, but this defect can be waived by the defendant.

A judgment must include the damages found and the costs awarded by the jury.

BL MS. Add. 35961, f. 64v, pl. 29

[In a case] between Dole and Mulleyn in [a writ of] error [entered] Hil. 2 [Car. I, rot.] 597, the first error was assigned because he declared upon an obligation and did not say *et profert hic in curia profert*. And this was held for error and how it was held [to be a] verdict not aidable by any statute because it is, as JONES said, a matter of substance, and, on account of this, it is not aided, as Dr. Leifield's case, C. 10, 62, was.[3] And thus, it has often times been ruled, as JONES said.

---

[1] YB 36 Hen. VI, f. 26, pl. 26 (1457 x 1458); *Regina v. Earl of Northumberland* (1567), 1 Plowden 310, 323, 75 E.R. 472, 492; YB Mich. 3 Hen. VII, f. 15, pl. 29 (1487).

[2] *Holmes v. Winegreen* (1627), BL MS. Add. 35961, f. 77, pl. 16, BL MS. Lansd. 1083, f. 133v, pl. 16 (Widdrington's reports).

[3] *Layfield v. Hillary* (1611), 10 Coke Rep. 88, 77 E.R. 1057, also Cro. Jac. 317, 79 E.R. 272, 1 Bulstrode 154, 80 E.R. 846.

But Serjeant *Hitcham* said that true it is that *prima facie* it is a material error, but, if afterwards the defendant comes and confesses the deed, this aids the non showing. And here, he has so done because the defendant was against the administrator on the obligation of the intestate, who came and pleaded *plene administravit*, by which he confessed the bond. And he cited Dy. 115,[1] where letters patent were pleaded without a showing and, because the plaintiff pleaded in avoidance of them, it was good (but JONES said that it passed *sub silentio*), and 6 Edw. IV, 2,[2] where one brought [an action of] debt upon a bond and did not show it, the defendant pleaded performance of the condition and, by the pleading, the showing [was] helped.

But DODDERIDGE granted it because, there, there was a full confession of it, but, here, the plea of *plene administravit* is not a confession etc.

And they were, in truth, to have given a day until next term but that two apparent errors were moved, first, that the jury found for the plaintiff and assessed damages and costs and the judgment is *quod recuperet debitum* [. . .] *damna de incremento* omitting the damages and costs by the jury, and this was held error clearly.

Also, the judgment was *ideo concessum est per consideratum*. And *Hitcham*, being asked what he [would] say to them, said that, if it be thus, he could say nothing. On account of this, it was reversed.

Query whether the plea of *plene administravit* confessed the deed because this was the doubt.

[Other reports of this case: Godbolt 399, 78 E.R. 235.]

280

Whitton v. Weston

(Part 4)
(K.B. Pas. 3 Car. I, 1627)

BL MS. Add. 35961, f. 65, pl. 30

And now, the case of Whitton and Weston was argued again (of which, see before f. 7b, pl. 9, f. 47, pl. 92)[3] by *Noy* for the plaintiff and Serjeant *Crawley* for the defendant. And because the argument of Noy was to the same intent as his former argument, I will only sum up the heads of his argument.

First, he argued that the lands of the Hospitalers were not discharged of tithes in the hands of the patentees of the king by the Statute of 31 Hen. VIII[4]

---

[1] *Regina v. Austin* (1556), 2 Dyer 115, 73 E.R. 252.
[2] YB Mich. 6 Edw. IV, ff. 1, 2, pl. 4 (1466).
[3] For earlier proceedings in this case, see above, Nos. 29, 31, 225.
[4] Stat. 31 Hen. VIII, c. 13 (*SR*, III, 733–739).

because this house was not dissolved by this Statute and, on account of this, the clause within this Statute of exemption of tithes does not extend to it because no lands are discharged of tithes by this Statute but those that came to the king by this Statute. And that the Hospitalers were not dissolved by this Act appears, first, because it dissolved only such houses which were both religious and ecclesiastical, but these were not both because, though religious, yet not ecclesiastical. And here, it is not averred that they were ecclesiastical. And on account of this, if they were, the judges will not to take notice of it nor *revera* they were. And on account of this, the books of *Triall*, 99; 21 Hen. VII, 7; and 2 Ric. III, 4,[1] which prove them [to be] religious, are not against it because they could [be] and they were thus and yet not [be] ecclesiastical. And the word in the Statute of 17 Edw. II,[2] where it is said that they were *canonice*, was not against this because it signifies only that they were entered in a rule and order; thus, [they were] religious. And thus is *Nonability*, 4, and *Feffments*, 68.[3] But yet, they were religious lay[men] and not religious ecclesiastical [men].

And it could be objected against it of the form of the summons to Parliament because temporal lords are summoned *in fide et legeancia* but spiritual lords *in fide et electione* and thus was the summons of the prior of St. John's. But to this he answered that the reason of it was because their tenure was in frankalmoign and this [is] the stronger reason that they were spiritual. And that they were not ecclesiastical is shown by things incomparable to the ecclesiastics: first, their profession was *vivere in armis et agere in sanguine*, which was prohibited by the canons to all ecclesiastics. Second, [there] were more ceremonies at the initiation of many lay orders and fraternities, as of the knights of the bath and of the garter etc., which are not but mere lay orders, but for these, they are but the putting on of a robe etc. And [in] 44 Ass. 9,[4] it appears that the prior and confreres of the *domus leprosorum* were religious because the prior sued alone and the others [were] dead persons [civilly] and yet they were lay[men] and not ecclesiastics, as is admitted there.

Also ecclesiastical profession is triable by the ordinary, but the profession here is not triable but by jury, as appears [in] 2 Ric. III, 4; 21 Hen. VII, 7; and *Triall*, 99. Therefore, it was not ecclesiastical because they have ecclesiastical privileges. This was not against it because so could a layman by a special grant or prescription. And by J. Selden's *Tithes*, 121, it appears that in all of the courts beyond the seas, they were adjudged to be mere laymen. But this is not material unless they were so accounted with us in this realm. And on account of this, in

---

[1] Mich. 31 Edw. I, Fitzherbert, Abr., *Triall*, pl. 99 (1303); YB Hil. 21 Hen. VII, ff. 6, 7, pl. 5 (1506); *Sondes v. Peckam* (1484), YB Mich. 2 Ric. III, ff. 3, 4, pl. 8.

[2] Stat. 17 Edw. II, stat. 2 (*SR*, I, 194–196).

[3] *Cernyngton v. Prioress of Bokland* (1388), YB Pas. 12 Ric. II, Ames Found., vol. 6, p. 150, pl. 5, Fitzherbert, Abr., *Nonhabilite*, pl. 4; YB Mich. 19 Edw. III, Rolls Ser. 31b, vol. 13, p. 353, pl. 27 (1345), Fitzherbert, Abr., *Feffements & faits*, pl. 68.

[4] YB 44 Edw. III, Lib. Ass., p. 284, pl. 9 (1370).

11 Edw. I and in Edw. II, when all of the clergy were taxed to tithes by bulls of the pope, they were not ecclesiastical.

Another reason for which they were not within the Statute of 31 [Hen. VIII] is because there were three separate dissolutions. The first was of 27 Hen. VIII[1] of the small houses upon the pretense that they were a disgrace to the other great houses and [were] not sufficient to support the estate of the monks. The second was of 31 Hen. VIII, and this was upon the pretense of their vicious living because the commissions being returned they were, that in such an abbacy *talis habet tres concubinas, talis sex* and in such a nunnery *talis sexies peperit, talis septies etc.* And lastly, the dissolution of this house in 32 Hen. VIII,[2] and the pretense of it was to eradicate all of the adherents of the pope. And on account of this, having all the several pretenses and several acts, there could not be one within the Statute of Monasteries.

Another reason that it will not be within [the Statute of] 31 [Hen. VIII] is because the Statute of 32 [Hen. VIII] says that it will be in the king by virtue of this Act. And on account of this, it cannot be by virtue of 31 [Hen. VIII] because, though it had been before 31 [Hen. VIII] by virtue of it, yet when 32 [Hen. VIII] came, it controlled the former act. And he said that it will be in the king by virtue of 32 [Hen. VIII]. And he put the case put, of C. 2, 46b,[3] upon this ground, and the case that one will not be remitted against the Statute of Uses[4] because the Statute says that he will be in of such an estate.

And another reason was because it coming by Parliament to the king, being superior to all the ways nominated, it will not be within the general words of 'any other means'. And he put the case there also put upon this ground, that a bishop is not within [the Statute of] 13 Eliz. 10.[5] And on account of this, he could make current leases, as was adjudged in Colyer's case[6] in the exchequer chamber, and 18 Jac., in Wright's case, in the [court of] common bench,[7] it was adjudged that the priory of Hatfield, being dissolved by [the Statute of] 27 Hen. VIII, was not within [the Statute of] 31 [Hen. VIII] to be discharged of tithes because not by Parliament and, on account of this, not within [the Statute of] 31 [Hen. VIII] and those that did not come to the king by this are not discharged by it.

Then, it is to see whether it be discharged by the Statute of 32 [Hen. VIII], which is the Statute that dissolved this hospital. And it is not [discharged]

---

[1] Stat. 27 Hen. VIII, c. 28 (*SR*, III, 575–578).

[2] Stat. 32 Hen. VIII, c. 24 (*SR*, III, 778–781).

[3] *Green v. Balser* (1596), 2 Coke Rep. 46, 76 E.R. 519, 1 Gwillim 189, 1 Eagle & Younge 113.

[4] Stat. 27 Hen. VIII, c. 10 (*SR*, III, 539–542).

[5] Stat. 13 Eliz. I, c. 10 (*SR*, III, 544–545).

[6] *Fox v. Collier* (1579), Moore K.B. 107, 72 E.R. 472.

[7] *Wright v. Gerrard* (1618), Cro. Jac. 607, 79 E.R. 518, Hobart 306, 80 E.R. 449, W. Jones 2, 82 E.R. 2, 1 Gwillim 375, 1 Eagle & Younge 289.

because, if this immunity is given to the king, it is by words of right and interest. And it is not because, then, all of the lands of the houses dissolved by [the Statute of] 27 [Hen. VIII] will be discharged because it gives to the king all of the rights and interests of the houses by the word 'privilege'. But it is not this because these words are in [the Statute of] 31 Hen. VIII and yet they have a particular clause of discharge.

And also the Statutes of 27 Hen. VIII and 1 Edw. VI[1] give to the king the privileges, but, as for the privilege of discharge, it did not pass. And the reason is because it is a personal privilege and, on account of this, it was not given to the king. And he put the cases of C. 7, 12 and 13, of personal privileges.[2]

But though it be admitted that the king is capable of discharge of tithes because he will not pay tithes but where they [are] granted as *de aequitibus de venacaribus et de forestis*, as are many patents of it, which proves that, without a grant, they will not pay, yet on account of this, it does not follow that his patentee will have the same advantage because conditions are by the Statute of Dissolutions given to the king and yet he does not have by it all conditions and those that he has do not pass to his patentee. Yet the Statute of 32 Hen. VIII was to this purpose.

And then, he cited Quarles' case and Wright's case,[3] before cited, and he endeavored an answer to 10 Eliz.[4] And he argued as he had done before that the defendant had not applied in pleading the privilege, which exception the court disallowed.

And thus he concluded.

Serjeant *Crawley, contra*: And the state of his argument was, first, that they are ecclesiastical because they have impropriations. 3 Edw. III, 11,[5] in [an action of] annuity brought against them; where they are parsons impropriate, they must be called parsons. 22 Edw. IV, 4; 42 Edw. III, 22; 33 Hen. VI, 56.[6] It is said that they [were] seised *in jure ecclesiae*; therefore, [they are] ecclesiastics. Linwood, [*Provinciale*], lib. 2, fo. 47, [says] that they are ecclesiastical.

Second, he argued that, by [the Statute of] 32 [Hen. VIII], they are discharged because this gives not only all privileges but all of whatever nature,

---

[1] Stat. 1 Edw. VI, c. 14 (*SR*, IV, 24–25).

[2] *Regina v. Englefield* (1591), 7 Coke Rep. 11, 77 E.R. 428, also 1 Anderson 293, 123 E.R. 480, Popham 18, 79 E.R. 1139, Moore K.B. 303, 72 E.R. 595, 4 Leonard 135, 170, 74 E.R. 779, 800.

[3] *Quarles v. Spurling* (1602), Moore K.B. 913, 72 E.R. 993, *sub nom. Cornwallis v. Spurling*, Cro. Jac. 57, 79 E.R. 48, 1 Gwillim 224, 1 Eagle & Younge 157; *Wright v. Gerrard* (1618), *ut supra*.

[4] *Stathome's Case* (1568), 3 Dyer 277, 73 E.R. 621, 1 Gwillim 132, 1 Eagle & Younge 59.

[5] YB Pas. 3 Edw. III, f. 11, pl. 1 (1329).

[6] *Prior of the Hospital of St. John v. J.* (1368), YB Trin. 42 Edw. III, f. 21, pl. 1; *Bishop of Winchester v. Prior of St. John of Jerusalem* (1457), YB Pas. 35 Hen. VI, f. 56, pl. 2.

named or condit[ional]. Therefore, this includes both *privilegium* but *privata lex* or *privatio legis*. And there is a difference between a gift of all but trees and of all but goods because, in the first case, apple trees and fruit trees do not pass and, in the second, but clothes. But, if it be with such an addition as here, it would pass. 14 Hen. VIII, 2; C. 3, Twyne's case.[1]

And because he objected that knighthood is not consistent with ecclesiastical possession, it is not so because he said that, here, Popham said that he had seen a commission to a bishop to make all the priests within his diocese knights and of this came Sir John and Sir Thomas ordinary in their appellations.

And this was the effect of his argument because he, as all who argued, insisted much upon 10 Eliz., Dy. 277, and Quarles' and Boyer's case,[2] which see before etc.

More 139b.[3]

[Other reports of this case: Benloe 168, 185, 73 E.R. 1031, 1043, BL MS. Gg.2.30, ff. 59v, 68; J. Bridgman 32, 123 E.R. 1179; Godbolt 392, 78 E.R. 231; W. Jones 182, 82 E.R. 96, BL MS. Hargr. 317, f. 181; Latch 89, 82 E.R. 289, HLS MS. 1235, f. 33; 1 Gwillim 410; 1 Eagle & Younge 340; H. Winch, *Le Beau Pledeur: A Book of Entries* (1680), p. 342; BL MS. Hargr. 38, ff. 26, 104v, 106v, 221; BL MS. Lansd. 1092, f. 60; CUL MS. Hh.2.1, f. 235v; CUL MS. Ll.3.13, f. 70.]

[This case is cited in Star v. Ellyot (Ex. 1680), 1 Freeman 299, 22 E.R. 1236, 89 E.R. 217, Dodd 288.]

281

Hamond v. Slade

(K.B. Pas. 3 Car. I, 1627)

An obligee can sue an action of debt without having first made a formal demand for payment.

---

[1] *King's College, Cambridge v. Hekker* (1522), YB Mich. 14 Hen. VIII, f. 2, pl. 2, 119 Selden Soc. 98; *Attorney General v. Twyne* (1601), 3 Coke Rep. 80, 76 E.R. 809, also Moore K.B. 638, 72 E.R. 809.

[2] *Stathome's Case* (1568), 3 Dyer 277, 73 E.R. 621, 1 Gwillim 132, 1 Eagle & Younge 59; *Quarles v. Spurling* (1602), *ut supra*; *Urrey v. Bowyer* (1611), 2 Brownlow & Goldesborough 20, 123 E.R. 791, 1 Gwillim 250, 1 Eagle & Younge 214, BL MS. Hargr. 385, f. 80 (Calthorpe's reports).

[3] *Whitton v. Weston* (1628), BL MS. Add. 35961, f. 203, pl. 26, BL MS. Lansd. 1083, f. 295v, pl. 26 (Widdrington's reports).

BL MS. Add. 35961, f. 65v, pl. 31

Between Hammond and Slade, *quod intratur* Hil. 2 [Car. I], rot. [*blank*], one was bound to pay so much upon the return of such a ship. And the obligee brought [an action of] debt for it. And he showed that the ship was returned, but he did not show that he gave notice of it to the obligor. And this [was] moved in arrest of judgment.

And [it was] ruled that notice was not necessary.

And JONES remembered the case of Hodges and More, before [. . .],[1] and he said that thus it was ruled then.

282

Jacob v. Alden

(K.B. Pas. Car. I, 1627)

An amendment to the record can be made to correct a clerical negligence but not a clerical ignorance.

BL MS. Add. 35961, f. 65v, pl. 32

Between Jacob and Alden in [an action of] debt against the heir, the bill upon the file was *debet et detinet*, but all of the other records, *viz.* the plea roll and *nisi prius* roll, were *detinet tantum*, and it was because, as the attorney confessed, after he had filed the bill, he enquired whether it was good in the *debet et detinet* and, by the advice of the other attorneys, he altered it and all of the other process. And because this here was not the negligence of the clerk, but the ignorance, and that it was not a slip but *ex proposito*, it could not be amended; otherwise if it had not been *ex consulto*. See C. 5, 36a, Walcot's case,[2] that such a slip is not amendable.

And query if it be not to be intended there as the bill upon the file and all are false because, often, the amendment is in a matter of substance if, by the paper book or precedent records, it appears to be the omission of the clerk who transcribed it.

[Other reports of this case: Latch 203, 82 E.R. 346, HLS MS. 1235, f. 94v; BL MS. Lansd. 1092, f. 186v.]

---

[1] *Hodges v. Moore* (1626), above, Nos. 65, 71.

[2] *Lloyd v. Walcot* (1588), 5 Coke Rep. 36, 77 E.R. 108, also 3 Leonard 206, 74 E.R. 635.

283

Anonymous

(K.B. Pas. Car. I, 1627)

The court of king's bench has the jurisdiction to punish disturbances and disruptions of leets.

BL MS. Add. 35961, f. 65v, pl. 33

It was moved for an attachment against certain bailiffs who arrested one who was sworn in a leet so that no verdict could be given nor presentment made. And [it was] said that it belonged to this court of which the leet is derived to punish all disturbances done to the service of the king, as a leet is etc., which was granted by the court. But they said that they must have some matter of record to ground the attachment upon and not to award it upon a bare surmise. And on account of this, it was said to the counsel to procure the attorney of the king to inform against them for this matter. And upon this, and attachment will issue.

[Other reports of this case: Latch 198, 82 E.R. 344.]

284

Payman v. Brantingham

(K.B. Pas. Car. I, 1627)

Where a husband and wife jointly made a lease, they can sue jointly as co-plaintiffs in an action of debt to recover the unpaid rent.

BL MS. Add. 35961, f. 65v, pl. 34

In [a writ of] error between Payman and Brantingham of Gray's Inn, *quod intratur* Trin. 20 Jac. [I, rot.] 101, the error assigned was because the action of debt for rent reserved upon a lease made by a husband and wife was brought by both.

And *Brantingham* cited 7 Edw. IV, 6,[1] upon which he said that he relied when he brought the action.

And thus the court conceived that there was no error because he can join with his wife or otherwise at his pleasure. Both ways are good enough.

Here follow three cases moved one day when I was absent.

---

[1] YB Pas. 7 Edw. IV, f. 5, pl. 16 (1467).

285

Gunter v. Gunter

(K.B. Pas. Car. I, 1627)

A writ of error must show the authority of the lower court unless the lower court is one whose jurisdiction is a matter of judicial notice.

BL MS. Add. 35961, f. 65v, pl. 35

Between Grinter and Grinter in [a writ of] error of a judgment given in the court of the Isle of Ely, the main exception was upon the style of the court, which was *placita tenta coram Thomae Athow, capitalis justiciariis infra Insulam praedictam*. And it did not show by what authority the court was held, *virtute litterarum patentium* or otherwise. And it was held error because, even though the entry paravail need not be otherwise, yet, when any plea is certified from an inferior court, it must also show their authority to hold the plea and this difference answers the precedents of such entry in the court of Ely. But, if the court paravail be such of which jurisdiction the court takes notice, the recital of authority is not necessary, as a county palatine and the court of great sessions in Wales, which was constituted by Parliament, and Ely is not now, though it could be that it was, a county palatine in ancient times because it does not have exclusive power as a county palatine and things done there can be tried *in corpore comitatus*, and the recovery of land there in the [court of] common pleas is good. And yet a writ of error there is directed *capitali justiciario* of Ely, but this is by the Statute of 27 Hen. VIII[1] etc. And [for] this cause, the judgment was reversed if cause not be shown to the contrary.

[Other reports of this case: Godbolt 380, 78 E.R. 224; Latch 180, 82 E.R. 335, HLS MS. 1235, f. 81; Noy 90, 74 E.R. 1056; BL MS. Lansd. 1092, f. 151v; CUL MS. Ll.3.13, f. 193v.]

---

[1] Stat. 27 Hen. VIII, c. 24, s. 18 (*SR*, III, 557–558).

286

Taylor v. Hodgekin

(K.B. Pas. Car. I, 1627)

This case involved the construction of a will.

BL MS. Add. 35961, f. 65v, pl. 36

Between Taylor and Hodgekin in [an action of] *ejectione firmae, quod intratur* Trin. 1 Car. [I, rot.] 189, upon a special verdict, the case was thus. One Moye, tenant in fee of certain lands held in socage, had no issue, but he had four persons who are his heirs at common law, *viz.* M., A., D., [and] E.; M. died having issue M., her daughter, who, with her husband, is the lessor of the plaintiff. Moye, by his testament, devised the lands to Susan, his wife, for life and, after her death, the remainder to be equally divided among his sisters and their heirs. And whether M., the daughter, will have one part was the sole question.

And *Whitfield* of Gray's Inn argued for the daughter that she will have [it] because it appears in Butler's case, C. 3, and C. 10, 76,[1] that wills will be taken according to the intent of the devisor. And this is the reason of 7 Edw. VI, B., *Demise*, 39,[2] that a devise to give or to sell and to do [it at] his pleasure is a fee simple. And the intent here appears that the daughter of M. will have one part or otherwise the words 'heirs' will be merely idle. And the rule is given [in] C. 1, 95,[3] that such a construction is to be made that all of the parts can take effect according to the intent of the party and without rejecting any; this [is] of conveyances, *a fortiori* in this of a will. And it was not requisite to add those words 'or their heirs' to make the sisters, who then were living, take. Therefore, that was only to the intent to make the daughter to take what otherwise she could not have taken. And the particle 'or' will be taken as the copulative for 'and' as in Malory's case, C. 5.[4] And thus it will be divided among the sisters who are living and the heir of M., who is [*blank*].

[In] Trin. 7 Jac., one was bound in an obligation to one upon a condition that he will allow his wife to devise £500 of goods to her son or daughter, and the wife devised £500 to the son and daughter, and she died. And it was resolved that it

---

[1] *Butler v. Baker* (1591), 3 Coke Rep. 25, 76 E.R. 684, also Popham 87, 79 E.R. 1199, 1 Anderson 348, 123 E.R. 510, Moore K.B. 254, 72 E.R. 563, Gouldsborough 84, 75 E.R. 1011, 3 Leonard 271, 74 E.R. 678; *The Chancellor of Oxford's Case* (1613), 10 Coke Rep. 53, 56, 77 E.R. 1006, 1010.

[2] 7 Edw. VI, Brooke, Abr., *Devise*, pl. 39 (1553).

[3] *Wolfe v. Shelley* (1579–1581), 1 Coke Rep. 88, 95, 76 E.R. 199, 212–213, also 1 Anderson 69, 123 E.R. 358, Moore K.B. 136, 72 E.R. 490, Jenkins 249, 145 E.R. 176, 3 Dyer 373, 73 E.R. 838.

[4] *Mallory v. Payn* (1601), 5 Coke Rep. 111, 77 E.R. 228, also Cro. Eliz. 805, 832, 78 E.R. 1033, 1058.

was a good prosecution or the condition. And there, '*aut*' was taken for '*et*'. And there, Warburton said, if one devise all of his goods in Dale or Sale and he dies, it is good for all in Dale and Sale.

And thus he concluded.

Justice JONES: If one devise land to his sisters equally to be divided, what estate have they? Certainly, but for life. Thus, the word 'heir' is to limit the estate to be a fee simple, and so to make the disjunctive here for a copulative makes it more strong against the plaintiff.

Note: Here, he devised to his sisters, being his heirs; the averment [was] good.

[See] after, 93, more of this.[1]

[Other reports of this case: Godbolt 362, 78 E.R. 213; BL MS. Hargr. 38, f. 179.]

287

Ashfield v. Ashfield

(Part 3)
(K.B. Pas. Car. I, 1627)

BL MS. Add. 35961, f. 65v, pl. 37

The case of Ashfield and Ashfield, of which see before, 26, p. 28,[2] was now argued again by Serjeant *Crawley* on the side of the plaintiff. And he made one sole question of it, if an infant copyholder of inheritance makes a lease for sixty years orally rendering rent and, at full age, accepts the rent, whether this lease and acceptance will bind the infant. And he thought the lease simply void and thus his acceptance could not make it good. And he took this ground, that an infant cannot do an act by a contract, be it orally or written, that can be a wrong to another or a prejudice to himself. And this lease for years is a wrong to the lord and a prejudice to the infant because, by it, he forfeits a copyhold of inheritance and the lord, by it, [is] entitled to have an assize. First, the infant will not be bound by acts that are a prejudice to himself by which, if an infant command another to disseise J.S. who does it, the infant is not a disseisor. Thus, if one disseise one to the use of an infant who afterwards agrees, this does not make him a disseisor. And an infant by a nude deed cannot prejudice himself. And for this [is] 26 Hen. VIII, 2;[3] if an infant grants an advowson and, at full age, confirms the estate of

---

[1] *Taylor v. Hodgekin* (1627), BL MS. Add. 35961, f. 99, pl. 8, BL MS. Lansd. 1083, f. 169, pl. 8 (Widdrington's reports).

[2] For earlier proceedings in this case, see above, Nos. 172, 189.

[3] YB Trin. 26 Hen. VIII, f. 2, pl. 1 (1534).

the grantees, it is a void confirmation. 4 Edw. II, F., *Release* 49;[1] [where there are] two joint tenants under age [and] one releases to the other, it is void. 18 Edw IV, 2;[2] [where an] infant leases for years without a deed, it [is] simply void. And [see] another case put there. And, if a contract be made by an infant that has a mixture[3] [to] the prejudice to the infant, it is void, as 5 Jac., between Bendloes and Holliday; an obligation upon a condition by an infant, though it be for apparel, [was] void by reason of a penalty; [it is] otherwise for a single obligation.

And here, the infant did a wrong to the lord also because, being in the manor only as a tenant at will, he made a lease for years, which was a disseisin at common law before the Statute of Westminster II, c. 25,[4] as appears [by] 3 Edw. IV, 17; 2 Edw. IV, 10; 10 Edw. IV, 18,[5] by which, upon the whole matter, the lease is void and the acceptance cannot make a void lease good.

If, in this case, he had made a feoffment in fee that will pass by livery, perhaps, it had been but a defeasible forfeiture.

And on the other side, it was argued that, if it had not been of copyhold land, but of other land, that a lease for years rendering rent clearly is not void, but solely voidable, and this was granted by the whole court, as appears [by] 7 Edw. IV, 6; 18 Edw. IV, 2; 9 Hen. VI, 5; and C., Paramor's case; and L. 547.[6] [Where] the lessee of an infant for twenty years leased for ten years, the infant, at full age, confirmed the estate of the second lessee, that, there the confirmation [was] good, which proves [that] the lease made by the infant is not void, but voidable and rendering rent is to be intended. And for the case of 13 Hen. VII, 17,[7] by Keble, upon a command by an infant to make a disseisin to his use, there, there cannot be intended any recompense to the infant; thus, the matter is whether the infant's being a copyholder would alter it. And he thought not because the lease made by him was a forfeiture, which proves that the lease was once good because the mere attempting was not a forfeiture if it not be by matter of record. Hil. 37 Eliz., rot. 99, [in the] king's bench;[8] a copyholder leased for three years to begin [at] Michaelmas, and it was oral; this was a forfeiture though it be *in futuro*; and, to the

---

    [1] *Ingelose v. Spytling* (1310), YB Mich. 4 Edw. II, Selden Soc., vol. 22, p. 140, pl. 36, YB Mich. 4 Edw. II, p. 84, Fitzherbert, Abr., *Reless*, pl. 49.

    [2] YB Pas. 18 Edw. IV, ff. 1, 2, pl. 7 (1478).

    [3] Sic in MS.

    [4] Stat. 13 Edw. I, Stat. of Westminster, c. 25 (*SR*, I, 84–85).

    [5] YB Mich. 3 Edw. IV, f. 17, pl. 12 (1463); YB Mich. 12 Edw. IV, f. 12, pl. 5 (1472); YB Mich. 10 Edw. IV, 49 Hen. VI, f. 18, pl. 22, 47 Selden Soc. 160 (1470 x 1471).

    [6] YB Pas. 7 Edw. IV, f. 5, pl. 16 (1467); YB Pas. 18 Edw. IV, f. 1, pl. 7 (1478); YB Pas. 9 Hen. VI, f. 5, pl. 14 (1431); *Paramour v. Yardley* (1579), 2 Plowden 539, 75 E.R. 794; T. Littleton, *Tenures*, sect. 547.

    [7] YB Hil. 13 Hen. VII, f. 17, pl. 21 (1498).

    [8] *East v. Harding* (1595–1597), Moore K.B. 392, 72 E.R. 648, Owen 63, 74 E.R. 901, Cro. Eliz. 292, 498, 78 E.R. 546, 749.

same purpose, it was agreed [in] Trin. 36 Eliz. in one Browning's case. And such a lessee for years of a copyhold can maintain [an action of] *ejectione firmae*.

And Justice JONES said that thus it was resolved in one Petre's case in the [court of] common pleas when he was there.

Hil. 38 Eliz., Haddon and Arrowsmith's case;[1] the lord of a copyholder licensed him to make a lease for two years *si tam diu vixerit*; he leased for two years absolute, and [it was] adjudged no forfeiture because it was included that, by his death, it was gone. And the case of an infant is not excepted out of this ground because, here, there was a recompense to the infant. And I conceive that the lease here made by the infant was not a forfeiture because, though it draws the inheritance out of the lord, yet, upon the entry of the infant, it is reducible [?]. The infant will be bound by the conditions in a deed, 31 Ass. 17b, *Coverture*, 17,[2] but he will not be bound by conditions in law that are easily[3] annexed to his estate. C. 8, 44b;[4] an infant tenant for life made a feoffment; this was not a forfeiture; *contra* if he levied a fine, if he did not reverse it during his nonage, it is a forfeiture. 9 Hen. VII, 24;[5] a woman infant [was] disseised; she took a husband [. . .][6] did not prejudice him, by which etc.

And afterwards, judgment was given for the plaintiff.

[Other reports of this case: Benloe 188, 73 E.R. 1046, CUL MS. Gg.2.30, f. 69v; Godbolt 364, 78 E.R. 214; W. Jones 157, 82 E.R. 84; Latch 199, 82 E.R. 344, HLS MS. 1235, f. 93; Noy 92, 74 E.R. 1058; BL MS. Hargr. 38, ff. 124v, 147v; BL MS. Lansd. 1092, f. 182v; CUL MS. Ll.3.13, f. 229v.]

---

[1] *Haddon v. Arrowsmith* (1596), Cro. Eliz. 461, 78 E.R. 699, Owen 72, 74 E.R. 910, Popham 105, 79 E.R. 1214.

[2] YB 31 Edw. III, Lib. Ass., p. 188, pl. 17 (1357), Brooke, Abr., *Coverture & Infancie*, pl. 71.

[3] silently [?].

[4] *Whittingham's Case* (1603), 8 Coke Rep. 42, 77 E.R. 537.

[5] YB Pas. 9 Hen. VII, f. 24, pl. 10 (1495).

[6] discent est ject *MS.*

Index of Names
of Persons and Places

[These references are to case numbers, not page numbers.]

Andrews, barrister, 262, 265

Ashley, Francis, serjeant, 61, 144

Askwith, W., 101

Athow, Thomas, serjeant, 49, 160, 215, 227, 263, 285

Audley, town clerk of Bedford, 80

Ayleworth, Umfry, Dr., 269

Baker, George, 82

Baker, Thomas, 82

Bankes, John, barrister, 26, 27, 39, 55, 101, 143, 152, 158, 161, 175, 196, 229, 252, 264

Barksdale, barrister, 168

Beddingfield, Thomas, barrister, 73

Bedford, town of, 80

Beneham, manor of, 211

Blackston, Sir William, 39

Bowyer, Sir William, 26

Bramston, John, serjeant, 61, 106, 225, 249

Brantingham, barrister, 284

Bridgman, John, serjeant, 9, 30, 31

Bridgnorth, Shropshire, 45, 127

Bristol, bishopric of, 101

Brome, secondary, 210

Browne, clerk, 85, 130

Browne, Sir Robert, 188

Bulstrode, Edward, barrister, 87

Bury St. Edmunds, Suffolk, 251

Button, Sir William, 108

Calfe, Benjamin, 149

Calfe, Joshua, 149

Calthorpe, Sir Henry, barrister, 39, 73, 98, 102, 149, 152, 235, 257, 262, 265, 278

Camberwell, Kent, 5

Carlisle, dean of, 266

Clarke, Nicholas, 118

Clarke, Sir Simon, 14

Cokersand Abbey, Lancashire, 27

Crawley, Francis, serjeant, 137, 280, 287

Crewe, Sir Thomas, king's serjeant, 7, 10, 54, 61, 70, 115, 206

Davenport, Humphrey, serjeant, 88, 94, 225, 239, 266, 271

Davies, Sir John, king's serjeant, 27

Dawberne, attorney, 81

Deanfield, 181

Dixon, bailiff of Whitechappel, 228

Dorrell, barrister, 69

Duck, Arthur, Dr., 135, 226

Eden, barrister, 226

Ely, Isle of, 285

Finch, Sir Henry, king's serjeant, 13; recorder, 131

Fish, Sir William, 252

Fortescue, Sir John, 3

Fox, Ulysses, 61

Gouldsmith, barrister, 26

Gransgrove, 182

Hales Hall, Norfolk, 12

Hamond, James, 12

Harding, manor of, 3

Hardington, Somerset, 118

Harris, alderman of Oxford, 270

Harvey, Sir Francis, 143, 197

Heath, Robert, attorney general, 133

Henden, Edward, serjeant, 52, 82, 131, 178, 213, 217, 263

Hetley, Thomas, serjeant, 3, 94, 140
Hitcham, Robert, serjeant, 12, 44, 134,
    159, 261, 274, 279
Holborn, barrister, 264
Hubard, Anthony, 12
Hubard, James, 12
Huntington, earl of, Henry, 54
Hutton, Matthew, archbishop of York, 101
Isley, Henry, 264
Isley, John, 264
Jermyn, Philip, barrister, 103, 153, 168
Jesson, sheriff of Sarum, 72
Jones, Griffith, 186
Kedgewin, Sir William, 4
Keeling, clerk, 269
Kellie, Lord, 211
Langhorne, barrister, 252
Limerick, bishopric of, 101
Littleton, Edward, barrister, 142, 230, 270
Maidstone, Kent, 131
Martin, mayor of Northampton, 42
Matthew, Toby, archbishop of York, 101
Molineux, Lady, 13
Murray, earl of Tullibardine, 141, 260
Newton Flotman, Norfolk, 233
Norris, Lord, 211
Northampton, Northants., 137, 233
Norwich, deanery of, 73
Noy, William, barrister, 8, 29, 44, 71, 75,
    80, 101, 118, 131, 145, 147, 154,
    157, 162, 175, 196, 270, 280
Orford, Suffolk, 200
Oxford, City of, 54, 270
Plowden, Edmund, 215
Poynes, Sir John, 118
Poynes, Robert, 118
Reynells, Sir George, 67, 136
Richardson, Sir Thomas, king's serjeant,
    26, 132, 155, 193
Rivet, Sir Thomas, 26

St. Neots, Huntingdonshire, 179
Saul, Thomas, 118
Savile, Sir Thomas, 129
Sheires, John, 52
Shelley, Sir John, 3
Shelley, William, 3
Stone, John, barrister, 76, 220
Strowde, Sir Richard, 188
Sudbury, borough of, 244
Sundridge, Kent, 264
Sutton, Dr., chancellor of Gloucester, 267
Sydenham, Alexander, 118
Sydenham, Elizabeth, 118
Sydenham, Joan, 118
Sydenham, John, 118
Sydenham, Maude, 118
Taverham, manor of, 73
Thornborough, John, dean of York, 101
Thynne, Egremond, serjeant, 259
Towse, William, serjeant, 93
Upley, Agnes, 52
Upley, John, 52
Upley, William, 52
Vanlore, Sir Peter, 211
Wade, Lady, 60
Wade, Sir William, 60
Walden, sheriff of Sarum, 72
Ward, John, 4
Weston, Sir William, 29
Whistler, barrister, 139
Whitfield, barrister, 286
Whitton, parson of Marrow, 29
Whitwell, barrister, 92
Wiltshire, undersheriff, 237
Windsor, Berkshire, 95, 173
Woolrich, barrister, 140, 236
Wortley, knight, 129
Yelverton, Henry, barrister, 3
York, deanery of, 101

Subject Index

[These references are to case numbers, not page numbers.]

Abuse of Process, 42, 199
Account, Writs of
    Infants, against, 238
    Necessaries, for, 238
Adjournment to Reading, 19
Administrators, *See* Executors
Admiralty, Court of
    Maritime contracts, 56, 58, 262
    Prohibition, writs of, 32
Appeals, *See* Error, Writs of
Arbitration, 188
Arrest
    Common bad fame, 110
    Demise of the crown, 201
    Victim, by, 110
Assaults
    Punishment for, 129
    Royal palace, in, 129
Assignments
    See also Powers of Appointment
    Crown, of, 3
    Rents, 30
Assize Justices, Powers of, 209
Assumpsit, Writs of
    Breach alleged, 145
    Conditions pleaded, 65
    Consideration, 134, 142, 164
    Contracts not to sue, 76, 142, 164
    Fraud, 240
    Indemnity bonds, 45
    Infant, against, 111
    Marriage, for, 65
    Necessaries, for, 111
    Non-payment, for, 140
    Notice pleaded, 65

    Payee not pleaded, 140
    Payment demanded, 24
    Pleaded sufficiently, 111, 134
    Releases, 223
    Sheriffs, 1
    Value, 240
    Warranties, express, 240
Attorneys-at-law and Barristers
    Defamation of, 81, 128
    Malpractice of, 116
    Struck off roll, 43
Attorneys-in-fact
    Barretry, 40, 276
    Generally, 262
Audita Querela, Writs of
    Bail, 46
    Executors, by, 77
    Generally, 15, 114, 116
Avowry, 60, 68, 213
Bail
    Appeal pending, 157
    Audita querela, 46
    Discharged by death, 149
    Extent of liability, 85
    Generally, 62, 85, 141, 149, 252
    Malicious prosecution, 199
Bailiffs, *See* Sheriffs
Barretry, 40, 276
Barristers, *See* Attorneys-at-law
Bastards, Support of, 78
Battery, 277
Bells, 182
Bequests, *See* Executors
Bishops, 101

Bonds
  See also Contracts; Creditors
  Bastards, support of, 78
  Estoppel by, 78
  Payable, date, 162
  Peace, 90
Box of Charters, 248
Brasenose College, 54
Bridges, Repair of, 179
Burglary, 102
Canon Law, 107, 255, 267
Capias ad Satisfaciendum, 1, 149
Capias Utlagatum, 1
Capias, Writs of
  Demise of the crown, 201
  Generally, 55
Case, Writs of
  See also Assumpsit
  Battery, 277
  Commons, tort to, 139
  Co-plaintiffs, 139
  Defamation, 2, 47, 108, 146, 153, 244,
    247, 261, 277
  Detinue, 248
  Easements, for, 69
  Escapes, for, 228
  False arrest, for, 110
  Forbearance to sue, 164
  Fraud, 116, 240
  Generally, 63
  Infants, against, 154
  Innkeepers, against, 87
  Malicious prosecution, 199
  Non-feasance of officer, 237
  Pleadings insufficient, 76, 154
  Process upon, 275
  Releases, 79
  Reliefs, for, 98
  Riparian rights, 69
  Sheriffs, against, 237
  Survivability of, 228
  Usury, 123
  Way, rights of, 181
  Wife, torts to, 277
Cattle Damage Feasant, 59
Certiorari, See Error, Writs of

Chancery, Court of
  Affidavits false, 93
  Commissioners murdered, 57
  Depositions not records, 254
  Interrogatories, 105
  Masters, 93, 105
  Oath false, 105
  Open always, 55
  Original writs, 55
  Pleadings not records, 254
  Sharp practices in, 219
Charitable Uses, 54
Charters, 248
Churches
  See also Tithes
  Advowsons, 268
  Bells, 182
  Chancellors, 267
  Commendams, 101
  Corporations, 73
  Deans and chapters, 60, 73, 101
  Disturbances in, 51
  Incumbents, 126
  Leases, 73, 101, 234
  Misnomers, 73
  Mortuaries, 191
  Parish boundaries, 99
  Patronages, 126
  Pensions, 92
  Presentations revoked, 255
  Rectories, 69
  Repairs to, 38, 182
  Seats in, 51
Cities and Towns, 80, 97, 270
Civil Law, Two-Witness Rule, 53, 74
Commendams, 101
Conditions
  Contractual, 58, 65
  Conveyances, in, 54
  Generally, 86
  Personal, 3
  Pleaded, 65
Conspiracy, Actions of, 20
Consultation, Writs of, *See* Prohibition
Contempt of court, 221

Contracts
  See also Debts, Writs of
  Bonds, 1, 4
  Breach of, 216
  Conditions, 58, 65
  Consideration, 76, 134, 164, 223
  Construed, 208
  Conveyance, to make, 241
  Co-obligees, 58
  Debts, 1, 4
  Demand for payment, 161
  Estoppel by, 78
  Executory, 188
  Forbearance to sue, 164
  Fraud as to value, 240
  Freight, 262
  Further assurances, 241
  Horses, 240
  Incumbrances on land, 190
  Infants, by, 111, 238
  Intent of parties, 208
  Joint and several, 58
  Jointures, 216
  Maritime, 56, 58, 262
  Marriage, 145
  Necessaries, for, 111, 238
  Non-payment, 140
  Not to sue, 76
  Obligors, joint, 114
  Performance of, 3, 58
  Personal, 205
  Pleading of, 58, 65
  Release of claims, 223
  Rent, to pay, 161, 259
  Sheriffs, 1
  Statutes, 15
  Survivability, 205
  Value, 240
  Void, 1
  Warranties, 240
Conveyances
  See also Powers of Attorney; Trusts
  Attorneys-in-fact, 54, 73
  Charitable uses, 54
  Conditions, 54
  Contract to make, 241

Copyholds
  Generally, 12
  Reliefs, 98
  Crown, from, 211
  Dedimus potestatem, 241
  Disseisin, after, 211
  Enrollments, 156
  Fines, 118
  Form of, 86
  Fraudulent, 133
  Further assurances, 241
  Leases
    Generally, 156
    Reservations, 73
  Manors exchanged, 188
  Misnomers, 73
  Reservations, 73
  Reversions, of, 156
  Roman Catholics, by, 133
  Title after disseisin, 211
  Validity of, 118
Coroners' inquests, 230
Corporations
  See also Churches
  Cities and Towns, 80, 97, 270
  Misnomer, 73
Costs, Court
  See also Fees
  Discontinuances, 148
  Filing fees in trover, 130
  Generally, 239
  Pardoned, 132, 155
  Statutory, 18
Counties, Repair of Bridges, 179
County Courts, 272
Covenant, Writs of
  Breach pleaded, 216
  Charter parties, 58
  Conveyance, to make, 241
  Co-obligees, 58
  Exchange of lands, 188
  Executory contract, 188
  Further assurances, 241
  Marriage contracts, 205
  Powers of attorney, 205
  Promise to pay, 176

Creditors
 See also Bonds; Executions; Sheriffs
 Bail sued, 199
 Capias ad satisfaciendum, 1, 149
 Judgments
  Confession of, 16
  Outlawry quashed, 66
 Judgment debtor released, 41
 Liens, 15
 Priorities of, 77
 Statutes acknowledged, 15
Crimes, *See* individual crimes
Crown
 Assignee of condition, 3
 Demise of, 13, 22, 49, 197, 201, 202
 Judgments absolute, 220
 Patents, 211
 Presentations revoked, 255
 Protections, 13
 Receiver of customs, 246
Customs, Local, 119
Deans and chapters, 60, 73, 101
Debt, Writs of
 Administrator, against, 166
 Bond to sheriff, 67
 Co-plaintiffs, 284
 Concessit solvere, 119
 Conditions, 86
 Court baron, in, 183
 Date payable, 162
 Debet et detinet, 4
 Demand for payment, 161, 281
 Detinet tantum, 4
 Escape, upon, 136, 170
 Executions upon, 72, 252
 Executors, 77, 82, 114, 127
 Foreign money, for, 4
 Generally, 66, 251
 Heirs, against, 26
 Insufficient pleading, 259, 282
 Judgments, on, 183
 Middlesex, bills of, 159
 Obligation, upon, 86
 Payment demanded, 24
 Performance, 86
 Place fictitious, 4
 Pleading, 4, 180

Record, on, 214
Records, 282
Rent, for, 124, 156, 161, 242, 259, 284
Third persons, 242
Tithes, for, 29, 112
Variances, 269
Wager of law, 183
Wife's joint action, 284
Defamation
 Adultery, 2
 Allegations of, 108
 Attorneys-at-law, 81, 128
 Bankrupt, 47, 146
 Clergyman, 2, 107
 Ecclesiastical courts, 155
 Diseased, 2
 Felony, accusation of, 153, 233, 247
 Infant, by, 261
 In mitiori sensu, 233
 Justices of peace, of, 108
 Murder accusation, 153
 Official malfeasance, 108
 Pander, 155
 Perjury, charge of, 254
 Reproachful words, 81
 Scandal, 14
 Trade, one's, 244
 Tradesman bankrupt, 146
 Venue, 247
Delegates, Court of, 255
Demurrers
 Generally, 37, 58, 59, 68, 72, 78, 124,
  161, 172, 176, 202, 216
 Pleading indefinite, 60
 Pleas, to, 10
Depositions
 Admissible, not, 23
 Perpetuate testimony, 23
Detinue, Writs of
 Box of charters, 248
 Debt as defense, 258
 Possession of goods, 48
 Rebail, failure to, 258
Devises, *See* Executors
Dogs, 59
Durham, County Palatine, 147

Ecclesiastical Courts
  See also Prohibition; Tithes
  Appeals in, 8, 132
  Canon law, use of, 107
  Costs, court, 132
  Evidence in, 250
  Jurisdiction
    Administrators, 256
    Classified, 155
    Clergy competence, 267
    Defamation, 107
    Disturbances in churches, 51
    Estate of decedent, 256
    Laymen, over, 107
    Mortuaries, 191
    Parish boundaries, 99
    Patronages, 126
    Pensions, 92
    Repair of churches, 182
    Seats in churches, 51
    Tithes, 8, 74, 99
  Legacies, 21
  Pardons, 155
  Two-witness rule, 53, 74
  Witnesses refused in, 250
Ejectment, Writs of
  Allegations insufficient, 184
  Ancient demesne, 7
  Co-defendants, 239
  Disseisin, 211
  Forfeitures, 12
  Generally, 3, 52, 118, 210
  Holdover lessees, 211
  Land devised badly, 173
  Leases, 54
  Place of ejectment, 184, 198
  Releases of claims, 223, 239
  Testator's intent, 286
  Title in issue, 211
Error, Writs of
  Appearance cures error, 122
  Authority of lower court, 285
  Bail, 157
  Box of charters, 248
  Certiorari, writs of, 57, 127, 147, 221
  Clerical errors, 197, 210, 213
  Co-plaintiffs, 284

Coram nobis, 117, 252
Customs, local, pleaded, 119
Dates of, 117
Declaration indefinite, 232
Defamation, 244, 261, 277
De minimis, 204
Diminution of record, 63
Durham, to, 147
Ejectment badly pleaded, 198
Executions, 157
Generally, 45
Imprisonment during, 149
Infants' contracts, 238
In nullo est erratum, 119, 127, 171
Joinder in error, 119, 127
Judgment
  Below bad, 120
  Damages, for, 231
  Executed, how, 266
Lower court's jurisdiction, 221
Misnomers, 197
Outlawries reversed, 264, 269, 272
Party dead, 171
Pleadings below, 180, 269
Process
  Cured, 275
  Lacking, 55
Proffer of deeds
  Generally, 63, 143, 266, 279
  Insufficient, 127, 285
Record amended, 143, 210
Release of claims, 223
Rent, 259, 284
Rider to record, 127
Scire facias, writs of, 127
Supersedeas, writs of, 16
Variances, for, 63
Venue, 57, 63
Verdict defective, 125, 251
Warranty, 240
Wife
  Suit for rent, 284
  Torts to, 277
Estoppel *in Pais*, 78
Evidence
  Affidavits, 148
  Depositions, 23

Intent of testator, 253
Judicial notice, 197
Perjured, 273
Two-witness rule, 53, 74
Witnesses in ecclesiastical courts, 250
Exchequer, Court of, 246
Executions
    See also Judgments; Sheriffs
    Bail pending appeal, 157
    Capias ad satisfaciendum, 1, 149
    Generally, 15, 131, 266
    Heirs, against, 26
    Protections, 141
    Scire facias, 26
Executors and Administrators
    Accounts of, 53
    Audita querela, 77, 114
    Escape of decedent's debtors, 228
    Heirs liable, 26
    Parties, as, 60
    Plene administravit, 21
    Powers of appointment, 52
    Renunciation of administration, 166
    Sheriff liable to, 228
    Suits against, 77, 82, 127, 279
    Suits by, 114
    Testator's intent, 52, 173, 253, 286
    Waste, liable for, 166
    Wills and devises
        Chattels, 253
        Legacies, 21
        Oral, 253
        Testator's intent, 52, 173, 253, 286
False Arrest, 42
False Imprisonment, 201
Fees
    See also Costs
    Filing for trover declarations, 130
    Jailer, of, 178
    Official, 72
Felony, Suspicion of, 110
Forcible Entries
    Copyholders, 215, 243
    Disseisin not alleged, 215
    Indictment defective, 34
    Moiety of a manor, 28

Restitution, 243
Tenants at will, 243
Fraud, 116, 219
Fraudulent Conveyances, 133
Gaolers, *See* Sheriffs
Habeas Corpus, Writs of
    Durham, into, 147
    Errors, to assign, 196
    House of Lords, by, 136
    Jailer's fees, 178
Heirs, *See* Executors
High Commission, Court of
    Church repairs, 38
    Clergy competence, 267
Homicide, 84
Horses, Sale of, 240
Imparlances, 7, 158, 201, 236
Imprisonment
    See also Sheriffs
    False arrest, for, 42, 201
Indictments
    Defective, 34, 35, 36, 105, 137, 160,
        222, 273, 276
    Sufficient, 40
    Treason, of, 20
Infants
    Contracts of, 238
    Copyholders, 172
    Defamation, 261
    Executors of, 154
    Guardians of, 154, 209, 261
    Leases by, 172
    Necessaries of, 111, 238
    Nonage pleaded, 154
    Suits against, 111, 154
    Venue, 261
Informations, 179
Innkeepers, 87
Jailers, *See* Sheriffs
Jesuits, 14
Judgments
    See also Errors, Writs of; Executions
    Arrest of, 2, 47, 65, 67, 76, 82, 87, 98,
        134, 138, 142, 145, 153, 154, 159, 162,
        169, 184, 233, 237, 259, 279, 281
    Audita querela, 15

Confession, by, 16
Damages, for, 231
Date of, 17, 113
Default, 98
Defeasible, 16
Form of, 231, 244, 269
Heirs, against, 26
Jeofails helps, 269
Liens, 15
Nihil dicit, 98, 261, 269
Non sum informatus, 55
Pleas, false, upon, 26
Recitals necessary, 45, 120
Reduced in London, 220
Stayed by court, 131, 136, 219
Supersedeas, 16
Juries, *See* Procedure
Jury, Grand, *Ignoramus*, 20
Justices of Peace, Award of Support by, 78
King, *See* Crown
Lawyers, *See* Attorneys-at-law
Leases, *See* Conveyances; Real Property
Leets, Disturbances in, 283
Libel, *See* Defamation
Liens
    See Judgments
    Heirs, binding, 26
London, City of
    Courts, 220
    Foreign attachments, 258
    Venue fictitious, 4
Maidstone, town of, 131
Malicious Prosecution, 199
Malpractice of Attorney, 116
Mandamus, Writs of
    Generally, 270
    Restitution, 80, 97
    Return false, 97
Maritime Contracts, 56, 58, 262
Marshals, *See* Sheriffs
Middlesex, Bills of, 159, 228
Misnomers
    Cured by amendment, 143
    Generally, 73, 269
Monstrans de droit, 3
Moritur cum persona, 228

Murder
    Bail, 57
    Generally, 230
    Homicide conviction, 84
    Venue impartial, 57
Nightwalking, 137
Nuisance
    Generally, 222
    Way, rights of, 36
Oaths, *See* Perjury
Obligations, *See* Contracts; individual
    torts
Officers, *See* Persons; Sheriffs
Outlawries Reversed, 66, 264
Oxford, City of, 270
Oxford University, 54
Pardons
    Costs, court, 132, 155
    Ecclesiastical courts, 155
    Generally, 95, 129
    Private prosecutions, 155
Parliament, Privilege of, 121
Parties
    See also Attorneys; Infants
    Additions, 159
    Co-defendants, 239
    Conspirators, 84
    Co-obligees, 58
    Co-plaintiffs, 139, 284
    Death of, 149, 171
    Disability, 158
    Heirs, 264
    Joint lessors, 284
    Joint tortfeasors, 262
    Judgment creditors, 66
    Outlawry quashed, 66, 264
    Rent reserved, 242
    Sheriffs as, 237
    Standing, lack of, 158
    Tenants in common, 139, 263
    Terre tenants, 264
    Tinners, 214
    Tort to wife, 277
    Trespass to land, 33
    Wife as lessor, 284
Patents, *See* Conveyances; Crown

Peace
    Breach of, in palace, 129
    Contra pacem, allegation of, 169
    Peace bonds, 90
Pensions, 92
Perjury
    Defamation, as, 254
    False affidavits, 93
    Generally, 273
    Indictment quashed, 105
    Oath in chancery, 105
Personal Property, *See* Detinue; Replevin;
    Trover
Persons
    See also Creditors; Crown; Executors;
        Infants; Parties; Sheriffs; Women
    Additions, 269
    Attorneys-at-law
        Defamation of, 81, 128
        Generally, 116
        Struck off roll, 43
    Attorneys-in-fact, 262
    Bankrupt, Defamation of, 47, 146
    Bastards, Support of, 78
    Bishops, 101
    Chancellors to bishops, 267
    Clergymen, Defamation of, 2, 107
    Commissioners in chancery killed, 57
    Deans and chapters, 60, 73, 101
    Incumbents of churches, 126
    Innkeepers, 87
    Jesuits, 14
    Masters in chancery, 93, 105
    Misnomers
        Cured by amendment, 143
        Generally, 73, 197, 269
    Officials of towns, 270
    Roman Catholics, 14, 133, 158
    Tailors, 111
    Tinners, 214
Pleas
    Ancient demesne, 6, 7
    Conclusions of, 7, 149, 158
    Consideration lacking, 164
    Double, 149
    False, 26
    General issue, 54, 118, 169

Imparlances, after, 7
Infancy, 238
In nullo est erratum, 119, 127, 171
Insufficient, 258
Justification, 5, 10, 202, 254
Ne unques administrator, 26
New promise, 45
Nihil debet, 156
Non assumpsit, 76, 142, 145
Non detinuit, 248
Non est factum, 82, 251
Not guilty, 3, 10, 12, 101, 139, 181,
    211, 228, 262
Nul tiel record, 214, 254
Pardons, 95, 129
Permission, of, 125
Pleading mercantile terms, 58
Plene administravit, 21, 127, 279
Protections, 13, 141
Puis darein continuance, 113
Releases, 45
Render to prison, 149
Res judicata, 102
Riens per descent, 26
Self defense, 5
Solvit ad diem, 162
Specificity of, 60
Sufficiency of, 176
Sworn, when, 247
Tender, 176
Traverses, 37
Venue waived by delay, 45
Void, 125
Powers of Appointment
    Assignments of, 3
    Married women, 52
    Widows, to, 52
Powers of Attorney, *See* Attorneys-in-fact;
    Real Property
Praemunire, 62
Privilege of Parliament, 121, 136
Procedure
    See also Bail; Costs; Demurrers; Error;
        Evidence; Executions; Judgments;
        Parties; Pleas; Venue; Verdicts
    Abatement, cured by imparlance, 158
    Affidavits, 93

Amendments, 282
Appearances
 Attorney, by, 171
 Dead person, 171
 Defects cured by, 122
 Generally, 55, 275
Arbitration, 124, 188
Avowry, 60, 68, 213
Capias, writs of, 1, 55, 201
Clerical errors, 244, 282
Contempt of court, 221
Continuances, 113
Craving oyer, 236
Criminal bail, 57
De injuria sua propria, 5, 125
Discontinuances, 108, 122, 148
Errors cured, 55
Executions
 Affirmation, after, 252
 Capias, by, 252
 Generally, 72
 How done, 266
Fees of officials, 72
Fictions, 159
Filing fees, 130
Filing in bad faith, 116
Guardians *ad litem*, 209
Imparlances, 7, 158, 201, 236
Issue joined, 82
Jeofails, 154, 261
Judicial notice, 197, 285
Juries, foreign, 57
Jurisdictional fictions, 159
Latitat, writs of, 237
Nonsuits, 108, 239
Outlawries reversed, 264, 269, 272
Peace bonds, 90
Pleadings cured, 154
Privilege, writs of, 121
Process, 55
Proffer of deeds, 279
Records amended, 282
Releases, 79, 223, 239
Repleader, 254, 261
Replies
 De injuria sua propria, 5, 125
 Generally, 111, 124, 254

Traverses, 5
Res judicata, 102
Respondeat ouster, 158
Standing to sue, 158
Variances, 63, 269
Verdicts amended, 213
Wager of law, 183
Prohibition, Writs of
 Admiralty pleadings, 32
 Canon law not applicable, 107
 Clergy competence, 267
 Consultation, after, 8, 132
 Debt on a record, 214
 Estates of decedents, 256
 Evidence refusal, 250
 Expiration of, 22, 49
 High commission, to, 38
 Leases, 96
 Libel withheld, 32
 Mortuaries, 191
 Pardon of offense, 155
 Parish boundaries, 99
 Patronages, 126
 Pensions, 92
 Presentations revoked, 255
 Refusal to allow plea, 21
 Repairs of churches, 182
 Requests, court of, 96
 Seats in churches, 51
 Stannary court, 214
 Tithes, 25, 27, 200
 Two-witness rule, 53, 74
 Wales, court of marches, 253
 Wills of chattels, 253
Property, *See* Conveyances; Detinue; Real
  Property; Replevin; Trover
Prostitution, Houses of, 137
Protections
 Attorney of court, by, 43
 Expiration of, 13
 Parliamentary, 43
 Pleaded, 141
 Security put in, 141
Quare impedit, Writs of, 255
Queen, *See* Crown
Quo warranto, Writs of, 131
Rabbits, 83

Reading, Adjournment to, 19
Real Property
    See also Churches; Conditions; Con-
      veyances; Ejectment; Executors;
      Forcible Entries; Tithes
    Advowsons, 268
    Ancient demesne, 6, 7
    Bailiff, 60
    Cattle damage feasant, 59
    Common
      Disturbed, 139
      Generally, 30
      Moors, 194
    Copyholders
      Forcible entries, 215, 243
      Forfeitures, 172
      Infants, 172
      Leases of, 172
      Reliefs, 98
      Rent unpaid, 61
    Disseisors, 211
    Easements, 69, 103
    Entails by copyholders, 212
    Entry denied, 123
    Forcible entries, 28, 34, 215, 243
    Forfeitures, 12, 61, 172
    Hedgebote, 25
    Houses, 124
    Incumbrances, leases as, 190
    Jointures, 216
    Leases
      Attornment, 96, 156
      Broken, 123
      Copyholds, of, 172
      Entry denied, 123
      Generally, 60
      Holdover lessees, 211
      Houses, of, 123
      Incumbrance, as, 190
      Infants, by, 172
      Joint lessors, 284
      Payments, 83
      Rent, 96
      Reservations, 73, 83
      Trees, 177
      Warrens, 83

Lessee as disseisor, 211
Liens on, 15
Life tenants, 177
Manors
    Advowsons, 268
    Customs of, 12, 212
    Entails, 212
    Exchange of, 188
    Forcible entries, 215, 243
    Forfeitures, 12, 61
    Moiety of, 28
    Reliefs, 98
Moors, 194
Nuisances, 222
Powers of appointment, 52
Powers of attorney, 205
Prescription, 69, 103, 181, 194
Privity of estate, 118
Purchasers, subsequent, 15
Re-entry, 263
Releases, 52
Reliefs, 98
Rents
    Attornment, 156
    Assignments, 30
    Date due, 156
    Demand for, 161
    Due, 98
    Lessor's death, 68
    Reserved, 30, 68, 242, 284
    Survivability, 30, 68
    Unpaid, 61
Reversions, sale of, 156
Riparian rights, 69
Roman Catholics, 133
Seats in churches, 51
Seisin pleaded, 60
Tenants at will, 243
Tenants in common, 139, 263
Trees, 177
Trusts, 3
Unity of possession, 69, 103
Warranties, 52, 118
Waste, 177
Water rights, 69
Way, rights of
    Generally, 36, 222

Termini of, 181
Unity of possession, 103
Widows, 52
Woods, 73
Receivers of Customs, 246
Records, *See* Error, Writs of; Procedure
Releases of Claims, 41, 79, 223, 239
Replevin, Writs of
  Avowry, 60, 213
  Generally, 68, 197
  Rents, 213
Requests, Court of, 96
Res judicata, 102
Restitution, *See Mandamus*
Restoration to Public Office, 270
Roman Catholics, 133, 158
Scire facias, Writs of
  Audita querela, 15
  Bail, 149
  Execution, for, 26
  Generally, 77, 141, 252
  Heirs, against, 26
  Wrongful, 199
Self Help for Cattle Damage Feasant, 59
Sewers, Commission of, 202
Sharp Practices, 219
Sheep Damage Feasant, 59
Sheriffs
  Arrest by, 110
  Bail, 46, 57
  Bailiffs, 1, 11, 144, 196, 201, 237, 282
  Bonds, 67
  Capias ad satisfaciendum, 149
  Contracts with, 1
  Duties of, 1
  Escapes, 136, 170, 228
  Executions released, 41, 223
  Fees, 72, 178
  Habeas corpus, 178
  Non-feasance, 237
  Prisoners of, 67
  Prisoners released, 41, 46
  Recaptures, 170
  Rescues, 11, 144, 196, 207
  Returns
    False, 237

Generally, 1, 11, 144, 149
Insufficient, 196, 207
Suits against, 237
Slander, *See* Defamation
Stannary Court, 214
Star Chamber, Court of, 219
Statutes Construed, 18
Supersedeas, Writs of, 16
Tailors, 111
Tithes
  Compounded for, 74
  Discharged, 27, 29
  Distrained wrongfully, 37
  Fish, 200
  Hospitaler land, 29
  Lambs, 8
  Leased, 234
  Modus decimandi, 8
  Oats, 37
  Oysters, 200
  Parish boundaries, 99
  Premonstratensian land, 27
  Shared, 112
  Wheat, 29
  Wood, 25
  Wool, 8
Torts, *See* individual torts
Treason
  Bail, 62
  Indictments of, 20
  Matchet, 62
  Shelley, William, 3
Trespass, Writs of,
  Ancient demesne, 6
  Assault, 5, 148
  Battery, 5, 138
  Cattle, 202
  Commons, 194
  Continuances, 148
  Contra pacem, 169
  Costs, court, 148
  Distress wrongful, 37
  Dogs, trespass by, 59
  Justification, 5
  Land, to, 6, 33, 59, 73, 101, 102, 125, 172
  Lessees, 5

Moors, 194
Parties, 33
Place where not alleged, 138
Self defense, 5
Settlements of, 50
Sewers, commissioners of, 202
Tithes, to, 37
Trees, 177
Way, rights of, 103
Trover, Writs of
    Fees for filing, 130
    Possession of goods, 48
    Tithes, 234
Trusts, 3
Universities, 54
Uses, 3
Usury, 95, 123
Venue
    Administration of estate, 127
    Change of, 57
    Defamation, 247
    Fictitious pleading, 4
    Foreign jury, 57
    Improper cured, 63
    Infancy, 261
    Lease of warren, 83
    Murder, 57
    Plea sworn, 247
    Waived by delay, 45

Verdicts
    Ignoramus, 20
    Issue
        Based on, 251
        Not based on, 248
        Special, 3, 12, 52, 73, 118, 179, 286
        Sufficient, 180
Wager of Law, 183
Wales, Court of Great Sessions, 117
Wales, Court of the Marches, 23
Waste
    Executors liable for, 166
    Trees, 177
Wills, *See* Executors
Witchcraft, 160, 192
Witnesses, *See* Evidence
Women
    Jointures, 216
    Lessors, 284
    Powers of appointment, 52
    Torts to, 277
    Widows, 52
Wood and Trees
    Tithes, 25
    Waste, 177